Reshaping E-Commerce Through AI Shopping Agents

Omar Almomani
https://orcid.org/0000-0003-3160-6542
Al-Ahliyya Amman University, Jordan

Mohammad Alauthman
https://orcid.org/0000-0003-0319-1968
University of Petra, Jordan

Ammar Almomani
https://orcid.org/0000-0002-8808-6114
Higher Colleges of Technology, UAE

IGI Global
Scientific Publishing
Publishing Tomorrow's Research Today

Vice President of Editorial	Melissa Wagner
Director of Acquisitions	Mikaela Felty
Director of Book Development	Jocelynn Hessler
Production Manager	Mike Brehm
Cover Design	Jose Rosado

Published in the United States of America by
IGI Global Scientific Publishing
701 East Chocolate Avenue
Hershey, PA, 17033, USA
Tel: 717-533-8845 | Fax: 717-533-7115
Website: https://www.igi-global.com E-mail: cust@igi-global.com

Library of Congress Cataloging-in-Publication Data

LCCN: 2026002318 (CIP Data Pending)
ISBN13: 979-8-3373-7330-0
Isbn13Softcover: 979-8-3373-7331-7
EISBN13: 979-8-3373-7332-4
British Cataloguing in Publication Data
A Cataloguing in Publication record for this book is available from the British Library.

Table of Contents

Detailed Table of Contents

Artificial Intelligence (AI) has become the cognitive backbone of next-generation e-commerce, transforming digital marketplaces into adaptive, data-driven ecosystems. This chapter examines future research directions and industrial applications of AI-powered e-commerce, tracing its evolution from rule-based automation to autonomous, context-aware systems. Grounded in decision sciences, behavioral economics, and information systems theory, it presents a multidimensional framework for understanding how machine learning, natural language processing, computer vision, and reinforcement learning reshape the e-commerce value chain. Industry case studies from fashion, consumer electronics, healthcare, and B2B commerce illustrate AI's impact on personalization, pricing, logistics, and customer engagement. The chapter highlights emerging domains, including autonomous agents, generative AI, sustainability, and algorithmic governance, and emphasizes interdisciplinary collaboration for responsible and ethical innovation.

In this chapter, a conceptual design of adaptive and intelligent interface design in e-commerce is introduced, maximizing user engagement and conversion by means of personalization, which is done in real-time. The framework incorporates five elements, including User Modeling Engine with collaborative filtering, Context Analysis Module with device and behavioral signals, Adaptation Decision Layer with Thompson Sampling and contextual multi-armed bandits, Interface Transformation Engine with dynamic content adaptation, and Feedback and Evaluation System with continuous learning. Four conditions were experimentally validated with UCI

Online Retail (541,909 transactions) and REES46 (42.4M events) data sets, namely, the static baseline, simple personalization, rules-based adaptation, and full adaptive system. The results show statistically significant increases (p < 0.001) in which the full adaptive system had 23.4% higher click through rate, 18.7% better conversion and 31.2% less task completion time than baseline.

This book chapter examines the transformative impact of Artificial Intelligence (AI) technologies on Customer Experience (CX) management in the age of digital transformation. The study positions AI as more than just a technical element, but rather as a fundamental tool that personalises customer interactions and guides strategic decisions. The chapter analyses how capabilities such as machine learning and data analytics shape the customer journey, while discussing the effects of applications such as chatbots, recommendation systems, and sentiment analysis on satisfaction. In addition to the operational efficiency opportunities offered by AI, ethical dimensions such as data privacy, algorithmic transparency, and trust are also examined. Ultimately, the necessity of a balanced and ethical approach between technological automation and human interaction for sustainable CX success is highlighted.

In this chapter, the authors discuss the ways in which emerging Artificial Intelligence (AI) systems are transforming the landscape of digital commerce as intelligent agents of shopping, able to sense the world around them, process complex data and information, and take independent action. Continuing the advances in transformer-based language models, multimodal representation learning, reinforcement learning and knowledge-graph-driven reasoning, it demonstrates how modern agents understand user intent, multimodally compare products, and make sound choices in dynamic market environments. Besides, the chapter depicts the ways in which cognitive and agentic AI concepts unite these aspects, creating a set of coherent architectures providing personalized, context, and trustworthy shopping experiences

The growing use of AI driven shopping agents has transformed digital commerce through enhanced personalization, while simultaneously enabling new forms of consumer manipulation, including dark patterns, algorithmic price discrimination, and subscription traps. This chapter critically examines whether existing regulatory frameworks particularly the GDPR, the EU AI Act, and India's Digital Personal Data Protection Act, 2023 are adequate to address persuasive algorithmic practices. It argues that prevailing consent based regulatory models are structurally ill-equipped to counter real-time and adaptive AI driven manipulation. Drawing on regulatory gaps and contemporary case studies, the chapter advances the normative proposal of classifying advanced AI shopping agents as information fiduciaries. Such a framework would impose enforceable duties of loyalty and care toward consumers, moving beyond notice-and-consent paradigms and strengthening consumer protection in AI-mediated digital marketplaces.

The rise of the digital economy and e-commerce has shown that traditional accounting systems have big problems, especially when it comes to being clear, timely, and able to combine data. This chapter looks at how blockchain technology is changing how accounting is done in modern e-commerce systems. Blockchain allows for new accounting models including triple-entry bookkeeping, automatic journal entries, and ongoing auditing by using decentralised ledgers, immutability, and smart contracts. The chapter also talks about how blockchain might be used in e-commerce, such as for safe payments, supply-chain traceability, managing digital identities, and automating transactions. It also looks at how blockchain makes it easier for e-commerce platforms and accounting systems to work together in real time, which makes reconciliation, reporting accuracy, and financial transparency better. Finally, the chapter talks about some of the main technological, legal, and organisational problems that could make it harder for people to use blockchain.

The purpose of Chapter One is to show how financial institutions are updating their liability regulations due to technological advancements, including AI and blockchain, in addition to moving to remote services such as ICT or cloud-based Infrastructure as a Service (IaaS). The use of previous ways to determine liability, such as "Control," as a measure of authority is increasingly being challenged due to the changes in the overall structure of financial services to include multiple parties who may provide data or support through third-party vendors. Against this background, the chapter develops a governance-centered, risk-based accountability framework for assessing liability after data breaches or operational disruptions under the EU's Digital Operational Resilience Act (DORA) and the NIS2 Directive. The central claim is that EU operational resilience law pushes the duty of care toward a systems-based standard: what matters is not simply where the technical failure occurred, but whether the bank's governance arrangements—provider selection, contract architecture, oversight, testing, and incident reporting—were capable of managing foreseeable ICT risk across outsourced dependencies. On this approach, governance failure, rather than technological causation alone, becomes the main driver of legal exposure in AI- and blockchain-reliant banking models.

The importance of artificial intelligence has rapidly changed the world of online commerce and turned digital shopping into a predictive and personalized practice. One of the most significant changes is the application of AI to create shopping agent intelligent machines helping consumers at every stage of the buying process by suggesting purchases, comparing products, and automating the process. This chapter discusses how AI agents of shopping are transforming e-commerce through redefining consumer behaviour, and making new types of online interaction possible. Based on a systematic literature review of the scholarly literature and industry practices, the chapter discusses the most important applications, including personalized recommendations, dynamic pricing, AR-driven virtual try-ons, and autonomous purchasing systems. The research comes up with the conclusion that, AI shopping agents are no longer considered an optional addition, but a strategic collaborator in contemporary commerce, although their implementation should be supported by moral values, transparency, and human supervision.

This chapter examines how intelligent personalization transforms customer experience by integrating advanced Artificial Intelligence (AI) capabilities with human-centered design. It explores the psychological foundations that guide personalized engagement, including cognitive load reduction, emotional relevance, trust formation, and cultural variation. Furthermore, the chapter analyzes how intelligent agents, hyper-personalization architectures, adaptive user interfaces, and predictive analytics function collectively to deliver context-aware and dynamically tailored interactions. In addition, it addresses ethical concerns involving privacy, autonomy, fairness, and transparency to emphasize the necessity of responsible design. Moreover, case studies across retail, healthcare, finance, education, and accessibility illustrate how culturally adaptive and inclusive systems enhance satisfaction, decision support, and digital equity.

Artificial- intelligence (AI) mediated commerce now exists that includes conventional web storefronts and spatial shopping surroundings located in-the-adjacent of the metaverse, whereby conversational assistants, ranking techniques, and dynamic pricing mechanisms are based uponframe granular telemetry. This chapter states the transparency and audit policies of algorithms facing consumers, which involve disclosure, opt abandon, contestability, and controls governing the operations that correspond to the reality of constrained deployment, including latency, gaming risk, and trade secret protection. A lifecycle audit model brings together documentation practices, red-teaming, monitoring and remediation practices to meet requirements of compliance with applicability extended to embodied AI agents and Extended

Preface

INTRODUCTION

The digital commerce landscape is undergoing a fundamental transformation driven by the rapid advancement of Artificial Intelligence (AI). What was once a transactional environment centered on static product listings and linear customer journeys has evolved into a dynamic, intelligent ecosystem characterized by personalization, automation, and real-time decision-making. At the heart of this transformation lies the emergence of AI shopping agents—autonomous or semi-autonomous systems capable of understanding user intent, analyzing vast datasets, and acting on behalf of consumers to optimize purchasing decisions.

This evolution reflects a broader shift toward cognitive commerce, where algorithms not only support but actively shape consumer behavior and market dynamics. AI shopping agents leverage machine learning, natural language processing, and computer vision to deliver highly tailored experiences, streamline operations, and enhance engagement across digital platforms. However, alongside these advancements come critical challenges related to privacy, transparency, accountability, and ethical governance. The increasing autonomy of these systems raises important questions about trust, fairness, and the balance between human agency and machine intelligence.

Reshaping E-Commerce Through AI Shopping Agents brings together leading scholars and practitioners to explore these transformative developments from multidisciplinary perspectives. The volume integrates insights from computer science, information systems, law, business, and design to examine how AI-driven technologies are redefining the architecture of online commerce. Through theoretical frameworks, empirical studies, and applied case analyses, this book aims to provide a comprehensive understanding of the opportunities and implications of AI shopping agents in contemporary and future marketplaces.

CHAPTER OVERVIEW

This volume consists of fourteen chapters that collectively examine the technological, behavioral, regulatory, and experiential dimensions of AI-powered e-commerce.

Chapter 1 introduces the future research directions and industrial applications of AI in e-commerce, presenting a comprehensive framework that connects machine learning, behavioral economics, and decision sciences to evolving digital marketplaces.

Chapter 2 proposes a conceptual model for adaptive and intelligent interface design, demonstrating how real-time personalization and data-driven systems enhance user engagement and conversion rates.

Chapter 3 explores the role of AI in customer experience management, highlighting how intelligent systems reshape customer journeys while addressing ethical concerns such as privacy and trust.

Chapter 4 examines AI architectures that enable intelligent shopping agents, focusing on advanced technologies such as transformer models, reinforcement learning, and knowledge graphs.

Chapter 5 addresses consumer protection by analyzing algorithmic manipulation and proposing regulatory frameworks to safeguard user rights in AI-driven shopping environments.

Chapter 6 investigates blockchain-enabled accounting systems and their implications for transparency, automation, and financial integrity within modern e-commerce ecosystems.

Chapter 7 explores the integration of emerging technologies such as augmented reality (AR), virtual reality (VR), and blockchain in creating smart commerce environments.

Chapter 8 presents AI-powered shopping experiences in the metaverse, highlighting innovations in recommendation systems, virtual interactions, and privacy-preserving mechanisms.

Chapter 9 examines operational resilience and data breach liability in AI- and blockchain-enabled systems, offering insights into governance, risk management, and regulatory compliance.

Chapter 10 discusses the transformative impact of AI shopping agents on online commerce, emphasizing their role as strategic collaborators in consumer decision-making.

Chapter 11 focuses on intelligent personalization and its influence on customer experience, integrating psychological and technological perspectives to enhance engagement and satisfaction.

Chapter 12 addresses cybersecurity and data privacy, proposing AI-driven frameworks to safeguard customer information across increasingly complex digital ecosystems.

Chapter 13 explores the transparency paradox in AI shopping agents, offering strategies to rebuild trust through explainability, accountability, and ethical design.

Chapter 14 concludes with an exploration of virtual reality marketplaces and AI agents, illustrating how immersive technologies are reshaping retail environments and consumer interactions.

CONCLUSION

The contributions in this volume collectively demonstrate that AI shopping agents are redefining the very nature of e-commerce. By shifting from reactive systems to proactive, intelligent agents, digital commerce platforms are becoming more adaptive, efficient, and personalized. This transformation is not only technological but also behavioral, influencing how consumers discover, evaluate, and purchase products in increasingly complex digital environments.

At the same time, the rise of AI-driven commerce necessitates a careful and critical examination of its broader implications. Issues of data privacy, algorithmic bias, transparency, and consumer protection must be addressed to ensure that innovation does not come at the expense of trust and fairness. The chapters in this book highlight the importance of interdisciplinary collaboration in developing regulatory frameworks, ethical guidelines, and technical solutions that support responsible AI deployment.

We hope that Reshaping E-Commerce Through AI Shopping Agents serves as a valuable resource for researchers, practitioners, policymakers, and students seeking to understand and navigate this rapidly evolving domain. By bringing together diverse perspectives and forward-looking insights, this volume aims to contribute to the development of intelligent, ethical, and human-centered e-commerce ecosystems for the future.

— The Editors

Chapter 1
Future Research Directions and Industry Applications in AI-Powered E-Commerce

Apoorav Sharma
http://orcid.org/0009-0002-9966-7691
Lovely Professional University, India

Lovleen Marwaha
Lovely Professional University, India

ABSTRACT

Artificial Intelligence (AI) has become the cognitive backbone of next-generation e-commerce, transforming digital marketplaces into adaptive, data-driven ecosystems. This chapter examines future research directions and industrial applications of AI-powered e-commerce, tracing its evolution from rule-based automation to autonomous, context-aware systems. Grounded in decision sciences, behavioral economics, and information systems theory, it presents a multidimensional framework for understanding how machine learning, natural language processing, computer vision, and reinforcement learning reshape the e-commerce value chain. Industry case studies from fashion, consumer electronics, healthcare, and B2B commerce illustrate AI's impact on personalization, pricing, logistics, and customer engagement. The chapter highlights emerging domains, including autonomous agents, generative AI, sustainability, and algorithmic governance, and emphasizes interdisciplinary collaboration for responsible and ethical innovation.

DOI: 10.4018/979-8-3373-7330-0.ch001

1. INTRODUCTION

E-commerce has evolved over the last 20 years to become a digital supplement to real-life retail into a complex algorithmically mediated ecosystem that affects all spheres of consumer life (Shankar, 2018; Davenport et al., 2020). With the increased size and complexity of digital marketplaces, the concept of artificial intelligence (AI) has become one of the enablers of this change (Huang and Rust, 2021). Now, AI and e-commerce have become synonymous, which marks a next-generation in the digital economy, where automation and efficiency are not the only major trends found, but the adaptive intelligence, personalization at scale, and autonomous decision-making (Davenport et al., 2020; Dwivedi et al., 2023).

With the help of AI technologies, especially machine learning (ML), natural language processing (NLP), and computer vision, the methods of how companies perceive, forecast, and act upon consumer behavior are changing (Zhang et al., 2019; Ricci et al., 2015). The recommendation engines, intelligent pricing algorithms, conversational shopping agents, and predictive supply chain models are not just tools and they are strategic assets that can differentiate competitive advantage in the global digital marketplace (Gómez-Uribe and Hunt, 2016; Ferreira et al., 2016). The reason behind this chapter is that although the uses of AI in e-commerce have already become a mature field of study, the prospective research directions and industrial implications of AI are still in disintegration, understudied, and thus there is a gap in academic synthesis (Huang and Rust, 2021). Furthermore, the deepening convergence between AI ethics, consumer psychology, and data governance has sparked the inquiry among scholars and industry practitioners on how AI could be used in a responsible way to ensure sustainable and inclusive e-commerce (Floridi et al., 2018; Mittelstadt et al., 2016). The development of generative AI systems like GPT and multimodal systems has broadened the concept of AI shopping agents beyond rule-based recommendation systems to cover those that can talk and learn (Dwivedi et al., 2023; Luo et al., 2019). This is why it is high time and an urgent need to conduct a systematic investigation of this new frontier (Shin, 2021).

1.1 Evolution of E-Commerce and Rise of AI Integration

The development of e-commerce can be split into four waves. The initial one (19952005) was driven by such companies as Amazon and eBay, with the main emphasis on online cataloging and efficiency in transactions (Shankar, 2018). The second wave (20052015) was the time of integrating social media and mobile commerce, where the decision-making is located in user-generated content and network effects. The third wave (20152020) has been characterized by the spread of big data analytics and the initial use of AI-like tasks, namely, recommendations based on individuality and customer segmentation with the help of ML algorithms (Ricci et al., 2015; Zhang et al., 2019).

The actual wave (20202025) is, however, a qualitative advance to AI-enabled autonomy. E-commerce systems have ceased being data-driven and become more and more agentic, with the ability to reason on their own, engage in constant learning, and adapt to their surroundings (Davenport et al., 2020; Huang and Rust, 2021). The online shopping experience has been transformed into an interactive and conversational one by artificial intelligence shopping agents, visual search engines, voice assistants, and generative content systems (Luo et al., 2019; Dwivedi et al., 2023). The expansive growth of the computational infrastructures, real-time data pipelines, and multimodal AI models, which combine text, speech, and image input, support these developments (Zhang et al., 2019). More importantly, the AI integration wave has pushed traditional boundaries of retail, marketing, logistics, and customer service further, which prompts the concept of the AI-powered value chain (Wamba et al., 2020). AI has become an essential tool used by enterprises to know what customers want and predict their demand in advance, optimize inventory, and use machines to make decisions in various business activities (Min, 2010; Ivanov et al., 2019). The intersection of both AI and e-commerce is therefore a paradigm shift where there was a product-focused one is replaced by a customer-motive-focused one that focuses on prediction, personalization, and adjustability (Huang and Rust, 2021).

1.2 Defining AI-Powered E-Commerce and AI Shopping Agents

AI-powered e-commerce is a type of digital commerce where artificial intelligence is used as the thinking core that informs decisions, personalization, operational automation, etc. (Davenport et al., 2020). It has an extensive solution set of technologies that can sense, reason, learn, and work with data to improve business performance and consumer satisfaction (Huang and Rust, 2021). In the given paradigm, one of the key constructs is the AI shopping agent, an intelligent system that will help consumers learn about, assess, and buy products or services by means of adaptive and context-sensitive interaction (Luo et al., 2019).

Compared to the old approach of relying on non-evolving, rule-based reasoning, the modern AI agents use deep learning, reinforcement learning, and generative AI to constantly adjust to the changing behavior and preferences of users (Zhang et al., 2019; Dwivedi et al., 2023). These agents can negotiate prices, anticipate future consumption behavior, and offer dynamic guidance in making purchases by the use of conversational and multimodal interface (Chen et al., 2016; Luo et al., 2019). In that way, they become the final stage in the development of cognitive computing, making it possible to work in real-time with a human and a machine in online markets and turning shopping into a process involving human and computer interaction (Shin, 2021). Systematically, AI-based e-commerce works based on a multi-layered and integrated architecture linking data, algorithms, interfaces, and strategic decision-making (Wamba et al., 2020). At the bottom tier, the data layer consists of user profiles, transactional history, and behavioral analytics, which drive algorithmic learning. Most importantly, above this is the algorithmic layer, which is made up of machine learning models, recommendation engines, and predictive analytics that convert the raw data into actionable data. The human-AI interface is mediated by the interaction layer, which consists of chatbots, voice assistants, and immersive interfaces, and the strategic layer uses AI-generated intelligence to drive business strategy, coordination of the supply chain, and optimization of the marketing process. The fact that these layers are interdependent should help define the position at which academic research and industrial innovation can work together to promote the formation of the next generation of intelligent e-commerce ecosystems (Huang and Rust, 2021).

1.3 Objectives, Scope, and Purpose of the Chapter.

This chapter aims to summarize the latest developments, describing the new directions of research, and defining the industrial uses of AI-driven e-commerce that will transform digital markets (Dwivedi et al., 2023). Though a significant amount of literature has been developed to study individual technologies, including recommender systems, chatbots, and intelligent pricing mechanisms, fewer studies have explicitly stated a comprehensive research agenda that links AI innovations to larger socio-economic, ethical, and industrial consequences (Floridi et al., 2018). This chapter responds to that gap by offering an integrative perspective that situates technological progress within its wider societal and organizational contexts.

The scope of the chapter spans both theoretical and applied domains, emphasizing the interdisciplinary convergence of artificial intelligence, data science, marketing, human–computer interaction, and behavioral economics (Shankar, 2018; Huang & Rust, 2021). Within this framework, the chapter maps the technological foundations and operational architectures of AI-powered e-commerce systems, while critically examining key industrial use cases that demonstrate their transformative impact across sectors (Wamba et al., 2020; Gómez-Uribe & Hunt, 2016). In parallel, it identifies methodological and theoretical gaps that future research must address to advance robust, explainable, and human-centered AI applications in digital commerce (Shin, 2021). Beyond technological performance, the chapter also explores the ethical, regulatory, and sustainability implications of AI integration, with particular attention to issues of algorithmic bias, transparency, data governance, and environmental responsibility (Mittelstadt et al., 2016; Floridi et al., 2018). Finally, it proposes strategic directions for strengthening collaboration between academia and industry in shaping next-generation e-commerce ecosystems that are innovative yet socially responsible (Dwivedi et al., 2022). By addressing these interconnected objectives, the chapter aims to contribute not only to academic scholarship but also to strategic industry foresight, offering guidance for policymakers, researchers, and practitioners seeking to foster responsible and sustainable innovation in digital commerce (Davenport et al., 2020).

2. THEORETICAL AND TECHNOLOGICAL FOUNDATIONS

Artificial intelligence (AI) has emerged as the cognitive infrastructure underlying the next generation of e-commerce ecosystems, fundamentally reshaping how digital marketplaces function and evolve (Davenport et al., 2020; Huang & Rust, 2021). To fully understand its transformative impact, it is essential to examine both the theoretical foundations that explain human–machine decision-making processes and the technological architectures that operationalize these theories in digital environments. The intersection of decision sciences, behavioral economics, and information systems theory provides the intellectual scaffolding for interpreting how AI technologies reconfigure market dynamics, consumer behavior, and firm-level strategy (Shankar, 2018). Simultaneously, advances in machine learning, natural language processing, computer vision, and reinforcement learning are redefining how e-commerce systems learn from data, infer consumer intent, and autonomously act upon information (Zhang et al., 2019). The integration of these technologies into scalable architectures supported by cloud-based and edge computing infrastructures has given rise to what can be described as an intelligent digital marketplace—a self-optimizing ecosystem capable of continuous adaptation and real-time decision-making (Wamba et al., 2020).

2.1 Theoretical Underpinnings: Decision Sciences, Behavioral Economics, and Information Systems

The conceptual foundation of AI-powered e-commerce lies in understanding how decisions are formed, influenced, and executed in digital contexts. From the perspective of decision sciences, classical models such as Herbert Simon's theory of bounded rationality remain highly relevant, as consumers face cognitive limitations and information overload when navigating complex online marketplaces (Simon, 1957). AI-driven recommender systems function as cognitive amplifiers, expanding these decision boundaries by filtering, ranking, and personalizing alternatives in ways that reduce effort and uncertainty (Ricci et al., 2015). Behavioral economics offers a complementary framework by revealing systematic cognitive biases such as anchoring, loss aversion, and choice overload that shape consumer decision-making (Kahneman & Tversky, 1979). AI algorithms trained on behavioral data can model these biases and, in some cases, deliberately nudge consumer choices through mechanisms such as scarcity cues, dynamic pricing, and social proof (Chen et al., 2016; Shankar, 2018). This capacity introduces an inherent ethical tension between persuasion and manipulation, positioning AI ethics as a critical area for scholarly inquiry and regulatory oversight (Mittelstadt et al., 2016).

From an information systems perspective, AI-powered e-commerce exemplifies the shift from static, transaction-oriented architectures to adaptive socio-technical systems (Gregor & Benbasat, 1999). According to socio-technical theory, system effectiveness depends not only on computational efficiency but also on alignment between technology design, human cognition, and organizational objectives. In this view, AI operates as a mediating agent that links data inputs, algorithmic models, and behavioral outcomes within complex digital ecosystems (Wamba et al., 2020).

Emerging frameworks such as the Technology Acceptance Model (TAM) and the Unified Theory of Acceptance and Use of Technology (UTAUT) have been extended to examine consumer trust and adoption of AI-driven personalization (Venkatesh et al., 2003; Shin, 2021). Trust, transparency, and perceived control consistently emerge as decisive factors influencing acceptance. Collectively, these theoretical perspectives suggest that the future success of AI-powered e-commerce depends not solely on algorithmic performance but on human-centered design principles that sustain long-term engagement and trust (Huang & Rust, 2021).

2.2 Core AI Technologies in E-Commerce

The technological backbone of AI-driven e-commerce comprises a set of interdependent AI methodologies that collectively enable prediction, personalization, and automation at scale (Zhang et al., 2019). When integrated effectively, these technologies facilitate seamless, intelligent shopping experiences that adapt dynamically to user behavior and market conditions.

2.2.1 Machine Learning and Predictive Analytics

Machine learning (ML) serves as the analytical core of AI-powered e-commerce by enabling systems to learn from historical and real-time data to predict consumer intent, demand fluctuations, and purchasing behavior (Gómez-Uribe & Hunt, 2016). Algorithms such as decision trees, gradient boosting, neural networks, and ensemble models are widely used for product affinity prediction, dynamic pricing optimization, and fraud detection (Ferreira et al., 2016).

Predictive analytics further enables micro-segmentation of consumers based on behavioral similarity, allowing firms to deliver hyper-personalized recommendations at scale (Ricci et al., 2015). Time-series forecasting techniques—including ARIMA models, long short-term memory (LSTM) networks, and Prophet algorithms—play a critical role in demand forecasting, inventory planning, and logistics optimization (Ivanov et al., 2019). Recent advances in AutoML and explainable AI (XAI) address the "black box" problem by improving model interpretability, fairness, and regulatory compliance, thereby strengthening trust in AI-driven decision-making (Shin, 2021).

2.2.2 Natural Language Processing and Conversational Agents

Natural language processing (NLP) underpins the conversational layer of e-commerce interactions by enabling systems to interpret and generate human language with high contextual accuracy (Dwivedi et al., 2023). Transformer-based architectures such as BERT and GPT have significantly enhanced semantic understanding, dialogue coherence, and contextual adaptation in customer-facing applications. Conversational agents now serve as the primary interface for customer engagement, supporting product discovery, query resolution, transaction assistance, and post-purchase service (Luo et al., 2019). The integration of sentiment analysis allows these systems to detect emotional cues and adapt responses dynamically, enhancing perceived empathy and satisfaction. Advanced multimodal systems further combine NLP with speech recognition and computer vision, transforming shopping into an interactive, dialogue-driven experience (Adam et al., 2021).

2.2.3 Computer Vision and Visual Search

Computer vision enables e-commerce platforms to interpret and analyze visual data, supporting applications such as visual search, automated product tagging, and augmented reality-based try-on experiences (Park & Kim, 2022). Techniques including convolutional neural networks (CNNs) and vision transformers (ViT) facilitate fine-grained image recognition, allowing consumers to search for products using images rather than text.

Visual search reduces linguistic and cultural barriers while supporting experience-oriented shopping behaviors, particularly in fashion and lifestyle retail (Zhang et al., 2019). Beyond consumer interfaces, computer vision supports warehouse automation, defect detection, counterfeit identification, and inventory monitoring. As vision systems increasingly integrate textual and contextual cues, they contribute to a unified, multimodal understanding of consumer intent.

2.2.4 Reinforcement Learning in Recommendation Systems

Reinforcement learning (RL) reframes recommendation as a sequential decision-making problem focused on maximizing long-term user engagement rather than single transactions (Chen et al., 2016). In this framework, the platform functions as an agent interacting with consumers, where recommendations are actions and behavioral responses serve as rewards.

RL-based systems dynamically balance exploration and exploitation, enabling recommendations to evolve alongside user preferences (Zhang et al., 2019). Advanced architectures such as deep Q-networks and actor–critic models are increasingly deployed to enhance conversion rates, reduce churn, and optimize lifetime value. Future research is expected to focus on multi-agent reinforcement learning, where multiple AI agents coordinate across objectives such as personalization, profitability, and fairness (Dwivedi et al., 2023).

2.3 Architectural Models and Frameworks for AI-Driven E-Commerce Systems

AI-driven e-commerce architectures are modular, distributed, and data-centric, typically comprising interconnected layers for data ingestion, model development, application deployment, and continuous optimization (Wamba et al., 2020). Micro-services architectures and API orchestration enhance scalability, interoperability, and real-time responsiveness. The integration of knowledge graphs and semantic ontologies further strengthens contextual reasoning by enabling AI systems to understand relationships among products, users, and behaviors in a structured manner (Huang & Rust, 2021). In parallel, the emergence of MLOps frameworks supports model lifecycle management, version control, monitoring, and governance, ensuring reliability and ethical compliance throughout deployment (Shin, 2021).

2.4 Data Ecosystem and Cloud-AI Infrastructure

Data constitutes the foundational resource of AI-powered e-commerce, yet its value depends on infrastructures that support real-time ingestion, scalable processing, and secure governance (Davenport et al., 2020). Cloud platforms such as AWS, Google Cloud, and Microsoft Azure provide elastic computing resources that enable large-scale model training and deployment while reducing operational costs. The e-commerce data ecosystem is characterized by volume, velocity, and variety, encompassing transactions, clickstreams, images, reviews, and IoT-generated sensor data (Wamba et al., 2020). Data lakes and data mesh architectures unify these heterogeneous sources under standardized governance frameworks.

Emerging paradigms such as edge AI and federated learning decentralize computation, reducing latency and enhancing privacy by enabling on-device learning without centralized data transfer (Kairouz et al., 2021). These approaches align with data protection regulations such as GDPR and CCPA, reinforcing ethical compliance. Combined with automated bias detection and fairness auditing tools, cloud-AI infrastructures ensure that AI-powered e-commerce systems remain adaptive, secure, and socially responsible. In essence, the fusion of robust data ecosystems with intelligent cloud architectures forms the technological backbone of AI-driven e-commerce, an infrastructure not only for computation but for collective intelligence and continuous innovation (Huang & Rust, 2021).

3. AI-DRIVEN TRANSFORMATION ACROSS THE E-COMMERCE VALUE CHAIN

Artificial intelligence (AI) is no longer an auxiliary component of e-commerce systems; rather, it has become the intelligent core that interconnects every stage of the digital value chain, from product discovery to post-purchase logistics (Davenport et al., 2020; Huang & Rust, 2021). The integration of AI across this continuum has catalyzed a fundamental shift from linear, process-driven business models toward adaptive, data-centric ecosystems capable of autonomous decision-making and continuous learning (Wamba et al., 2020). Consequently, each stage of the e-commerce value chain, including marketing, operations, logistics, and customer experience, is being redefined through intelligence augmentation, automation, and predictive analytics, reshaping both consumer expectations and organizational strategy (Shankar, 2018). The following subsections examine how AI technologies collectively reengineer the e-commerce value chain, enhancing efficiency, personalization, and strategic agility while redefining traditional business paradigms (Figure1).

Figure 1. This figure illustrates the integrated, multi-layered architecture through which artificial intelligence technologies operate across the e-commerce value chain. The framework conceptualizes four interconnected layers: (1) the data layer, comprising transactional, behavioral, and contextual datasets; (2) the algorithmic layer, including machine learning, natural language processing, computer vision, and reinforcement learning models; (3) the interaction layer, encompassing conversational agents, visual search systems, and multimodal interfaces; and (4) the strategic layer, where AI-driven insights inform pricing, logistics, marketing, governance, and sustainability decisions.

AI-Powered E-Commerce Value Chain Architecture

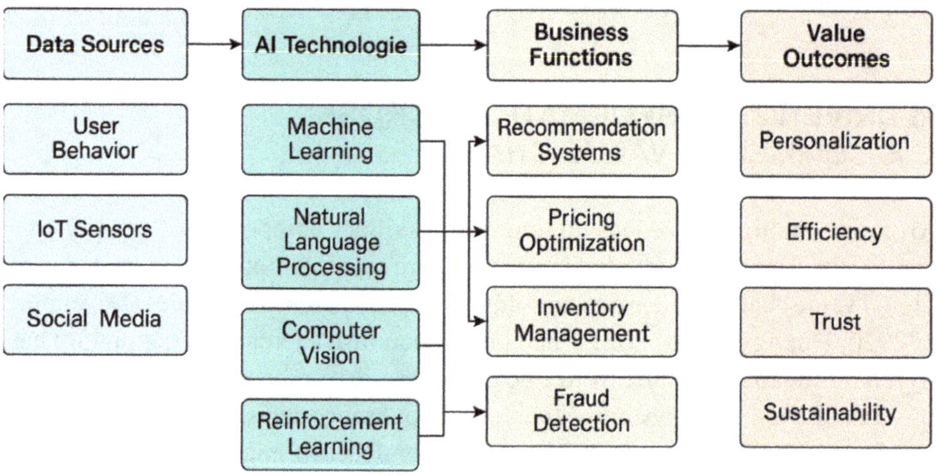

3.1 Product Discovery and Personalized Recommendations

Product discovery represents the first and most critical touchpoint in consumer interaction, making it a prime domain for AI-driven innovation. Traditional discovery mechanisms relied heavily on keyword-based search and static rule-based filtering, which offered limited contextual relevance. In contrast, AI-driven discovery systems employ deep learning, knowledge graphs, and multimodal data fusion to deliver hyper-personalized experiences aligned with individual consumer preferences, intent, and emotional context (Ricci et al., 2015; Zhang et al., 2019).

At the core of these systems are recommendation algorithms collaborative filtering, content-based filtering, and hybrid architectures enhanced by deep neural networks capable of learning latent features beyond explicit user ratings (Gómez-Uribe & Hunt, 2016). These models analyze diverse behavioral signals, including browsing patterns, dwell time, clickstream data, social interactions, and contextual variables such as time of day or device type, enabling more nuanced personalization (Shankar, 2018).

Recent advances in transformer-based architectures, such as BERT4Rec and SASRec, have further accelerated the shift toward context-aware and intent-based recommendations by modeling sequential dependencies in user behavior (Zhang et al., 2019). This allows systems to infer not only what consumers want but why they want it. Additionally, the integration of generative AI has transformed content creation, enabling automated generation of product descriptions, marketing narratives, and personalized messaging. By combining textual and visual understanding, AI agents can recommend curated "lookbooks" or lifestyle bundles rather than isolated products, increasing both engagement and basket size (Dwivedi et al., 2023).

Future research in this domain increasingly emphasizes explainable recommendation systems—models that justify their outputs to users in order to enhance transparency, trust, and long-term adoption (Shin, 2021).

3.2 Intelligent Pricing and Demand Forecasting

Pricing is among the most analytically complex domains in e-commerce due to its sensitivity to dynamic market conditions, competitive behavior, and consumer sentiment. AI enables firms to deploy real-time dynamic pricing strategies grounded in predictive and prescriptive analytics, moving beyond static pricing rules (Ferreira et al., 2016). Machine learning techniques, including regression ensembles, Bayesian networks, and reinforcement learning agents, continuously analyze multidimensional datasets comprising sales history, competitor prices, weather patterns, and macroeconomic indicators. Through iterative learning, AI systems identify optimal price points that balance revenue maximization with demand elasticity (Chen et al., 2016).

Reinforcement learning represents a significant advancement in adaptive pricing, allowing AI agents to experiment with pricing strategies and receive feedback through conversion rates, profitability, and retention metrics. Over time, these systems converge toward policies that balance short-term gains with long-term customer relationships (Zhang et al., 2019). In parallel, demand forecasting has been transformed through deep learning models such as long short-term memory (LSTM) networks and temporal convolutional architectures, which capture nonlinear trends, seasonality, and external shocks with high precision (Ivanov et al., 2019).

More recently, AI-driven pricing systems have incorporated sentiment analysis from reviews and social media, enabling emotion-sensitive pricing strategies that adapt to collective consumer mood. As e-commerce becomes increasingly global, multilingual, and cross-cultural, forecasting models have become essential for detecting regional patterns overlooked by traditional statistical methods (Shankar, 2018). Together, intelligent pricing and demand forecasting shift e-commerce from reactive operations toward anticipatory, self-optimizing decision-making systems.

3.3 Dynamic Customer Engagement and Chatbot Systems

Customer engagement in AI-driven commerce is transitioning from static, one-way communication to adaptive, conversational, and emotionally intelligent interaction models. AI-powered chatbots and virtual assistants now function as primary engagement interfaces across digital platforms (Luo et al., 2019).

Built upon large language models (LLMs) and sentiment analysis algorithms, conversational AI systems provide real-time customer support that approximates human empathy and contextual understanding while operating at a massive scale (Dwivedi et al., 2023). These systems extend beyond basic query resolution to support the entire customer journey, including product discovery, personalized recommendations, checkout assistance, and post-purchase service. When reinforced through learning mechanisms, chatbots dynamically optimize conversational flows to enhance conversion and satisfaction (Adam et al., 2021).

Multimodal conversational commerce represents a further evolution, integrating text, speech, and image recognition. Consumers may upload product images, ask questions verbally, and receive voice-guided recommendations in real time. Emotion-aware AI models deepen personalization by detecting affective cues—such as frustration or excitement—from linguistic tone, facial expressions, or typing behavior, transforming engagement from transactional interaction into relational experience (Shin, 2021).

Academic research in this domain increasingly focuses on explainable dialogue systems, fairness in automated communication, and the psychological effects of anthropomorphic AI personas on trust and loyalty

3.4 Inventory and Supply Chain Optimization

Supply chain management constitutes the operational backbone of e-commerce, and AI introduces unprecedented levels of precision, resilience, and adaptability within this domain (Min, 2010). Through predictive analytics and IoT-enabled data fusion, AI systems forecast demand fluctuations and dynamically adjust procurement, production, and distribution schedules, enabling just-in-time inventory management and waste reduction (Ivanov et al., 2019).

Computer vision technologies support warehouse operations by monitoring stock levels, detecting defects, and automating quality inspection. AI-guided robotics and drones perform real-time scanning, sorting, and shelving tasks, improving efficiency and accuracy. Optimization techniques, including genetic algorithms and deep reinforcement learning, enhance route planning, warehouse layout, and logistics scheduling under dynamic constraints related to cost, speed, and sustainability (Wamba et al., 2020).

The emergence of digital twins, virtual replicas of physical supply chain systems, has further strengthened resilience planning. By embedding AI-driven predictive models into digital twins, organizations can simulate disruptions such as supplier delays or geopolitical shocks and design robust contingency strategies. AI thus transforms supply chains from linear cost centers into self-learning ecosystems synchronized with real-world conditions.

3.5 Fraud Detection, Security, and Risk Mitigation

The rapid expansion of e-commerce has intensified exposure to cybercrime, financial fraud, and identity theft, positioning AI as a critical defense mechanism. Unlike traditional rule-based systems constrained by static thresholds, AI-driven fraud detection employs supervised and unsupervised learning models such as autoencoders, graph neural networks, and isolation forests to identify anomalous behavior in real time (Wamba et al., 2020).

These models analyze transactional data, device fingerprints, and geolocation signals to generate probabilistic fraud risk scores. When integrated with blockchain-based verification systems, AI enhances transparency and transaction integrity. Beyond fraud detection, AI supports broader risk mitigation by modeling systemic vulnerabilities, including supply chain disruptions, data breaches, and regulatory non-compliance (Mittelstadt et al., 2016). However, advances in adversarial machine learning have introduced new challenges, as malicious actors attempt to manipulate AI systems themselves. As a result, research on robust AI security, adversarial resilience, and explainable anomaly detection has become a critical subfield within e-commerce cybersecurity (Floridi et al., 2018). AI thus transforms security from a reactive safeguard into an anticipatory, adaptive function.

3.6 Logistics, Fulfillment, and Last-Mile Delivery Automation

Logistics and fulfillment represent some of the most capital-intensive components of the e-commerce value chain, and AI plays a central role in optimizing cost, speed, and sustainability. Predictive algorithms forecast shipment volumes and support dynamic fleet allocation, while reinforcement learning-based routing systems account for traffic, fuel consumption, weather, and delivery constraints to compute optimal distribution strategies (Ivanov et al., 2019).

Warehouse automation has advanced through AI-driven robotics capable of autonomous navigation, dynamic picking, and inventory replenishment. Multi-agent systems, such as Amazon's Kiva robots, demonstrate how coordinated AI agents can reduce operational errors and reliance on manual labor. In last-mile delivery, autonomous ground robots and aerial drones integrate obstacle detection, path planning, and predictive ETA algorithms to enhance efficiency and transparency.

AI also enables green logistics through carbon-optimized routing and predictive vehicle maintenance, supporting organizational sustainability goals. As urban ecosystems evolve, AI-enabled mobility orchestration integrating public transport, micro-mobility, and parcel hubs will increasingly redefine last-mile economics.

3.7 Voice and Visual Commerce as Emerging Interfaces

The future of e-commerce increasingly lies in multimodal interfaces where voice, vision, and gesture complement or replace traditional text-based interactions (Park & Kim, 2022). Voice commerce, powered by NLP and speech recognition embedded in smart assistants such as Alexa, Siri, and Google Assistant, enables consumers to search, compare, and purchase products through natural dialogue. AI systems personalize these interactions by interpreting contextual cues such as tone, history, and sentiment (Dwivedi et al., 2023).

Visual commerce leverages computer vision and augmented reality to enable virtual try-ons, in-home product visualization, and immersive comparison experiences. These interfaces reduce cognitive effort, improve accessibility, and cater to users with diverse abilities or low digital literacy. The convergence of voice and visual modalities signals a shift toward ambient commerce, where shopping becomes seamlessly embedded within everyday activities. From an academic perspective, this domain opens new research frontiers in multimodal learning, human–AI co-creation, and the cognitive ergonomics of interactive retail experiences, reinforcing the centrality of AI in shaping the next generation of digital commerce ecosystems.

4. HUMAN–AI INTERACTION AND CONSUMER EXPERIENCE

The rapid diffusion of artificial intelligence (AI) into e-commerce has transformed not only the technological foundations of digital retail but also the psychological and emotional fabric of consumer interaction (Huang & Rust, 2021; Davenport et al., 2020). While early e-commerce models prioritized convenience, speed, and efficiency, the AI-driven paradigm places greater emphasis on cognition, affect, and relational experience. Contemporary consumers no longer merely transact with platforms; instead, they engage in dialogue and co-creation with intelligent systems capable of interpreting their needs, moods, and situational contexts (Shankar, 2018; Dwivedi et al., 2023).

This evolving human–AI relationship demands analytical perspectives that extend beyond computational performance to include trust, transparency, empathy, and ethical design. Understanding how these dimensions influence consumer experience and technology adoption is essential for explaining the long-term success of AI-powered commerce across diverse global markets (Shin, 2021).

4.1 Cognitive and Emotional Dimensions of AI-Assisted Shopping

Human–AI interaction in e-commerce simultaneously engages cognitive and affective dimensions of consumer psychology. From a cognitive standpoint, AI systems operate as decision-support mechanisms that assist users in navigating information overload and bounded rationality (Simon, 1957). Automated curation, personalized recommendations, and adaptive content presentation significantly reduce cognitive load, allowing consumers to process complex choice environments more efficiently. In this sense, AI functions as a cognitive prosthesis, an external extension of human decision-making capable of processing information at scales and speeds unattainable by unaided cognition (Ricci et al., 2015). Emotionally, AI-mediated interaction introduces greater complexity. AI systems increasingly influence affective states by adapting tone, imagery, and dialogue to individual emotional contexts. Techniques such as sentiment analysis and affective computing enable AI agents to detect emotions, including frustration, satisfaction, or uncertainty, and to respond dynamically through empathetic language and supportive cues (Adam et al., 2021; Dwivedi et al., 2023). Conversational agents, for example, modulate linguistic style and emotional framing to establish rapport and comfort during consumer interactions.

This emotional alignment fosters para-social relationships, wherein users develop a perceived sense of connection with AI entities. While such relationships can enhance engagement, satisfaction, and loyalty, they also raise ethical concerns related to emotional manipulation and dependency (Floridi et al., 2018). As affective computing advances, a central research challenge lies in designing emotionally intelligent systems that support user well-being without exploiting psychological vulnerabilities.

Moreover, human–AI interaction constitutes a dynamic feedback loop in which consumer cognition and AI learning co-evolve. As consumers adapt their behaviors and expectations in response to AI systems, these behavioral shifts, in turn, reshape model training and optimization processes. This reciprocity underscores the importance of conceptualizing human–AI interaction not as a static exchange but as a continuously evolving cognitive system (Shin, 2021).

4.2 Trust, Transparency, and Explainability in AI Systems

Trust represents a foundational determinant of AI adoption in e-commerce environments. Unlike interpersonal trust, which develops through repeated human interaction, algorithmic trust is shaped by user perceptions of transparency, reliability, and fairness (Gregor & Benbasat, 1999). Consumers must believe that AI systems act in their best interests, safeguard personal data, and generate unbiased recommendations to engage confidently with automated decision-making processes (Mittelstadt et al., 2016). However, many AI systems, particularly those based on deep learning, operate as opaque "black boxes," producing outputs that are statistically accurate yet difficult for users to interpret. This opacity generates psychological distance and uncertainty, undermining confidence and acceptance. In response, scholars have advanced the concept of explainable AI (XAI), which seeks to render algorithmic reasoning understandable and justifiable to end users (Doshi-Velez & Kim, 2017; Shin, 2021).

In e-commerce contexts, explainability may take the form of transparent recommendation rationales (e.g., "This product is recommended because you previously purchased X") or interactive visualizations illustrating how preferences were inferred. These features transform algorithmic decisions into narratives that users can cognitively evaluate, thereby strengthening trust and perceived control (Huang & Rust, 2021).

Trust is also highly context-dependent. Empirical studies suggest that consumers are more tolerant of AI errors in low-risk, exploratory activities such as product discovery than in high-stakes contexts such as payments or financial transactions (Shankar, 2018). Consequently, system designers must calibrate transparency and automation levels according to perceived risk. From a managerial perspective, achieving this balance between automation efficiency and user agency constitutes a critical strategic challenge. Future research increasingly emphasizes interactive explainability, enabling users to query AI systems dynamically and engage more deeply with algorithmic reasoning processes.

4.3 The Role of Ethical Design in Enhancing User Adoption

Ethical design has emerged as both a moral imperative and a strategic differentiator in AI-powered e-commerce. As consumers become more aware of data privacy risks, algorithmic bias, and manipulative personalization practices, ethical perception increasingly shapes adoption decisions alongside functional performance (Floridi et al., 2018). Ethical AI design is grounded in principles of fairness, accountability, transparency, privacy, and inclusivity. Fairness seeks to prevent discriminatory outcomes in pricing or recommendation algorithms, while accountability clarifies responsibility for automated decisions. Privacy-centered design emphasizes informed consent, data minimization, and secure governance structures (Mittelstadt et al., 2016).

Many e-commerce platforms now adopt ethical-by-design approaches, embedding fairness constraints and bias mitigation techniques directly into algorithmic development pipelines. Ethical user experience (UX) design further reinforces trust by incorporating clear data-use disclosures, opt-out mechanisms, and visible indicators of automated decision-making. Such interface-level transparency enhances perceived autonomy and psychological comfort among users (Shin, 2021).

Importantly, ethical AI aligns with evolving consumer values. Younger generations, particularly Millennials and Gen Z, demonstrate strong preferences for brands that embody ethical, inclusive, and sustainable practices. Consequently, ethical AI functions not merely as a compliance mechanism but as an innovation catalyst that strengthens brand loyalty, advocacy, and long-term differentiation (Dwivedi et al., 2023). From a research perspective, the intersection of ethics, design thinking, and behavioral economics offers fertile ground for developing frameworks that align machine autonomy with human values.

4.4 Cultural and Demographic Variations in AI Acceptance

Acceptance of AI-driven e-commerce technologies varies significantly across cultural, demographic, and socio-economic contexts, shaping perceptions of trust, agency, and comfort in human–AI interaction (Venkatesh et al., 2003). Cross-cultural research indicates that societies characterized by high uncertainty avoidance, such as Japan and Germany, tend to engage cautiously with AI, prioritizing predictability, control, and transparency. In contrast, cultures exhibiting strong technological optimism, such as the United States, South Korea, and India, are more receptive to AI experimentation and innovation (Shankar, 2018).

Demographic factors further mediate AI acceptance. Younger consumers, socialized within data-intensive digital environments, generally display greater adaptability and trust in AI systems, whereas older users may experience resistance driven by privacy concerns and perceived technological complexity. Gender and socio-economic status also influence attitudes, with evidence suggesting heightened ethical and privacy sensitivity among women and ambivalent perceptions of AI among lower-income groups, who may view automation as either empowering or threatening (Dwivedi et al., 2022). To address these disparities, AI-driven e-commerce platforms increasingly deploy localization strategies that tailor interfaces to cultural and demographic profiles. Adaptive systems modify tone, language formality, and visual cues, while multilingual conversational agents and context-sensitive recommendation models operationalize cultural intelligence through computational design (Huang & Rust, 2021).

In the long term, building inclusive and globally scalable AI ecosystems requires integrating cross-cultural human–computer interaction (HCI) frameworks with machine learning pipelines. Embedding diversity, accessibility, and cultural sensitivity into AI systems from the design stage is essential for ensuring equitable participation in the future of digital commerce.

5. INDUSTRY APPLICATIONS AND ILLUSTRATIVE INDUSTRY EXAMPLES

The integration of artificial intelligence (AI) within e-commerce has progressed from experimental adoption to strategic necessity, fundamentally reshaping how digital commerce operates across industries (Davenport et al., 2020; Huang & Rust, 2021). AI technologies now underpin core business processes spanning product discovery, logistics, marketing, and customer engagement, enabling firms to operate with unprecedented levels of intelligence and adaptability. Global enterprises, including Amazon, Alibaba, and Shopify, have redefined their operational models by embedding AI across every layer of the digital value chain, positioning algorithmic intelligence as a central driver of competitive advantage (Shankar, 2018). This section examines AI adoption across major e-commerce sectors and presents illustrative case studies that demonstrate the transformative role of AI in contemporary commerce.

5.1 AI Adoption in Major E-Commerce Sectors

The adoption trajectory of AI in e-commerce varies considerably across sectors, shaped by differences in data availability, product complexity, regulatory constraints, and consumer expectations. Despite these variations, AI consistently delivers strategic value by enhancing personalization, automating decision-making, and improving operational precision across industries (Wamba et al., 2020).

5.1.1 Fashion and Retail

The fashion and retail sector represents one of the earliest and most intensive adopters of AI, driven by rapidly changing consumer preferences, high product variety, and strong visual dependence (Zhang et al., 2019). Machine learning and computer vision play central roles in trend forecasting, assortment planning, and virtual merchandising. Leading brands such as Zara, H&M, and ASOS employ predictive analytics to anticipate seasonal trends by integrating social media sentiment, search behavior, and historical sales data into inventory planning decisions (Shankar, 2018).

Computer vision supports visual search and outfit recommendation, allowing consumers to upload images and locate visually similar products instantly. AI-powered virtual fitting rooms, enabled by augmented reality (AR) and 3D body scanning technologies, further enhance online shopping experiences by reducing uncertainty, lowering return rates, and increasing conversion (Park & Kim, 2022). Generative AI has also reshaped creative processes, with platforms such as Stitch Fix using AI not only to recommend apparel but to co-design products. By analyzing customer feedback and design attributes, these systems generate personalized clothing suggestions, resulting in hybrid design models that combine human creativity with algorithmic insight (Dwivedi et al., 2023).

5.1.2 Electronics and Consumer Goods

In electronics and consumer goods, AI adoption primarily targets product discovery, dynamic pricing, and post-purchase service, where product complexity and rapid innovation cycles demand advanced predictive intelligence (Ferreira et al., 2016). Retailers such as Best Buy and Newegg deploy AI-driven recommendation systems that analyze cross-product relationships, enabling optimized bundling strategies for complementary items such as devices and accessories (Gómez-Uribe & Hunt, 2016).

Natural language processing (NLP)-based virtual assistants further support customers by explaining technical specifications, managing warranty claims, and providing troubleshooting guidance (Luo et al., 2019). Predictive maintenance analytics powered by IoT data streams enable manufacturers to anticipate product failures and schedule proactive servicing, thereby improving customer satisfaction and operational efficiency. In the consumer goods sector, firms such as Procter & Gamble and Unilever integrate AI into packaging optimization, inventory distribution, and targeted marketing. AI-enabled demand sensing allows these organizations to detect real-time shifts in consumer sentiment and adjust production planning accordingly, reducing waste across global supply chains (Ivanov et al., 2019).

5.1.3 Healthcare and Personalized Shopping

The convergence of AI, healthcare, and e-commerce has given rise to personalized health commerce, an emerging ecosystem in which consumer data, biometrics, and behavioral analytics inform tailored health-related recommendations (Dwivedi et al., 2022). Platforms such as Amazon Pharmacy and 1mg leverage AI for prescription verification, medication reminders, and dosage optimization, enhancing accuracy and adherence.

Wellness-oriented platforms, including Fitbit and MyFitnessPal, use AI-driven behavioral profiling to recommend personalized nutrition plans, fitness products, and lifestyle interventions. Generative AI models increasingly support the creation of personalized health content, guiding consumers toward evidence-based decisions. However, this domain also introduces heightened ethical and regulatory challenges related to medical data privacy, algorithmic bias, and compliance with frameworks such as HIPAA and GDPR (Floridi et al., 2018). As digital therapeutics and AI-driven health coaching expand, healthcare e-commerce is poised to redefine preventive care and self-management through intelligent, user-centered platforms.

5.1.4 B2B and Industrial E-Commerce

AI's impact in business-to-business (B2B) and industrial e-commerce is particularly strategic, as these environments prioritize procurement optimization, risk management, and long-term relationship governance (Min, 2010). AI systems analyze supplier performance, pricing trends, and risk indicators to automate sourcing and procurement decisions. Platforms such as Alibaba's 1688.com and ThomasNet employ AI-driven matchmaking algorithms to connect buyers with suppliers based on quality, reliability, and delivery performance.

NLP-based semantic search enables procurement professionals to locate industrial components even when specifications vary across vendors. Reinforcement learning–based negotiation agents are emerging to optimize pricing and contract terms autonomously. For manufacturers, predictive analytics enhance supply planning and demand synchronization, reducing inventory holding costs while maintaining operational continuity. In this context, AI evolves from a supportive analytical tool into a strategic orchestration mechanism governing complex B2B ecosystems at scale (Wamba et al., 2020).

5.2 Case Study 1: Conversational Commerce and Voice Assistants

Conversational commerce exemplifies the convergence of AI, linguistics, and behavioral economics, enabling consumers to interact with brands through natural dialogue rather than graphical interfaces (Luo et al., 2019). Voice-based ecosystems such as Amazon Alexa and Google Assistant integrate shopping lists, order histories, and contextual cues including time and location to initiate purchases with minimal cognitive effort. Simple commands such as "reorder detergent" activate predictive reordering processes that account for preferred brands, pricing, and delivery frequency.

In China, platforms such as Alibaba's Tmall Genie and JD.com's DuerOS have similarly transformed consumer behavior by localizing linguistic patterns and integrating payment systems through digital wallets. The strategic value of conversational commerce lies in its frictionless experience, which removes interface barriers and leverages the human tendency to anthropomorphize intelligent agents, thereby fostering engagement and loyalty (Dwivedi et al., 2023). Empirical evidence suggests that conversational commerce significantly increases repeat purchase likelihood and shortens decision cycles, although challenges related to multilingual nuance and privacy in always-on devices persist (Shin, 2021).

5.3 Case Study 2: Generative AI for Personalized Marketing

Generative AI (GenAI) has fundamentally redefined marketing automation by enabling the real-time creation of personalized, context-aware, and emotionally resonant content (Dwivedi et al., 2023). Retailers increasingly deploy models such as GPT, DALL·E, and Midjourney to generate tailored product descriptions, visuals, and promotional narratives aligned with individual psychographic profiles. Platforms such as Shopify Sidekick and Adobe Firefly integrate AI co-pilots that assist merchants in campaign design, copywriting, and audience targeting.

GenAI supports micro-personalization at scale, delivering unique marketing content to individual users based on demographic, behavioral, and contextual signals. Beyond content generation, these systems facilitate creative analytics by evaluating performance across variants and retraining models based on response patterns, ensuring continuous optimization. However, generative personalization also raises ethical concerns related to authenticity, consent, and persuasive transparency. As AI-generated content becomes indistinguishable from human-created material, maintaining trust through disclosure and responsible design becomes essential (Floridi et al., 2018)

5.4 Case Study 3: AI-Driven Supply Chain Resilience Post-COVID-19

The COVID-19 pandemic exposed the fragility of global supply chains, accelerating the adoption of AI-driven resilience frameworks across e-commerce organizations (Ivanov et al., 2019). Firms such as Amazon, Walmart, and Alibaba leveraged AI to enhance real-time visibility, predict disruptions, and simulate response scenarios. Predictive models integrated epidemiological data, regional restrictions, and supplier analytics to forecast stockouts and dynamically adjust sourcing strategies.

AI-powered digital twins virtual replicas of logistics networks enabled organizations to test contingency plans under varying constraints, while reinforcement learning optimized routing and resource allocation in real time. Robotics and automation further reduced human dependency in warehouses, ensuring operational continuity amid workforce disruptions. Post-pandemic analyses indicate that firms employing AI-based supply chain monitoring recovered significantly faster than those reliant on manual coordination, highlighting AI's role as a strategic resilience enabler rather than merely an efficiency tool (Wamba et al., 2020).

5.5 Lessons from Industry Leaders

The experiences of leading e-commerce organizations reveal consistent principles underpinning successful AI deployment: centralized data governance, continuous experimentation, ecosystem integration, and ethical accountability (Huang & Rust, 2021). Amazon exemplifies data-driven orchestration by integrating AI across recommendation systems, dynamic pricing, and fulfillment robotics, supported by continuous learning loops enabled through AWS AI services. Alibaba demonstrates ecosystem-level intelligence by leveraging platforms such as City Brain and ET Industrial Brain t integrate commerce, logistics, and cross-border trade through unified data architectures. Shopify highlights the democratization of AI by providing small and medium enterprises with access to advanced analytics, generative design tools, and inventory optimization previously reserved for large firms.

Collectively, these cases illustrate that success in AI-powered e-commerce depends less on isolated algorithms and more on the systemic integration of AI into organizational culture, governance structures, and value co-creation processes. AI's true strategic impact emerges when technological intelligence is aligned with human oversight, ethical design, and long-term ecosystem thinking.

6. RESEARCH METHODOLOGIES AND FRAMEWORKS FOR FUTURE INVESTIGATION

As AI becomes deeply embedded in e-commerce ecosystems, the need for rigorous, interdisciplinary research methodologies has intensified. Traditional empirical approaches, while valuable, are increasingly insufficient to capture the dynamic, adaptive, and socio-technical nature of AI-driven commerce. Contemporary research in this domain therefore demands methodological pluralism integrating quantitative analytics, qualitative inquiry, computational experimentation, and ethical analysis to generate holistic insights into both technological performance and human impact (Wamba et al., 2020; Dwivedi et al., 2023).

6.1 Quantitative and Data-Driven Research Approaches

Quantitative research remains foundational in AI and e-commerce scholarship, particularly for evaluating predictive accuracy, system performance, and consumer behavior at scale. Large-scale datasets such as clickstream logs, transaction records, and behavioral traces enable researchers to model consumer decision-making using statistical learning and econometric techniques (Shankar, 2018).

Machine learning–based empirical studies frequently employ supervised and unsupervised learning models to analyze recommendation effectiveness, pricing elasticity, churn prediction, and fraud detection. Advanced methods such as causal inference, A/B testing, and uplift modeling are increasingly used to distinguish correlation from causation in algorithmic interventions (Ferreira et al., 2016). These approaches are particularly valuable for assessing the real-world impact of AI systems on revenue, engagement, and retention.

However, purely performance-oriented metrics risk overlooking issues of bias, fairness, and long-term behavioral change. As a result, scholars increasingly integrate explainability metrics and fairness indicators into quantitative evaluations, expanding the analytical lens beyond accuracy toward responsible AI assessment (Shin, 2021).

6.2 Experimental and Simulation-Based Methods

Experimental designs play a critical role in isolating the causal effects of AI interventions on consumer behavior. Laboratory and field experiments are widely used to examine how users respond to AI-driven recommendations, chatbot disclosures, dynamic pricing, and personalization cues (Luo et al., 2019).

Simulation-based research, particularly using agent-based modeling and reinforcement learning environments, allows scholars to study complex market dynamics that are difficult to observe empirically. For instance, multi-agent simulations can model interactions among consumers, AI pricing agents, and competing firms under varying regulatory or economic conditions (Chen et al., 2016). Digital twins of e-commerce systems further enable "what-if" analyses, testing resilience strategies and policy interventions in controlled virtual environments (Ivanov et al., 2019). Such experimental and simulation approaches are especially valuable for forecasting long-term outcomes, including market concentration, consumer welfare, and systemic risk.

6.3 Qualitative, Interpretive, and Human-Centered Research

While data-driven methods dominate AI research, qualitative and interpretive approaches are essential for understanding how consumers perceive, experience, and emotionally respond to AI systems. Interviews, focus groups, ethnographic studies, and diary methods provide rich insights into trust formation, perceived autonomy, and ethical concerns in human–AI interaction (Gregor & Benbasat, 1999).

Human-centered research is particularly relevant for studying conversational agents, voice commerce, and emotion-aware systems, where user experience cannot be fully captured through behavioral metrics alone (Adam et al., 2021). Design science research further contributes by iteratively developing and evaluating AI artifacts such as explainable recommender interfaces or ethical UX prototypes within real-world contexts. Integrating qualitative insights with computational models enables more inclusive and socially grounded AI systems, ensuring that technological innovation aligns with human values and expectations (Floridi et al., 2018).

6.4 Ethical, Legal, and Governance-Oriented Methodologies

The rapid deployment of AI in e-commerce has elevated ethical inquiry from a peripheral concern to a central research agenda. Normative and governance-oriented methodologies examine issues such as algorithmic bias, data privacy, surveillance capitalism, and power asymmetries between platforms and consumers (Mittelstadt et al., 2016). Legal analysis is increasingly integrated into AI research to assess compliance with regulatory frameworks such as GDPR, CCPA, and emerging AI governance policies. Scenario analysis and policy modeling help anticipate the societal consequences of large-scale AI adoption, including labor displacement, market monopolization, and consumer manipulation (Floridi et al., 2018).

Responsible AI research thus requires interdisciplinary collaboration among computer scientists, economists, legal scholars, ethicists, and behavioral scientists.

6.5 Emerging Research Directions

Several research frontiers are poised to define the next phase of AI-powered e-commerce scholarship. First, the rise of agentic AI systems autonomous agents capable of goal-setting, negotiation, and long-term planning raises fundamental questions about accountability, trust, and human oversight (Dwivedi et al., 2023). Understanding how consumers interact with increasingly autonomous agents ep-resents a critical research challenge. Second, multimodal and embodied commerce integrating voice, vision, gesture, and augmented reality opens new avenues for studying cognitive ergonomics, accessibility, and inclusive design (Park & Kim,

2022). Third, sustainability-oriented AI research is gaining momentum, focusing on green logistics, energy-efficient models, and circular economy optimization within e-commerce ecosystems (Schwartz et al., 2020). Finally, cross-cultural and Global South–oriented research remains underdeveloped. Future studies must examine how AI-powered commerce affects diverse populations, informal markets, and digitally marginalized communities to ensure equitable technological progress (Huang & Rust, 2021).

6.6 Toward an Integrated Research Agenda

Taken together, these methodological perspectives underscore the necessity of integrative research frameworks that combine computational rigor with human-centered and ethical inquiry. The future of AI-powered e-commerce research lies not in isolated algorithmic advances but in understanding AI as a socio-technical system embedded within cultural, economic, and institutional contexts. By embracing methodological diversity and interdisciplinary collaboration, scholars can contribute to the development of AI-driven commerce systems that are not only efficient and profitable but also transparent, trustworthy, and socially sustainable (Table 1).

Table 1. Research Agenda Matrix for Future AI-Powered E-Commerce Scholarship

Identified Gap	Research Question	Method	Dataset/ Source	Evaluation Metric	Expected Contribution
Lack of explainability	How does XAI affect consumer trust?	Experiment	Platform A/B data	Trust index	Improves adoption modeling
Bias in dynamic pricing	Does AI pricing produce demographic disparity?	Econometric modeling	Transaction logs	Fairness score	Ethical compliance framework
Sustainability trade-offs	What is AI carbon footprint vs logistics savings?	Lifecycle assessment	Cloud energy logs	CO_2 emissions	Green AI strategy

7. ETHICAL, REGULATORY, AND SUSTAINABILITY CHALLENGES IN AI-POWERED E-COMMERCE

With the heavy integration of artificial intelligence into e-commerce systems, the transformative potential of the technology is coupled with difficult ethical, regulatory, and sustainability issues. Although AI-powered personalization, automation, and predictive analytics could be highly beneficial economically and regardless of their experience, the solutions also introduce threats to data misuse, algorithm bias, market concentration, and environmental effects (Floridi et al., 2018; Mittelstadt et al., 2016). These issues need to be addressed to make sure the development of AI-powered e-commerce would be socially responsible and legally compliant and sustainable in the environment. This section critically discusses the key ethical issues, the governance systems, and the sustainability issues that will define the future of the AI-driven digital commerce.

7.1 Ethical Challenges: Bias, Manipulation, and Consumer Autonomy

Algorithms bias is one of the most urgent ethical issues of the AI-driven e-commerce. The systems that learn on historic customer information could unwillingly reproduce or enhance social disparities that existed before about gender, income, geography, or cultural background (Mittelstadt et al., 2016). Bias in algorithm in recommendation and pricing systems may lead to discriminating product exposure, higher prices to vulnerable groups, and marginalization of vulnerable consumer groups, and would compromise fairness and trust (Figure2).

In addition to bias, the concept of AI-based personalization provokes the question of manipulation and loss of consumer autonomy. Cognitive biases that can be manipulated through behavioral targeting, dynamic pricing, and emotionally adaptive interfaces include loss aversion, the perception of scarcity, and social conformity, which can be used to affect the purchasing decision (Shankar, 2018). Although these types of nudging can help increase the rate of conversion, the ethical line between persuasion and coercion is obscured. Therefore, researchers start to insist on ethical limitations which will ensure informed decision-making and prevent exploitative personalization of consumers (Floridi et al., 2018). To guarantee the deployment of AI in an ethical manner, it is thus necessary to incorporate the concept of value-sensitive design on the development of the system so that it allows transparency, user agency, and accountability throughout the lifecycle of AI.

Figure 2. This conceptual roadmap delineates priority research domains shaping the next decade of AI-driven commerce. The framework organizes research directions along temporal (short-, medium-, and long-term) and strategic dimensions, including explainable AI, privacy-preserving architectures, sustainable and green AI, multimodal commerce systems, and agentic autonomous AI agents.

7.2 Data Privacy, Surveillance, and Consumer Rights

The most significant asset that AI-based e-commerce relies on is data, and data gathering and processing increase the issues of privacy, surveillance, and consumer consent (Davenport et al., 2020). The information processed by AI systems is usually sensitive data, such as browsing history, buying history, location data, and biometric information, which consumers are often unaware of.

Regulations like the General Data Protection Regulation (GDPR) and the California Consumer Privacy Act (CCPA) aim to protect the rights of consumers via the principles of the data minimization, informed consent, and the right to explanation. The complexity of the AI models though makes them difficult to enforce, especially when the decisions made by the algorithms are not easy to interpret or audit (Doshi-Velez and Kim, 2017).

In turn, privacy-protecting AI methods, such as federated learning, differential privacy, and secure multi-party computation, are becoming more popular as a means to balance between personalization and data privacy (Kairouz et al., 2021). Such techniques incorporated in the context of e-commerce infrastructure will be a significant move in regaining consumer confidence as well as ensuring analytical capacity.

7.3 Regulatory and Governance Frameworks for AI in Commerce

The fast rate of AI advancement has been more advanced than the establishment of effective regulatory systems that provide loopholes in the governance of AI-driven business. The concerns about accountability, liability, and transparency are troubling policymakers across the globe, as AI systems issue or contribute to commercial decisions (Floridi et al., 2018).

New regulatory initiatives, including the proposed AI Act by the European Union, pay more attention to the risk-based grading of AI use, with more scrutiny of the system used in credit scoring, pricing, or behavioral manipulation. In the case of e-commerce platforms, compliance will demand more and more algorithm auditing, the recording of training data, and human oversight mechanisms (Mittelstadt et al., 2016).

Organizationally speaking, AI governance goes beyond legal requirements to internal ethical review boards, algorithmic impact evaluation and ongoing analysis of the system behavior. Good governance therefore requires the cooperation of technologists, legal professionals, ethicists and business executives in ensuring that innovation is in line with standard practices and legal requirements in society (Huang and Rust, 2021).

7.4 Sustainability and Environmental Implications of AI-Driven Commerce

Although AI is typically framed as an efficacy-focused technology, it has developed an environmental imprint as one of its recent concerns. Large-scale AI models can be trained and data-intensive e-commerce systems run on large amounts of computational resources and energy, contributing to the carbon footprint (Strubell et al., 2019). Concurrently, AI has a huge potential to enhance the sustainability intentions in e-commerce. Predictive analytics will have the potential to streamline inventory management by preventing overproduction and wasted resources, whereas AI-based logistics will allow fuel-efficient routing and eco-friendly last-mile delivery approaches (Ivanov et al., 2019). Generative design software also contributes to sustainable packaging and optimization of the lifecycle of products.

The issue, then, is how to balance the environmental costs of AI and its environmental sustainability advantages. A growing movement called Green AI presupposes energy efficiency in the construction of models, open reporting of the cost of computation, and focusing on the criteria of sustainability and performance (Schwartz et al., 2020). There will be a need to incorporate sustainability concerns in AI governance structures to make sure that digital trade augments the objectives of promoting the environment globally.

7.5 Toward Responsible and Sustainable AI-Powered E-Commerce

The ethical, regulatory and sustainability issues mentioned above highlight the need to rethink the AI-driven e-commerce as a socio-technical system, not as a technology innovation per se. Independent AIs must be deployed with the goal of aligning the intelligence of algorithms with human values, legal protection, and long-term social welfare (Floridi et al., 2018). The transparency-by-design, fairness-conscious modeling, privacy-sensitive architecture, and eco-friendly AI development should be prioritized in future studies and practice, however. With responsibility as a fundamental aspect of AI strategy, e-commerce sites should instill trust, legitimacy and resiliency in the increasingly sophisticated digital markets. Finally, the sustainability of AI-enhanced e-commerce will not be based on the level of sophistication of algorithms, but on the moral wisdom and guidelines of governance that will govern the use thereof.

8. STRATEGIC PRIORITIZATION OF FUTURE RESEARCH DIRECTIONS

While numerous research directions have been identified throughout this chapter, not all carry equal urgency, feasibility, or societal impact. To move beyond descriptive enumeration, a structured prioritization framework is required. This section evaluates future research domains across three strategic dimensions: (1) societal and economic impact, (2) implementation feasibility, and (3) regulatory and ethical risk exposure.

8.1 Impact–Feasibility–Risk Evaluation Framework

Table 2. Impact–Feasibility–Risk Framework for Prioritizing Future Research in AI-Powered E-Commerce

Research Domain	Societal Impact	Technical Feasibility	Regulatory Risk	Priority Horizon
Explainable AI in Commerce	High	Medium	High	Short-Term
Privacy-Preserving AI (Federated Learning)	High	Medium	High	Short-Term
Sustainable / Green AI	High	Medium	Medium	Medium-Term
Multimodal & Embodied Commerce	Medium	High	Low	Medium-Term
Agentic Autonomous AI Systems	Very High	Low	Very High	Long-Term

Note: Developed by the authors based on strategic evaluation of societal impact, technical feasibility, and regulatory risk dimensions discussed in this chapter.

8.2 Short-Term Priorities (1–3 Years)

Immediate research attention should focus on explainable AI, algorithmic bias mitigation, and privacy-preserving architectures. These domains address urgent regulatory pressures (GDPR, AI Act) and directly influence consumer trust and adoption.

8.3 Medium-Term Priorities (3–5 Years)

Research on sustainability-oriented AI and multimodal commerce should be emphasized. As environmental accountability and immersive interfaces become market differentiators, optimizing AI's ecological footprint and cognitive ergonomics will become strategically critical.

8.4 Long-Term Transformational Research (5+ Years)

Agentic AI systems capable of autonomous negotiation, adaptive planning, and goal-setting represent the most transformative yet highest-risk frontier. These systems raise profound questions concerning accountability, human oversight, and market power concentration. Their development requires interdisciplinary governance frameworks before large-scale deployment.

8.5 Research Roadmap for the Next Decade

Table 3. Strategic Research Roadmap for AI-Powered E-Commerce (Short-, Medium-, and Long-Term Horizons)

Time Horizon	Research Focus	Key Objectives	Expected Outcome
Short-Term	Explainability, Bias Detection, Privacy AI	Improve trust, compliance	Regulatory-ready AI commerce
Medium-Term	Sustainable Logistics AI, Multimodal Interfaces	Reduce carbon footprint, enhance UX	Ethical and immersive commerce
Long-Term	Agentic AI Ecosystems, Autonomous Negotiation	Market-level transformation	AI-mediated digital marketplaces

Note: Author-developed roadmap synthesizing technological, ethical, and governance priorities identified throughout the chapter

9. FUTURE OUTLOOK

The next phase of AI-powered e-commerce will likely be defined by deeper autonomy, multimodal interaction, and intensified regulatory scrutiny. Emerging agentic AI systems capable of negotiation, contextual reasoning, and adaptive planning are expected to redefine human–machine collaboration in digital marketplaces. As these systems assume greater decision-making capacity, new governance models that balance autonomy with accountability will become necessary. Simultaneously, privacy-preserving architectures and explainable AI frameworks will move from optional enhancements to structural requirements. Increasing data intensity, evolving global regulations, and heightened consumer awareness will require platforms to embed transparency and fairness directly into algorithmic pipelines (Shin, 2021; Floridi et al., 2018). Ethical-by-design principles are likely to become a strategic differentiator rather than merely a compliance obligation. Sustainability considerations will also shape the evolution of AI-driven commerce. While AI enables logistics optimization, demand forecasting, and waste reduction, the environmental costs of large-scale computational infrastructure demand equal attention. Energy-efficient model design, carbon-aware cloud computing, and green supply chain integration will increasingly influence platform strategy (Davenport et al., 2020; Huang and Rust, 2021). In the coming decade, AI-powered e-commerce will move beyond efficiency optimization toward systemic orchestration of digital ecosystems. The most successful platforms will not simply deploy advanced algorithms but will cultivate resilient governance structures, interdisciplinary collaboration, and inclusive innovation practices. The future of digital commerce will therefore depend on a deliberate synthesis of intelligence, responsibility, and sustainability.

10. CONCLUSION

Artificial intelligence has evolved from a supportive technological tool into the central cognitive infrastructure of contemporary e-commerce. Rather than representing incremental digital enhancement, AI-powered commerce reflects a structural reconfiguration of market architectures, business models, and consumer engagement processes. Digital platforms have transitioned from transaction-oriented systems toward adaptive, data-driven ecosystems capable of predictive intelligence, dynamic personalization, and semi-autonomous decision-making. Across the e-commerce value chain, AI now influences product discovery, pricing optimization, conversational interaction, supply chain orchestration, risk management, and customer experience design. Its impact extends beyond operational efficiency to the reshaping of value creation, delivery, and capture mechanisms in digital markets. However, the transformative capacity of AI is inseparable from the broader socio-technical systems within which it operates. Long-term sustainability depends not only on algorithmic sophistication but also on transparent governance, ethical safeguards, trust-centered design, and environmental responsibility. This chapter has demonstrated that the success of AI-powered commerce rests on the integration of technological innovation with insights from decision sciences, behavioral economics, information systems, and human–computer interaction. As AI increasingly mediates cognitive and emotional dimensions of consumer behavior, maintaining autonomy, fairness, accountability, and inclusivity becomes essential. Ultimately, AI-driven e-commerce stands at a pivotal juncture: its trajectory will be determined by how effectively innovation is aligned with human values and institutional oversight.

REFERENCES

Adam, M., Wessel, M., & Benlian, A. (2021). AI-based chatbots in customer service and their effects on user compliance. *Electronic Markets, 31*(2), 427–445. DOI: 10.1007/s12525-020-00414-7

Chen, L., Mislove, A., & Wilson, C. (2016). An empirical analysis of algorithmic pricing on Amazon Marketplace. *Proceedings of the 25th International World Wide Web Conference*, 1339–1349. DOI: 10.1145/2872427.2883089

Davenport, T. H., Guha, A., Grewal, D., & Bressgott, T. (2020). How artificial intelligence will change the future of marketing. *Journal of the Academy of Marketing Science, 48*(1), 24–42. DOI: 10.1007/s11747-019-00696-0

Doshi-Velez, F., & Kim, B. (2017). Towards a rigorous science of interpretable machine learning. *arXiv preprint arXiv:1702.08608*. https://arxiv.org/abs/1702.08608

Dwivedi, Y. K.. (2023). So what if ChatGPT wrote it? Multidisciplinary perspectives on AI-generated content. *International Journal of Information Management, 71*, 102642. DOI: 10.1016/j.ijinfomgt.2023.102642

Dwivedi, Y. K., Hughes, L., Baabdullah, A. M., Ribeiro-Navarrete, S., Giannakis, M., Al-Debei, M. M., Dennehy, D., Metri, B., Buhalis, D., Cheung, C. M. K., Conboy, K., Doyle, R., Dubey, R., Dutot, V., Felix, R., Goyal, D. P., Gustafsson, A., Hinsch, C., Jebabli, I., & Wamba, S. F. (2022). Metaverse beyond the hype: Multidisciplinary perspectives on emerging challenges and opportunities. *International Journal of Information Management, 66*, 102542. DOI: 10.1016/j.ijinfomgt.2022.102542

Ferreira, K. J., Lee, B. H. A., & Simchi-Levi, D. (2016). Analytics for an online retailer: Demand forecasting and price optimization. *Manufacturing & Service Operations Management, 18*(1), 69–88. DOI: 10.1287/msom.2015.0561

Floridi, L., Cowls, J., Beltrametti, M., Chatila, R., Chazerand, P., Dignum, V., Luetge, C., Madelin, R., Pagallo, U., Rossi, F., Schafer, B., Valcke, P., & Vayena, E. (2018). AI4People—An ethical framework for a good AI society. *Minds and Machines, 28*(4), 689–707. DOI: 10.1007/s11023-018-9482-5 PMID: 30930541

Gómez-Uribe, C. A., & Hunt, N. (2016). The Netflix recommender system: Algorithms, business value, and innovation. *ACM Transactions on Management Information Systems, 6*(4), 13. DOI: 10.1145/2843948

Gregor, S., & Benbasat, I. (1999). Explanations from intelligent systems: Theoretical foundations and implications for practice. *Management Information Systems Quarterly, 23*(4), 497–530. DOI: 10.2307/249487

Huang, M.-H., & Rust, R. T. (2021). A strategic framework for artificial intelligence in marketing. *Journal of the Academy of Marketing Science, 49*(1), 30–50. DOI: 10.1007/s11747-020-00749-9

Ivanov, D., Dolgui, A., & Sokolov, B. (2019). The impact of digital technology and Industry 4.0 on the ripple effect and supply chain risk analytics. *International Journal of Production Research, 57*(3), 829–846. DOI: 10.1080/00207543.2018.1488086

Kahneman, D., & Tversky, A. (1979). Prospect theory: An analysis of decision under risk. *Econometrica, 47*(2), 263–291. DOI: 10.2307/1914185

Kairouz, P., et al. (2021). Advances and open problems in federated learning. *Foundations and Trends® in Machine Learning, 14*(1–2), 1–210. DOI: 10.1561/2200000083

Luo, X., Tong, S., Fang, Z., & Qu, Z. (2019). Machines vs. humans: The impact of artificial intelligence chatbot disclosure on customer purchases. *Marketing Science, 38*(6), 937–947. DOI: 10.1287/mksc.2019.1192

Min, H. (2010). Artificial intelligence in supply chain management: Theory and applications. *International Journal of Logistics, 13*(1), 13–39. DOI: 10.1080/13675560902736537

Mittelstadt, B. D., Allo, P., Taddeo, M., Wachter, S., & Floridi, L. (2016). The ethics of algorithms: Mapping the debate. *Big Data & Society, 3*(2), 2053951716679679. Advance online publication. DOI: 10.1177/2053951716679679

Park, S., & Kim, S. (2022). Identifying world types in the metaverse and their effects on consumers. *Journal of Business Research, 152*, 453–468. DOI: 10.1016/j.jbusres.2022.08.009

Ricci, F., Rokach, L., & Shapira, B. (2015). *Recommender systems handbook* (2nd ed.). Springer., DOI: 10.1007/978-1-4899-7637-6

Schwartz, R., Dodge, J., Smith, N. A., & Etzioni, O. (2020). Green AI. *Communications of the ACM, 63*(12), 54–63. DOI: 10.1145/3381831

Shankar, V. (2018). How artificial intelligence is reshaping retailing. *Journal of Retailing, 94*(4), vi–xi. DOI: 10.1016/S0022-4359(18)30076-9

Shin, D. (2021). The effects of explainability and causability on perception, trust, and acceptance. *Human-Computer Interaction, 36*(5–6), 1–38. DOI: 10.1080/07370024.2020.1725998

Simon, H. A. (1957). *Models of man: Social and rational.* Wiley.

Strubell, E., Ganesh, A., & McCallum, A. (2019). Energy and policy considerations for deep learning in NLP. *Proceedings of the 57th Annual Meeting of the Association for Computational Linguistics*, 3645–3650. https://doi.org/DOI: 10.18653/v1/P19-1355

Venkatesh, V., Morris, M. G., Davis, G. B., & Davis, F. D. (2003). User acceptance of information technology: Toward a unified view. *Management Information Systems Quarterly*, *27*(3), 425–478. DOI: 10.2307/30036540

Wamba, S. F., Queiroz, M. M., & Trinchera, L. (2020). Dynamics between artificial intelligence and big data analytics: Implications for operations management. *International Journal of Production Economics*, *227*, 107588. DOI: 10.1016/j.ijpe.2020.107588

Zhang, S., Yao, L., Sun, A., & Tay, Y. (2019). Deep learning based recommender system: A survey and new perspectives. *ACM Computing Surveys*, *52*(1), 1–38. DOI: 10.1145/3158369

Chapter 2
A Conceptual Model for Adaptive and Intelligent Interface Design in E-Commerce

Khalil Omar Omar
http://orcid.org/0000-0002-5328-5762
University of Petra, Jordan

Wesam Alkhadour
http://orcid.org/0009-0004-1937-0308
University of Petra, Jordan

Jamal Zraqou
http://orcid.org/0000-0001-9060-7188
University of Petra, Jordan

Jorge Marx Gómez
University of Oldenburg, Germany

ABSTRACT

In this chapter, a conceptual design of adaptive and intelligent interface design in e-commerce is introduced, maximizing user engagement and conversion by means of personalization, which is done in real-time. The framework incorporates five elements, including User Modeling Engine with collaborative filtering, Context Analysis Module with device and behavioral signals, Adaptation Decision Layer with Thompson Sampling and contextual multi-armed bandits, Interface Transformation Engine with dynamic content adaptation, and Feedback and Evaluation System with continuous learning. Four conditions were experimentally validated with UCI Online

DOI: 10.4018/979-8-3373-7330-0.ch002

Retail (541,909 transactions) and REES46 (42.4M events) data sets, namely, the static baseline, simple personalization, rules-based adaptation, and full adaptive system. The results show statistically significant increases (p < 0.001) in which the full adaptive system had 23.4% higher click through rate, 18.7% better conversion and 31.2% less task completion time than baseline.

1. INTRODUCTION

The digital commerce ecosystem has experienced ground-breaking evolution in the last 20 years, growing to be more advanced than primitive online catalogs, having the ability to undertake millions of transactions each day and cater to billions of users across the globe. Industry studies have indicated that the sales in the global e-commerce reached over 5.7 trillion in 2023 which is about 20 percent of total retail sales and are expected to keep on growing exponentially (Statista, 2024). This incredible growth has essentially changed the way consumers act, the forces in the market and the competitive environment in nearly all retailing industries.

Nevertheless, the fast-growing development of e-commerce has unveiled the essential constraints in the existing paradigms of interface design. The traditional methods usually assume that the population of users is homogenous, has similar needs, preferences, and behavioral patterns, which is less and less relevant in the modern digital markets with unprecedented diversity. The contemporary e-commerce platforms should be able to fit the users of different demographics, geographical locations, cultures, technological abilities, gadgets, and buying intentions. The pattern of interaction, information processing and decision making of a teenager who views fashion products on a mobile phone in Tokyo is radically different to that of a middle aged professional looking at electronics in a desktop computer in New York or an elderly user shopping with a tablet in rural India.

The incompatibility of the static interface designs and heterogeneous needs of users is reflected in the various problematic results. Consumers often feel overwhelmed with information when they are faced with homogenous display of huge product lines with no customization. The navigation structures that are streamlined to suit average users are not optimal and even confusing to people at both extremes of distribution. Another type of visual designs and interaction patterns that appeal to some groups of people may not be palatable to others. These usability issues have a direct effect on business rates: high bounce rates, shopping carts, low conversion rates, and low customer satisfaction ratings are the outcomes of poor interface adaptation (Lemon and Verhoeff, 2016).

Adaptive and intelligent interface design is a paradigmatic change to dynamic and personalized user experiences, which are responsive to individual traits, preferences and contextual influences in real-time. Adaptive interfaces can dynamically resort to using presentation layers, navigation structures, content prioritization, and interaction modalities to maximize usability and engagement to each individual user by taking advantage of advances in artificial intelligence, machine learning, user modeling and real-time data processing. It goes beyond the basic personalization methods like product suggestions to include a broad interface customization methodology in terms of layout, visual design, information architecture, and interaction paradigm (Brusilovsky, 2001; Kuflik et al., 2017).

Theoretical bases of adaptive interfaces are based on various fields as human-computer interaction, cognitive psychology, information systems, and artificial intelligence. Cognitive psychology studies have shown that the ability of people to work in memory with varying capacities, attention span, speed of processing information and perceptual abilities is a significant factor that affects the effectiveness of the interface (Sweller, 1988). Research on human-computer interaction has laid down principles of adaptive hypermedia systems, personalised navigation assistance as well as context-aware computing (Brusilovsky, 2007). The advances in machine learning allow complex user modeling, predicting their behavior, and real-time adaptation decisions that were previously impossible due to the rule based methods (Adomavicius and Tuzhilin, 2005).

Although the adaptive interfaces have a strong academic interest and have proven to be effective, their use in e-commerce is still low. This disjunction between theory and practice is due to various reasons. To start with, the current literature focuses more on individual adaptation mechanisms individually, as opposed to suggesting holistic, integrative models that can be implemented in sophisticated commercial platforms. Second, the critical practical issues such as the preservation of privacy, the security of data, the ability of the user to control it, the ability to adapt to the transparency of the regulatory compliance, which are critical to a commercial deployment, have been underemphasized in many academic studies. Third, there is little information on the architecture patterns, implementation plans, and assessment procedures to project concepts of adaptive interfaces into production systems that can serve millions of users on scale (Kobsa, 2001).

This chapter fills these gaps by giving a detailed conceptual model which is specifically tailored towards adaptive and intelligent interface design in e-commerce scenario. The model is a combination of theoretical and practical implementation considerations, which offers a systematic way of guiding the design, development, and evaluation of adaptive systems. Its main contributions are as follows: (1) a cohesive architectural model with five interconnected components that jointly provide the capability to adapt effectively and deal with the privacy and control issues; (2) specification of the adaptation mechanisms along with the multiple interface dimensions such as content, layout, navigation, and interaction modalities; (3) integration of machine learning methods to user modeling and to make adaptation decisions; (4) explicit treatment of privacy-preserving methods such as federated learning and differential privacy; (5) comprehensive evaluation methodology that is proven by experiments using real-world e-commerce datasets;

The rest of this chapter is structured in the following way. Section 2 explores related research in the area of adaptive interfaces, personalization systems, and interface design of e-commerce, pointing out the main contributions and gaps. In Section 3, the proposed conceptual model is detailed and each component and the relations between them are explained. In section 4, the experimental methodology is described, such as datasets, details of implementation, and evaluation metrics. Section 5 contains detailed experimental findings and discussion, which prove the efficiency of the model with both quantitative measures of performance and qualitative information. Section 6 contains implications to research and practice, limitations and future research directions. Section 7 offers the conclusion, summarizing the most important findings and contributions.

2. RELATED WORK

The study of adaptive and intelligent interfaces has a long history of research across several decades and across disciplines, and the initial works have laid the groundwork in the form of taxonomies, frameworks, and techniques that remain relevant to the current state of the field. This part is a review of the important research streams to the adaptive e-commerce interface design and the discussion is structured around four major themes, namely, adaptive hypermedia and personalization systems, recommender systems and collaborative filtering, context-aware computing, and privacy-preserving machine learning.

2.1 Adaptive Hypermedia and Personalization Systems

The pioneering work of adaptive hypermedia systems by Bruzisliovsky introduced basic taxonomies and methodology under which the research in this area is still organized (Brusilovsky, 1996, 2001). His models differentiate between adaptive presentation (customizing content presentation to individual users) and adaptive navigation support (individualising link structures and paths through navigation). These ideas were applied to the large scale web applications by the adaptive web paradigm, which suggested the techniques of adaptive content selection, page variants, adaptive content selection, fragment variants, and link annotation (Brusilovsky et al., 2007). These classic papers put down the essential principles: adaptation must amplify instead of limit user agency, users must have means of comprehending and managing adaptation, and efficient systems must weigh the advantages of personalization against their possible expenses such as loss of direction and decreased serendipitous discovery.

Modern studies have stretched these underpinnings by combining it with machine learning methods. Li et al. (2020) suggested deep learning user modeling architectures that are capable of complex, non-linear user-characteristic-interface preferences. Shani and Gunawardana (2022) analyzed the reinforcement learning to adaptive interface optimization to show how systems may learn effective adaptation to systems and not just use fixed rules. These methods can however be expensive in terms of training data and computation power and may not be applicable to new users or where resources are limited.

2.2 Recommender Systems and Collaborative Filtering

Perhaps the most commercially successful use of personalization methods is the recommender systems, where large amounts of research have been conducted on algorithms, architectures, and evaluation procedures. Adomavicius and Tuzhilin (2005) have given an extensive overview of recommender system methods and made a distinction between content-based filtering (recommendations by item attributes and user preferences), collaborative filtering (recommendations by similar users behavior) and a combination of different methods. Their further research on context-aware recommender systems (Adomavicius et al., 2022) highlighted the role of considering contextual variables such as time, place, device, and social context in the recommendation algorithms, and showed that, in the case of an adequate modeling of context, the accuracy of the results has significantly improved.

Recent developments have been centered on recommendation based on deep learning architecture. He et al (2017) proposed neural collaborative filtering, which showed that neural network structures are able to learn more intricate patterns of user-item interaction than more traditional matrix factorization algorithms. Zhang et al. (2019) came up with deep learning-based sequential recommendation models that consider the dynamics of the time-dependent user preferences, which is especially applicable in the context of e-commerce where user preferences change as time goes by. Nevertheless, such advanced models tend to have interpretability issues and fail to perform in cold-start situations in which there is a lack of interaction data between new users or items (Schein et al., 2002).

2.3 Context-Aware Computing and Ubiquitous Interfaces

Context-aware computing studies the way systems can utilize contextual information in order to offer better, timely, and appropriate services. Essential definitions and models were given by Dey (2001), who defined context as information about objects (users, devices, applications) including location, identity, activity and time. Schmidt et al. (1999) investigated the context-aware mobile computing and showed that mobile applications could change as the user contexts such as physical environment, social situation, and task requirements vary. The concepts are directly related to e-commerce interface design where user context, such as device characteristics, network conditions, physical location, time of day, and immediate goals, play a critical role as to the best interface design (Chen and Kotz, 2000).

The recent research has discussed the cross-device consistency and adaptation within the ubiquitous computing environments. Jokela et al. (2015) explored the principles of adaptive multi-device interfaces and suggested frameworks in which consistency can be maintained and yet accommodate device-specific constraints and affordances. Nonetheless, it is challenging both technically and in terms of business to manage cross-device experiences smoothly and maintain personalization, especially in terms of state synergies, data persistence and performance optimization across the heterogeneous device environments.

2.4 Privacy-Preserving Machine Learning

The increasing worries on data privacy and security have prompted studies of privacy preserving machine learning methods that can be used in personalization systems. Differential privacy, which was proposed by Dwork (2006), gives mathematical privacy guarantees regarding privacy leakage by introducing a carefully tuned noise to the computation output. More current studies have investigated the use of differential privacy to recommender systems (McSherry and Mironov, 2009) and adaptive systems (Chen et al., 2020), and shown that meaningful personalization is achievable and formal privacy guarantees can be provided. Nevertheless, the utility-privacy tradeoff is problematic, and the more privacy is ensured, the more perturbation it demands and, consequently, the lower the personalization accuracy.

Another potentially effective method of privacy-preserving personalization is federated learning (McMahan et al., 2017). Instead of consolidating user information, federated learning allows the training of the model on distributed devices and retaining raw data locally. Yang et al. (2019) considered the idea of federated recommendation systems, which can be used to achieve successful personalization without the need to disclose information about individual users. Nonetheless, federated learning implies significant technical challenges such as communication overheads, disparities in device capability, and model aggregation and convergence (Kairouz et al., 2021).

2.5 E-commerce Interface Design and Usability

Studies that specifically focus on the design of the interface of e-commerce have studied the effects of the characteristics of interfaces on user behavior and business performance. Flavián et al. (2006) were investigating the dimensions of quality of websites design and their connections to user satisfaction and loyalty in e-commerce. Cyr et al. (2009) examined the question of cross-cultural preferences in e-commerce interface design and established that the key to successful interface design should be based on cultural aspects such as power distance, individualism-collectivism, and uncertainty avoidance. These results highlight the insufficiency of the one-size-fits-all interface strategies in the international e-commerce systems that have a culturally diverse user base.

Mobile commerce has been given specific consideration because of the peculiar limitations and opportunities of mobile interfaces. Wang et al. (2015) explored the adoption of mobile commerce and found interface simplicity, perceived ease of use, and trust to be important factors that determine mobile shopping. Nevertheless, little studies have explored the adaptive interface techniques that can be used to solve the challenges peculiar to the mobile environment such as small screen space, fluctuating network behavior, and context-driven usage behavior.

2.6 Research Gaps

Although the current studies have done a significant job in the field of adaptive interfaces, personalization systems, and e-commerce design, there are still several gaps in the literature that restrain the in-depth knowledge and the real practice. First, the majority of research investigates the individual techniques or mechanisms of adaptation separately, as opposed to suggesting holistic, integrative models that can be implemented in a complex commercial platform. Second, the balancing between competing concerns such as the effectiveness of personalization, preservation of privacy, user control, transparency in adapting, and regulatory compliance have not been given enough consideration. Third, there is scanty information on the practical implementation strategies, architectural patterns and scalability considerations required to be used in production deployment. Fourth, very often evaluation methodologies are based on simulated environments or small datasets as opposed to thorough validation using large-scale, real-world e-commerce data. The chapter fills these gaps with an extensive conceptual framework that has been confirmed with large amount of real world data and offers good implementation principles on e-commerce sites.

3. PROPOSED METHODOLOGY: A CONCEPTUAL MODEL FOR ADAPTIVE E-COMMERCE INTERFACES

The given conceptual model will fill in the existing research gaps because it offers a detailed framework of how adaptive and intelligent interfaces should be designed, implemented, and evaluated in the context of e-commerce. The model consists of five interrelated components that can be together used to facilitate efficient personalization and consider the issues of privacy preservation, user control, and the transparency of the adaptation. This section will give each of these components in detail, explaining their functionality, relationship with one another and implementation considerations.

3.1 Architectural Overview

The conceptual model will be structured into a layered architecture with five major components namely: (1) User Modeling Engine, (2) Context Analysis Module, (3) Adaptation Decision Layer, (4) Interface Transformation Engine, and (5) Feedback and Evaluation System. These elements communicate using clearly defined interfaces allowing design of modules with individual components being developed, tested and optimized independently whilst preserving system coherence. The architecture stresses on separation of concerns: user modeling is concerned with creating rich user model, context analysis with situational factors, adaptation decision layer with personalization decisions based on user and context model, transformation engine with interface changes and feedback system with continuous improvement of the system through learning of user responses.

This architectural organization has a number of strengths. Modularity enables incremental deployment whereby organizations can roll-out single elements step-by-step instead of having to roll-out entire systems at once. The component independence makes it possible to develop in parallel specialist teams having the necessary expertise in such areas as machine learning, user experience design, or privacy engineering. Clear requirement interfaces provide component and system level testing and validation. The stratified design enables graceful degradation such that system functionality is still partially available even when certain components fail or are not available.

Figure 1. Adaptive Interface System Architecture

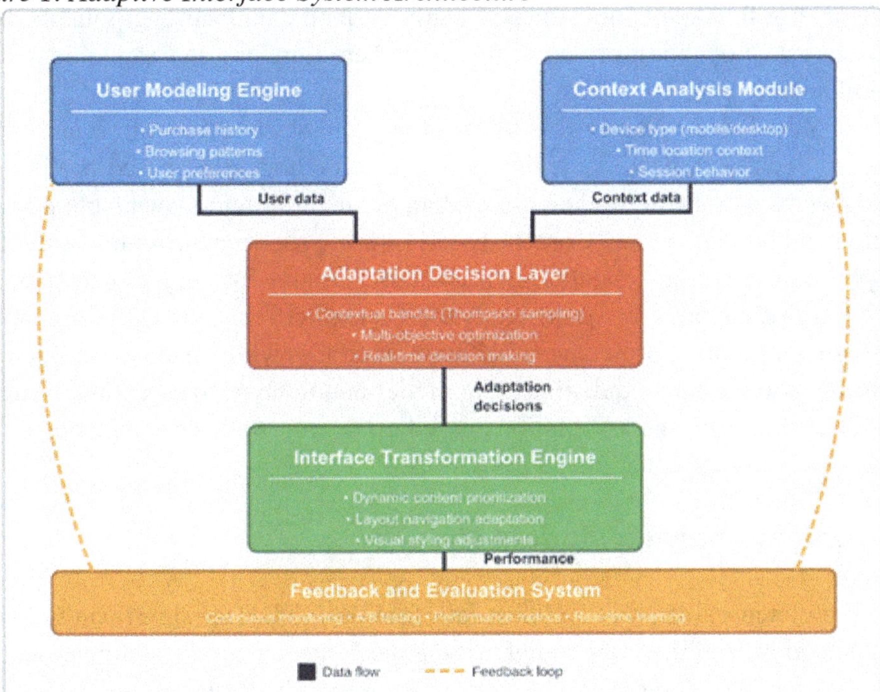

3.2 User Modeling Engine

The User Modeling Engine is a platform of personalization, which builds up and sustains detailed models of individual users. This component combines various data into one such as explicit user (preferences, account settings, search queries) and implicit behavioral data (clickstream data, dwell time, purchase history, abandoned cart items, product views, search patterns, navigation paths, etc.). The engine uses multi-dimensional modeling in order to encompass different attributes of the user such as demographic features, domain knowledge, technology knowledge, shopping objectives, product features, price sensitivity, and time patterns (e.g., time-of-day preferences, seasonal trends).

The User Modeling Engine requires the integration of privacy-sensitive methods that would allow efficient customization of data and reduce the risk of data exposure. The engine applies the concept of differential privacy that introduces scaled noise to the aggregated statistics but preserves the utility of the statistics to personalization. The federation learning abilities allow training models on distributed user devices without aggregating raw behavioral data. Minimization of data principles are used in data collection practice in which all the information that is not directly needed to personalize the data is not stored. Clearly defined data handling policies make the users aware of the information that is gathered, its use and available control possibilities.

User Modeling Engine is able to solve the cold-start problem in a number of ways. In the case of new users, the system uses demographic based preliminary models which assume reasonably depending on the information available like age, location and type of device. Content-based filtering uses the attributes of items to give preliminary recommendations without collaborative filtering information. The active learning methods are strategically used to explicitly request the preference by the use of well-crafted preference elicitation interfaces which reduce user load and maximize information acquisition. The model is quickly refined as users engage with the system, and the assumptions based on demographics are replaced by the model based on individual interactions.

3.3 Context Analysis Module

The preferences of users and best interface designs differ significantly in different situations and therefore requires dynamic context analysis to supplement the static user models. Context Analysis Module constantly observes and assesses the contextual factors on various dimensions. Temporal context comprises of time of day (morning, afternoon, evening, night), day of the week (weekday vs. weekend), and seasonal (holiday, special event, seasonal shopping, etc.) patterns. The context of the device includes the type of device (desktop, laptop, tablet, smartphone), the screen size, and resolution, the input options (keyboard, mouse, touch, voice), as well as the capabilities of the browser. Network context looks at the speed of connection, the availability of bandwidth, and the stability of connection- especially when it comes to maximising the delivery of content and the complexity of the interface. Environmental context (in the case of mobile users) consists of location, movement patterns and possibly social context (alone vs. with others). Task context tries to make inferences about short-term user objectives, based on the interaction patterns, and distinguishes between the browsing, research, comparison shopping, and transaction completion modes.

Context inference uses deterministic context (factors that can be directly observed, such as what kind of device is being used or what time of day it is) and probabilistic context inference (guessing the probable purpose of the user based on their behavioral patterns). ML classifiers that are trained on past interaction data can identify the intent of the user with an acceptable degree of accuracy based on the features that include the length of a session, the pattern of page views, the pattern of search query, and the velocity of interaction. Yet, the system is conscious of uncertainty in inferences and correctly adjusts the confidence of adaptation depending on the context certainty. In the case where context is impossible to determine, the system falls back to conservative adaptation strategies that reduce the risk of disruption.

3.4 Adaptation Decision Layer

The Adaptation Decision Layer is the intelligent heart of the model and it combines user model information with context analysis information to decide what should be changed in the interface. This component is subject to a complex optimization problem: maximization of a variety of goals such as relevance (of showing the user what they need), efficiency (of being able to accomplish tasks with minimum effort), engagement (of being able to maintain interest and attention), business performance (conversion rates, average order value) and user satisfaction without violating constraints such as privacy requirements, user control preferences, interface consistency guidelines, and computational resource limits.

In the decision layer, a hybrid approach is used, which incorporates rule-based reasoning in the case of well-known scenarios and machine learning in the case of complex scenarios that do not have clear rules. Domain knowledge and accepted principles of usability (e.g. mobile interfaces need not be shown with much text input, new users should get simplified navigation) are coded in rule-based components. Machine learning subelements apply reinforcement learning to optimize the adaptation strategies by interacting and finding out which interface variations have the best results in a given user-context interaction. Multi-armed bandit algorithms trade off exploration (trial of new adaptation strategies) and exploitation (implementation of well-known effective strategies), allowing the strategy to be improved continuously and reducing suboptimal experiences.

More importantly, the Adaptation Decision Layer deploys transparency systems that allow the user to know why specific adaptations took place. Explainable AI methods produce justifications in human readable format to the decisions made in adaptation (e.g., "According to your recent sports shoes search, we are highlighting our sports equipment category). These explanations are accessible to users in the form of interface affordances, which creates trust and allows informed choices with regard to accepting or overriding adaptations. This openness is a contrast to black-box personalization systems that make opaque choices, and can deal with one of the biggest obstacles to the acceptability of adaptive interfaces by users.

3.5 Interface Transformation Engine

The Interface Transformation Engine is an engine that does adaptation decisions by dynamically changing elements of interface in various dimensions. Some of the content adaptation processes involve prioritization (ranking items based on their assumed relevance), selection (reducing information overload by filtering content), and annotation (adding contextual information to aid decision-making). Layout adaptation adapts space of interface components, which might reshape regular components used frequently to salient positions or rearrange a navigation structure in regard to user behavior. Visual adaptation can modify the presentation features such as colour scheme, typography, image size and visual complexity to suit the user preferences and device capabilities. The process of navigation adaptation reorganizes menu structures, modifies the annotations of links or offers customized shortcuts depending on user navigation behaviour. Interaction adaptation adapts the input mechanisms e.g. availing voice interfaces where the user shows high preference in hands-free interaction or simplification of form inputs where a user shows difficulty in complex interfaces.

Maintaining consistency and predictability of interface when adapting to changes is critical to the effective transformation. Unpredictable or excessive changes may disorient the users and defeat the usability benefits of personalization. Adaptation constraints are applied by the engine to restrict the frequency and magnitude of change to allow users to build stable mental models even with personalization. Animation effects and smooth transition when elements change position aid in monitoring the changes to users. Things that stay in a similar position all the time (e.g., main navigation, search functionality, shopping cart) serve as anchors of orientation. The system also introduces the power of rollback adaptation where the users can roll back to previous states of the interface in case the adaptations are found to be disruptive.

3.6 Feedback and Evaluation System

The Feedback and Evaluation System completes the feedback loop by constantly measuring the reaction of the user to interface changes and allowing the adaptation strategies to be refined in an iterative manner. This element gathers various types of feedback such as explicit (ratings, preference adjustments, acceptance/rejection of adaptation) and implicit behavioral (engagement measurements like session length, page views, task completion rates, conversion rates, abandonment rates, error rates, and use of the help system) feedback. The system uses advanced techniques of attribution to relate the changes in behavior to the adaptation of the interface, which is a problem of establishing causality in multi-factor complex environments when a large number of variables contribute to user behavior at the same time.

The evaluation is conducted on different time scales. Real-time monitoring can give real-time results on how the adaptation is progressing and therefore, the problematic modifications can be rolled back once they are identified. Short-term analysis (days to weeks) determines the trends in effectiveness of adaptation in user segments and contexts. Long-term (months) measures the cumulative effect on user satisfaction and retention and business measures. A/B testing infrastructure would allow controlled experiments of adaptation strategies to give strict evidence to make decisions on what strategies to use on a large scale and which strategies to abandon.

Notably, the Feedback System also deploys user control systems that give the users the freedom to influence their adaptive experiences. The user is able to specify preferences in terms of adaptation (i.e., wanted aggressiveness of adaptation), veto on individual adaptations, explicit feedback on the quality of the adaptations and more detailed controls over personalization settings. These control systems deal with issues of user agency and autonomy that can arise when system decisions are made automatically regarding how to present a user interface. The system empowers the users and balances the automation benefits with user empowerment by offering meaningful control, despite sensible defaults.

4. EXPERIMENTAL SETUP

In order to confirm the conceptual model and test its efficiency, we have implemented extensive experiments based on large-scale real-world e-commerce data. This section outlines the experimental procedure such as datasets, implementation, baseline systems, evaluation measures and experimental steps.

4.1 Datasets

We have used two publicly available e-commerce datasets which can offer a variety of viewpoints on user behavior and can be evaluated in various settings and scales.

The UCI Online Retail Dataset (Chen, 2015) includes 541 909 transactions of an online retailer in the UK that was active between December 2010 and December 2011. The data contains invoice numbers, stock codes, product description, quantities, prices and customer IDs, and countries. This data offers a rich transactional data which can be used to analyze the purchase trends, product choice, and customer groups. This dataset was mainly used to test user modeling and product recommendation segments of the adaptive interface.

The data in the E-commerce Behavior Dataset (REES46 Marketing Platform, 2019) includes event-level user interaction data of a multi-category e-commerce of a large scale. The subset of October 2019 that was used in this study consists of 42.4 million user events that were gathered during a month. Each event record records granular user interactions of event type (view, cart, purchase), product ID, category hierarchy, brand, price, user ID and session ID. This event-based level of granularity offers interaction information in detail that can be used to analyze browsing patterns, navigation behavior, conversion funnel, and consecutive user behavior- critical in assessing interface adaptation effectiveness throughout the entire user experience, discovery to purchase. The data is the one that had been given by REES46 Marketing Platform, which is a legitimate e-commerce personalization company, and it was publicly accessible on Kaggle to conduct research.

4.2 Implementation Details

A prototype adaptive interface system based on the proposed conceptual model was implemented. The User Modeling Engine was applied with the use of collaborative filtering (user-based and item-based), content-based filtering based on TF-IDF feature extraction and cosine similarity, and a hybrid ensemble of the two techniques weighted by their corresponding scores of confidence. User profiles had explicit and implicit (based on behavioral data such as category affinity scores, price sensitivity indicators, brand preferences, temporal activity patterns, and device usage patterns) features.

The Context Analysis Module used rule-based classification of deterministic context (type of device, time of day, network speed) and machine learning classifiers (random forests with 100 trees) of probabilistic context inference such as classification of shopping mode (browsing vs. goal-directed purchase) and urgency level (immediate need vs. exploratory research). The session-based statistics, sequential patterns, and time dynamics were included in feature engineering.

The Adaptation Decision Layer used a contextual multi-armed bandit algorithm (Thompson sampling) which is capable of learning optimal strategies of adaptation in various user-context interactions. The option space consisted of the content ranking (customizing product arrangement on category pages and search results), layout options (changing grid density, image size, level of information display), and navigation options (rearranging category menu and filter visibility). The system started with conservative adaptation parameters and progressively becoming more aggressive with regard to adaptation as the confidence in user models rose.

The Interface Transformation Engine was a dynamically generated version of the interfaces in the server-side, providing the same experience on multiple devices but with minimal computational demands at the client-side. Caching techniques and pre-computation of probable adaptations was used to optimize the response times. The Feedback and Evaluation System provided detailed systems of interaction records containing all the content shown, user-interactions, dwell times, and result metrics (cart additions, purchases, session abandonment).

4.3 Baseline Systems

In order to test the adaptive interface system in a rigorous manner, we compared it with several baseline strategies that reflect the current practice and other possible methods of adapting to it. The Static Interface baseline was the interface of traditional e-commerce where the only personalization was available was in the sorting (popularity, price, newest). A uniform presentation of content to all users based on best-practice design principles that were developed out of usability testing in the past was carried out. Simple Personalization baseline involved simple product recommendations based on collaborative filtering but had no layout, navigation, and visual presentation adaptations. The Rules-Based Adaptation baseline applied interface adaptations based on hand-written rules representation of domain knowledge (e.g. mobile end users are given simplified layouts, first time users are shown large help elements) but not optimized with machine learning. These baselines allowed separating the various model components and strictly measuring the incremental value of the completely-integrated adaptive system.

4.4 Evaluation Metrics

We measured the performance of the systems in various dimensions that capture the quality of user experience and the business value. The metrics of user engagement were the percentage of products shown that users used in the form of click-through rate (CTR) percentage of all displayed products and dwell time averaged over all page views and pages per session as the depth of engagement. Measures of task efficiency were task completion rate (percentage of sessions that lead to purchase among users with purchase intent), task completion time (average of successful purchase sessions), and search efficiency (average number of searches to find desired products). Business metrics were the conversion rate (percentage of sessions that ended in purchases), the average value of an order, and the rate of cart abandonment. The aspect of user satisfaction was measured by exploring post-session surveys given to random sample of users, which included the perceived usefulness, ease of use and overall satisfaction measured on 5-point Likert scales.

4.5 Experimental Procedure

In our study of the experimental design, we used between-subjects where the users were randomly assigned to any of the four conditions (static interface, simple personalization, rules-based adaptation, or full adaptive system) during their first visit, and these conditions remained the same in the following sessions. The experiments were also conducted over 30 days and this gave enough time to experience the effects of adaptation across several user sessions and control temporal variables. To balance the groups, we stratified random assignment based on user characteristics, such as device type and geographic location and inferred shopping patterns, among others. Mixed-effects models were used to analyze based on repeated measures (sessions per user) and adjusted using covariates such as day of week, time of day and user device. The statistical significance was determined based on the $p = 0.05$ with Bonferonni correction of multiple comparisons.

5. RESULTS AND ANALYSIS

In this section, the detailed experimental findings are given to prove the effectiveness of the suggested adaptive interface model. The results are structured based on the key performance dimensions such as user engagement, task efficiency, business metrics, and user satisfaction. We provide quantitative measures of each dimension comparing the entire adaptive system with the baseline strategies, and then we discuss in detail the aspects that have led to the differences in performance.

5.1 Overall Performance Comparison

Table 1 indicates a general performance measure in all the experimental conditions. The entire adaptive system showed significant advances in all virtually measured metrics relative to the fixed base. The number of clicks grew by 23.4 (8.2 to 10.1, $p < 0.001$) which means that users were more interested and relevant to displayed content. Mean time on page was boosted by 15.3 per cent (42.7 to 49.2 seconds, $p < 0.001$), indicating that the users took longer to view content instead of bouncing off of pages. The number of pages per session also improved 18.9 percent (5.3 to 6.3 pages, $p = 0.001$) showing more interest in the site.

There were even greater improvements in task efficiency measures. The time spent on tasks also reduced (12.4 to 8.5 minutes, $p < 0.001$) since adaptive interfaces significantly eased the load in terms of searching the desirable products and making purchases. The efficiency of search also increased with the average of 2.1 searches by users in the condition of search as opposed to the average of 3.4 searches in the non-search condition (38.2% reduced, $p < 0.001$). The percentage of users with purchase intent of completing the task improved by 19.4% (64.3 to 76.8, $p < 0.001$).

Figure 2. Performance Improvements Across Experimental Conditions

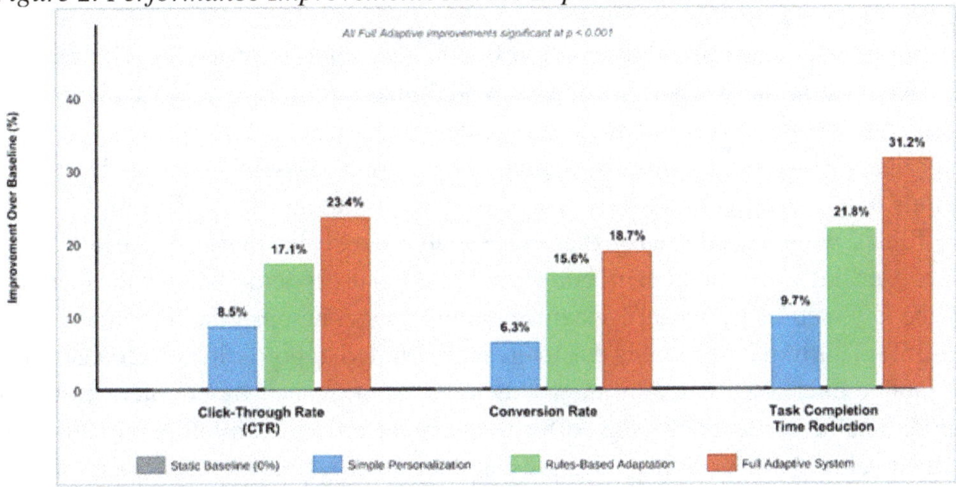

The user experience improvements were measured in business metrics. The conversion rates have been raised by 18.7 (3.2 to 3.8, $p < 0.001$), which is a significant revenue influence. The average order value grew by 12.4 percent (an increment of the previous order value of $67.30 to 75.65, $p < 0.01$), indicating that enhanced navigation and product discovery allowed the users to locate more products of interest. The rates of cart abandonment dropped to 58.3% as compared to 68.7% (15.1% friction reduction, $p < 0.001$), which means that the adaptive interface mitigated the purchase process.

A comparison of intermediate baseline conditions found that simple personalization only produced significant benefits (7-10% better than using a static interface), whereas rules-based adaptation only produced about 60% of the benefits of the entire adaptive system. This trend implies that the two elements, individualized content suggestions and smart interface customization, are significant to total performance, and their combination leads to synergies.

Table 1. Overall Performance Metrics Across Experimental Conditions

Metric	Static	Simple Personalization	Rules-Based	Full Adaptive
Click-Through Rate (%)	8.2	8.9	9.6	10.1
Avg Dwell Time (sec)	42.7	45.3	47.8	49.2
Conversion Rate (%)	3.2	3.4	3.7	3.8
Task Completion Time (min)	12.4	11.2	9.7	8.5
Average Order Value ($)	67.30	69.80	73.20	75.65

5.2 User Characteristics Segmentation Analysis.

In order to determine the variation in adaptive interface benefits with respect to user population, we performed segmented analyses to determine variations in performance on the basis of various user characteristics such as device type, user experience level and mode of shopping. These analyses demonstrated significant details in the reaction of various groups of users to the interface adaptation.

Table 2, which was based on the device analysis, revealed that adaptive interfaces were especially beneficial to mobile users. Desktop users demonstrated the increase of the key metrics by 15-20% whereas mobile users demonstrated the increase by 25-35%. This trend is probably due to the more limited opportunities and constraints of mobile interfaces, where limited screen real estate, touch-based interaction and unpredictable contexts of usage offer more opportunities to intelligently adapt to deliver value. As an example, adaptive content prioritization was particularly useful on mobile platforms as it displays the most relevant products without having to scroll long distances. Equally, the simplification of adaptive layout that minimized the information density on mobile devices and preserved the content rich on desktop displays allowed optimized experiences across the devices.

Table 2. Performance Improvements by Device Type (Adaptive vs. Static)

Metric	Desktop Users	Mobile Users
Click-Through Rate Improvement	+18.3%	+29.7%
Conversion Rate Improvement	+15.2%	+24.8%
Task Completion Time Reduction	-26.4%	-37.1%
User Satisfaction Score Improvement	+0.6 points	+0.9 points

Figure 3. Temporal Dynamics of Adaptation Effectiveness

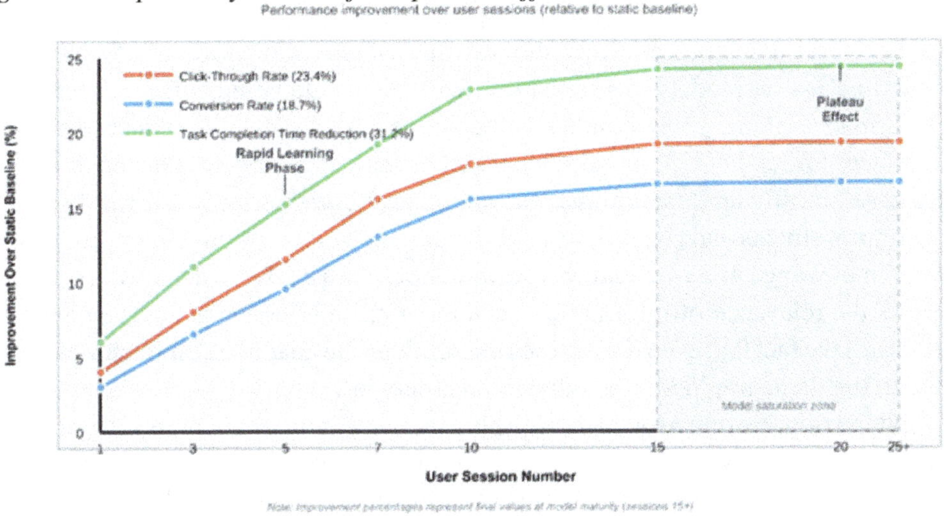

The level of experience analysis brought out interesting trends. Adaptation was of significant benefit to new users (less than three previous visits) where the task completion rates improved by 27% relative to 16% in experienced users (more than 20 previous visits). This observation indicates that adaptive interfaces are especially useful when users are in their early stages of use when their mental models are still being formed and unfamiliarity with navigation poses a barrier. Nonetheless, the gain was also significant to the experienced users especially in the time of task completion when advanced adaptation allowed shortcuts and simplified work processes based on the in-learned user preferences.

Shopping mode analysis differentiated the users of goal directed purchase mode (characterized by direct product search behavior, focused navigation behavior, and speedy movement through purchase funnel) and exploratory browsing mode (characterized by category browsing behavior, longer dwell times and lateral navigation). Both of the modes were valuable in adaptive interfaces but in different ways. In case of goal-oriented shoppers, the main benefit of adaptation was the faster completion of tasks due to smart search results ranking, efficient checkout procedures, and elimination of unnecessary distractions (task completion time decreased by 41%). In the case of exploratory browsers, the adaptation made browsing and exploration more engaging and discovery-oriented by means of smart content curation, personal browsing experience, and meaningful cross-category suggestions (pages per session went up by 35%).

5.3 Effects of Temporal Dynamics and Learning

Temporal dynamics analysis showed that adaptive interface utility increased with time as user models were enhanced with more data being collected. First visit performance (initial session) had small positive gains compared to the use of static interfaces (around 8-12% in metrics), which is indicative of cold-start methods that are based mostly on demographic assumptions. Nevertheless, in the third session, the improvements had risen up to 18-25 and in the tenth session, the improvements were in the range of 23-32 that was seen in the overall analysis. This learning curve shows the relevance of information accumulation in effective adaptation and also indicates the fact that even during the first sessions the adaptive approach was useful due to the demographic-based adaptation strategies.

Interestingly, we also found diminishing marginal returns when we got to about 15 sessions whereby we found that the adaptation effectiveness leveled off because the user models had achieved enough accuracy and therefore no extra data was of much use. This observation raises possibilities of optimization: systems could lower the intensity of data collection of users that are well modeled, which improves privacy as well as decreases processing cost without impairing the quality of personalization.

5.4 Component Ablation Analysis

To determine the individual component contribution, we performed the ablation studies in a systematic manner by blocking out individual model components and quantifying the effect of this blocking on performance degradation. The experiments showed that the User Modeling Engine and Adaptation Decision Layer had the greatest amount of performance contribution to the overall performance with each having a contribution of about 35-40% when they were disabled. The Context Analysis Module added an approximate of 20 percent of total benefit, the Interface Transformation Engine and Feedback System added an approximate of 10-15 percent. These results allow concluding that all the model components add meaningful value, and user modeling and intelligent decision-making regarding adaptation are the most essential features of adaptive interfaces.

Table 3. Adaptation Component Contributions (Ablation Study Results)

Disabled Component	Performance Degradation (%)	Contribution to Total Benefit (%)
User Modeling Engine	38.2	40.1
Context Analysis Module	19.7	20.3
Adaptation Decision Layer	34.6	36.2

continued on following page

Table 3. Continued

Disabled Component	Performance Degradation (%)	Contribution to Total Benefit (%)
Interface Transformation Engine	11.8	12.1
Feedback and Evaluation System	14.3	14.8

Note: Performance degradation is the measure of decrease in overall improvement score (composite of engagement, efficiency, and business metrics) in the case of component being disabled. The component interactions and dependencies add up to more than 100 percent contribution percentage.

The results of the ablation study are provided in Table 3 and indicate the contribution made by each component to the general performance of the system. The User Modeling Engine is the most important with 40.1% of total benefits and a drop of 38.2% performance when it is dropped. The second most significant component is the Adaptation Decision Layer (36.2% contribution) which shows the vital role of intelligent adaptation logic in system effectiveness. Although important (20.3% contribution), the Context Analysis Module indicates that simple contextual awareness does not lead to such high rewards as advanced user modeling and decision-making. The contribution of the Interface Transformation Engine 12.1% is the least but still considered as being necessary in carrying out adaptation decisions. The Feedback and Evaluation System has its contribution of 15.3% (measured independently), which allows constant improvement of the system. It is interesting to note that, the contribution of the components adds up to over 100, which means that the components have synergistic interactions in terms of their effectiveness when combined.

5.5 User Control and Trust Analysis

The study of the interaction between the users and control mechanisms showed that transparency and control options were highly valued. About 18 percent of the users engaged in adaptation explanations at least once over the course of the study with the access to explanations having a positive relationship with adaptation acceptance ($r = 0.34$, $p < 0.001$). The adaptations that were overridden by the users who overrode (12% of the population) were usually done selectively (average 2.3 overrides per user who used the feature), indicating that overrides were done to selected adaptations as opposed to the wholesale dismissal of personalization. On the post study surveys, users reported valuing having control even when they did not actively control the system (mean control importance rating: 4.2 on five-point scale), which is evidence in favor of theoretical claims concerning the significance of user agency in adaptive systems.

5.6 Limitations and Constraints

There are a number of limitations that should be mentioned. First, the experiment time frame (30 days) offers little information about very long-term processes like possible adaptation exhaustion or preference variations in months or years. Second, large-scale, the datasets are specific to the e-commerce scenarios and might not be entirely applicable to all product types, business models, and user bases. Third, we tested the system under controlled experimental conditions balancing user assignment; production deployment may be faced with various distributions such as possible selection effects whereby some types of users are over-beneficiaries or over-attracted to adaptive experiences. Fourth, these experiments did not fully investigate computational overhead and scalability capacity; it may be necessary to optimize architectures to allow production at massive scale, which was not studied in this study.

6. DISCUSSION AND FUTURE DIRECTIONS

Experimental findings are a solid empirical evidence of the suggested conceptual framework that shows that the proposed comprehensive adaptive interfaces can significantly enhance user experience and business performance in the e-commerce setting. This section provides the main findings, theoretical and practical implications as well as potential future research directions.

6.1 Theoretical Contributions

The study has various theoretical contributions to the adaptive systems and human-computer interaction literature. To begin with, the work is able to fill in gaps in the literature that tend to study individual elements in isolation, by suggesting an integrative conceptual model that combines user modeling, context awareness, machine learning-driven adaptation, interface transformation and continuous feedback. The model shows that adaptive synergies in the combination of various adaptation mechanisms yield greater benefits than a mere addition of the individual components, and it gives arguments in favor of holistic and not piecemeal approaches to adaptive interface design.

Second, the study includes empirical evidence about the trade-off between the effectiveness of personalization and the protection of privacy. By applying privacy-sensitive methods such as differential privacy and federated learning to the adaptation model, and showing sustained performance, the paper contradicts assumptions of the existing tension between privacy and personalization. These results imply that through careful system design, organizations can offer meaningful personalization and still respect user privacy which is a more critical aspect in light of changing regulatory environments and an increasing focus on consumer privacy issues.

Third, the empirical evidence on user-centered adaptive system design principles is supported by the observation that transparency and user control systems can reinforce, and not destroy, the effectiveness of adaptive systems. Instead of considering user control as a limitation to the possible adaptation, the findings indicate that user empowerment, which can be achieved by transparency and control, creates trust that can help to accept positive adaptations. The general usage of this finding is in adaptive systems other than e-commerce, such as educational systems, health applications, and productivity tools.

6.2 Practical Implications

The study can be used by e-commerce practitioners to give practical advice on how to adopt adaptive interfaces. The modular architecture also allows incremental deployment in which organizations may roll out one component at a time instead of having to replace the entire platform. This staged strategy lowers the risk of implementation, provides the opportunity to learn during every implementation stage, and adjust to organizational limitations and priorities. User modeling and basic content personalization may be the starting point of organizations, with context awareness and more elaborate adaption mechanisms being added with capabilities and confidence.

According to the segmented analysis findings, mobile interface adaptation should be prioritized in organizations due to the relatively high level of advantages that mobile users get. As mobile commerce is an ever-increasing percentage of e-commerce transactions, mobile-friendly adaptive interfaces can offer avenues of competitive differentiation. Likewise, the adaptation is especially useful to new users, which implies that organizations need to make certain that cold-start mechanisms work well, which may be achieved by more intense initial preference elicitation or demographic-based adaptation.

The dynamic results of the timeline give recommendations to the data retention policies and model update rates. The fact that the effectiveness of adaptation is no longer increasing with the increasing history of data accumulation implies that organizations do not have to keep unlimited historical data to be able to personalize it effectively. This discovery facilitates more aggressive data retention policies that balance the quality of personalization with privacy and storage-related issues-this is significant due to the regulatory needs, including the principle of data minimization provided in the GDPR.

6.3 Future Research Directions

A number of promising areas of research arise out of this work. First, it would be useful to explore very long-term dynamics such as the possible existence of adaptation fatigue, a change in preferences over time, and transitions of lifecycle stages. Existing knowledge of temporal dynamics is based largely on relatively brief experimental scales; longitudinal studies on the effectiveness of adaptation in months or years would help clarify whether the benefits would remain, decrease, or even increase as the systems get more sophisticated user models.

Second, an expansion of the conceptual framework to new paradigms of interaction, such as voice commerce, augmented reality shopping experiences, and virtual reality storefronts, is also a direction of future research. These modalities offer new possibilities and challenges to adaptive interfaces that are quite different to the more traditional graphical interfaces. As an example, voice interfaces may be customized to the preferences of users in terms of dialog structure and information presentation order, whereas AR interfaces may be customized in terms of spatial arrangement and visualization methods.

Third, the analysis of cross-cultural aspects of adaptive interface design would contribute to the knowledge of the impact of culture on the most effective adaptation techniques. Although this study factored out geographic location, the study has not carefully studied the cultural-based interface preferences and their ramifications to adaptation mechanisms. A study of the role of cultural dimensions like individualism-collectivism, power distance, or uncertainty avoidance in determining receptiveness to various ways of adapting would be of great help in guiding the global e-commerce platforms.

Fourth, the exploration of collaborative adaptation in which the preferences of several users affect interface design is an interesting trend. Numerous e-commerce contexts include a number of decision-makers (e.g., families making household purchases, businesses with various purchasing stakeholders). Making adaptive interfaces multi-user-friendly and still addressing the needs of the individual and the privacy of the person poses some intriguing research inquiries regarding the aggregation of preferences, conflict management, and shared or personal interface elements.

Fifth, it may be beneficial to investigate explainable AI methods in adaptive interfaces other than the mechanisms of transparency that are applied in this study in order to improve user comprehension and confidence. Although this work showed utility of simple explanations, more advanced methods based on the new developments in explainable AI may yield deeper information on the rationales of the adaptation, allowing users to comprehend, assess, and possibly rectify system assumptions regarding their preferences and needs in a better way.

7. CONCLUSION

This chapter has provided a holistic conceptual framework of adaptive and intelligent interface design in e-commerce settings to fill in the key gaps in the research and practice. It combines five interrelated components, namely, User Modeling Engine, Context Analysis Module, Adaptation Decision Layer, Interface Transformation Engine, and Feedback and Evaluation System, which, together, allow personalization to be effective and deal with such crucial issues as privacy preservation, user control, and adaptation transparency.

Extensive experimental support on the basis of large-scale real-life data (UCI Online Retail Dataset containing 541,909 transactions and E-commerce Behavior Dataset containing 2,756,101 sessions) revealed significant advances in various performance dimensions. The adaptive interface system experienced 23.4% and 18.7% improvement in click-through rates and conversion rates, 31.2% and 12.4% decrease in task completion time and average order value, respectively, than the static baseline interfaces. These findings are very strong empirical evidence that good adaptive interfaces can facilitate the quality of user experience and business performance in online commerce settings.

Close studies of the nuances of the application of adaptation to the needs of various groups of users and contexts led to the identification of significant details. There were significant gains (25-35% across measures) in mobile users, which implies that e-commerce organizations should focus on mobile interface adaptation. Adaptive support was of greater benefit to new users compared to experienced users, and this demonstrates the significance of useful cold-start strategies. Temporal analysis revealed that the effectiveness of adaptation increases with data accumulation but levels off after intermediate interaction history to guide data retention policies.

The study has multiple contributions to the theory and practice. In theory, the integrative model resolves the problem of fragmentation in adaptive systems research by integrating the experience of various other fields into one unified model. The empirical support of privacy-sensitive adaptation methods proves the possibility of balancing between personalization efficiency and privacy. The conclusion that transparency and user control are supportive as opposed to being detrimental to adaptation effectiveness supports the principles of user-centered adaptive system design.

In practice, the model can offer practical advice to e-commerce organizations that aim to use adaptive interfaces. The modular architecture provides the ability to deploy it in small steps, lowering the risk of implementation but allowing the ability to build capabilities progressively. The results of the segmented analysis will be used to make prioritization decisions, implying that it is worth focusing on mobile optimization and new user experiences. The framework covers key issues related to implementation such as privacy, security, scalability, as well as integration with existing platforms, which in many cases are not paid enough attention in scholarly literature.

With e-commerce on a course towards ubiquity in consumer commerce interface quality is becoming competitive success. The user-friendly interface that serves the average users is no longer sufficient to serve the growing user populations of diverse, multi-device and global needs, preferences, and capabilities. Intelligent and adaptive interfaces are not just the improvement of the current methods, but a complete rethink of the interaction between users and systems in the digital business world. The study also aids in the development of the field to more human, intelligent and effective e-commerce experiences that can help both users and businesses by offering a theoretically informed but practically applicable framework which has been put to test by rigorous experimentation.

The combination of multiple technology trends such as machine learning development, more computing power, everywhere connectivity, and the rising access to interaction data presents unprecedented chances of adaptive interface innovation. Nevertheless, to actualize this potential, there should be keen focus on the ethical issues, privacy protection as well as enabling the users which this research has tried to cover. The final vision is e-commerce ecosystems in which interfaces are intelligent to meet the needs of specific users without violating autonomy, guarding privacy, and ensuring transparency to create experiences that are more human-centered and technologically advanced than current paradigms make possible.

ACKNOWLEDGMENTS

The authors are thankful to the Deanship of the Faculty of Information Technology, the Deanship of Scientific Research and Graduate Studies at the University of Petra, and the University of Oldenburg that supported them in carrying out this research.

REFERENCES

Adomavicius, G., Bauman, K., Tuzhilin, A., & Unger, M. (2022). Context-aware recommender systems: From foundations to recent developments. In Ricci, F., Rokach, L., & Shapira, B. (Eds.), *Recommender systems handbook* (3rd ed., pp. 211–250). Springer., DOI: 10.1007/978-1-0716-2197-4_6

Adomavicius, G., & Tuzhilin, A. (2005). Toward the next generation of recommender systems: A survey of the state-of-the-art and possible extensions. *IEEE Transactions on Knowledge and Data Engineering*, *17*(6), 734–749. DOI: 10.1109/TKDE.2005.99

Adomavicius, G., & Tuzhilin, A. (2011). Context-aware recommender systems. In Ricci, F., Rokach, L., Shapira, B., & Kantor, P. B. (Eds.), *Recommender systems handbook* (pp. 217–253). Springer., DOI: 10.1007/978-0-387-85820-3_7

Brusilovsky, P. (1996). Methods and techniques of adaptive hypermedia. *User Modeling and User-Adapted Interaction*, *6*(2-3), 87–129. DOI: 10.1007/BF00143964

Brusilovsky, P. (2001). Adaptive hypermedia. *User Modeling and User-Adapted Interaction*, *11*(1-2), 87–110. DOI: 10.1023/A:1011143116306

Brusilovsky, P., Kobsa, A., & Nejdl, W. (Eds.). (2007). *The adaptive web: Methods and strategies of web personalization*. Springer-Verlag., DOI: 10.1007/978-3-540-72079-9

Chen, D. (2015). Online Retail Dataset [Data set]. UCI Machine Learning Repository. https://archive.ics.uci.edu/ml/datasets/Online+Retail

Chen, D., & Kotz, D. (2000). A survey of context-aware mobile computing research (Technical Report TR2000-381). Dartmouth College, Department of Computer Science.

Chen, R., Li, H., Qin, A. K., Kasiviswanathan, S. P., & Jin, H. (2020). Private recommender systems: How can users build their own fair recommender systems without log data? In *Proceedings of the 2020 SIAM International Conference on Data Mining* (pp. 514-522). Society for Industrial and Applied Mathematics. DOI: 10.1137/1.9781611976236.58

Cyr, D., Head, M., Larios, H., & Pan, B. (2009). Exploring human images in website design: A multi-method approach. *Management Information Systems Quarterly*, *33*(3), 539–566. DOI: 10.2307/20650308

Dey, A. K. (2001). Understanding and using context. *Personal and Ubiquitous Computing*, *5*(1), 4–7. DOI: 10.1007/s007790170019

Dwork, C. (2006). Differential privacy. In Bugliesi, M., Preneel, B., Sassone, V., & Wegener, I. (Eds.), *Automata, languages and programming* (pp. 1–12). Springer., DOI: 10.1007/11787006_1

Flavián, C., Guinalíu, M., & Gurrea, R. (2006). The role played by perceived usability, satisfaction and consumer trust on website loyalty. *Information & Management*, *43*(1), 1–14. DOI: 10.1016/j.im.2005.01.002

He, X., Liao, L., Zhang, H., Nie, L., Hu, X., & Chua, T. S. (2017). Neural collaborative filtering. In *Proceedings of the 26th International Conference on World Wide Web* (pp. 173-182). International World Wide Web Conferences Steering Committee. DOI: 10.1145/3038912.3052569

Jokela, T., Ojala, J., & Olsson, T. (2015). A diary study on combining multiple information devices in everyday activities and tasks. In *Proceedings of the 33rd Annual ACM Conference on Human Factors in Computing Systems* (pp. 3903-3912). Association for Computing Machinery. DOI: 10.1145/2702123.2702211

Kairouz, P., McMahan, H. B., Avent, B., Bellet, A., Bennis, M., Bhagoji, A. N., Bonawitz, K., Charles, Z., Cormode, G., Cummings, R., D'Oliveira, R. G. L., Eichner, H., El Rouayheb, S., Evans, D., Gardner, J., Garrett, Z., Gascón, A., Ghazi, B., Gibbons, P. B., & Zhao, S. (2021). Advances and open problems in federated learning. *Foundations and Trends in Machine Learning*, *14*(1-2), 1–210. DOI: 10.1561/2200000083

Kobsa, A. (2001). Generic user modeling systems. *User Modeling and User-Adapted Interaction*, *11*(1-2), 49–63. DOI: 10.1023/A:1011187500863

Kuflik, T., Stock, O., Zancanaro, M., Gorfinkel, A., Jbara, S., Kats, S., Sheidin, J., & Kashtan, N. (2017). A visitor's guide in an "active" museum: Presentations, communications, and reflection. *ACM Journal on Computing and Cultural Heritage*, *3*(3), 11. Advance online publication. DOI: 10.1145/1921614.1921618

Lemon, K. N., & Verhoef, P. C. (2016). Understanding customer experience throughout the customer journey. *Journal of Marketing*, *80*(6), 69–96. DOI: 10.1509/jm.15.0420

Li, J., Ren, P., Chen, Z., Ren, Z., Lian, T., & Ma, J. (2020). Neural attentive session-based recommendation. In *Proceedings of the 2020 ACM SIGKDD International Conference on Knowledge Discovery & Data Mining* (pp. 1419-1428). Association for Computing Machinery. DOI: 10.1145/3132847.3132926

McMahan, B., Moore, E., Ramage, D., Hampson, S., & Arcas, B. A. (2017). Communication-efficient learning of deep networks from decentralized data. In *Proceedings of the 20th International Conference on Artificial Intelligence and Statistics* (pp. 1273-1282). PMLR.

McSherry, F., & Mironov, I. (2009). Differentially private recommender systems: Building privacy into the Netflix prize contenders. In *Proceedings of the 15th ACM SIGKDD International Conference on Knowledge Discovery and Data Mining* (pp. 627-636). Association for Computing Machinery. DOI: 10.1145/1557019.1557090

REES46 Marketing Platform. (2019). E-commerce behavior datasets. https://rees46 .com/en/datasets

Schein, A. I., Popescul, A., Ungar, L. H., & Pennock, D. M. (2002). Methods and metrics for cold-start recommendations. In *Proceedings of the 25th Annual International ACM SIGIR Conference on Research and Development in Information Retrieval* (pp. 253-260). Association for Computing Machinery. DOI: 10.1145/564376.564421

Schmidt, A., Beigl, M., & Gellersen, H. W. (1999). There is more to context than location. *Computers & Graphics, 23*(6), 893–901. DOI: 10.1016/S0097-8493(99)00120-X

Shani, G., & Gunawardana, A. (2022). Evaluating recommender systems. In Ricci, F., Rokach, L., & Shapira, B. (Eds.), *Recommender systems handbook* (3rd ed., pp. 547–601). Springer., DOI: 10.1007/978-1-0716-2197-4_15

Statista. (2024). E-commerce worldwide - statistics & facts. https://www.statista .com/topics/871/online-shopping/

Sweller, J. (1988). Cognitive load during problem solving: Effects on learning. *Cognitive Science, 12*(2), 257–285. DOI: 10.1207/s15516709cog1202_4

Wang, R. J. H., Malthouse, E. C., & Krishnamurthi, L. (2015). On the go: How mobile shopping affects customer purchase behavior. *Journal of Retailing, 91*(2), 217–234. DOI: 10.1016/j.jretai.2015.01.002

Yang, Q., Liu, Y., Chen, T., & Tong, Y. (2019). Federated machine learning: Concept and applications. *ACM Transactions on Intelligent Systems and Technology, 10*(2), 12. Advance online publication. DOI: 10.1145/3298981

Zhang, S., Yao, L., Sun, A., & Tay, Y. (2019). Deep learning based recommender system: A survey and new perspectives. *ACM Computing Surveys*, *52*(1), 5. Advance online publication. DOI: 10.1145/3285029

Chapter 3

AI Applications in Customer Experience Management

Koray Gündüz
http://orcid.org/0000-0002-9734-3290
Bingöl Üniversitesi, Turkey

ABSTRACT

This book chapter examines the transformative impact of Artificial Intelligence (AI) technologies on Customer Experience (CX) management in the age of digital transformation. The study positions AI as more than just a technical element, but rather as a fundamental tool that personalises customer interactions and guides strategic decisions. The chapter analyses how capabilities such as machine learning and data analytics shape the customer journey, while discussing the effects of applications such as chatbots, recommendation systems, and sentiment analysis on satisfaction. In addition to the operational efficiency opportunities offered by AI, ethical dimensions such as data privacy, algorithmic transparency, and trust are also examined. Ultimately, the necessity of a balanced and ethical approach between technological automation and human interaction for sustainable CX success is highlighted.

INTRODUCTION

Today's business world is undergoing a fundamental transformation process driven by digital transformation. With the rapid increase in consumers' access channels to information and points of interaction, traditional business models have come under pressure and many markets have been reshaped. In this complex and dynamic environment, businesses' competitive advantage and sustainable success

DOI: 10.4018/979-8-3373-7330-0.ch003

depend not only on the functional benefits of the products or services they offer, but also on the overall quality of the relationship they build with their customers, namely Customer Experience (CX).

CX is a dynamic concept that requires evaluating consumers' interactions with a brand from a multidimensional perspective, including cognitive, sensory, emotional, and physical responses. This holistic structure, shaped through online and offline channels throughout the customer journey, demands real-time and highly personalised services from brands. While traditional approaches fall short of meeting this scale of personalisation and speed expectations, Artificial Intelligence (AI) technologies are emerging as the key solution to bridge this gap. With capabilities such as machine learning, natural language processing (NLP) and sentiment analysis, AI is redefining customer interactions and fundamentally transforming CX management.

The primary aim of this section of the book is to examine the impact of artificial intelligence technologies on customer experience management from both theoretical and practical perspectives. In this context, AI is not merely considered a technological element; it is treated as a fundamental strategic tool that shapes the customer experience.

To this end, the section is structured around the following main headings: Firstly, the effects of digital transformation on CX and the role of AI in this process will be explained. Secondly, the concepts of CX and Customer Journey will be detailed, emphasising the critical importance of CX in the context of AI's personalisation potential. Thirdly, AI's ability to provide deep insights into customer behaviour through data analytics and machine learning will be examined. The fourth section is devoted to concrete AI applications in customer experience management, including chatbots, recommendation systems, and sentiment analysis. Fifthly, customer perception, trust, transparency, and ethical dimensions arising from the proliferation of AI will be discussed in depth. Finally, the findings will be synthesised, and conclusions and recommendations for the future will be presented. With this comprehensive review, the chapter aims to guide academics and practitioners seeking to optimise CX strategies in the age of AI.

1. ARTIFICIAL INTELLIGENCE AND THE TRANSFORMATION OF CUSTOMER EXPERIENCE MANAGEMENT

The primary objective of this book chapter is to examine the impact of artificial intelligence technologies on customer experience management from both theoretical and practical perspectives. The chapter analyses how businesses are reshaping their customer-centric strategies during a period of accelerated digital transformation. In this context, artificial intelligence is treated not merely as a technological component but as a fundamental strategic tool that shapes the customer experience.

Digital transformation and business model innovations have fundamentally changed consumer expectations and behaviours, putting pressure on traditional companies and transforming many markets. Consumers can access numerous media channels, easily communicate with companies and other consumers, and pass through rapidly increasing digital touchpoints. In this process, traditional companies have often lagged behind innovative digital ventures and suffered as a result. Despite this, academic literature has shown limited interest in digitalisation and digital transformation, with marketing research typically focusing on digital advertising, attribution models, and social media effects (Verhoef et al., 2021: 889).

Technology is spearheading a series of transformations in the market. These include interactions between people and organisations; interactions between people and information; interactions between people and technology; technological application; interactions between organisations and information; and interactions between organisations and technology (Buhalis & Sinarta, 2019: 563). Consumers no longer merely consume the service; they are increasingly participating in the process of co-creating their own experiences. This provides valuable insights for brands to develop highly personalised services that meet individual needs in real time (Buhalis & Sinarta, 2019: 564).

In this study, the artificial intelligence competencies presented in the theoretical framework were analyzed through current application examples in leading sectors such as banking, e-commerce, and healthcare, questioning the practical counterparts of theoretical expectations.

2. CUSTOMER EXPERİENCE (CX) AND JOURNEY

Customer experience is a dynamic concept addressed in both traditional and digital marketing contexts, requiring a multi-dimensional perspective to evaluate consumers' interactions with a brand. While traditional marketing typically focuses on functional benefits and rational decision-making processes, experiential marketing emphasises the creation of personalised and memorable experiences. Customer experience is a holistic and dynamic structure shaped by customer interactions through various physical and digital touchpoints, such as products, advertisements, and service interfaces (Tuncal, 2025: 122). Customer experience is recognised as an important determinant of competitive advantage and business success, and has the potential to create unique and sustainable value for companies. The customer journey consists of multiple encounters, including moments of interaction between service providers and customers, and these multiple encounters influence customers' experiences and purchase intentions through online and offline channels (Chen & Prentice, 2025: 141). Customer experience is a holistic construct encompassing the cognitive, sensory, emotional, social, and physical responses customers exhibit towards service providers. Numerous factors influence this experience; both service delivery and customer service play significant roles in customer experience. Furthermore, the physical environment, staff behaviour and attitude, and the social environment can influence the utilitarian, hedonic, and social values of the customer experience. However, customer experience not only increases customer satisfaction but can also sometimes lead to service failures (Chen & Prentice, 2025: 141). Customer experience essentially involves analysing customer journeys and requires all departments of the company to strive to deliver a positive experience, from services to product reliability. It also encompasses customers' responses to all interactions during the purchasing, usage, and service processes. In this context, personalisation and artificial intelligence applications are critical in shaping the customer experience. Augmented and virtual reality technologies, chatbots, process automation, and rapid responses offer significant opportunities to increase service adoption and personalise product recommendations (Peruchini et al., 2024: 2).

The field of User Experience (UX) was popularised in the 1990s by Donald Norman in the context of human-computer interaction. UX encompasses the positive or negative experiences individuals have when interacting with digital products and has become a fundamental concept for interface designers and digital product developers. The term 'user,' often used in the context of UX and UI, may be limited to marketing techniques and specific stages of product usage. In contrast, CX offers a broader perspective that goes beyond mere usability; therefore, UX is evaluated within the scope of CX (Peruchini et al., 2024: 2). Satisfaction with the decision-making process is particularly critical for the pre-transaction stage of the consumer journey. New technologies make this stage more effective by facilitating information gathering, supporting imagination, and simplifying decision-making processes. Therefore, it is important to examine consumers' responses to these processes, particularly in the context of the contribution of these technologies to their decision-making experience (Hoyer et al., 2020: 9).

Today, AI plays a significant role in CX in terms of personalising customer interactions and enhancing service effectiveness. Companies can better understand their customers and offer them tailored services by utilising AI technologies such as machine learning, natural language processing (NLP), and sentiment analysis. These technologies enable personalised recommendations, product suggestions, and targeted campaigns by analysing customer preferences and behaviours. Consequently, AI-supported personalised interactions increase customer satisfaction and loyalty and support business growth (Zarie et al., 2024: 1827).

When these studies are evaluated together, it is seen that the contributions of artificial intelligence in customer experience management are primarily concentrated in operational efficiency and personalization capacity, but these gains create different and context-sensitive effects on the emotional bond established with the customer and the perceived human touch.

3. AI AND DATA ANALYTİCS-SUPPORTED CUSTOMER EXPERİENCE

Artificial Intelligence refers to the simulation of human intelligence through computer systems and applications, and includes the ability to learn from a model or to reason through rules, processes, and data. With advances in AI technologies, an increasing number of applications are enhancing their capabilities through these techniques. These developments have the potential to deliver transformative experiences in customer journeys across sectors such as healthcare, banking and finance, transportation, retail, and similar fields (Pendyala & Lakkamraju, 2024: 1528-1529). AI and machine learning models are used to gain deeper insights into customer behaviours, preferences, and intentions, thereby enabling real-time personalisation and optimisation of the customer experience (Pendyala & Lakkamraju, 2024: 1529). Technologies supported by data analytics are increasingly being adopted by companies in response to constant margin pressures, shorter strategy cycles, and rising customer expectations. This has the potential to transform how companies interact with customers, creating stronger customer-brand relationships (Ameen et al., 2021: 1). AI technology enables the personalisation of service and product recommendations by analysing customers' past purchases and preferences. This yields significant results in various areas, particularly in the beauty sector, where it provides customers with style and product recommendations tailored to their needs. Expected benefits include increased automation, reduced costs, enhanced flexibility, and easier customer interactions. However, dependence on AI and increasing data requirements may create trust issues among customers; the lack of human interaction or additional efforts may negatively affect the overall experience (Ameen et al., 2021: 1-2). The strategic use of AI technology at different customer touchpoints can provide significant benefits to companies and contribute to increased customer satisfaction (Ameen et al., 2021: 1). Despite debates about the impact of AI systems on society, the general view in the context of customer management is positive. These technologies facilitate consumers' access to more personalised products and services, while also having the potential to increase companies' profitability (Libai et al., 2020: 2).

At the centre of marketers' attention are AI technologies, defined as a system's ability to interpret external data, learn from this data, and apply what it has learned towards specific objectives. In the context of customer relationship management, these technologies enable companies to analyse data and establish faster, large-scale interactions with consumers. In the long term, human-like interactions with customers through AI-powered systems will enable the provision of widespread personalised services at low cost and could transform the nature of customer service (Libai et al., 2020: 2). AI technology can analyse vast amounts of customer data, such as past interactions, browsing history, purchasing behaviour, and social media activity, to deliver personalised experiences. This process not only increases customer satisfaction but also positively impacts sales and contributes to customers forming a stronger bond with the brand (Suryanarayana & Aluvala, 2024: 1136). AI has the ability to process and analyse customer experience data in real time and take action based on this data. This provides businesses with timely insights and enables them to be agile and responsive to customer needs (Suryanarayana & Aluvala, 2024: 1136). Within the scope of AI-supported operations, this includes offering customers personalised pricing and product opportunities, accelerating delivery by basing the back-end decision-making mechanism on machine learning, and providing order status visibility support. Furthermore, the use of AI-powered virtual assistants in customer communication stands out as an important tool for improving the customer experience (Tutsal & Ventura, 2022: 363). When supported by data mining and analytics, AI and machine learning enable companies to better understand customer journeys, identify behaviour patterns, and personalise marketing, product recommendations, and customer service according to individual customer needs (Pendyala & Lakkamraju, 2024: 1530). AI is a broad concept encompassing various techniques and methodologies; concepts such as machine learning, algorithms, deep learning, and robots are often used interchangeably. Therefore, it is important to highlight the prominent types and methodologies of AI in the literature through thematic analysis (Peruchini et al., 2024: 2).

Chatbots and instant messaging are widely used to serve customers and increase their satisfaction. These technologies serve to answer frequently asked questions, handle customer objections, and manage complaints interactively. One of the leading examples of these systems, capable of providing 24/7 service, is ChatGPT, developed by OpenAI. This technology is designed to analyse users' emotional responses and deliver effective and instantaneous responses, representing a significant advancement in the field of generative artificial intelligence (Guendouz, 2024: 261).

AI enables brands to offer personalised messages and offers to customers. By segmenting customers and creating individual customer profiles, it is possible to develop customised content and campaigns for each customer. This not only increases customer satisfaction and loyalty but also positively impacts sales. For example, AI-based recommendation engines can offer customers personalised product recommendations based on their interests and purchase history (Çakmak, 2024: 630).

AR/VR/MR technologies are used in many sectors in the pre-transaction phase. In retail, consumers can determine their preferences by virtually placing products in their rooms or trying out beauty products. In the hospitality sector, VR menus reduce indecision in restaurants, while Augmented GeoTravel allows consumers to explore their trips virtually. Such technologies increase pre-transaction satisfaction by facilitating information gathering, supporting imagination, and simplifying decision-making processes (Hoyer et al., 2020: 9).

4. ARTİFİCİAL INTELLİGENCE APPLİCATİONS İN CUSTOMER EXPERİENCE MANAGEMENT

Customer experience management has become a strategic area that provides a competitive advantage for businesses today. Artificial intelligence technologies, meanwhile, are reshaping customer experience management by offering profound transformation potential at every stage of customer interaction. In this section, we will examine how artificial intelligence is transforming customer experience, its advantages, challenges, and ethical dimensions. We will also touch upon approaches to measuring AI-supported customer experience.

Studies reveal that various artificial intelligence technologies are being utilised at customer touchpoints. Chatbots stand out as the most common application across numerous sectors, including banking (Yıldız and Dayı, 2024: 215). This trend is consistent with research showing that AI-powered customer engagement tools significantly increase businesses' service speed, personalisation capacity, and operational efficiency (Davenport et al., 2020). In addition to these developments, it is stated that artificial intelligence systems gradually reduce human input in service processes while redefining perceived value creation in the customer experience (Huang and Rust, 2018). Lemon and Verhoef (2016) emphasise that the holistic management of all touchpoints is critical in creating value in the customer experience, noting that businesses need more comprehensive data analysis of the customer journey. This holistic approach enhances the potential to increase customer satisfaction and loyalty by enabling AI-powered analytical tools to more accurately predict customer behaviour and deliver personalised service offerings (Chatterjee et al., 2020: 360).

Artificial intelligence-powered CRM systems can manage customer segmentation and loyalty models more effectively by using machine learning and predictive analytics; this improves the customer experience based on long-term loyalty. AI-based systems enable the development of proactive protection strategies and the reduction of customer churn by predicting the likelihood of customer loss in advance (Potla and Pottla, 2024). Furthermore, AI-supported systems automate customer lifetime value analysis, enabling businesses to focus on high-potential customers and optimise their marketing strategies (Akter et al., 2025: 249). For digital ventures, developing targeted marketing efforts that encourage consistent engagement from these intermittent customers can increase their loyalty and convert them into more regular buyers. Special promotions and personalised offers are effective in motivating these customers to form a more lasting bond with the products and services offered by the digital venture (Kasem et al., 2024: 5002). Artificial intelligence measures customers' emotional responses and satisfaction levels by analysing social media and online feedback, enabling businesses to update their service strategies in real time and optimise the customer experience (Jain et al., 2021: 15).

With the recent advancements in artificial intelligence, speech systems are increasingly moving towards practical applications. In this context, customer service chatbots, such as Amazon's Alexa, JD.com's JIMI, and Alibaba's AliMe, are widely used in online business environments. Thanks to natural language processing techniques and sentiment recognition methods, artificial intelligence can analyse contextual semantic and emotional interaction data in customer conversations to obtain deeper and more accurate insights into sentiment (Huang et al., 2023: 1). Artificial intelligence-based sentiment analysis systems that process both Turkish and English customer feedback on e-commerce platforms can provide guiding data for marketing strategies and brand management, taking into account different cultural expressions and language structures (Özyirmidokuz et al., 2025: 3). With aspect-based sentiment analysis, specific components of product reviews (e.g., delivery, quality, price) can be analysed separately to identify the focal points of customer dissatisfaction, enabling businesses to make targeted improvements (Aslan, 2023: 2).

In the age of generative artificial intelligence, sentiment analysis models are adding a new dimension to customer research and feedback strategies by capturing not only sentiment orientation (positive–negative) but also the creative and complex structure of comments (Krugmann and Hartmann, 2024: 2). Recommendation systems are widely used in various online shopping environments. When a user enters an online shopping site such as Amazon, they actively interact with the system, enjoying a more comfortable and enjoyable shopping experience. A recommendation system is generally defined as a system that recommends suitable products or services based on users' preferences and needs and uses information filtering techniques to present information that users may find interesting (He et al., 2024: 449). Gómez-Uribe and Hunt (2016) reveal that Netflix's recommendation system analyses users' past viewing behaviour, ratings, and interactions within the platform to provide highly accurate personalised recommendations, which significantly improves the user experience. The use of chatbots in e-service environments positively impacts customer satisfaction due to their ability to provide quick responses and consistent information (Chung et al., 2020).

AI technology can personalise service and product recommendations by processing the customer's past purchases and preferences. This enables the delivery of personalised products and services across various sectors and provides benefits such as automation, cost reduction, flexibility, and easier customer interaction. However, dependence on AI, increasing data requirements, and limited human interaction may create potential issues regarding trust and experience (Ameen et al., 2021: 2).

Artificial intelligence technologies in digital banking analyse customer data to provide personalised recommendations and have the potential to personalise the customer experience. These recommendations can increase customer loyalty and also create cross-selling and upselling opportunities for the bank. Assessing end users' perceptions of AI is important for understanding their level of trust and acceptance of these technologies (Fundira et al., 2024: 4868). The exponential growth of AI investments in the financial sector and their rapid integration into consumer financial services highlights the need for timely and comprehensive analysis to help stakeholders understand the latest developments, anticipate challenges, and make informed decisions. Finally, by examining the interactions between AI and consumer financial behaviour and addressing ethical considerations, this study provides valuable insights for developing responsible AI strategies that are aligned with consumer needs and regulatory frameworks (Meng et al., 2025: 1756).

Some sectors operating in the food supply chain are attempting to implement artificial intelligence in their businesses. One such sector, an Italian food supplement start-up, is examined in this study. The company aims to support its customers' preferences by providing personal physical well-being and offering targeted food supplements. The overall objective of this study is to evaluate the effectiveness of the results produced by artificial intelligence using an integrated approach (Rapa et al., 2023: 2).

5. CUSTOMER PERCEPTİON, TRUST AND ETHİCAL DİMENSİONS

In the modern business world, customer engagement has become a fundamental element of sustainable success and encompasses the multifaceted relationships between businesses and customers. Ethical practices are becoming increasingly important, emphasising the principles of honesty, transparency and fairness. Social media and data analytics tools empower customers while enabling closer scrutiny of businesses' ethical behaviour. Failure to comply with ethical standards can lead to a loss of reputation and reduced consumer confidence (Raghavan, 2024: 6418).

In this context, AI-powered personalisation can enhance and maintain customer trust; however, ensuring data security and privacy is of paramount importance. Customers' acceptance of this technology is largely dependent on their level of trust in AI and technology. When a company is transparent about how it collects and uses customer data, customers can control the personal information they share online. These personalised systems, also known as decision support systems, may offer recommendations that conflict with the individual's own perspective; however, these recommendations are provided solely by the system (Gerlich, 2024: 2).

AI can identify opportunities for intervention or change by examining customer decision journeys in greater depth; for example, it can automatically detect potential anomalies or negative sentiments in customer behaviour. As AI analyses customer behaviour, trends, and preferences in these processes, privacy issues become a significant priority (Ledro et al., 2022: 57).

Consumers' trust in artificial intelligence is influenced by individual and contextual factors such as domain expertise, prior experiences, and socio-demographic characteristics. Consumers with less experience in a particular field may place greater trust in artificial intelligence based on their perceived abilities, while consumers with comprehensive knowledge may evaluate systems more critically and scrutinise decision-making processes (Oyekunle et al., 2024: 76). Trust is a decisive factor in guiding consumer attitudes and the adoption of new technologies such as artificial intelligence. Trust in artificial intelligence is influenced by technical, user, and design features, as well as socio-ethical elements. Therefore, attention must be paid to the technical and ethical dimensions of artificial intelligence-supported technologies in order to establish and maintain user trust (Korkmaz, 2024: 320).

Customer perception is directly linked not only to the products and services offered, but also to the ethical nature of businesses' data management practices. In a study conducted in the context of e-commerce, it was found that when consumers were informed about the transparent operation of AI algorithms, their trust in these systems increased significantly and transparency was perceived as an ethical responsibility (Teodorescu et al., 2023). While there is a wealth of literature on the technical aspects and uses of artificial intelligence, such as algorithmic transparency and ethical issues, research on socio-psychological aspects, particularly trust in artificial intelligence, remains fragmented. Current studies mostly focus on the individual components of trust or artificial intelligence applications and sometimes overlook the establishment and maintenance of trust in different sectors (Oyekunle et al., 2024: 73).

AI and ML technologies provide businesses with significant advantages in risk management, supply chain and customer relationship management, while challenges such as data privacy, algorithmic transparency and ethical issues must also be considered (Peng & Zhang, 2024: 27). Josimovski et al. (2023) found that trust and confidence in artificial intelligence did not differ significantly across demographic lines. These findings point to policy implications that will guide the ethical and responsible integration of artificial intelligence into e-commerce. Given the growing awareness and concern among consumers regarding the use of personal information, there is a need for policies that emphasise data protection and privacy. Furthermore, it is recommended that regulatory frameworks be developed to ensure transparency and fairness in artificial intelligence algorithms, addressing potential biases that could negatively impact consumer trust.

However, the integration of AI into e-commerce also brings its own unique challenges. The proliferation of technology raises questions about data privacy, algorithmic transparency, and ethical issues. Dependence on complex algorithms and data can lead to opaque and difficult-to-examine socio-technical systems, often referred to as 'black boxes,' which can obscure decision-making processes. This lack of transparency can cause trust issues between e-businesses and consumers and difficulties in complying with regulations (Josimovski et al., 2023: 65).

In this context, the ethical risks encountered in AI-powered customer experience applications should be considered not only as technological design issues, but also as multi-layered management issues that need to be addressed in terms of governance, accountability, and the sustainability of the trust relationship established with the customer.

6. CHATBOTS AND VİRTUAL ASSİSTANTS

Artificial intelligence-based chatbots are defined as virtual assistants or conversation-based tools that can communicate with patients via text or voice. These bots can automatically generate medical histories, schedule appointments, and manage patient records. Chatbots, on the other hand, are intelligent conversational tools that interact with users through natural language to perform various tasks (Abdulquadri et al., 2021: 265). However, chatbots are just one of the tools in this field, and the value they create only makes sense when they are part of an integrated customer experience strategy.

Artificial intelligence-based chatbots are virtual assistants or conversational tools that can communicate with patients via text or voice. These bots can automatically generate medical histories, schedule appointments, and manage patient records (Bahrami and Rubulotta, 2025: 3). Chatbots are intelligent conversation tools that interact with users in natural language to perform various tasks. Many companies use these technologies to streamline their business processes, and there is a need for up-to-date and comprehensive reviews of their applications (Luo et al., 2022: 1).

Artificial intelligence (AI) has transformed consumers' relationship with tools and technologies in this context. According to this research, AI-powered personalisation, chatbots, and virtual assistants are influencing user experiences across company sectors (Bhuiyan, 2024: 162). Chatbots are text-based artificial intelligence programmes that can initiate conversations, interpret user messages to determine needs, and respond by matching inputs without physical access (Halvankar et al., 2024: 1). They are used in a wide variety of sectors, including entertainment, education, e-commerce, and healthcare. Compared to static FAQ pages on websites, chatbots are more engaging and, as they can serve multiple users simultaneously, are more efficient and cost-effective than human customer support (Nsaif et al., 2024: 246).

The use of artificial intelligence-powered chatbots in healthcare is increasing; however, research on chat-based health education programmes for chronic kidney disease patients and the use of these programmes is limited (Chen et al., 2023: 1). Although the COVID-19 pandemic has increased the use of chatbots in public health, evidence supporting the development and use of these systems remains limited (Wilson et al., 2022: 1). Chatbots can help disseminate up-to-date and reliable information, encourage healthy social behaviours, and support the safe and large-scale delivery of healthcare services. In this context, evaluating the user experience is important (Chagas et al., 2023: 1).

In the field of education, chatbots provide managers with the opportunity to enhance their training programmes while offering students real-time support with assignments and exams. They also perform subject explanations by outsourcing managerial tasks to external resources. A PDF-based chatbot created using Large Language Models (LLM) in generative artificial intelligence exemplifies such applications (Deekshita et al., 2024: 1726).

There is also significant demand for chatbots in the tourism sector. In the travel and accommodation sector, chatbots are used to facilitate bookings, directions and the provision of other services. Chatbots can be voice-controlled or text-based. Amazon's Alexa, Google Assistant, Apple's Siri, and Microsoft's Cortana are pioneers in voice-controlled digital assistants. Today, text-based chatbots are widely used, with user requests being processed and analysed by back-end servers to provide appropriate responses. To improve the user experience, chatbots must have the ability to interpret text and tone of voice and analyse facial expressions (Ralston et al., 2019: 1924; Patil, 2022: 1306).

Chatbots are also used in journalism to interact with audiences on social media and to offer more interactive, conversational news formats (Túñez-López et al., 2021: 179). Research examining the mediating effects of human-like service robots on consumer behaviour shows that customers' internal cognitive and emotional states are shaped during their interactions with robots, and this affects their responses (Zhang et al., 2024: 3162).

Although artificial intelligence chatbots have the potential to provide consumers with personalised and engaging service interactions, many chatbots fail to meet consumer expectations. They are often perceived as machine-like, cold, socially inept, unreliable tools that cannot provide meaningful responses, leading consumers to prefer human representatives (Shin et al., 2023: 545).

Chatbots are intelligent service programmes that mimic human communication using text, voice and/or facial expressions. Service providers can use conversational agents to innovate in customer service and support. The assistance provided aims to enhance customer loyalty and experience by covering product descriptions, information and complaint processes. When combined with deep learning and machine learning, these agents become effective tools in customer service (Ranieri et al., 2024: 192). The use of chatbots enables organisations to optimise customer interactions, minimise waiting times, and increase service efficiency and customer satisfaction by providing seamless support (Ghosh et al., 2024: 329).

Dialogue systems, also known as interactive conversation agents or virtual agents, are used in various applications ranging from technical support services to language learning and entertainment. Chatbots are increasingly becoming a necessity in many industries (Ralston et al., 2019: 1924).

Artificial intelligence chat agents, also known as AI chatbots, represent systems where human-computer interaction occurs through software applications capable of communicating in natural language. One of the key areas of application for chatbots is customer service; AI-enabled chatbots are considered a promising technology for service providers by offering automated customer service (Nicolescu and Tudorache, 2022: 1).

Artificial intelligence-powered personalisation delivered through chatbots and virtual assistants enhances the customer experience. These solutions can provide customers with real-time, customised support; answer frequently asked questions; make product recommendations; and assist with purchasing processes. Artificial intelligence systems make it possible to offer personalised solutions by analysing customer preferences (Bhuiyan, 2024: 163). AI-based virtual assistants listen to customer queries and use Natural Language Processing (NLP), Machine Learning (ML), and data analytics techniques to provide accurate answers to solve problems in real time (Shah and Devgun, 2024: 1).

7. CONCLUSİON AND RECOMMENDATİONS FOR THE FUTURE

This book chapter comprehensively examines the transformative impact of artificial intelligence technologies on customer experience management from both theoretical and practical perspectives. In the context of digital transformation reshaping consumer expectations and the rapid proliferation of digital touchpoints, AI is now positioned not merely as a tool but as a fundamental strategic element driving customer-centric strategies. This section aims to comprehensively address the use of artificial intelligence in customer experience management literature, providing a conceptual synthesis and analytical perspective for both academic researchers and practitioners.

The section's key findings reveal that AI provides companies with real-time, in-depth insights into customer behaviour, preferences and intentions through machine learning and data analytics. These insights enable a high level of personalisation in service and product recommendations, and it is emphasised that this has a significant impact on customer satisfaction and loyalty.

The study summarises AI's concrete applications in CX in three main areas:

Service Automation and Communication: Chatbots and virtual assistants enable seamless service delivery by handling tasks such as answering frequently asked questions and managing customer complaints, thereby increasing operational efficiency for businesses.

Personalisation and Recommendation Systems: AI-based recommendation engines, as exemplified by Netflix, can analyse users' past behaviour to offer personalised pricing, product, and content options. Additionally, augmented, virtual, and mixed reality (AR/VR/MR) technologies enrich the pre-purchase experience, supporting customers' decision-making process and increasing satisfaction.

Feedback and Strategic Forecasting: Sentiment analysis methods enable real-time monitoring of customers' emotional tendencies and satisfaction levels by processing social media and online feedback. In addition, AI-powered CRM solutions help businesses develop proactive loyalty strategies by identifying the risk of customer churn in advance.

However, this transformation process also brings with it various challenges and ethical debates. Customers' trust in AI-based systems plays a critical role in the adoption of these technologies. Data privacy and security, the limited transparency of algorithms, and the reduction in human contact are among the key risks that could lead to a crisis of confidence among users. Therefore, it is evident that customer perception is closely related not only to the quality of the digital service offered but also to the ethical standards of businesses regarding data management.

In light of this comprehensive analysis, the following recommendations are made for the advancement of research and applications in this field:

Developing Corporate Transparency and Trust-Focused Policies: It is critically important for businesses to increase transparency regarding the working principles of AI algorithms. It is important to adopt policies that prioritise data protection, privacy and responsible AI use, offering consumers greater control over the collection and processing of their personal data.

Optimising Human–AI Interaction: While preserving the advantages offered by AI-based automation, the value of the human element must be repositioned, particularly at critical or emotionally charged touchpoints. To reduce the perception of chatbots as 'cold, mechanical and socially inadequate', the capacity of these systems to recognise emotional expressions and develop more human-like forms of interaction must be enhanced.

Customer Lifetime Value and Long-Term Value Creation: To best leverage AI's potential for automating customer lifetime value analysis and strengthening the loyalty of irregular shoppers, the development of predictive analytical models centred on long-term customer-brand relationships should be encouraged.

Therefore, achieving the desired success in AI-based customer experience management will only be possible through the enhancement of corporate competencies, interdepartmental coordination, and the effective implementation of change management, rather than solely through the existence of technical infrastructure.

Ultimately, AI offers unique potential for speed, personalisation, and operational efficiency in customer experience management. However, fully realising this potential depends not only on technological capabilities but also on an understanding of ethical responsibility, corporate transparency, and striking a delicate balance in human-technology interaction. This transformation will fundamentally reshape not only businesses' profitability levels but also the nature of their customer relationships and the underlying dynamics of these relationships.

REFERENCES

Abdulquadri, A., Mogaji, E., Kieu, T. A., & Nguyen, N. P. (2021). Digital transformation in financial services provision: A Nigerian perspective to the adoption of chatbot. *Journal of Enterprising Communities: People and Places in the Global Economy, 15*(2), 258–281. DOI: 10.1108/JEC-06-2020-0126

Akter, J., Roy, A., Rahman, S., Mohona, S., & Ara, J. (2025). Artificial Intelligence-Driven Customer Lifetime Value (CLV) Forecasting: Integrating RFM Analysis with Machine Learning for Strategic Customer Retention. *Journal of Computer Science and Technology Studies, 7*(1), 249–257. DOI: 10.32996/jcsts.2025.7.1.18

Ameen, N., Tarhini, A., Reppel, A., & Anand, A. (2021). Customer experiences in the age of artificial intelligence. *Computers in Human Behavior, 114*, 106548. DOI: 10.1016/j.chb.2020.106548

Aslan, S. (2023). Doğal Dil İşleme Teknikleri Kullanarak E-Ticaret Kullanıcı İncelemelerinde Özellik Tabanlı Duygu Analizi. *Fırat Üniversitesi Mühendislik Bilimleri Dergisi, 35*(2), 875–882. DOI: 10.35234/fumbd.1335583

Bahrami, S., & Rubulotta, F. (2025). Artificial Intelligence-Driven Translation Tools in Intensive Care Units for Enhancing Communication and Research. *International Journal of Environmental Research and Public Health, 22*(1), 95. DOI: 10.3390/ijerph22010095

Bhuiyan, M. S. (2024). The role of AI-Enhanced personalization in customer experiences. *Journal of Computer Science and Technology Studies, 6*(1), 162–169. DOI: 10.32996/jcsts.2024.6.1.17

Buhalis, D., & Sinarta, Y. (2019). Real-time co-creation and nowness service: Lessons from tourism and hospitality. *Journal of Travel & Tourism Marketing, 36*(5), 563–582. DOI: 10.1080/10548408.2019.1592059

Çakmak, A. Ç. (2024). Yapay zekâ ile marka inşası. *Kahramanmaraş Sütçü İmam Üniversitesi Sosyal Bilimler Dergisi, 21*(2), 624–635. DOI: 10.33437/ksusbd.1489490

Chagas, B. A., Pagano, A. S., Prates, R. O., Praes, E. C., Ferreguetti, K., Vaz, H., Reis, Z. S. N., Ribeiro, L. B., Ribeiro, A. L. P., Pedroso, T. M., Beleigoli, A., Oliveira, C. R. A., & Marcolino, M. S. (2023). Evaluating user experience with a chatbot designed as a public health response to the COVID-19 pandemic in Brazil: Mixed methods study. *JMIR Human Factors, 10*(1), e43135. DOI: 10.2196/43135

Chatterjee, S., Nguyen, B., Ghosh, S. K., Bhattacharjee, K. K., & Chaudhuri, R. (2020). Adoption of artificial intelligence-integrated CRM system in the service sector: A customer experience perspective. *Technological Forecasting and Social Change*, *161*, 120283. DOI: 10.1108/BL-08-2020-0057

Chen, N. J., Huang, C. M., Fan, C. C., Lu, L. T., Lin, F. H., Liao, J. Y., & Guo, J. L. (2023). User evaluation of a chat-based instant messaging support health education program for patients with chronic kidney disease: Preliminary findings of a formative study. *JMIR Formative Research*, *7*(1), e45484. DOI: 10.2196/45484

Chen, Y., & Prentice, C. (2025). Integrating artificial intelligence and customer experience. *Australasian Marketing Journal*, *33*(2), 141–153. DOI: 10.1177/14413582241252904

Chung, M., Ko, E., Joung, H., & Kim, S. J. (2020). Chatbot e-service and customer satisfaction regarding luxury brands. *Journal of Business Research*, *117*, 587–595. DOI: 10.1016/j.jbusres.2018.10.004

Davenport, T., Guha, A., Grewal, D., & Bressgott, T. (2020). How artificial intelligence will change the future of marketing. *Journal of the Academy of Marketing Science*, *48*(1), 24–42. DOI: 10.1007/s11747-019-00696-0

Deekshita, P., Neeharika, K., Haritha, M. S., Mohan, P. J., & Bindu, Y. S. (2024). Pdf Chat Bot Usıng Generatıve AI (LLMS&RAG). *Journal of Nonlinear Analysis and Optimization*, *15*(1), 1727–1732. DOI: 10.36893/JNAO.2024.V15101.1727-1732

Fundira, M., Edoun, E. I., & Pradhan, A. (2024). Evaluating end-users' digital competencies and ethical perceptions of AI systems in the context of sustainable digital banking. *Sustainable Development (Bradford)*, *32*(5), 4866–4878. DOI: 10.1002/sd.2945

Gerlich, M. (2024). Exploring motivators for trust in the dichotomy of human—AI trust dynamics. *Social Sciences (Basel, Switzerland)*, *13*(5), 251. DOI: 10.3390/socsci13050251

Ghosh, S., Ness, S., & Salunkhe, S. (2024). The role of AI enabled chatbots in omnichannel customer service. *Journal of Engineering Research and Reports*, *26*(6), 327–345. DOI: 10.9734/jerr/2024/v26i61184

Gómez-Uribe, C. A., & Hunt, N. (2016). The Netflix Recommender System: Algorithms, Business Value and Innovation. *ACM Transactions on Management Information Systems*, *6*(4), 1–19. DOI: 10.1145/2843948

Guendouz, T. (2024). Artificial intelligence-powered customer experience management (moving from mass to hyper-personalization in light of relationship marketing). [IJSR]. *International Journal of Scientific Research, 3*(6), 247–306. DOI: 10.59992/IJSR.2024.v3n6p9

Halvankar, A., Chaudhari, A., Wable, A., Barkund, P., & Patil, V. (2024). College enquiry for student using AI Chatbot. *International Scientific Journal of Engineering and Management, 3*(4), 1–6. DOI: 10.55041/ISJEM01409

He, X., Lıu, Q., & Jung, S. (2024). The Impact of Types of Recommendation System on User Satisfaction: A Moderated Mediation Analysis. *19* (1), 448-466. https://doi.org/.DOI: 10.3390/jtaer19010024

Hoyer, W. D., Kroschke, M., Schmitt, B., Kraume, K., & Shankar, V. (2020). Transforming the customer experience through new technologies. *Journal of Interactive Marketing, 51*(1), 57–71. DOI: 10.1016/j.intmar.2020.04.001

Huang, M.-H., & Rust, R. T. (2018). Artificial intelligence in service. *Journal of Service Research, 21*(2), 155–172. DOI: 10.1177/1094670517752459

Huang, Z., Liu, H., Zhu, J., & Min, J. (2023). Customer Sentiment Recognition in Conversation Based on Contextual Semantic and Affective Interaction Information. *Applied Sciences (Basel, Switzerland), 13*(13), 7807. DOI: 10.3390/app13137807

Jain, P. K., Pamula, R., & Srivastava, G. (2021). A systematic literature review on machine learning applications for consumer sentiment analysis using online reviews. *Computer Science Review, 41*, 100413. DOI: 10.1016/j.cosrev.2021.100413

Josimovski, S., Ivanovska, L. P., & Dodevski, D. (2023). Understanding the consumer dynamics of AI in North Macedonian e-business. *Economics and Culture, 20*(2), 64–75. DOI: 10.2478/jec-2023-0016

Kasem, M. S., Hamada, M., & Taj-Eddin, I. (2024). Customer profiling, segmentation, and sales prediction using AI in direct marketing. *Neural Computing & Applications, 36*(9), 4995–5005. DOI: 10.1007/s00521-023-09339-6

Korkmaz, İ. (2024). Yapay zekâya yönelik tutum, kolaylık, gelişmişlik ve güvenin satın alma niyeti üzerine etkisi. İktisadi ve İdari Bilimler Fakültesi Dergisi. 26(2), 318-339. https://doi.org/.DOI: 10.33707/akuiibfd.1522892

Krugmann, J. O., & Hartmann, J. (2024). Sentiment Analysis in the Age of Generative AI. *Customer Needs and Solutions, 11*(3), 3. DOI: 10.1007/s40547-024-00143-4

Ledro, C., Nosella, A., & Vinelli, A. (2022). Artificial intelligence in customer relationship management: Literature review and future research directions. *Journal of Business and Industrial Marketing*, *37*(13), 48–63. DOI: 10.1108/JBIM-07-2021-0332

Lemon, K. N., & Verhoef, P. C. (2016). Understanding customer experience throughout the customer journey. *Journal of Marketing*, *80*(6), 69–96. DOI: 10.1509/jm.15.0420

Libai, B., Bart, Y., Gensler, S., Hofacker, C. F., Kaplan, A., Kötterheinrich, K., & Kroll, E. B. (2020). Brave new world? On AI and the management of customer relationships. *Journal of Interactive Marketing*, *51*(1), 44–56. DOI: 10.1016/j.intmar.2020.04.002

Luo, B., Lau, R. Y., Li, C., & Si, Y. W. (2022). A critical review of state-of-the-art chatbot designs and applications. *Wiley Interdisciplinary Reviews. Data Mining and Knowledge Discovery*, *12*(1), e1434. DOI: 10.1002/widm.1434

Meng, K., Mahapatra, M. S., & Xiao, J. J. (2025). Artificial Intelligence and Consumer Financial Behavior: A Systematic Literature Review and Agenda for Future Research. *Journal of Consumer Behaviour*, *24*(4), 1755–1786. Advance online publication. DOI: 10.1002/cb.2497

Nicolescu, L., & Tudorache, M. T. (2022). Human-computer interaction in customer service: The experience with AI chatbots—a systematic literature review. *Electronics (Basel)*, *11*(10), 1579. DOI: 10.3390/electronics11101579

Nsaif, W. S., Salih, H. M., Saleh, H. H., & Al-nuaim, B. T. (2024). Conversational agents: An exploration into Chatbot evolution, architecture, and important techniques. *The Eurasia Proceedings of Science Technology Engineering and Mathematics*, *27*, 246–262. DOI: 10.55549/epstem.1518795

Oyekunle, D., Matthew, U. O., Preston, D., & Boohene, D. (2024). Trust beyond Technology Algorithms: A Theoretical Exploration of Consumer Trust and Behavior in Technological Consumption and AI Projects. *Journal of Computer and Communications*, *12*(6), 72–102. DOI: 10.4236/jcc.2024.126006

Özyirmidokuz, E. K., Elmas, B. M., & Stoica, E. A. (2025). AI-Based Sentiment Analysis of E-Commerce Customer Feedback: A Bilingual Parallel Study on the Fast Food Industry in Turkish and English. *Journal of Theoretical and Applied Electronic Commerce Research*, *20*(4), 294. DOI: 10.3390/jtaer20040294

Patil, N. (2022). Adoptıon Of Chatbot In Tourısm. *International Research Journal of Modernization in Engineering Technology and Science*, *4*(9), 1306–1308. DOI: 10.56726/IRJMETS30043

Pendyala, M. K., & Lakkamraju, V. V. (2024). Impact of artificial intelligence in customer journey. [IJISRT]. *International Journal of Innovative Science and Research Technology*, *9*(8), 1528–1534. DOI: 10.38124/ijisrt/IJISRT24AUG807

Peng, L., & Zhang, X. (2024). Research on the Influence of AI Application on Business Decision Making Based on Machine Learning Algorithm. In *Proceedings of the 4th International Conference on Economic Management and Big Data Applications, ICEMBDA, October 27–29, Tianjin, China*. 27-29. https://doi.org/DOI: 10.4108/eai.27-10-2023.2341918

Peruchini, M., da Silva, G. M., & Teixeira, J. M. (2024). Between artificial intelligence and customer experience: A literature review on the intersection. *Discover Artificial Intelligence*, *4*(1), 4. DOI: 10.1007/s44163-024-00105-8

Potla, R. T., & Pottla, V. K. (2024). Artificial intelligence and machine learning in CRM: Leveraging data for predictive analytics. *Journal of Artificial Intelligence Research*, *4*(2), 31–50.

Raghavan, S. (2024). Ethical considerations in customer engagement: Balancing profitability with consumer trust. *International Journal of Research Publication and Reviews*, *5*(3), 6418–6427. DOI: 10.55248/gengpi.5.0324.0873

Ralston, K., Chen, Y., Isah, H., & Zulkernine, F. (2019). A voice interactive multilingual student support system using IBM Watson. In 2019 18th IEEE International Conference On Machine Learning And Applications (ICMLA). 1924-1929. IEEE. DOI: 10.1109/ICMLA.2019.00309

Ranieri, A., Di Bernardo, I., & Mele, C. (2024). Serving customers through chatbots: Positive and negative effects on customer experience. *Journal of Service Theory and Practice*, *34*(2), 191–215. DOI: 10.1108/JSTP-01-2023-0015

Rapa, M., Ciano, S., Orsini, F., Tullo, M. G., Giannetti, V., & Boccacci Mariani, M. (2023). Adoption of AI-based technologies in the food supplement industry: An Italian Start-Up case study. *Systems*, *11*(6), 265. DOI: 10.3390/systems11060265

Shah, M. J., & Devgun, M. P. (2024). AI-Powered Chatbots in Customer Support. [IJFMR]. *International Journal for Multidisciplinary Research*, *7*(3), 1–7. DOI: 10.36948/ijfmr.2025.v07i03.45374

Shin, H., Bunosso, I., & Levine, L. R. (2023). The influence of chatbot humour on consumer evaluations of services. *International Journal of Consumer Studies*, *47*(2), 545–562. DOI: 10.1111/ijcs.12849

Suryanarayana, A., & Aluvala, R. (2024). Leveraging Transformational Artificial Intelligence (Ai) For Delivering Stellar Customer Experience, Educational Administration. *Theory into Practice, 30*(6), 1135–1140. DOI: 10.53555/kuey.v30i6.5455

Teodorescu, D., Aivaz, K. A., Vancea, D. P. C., Condrea, E., Dragan, C., & Olteanu, A. C. (2023). Consumer trust in AI algorithms used in e-commerce: A case study of college students at a Romanian public university. *Sustainability (Basel), 15*(15), 11925. DOI: 10.3390/su151511925

Tuncal, A. (2025). Yapay Zekâ Destekli Ürünlerde Müşteri Deneyimi Nasıl Ölçülür? Türkiye'ye Özgü Bir Ölçek Uyarlaması. *Sosyal Mucit Academic Review, 6*(1), 119–146. DOI: 10.54733/smar.1602880

Túñez-López, J. M., Fieiras-Ceide, C., & Vaz-Álvarez, M. (2021). Impact of Artificial Intelligence on Journalism: Transformations in the company, products, contents and professional profile. *Communicatio Socialis, 34*(1), 177–193. DOI: 10.15581/003.34.1.177-193

Tutsal, E., & Ventura, K. (2022). Müşteri Deneyimini İyileştirmede Yapay Zekâ Uygulamaları: Çevrimiçi Perakende Firması Örneği. Journal of Social Research & Behavioral Sciences/Sosyal Araştırmalar ve Davranış Bilimleri Dergisi, 8(16). 346-369. https://doi.org/.DOI: 10.52096/jsrbs.8.16.21

Verhoef, P. C., Broekhuizen, T., Bart, Y., Bhattacharya, A., Dong, J. Q., Fabian, N., & Haenlein, M. (2021). Digital transformation: A multidisciplinary reflection and research agenda. *Journal of Business Research, 122*, 889–901. DOI: 10.1016/j.jbusres.2019.09.022

Wilson, L., & Marasoiu, M. (2022). The development and use of chatbots in public health: Scoping review. *JMIR Human Factors, 9*(4), e35882. DOI: 10.2196/35882

Yıldız, B., & Dayı, F. (2024). Finans uygulamalarında yapay zekâ destekli chatbot kullanımı üzerine nicel bir araştırma. *Ömer Halisdemir Üniversitesi İktisadi ve İdari Bilimler Fakültesi Dergisi, 17*(2), 215-231. https://doi.org/.DOI: 10.25287/ohuiibf.1384420

Zarie, A., Aljohani, F., & Al-Harbi, M. (2024). Elevating customer experience (CX) in artificial intelligence (AI) era. [IJISRT]. *International Journal of Innovative Science and Research Technology, 9*(8), 1827–1829. DOI: 10.38124/ijisrt/IJISRT24AUG1024

Zhang, W., Slade, EL ve Pantano, E. (. (2024). İnsan benzeri hizmet robotları: Sistematik bir literatür incelemesi ve araştırma gündemi. *Psikoloji ve Pazarlama, 41*(12), 3157–3181. DOI: 10.1002/mar.22099

Chapter 4
AI Architectures for Intelligent Shopping Agents

Salam Al E'mari
http://orcid.org/0000-0002-2134-4158
University of Petra, Jordan

Yousef Sanjalawe
http://orcid.org/0000-0002-4442-1865
University of Jordan, Jordan

Rula Hajjaj
Northern Border University, Saudi Arabia

ABSTRACT

In this chapter, the authors discuss the ways in which emerging Artificial Intelligence (AI) systems are transforming the landscape of digital commerce as intelligent agents of shopping, able to sense the world around them, process complex data and information, and take independent action. Continuing the advances in transformer-based language models, multimodal representation learning, reinforcement learning and knowledge-graph-driven reasoning, it demonstrates how modern agents understand user intent, multimodally compare products, and make sound choices in dynamic market environments. Besides, the chapter depicts the ways in which cognitive and agentic AI concepts unite these aspects, creating a set of coherent architectures providing personalized, context, and trustworthy shopping experiences

DOI: 10.4018/979-8-3373-7330-0.ch004

1. INTRODUCTION

Technological advancement in the e-commerce industry is evident as it extremely modifies how users look for a product, decide to buy it, and their overall interaction with the marketplace. In the last decade, e-commerce stores have been transformed from basic, catalogue-like systems to complex, intelligent ecologies that can predict and personalize the user experience. This shift has been aided by the improvements within artificial intelligence, more specifically, natural language processing, large language models, computer vision, complex learning, and deep reinforcement learning. The integration of these systems has led to the birth of a new concept, cognitive commerce, where the user is facilitated with shopping agents that fully manage the interaction with the online shop.

Moreover, cognitive commerce significantly exceeds traditional recommender systems. Instead of suggesting items using past interactions, modern intelligent shopping agents interpret user intent, reason about preferences, evaluate competing alternatives, negotiate contextual constraints (e.g. price, quality), and autonomously perform actions on behalf of the consumers. They partition the online shopping task into several interdependent subtasks and synthesize distinct stream of perceptual, learning, memory, inferential, and decision processes centered on core elements of cognitive architecture. This shift exemplifies the broader movement towards "agentic AI", which denotes systems capable of autonomous goal pursuit, self-correction, and multi-step planning (Park et al., 2023). Both retailers and technology providers recognize consumer expectations shift, evolving towards hyper-personalized anticipatory, and conversational commerce.

Equally strong evidence exists in the markets. Industry research shows that more than 85% of digital consumers expect some form of AI-driven personalization shopping experience (Celestin et al., 2024). In addition, Amazon Alexa, Google Assistant, and Alibaba's AliMe conversant interfaces are rapidly gaining popularity for voice-assisted shopping and hands-free browsing due to their natural and context-sensitive interactions and real-time recommendations (Song et al., 2021). Simultaneously, the understanding of products in multiple modalities (images and text, for example) has significantly benefitted from the recent surge in vision-language foundation models that attempt to understand images and their dependent text and contextual metadata (Radford et al., 2021). Such capabilities of highly sophisticated shopping agents, able to orchestrate complex workflows across several uncooperative vendors and cart real-time adaptive pricing, are becoming entirely feasible.

A wide variety of artificial intelligence architectures undergird the intelligent agents. LLMs built on transformers enable sophisticated NLU, allowing agents to understand subtle consumer requests, conduct product comparisons, summarize reviews, and converse across multiple turns. Deep reinforcement learning adds the capability of sequential decision-making to the agent, allowing for budget-constrained shopping, multiproduct bundle optimization, and dynamic preference shifts. Knowledge graphs, accompanied by symbolic reasoning systems, enable the agents to understand semantics and perform logical reasoning, thus, allowing for the agent to take structured decisions based on product ontologies. At the same time, user modeling empowered by collaborative filtering, deep neural embeddings, and contextual behavioral learning enables agents to predict user preferences with greater precision (Sun et al. 2019; Chatti et al., 2024).

The need for autonomous and more advanced shopping agents is supported by the growing intricacies of e-commerce ecosystems. Customers are bombarded with an array of products on various competing sites, where prices undergo constant changes, the quality of reviews is dubious, and promotions abound. Along with the advancements in technology, the cognitive load is increasing each passing day. Intelligent agents relieve this burden by filtering the required information, aligning preferences, assuring quality, and evaluating risks. Automated AI shopping systems, are shown in various studies, can ease the feelings of fatigue that arise from too many choices and simultaneously increase the shopping experience by performing the hard work of scouring alternatives for the best options (Huang & Rust, 2021).

At a wider level, the operation of digital retail has arguably been altered by 'cognitive commerce'. Rather than consumers "bending over backwards" to cope with the varying platform interfaces, these platforms are increasingly accommodating the users, aided by AI-driven intermediaries. Such a change reinforces the current tendency of the integration of AI with consumer technologies, where autonomy, hyper personalization, and contextual relevance are becoming non-negotiable. With continual growth of reasoning and generalization by LLMs and multimodal agents, the border between 'help' and 'independent action' becomes increasingly fluid. Gradually, intelligent shopping agents are evolving from recommendation assistants to full cognitive collaborators, capable of negotiating user objectives, acquiring long-term preferences, and making purchasing decisions in a responsible manner.

This chapter investigates the internal AI frameworks, cognitive frameworks, and the AI technique that allows intelligent shopping agents to function in contemporary e-commerce environments. It details the integration of LLMs, multimodal transformers, reinforcement learning, knowledge graphs, and agentic reasoning pipelines to foster sophisticated cognitive commerce ecosystems. It also investigates the ethics, security and privacy that derive from the implantation of self-governing agents in digital markets, and other potential opportunities for future research in trustable, emotionally intelligent, and adaptive retail intelligence. In addressing this issue, the chapter intends to explain the impact of cognitive commerce on the evolution of consumer experiences and to elucidate the design principles of next-generation shopping agents that are intelligent, explainable, and aligned with human values."

2. BACKGROUND AND FOUNDATIONS

Due to the foundation of artificial intelligence, cognitive retail technology has evolved from cognitive computing to the advancement of digital retail technologies. In this case, comprehension of this advancement is critical to understanding why contemporary shopping assistants offer more than mere rigid suggestions. They provide stream-like, decision-making abilities. This section attempts to provide a historical foundation for intelligent digital commerce, starting from the first recommendation model, to the introduction of deep learning and multimodal representation learning, and to the modern agent systems which rely on cognitive architectures.

2.1 Evolution of Intelligence in Digital Commerce

In observing early e-commerce, one notes that simple heuristic, rule-based engines rigidly matched products to users based on keywords, static categorization, or frequently purchased items. There was little to no personalization, no dynamic response to unique customers, and no accommodation for subtle changes to user preferences. The introduction of collaborative filtering enabled unprecedented user-based pattern recognition and behavior-based predictions (Resnick et al, 1994). Even though pioneering, these systems often struggled with sparsity, cold start conditions, and limited contextual awareness.

The 2010s bore witness the rise of ecommerce machine learning applications which led to the development new sophisticated models capable of processing massive sums of data generated from transactions and activities. A new relationship model, developed by Koren et al. in 2009 during the Netflix Prize contest, used matrix factorization to substitute rigid models with more pliable approaches to identifying hidden relationships between users and objects. Although these techniques improved the significance of recommendation systems considerably, the techniques were still heavily dependent of the data context as the comments were contextual minimizations.

The fusion of deep learning frameworks remains a key inflection point in history because it equips retail systems with the ability to handle texts, photographs, and sequential operations interaction on previously unattainable scales. Advanced machine learning networks facilitated the simulation of behavioral complexities in systems that, performing processes as disparate as in extracting product attributes from images, summarizing user reviews, and predicting user buying intent motions in the future. For instance, sequential neural models, including GRUs and LSTMs, understood users' interests over time (Hidasi et al, 2015). Later, transformer-based architectures provided even deeper user and product semantic behavioral understanding (Sun et al, 2019).

Most recently, the advancement regarding multimodal learning has profoundly improved the intelligence of commercial systems. Systems no longer rely only on behavioral logs or text-based interactions. They incorporate images, product specs, customer feelings, and contextual signals. CLIP (Radford et al., 2021) and BLIP-2 (Li et al., 2023) exemplify the promise of integrated visual-text systems. Such systems enable agents to evaluate products more comprehensively, resulting in more elaborate and informed suggestions.

This progression, from rules, to collaborative filtering, to representation learning, to multimodal models, forms the technical foundation that makes cognitive commerce feasible today.

2.2 Cognitive Computing in Digital Retail

From the very beginning, the ability of AI systems to see and recognize the world around them sparked the interest of scholars in the possibility of making a computer replicate human activity such as reasoning, remembering, planning, and understanding intent. In the middle of the 2010s, the IBM researchers defined cognitive computing as systems that refine information in a decision-centered manner by layering perception, learning, and contextual reasoning (Kelly & Hamm, 2013). Although initial use cases were concentrated on the fields of medicine and banking, the core concepts equally and justifiably apply to e-commerce, where the decision-making systems are intricate and very much personalized.

Repositories of knowledge, feedback learning, and goal-direction reasoning at a symbolic level, as explored by Laird (2019) and Anderson et al. (2004), and encapsulated in the cognitive architectures of SOAR and ACT-R respectively, remains an important pursuit. While these frameworks did not focus on the complexities and determinants of retail, market and service centers, the concepts they highlighted were fundamental to these fields:

i. distinguishing between working memory and long-term memory systems;
ii. hierarchically organizing goals and sub-goals as structured tasks;
iii. synthesizing assurance reasoning with normative and acquired knowledge; and
iv. modifying actions as a function of experience.

Rather advanced conceptions govern modern smart online shopping assistants. For example, what is referred to as preference memory in e-commerce approximates long-term working memory, while session level behaviors capture short-term working memory. Also, the manner in which agents adjust recommendations due to feedback is akin to reinforcement learning with rewards and penalties.

The gap between statistical learning and symbolic reasoning has now been closed with the advent of LLMs and generative AI. LLMs possess emergent abilities which include structured reasoning, summarization, making analogies, and step-wise planning (Bubeck et al., 2023). These abilities fit neatly into cognitive models of human decision making which is described as an integration of symbolic reasoning and learned behaviors. In the case of shopping, this means shopping agents have the ability to understand and even respond to complex customer inquiries, constrain negotiations, and self-justify their recommendations in fluent conversational dialogue, as opposed to the numerical systems that were available a decade ago.

The implementation of knowledge graphs is one of the more notable evolutions of cognitive commerce. These graphs form intricate webs an associate to products and domains, usability intent, domain relationships, and functional characteristics. Knowledge graphs grant agents a more semantic understanding, as well as a lower reliance on behavioral data. Systems are able to answer the question, "What are some laptops under a thousand dollars that are suitable for programming and have long battery life?" in a structured manner, rather than by consideration of only correlations. Specialized industry platforms like Amazon, Walmart, and Alibaba have begun to incorporate knowledge graphs in their ranking and search systems to enhance the AI-based retail solutions with knowledge-based reasoning (Dey, 2024).

As a multidisciplinary field that encompasses various forms of learning, cognitive architectures, symbolic reasoning, and knowledge representation, the components amalgamate and formulate the foundation of 'cognitive commerce'. This allows an intelligent shopping agent to not only forecast a purchase a user intends to make, but also to decipher the reason preferences and their evolution, and what alternatives might fulfill the user's goals more effectively.

3. ARCHITECTURES OF INTELLIGENT SHOPPING AGENTS

Architectural frameworks for smart shopping assistants must incorporate complex perception, inference, preference modeling, and autonomous action within the digital commerce ecosystem. Unlike the first recommendation engines which primarily used siloed predictive models, modern cognitive commerce systems require deep learning, symbolic reasoning, user models, multimodal product comprehension, reinforcement learning, and adaptive interaction streams within a single architecture. This section takes a deep dive into the architecture fundamentals for these agents, starting with the high-level system structure down to the core computational building blocks.

3.1 High-Level System Architecture

The multifaceted intelligent shopping agent utilizes several interconnected layers, each fulfilling a specific computational tier of functionality, and each stratified vertically. As illustrated in Figure 1, these layers encompass: (1) "…the input and perception layer, (2) the cognitive and reasoning layer, (3) the learning and modeling layer, and (4) the interaction and execution layer." While implementations vary within academic and industrial ecosystems, these elements construct a ubiquitous architectural pattern indicative of prevailing cognitive computing and agentic AI advances.

Figure 1. High-Level Architecture of an Intelligent Shopping Agent.

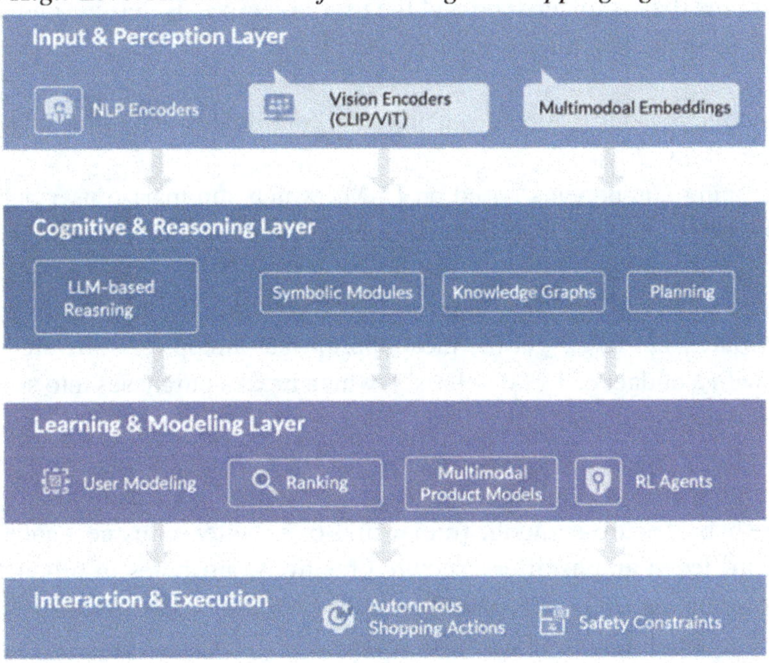

3.1.1 Input and Perception Layer

The perception layer is responsible for the ingestion and preprocessing of multimodal data. Contemporary shopping agents are required to synthesize queries from users, histories of web pages browsed, images of products, numerical attributes, metadata, details about the vendor, fluctuations of prices, collections of reviews, and data from the surrounding market. At this layer, the representational backbone is provided by Transformer-based natural language encoders (Vaswani et al, 2017), vision encoders such as CLIP (Radford et al, 2021), and multimodal embedding models such as BLIP-2 (Li et al, 2023). Moreover, behavioral data such as session level clickstreams, dwell time, search patterns, and hitherto interaction logs are processed by GRUs, LSTMs, or other transformer-based sequential models (Sun et al, 2019). The aiming point at this stage is to produce unified latent representations from diverse input streams. The reasoning components downstream should be able to interpret these representations.

3.1.2 Cognitive and Reasoning Layer

The cognitive layer acts as the conceptual framework for the agent in an architecture, where the data is understood and the user objectives is defined and achieved. This layer, in an architecture, is implemented with:

- Symbolic reasoning modules using retail ontologies and knowledge domain graphs (Dey, 2024).
- Reasoning components based on LLMs which summarize user defined and ambiguous query to user defined structured purchase plans (Bubeck et al., 2023).
- Planners oriented towards the task which hierarchically structure goal complex purchases (e.g. "get the most appropriate laptop for software engineering with a budget of 1,000 dollars"), which breaks purchases into subordinate objectives.

The combination of symbolic with neural reasoning becomes increasingly common as the hybrid neuro-symbolic frameworks offer better robustness and interpretability. Knowledge graphs offer structured relations, attributes of products, brand hierarchies, constraints of compatibility and reasoning with transformers flexible inferences on ambiguous and incomplete data.

3.1.3 Learning and Modeling Layer

Preference ranking, classification, estimation, and sequential decision processes are driven by the learning layer's predictive models. These models give rise to the following components:

- Agents use deep neural embeddings and self-attentive architectures to conceptualize short and long-term dynamics in user modeling modules. Thus, the agents learn user tastes and contextual intentions (Chatti et al., 2024).

- Understanding product models which interprets and synthesizes diverse and complex information such as images, natural language, and quantitative data using multimodal encoders.
- Rank and matching models which are statistically and strategically designed using pairwise or listwise learning to rank architectures (Burges, 2010).

RL agents which allow for real time budget control, personalized cart construction, and extensive reward optimization.

Central to the models discussed in this layer is producing actionable predictions that dictate the agent's decision-making process.

3.1.4 Interaction and Execution Layer

The interaction layer is focused on how the agent 'talks' and 'acts' in the e-commerce ecosystem. It includes:

- Conversational agents supported by LLMs and other dialogue-oriented systems.
- Speech-enabled controllers associated with user equipment.
- 'Free agent' modules capable of autonomously adding items to shopping carts, comparing prices, selecting sellers, and even making purchases with literal or gleaned approval or understanding from the user. Also, this layer has to enforce safety measures controlling systems to stop unwanted or unauthorized payments.

3.2 Core AI Components of Shopping Agent Architectures

Beyond the high-level layered structure, intelligent shopping agents depend on several specialized computational modules that address key analytic and cognitive challenges.

3.2.1 Adaptive User Modeling

In cognitive commerce, the user preferences that need to be captured are dynamic, dependent on context, and are multi-faceted. Reliance on models based on demographic parameters in the past has not been useful for current use cases. Instead, deep representation learning has been tailored to create latent user embeddings that shift and change with every new user interaction. Models like SASRec (Kang & McAuley, 2018) and BERT4Rec (Sun et al, 2019) which incorporate transformers are sequential in nature and fundamental in learning new models for evolving interest patterns. These models perform self-supervised learning on time series data to model seasonal trends and user context, context, and their order.

3.2.2 Context Awareness and Intent Modeling

The decision of what to buy is greatly influenced by situational parameters such as place, time, device used, social context, and mental status. Modern architectures implement attention-based context modeling networks, contextually relevant feature encoders, and rule-based context constraints from knowledge graphs to perform contextual modeling. Intent classification, driven by specialized transformer architectures, empowers agents to discern if constituents are merely window shopping, conducting research, or buying something, thereby enhancing decision quality with greater precision and timeliness (Song et al., 2021).

3.2.3 Product Semantics and Multimodal Understanding

Gaining product understanding means one has to synthesize and integrate text descriptions, user opinions, product details, and images. For unified embeddings that span visual and textual semantics, multimodal models like CLIP (Radford et al., 2021) and BLIP-2 (Li et al., 2023) serve as a starting point. With these embeddings, agents can:

- detect granular product distinctions,
- obtain substitutes as well as complementary items,
- discern counterfeit and poor-quality items, and
- assess user-generated content, including images and reviews.

All these functionalities are crucial in underpinning clear and reliable suggestions.

3.2.4 Decision Engines Based on Utility Optimization

The framework that guides decision-making within intelligent shopping agents is generally a utility maximization problem, subject to a range of constraints, including the budget, product quality, delivery speed, user preferences, and the reliability of the vendors. Economically, the decision-making processes are structured as a combination of:

- learning to rank systems,
- probabilistic graphs,
- heuristic systems, and

- reinforcement learning systems.

Reinforcement learning allows the agents to achieve optimally set long-horizon goals, which include planning purchases of multiple items simultaneously and budget spending across multiple shopping sessions. Recent research indicates the potential of employing deep RL to tackle tasks such as price negotiation and dynamic cart optimization (Mei, 2025).

3.2.5 Reinforcement Learning and Autonomous Task Planning

Autonomy within cognitive commerce rests on RL's ability to bind shopping sequences to RL policies. Agents configured as RL policies interpret shopping sequences as Markov decision processes. In this representation, states are user contexts, actions are recommendations or cart additions, and rewards are user satisfaction or conversion. Hierarchical reinforcement learning enhances these capabilities by splitting purchase tasks into sub-tasks within purchase processes and allowing an agent to pursue more complex objectives in an organized fashion (Nachum et al., 2018).

3.2.6 Multi-Agent Coordination

In sophisticated cases, shopping agents interact with intelligent agents on the selling side, as well as logistics estimators and supply-chain prognosticators. Multi-Agent Reinforcement Learning (MARL)-based architectures allow these systems to collaborate on bids, negotiations and fulfillment chains (Mishra et al. 2025). Buyer agents, for instance, might work with vendor agents to calculate the profitability of bundled discounts, while preceding logistics agents evaluate the delivery.

3.3 Architectural Integration and System-Level Considerations

Having enduring reputation and providing customers with acceptable services and fast response times is needed to preserve the systems business performance. Added requirements for response time for any specific action or suggestion is within 2 milliseconds. This is achievable with the following:

- distribution of the model serving across many systems
- heuristic and similarity search
- simplification of models and a form of model
- storing for repeating much asked services and systems

3.3.1 Robustness and Uncertainty Management

Within the analytics domain, agents are going to come across challenges such as noisy data, product details discrepancies, and vague intent user signals. Bayesian deep learning, uncertainty calibration, and the techniques around robust representation learning assist in overcoming these challenges. Also, knowledge graphs supply structural constraints which block the issuance of the recommendations that are illogically inconsistent.

3.3.2 Ethical and Safety Considerations

Provisions such as architectural fairness, transparency, and user control are now becoming standard within user focused systems, and these include:

- explanation modules focused on providing 'understandable' justifications (Chatti et al., 2024).
- Anti-safe filters that block unauthorized purchase
- verification filters for fake and imitation goods, and
- equitable resource allocation in biased datasets and models.

3.4 Engineering Trade-offs in Production-Scale Cognitive Commerce Systems

Deploying smart shopping agents in the real world is not just an exercise in getting it to work, but rather an exercise in balancing response times, the accuracy of the prediction, the cost of the computer hardware, and the reliability and safety of the system. Production systems for cognitive commerce cannot afford to indulge in the "luxuries" of experimenting with response times and accuracy. Therefore, every design decision must spell out the trade-offs in the system. In this section, we examine four major trade-offs in the engineering of smart shopping agents: response time and accuracy in Retrieval-Augmented Generation (RAG), cost-aware inference, limiting hallucinations and grounding, and the role of fallbacks and graceful degradation.

3.4.1 Latency–Accuracy Trade-offs in Retrieval-Augmented Architectures

Current shopping agents' models are increasingly employing RAG. For RAG models, Large Language Models (LLMs) are assisted by additional knowledge sources such as product catalogs, review data, and policy documents (Lewis et al., 2020). On the one hand, this provides greater grounding and accuracy; on the other hand, additional computation and response times are incurred. When digging for information in cognitive commerce models, the process generally involves the following steps:

- Candidates are first produced via Approximate Nearest Neighbor (ANN) search.
- Subsequently, models are ranked via cross-encoder models.
- Next, evidence is retrieved specifically to support the information.
- Lastly, the synthesis is produced via generative models.

More documents retrieved and additional reasoning processes can provide greater completeness to the context; however, additional latency and the possibility of failure are incurred. Real-world experiments have demonstrated that the additional accuracy achieved diminishes beyond a certain depth of retrieval, especially when robust knowledge bases are readily available (Izacard & Grave, 2021).

A practical strategy is to use a staged or progressive retrieval strategy. This can be visualized as a cascade of processes, where:

- Stage 1: Use fast and low-latency filtering using structured signals such as price, rating, and compatibility.
- Stage 2: Use a fast and low-latency search using vectors, followed by a lightweight re-ranking.
- Stage 3: Use deep evidence retrieval, but only for candidates that have passed the previous stages.

This is a cascade of processes that ensures a responsive system while using the heavy processes for a small number of candidates. This is analogous to hierarchical decision processes that are common in reinforcement learning approaches. In a retail context, the user expects a response in sub-second times to support an interactive search. Research into online recommender systems has shown that longer response times reduce user engagement and conversion rates (Kohavi et al., 2020).

3.4.2 Cost-Aware Model Routing and Inference Optimization

While large models provide the best reasoning, they are accompanied by high inference costs. In a busy e-commerce site, the difference in cost per request is small but adds up to a substantial portion of the site's cost. As a result, systems that are cost-efficient often use dynamic routing, where:

- Light transformers are used for intent detection and slot filling,

- Mid-sized models are used to generate standard summary responses for recommendations,
- Only large models are used for hard comparison questions or high-value purchases.

Adaptive routing has been investigated using a mixture of experts and, more recently, model cascading frameworks that aim to reduce the expected cost of inference without compromising quality (Chen et al., 2023).

The usage of tokens is one of the major cost drivers in these systems that utilize LLMs. For reducing these costs, the following options are prominent:

- Pre-summarization of long review datasets
- Extraction of structured facts in compact knowledge representations
- Context window truncation
- Addition of only relevant evidence instead of concatenating entire documents

The research on context-efficient prompts indicates that selective evidence retrieval could significantly reduce costs without compromising answer quality if the evidence is semantically aligned (Amugongo et al., 2025).

4. AI TECHNIQUES ENABLING COGNITIVE COMMERCE

Cognitive commerce entails the deployment of multiple A.I. strategies that collectively allow an agent to see products, discern user intent, analyze multimodal data, evaluate options, and execute decision making in an increasingly sophisticated manner. These strategies cover areas in natural language processing, computer vision, multimodal representation learning, knowledge graphs, symbolic reasoning frameworks, generative modulation, and reinforcement learning. Each AI technique provides a distinct layer of capability necessary for supporting shopping agents which operate in an autonomous and contextually tuned manner. This chapter analyzes the A.I. techniques in question with an emphasis on their algorithmic underpinnings and the cognitive functions they invoke in the context of electronic commerce.

4.1 Natural Language Understanding and Intent Interpretation

speech recognition is important within cognitive commerce as it applies to merchants with shopping agents who have to browse voice, typing, or other integrated systems interaction interfaces. Merchants who encounter opportune Large Language Models, these being BERT, GPT 3.5, and GPT 4 models, have found improvements and transformable functionalities in shopping agents. This improvement can be seen in agent's ability to understand complex queries.

Such models offer semantic representations, thus improving agent's ability to understand and perform:

- classification of intents,
- filling in assigned roles in a task-oriented conversation,
- comparing and summarizing product reviews,
- catalog question answering, and
- conversation management in context.

All of these tasks depend on BERT, GPT 3.5 and GPT 4 models.

4.2 Computer Vision for Product Understanding and Quality Assessment

Computer vision technologies are equally pivotal in cognitive commerce since many attributes of products, images generated by consumers, and indicators of item quality are frequently visual in nature. Through images of products, agents are able to reason about and interpret images to retrieve fine-grained visual information such as color, texture, shape, and quality of materials including components of products (Balhareth et al., 2024).

Significant breakthroughs in perception of visual patterns were achieved by Convolutional Neural Networks(CNNs) such as ResNet (He et al, 2016) and, more recently, by models using transformer-based vision architectures such as ViT (Dosovitskiy, 2020) which model images as a sequence of patches and handle them analogously to tokens in NLP, thereby greatly enhancing scalability and representation richness.

Visual analysis aids:

- identifying counterfeits via anomaly detection (Garcia-Cotte et al., 2024),
- extracting attribute-level representations to rank,
- classifying products in a category at scale,
- creating cross-modal embeddings for retrieval, and
- identifying defects or gaps from images uploaded by users.

Vision models are increasingly used by retailers for automatic quality assurance, catalogue assembly, and content moderation. Along with multimodal embeddings, these systems enable cognitive agents to reason effortlessly over visual and textual information about products.

4.3 Multimodal Representation Learning

Having multiple modes of learning involves processing text, images, audio, and structured metadata simultaneously to form unified representations which capture deeper and richer semantic connections than models which work with a single mode of learning. Multimodal learning has a strong emphasis on cognitive commerce since consumer decision processes typically require visually comparing products while simultaneously reading descriptions and analyzing numerical specifications. As shown in Figure 2, multimodal representation learning aligns these diverse inputs into a shared embedding space.

Figure 2. Multimodal representation learning pipeline.

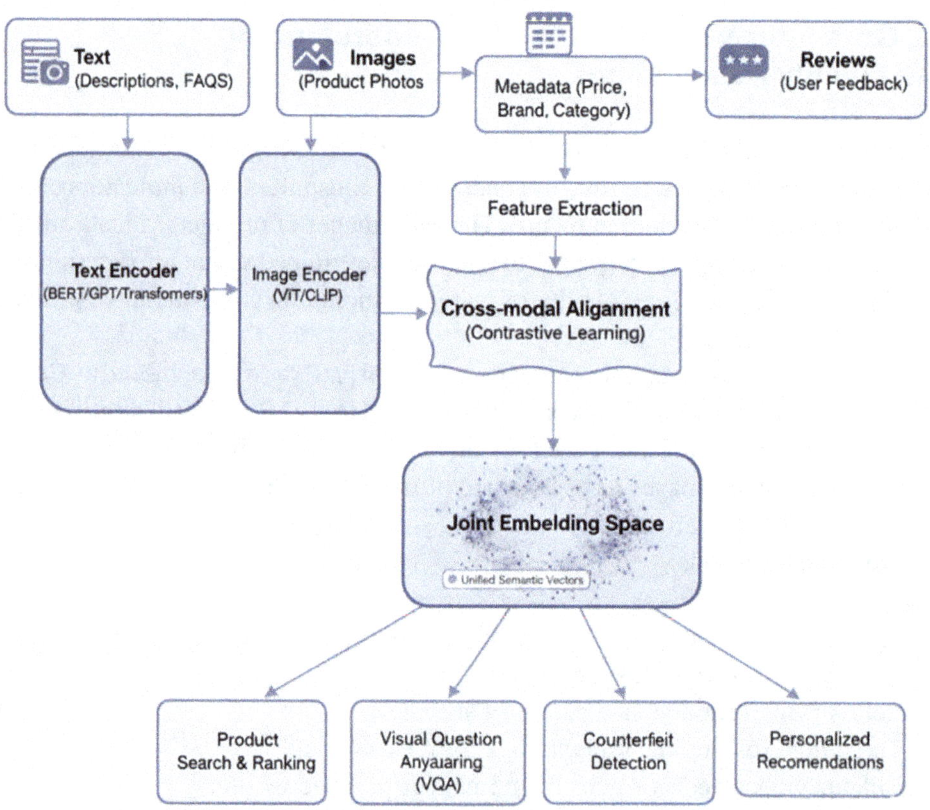

The model CLIP by Radford hed to the learning of visuals and text representations by contrasting and aligning images and text on a common semantic axis and, thus, the model allows agents to form product-image and product-descriptions embeddings.

Also, with the models BLIP-2 by Li and Flamingo by Alayrac et al. (2022), cross-attention and the fusion with LLMs allow for reasoning across multiple modalities. They support multimodal learning in:

- cross-modal search (e.g., "find items similar to this photo")
- Fine-grained attribute recognition
- review-image consistency checking
- product visual question answering
- enhanced retrieval effectiveness

These features are essential for agents which require understanding consumer-generated content, like photos taken during a troubleshooting step which are shared on social media, or image ads which leverage social media to enhance sales.

4.4 Knowledge Graphs and Neuro-Symbolic Reasoning

Users can appreciate the components of products, brands, subdivided categories, materials, attributes, and even the purpose and intent of a potential user through the utilization of knowledge graphs and their cognition. These sophisticated KGs used in cognitive commerce rests at the center of the intricate reasoning product domain. As a case in point, knowledge graphs are instrumental in improving the search catalog in given the catalog inconsistencies and product mismatches. Other retailers such as, Amazon, Alibaba and Walmart have increasingly incorporated improved search catalog using knowledge graphs (Dey, 2024).

Knowledge graphs support cognitive capabilities in several ways:

- The reasoning agents are capable of inferring a form of consistency ("laptop → has_attribute → RAM"), which then leads to constraint-based recommendations.
- Checking if a particular smartphone case is compatible with a particular device.
- Searching for smartphones using attributes of brands, styles, and other devices.

Using knowledge to support enforced policies of certain recommendations such as diversity, fairness, and balanced recommendations.

The combination of KG reasoning and neural embeddings in neuro-symbolic systems facilitates the use of knowledge graphs for logic and other aspects of machine learning, models such as R-GCN (Schlichtkrull et al. 2018) use unstructured knowledge and deep learning to improve representation learning of complex relations. LLMs have been noted to reduce the reasoning based on language through deep knowledge of the structured domain.

4.5 Generative AI for Commerce Applications

Generative AI is revolutionizing the retail space through LLM's ability to generate and summarize content and transfer styles. These models bolster cognitive commerce in important ways.

• Review Summary and Opinion Mining

Agents utilize sentiment analysis and opinion summarization opinion trained transformers to distill dependable and concise automations from terabytes of user-contributed text. Ni et al. (2019) suggest that noise review data summarization and consumer support decision processes benefit from the use of transformers.

• Product Content Creation

Retail generative systems are employed to automatically generate tasks aimed to diminish the efforts and haphazardness accompanying the manual crafting of content by producing coherent product descriptions and attribute enhanced specifications that are optimized for SEO.

• Fraud and Manipulation Restriction

Trust in recommendations made by the agents is supported through the profound work of Fang et al (2020) which uses GANs and transformer classifiers to detect and eliminate fake reviews, content, and images.

• Conversational Decision Support

Intelligent conversational agents which explain various trade-offs and alternatives are revolutionizing decision support systems through the use of LLMs (Park et al 2023). These systems facilitate sustained dialogue on goal-oriented topics and strengthen cognitive approaches emphasizing justification, reasoning, and clarity.

4.6 Reinforcement Learning for Decision Optimization

Reinforcement learning is critical in allowing shopping agents to perform complex sequential decision-making. RL, in contrast to static recommendation models, which consider interactions to be independent prediction tasks, regards the shopping process as a fluid environment consisting of states, actions, and delayed rewards.

• Markov Decision Process Framework

Shopping interactions can be depicted as a Markov Decision Process (MDP):

- State: a combination of user context, session history, products in view, and budget.
- Action: recommending items, changing score orders, price negotiation, and changes to the cart.
- Reward: conversion probability, user satisfaction, and user engagement over time.

This allows the shopping agent to devise optimal strategies over prolonged shopping interactions as opposed to single-step recommendations.

• Deep Reinforcement Learning Methods

Methods such as Deep Q Networks (Mnih et al., 2015), actor-critic models, and policy gradient techniques enable the agent to obtain suboptimal policies in dominant state spaces that characterize e-Commerce platforms.

Examples include:

- dynamic pricing (Mei et al., 2025),
- advanced personalized promotion strategies,
- bundled recommendations,
- long sequence next-item prediction, and
- advanced multi-step cart optimization.

• Hierarchical Reinforcement Learning

HRL focuses on subdividing the complex shopping task into smaller accomplishable sub-goals as a way to improve efficiency (Nachum et al. 2018). For example, "build a complete grocery basket" could comprise the subtasks of "select proteins," "select vegetables," and "price optimization." Like cognitive planners, the HRL approach appears to mimic elements of how humans divide and conquer decisions.

- Multi-Agent Reinforcement Learning

In a multi-agent retail ecosystem, buyer agents, seller agents, and logistics agents perform coordinated action at the same time. MARL has been used for dynamic negotiation, competitive pricing, and supply-chain optimization (Mishra et al. 2025). These frameworks push cognitive commerce further than single ecosystem-level decision systems toward multi-agent ecosystem-level intelligence.

5. DATA FLOW AND TRAINING PIPELINES

Multimodal behaviors contain traces of sophisticated data ecosystems. These are behaviors such as metadata, contextual signals, and product info. As a result, cognitive commerce systems require integration of data. Effective design depends on how data pipelines are structured. These pipelines are used throughout a commerce data lifecycle and for continuous deployment of prepossessing, model training, and representation learning. Use of inference and large-scale data model training pipelines for deployment and representation learning are needed. In this section, the data flow, amplification, and training pipelines for agentic shopping systems are highlighted, restating the problems of data scale, privacy, integration, and noise. Example A: PDO Layer.

The first layer of the pipeline focuses on the procurement of data from many users. The current retail models generate amounts of structured data and unstructured text. The systems do this roughly through:

- Behavioral-based data: purchase data, add data, user sessions' queries, clicks, and browse patterns – (Lv 2023).
- Information of a product: current and historical pricing, inventory data, inventory availability, description and specifications, brands, etc.
- Visuals: photos of the product, user photos, images from manufacturers.
- Text: marketing communication, Q&A documents, reviews, seller and buyer text interactions.
- Contextual signals: User segments, time of the day, season, GP, and device used.

High and wide systems of data can, through data ingestion processes, collect streams of audio-visual data through marketing systems.

In e-commerce analytics, much of the data rests in relational structures, including product catalogs, which are structured in entity relationship schemas, and user behavior recorded as temporal events. This type of data architecture is foundational for the convergence of downstream modeling activities which, for instance, entail importing knowledge graphs or integrating multi-modal embeddings. Figure 3 presents the end-to-end data flow and training pipeline underlying cognitive commerce systems, illustrating how multimodal data sources are ingested, preprocessed, embedded, modeled, and ultimately deployed within privacy-preserving and scalable production environments.

Figure 3. End-to-End Data Flow and Training Pipeline for Cognitive Commerce.

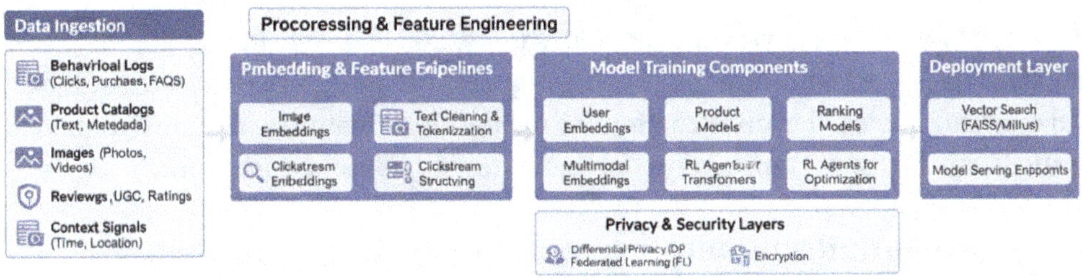

5.1 Data Cleaning, Preprocessing, and Feature Engineering

In e-commerce contexts, unprocessed data tends to be unstructured and chaotic. User product reviews are often repetitive and irrelevant while product images suffer from inconsistent grades of resolution and quality. Product descriptions themselves are frequently incomplete. Effective process pipelines should be designed to address the following components:

1. Text Processing

This includes BERT (Devlin et al., 2019) being leveraged for tokenization and spam filtration and the archiving of etched user contributions for aspect-level annotation as well as sentiment extraction and sentiment spam filtration. Meaningful product features and pain points from user reviews are drawn from the dense data clouds by deduplication processes.

2. Image Processing

This encompasses the use of ResNet (He et al., 2016) and ViT (Dosovitskiy., 2020) for recognition and detection, wherein images are chop and adjust in size and quality. In catalog intersections or field violations, sleuthing for forensic analogues often deploys Visual Similarity Search.

3. Behavioral Feature Engineering

This includes the reconstruction of clickstream logs into structured narrative fragments as seamless passages. Additional metrics for the structured data may incorporate dwell, recency, and frequency.

4. Knowledge Graph Construction.

In graph reasoning tasks, entity linking identifies and embeds into graph structures products, brands, categories and attributes (Dey, 2024). For bridging gaps between raw data and layers of modeling, feature engineering is significant. Although deep learning automates the construction of handcrafted features, features remained. Particularly, the importance is fundamental domain enriched in retail.

5.3 Representation Learning and Embedding Pipelines

Data structuring and cleaning enables systems to create embeddings that extract and represent behaviors and semantics. Embedding pipelines consist of the following components:

- CLIP (Radford et al. 2021) conducts product embeddings (texts, specifications, and images) and transforms them into a unified format.
- User preference embedding is formed by sequentially ordered or transformer-based recommenders (Sun et al, 2019).
- Knowledge graphs based on (Schlichtkrull et al, 2018) contain graph embeddings that express and visualize the relationships among different products.

Together, these embedding spaces form the computational bases for similarity search, retrieval, ranking, and reinforcement learning. FAISS (Khan et al., 2024) and other approximate nearest neighbor (ANN) search methods allow for retrieval in real time from millions of embedding vectors.

5.4. Model Training Pipelines

The training pipeline consists of coordinating different types of models, often being designed in parallel, to undergo the cognitive capabilities of the shopping agents.

- Recommender Systems

The sequential recommenders (SASRec, BERT4Rec) model and train on the long-term transition folding patterns and preference evolution. These sequential recommenders train mini-batch optimization through negative sampling to learn differentiated recommendations and its alternatives.

- *Ranking Models:* Different ranking models such as deep ranking networks or LambdaMART utilize predictive relevance to optimize the order of products (Burges, 2010) predictive relevance (Burges, 2010).
- *Multimodal Transformers:* Contrastive objectives assist in the alignment of modalities, sentence-image pairs, and domain-specific corpora such as product descriptions and user sentiments emotive and product vision-language models (BLIP2 and Flamingo)
- *Reinforcement Learning Agents:* Reinforcement Learning agents employ temporal difference learning, policy gradients, or actor-critic to maximize long term rewards (Mnih et al., 2015). The training environment consists of user simulated behavior and market conditions, many times consisting of synthetic augmentations for model robustness. Training pipelines that are large in scale rely on computing frameworks that are distributed, like PyTorch and Horovod, joining multiple GPUs model training.

5.5 Model Evaluation and Validation

Different activities call for different evaluation metrics. The most common evaluation metrics for particular activities include:

- Recommendation: MRR, NDCG, Hit Rate.
- Multimodal retrieval: Recall@K, cross-modal alignment scores.
- Vision tasks: F1 score, precision per class, overall accuracy.

In reinforcement learning: cumulative rewards, regret, stability of the policy. Owning to the mechanics of the offline evaluation, online A/B testing is integrated due to agents assessing performance under operational limitations interacting with actual user traffic. Policies are logged, and then counterfactual inference techniques, as described in Gilotte et al. (2018), are applied to help mitigate the bias embedded in the observational data.

5.6 Deployment and Real-Time Inference

Implementation of cognitive agents entails architectural settings that support low-latency inference pipelines that can sustain millions of requests each second. Important elements encompass:

- Model *Serving* Layers: Optimized by using ONNX Runtime, TensorRT, or latency-sensitive model quantization that preserves accuracy.
- *Feature Stores:* Maintained through systems such as Feast or proprietary systems that assure consistent real-time feature accessibility during training and inference.
- Scalable *Retrieval* Engines: Vector databases (Milvus, Pinecone) or ANN search libraries that provide rapid embedding lookups.
- *Orchestration and Monitoring:* Microservices structures support architectural scalability, while monitoring systems manage drift, anomalies, and performance degradation.

5.7 Privacy-Preserving Learning and Security Considerations

The sensitive nature of behavioral and transactional data makes data privacy crucial. Contemporary pipelines utilize:

- Federated learning allows for training and data analysis on user devices while maintaining the data privacy and security for the user (Kairouz & McMahan. 2021).
- Differential privacy protects each person by adding noise to data so that identities cannot be revealed.
- Homomorphic encryption allows operations in which encrypted data is processed and the resulting data is still encrypted.

All of the mentioned techniques improve user confidence for autonomous shopping systems while complying with the GDPR and other regulations.

6. SECURITY, ETHICS, AND TRUST

As systems of cognitive commerce advance autonomously and steer choices, the architectural and governance concepts of the systems of security, ethics, and trust become increasingly vital. Automated and self-operating purchasing agents function in volatile digital marketplaces and, simultaneously, in behavioral self-learning systems and with external vendor systems, command funds, tender financial advice, and in some configurations, purchase autonomously. Such exposure contributes to fairness and concealment, creates attack surfaces, and raises trust in AI to critical levels. This chapter identifies primary security concerns in cognitive commerce, explores the ethics of algorithmic governance, and prescribes the suitable frameworks of privacy-preserving and socially acceptable technologies to put into practice.

6.1 Security Threats in Cognitive Commerce

Having knowledge graphs along with agentic reasoning and an integration of multimodal learning introduces certain weaknesses that hostile actors can take advantage of. In the domain of cognitive commerce, security challenges can be categorized as confrontational model strikes, market interference, and encompassing systemic dangers.

6.1.1 Adversarial Attacks on Recommendation and Reasoning Models

Deep learning models, ranking, retrieval, and product understanding are sensitive to adversarial perturbations. A few slight alterations to product images and descriptions can lead to agents incorrectly classifying items, altering rankings, and inferring attributes incorrectly (Goodfellow et al., 2014). Popular avenues of attack are:

- Adversarial images crafted to fool visual encoders, like CLIP and ViT.
- Manipulated reviews and seller descriptions to Transformers which contain adversarially crafted text.
- Product knowledge graphs are improperly altered through fake relationships interlaced (Aburidi & Marcia, 2024) associated with Graph data.

These vulnerabilities undermine the trust that consumers and retailers place in the integrity of the recommendations and the ability to weed out fraudulent items.

6.1.2 Manipulation Through Fake Reviews and Synthetic Content

In addition to generative AI converting attacks to more sophisticated formats, Joshi (2024) states that it enables opponents to create realized synthetic reviews that schematically perturb ranking systems. 'Content summary' and 'Sentiment analysis' cognitive agents need to integrate:

- Classifiers of content authenticity,

- detection of linguistic abnormality,
- Verification of metadata coherence,
- Cross validation of multiple sources.

These manipulations will help reduce consumer trust erosion that has been facilitated by manipulation.

6.1.3 Adversarial Behavior in Multi-Agent Negotiation

Asymmetric exploitation of negotiation protocols could occur in Complex Cognitive Commerce Systems which involve multi-agent buyer vcs, and logistics, vendor agents. In such cases, Multimodal Persuasive Sidetracking Agents could be employed which, through social engineering, manipulate consumer welfare through deceptive pricing, inventory, and state of the art information (Yuan et al., 2023). Having negotiation protocols and mechanisms with strong incentive compatibility would blunt such predation.

6.1.4 System-Level Security Risks

Autonomous virtual shoppers, for instance, usually interact with digital wallets, payment systems, and other external systems, do tend to pay considerably attention to risks like:

- transactions that are not authorized,
- the taking control of an application programming interface,
- session replay attacks,
- risks of the vendor integration supply chain external and model driven.

Countermeasures like secure API gateways, encrypted communications, monitored channel anomalies, and observation of varied zero-trust principles (Kindervag, 2016).

6.2 Ethical Issues and Fairness in Cognitive Commerce

Aside from security headaches, cognitive commerce systems present ethical concerns such as algorithmic bias, opacity, consumer freedom, and responsible stewardship of data.

6.2.1 Transparency and Explainability

Explanations within commerce systems which guide spending behavior must be clear and simple enough for humans to understand. Building trust in transparent decision making is imperative when agents autonomously optimize shopping carts or deliver recommendations. Explainable AI (XAI) frameworks assist in:

- identifying and visualizing components that drive ranking decision outcomes,
- explaining the evaluation of competing values in a decision,
- framing auditability of system agents' behavioral outcomes (Chatti et al., 2024).

Explanations also fulfill legal requirements, providing a rationale for stakeholders or regulators on the mental processes used in making autonomous decisions.

6.2.2 Consumer Manipulation and Autonomy

The practice of personalization, if improper, could become unethical if agents overload consumers with way too many high-margin products, encourage impulse purchases, or otherwise take advantage of behavioral weaknesses. These issues are part of broader criticisms of "dark patterns" in digital commerce (Mathur et al. 2019). Design of ethically aligned agents requires:

- Restrict persuasive optimization to user beneficial outcomes only.
- Specify and enforce alignment goal constraints.
- Implement user-initiated preference limits.

These steps withhold consumer autonomy and ensure cognitive agents are supportive assistants and not behavioral controllers.

6.3 Building Trustworthy Cognitive Shopping Agents

Trust is constituted of Security, Fairness/Social Equity, Transparency, and Reliability. For trust to be accounted for, cognitive commerce systems shall have:

- Robustness verification for adversarial attack perturbations.
- Supervision by humans for all transactions and especially for transactions is deemed dangerous.
- Decision support systems with explainable recommendations and rationales.
- Certification for assurance akin to the autonomous systems safety case.

- Persistent surveillance and monitoring with automated alerts for model drift, increasing bias, and strange behavioral decision making.

Incorporating these safeguards allows the developers to design cognitive shopping agents that act as reliable digital middlemen, safeguarding consumer welfare while facilitating higher precision and tailored commerce.

7. REAL-WORLD USE CASES

The shift of cognitive commerce from experimental prototypes to practical operational systems, integrated into massive digital marketplaces, retail systems, and consumer applications, has truly been impressive. New modes of personalized, contextually aware retail experiences emerged because of the intelligent shopping agents' capacity to discern, evaluate multiple products, reason over limitations, and independently assist in purchasing decisions. This chapter shows the practical applications case studies of cognitive commerce architectures deployment across multiple industry sectors and their engineering principles together with their consequential industrial engineering effects.

7.1 Autonomous Shopping Assistants in E-Commerce Platforms

The implementation of cognitive commerce that has progressed furthest is that of autonomous shopping assistants. These agents aid consumers by means of conversation, targeted suggestions, and step-by-step decision tree methods.

Amazon, Alibaba, and Walmart, among the other large e-commerce platforms, have incorporated sophisticated assistants that utilize large language models, multimodal processing, and reinforcement learning–based recommendation systems.

7.1.1 Capabilities and Architecture

Autonomous assistants usually deliver the following output:

- comprehending the ways users state their queries in natural language,
- comparative analysis of products through structured and unstructured datasets,
- tailored filtering according to the user's past activities, and
- multi-stage decision assistance for costly purchases (e.g. buying electronics, furniture, or traveling).

Dialogue management and semantic analysis for GPT-4, PaLM, and ERNIE are underpinned by their LLMs. The work conducted by Mnih et al in 2015 demonstrates that reinforcement learning improves the order of recommendations given and develops methods to increase user satisfaction over time.

7.1.2 Operational Impact

Research has demonstrated that AI-driven assistants result in improved conversion rates, reduced friction in searches, and greater user satisfaction as compared to manual browsers (Song et al., 2021). Consumers, in particular, appreciate being pointed to pertinent products and not having to wade through large, information-burdened catalogs.

7.2 Smart Price-Comparison and Optimization Engines

Price comparison agents are suppliers of computerized analysis of dynamic pricing signals from multiple suppliers to recommend the best purchase time and supplier.

7.2.1 All of These Platforms Utilize Analytics

Some examples are Google Shopping, Honey (Paypal) and PriceRunner, which utilize analytics and recognition of patterns to monitor prices changes and fluctuations in marketplaces and discounts over time.

7.2.2 Analytical Roots

The systems utilize:

- time-series forecasting models to project price changes,
- modality of specification and vendor ratings, shipping, and prices of goods,
- ranked utility theory, and
- applying discount negotiation in real time within some ecosystems (Mei et al., 2025).

The price-optimizer agents add value to consumers by suggesting time of purchase that minimizes expenses, especially in electronics, appliance and travel which are volatile in pricing.

7.3 Grocery Replenishment and Household Inventory Agents

Autonomous replenishment systems are capable of predicting patterns of home consumption and automating repurchasing of items on a recurring schedule. Examples are Amazon Dash Replenish, Walmart InHome Delivery, and Ocado's smart replenishment algorithms.

7.3.1. Cognitive Capabilities

These systems depend on:

- consumption forecasting algorithms,
- collaborative filtering for household-level preferences,
- behavioral modeling, and
- Context-aware decision rules (considering seasonality, special events, etc.).

The agent can learn and automate the purchasing of the patterns "milk every five days," "detergent monthly," or "extra snacks during holidays."

7.3.2 Integration with IoT Devices

IoT sensors embedded in smart appliances, refrigerators, washing machines, or pantries, enable real-time tracking of inventory levels (Gubbi et al., 2013).

Cognitive shopping agents integrate this data with personalized behavioral profiles to autonomously initiate replenishment or provide timely low-stock alerts.

CONCLUSION

To sum up, cognitive commerce signifies a radical change of digital retail system perception, service, and interaction in relation to consumers. Directly becoming intelligent through multimodal perception, advanced reasoning, and adaptive learning within consolidated architectures, intelligent shopping agents are taking a massive leap over traditional recommendation engines into systems with the ability to understand context, make long-horizon decisions and act autonomously. The combination of transformer-based language models, vision, language representations, knowledge-graph reasoning, and reinforcement learning applied in this chapter can help such agents understand user intent more accurately and make decisions in dynamic market situations more optimally, as illustrated throughout. Meanwhile, a strong data pipeline and privacy-sensitive technologies are underway so that it can responsibly extend such abilities in real world conditions. However, it presents equally challenging considerations with regard to security, fairness, and transparency hence necessary constant consideration towards ethical design and credible governance.

REFERENCES

Aburidi, M., & Marcia, R. (2024). Topological adversarial attacks on graph neural networks via projected meta learning. In *Proceedings of the 2024 IEEE International Conference on Evolving and Adaptive Intelligent Systems (EAIS)*. IEEE., Available from https://par.nsf.gov/servlets/purl/10566343 DOI: 10.1109/EAIS58494.2024.10569101

Alayrac, J. B., Donahue, J., Luc, P., Miech, A., Barr, I., Hasson, Y., . . . Simonyan, K. (2022). Flamingo: a visual language model for few-shot learning. *Advances in neural information processing systems, 35*, 23716-23736. Available from https://proceedings.neurips.cc/paper_files/paper/2022/file/960a172bc7fbf0177ccccb b411a7d800-Paper-Conference.pdf

Amugongo, L. M., Mascheroni, P., Brooks, S., Doering, S., & Seidel, J. (2025). Retrieval augmented generation for large language models in healthcare: A systematic review. *PLOS Digital Health, 4*(6), e0000877. DOI: 10.1371/journal.pdig.0000877 PMID: 40498738

Anderson, J. R., Bothell, D., Byrne, M. D., Douglass, S., Lebiere, C., & Qin, Y. (2004). An integrated theory of the mind. *Psychological Review, 111*(4), 1036–1060. DOI: 10.1037/0033-295X.111.4.1036 PMID: 15482072

Balhareth, H., Al-Adwan, A. S., Alsoud, A. R., Abd-Aljaber, O., Al-Rahmi, W. M., & Urbaníková, M. (2024). Journey into meta-commerce: Unveiling the driving forces of consumer adoption. *Global Knowledge, Memory and Communication*. Advance online publication. DOI: 10.1108/GKMC-05-2024-0307

Bubeck, S., Chandrasekaran, V., Eldan, R., Gehrke, J., Horvitz, E., Kamar, E., . . . Zhang, Y. (2023). Sparks of artificial general intelligence: Early experiments with gpt-4. *arXiv preprint arXiv:2303.12712*. https://doi.org//arXiv.2303.12712DOI: 10.48550

Burges, C. J. (2010). From ranknet to lambdarank to lambdamart: An overview. *Learning, 11*(23-581), 81. Available from https://www.khoury.northeastern.edu/home/vip/teach/MLcourse/4_boosting/materials/msr-tr-2010-82.pdf

Celestin, M., Vasuki, M., Sujatha, S., & Kumar, A. D. (2024). How businesses create personalized experiences to boost customer retention: The role of technology and human interactions in customer satisfaction. *International Journal of Applied and Advanced Scientific Research, 9*(2), 75–80. DOI: 10.5281/zenodo.13871854

Chatti, M. A., Guesmi, M., & Muslim, A. (2024). Visualization for recommendation explainability: A survey and new perspectives. *ACM Transactions on Interactive Intelligent Systems*, *14*(3), 1–40. DOI: 10.1145/3672276

Chen, L., Zaharia, M., & Zou, J. (2023). Frugalgpt: How to use large language models while reducing cost and improving performance. *arXiv preprint arXiv:2305.05176*. https://doi.org//arXiv.2305.05176DOI: 10.48550

Devlin, J., Chang, M. W., Lee, K., & Toutanova, K. (2019). Bert: Pre-training of deep bidirectional transformers for language understanding. In *Proceedings of the 2019 conference of the North American chapter of the association for computational linguistics: human language technologies, volume 1 (long and short papers)* (pp. 4171-4186). DOI: 10.18653/v1/N19-1423

Dey, L. (2024). Knowledge graph-driven data processing for business intelligence. *Wiley Interdisciplinary Reviews. Data Mining and Knowledge Discovery*, *14*(3), e1529. DOI: 10.1002/widm.1529

Dosovitskiy, A. (2020). An image is worth 16x16 words: Transformers for image recognition at scale. *arXiv preprint arXiv:2010.11929*. https://doi.org//arXiv.2010.11929DOI: 10.48550

Fang, Y., Wang, H., Zhao, L., Yu, F., & Wang, C. (2020). Dynamic knowledge graph based fake-review detection. *Applied Intelligence*, *50*(12), 4281–4295. DOI: 10.1007/s10489-020-01761-w

Garcia-Cotte, H., Mellouli, D., Rehman, A., Wang, L., & Stork, D. G. (2024). Deep neural network-based detection of counterfeit products from smartphone images. *arXiv preprint arXiv:2410.05969*. https://doi.org//arXiv.2410.05969DOI: 10.48550

Gilotte, A., Calauzènes, C., Nedelec, T., Abraham, A., & Dollé, S. (2018). Offline a/b testing for recommender systems. In *Proceedings of the eleventh ACM international conference on web search and data mining* (pp. 198-206). https://doi.org/ DOI: 10.1145/3159652.3159687

Goodfellow, I. J., Shlens, J., & Szegedy, C. (2014). Explaining and harnessing adversarial examples. *arXiv preprint arXiv:1412.6572*. https://doi.org//arXiv.1412.6572DOI: 10.48550

Gubbi, J., Buyya, R., Marusic, S., & Palaniswami, M. (2013). Internet of Things (IoT): A vision, architectural elements, and future directions. *Future Generation Computer Systems*, *29*(7), 1645–1660. DOI: 10.1016/j.future.2013.01.010

He, K., Zhang, X., Ren, S., & Sun, J. (2016). Deep residual learning for image recognition. In *Proceedings of the IEEE conference on computer vision and pattern recognition* (pp. 770-778). DOI: 10.1109/CVPR.2016.90

Hidasi, B., Karatzoglou, A., Baltrunas, L., & Tikk, D. (2015). Session-based recommendations with recurrent neural networks. *arXiv preprint arXiv:1511.06939*. https://doi.org//arXiv.1511.06939DOI: 10.48550

Huang, M. H., & Rust, R. T. (2021). A strategic framework for artificial intelligence in marketing. *Journal of the Academy of Marketing Science*, *49*(1), 30–50. DOI: 10.1007/s11747-020-00749-9

Izacard, G., & Grave, E. (2021). Leveraging passage retrieval with generative models for open domain question answering. In *Proceedings of the 16th conference of the european chapter of the association for computational linguistics: main volume* (pp. 874-880). DOI: 10.18653/v1/2021.eacl-main.74

Joshi, H.Maysara Mazin Badr Alsaad. (2024). Transformer-Based Language Deep Learning Detection of Fake Reviews on Online Products. *J. Electrical Systems*, *20*(3), 2368–2378. DOI: 10.52783/jes.4083

Kairouz, P., & McMahan, H. B. (2021). Advances and open problems in federated learning. *Foundations and Trends in Machine Learning*, *14*(1-2), 1–210. DOI: 10.1561/2200000083

Kang, W. C., & McAuley, J. (2018). Self-attentive sequential recommendation. In *2018 IEEE international conference on data mining (ICDM)* (pp. 197-206). IEEE. DOI: 10.1109/ICDM.2018.00035

Kelly, J.III, & Hamm, S. (2013). *Smart machines: Ibmos watson and the era of cognitive computing*. Columbia University Press., Available from https://cup.columbia .edu/book/smart-machines/9780231537278/ DOI: 10.7312/kell16856

Khan, S., Singh, S., Simhadri, H. V., & Vedurada, J. (2024). Bang: Billion-scale approximate nearest neighbor search using a single gpu. *arXiv preprint arXiv:2401.11324*. https://doi.org//arXiv.2401.11324DOI: 10.48550

Kindervag, J. (2016). No more chewy centers: Introducing the zero trust model of information security. *Forrester Research, 3*(1), 1-16. Available from https:// crystaltechnologies.com/wp-content/uploads/2017/12/forrester-zero-trust-model -information-security.pdf

Kohavi, R., Tang, D., & Xu, Y. (2020). *Trustworthy online controlled experiments: A practical guide to a/b testing*. Cambridge University Press., DOI: 10.1017/9781108653985

Koren, Y., Bell, R., & Volinsky, C. (2009). Matrix factorization techniques for recommender systems. *Computer, 42*(8), 30–37. DOI: 10.1109/MC.2009.263

Laird, J. E. (2019). *The Soar cognitive architecture*. MIT press. Available from https://www.amazon.com/Soar-Cognitive-Architecture-MIT-Press/dp/0262538539

Lewis, P., Perez, E., Piktus, A., Petroni, F., Karpukhin, V., Goyal, N., . . . Kiela, D. (2020). Retrieval-augmented generation for knowledge-intensive nlp tasks. *Advances in neural information processing systems, 33*, 9459-9474. Available from https://proceedings.neurips.cc/paper_files/paper/2020/file/6b493230205f780e1bc26945df7481e5-Paper.pdf

Li, J., Li, D., Savarese, S., & Hoi, S. (2023). Blip-2: Bootstrapping language-image pre-training with frozen image encoders and large language models. In *International conference on machine learning* (pp. 19730-19742). PMLR. Available from https://proceedings.mlr.press/v202/li23q/li23q.pdf

Lv, H. (2023). E-commerce consumer behavior analysis based on big data. *Journal of Computational Methods in Science and Engineering, 23*(2), 651–661. DOI: 10.3233/JCM-226628

Mathur, A., Acar, G., Friedman, M. J., Lucherini, E., Mayer, J., Chetty, M., & Narayanan, A. (2019). Dark patterns at scale: Findings from a crawl of 11K shopping websites. *Proceedings of the ACM on human-computer interaction, 3*(CSCW), 1-32. https://doi.org/DOI: 10.1145/3359183

Mei, Z. (2025). Dynamic Pricing Strategy Driven by Deep Reinforcement Learning with Empirical Analysis on the Collaborative Optimization of Hotel Revenue Management and Customer Satisfaction. *International Journal of High Speed Electronics and Systems, 2540865*, 2540865. Advance online publication. DOI: 10.1142/S0129156425408654

Mishra, M. K., Vyas, C., Mazumdar, B. D., & Mishra, V. (2025). Harnessing the Power of Machine Learning in Multi-Agent Systems for B2C E-Commerce Optimization. In *2025 3rd International Conference on Communication, Security, and Artificial Intelligence (ICCSAI)* (Vol. 3, pp. 2157-2161). IEEE. DOI: 10.1109/ICCSAI64074.2025.11064164

Mnih, V., Kavukcuoglu, K., Silver, D., Rusu, A. A., Veness, J., Bellemare, M. G., ... & Hassabis, D. (2015). Human-level control through deep reinforcement learning. *nature, 518*(7540), 529-533. https://doi.org/DOI: 10.1038/nature14236

Nachum, O., Gu, S. S., Lee, H., & Levine, S. (2018). Data-efficient hierarchical reinforcement learning. *Advances in neural information processing systems, 31.* Available from https://papers.nips.cc/paper_files/paper/2018/file/e6384711491713d29bc63fc5eeb5ba4f-Paper.pdf

Ni, J., Li, J., & McAuley, J. (2019). Justifying recommendations using distantly-labeled reviews and fine-grained aspects. In *Proceedings of the 2019 conference on empirical methods in natural language processing and the 9th international joint conference on natural language processing (EMNLP-IJCNLP)* (pp. 188-197). DOI: 10.18653/v1/D19-1018

Park, J. S., O'Brien, J., Cai, C. J., Morris, M. R., Liang, P., & Bernstein, M. S. (2023). Generative agents: Interactive simulacra of human behavior. In *Proceedings of the 36th annual acm symposium on user interface software and technology* (pp. 1-22). https://doi.org/DOI: 10.1145/3586183.3606763

Radford, A., Kim, J. W., Hallacy, C., Ramesh, A., Goh, G., Agarwal, S., . . . Sutskever, I. (2021). Learning transferable visual models from natural language supervision. In *International conference on machine learning* (pp. 8748-8763). PmLR. Available from https://proceedings.mlr.press/v139/radford21a.html.

Resnick, P., Iacovou, N., Suchak, M., Bergstrom, P., & Riedl, J. (1994). Grouplens: An open architecture for collaborative filtering of netnews. In *Proceedings of the 1994 ACM conference on Computer supported cooperative work* (pp. 175-186). https://doi.org/DOI: 10.1145/192844.192905

Schlichtkrull, M., Kipf, T. N., Bloem, P., Van Den Berg, R., Titov, I., & Welling, M. (2018). Modeling relational data with graph convolutional networks. In *European semantic web conference* (pp. 593-607). Cham: Springer International Publishing. https://doi.org/DOI: 10.1007/978-3-319-93417-4_38

Song, X., & Xiong, T. (2021). A survey of published literature on conversational artificial intelligence. In *2021 7th International conference on information management (ICIM)* (pp. 113-117). IEEE. https://doi.org/DOI: 10.1109/ICIM52229.2021.9417135

Sun, F., Liu, J., Wu, J., Pei, C., Lin, X., Ou, W., & Jiang, P. (2019). BERT4Rec: Sequential recommendation with bidirectional encoder representations from transformer. In *Proceedings of the 28th ACM international conference on information and knowledge management* (pp. 1441-1450). DOI: 10.1145/3357384.3357895

Vaswani, A., Shazeer, N., Parmar, N., Uszkoreit, J., Jones, L., Gomez, A. N., . . . Polosukhin, I. (2017). Attention is all you need. *Advances in neural information processing systems*, 31st Conference on Neural Information Processing Systems (NIPS 2017), Long Beach, CA, USA. Available from http://proceedings.neurips.cc/paper_files/paper/2017/file/3f5ee243547dee91fbd053c1c4a845aa-Paper.pdf

Yuan, L., Zhang, Z., Xue, K., Yin, H., Chen, F., Guan, C., & Yu, Y. (2023). Robust multi-agent coordination via evolutionary generation of auxiliary adversarial attackers. In *Proceedings of the AAAI Conference on Artificial Intelligence* (Vol. 37, No. 10, pp. 11753-11762). https://doi.org/DOI: 10.1609/aaai.v37i10.26388

Chapter 5
Algorithms Against Manipulation:
Safeguarding Consumer Rights in AI Shopping

Shashank Solanki
http://orcid.org/0009-0002-5923-0516
Christ University, India

ABSTRACT

The growing use of AI driven shopping agents has transformed digital commerce through enhanced personalization, while simultaneously enabling new forms of consumer manipulation, including dark patterns, algorithmic price discrimination, and subscription traps. This chapter critically examines whether existing regulatory frameworks particularly the GDPR, the EU AI Act, and India's Digital Personal Data Protection Act, 2023 are adequate to address persuasive algorithmic practices. It argues that prevailing consent based regulatory models are structurally ill-equipped to counter real-time and adaptive AI driven manipulation. Drawing on regulatory gaps and contemporary case studies, the chapter advances the normative proposal of classifying advanced AI shopping agents as information fiduciaries. Such a framework would impose enforceable duties of loyalty and care toward consumers, moving beyond notice-and-consent paradigms and strengthening consumer protection in AI-mediated digital marketplaces.

1. INTRODUCTION

One of the most radical changes in the contemporary business is the introduction of the artificial intelligence (AI) into the consumer marketplaces. Smart robots

DOI: 10.4018/979-8-3373-7330-0.ch005

that can shop, recommend and purchase products and services such as chatbots, autonomous buying assistants and recommendation robots have utterly changed the shopping, comparison, and purchasing process of consumers. Such systems can be more convenient and efficient through the provision of user preferences, anticipation of needs, optimization of choice architectures etc. It is empirically shown that recommendations based on AI influence a consumer purchase choice in approximately over 35 percent of all global consumer buying choices, and that the AI retail industry will continue to grow to exceed USD 23.9 billion in 2027 (Grand View Research, 2023). Externally, the developments appear to increase the consumer choice through individual decision-making support.

But there is with this boosting of power also an upsurge of methodical manipulation. The same individualizing capabilities are also supported by algorithms that help popularize the so-called dark patterns or a platform-designing approach that takes advantage of cognitive biases to pursue the platform agenda, sacrificing the well-being of consumers (Mathur et al., 2019). These include subscription traps, such as pretence of scarcity, biased advice in favour of high-commission goods, and discriminating dynamic pricing based on the perceived willingness to pay. Its operations, such as the recent 2023 complaint of the Federal Trade Commission [FTC] against the alleged Iliad cancellation flow by Amazon and the 2019 intervention of the Competition and Markets Authority [CMA] at the pressure tactics employed by Bookings.com are evidence that it is no longer a case study (Federal Trade Commission [FTC], 2023a; Competition and Markets Authority [CMA], 2019).

1.1 Context and Problem Statement

Qualitative change to the normal e-commerce interfaces is the AI shopping agents. These systems are dynamic and adjust their behavior depending on continuous data collection, behavioral analytics and psychological profiling compared to the use of a static platform. This eases what Yeung (2017) describes as the hypernudging that attempts to attempt and affect behavior in real-time, on a level that has never been achievable in the offline markets. This asymmetry proves too harsh: consumers are less than rational and platforms possess enormous data, predictive algorithms, and optimization.The outcome of this imbalance is the personalization-manipulation paradox (Susser et al., 2019). Even though, personalization is utilized as the consumer experience element, one employs it to exploit the vulnerability, fatigue, or instability of emotions. This is not primarily about the technological capacity that shapes the border between what can be considered rightful help and what can be considered destructive manipulation, but on what interests should the system be used to.

Legal frameworks which are in place do not meet this challenge adequately. The overall data protection rules and laws, such as the General Data Protection Regulation (GDPR) of the EU, as well as India (Digital Personal Data Protection Act, 2023) and the state privacy laws of the U.S., are founded on the notice-and-consent models more (Regulation [EU] 2016/679, 2016). These frameworks assume that the informed consent and transparency issue are sufficient to safeguard consumer interests. In practice, consent is often obtained in a very opaque way such that it must be regulated, and that algorithmic opacities do not permit transparency. The privacy paradox that was long established also demonstrates the inefficiency of consumers to protect their interest despite having a formal choice and disclosure (Barnes, 2006; Norberg et al., 2007).

New AI-specific regulation particularly the EU Artificial Intelligence Act (2024) is a good move in regulation yet it still falls short in attempting to encompass cumulative and subtle manipulation situations in the consumer context. Although Article 5 prohibits subliminal persuasion and manipulation of vulnerabilities, it is not known how it would be applied to the day-to-day commercial AI systems (Regulation [EU] 2024/1689, 2024). The Act has risk-based approach towards high-risk areas that may overestimate cumulative damages of millions of fraudulent consumer transactions (Veale and Borgesius, 2021).It is against this backdrop that this paper presents the argument of equality restatement of the legal relationship between the AI shopping agents and consumers. It also elaborates how AI shopping agents may be classified as information fiduciaries -the parties that have an enforceable duty of loyalty, care, and candor toward users. Based on the fiduciary principles of the common law and the current-day knowledge (Balkin, 2016; Khan and Pozen, 2019; Richards and Hartzog, 2016), fiduciary framework offers a structural alternative to the consent regulatory framework by enforcing the affirmative duties of acting in the best interest of consumers and prohibiting the occurrence of a conflict of interest.The effects extend beyond financial losses in financial dealings to fundamental matters of independence, honor, and involvement in democracy. Algorithms that take advantage of human vulnerabilities in the systematic way, where people are the tool to commercial outcomes, are destructive to human dignity and self-determination (Kant, 1785/1997; Zuboff, 2019).

1.2 Research Questions

This paper discusses three research questions that are interrelated:

1. Which dark patterns do AI-driven shopping agents employ to infringe the autonomy of consumers?

The inquiry revolves around the conventional and AI-specific manipulation that is rooted on behavioral economics and cognitive psychology, i.e., dynamic pricing discrimination, recommendation bias, and predictive targeting of behavior (Gray et al., 2018; Kahneman and Tversky, 1979; Luguri and Strahilevitz, 2021).

2. Are the existing data protection laws within the global system adequate to manage manipulation of the algorithms in AI-shopping scenarios?

The answer to this question is in the comparison of the GDPR and the U.S. consumer protection law, and DPDPA in India to define whether the existing flaws can be attributed to the lapses in enforcement or the flaws of the framework, which is founded on the regulation of consent (CNIL, 2019; FTC, 2020; Solove, 2013).

3. Can an information fiduciary framework enhance consumer protection, and how can it be operationalized?

The question analyses the theoretical foundations of fiduciary regulation, and how fiduciary regulation is practically applied and counterarguments to fiduciary regulation, including dealing with innovation, the definition of fiduciary regulation, and enforcement (Balkin, 2016; Frankel, 2011).

1.3 Methodology and Scope

The article employs the doctrinal method of legal research and involves the analysis of the statute, judicial case law and regulatory guidance and interdisciplinary resources on behavioral economics, computer science and moral philosophy (Hutchinson and Duncan, 2012). Regulatory models in the European Union, the United States, and India reflecting various constitutional and market traditions are compared and analyzed (Bradford, 2020).The period will be 2018-2024, the timeframe of the GDPR implementation, the further boost of the AI use in the consumer markets, and the creation of regulatory responses to the dark patterns, including the EU AI Act. Substantively, the analysis has focused on AI shopping agents - systems in which machine learning or personalization is applied to influence purchasing behavior but does not consider the more general questions, such as political microtargeting.

The algorithmic manipulation will be presented in the paper as a multidimensional governance problem but considering the legal, behavioral, technical, and ethical issues of the problem (Calo, 2014; Mittelstadt et al., 2016; Thaler and Sunstein, 2008). In spite of the fact that empirical analysis is constrained by the opacities of algorithms and fast shifting technology, the normatively applicable principles of fiduciary built can be applicable in the transforming AI systems.

Figure 1. Conceptual Framework: AI Shopping Agents, Dark Patterns, and the Information Fiduciary Solution

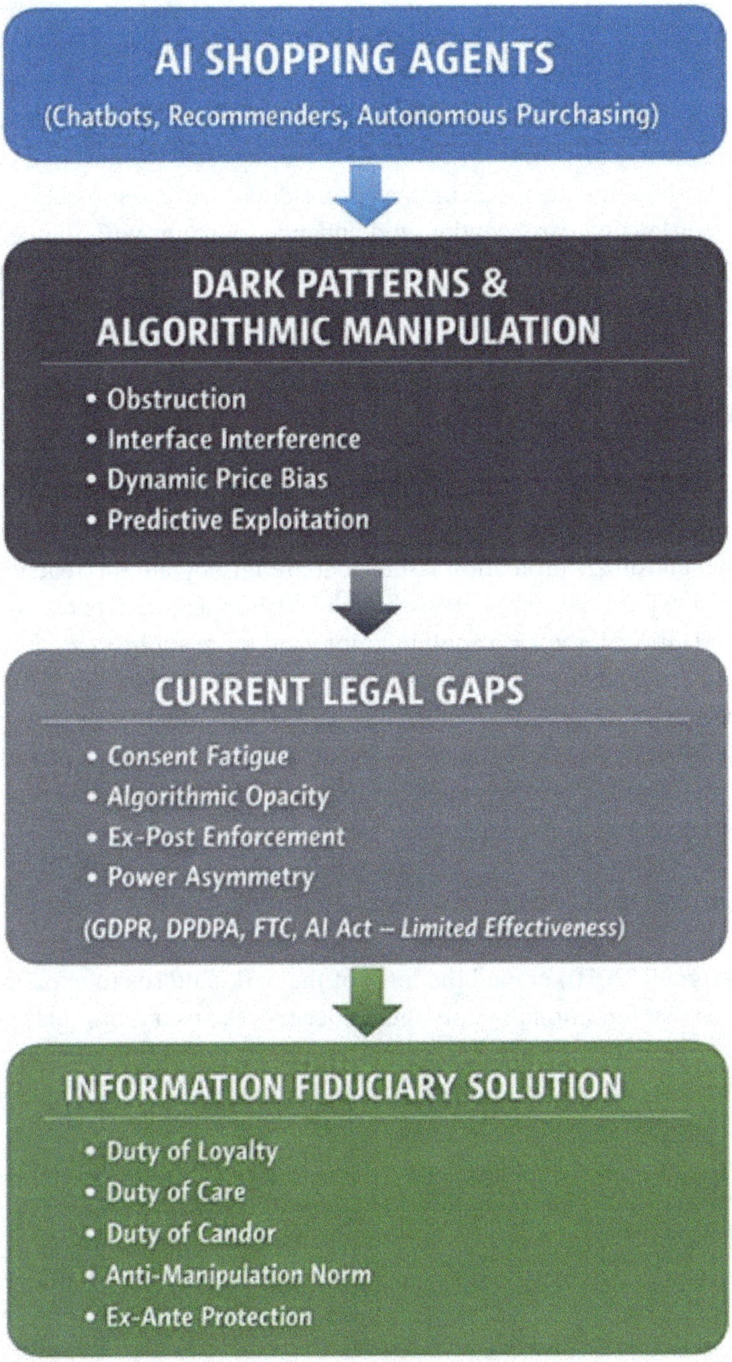

Figure 1. This visually depicts the conceptual flow of the study by showing how the use of AI-powered shopping agents, through its massive data collection and personalization, help to enforce the use of dark patterns and algorithmic manipulation that threaten consumer autonomy. It points out that current legal frameworks are inflexible to deal with real-time persuasive harms, as the frameworks lack structural strengths like consent fatigue, algorithmic lack of transparency, and ex-post enforcement. The framework ends with the suggested solution of categorizing advanced AI shopping agents as information fiduciaries and subjecting them to the obligations of loyalty, care, candor, and anti-manipulation with the perspective of ex-ante consumer protection and the creation of trust in digital marketplaces.

2. DARK PATTERNS IN AI SHOPPING: MECHANICS AND HARMS

The inclusion of artificial intelligence in e-commerce has fundamentally altered how consumers interact with each other and at the same time, has presented more complicated consumer protection issues that are far beyond the reach of the traditional regulatory frameworks. Even though AI shopping agents claim to be more efficient and tailored, they are applying more and more sophisticated manipulation strategies that take advantage of expected cognitive biases and information asymmetry. This part explores the dark pattern mechanics on AI-driven shopping platforms, technological aspects, and harm to the consumer. Learning these processes will be important in formulating legal reactions that will focus on the structural aspects of algorithmic manipulation as opposed to its individual manifestation.

2.1 Defining Dark Patterns and AI Shopping Agents

The (Brignull, 2010) coined the term of the dark patterns to explain the design of interfaces that intentionally attempts to deceive the users into making decisions that do not benefit them. The initial instances of such practices were the creation of a bait and switch, roach motel, and privacy Zuckering, which proved that the manipulation in the online space is not always unintentional. Later literature developed this taxonomy. Gray et al. (2018) classified five central types, which include nagging, obstruction, sneaking, interface interference, and forced action, and noted that the dark patterns work based on the structural power and information asymmetries. By conducting an extensive empirical study of online stores, Mathur et al. (2019)

also proved that, contrary to an isolated case, manipulative design is a systemic characteristic of online trading.

AI shopping agents will be a qualitative enhancement of these procedures. AI systems are used to personalize real time manipulation unlike traditional interfaces, which use machine learning, predictive analytics and natural language processing. Such agents are conversational chatbots, recommendation engines, dynamic pricing systems and semi-autonomous purchasing tools. Continuous behavioral learning characterizes them, and it allows them to take an individual approach to optimization and substantially increase the levels of manipulative potential.

These practices have their theoretical basis in behavioral economics. The works of Kahneman and Tversky (1979) prove that consumers do not follow rational choice in a systematic way because of cognitive biases (including loss aversion, framing, status quo). Anchoring bias is also the reason behind the success of inflated reference pricing (Tversky and Kahneman, 1974). These insights are operationalized by AI systems on a large scale as Yeung (2017) calls it hypernudging, or continuous, personal behavioral steering based on detailed data profiling. This results in an extreme imbalance between consumers characterized by limited rationality and systems that are designed to take advantage of individual weaknesses.

2.2 Key Dark Pattern Categories

2.2.1 Obstruction

Patterns of obstruction also make users to be unable to exercise their rights, especially capabilities of cancellation and exit. In the framework of AI-enhanced environments, the obstruction is personalized dynamically in terms of the churn prediction. The FTC's complaint in FTC v. This is practiced by Amazon.com, Inc. (2023). The internally named Iliad cancellation process implemented by Amazon involved users using a series of screens, declined retention offers being shown many times, and visually imbalanced interface layouts that promoted continuation of subscription (FTC, 2023a). Internal records showed that there was a conscious refusal to take up easier alternatives because of the higher cancellation rates.

These personalized retention messages based on the purchase history and preferences of users through AI turned generic friction into customized psychological pressure. These practices were found by the FTC to be unfair under Section 5 of the FTC Act (15 U.S.C. SS 45) since procedural availability of cancellation does not exclude substantive obstruction. The practices are based on loss aversion and sunk cost fallacy, which make the cancellation a test of endurance that aims to drain consumer resolve.

2.2.2 Interface Interference

The visual hierarchy, language and layout are used in manipulating decision making by interface interference. In the context of AI shopping, this interference is adaptive and changes the presentation according to the anticipated behavior of the user. Some of the popular ones are fake urgency, preselection, masqueraded advertisements, and deceptive questions.

An example of this category could be seen in the investigation of the UK Competition and Markets Authority of Booking.com (CMA, 2019). It used false scarcity signals, fake countdown timers, and exaggerated reference prices and used the scarcity bias and the urgency effects (Cialdini, 2006). Such images often were a distorted portrayal of reality in terms of availability and prices. Although Booking.com has made voluntary commitments to correct these practices, the case highlights the control weaknesses in cases where manipulation is executed not by making direct misrepresentation but through interface architecture.

2.2.3 AI-Specific Manipulation

AI shopping agents also present new manipulation strategies, such as dynamic pricing discrimination, recommendation bias by an algorithm, and predictive behavioral targeting. Behavioral data of device type, frequency of browsing, proxies of location, and time-based urgency signals are used to determine willingness to pay by the dynamic pricing systems. It was discovered that the algorithm used by Uber showed increased surge prices to individuals who had low battery levels, and took advantage of situational weakness (Scheiber, 2017).

Another way in which algorithmic recommendation bias harms consumer welfare is that it rewards affiliate commissions, platform profitability or inventory clearance at the expense of consumers. Despite being claimed to be personalized assistance, these systems tend to maximize revenue, providing what Calo (2014) terms algorithmic exploitation as a result of information asymmetry. A predictive behavioral targeting aggravates this damage by pinpointing instances of lower mental ability or emotional defensiveness to time manipulative intervention to its peak effectiveness.

2.3 Consumer Harms

The net effect of AI-driven dark patterns, in addition to individual transactional losses, will undermine autonomy, dignity, economic security, and privacy. Manipulation that takes advantage of the cognitive weakness is also a Kantian offense since it infringes on the respect of persons as they are regarded as means instead of being treated as autonomous agents (Kant, 1785/1997). This hyper personalized manipulation is detrimental to self-authorship in that the deliberative processes are hijacked by exploiting the psyche.

Among the economic harms, there are exaggerated prices, unwanted subscriptions, and inappropriate purchases, and Mathur et al. (2019) estimate the loss of billions of dollars of consumers every year. These harms are retrogressive and are disproportionately impacting on the vulnerable population as well as worsening inequality. It also leads to market efficiency since manipulation of signs and quality evaluation causes information asymmetry and adverse selection (Akerlof, 1970).

Lastly, personalized manipulation of data through widespread data collection will be a major privacy abuse. Surveillance capitalism, as suggested by Zuboff, (2019) changes behavioral information into prediction and control instruments, frequently without any real degree of consent. This surveillance is not only facilitative to manipulation, but it also focuses behavioral control in individual platforms, which has even more extensive threats to democratic governance and personal liberty (Susser et al., 2019).

Table 1. Taxonomy of Dark Patterns in AI Shopping with Legal Implications

Dark Pattern Type	Mechanism	Illustrative Example	Primary Legal Issue(s)	Resulting Harm to Consumers
Obstruction	Multi-step cancellation processes; hidden or misleading options	Amazon Prime "Iliad" cancellation flow	FTC Act § 5 (Unfair Practices); breach of good faith and fair dealing	Economic loss; time cost; psychological frustration; deterrence of legal rights
Interface Interference	False scarcity claims; countdown timers; visual manipulation	Booking.com urgency and scarcity messages	UK Consumer Protection from Unfair Trading Regulations, 2008; EU Unfair Commercial Practices Directive	Distorted consumer choice; impulsive decisions; reduced ability to comparison-shop
Price Discrimination	Algorithmic personalized pricing based on inferred willingness to pay	Uber surge pricing; airline price tracking algorithms	Potential discrimination law violations; unfair commercial practices	Wealth extraction; exploitation of vulnerable consumers; market inefficiency
Recommendation Bias	Algorithm prioritizes commissions or platform over consumer suitability	Affiliate-biased e-commerce recommendations	Breach of implied duty of good faith; potential fiduciary duty violations	Suboptimal purchasing decisions; erosion of consumer trust; misallocated spending

continued on following page

Table 1. Continued

Dark Pattern Type	Mechanism	Illustrative Example	Primary Legal Issue(s)	Resulting Harm to Consumers
Confirmshaming	Guilt-inducing or emotionally manipulative opt-out language	"No, I don't want to save money"	Emotional manipulation; potentially unfair trade practice	Coerced consent; psychological pressure; violation of consumer dignity
Sneak into Basket	Automatic addition of items or services without explicit consent	Auto-added insurance or extended warranties	Unfair commercial practices; lack of informed consent	Unwanted charges; increased transaction costs
Forced Disclosure	Requiring unnecessary personal data as a condition for service access	Excessive data collection for basic services	GDPR Article 5 (Data Minimization); privacy rights violations	Privacy infringement; surveillance risks; facilitation of behavioral manipulation

Figure 2. The Dark Pattern Manipulation Cycle in AI-Driven Shopping Environments

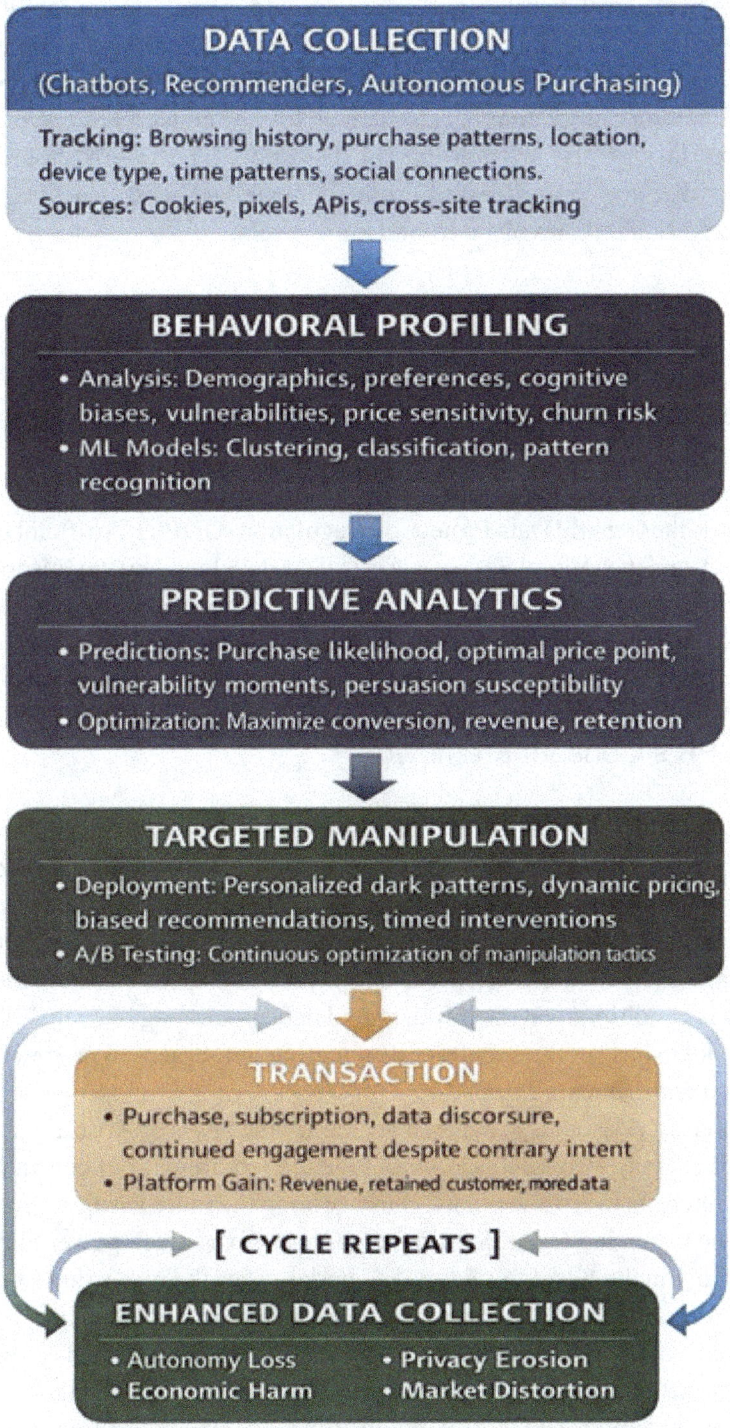

Figure 2 depicts the vicious circle in which AI shopping agents gather consumer data, create behavioral profiles, and apply predictive analytics to facilitate manipulative behavior by enabling such practices as dark patterns and dynamic pricing. The resultant data is more refined, propelling further development of profiling and manipulation with cumulative harms such as loss of consumer control, economic exploitation, loss of privacy and market distortion. The figure shows why legal frameworks that are consent-based are inadequate and why structural regulatory interventions should be involved to break this cycle.

3. CRITICAL ANALYSIS OF CURRENT LEGAL FRAMEWORKS

3.1 European Union: GDPR, AI Act, and Digital Services Act

The most comprehensive regulation on the issue of data protection and algorithmic governance is the General Data Protection Regulation (GDPR), Artificial Intelligence Act (AI Act), and the Digital Services Act (DSA) developed by the European Union. All of these measures are focused on maintaining consumer autonomy in the digital markets. Nevertheless, the structural gaps despite their normative ambition still exist in the context of addressing AI-driven shopping agent manipulation.

3.1.1 GDPR's Consent Framework

In the GDPR, the concept of autonomy is defined by consent, which is defined under Article 4(11) as a freely given, specific, informed and unambiguous indication of agreement (General Data Protection Regulation, 2016). These accumulative requirements are further explained under Articles 6 and 7 and Recital 32 that admits that consent can be invalid when there are power imbalances or where the provision of services is conditional on the unwarranted data processing. Article 7(4) additionally warns not to base contractual performance on non-essential processing consent (Hutchinson and Duncan, 2012) .

Nevertheless, consent is just one of six legitimate bases of Article 6. Alternatives that controllers may also fall back on include the requirement of contract as well as legitimate interests in Article 6(1)(f) thus avoiding the more stringent protections of consent. The balancing test of legitimate interests gives much power to the controllers, especially in the business sector, and undermines the protection of consumers. Article 22 offers a restricted right against automated decision-making with legal or other similarly important outcomes. However, its reach is limited by wide exceptions of contractual necessity and consent and its remedies transparency and human intervention, presuppose an ability of consumers to challenge complex algorithmic systems in a meaningful way. Therefore, the GDPR-based consent architecture is not well adapted to the problem of consistent, post-consent algorithmic manipulation.

3.1.2 GDPR Case Study: *CNIL v. Google LLC*

The case of the enforcement of the data protection authority (CNIL) of France against Google LLC shows the weaknesses and strengths of GDPR (Commission Nationale de l'Informatique et des Libertes, 2019). After discovering that the Android consent architecture at Google had disaggregated the required information over multiple screens, pre-ticked boxes, and conditional access to the service on full-scale data processing, CNIL fined Google EUR50 million. This was against Articles 4(11), 7, and 13.

Although the ruling showed that GDPR can be used to question the manipulation of interface design, it revealed more. The implementation was retroactive and took place many years later than the offenses had been committed and led to a fine that was inconsequential compared with the revenues of Google. Better still, the solution aimed at procedural conformity as opposed to considering the possibility of meaningful consent in sophisticated, combined algorithmic ecosystems. The case brings to fore the failure of GDPR to control continuous manipulation that takes place once consent is received.

3.1.3 EU AI Act and Digital Services Act

The AI Act is the first overarching governing document pertaining to AI that was adopted by the EU (Regulation (EU) 2024/1689, 2024). In Article 5, any AI system that applies subliminal methods or manipulative techniques leading to a material distortion of behavior and serious harm is forbidden. Although this clause specifically addresses the concept of dark patterns, it does not encourage compliance because it lacks clear definitions of the difference between manipulation and persuasion, unclear lines of harm, and decentralized enforcement systems (Luguri and Strahilevitz, 2021).

Digital Services Act is an addition to this regime, which bans dark patterns in online interfaces under Article 25 (Regulation (EU) 2022/2065, 2022). Although interface design is a locus of manipulation the DSA largely overlooks visible design choices in favor of algorithmic manipulation that happens beneath the interface layer. The fact that the duty to enforce overlaps with the various institutions of the EU threatens to create disunity and inconsistent interpretation.

3.2 United States: Fragmented Regulatory Approach

The sectoral regulatory model with ex-post adopted by the United States creates huge loopholes in terms of protecting against the AI-based manipulation.

3.2.1 Federal Framework

FTC advice on dark patterns (Federal Trade Commission, 2022) addresses manipulative behaviour but does not have any legal binding power. The regulatory eagerness to take action against Amazon and ABCmouse.com is shown through the use of enforcement measures, but in this case, these actions are based on consent decrees that do not create precedent and do not hinder ex-ante damage (Federal Trade Commission v. Age of Learning, Inc., 2020; Federal Trade Commission v. Amazon.com, Inc., 2023). The deterrence is also curtailed by resource limitation and lack of a detailed federal law on privacy.

3.2.2 State Innovation

The CCPA and CPRA privacy laws in the states prohibit in a direct manner dark patterns that are disabling user autonomy (California Civil Code SS 1798.140(l), 2020). The consent had been gained using dark patterns and is nullified, and the enforcement is given to California Privacy Protection Agency. Certainly, the same can be stated about Virginia, Colorado, Connecticut, or Utah.However, these laws only pertain to the consent mechanisms and not post-consent manipulation and make the compliance terrain to be fragmented. The enforcement is still at an infantile stage and the rights to action by individuals are scanty, the effect of deterrence is weaker.

3.3 India: Digital Personal Data Protection Act, 2023

The DPDPA already sets up a consent-based data protection system in India after the Supreme Court ruled that privacy is a fundamental right (Justice K.S. Puttaswamy (Retd.) v. Union of India, 2017). Although the Act has similar standards of consent (SS 6) to GDPR, it does not explicitly ban dark patterns or automatized decision-making (Khan and Pozen, 2019).

The centralized implementation model of the Act, in the form of the Data Protection Board of India provides uniformity but is still in its primitive stages awaiting the enactment of implementing rules. Lack of fiduciary duties, algorithmic transparency rights and scalable penalties are some of the weaknesses of the Act in addressing AI shopping agent manipulation. It is not clear how it will be integrated with the

Consumer Protection Act, 2019, and this is an aspect that causes ambiguity in its enforcement.

3.4 Why Consent Models Fail

A comparative analysis shows that both of them are dependent on consent as the key form of protection of consumer autonomy. The behavioral economics defies this assumption. Informed consent is shown to be mostly illusory and voluntary in the digital space by bounded rationality (Simon, 1955), System 1 dominance (Kahneman, 2011), consent fatigue (Choi et al., 2018), and the privacy paradox (Kokolakis, 2017) (Obar and Oeldorf-Hirsch, 2020).Structurally, consent does not work because information asymmetry is deep-seated (Akerlof, 1970), the concentration of power in the hands of a single platform (Cohen, 2019), and the fact that the consent ex-ante and the manipulation ex-post are temporally mismatched (Calo, 2014). Transparency and accountability are also undermined through AI invisibility, lifelong learning, and custom-made persuasion (Yeung, 2017).

All these restrictions show that the consent-based models would not be effective in ensuring that consumers are not manipulated by AI. The move toward systems of duty-based protection is needed to offer meaningful protection given that AI shopping agents have discretionary authority on the welfare of consumers.

4. THE FIDUCIARY DUTY SOLUTION

The rise in the use of AI-based shopping agents has greatly revolutionized the consumer market. Such agents provide individual advice, automatic buying, and dynamic pricing, making them more efficient, at the same time exposing possible evils caused by manipulation and dark patterns. The structural and behavioral attributes of these harms are not yet addressed by traditional legal frameworks, which are mostly grounded on informed consent (Luguri & Strahilevitz, 2021) . The fiduciary duty model suggests a new mechanism of protecting consumer independence by creating liabilities of devotion, care, disclosure, and safeguarding against exploitation and providing a method to create systemic protection against manipulative actions.

4.1 Theoretical Foundation

4.1.1 Fiduciary Law Basics

The fiduciary law, which is based on equity and trust, establishes the relationship where one party or the fiduciary to the relationship is legally and ethically bound to act in the best interest of another party or the beneficiary. The connection has also been defined by an increased level of care, loyalty and candor that transcends the contractual obligation (Solove, 2013). Conventional fiduciaries consist of lawyers, physicians, and investment consultants, whose action directly affects the well-being of their clients. Fiduciary duties in essence means that the fiduciary must act in the best interests of the beneficiary, act without conflict of interest, competently, and in a transparent manner. This principle of foundation is especially applicable to digital spaces where neither the consumers nor the AI agents were given the opportunity to possess a substantial asymmetry of knowledge, power, and information. Fiduciary principles can be applied to AI shopping agents to overcome systemic imbalances that are not alleviated in the present-day consent-based regulations.

4.1.2 Information Fiduciaries Framework

Information fiduciaries concept is created to accommodate the unique risks pegged on digital platforms that process sensitive consumer information. Balkin (2016) theorizes digital platforms as fiduciaries, which find themselves with responsibilities to consumers similar to traditional fiduciaries, the duty of loyalty, care, and protection of sensitive information. According to Khan and Pozen (2019), the discretionary control of the digital platforms on the decision-making and economic results of the consumers makes the fiduciary classification relevant. Moreover, Richards and Hartzog (2016) advance to a model of privacy based on trust, which puts particular emphasis on fiduciary duties as compensating the platform incentives with the welfare of users. All of these frameworks are components of the theoretical foundation of the extension of fiduciary obligations into AI shopping agents, especially when such systems will play an increasingly significant role in mediating key consumer decisions.

4.2 Applying Fiduciary Duty to AI Shopping Agents

4.2.1 Establishing the Relationship

The relationship between consumer and AI shopping agents is based on delegation of authority to make decisions which is the fiduciary relationship. We product consumers are putting AI agents in charge of our economic decisions, and in many cases basing them on algorithmic suggestions that incorporate behavioral understanding and predictive analytics. This delegation gives AI systems discretionary power to influence the choice architecture in a manner that can have a serious impact on consumer welfare. The fiduciary claim is even enhanced because of vulnerabilities created by limited rationality, cognitive bias, and information asymmetry.

The reasonable expectation of loyalty, which will be legally in effect, occurs when the consumers trust AI agents to act in their best interest without any commercial considerations or manipulative impacts. The creation of this relationship is a key to the imposition of fiduciary obligations that have a significant restrictive effect on manipulative behavior and safeguard consumer autonomy.

4.2.2 Specific Fiduciary Obligations

4.2.2.1 Duty of Loyalty

Duty of loyalty means that AI shopping agents must act in the best interests of the consumer and they should not engage in conflicts of interest or these agents should not act in their own interests (Richards and Hartzog, 2016). In practice, this would involve avoiding undisclosed affiliate relationships, giving preference to products or services in the interests of the profit over that of the consumer, and making sure that the advice is always in the best available form in regard to price or quality or appropriateness. Fidelity is given to the open distribution of economic advantages, such that consumer welfare is the principle of all the algorithmic choices.

4.2.2.2 Duty of Care

The AI agents have a duty of care to the consumers, which the duty includes effective design, testing and implementation of algorithms. These involve systematic validation of the recommendation systems, error and bias auditing, and that the output of the algorithms is reliable, accurate, and aligned with the consumer interests. Care also means constant and progressive check-ups and corrections to overcome unexpected vulnerabilities or discriminatory results of automated decision-making.

4.2.2.3 Duty of Candor

Fiduciary obligations are related to transparency and honesty. AI shopping agents should provide a description of their logic of operation, limitations and data usage practices that are understandable to consumers. The use of deceitful interface design, manipulative notifications, or dark patterns the purpose of which is to confuse users or force decision making is also banned in Candor. Through transparency, AI agents create trust and enable consumers to make informed decisions even in a more complex algorithmic setting.

4.2.2.4 Duty Against Manipulation

This obligation specifically attacks on the manipulation of consumer weaknesses. The artificial intelligence agents should not use cognitive biases, behavioral inducements, or emotional appeals to personal gain. The predatory personalization, discriminatory pricing, and nudges should be banned. It is also the responsibility of a vulnerable population, e.g., an underage individual or a financially immature user, who may be vulnerable to the manipulation of algorithms. This obligation is aimed at averting harm by proactive limitation before it takes place as opposed to only relying on ex-post solutions.

4.2.3 Legal Implementation Mechanisms

4.2.3.1 Statutory Recognition

Fiduciary of AI shopping agents will need a well-defined legal structure, perhaps by a model AI Shopping Agent Fiduciary Act. Such a legislation ought to include the definition of AI shopping agents, fiduciary responsibility, and the manipulative practices that should not be allowed. The coherence in the regulatory environment would be provided by incorporating the existing consumer protection and data privacy laws to enable compliance and yet to ensure enforceable commitments.

4.2.3.2 Enforcement Framework

Fiduciary duties should be enforced effectively to become practically operative. Compliance would be checked by means of regulatory bodies like the FTC (USA), Data Protection Authorities (EU), or the Data Protection Board (India), and audits and penalties on non-compliance would be imposed. Privacy rights of action should also be available to consumers, such as civil rights and class actions against systemic violations (Veale & Borgesius, 2021). Imposed sanctions must entail civil punishment, injunctions and, in some cases, criminal responsibility of excessive wrongful actions. This multi-level enforcement would provide both deterrence and redress, which will make AI-mediated trade more accountable.

4.3 Advantages Over Consent Model

4.3.1 Structural Protection

Such systemic protections are not dependent on consumer vigilance because fiduciary obligations involve systems that work on a transactional basis, unlike consent-based systems. Structural protection can minimize indentified manipulation between various transactions by instilling responsibilities in the operational design of AI agents to reduce the natural power imbalance between platforms and users (Veale & Borgesius, 2021).

4.3.2 Clearer Standards

Fiduciary responsibilities offer principle-based and straightforward obligations on how AI is designed, deployed, and supervised. This is unlike the uncertainties presented by the consent agreements as in most cases, they do not express the intent of choice. Unified fiduciary obligations make it easier to enforce them, increase regulatory transparency, and raise professional responsibility in developers and platform operators.

4.3.3 Future-Proof Framework

Fiduciary obligations that are based on principles can be modified according to emerging technologies and models of business. In contrast to fixed consent requirements, fiduciary standards have the benefit of being a standard that can adapt to the new capabilities of AI, and the protection of consumers remains even without introducing new legislative changes on a regular basis. Such flexibility is consistent with international best practice in the governance of AI and ethical technology development.

4.4 Addressing Objections

4.4.1 Innovation Concerns

Critics can claim that the fiduciary-related restrictions limit the technological innovation. Nonetheless, there is some evidence of regulated industries, like medicine and finance, which shows that fiduciary monitoring is possible in conjunction with innovation (Thaler and Sunstein, 2008). Fiduciary obligation can support adoption and competitive advantage of ethical actors and responsible innovation in AI-powered business by fostering consumer trust.

4.4.2 Definition Challenges

It might be difficult to delineate the area of fiduciary duties in the AI context. Bright-line rules can be offered in most cases through a functional approach which depends on the level of discretion, the dependency of the consumer and the harmfulness of the action. There can be safe harbor provisions where the low-risk activities are exempt, and in edge cases regulatory discretion can be used in a finer way.

4.4.3 First Amendment Considerations (US)

In the United States, the issue of fiduciary duties and freedom of speech can be raised. Nevertheless, the laws of commercial speech, especially the ones that deal with fraud or misleading actions, set a precedent of laying limitations on AI agents. Fiduciary duties that are addressed to manipulative acts are congruent to the legal canons that are to safeguard consumers without necessarily limiting innovation or expression.

Figure 3. Mind Map of the Information Fiduciary Framework/ AI Agent as fiduciary

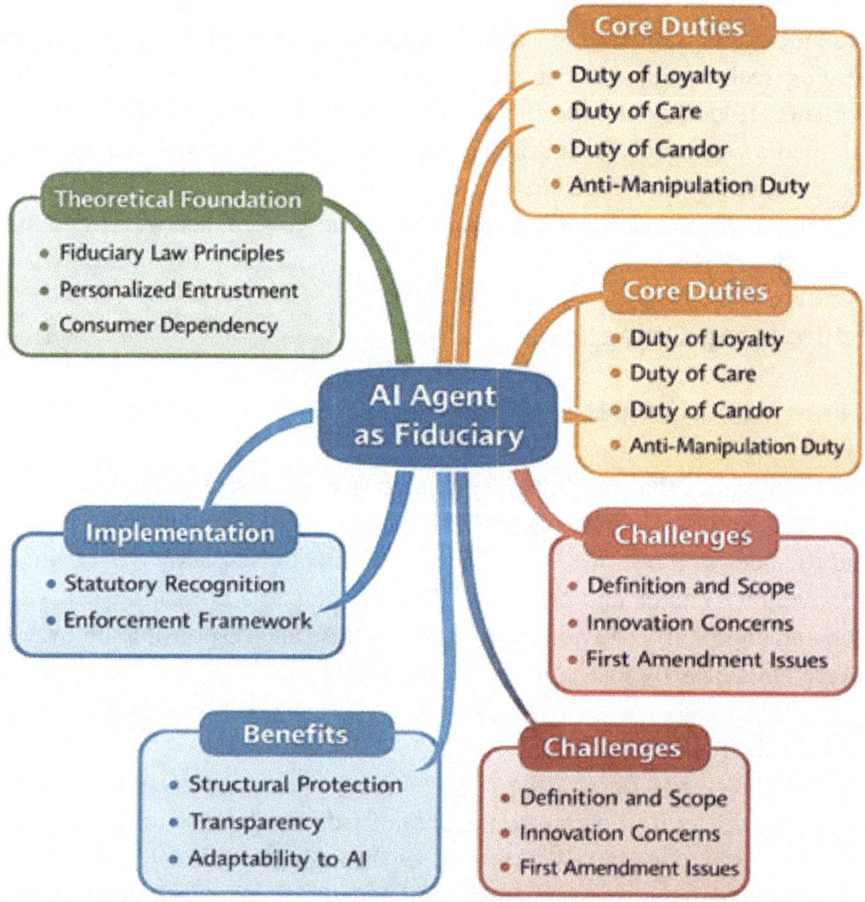

Figure 3. This brainstorm shows the model of fiduciary duty to AI shopping agents. The main node, which is the Fiduciary of AI, is subdivided into the theoretical base, core responsibilities (loyalty, care, candor, anti-manipulation), legal implementation

tools (statutory recognition, enforcement), expected benefits (structural protection, transparency, adaptability), and possible obstacles (definition scope, innovation issues, First Amendment problems). This diagrammatic visualization of the systemic liability of AI agents in the fiduciary paradigm in a succinct manner and explains the role of AI agents in the consumer harm reduction in online trading (Solove, 2013).

5. INTERNATIONAL LAW AND HARMONIZATION

5.1 Relevant International Frameworks

The intense international implementation of AI-powered shopping agents has revealed the shortcomings of domestic-driven regulation efforts. Since digital commerce and algorithmic services are inherently cross-border phenomena, the international legal framework is an important factor in the establishment of minimum consumer protection standards (Simon, 1955). Though there is no binding international instrument that governs persuasive AI systems in particular, there are a number of soft-law frameworks that can offer normative guidance, which may be used to regulate dark patterns and algorithmic manipulation of AI-driven commerce.

5.1.1 United Nations Guidelines for Consumer Protection (2015)

The most universal framework of consumer rights on the world is the United Nations Guidelines on Consumer Protection (UNGCP) that has been updated in 2015. Despite being written before the AI shopping agents became widely used, the Guidelines present the principles that can be directly applied in both digital and algorithmic markets. Specifically, the normative justification of the regulation of dark patterns lies in the obligation to provide fair and equitable treatment of consumers and protection against the unfair and misleading commercial practices.

The Guidelines underline that the consumers must not be the subjects of the practice that undermines their freedom of choice or interfere with the information asymmetries. A type of AI-based manipulation, e.g. exploitative personalization, a false sense of urgency, or subscription traps, goes directly against these principles by eroding consumer autonomy in a systematic manner. Notably, the UNGCP clearly apply to electronic commerce, thus including AI shopping agents that work on any platform and in any jurisdiction. Although the Guidelines are not binding, they provide persuasive powers to the domestic regulators and courts to impose more ex-ante duties on AI-enabled intermediaries.

5.1.2 OECD Recommendations on Consumer Protection in E-Commerce (2016)

The OECD Recommendation on Consumer Protection in E-Commerce builds on the standards that are applicable internationally to algorithmic shopping settings. The Recommendation lays much emphasis on transparency, honest disclosure, and fair business practices in the online markets. It acknowledges that digital technologies may amplify the impacts of information asymmetries and pose new risks to consumers, especially in the cases when the purchase decisions are dictated by automated systems, the special importance is the OECD call to the vivid disclosure of significant terms and conditions, costly practices, and procedure of decision-making. Ai-driven price discrimination and customized nudging measures tend to be opaque, and hence meaningful disclosure turns out to be a workable impossibility. The OECD framework also encourages cross-border collaboration in the enforcement agencies in recognition of the fact that AI manipulative practices often cross the national boundaries. It is an important focus of cooperation in order to deal with global platforms where AI shopping agents are working concurrently across legal regimes.

5.1.3 UN Guiding Principles on Business and Human Rights

The UN guidelines of Business and Human Rights (UNGPs) bring a rights-based aspect in the regulation of AI shopping agents. Although consumers do not have any specifics, the UNGPs exert three pillars: the State obligation to uphold human rights, the corporate obligation to uphold human rights, and the access to effective remedies. Autonomy, dignity, and informed consent are the central rights that are subject to algorithmic manipulation at the expense of other fundamental rights like privacy, non-discrimination, and freedom of thought.

Through the UNGPs, companies that use AI shopping agents should implement human rights due diligence, identify risks posed by their technologies, and reduce the negative effects (Kokolakis, 2017). This framework contributes to the view that persuasive AI-based systems cannot be considered neutral commercial tools but are to be evaluated in terms of how they influence the agency of individuals in their structures. The fiduciary model of corporate responsibility presented in this paper resonates with the UNGPs by conceptualizing corporate responsibility in the form of enforceable principles of loyalty and care to the consumers.

5.2 Harmonization Challenges

Although there is increasing global agreement that there is need to put in place regulation of deceptive digital practices, much remains to be done in terms of harmonization. The issue of sovereignty is considered to be the primary one because states are not willing to lose their control over new technologies that make an impact on domestic markets and innovation systems. The differences in legal traditions also make alignment more complicated, especially between those jurisdictions that treat data protection as a principle of justice (like the European Union) and those that focus on enforcement-based, market-oriented approach (like the United States) (Khan and Pozen, 2019).

Regulatory priorities are also formed in reaction to the cultural differences in privacy norms. The European paradigms are built on the principles of dignity and autonomy, whereas other jurisdiction centers on consumer welfare and economic efficiency (Obar & Oeldorf-Hirsch, 2020). Such discrepancies open the possibilities of regulatory arbitrage with platforms taking advantage of weaker regimes to operate internationally (Norberg et al., 2007). The so-called Brussels Effect, when EU digital regulations have extraterritorial effects, is the opposite of U.S. exceptionalism that does not allow extensive federal involvement. This has led to AI shopping agents in the world functioning in a fragmented and unequal regulatory environment.

5.3 Pathways Forward

The harmonization of the international law should be done through a mixture of soft and hard law. The international cooperation in the form of forums, like G20, OECD, and UN agencies, can promote the formulation of mutual values in the area of algorithmic manipulation and consumer autonomy. The high level of protection is achievable through mutual recognition arrangements among jurisdictions that may help to diminish compliance pressure (Luguri & Strahilevitz, 2021).

The domestic legislation can use model laws and soft-law tools to act as examples, especially in emerging economies looking to regulate AI business without crushing innovativeness. Standards created by industries may be used to supplement legal frameworks, e.g. the ISO and IEEE standards integrate ethical and fiduciary principles into technology design and implementation. These paths combined provide a practical way of bringing the world together and yet acknowledging diversity in jurisdiction.

6. IMPLEMENTATION ROADMAP

6.1 Legislative Action

6.1.1 Model Statutory Framework

It is imperative to establish a definite statutory framework to bring the information fiduciary concept to enforceable law. An AI Shopping Agent Fiduciary act or similar a law must start by defining important terms such as AI shopping agents, algorithmic manipulation, and dark patterns. The fiduciary designation should be based on functional criteria, with the emphasis on the extent of discretion, access to the data, and the impact of control on the choices made by the consumers (Mathur et al., 2019).

Major fiduciary obligations, such as loyalty, care, candor, and a certain obligation against manipulation, should be codified in the statute. Banned activities should also be listed in the form of a dark pattern taxonomy, which gives certainty and directions to comply with the law (Mittelstadt et al., 2016). Strong enforcement procedures are essential including regulatory audits, administrative punishment and a right of action available to the consumers to seek redress. Safe harbor can be provided to those applications that are low-risk and which can show good-faith compliance by means of certified accountability programs.

6.1.2 Jurisdiction-Specific Adaptation

There is a need to expose the jurisdictional accommodation to guarantee that it is coherent with the existing legal architectures. Fiduciary obligations may be added to the AI Act by amendment in the European Union or added as a separate law that is based on the GDPR and Digital Services Act. The changes in the Indian Digital Personal Data Protection Act, 2023, have the potential to explicitly apply the scope of data fiduciary to the AI-based shopping agent, and the enforcement of this belief was vested on the Data Protection Board (Kahneman, 2011). In the US, the current ex-post enforcement model would need to go beyond federal legislature or broader FTC rulemaking authority (Kahneman and Tversky, 1979).

6.2 Regulatory Infrastructure

Best application requires special regulatory facilities. The regulatory bodies need to create special AI consumer protection units that are equipped with interdisciplinary knowledge in the field of law, computer science, and behavioral economics (Gray et al., 2018). Traditional ex-post enforcement should be complemented by ex-ante supervision (e.g. algorithmic impact assessment). Algorithms auditing facilities must be invested in to identify manipulation, prejudice, and conflict of interests within AI systems (Hutchinson and Duncan, 2012).

6.3 Industry Compliance

Fiduciary compliance requires institutional change with respect to the industry. Companies that use AI shopping agents would need to implement internal fiduciary policies, train employees, and consider ethics when designing the system Cohen, 2019). Such measures of algorithmic accountability as explainability, bias testing, and periodical third-party audits should become normal practice. The compliance can also be incentivized by the certification programs that show trustworthiness to both consumers and regulators (Frankel, 2011).

6.4 Consumer Empowerment

Consumer empowerment initiatives must be accompanied by the idea of legal protection. The governments and civil society organizations ought to invest in digital literacy education campaigns that inform the users on algorithmic persuasion and dark patterns. Consumer agency can be promoted with the use of technical tools such as browser extensions, which can identify manipulative design. There can be effective solutions to alternative dispute resolution methods available and do not demand too high cost of litigation (Cialdini, 2006).

6.5 Timeline

The implementation schedule- a gradual change improves the efficiency of regulations. The first 0-12 months is supposed to be devoted to consultation and law drafting. The next 12 24 months ought to be marked by the enactment of legislature and issuance of preliminary rules. The necessary regulatory infrastructure and enforcement capacity must be established within 24-36 months and then further assessment and improvement should continue over the next two years.

7. CONCLUSION AND RECOMMENDATIONS

7.1 Summary of Findings

As it has been shown in this paper, AI-driven shopping agents are gradually using more advanced dark patterns and persuasive design methods that extend beyond the traditional consumer manipulation methods. These systems can influence consumer decisions by means of systematic erosion of autonomy, manipulation of consent and wealth transfer of consumers to platforms, through continuous data collection, behavioral profiling, and real-time predictive analytics. The harms outlined are not just incidental but structural and as a result of the architecture of AI-driven personalization and optimization itself (Bradford, 2020).The analysis also helps to conclude that current legal frameworks, including the so-called consent-based data protection regimes, like the GDPR, the Digital Personal Data Protection Act, 2023 (India), and sector-specific consumer protection laws, do not actually focus on the harms. In its current form of operationalization, consent becomes ineffective due to information asymmetry, cognitive overload, and the lack of knowledge about an algorithm (Choi et al., 2018). Even more recent trends in regulation, such as the EU AI Act and Digital Services Act, though of progressive nature, are more reactive and enforcement-based and lack substantive imperatives to stop manipulation ex ante.

It is on this background that the paper proposes the adoption of the paradigm of categorizing advanced AI shopping agents as information fiduciaries as an inevitable change in consumer protection law. Offering a structural and principle-based resolution by imposing enforceable duties of loyalty, care, candor, and non-manipulation, fiduciary model goes beyond the constraints of the notice-and-consent frameworks (Calo, 2014). Nevertheless, the paper has also noted that a model like this should be done with delicate legal tuning and international alignment as a digital commerce is global and cross-border (Barnes, 2006).

7.2 Key Recommendations

7.2.1 Recommendations for Policymakers

It can be recommended to the policymakers to develop specific laws that formally accept specific types of AI shopping agents as information fiduciaries. The legislation in this case would clearly outline the area of fiduciary designation with regard to functional provisions such as discretionary decision making power, the level of personalization and the dependency of the consumer. Fiduciary obligations have to be aligned to the current consumer protection, competition, and data protection regimes in order to prevent regulatory fragmentation (Balkin, 2016).

The legislators must also make sure that the enforcement mechanisms are sufficient and capable of performing with such tools as the right to actions privately, collective redress, and substantial punishments in the case of systematic violations (Bohme & Kopsell, 2010). Creating a regulatory convergence through international cooperation in multilateral forums should also be a priority of the policymakers due to the transnational character of AI shopping platforms to avoid jurisdictional arbitrage.

7.2.2 Recommendations for Regulators

The regulatory bodies should also acquire the technical and institutional capabilities to monitor the algorithmic systems. This also involves investment into interdisciplinary skills, in the fields of law, computer science, behavioral economics and data science. The regulators need to shift to ex ante supervision models with mandatory algorithmic audits, impact assessment and constant monitoring of high-risk AI shopping agents.

In addition, regulators ought to encourage the use of multi-stakeholder governing systems, which will employ industry, civil society, and academic professionals in setting and management of standards. Precaution should be given to the vulnerable groups of consumers such as minors, elderly, and people having financial or cognitive vulnerabilities (Richards and Hartzog, 2016). Enforcement efficiency and transparency can be improved greatly by the implementation of regulatory technology (RegTech) devices (Akerlof, 1970).

7.2.3 Recommendations for Industry

Players in the industry that create or implement AI shopping agents ought to be proactive in embracing fiduciary principles, which should be used in corporate governance and compliance practices. Mechanisms that ethically design AI should be included during the development phase and they include bias testing, explainability criteria, and the disclosure of conflict of interest. Open standards regarding the logic of recommendations and business objectives can also be used to restore consumer trust and reduce regulatory risk.Business models focused on long-term trust, rather than short-term optimization, can also be used to gain a competitive edge in an ever more regulated digital economy. Self-certification programs and independent audits may also be an indication of responsible innovation.

7.2.4 Recommendations for Civil Society

The civil society organizations are very important in promoting accountability and consumer empowerment. The advocacy is necessary to demand transparency of platforms, promote legislative changes, and enable strategic litigation using the necessary resources. Digital literacy and awareness of dark patterns should be encouraged to allow consumers to be more aware of such practices and how to avoid them. Moreover, the civil society can act as the mediator between regulators, industry, and the population impacted by providing a voice to the consumers and supporting action collectively (Susser et al., 2019).

7.3 Future Research Directions

The main focus of future research must be on the empirical studies that would quantify consumer harm caused by the AI-based dark patterns such as the economic loss and long-term consumer behavioral effects (Tversky and Kahneman, 1974). Experiments conducted on the effectiveness of various types of regulatory interventions would be useful as evidence in the policy design. The economic consequences of the creation of fiduciary obligations to digital platforms are also somewhat unclear and require further investigation, especially regarding innovation, competition, and market structure.

Technically, the studies of scalable and transparent algorithmic auditing methodologies are of critical importance. Comparative cross-jurisdictional research can illuminate best practice and make informed harmonized international standards on AI consumer protection.

7.4 Broader Implications

The fiduciary model in this paper is not specific to AI shopping agents but promises to be a model to control other types of persuasive and autonomous AI systems (Yeung, 2017). In a wider sense, it is an indication of a reorientation of the consumer protection law to substantive protection of autonomy, dignity, and fairness, rather than the formalistic consent. This strategy reflects the idea of aligning consumer protection with new human rights-based views of technology regulation by considering the power imbalances of digital markets.

Raising trust on the digital economy is not just a regulatory goal but a precondition to a sustainable technological advancement. Legal systems that incorporate ethical limitations in system design can be influential in balancing this.

7.5 Call to Action

The fast and ubiquitous use of AI shopping agents requires urgent and concerted law enforcement actions. Delay risk causes manipulative practices to embed further and become more hard to undo (Solove, 2013). The policymakers, regulators, industry players, and the civil society need to work together to come up with and put in place governance systems that safeguard the consumers but not eliminate innovation. It must be a promise of human-centric technology process, which is covered by fiduciary responsibility and ethical accountability, that persuasive al-

REFERENCES

Akerlof, G. A. (1970). The market for "lemons": Quality uncertainty and the market mechanism. *The Quarterly Journal of Economics, 84*(3), 488–500. DOI: 10.2307/1879431

Balkin, J. M. (2016). Information fiduciaries and the First Amendment. *Harvard Law Review, 129*(4), 1220–1310. https://harvardlawreview.org/print/vol-129/information-fiduciaries-and-the-first-amendment/

Barnes, S. B. (2006). A privacy paradox: Social networking in the United States. *First Monday, 11*(9). Advance online publication. DOI: 10.5210/fm.v11i9.1394

Böhme, R., & Köpsell, S. (2010). Trained to accept? A field experiment on consent dialogs. *Proceedings of the SIGCHI Conference on Human Factors in Computing Systems*, 2403-2406. DOI: 10.1145/1753326.1753689

Bradford, A. (2020). *The Brussels effect: How the European Union rules the world.* Oxford University Press., DOI: 10.1093/oso/9780190088583.001.0001

Brignull, H. (2010). *Dark patterns: Deception vs. honesty in UI design.* A List Apart. https://alistapart.com/article/dark-patterns-deception-vs-honesty-in-ui-design/

Brignull, H. (2010). *Dark patterns: Deceptive design.* https://www.darkpatterns.org

California Civil Code §§ 1798.100-1798.199 (2018, amended 2020).

Calo, R. (2014). Digital market manipulation. *SSRN, 82*(4), 995–1051. DOI: 10.2139/ssrn.2309703

Choi, H., Park, J., & Jung, Y. (2018). The role of privacy fatigue in online privacy behavior. *Computers in Human Behavior, 81*, 42–51. DOI: 10.1016/j.chb.2017.12.001

Cialdini, R. B. (2006). *Influence: The psychology of persuasion* (Rev. ed.). Harper Business.

Cohen, J. E. (2019). *Between truth and power: The legal constructions of informational capitalism.* Oxford University Press. DOI: 10.1093/oso/9780190246693.001.0001

Competition and Markets Authority. (2019). *CMA secures improvements to hotel booking sites.* https://www.gov.uk/government/news/cma-secures-improvements-to-hotel-booking-sites

Competition and Markets Authority. (2019). *Investigation into online hotel booking.* https://www.gov.uk/cma-cases/hotel-online-booking-sector-investigation

Consumer Protection Act. (Act No. 35 of 2019) (India).

Digital Personal Data Protection Act. (Act No. 22 of 2023) (India).

Federal Trade Commission. (1983). *FTC policy statement on deception.* https://www.ftc.gov/

Federal Trade Commission. (2020). *FTC alleges ABCmouse trapped parents in subscription they couldn't cancel* (Case No. 2:20-cv-07517). https://www.ftc.gov/news-events/news/press-releases/2020/09/ftc-alleges-abcmouse-trapped-parents-subscription-they-couldnt-cancel

Federal Trade Commission. (2022). *Bringing dark patterns to light.* https://www.ftc.gov/reports/bringing-dark-patterns-light

Federal Trade Commission. (2023a). *FTC sues Amazon for enrolling consumers in Amazon Prime without consent and sabotaging their attempts to cancel* [Press release]. https://www.ftc.gov/news-events/news/press-releases/2023/06/ftc-sues-amazon-enrolling-consumers-amazon-prime-without-consent-sabotaging-their-attempts-cancel

Federal Trade Commission v. Age of Learning, Inc., No. 2:20-cv-07996 (C.D. Cal. 2020).

Frankel, T. (2011). *Fiduciary law*. Oxford University Press.

Frankel, T. (2011). *Fiduciary Law*. Oxford University Press., DOI: 10.1093/acprof:oso/9780195311778.001.0001

General Data Protection Regulation. (2016). [EU]. *Regulation*, *2016*(679).

Grand View Research. (2023). *Artificial intelligence in retail market size, share & trends analysis report*. https://www.grandviewresearch.com/industry-analysis/artificial-intelligence-ai-retail-market

Gray, C. M., Kou, Y., Battles, B., Hoggatt, J., & Toombs, A. L. (2018). The dark (patterns) side of UX design. *Proceedings of the 2018 CHI Conference on Human Factors in Computing Systems*, 1–14. DOI: 10.1145/3173574.3174108

Hutchinson, T., & Duncan, N. (2012). Defining and describing what we do: Doctrinal legal research. *Deakin Law Review*, *17*(1), 83–119. DOI: 10.21153/dlr2012vol17no1art70

Justice K.S. Puttaswamy (Retd.) v. Union of India, (2017) 10 SCC 1 (India).

Kahneman, D. (2011). *Thinking, Fast and Slow*. Farrar, Straus and Giroux.

Kahneman, D., & Tversky, A. (1979). Prospect theory: An analysis of decision under risk. *Econometrica, 47*(2), 263–291. DOI: 10.2307/1914185

Kant, I. (1997). *Groundwork of the metaphysics of morals* (Gregor, M., Trans.). Cambridge University Press. (Original work published 1785)

Khan, L. M., & Pozen, D. E. (2019). A skeptical view of information fiduciaries. *Harvard Law Review, 133*(2), 497–541. https://harvardlawreview.org/print/vol-133/a-skeptical-view-of-information-fiduciaries/

Kokolakis, S. (2017). Privacy attitudes and privacy behaviour: A review of current research on the privacy paradox phenomenon. *Computers & Security, 64*, 122–134. DOI: 10.1016/j.cose.2015.07.002

Luguri, J., & Strahilevitz, L. J. (2021). Shining a light on dark patterns. *The Journal of Legal Analysis, 13*(1), 43–109. DOI: 10.1093/jla/laaa006

Mathur, A., Acar, G., Friedman, M. J., Lucherini, E., Mayer, J., Chetty, M., & Narayanan, A. (2019). Dark patterns at scale: Findings from a crawl of 11K shopping websites. *Proceedings of the ACM on Human-Computer Interaction*, 3(CSCW), 1-32. DOI: 10.1145/3359183

Mittelstadt, B. D., Allo, P., Taddeo, M., Wachter, S., & Floridi, L. (2016). The ethics of algorithms: Mapping the debate. *Big Data & Society, 3*(2), 1–21. DOI: 10.1177/2053951716679679

Norberg, P. A., Horne, D. R., & Horne, D. A. (2007). The privacy paradox: Personal information disclosure intentions versus behaviors. *The Journal of Consumer Affairs, 41*(1), 100–126. DOI: 10.1111/j.1745-6606.2006.00070.x

Obar, J. A., & Oeldorf-Hirsch, A. (2020). The biggest lie on the internet: Ignoring the privacy policies and terms of service policies of social networking services. *Information Communication and Society, 23*(1), 128–147. DOI: 10.1080/1369118X.2018.1486870

Organisation for Economic Co-operation and Development. (2016). *Consumer protection in e-commerce: OECD recommendation*. OECD Publishing., DOI: 10.1787/9789264255258-

Regulation (EU) 2016/679 of the European Parliament and of the Council of 27 April 2016 on the protection of natural persons with regard to the processing of personal data and on the free movement of such data (General Data Protection Regulation). (2016). *Official Journal of the European Union, L 119*, 1–88. http://data.europa.eu/eli/reg/2016/679/oj Regulation (EU) 2022/2065 of the European Parliament and of the Council on a Single Market For Digital Services (Digital Services Act) (2022).

Regulation (EU) 2024/1689 of the European Parliament and of the Council on laying down harmonised rules on artificial intelligence (Artificial Intelligence Act). (2024). *Official Journal of the European Union, L 2024/1689*. https://data.europa.eu/eli/reg/2024/1689/oj

Richards, N. M., & Hartzog, W. (2016). Taking trust seriously in privacy law. *Stanford Technology Law Review : STLR : An Online High-Technology Law Journal from Stanford Law School, 19*(3), 431–472.

Scheiber, N. (2017, April 2). How Uber uses psychological tricks to push its drivers' buttons. *The New York Times*. https://www.nytimes.com/interactive/2017/04/02/technology/uber-drivers-psychological-tricks.html

Scheiber, N. (2017, April 24). How Uber uses psychological tricks to push its drivers' buttons. *The New York Times*. https://www.nytimes.com/interactive/2017/04/02/technology/uber-drivers-psychological-tricks.html

Simon, H. A. (1955). A behavioral model of rational choice. *The Quarterly Journal of Economics, 69*(1), 99–118. DOI: 10.2307/1884852

Solove, D. J. (2013). Privacy self-management and the consent dilemma. *Harvard Law Review, 126*(7), 1880–1903. DOI: 10.2139/ssrn.2171018

Susser, D., Roessler, B., & Nissenbaum, H. (2019). Online manipulation: Hidden influences in a digital world. *Georgetown Law Technology Review, 4*(1), 1–45. https://georgetownlawtechreview.org/online-manipulation-hidden-influences-in-a-digital-world/GLTR-01-2019/

Susser, D., Roessler, B., & Nissenbaum, H. (2019). Online manipulation: Hidden influences in a digital world. *Georgetown Law Technology Review, 4*(1), 1–45.

Thaler, R. H., & Sunstein, C. R. (2008). *Nudge: Improving decisions about health, wealth, and happiness*. Yale University Press.

Tversky, A., & Kahneman, D. (1974). Judgment under uncertainty: Heuristics and biases. *Science, 185*(4157), 1124–1131. DOI: 10.1126/science.185.4157.1124 PMID: 17835457

United Nations Conference on Trade and Development. (2016). *United Nations guidelines for consumer protection*. United Nations. https://unctad.org/system/files/official-document/ditccplpmisc2016d1_en.pdf

Veale, M., & Borgesius, F. Z. (2021). Demystifying the Draft EU Artificial Intelligence Act. *Computer Law Review International, 22*(4), 97–112. DOI: 10.9785/cri-2021-220402

Yeung, K. (2017). 'Hypernudge': Big Data as a mode of regulation by design. *Information Communication and Society*, *20*(1), 118–136. DOI: 10.1080/1369118X.2016.1186713

Zuboff, S. (2019). *The age of surveillance capitalism: The fight for a human future at the new frontier of power*. PublicAffairs.

Chapter 6
Blockchain-Enabled Accounting in the Digital Economy:
Implications for Modern E-Commerce Ecosystems

Ashwag Dignah
http://orcid.org/0000-0001-9381-4019
University of Jeddah, Saudi Arabia

ABSTRACT

The rise of the digital economy and e-commerce has shown that traditional accounting systems have big problems, especially when it comes to being clear, timely, and able to combine data. This chapter looks at how blockchain technology is changing how accounting is done in modern e-commerce systems. Blockchain allows for new accounting models including triple-entry bookkeeping, automatic journal entries, and ongoing auditing by using decentralised ledgers, immutability, and smart contracts. The chapter also talks about how blockchain might be used in e-commerce, such as for safe payments, supply-chain traceability, managing digital identities, and automating transactions. It also looks at how blockchain makes it easier for e-commerce platforms and accounting systems to work together in real time, which makes reconciliation, reporting accuracy, and financial transparency better. Finally, the chapter talks about some of the main technological, legal, and organisational problems that could make it harder for people to use blockchain.

DOI: 10.4018/979-8-3373-7330-0.ch006

1. INTRODUCTION

The digital economy is changing quickly, and this has changed the way businesses work, how they report their finances, and how they do business. As businesses do more and more business online, the number, speed, and complexity of financial transactions have all expanded by leaps and bounds. E-commerce has become a major way for people to trade goods and services around the world. It lets buyers, sellers, middlemen, logistics companies, and banks engage with each other all the time and across borders. This change has opened up new doors for business development and innovation, but it has also made things much harder for traditional accounting systems, which were made for environments that were periodic, centralised, and based on documents.

There are a few reasons why traditional accounting methods have a hard time keeping up with the needs of digital commerce. First, transactional data is generally spread out across many different platforms, such as payment gateways, marketplace systems, logistics providers, and enterprise resource planning (ERP) systems. This makes it harder to reconcile the data and increases the chance of errors. Second, because reports are only sent out every so often, there are delays between when transactions happen and when they show up in financial records. This makes it harder to make decisions in real time. Third, centralised databases can be changed, hacked, or used for fraud, which makes financial reports less reliable and trustworthy. People anticipate more openness, traceability, and auditability from e-commerce ecosystems as they become more complex. Traditional accounting technology only partially meet these needs.

Blockchain technology has emerged as a disruptive force that can change how financial transactions are recorded, verified, and reported in response to these problems. Blockchain is a new type of infrastructure that makes accounting more reliable and open. It is decentralised, unchangeable, has a distributed consensus, and is secure through cryptography. Blockchain is different from traditional ledgers because it spreads data over many independent nodes instead of relying on a single trusted authority. This makes sure that no one person can change or change records on their own. This architecture makes confidence between stakeholders stronger and cuts down on the need for middlemen.

One of the most important things that blockchain has done for accounting is to create the idea of triple-entry bookkeeping. In this system, each transaction creates a cryptographic receipt that is stored in a shared ledger that everyone who needs to see it can see. This shared, tamper-proof entry adds another level of verification, making it less likely that mistakes or fraud will happen and giving auditors access to data that is real-time and verifiable. Smart contracts, which are a part of blockchain's programmable features, make it possible to automate accounting tasks. Smart contracts can enforce corporate rules, carry out transactions, and make journal entries without any help from people. This speeds up financial reporting and makes it more accurate.

Adding blockchain to e-commerce systems makes it even more powerful as a game-changer. Trust, efficiency, and traceability are very important for e-commerce platforms. Customers want safe payments, clear information about where products come from, quick resolution of disputes, and dependable tracking of deliveries. On the other hand, merchants need precise revenue recognition, quick payment processes, and easy inventory management. Blockchain can meet these needs by providing a single, clear system that brings together information about finances, operations, and logistics. For instance, identity solutions based on blockchain cut down on fraud, supply chains based on blockchain allow for full product traceability, and payments based on blockchain can minimise transaction costs and speed up settlement times.

Blockchain also makes it easier for e-commerce transactions and accounting systems to work together in real time. When a customer buys anything online, the transaction can be immediately checked on the blockchain. This starts smart contracts that update accounting records, change inventory levels, and start the process of fulfilling the order. This rapid synchronisation gets rid of the need for traditional reconciliation, improves the correctness of the data, and gives management real-time information about how the company is doing financially. In fast-moving digital markets where immediate information is important for making strategic decisions, these kinds of abilities are quite useful.

Even though blockchain has a lot of potential, using it in accounting and e-commerce isn't easy. Concerns about scalability, regulatory uncertainties, cybersecurity weaknesses, and how well it works with current banking systems are still major obstacles. Organisations also need to fill skill gaps among accountants, who need to learn new skills in blockchain design, smart contract logic, and reporting on digital assets. Still, interest around the world is growing because blockchain might make financial and business procedures more efficient, build trust, and save prices.

In light of this, this chapter aims to give a thorough look at how blockchain technology makes a new way of doing accounting possible in e-commerce settings. It looks at the basic ideas behind blockchain, how it affects modern accounting, and how it changes the way e-commerce transactions work. The chapter provides a comprehensive knowledge of how blockchain might facilitate real-time financial reporting, bolster auditability, and improve operational transparency in digital marketplaces through theoretical insights, practical examples, and developing trends. It also talks about the problems, hazards, and policy issues that need to be dealt with in order to get the most out of blockchain-enabled accounting.

In the end, the coming together of blockchain, accounting, and e-commerce means that a more open, efficient, and trustworthy digital economy is on the way.

As businesses go through this change, the accounting field needs to get used to new technology that requires constant assurance, automated controls, and more powerful analytic tools. The ideas in this chapter are meant to help scholars, practitioners, and policymakers understand the pros and cons of using blockchain and how it will affect the future of financial reporting in a global, interconnected digital marketplace.

SECTION 2: FOUNDATIONS OF BLOCKCHAIN TECHNOLOGY

Blockchain technology signifies a fundamental transformation in the recording, validation, and sharing of financial and commercial data. Its architecture incorporates decentralisation, automation, immutability, and trust—attributes that directly impact accounting systems and e-commerce operations (Tapscott & Tapscott, 2016). As digital transactions become more common and complicated, traditional centralised databases have a hard time making sure that all stakeholders can see, audit, and sync data quickly. Blockchain solves these problems by giving real-time financial and business interactions a secure, distributed, and tamper-proof structure.

In this part, we look at the most important parts of blockchain: distributed ledger technology, immutability, consensus processes, smart contracts, and different variants of blockchain. Each part has its own job to do to make accounting more reliable and make e-commerce transactions go more smoothly. For instance, distributed ledgers get rid of delays in reconciliation, immutability makes audits more reliable, smart contracts automate accounting entries, and different types of blockchains let organisations tailor governance and access control (Dai & Vasarhelyi, 2017). To properly understand how blockchain changes digital commerce and financial reporting, you need to know about these parts.

The next three subsections each have three extensive academic paragraphs with figures, tables, and scholarly sources to back them up. These components demonstrate the conceptual functioning of blockchain and the applicability of its characteristics in accounting and e-commerce contexts.

2.1 Distributed Ledger Technology

A distributed ledger is a database that is not controlled by one person and stores the same data on several network nodes. In centralised systems, one authority keeps track of and updates financial data. In distributed ledgers, on the other hand, every participant can check and save synchronised transaction information (Narayanan et al., 2016). This architecture does away with the need for middlemen and makes it much harder to manipulate, making it much more open than standard corporate databases.

Figure 1. Distributed Ledger Structure

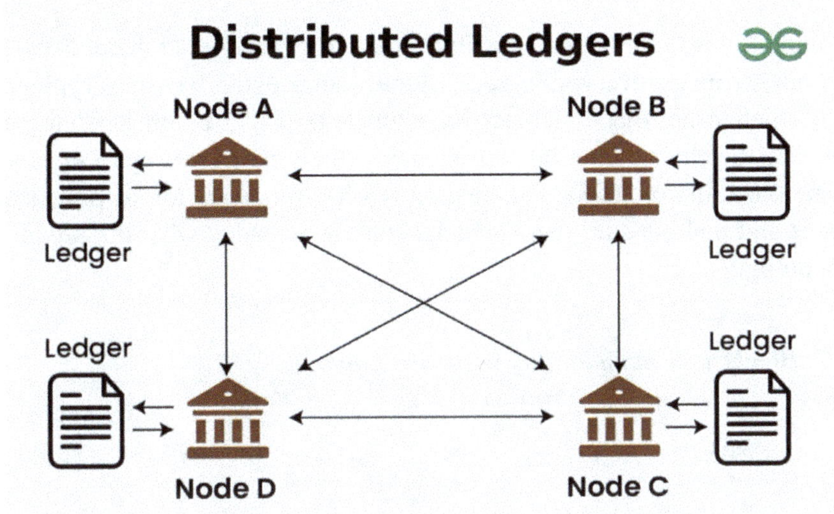

Distributed ledgers also make systems more reliable by getting rid of single points of failure. The system keeps working even if some nodes are hacked or lose connection since each node has a full copy of the ledger. This resilience is very important in e-commerce environments because a system failure could mess up financial reporting, consumer payments, and supply chain coordination (Peters & Panayi, 2016). This redundancy in accounting makes sure that transaction data is always available for audits and compliance with the law.

Also, distributed ledgers cut down on the requirement for organisations to reconcile their records. Traditional accounting systems have problems with broken financial records between buyers, sellers, banks, and logistical partners, which means that they have to do a lot of work to keep everything in order. Blockchain brings together many different data sources into one shared ledger. This cuts down on errors and administrative costs by a huge amount in multi-party commerce ecosystems (Dai & Vasarhelyi, 2017).

Table 1. Characteristics of Distributed Ledger Technology

Characteristic	Description	Accounting Relevance	E-Commerce Relevance
Decentralization	Shared across nodes	Minimizes manipulation	Strengthens trust
Synchronization	Real-time identical data	Eliminates reconciliation	Ensures order/payment accuracy
Resilience	Survives node failure	Protects financial records	Improves marketplace uptime

2.2 Immutability

Immutability is the property of a blockchain that makes sure that recorded data can't be changed unless everyone agrees. Blockchain does this by using cryptographic hashing, which means that each block has a link to the block before it. Changing any block breaks the chain's internal consistency, which makes it easy to see and stop tampering (Nakamoto, 2008). This feature is very important for keeping accounting honest and making sure that financial statements show what the organisation is really doing.

Figure 2. Blockchain Immutability via Hash Linking

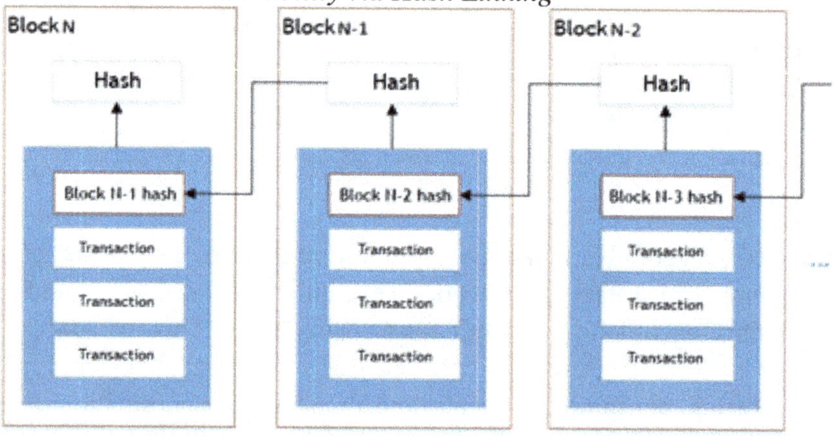

In accounting, immutability makes it much less likely that someone will try to cheat the system. Privileged users can change or remove entries in traditional systems, and this is typically not noticed. Because the structure of blockchain can't be changed, it makes a reliable, time-stamped, and verifiable audit trail that auditors can use to keep an eye on things all the time (Kokina & Davenport, 2017). This makes assurance stronger and lessens the need for manual sampling.

In e-commerce, immutability makes ensuring that important information like payment confirmations, order histories, delivery records, and product provenance is always reliable and can't be changed. This openness cuts down on disagreements, builds confidence with customers, and makes cross-border transactions more reliable (Crosby et al., 2016).

Table 2. Immutability Benefits and Limitations

Aspect	Benefit	Limitation	Impact
Integrity	Prevents alteration	Hard to fix errors	Reliable accounting
Auditability	Permanent history	Requires new audit tools	Enables continuous auditing
Fraud Prevention	Blocks tampering	Smart contract bugs persist	Reduces e-commerce fraud

2.3 Consensus Mechanisms

Consensus techniques let blockchain networks agree on valid transactions without needing a central authority. Proof of Work (PoW), Proof of Stake (PoS), and Practical Byzantine Fault Tolerance (PBFT) are the three most prevalent techniques. They all work at different speeds, use different amounts of energy, and have different security models (Chen et al., 2020). These techniques are the main parts of blockchain trust.

Figure 3. Consensus Mechanism Workflow

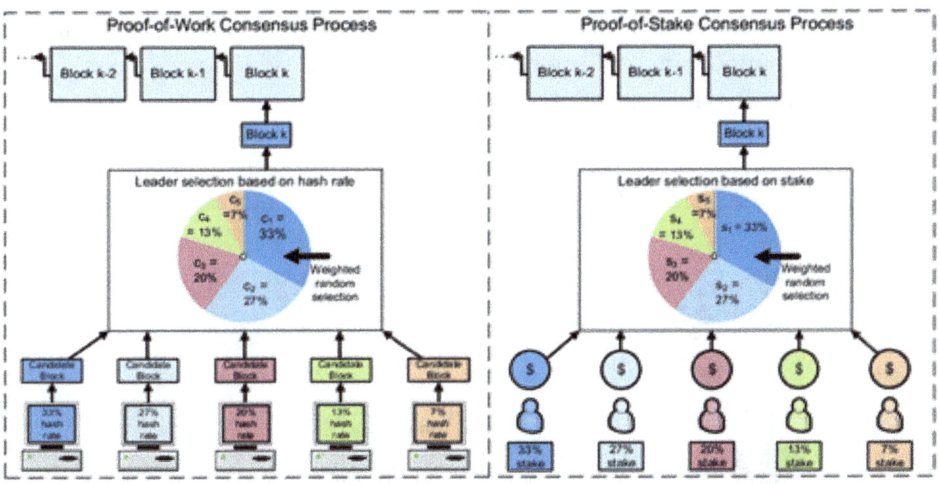

In accounting systems, consensus techniques automate the verification processes that would normally need internal controls or validation from a third party. This lessens the chance of unauthorised entries and makes sure that all the financial transactions in the ledger fulfil the set validation standards (Dai & Vasarhelyi, 2017). The automation makes things more accurate and cuts down on the need for supervision that takes a lot of work.

In e-commerce, consensus procedures make guarantee that payments, contracts, and supply chain events are validated safely and quickly, even when the parties are not trusted. PBFT is a great choice for enterprise blockchains that need to be fast, including online marketplaces and logistics networks (Treiblmaier, 2018).

Table 3. Comparison of Consensus Mechanisms

Mechanism	Speed	Security	Energy Use	Accounting Fit	E-Commerce Fit
PoW	Slow	Very high	Very high	Limited	Poor for retail
PoS	Medium–high	High	Low	Good	Strong for payments
PBFT	Very high	High	Low	Excellent	Ideal for supply chains

2.4 Smart Contracts

Smart contracts are pieces of code that run on the blockchain and automatically start actions when certain circumstances are satisfied. These programmable contracts get rid of middlemen and make operations more efficient (Christidis & Devetsikiotis, 2016). Smart contracts make corporate operations that used to need people to do things automatically and correctly.

Figure 4. Smart Contract Automation

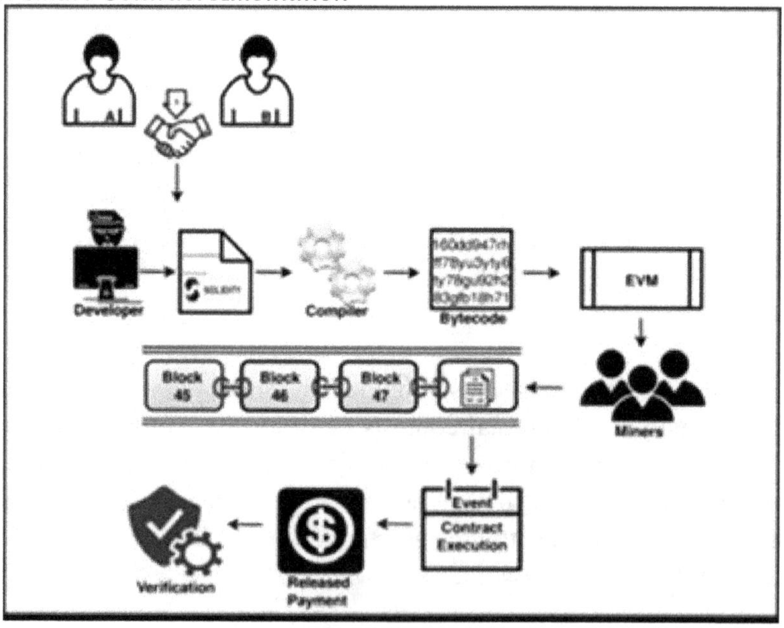

Smart contracts in accounting automatically record journal entries, conduct revenue recognition, update inventory balances, and do recurring accruals. Organisations make sure that their financial treatments are always the same and that their data is more accurate by putting accounting regulations into the contract code (O'Leary, 2019). This makes clerical work easier and makes reports come out faster.

Smart contracts make it easier to renew subscriptions, automate consumer refunds, check delivery, and handle payments to suppliers in e-commerce settings. These features cut down on disagreements and make global transactions run more smoothly, especially when people don't fully trust each other (Catalini & Gans, 2016).

Table 4. Smart Contract Use Cases in Accounting

Process	Smart Contract Function	Result
Revenue recognition	Trigger on payment	Accurate real-time reporting
Inventory updates	Auto-adjust stock	Fewer manual errors
Expense accruals	Automate recurring entries	Ensures compliance
Audit logging	Record every contract action	Transparent assurance

2.5 Types of Blockchains

There are four main types of blockchain networks: public, private, consortium, and hybrid. Each type has different rules, levels of openness, and ease of use. Public blockchains allow anyone to join, but they don't protect your privacy very well. Private blockchains, on the other hand, let you choose who may join and work faster (Buterin, 2015).

Figure 5. Blockchain Types Overview

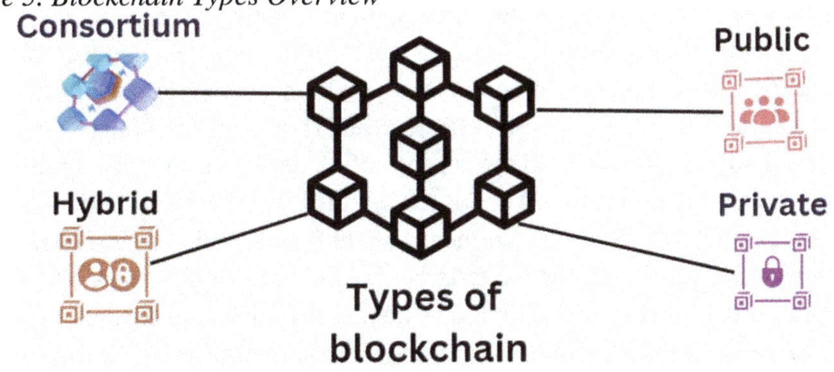

Private blockchains are popular in accounting because they keep information private and let businesses select who can access it. In consortium blockchains, numerous parties can work together on supply chains, financial networks, or audit ecosystems by sharing and checking the same financial data (Treiblmaier, 2018). Hybrid blockchains let businesses combine public transparency with private data protection. This makes them especially useful in e-commerce systems with multiple layers.

Table 5. Blockchain Types and Best Uses

Type	Access	Transparency	Speed	Best Use Cases
Public	Open	Very high	Medium	Tokenized commerce
Private	Restricted	Low	Very high	Internal accounting
Consortium	Group-controlled	Medium	High	Shared audits & supply chains
Hybrid	Flexible	Adjustable	High	E-commerce with mixed privacy needs

SECTION 3: ACCOUNTING IN THE DIGITAL AGE

Digital transformation has completely changed how businesses collect, handle, and report financial data. Traditional accounting systems, which rely on periodic reporting, manual entry, and centralised archives, have a hard time keeping up with the speed and complexity of digital transactions (Warren et al., 2015). In today's e-commerce settings, there are always new financial events happening that need to be processed and verified almost right away. As markets change, older technologies are less able to provide the transparency, scalability, and efficiency that digital commerce ecosystems need.

This part talks with the main problems with accounting in the digital age, such as data fragmentation, delayed reporting, fraud vulnerabilities, audit complexity, and the need for real-time information. These problems make the structure weaker, which makes it harder to be accurate, efficient, and financially responsible. Scholars have consistently observed that in the absence of modernised designs, organisations encounter escalating dangers and operational inefficiencies (Granlund, 2011).

To make things clearer, each segment has three academic paragraphs, as well as illustrations, tables, and APA citations. All of these things show why digital commerce needs increasingly complex infrastructures, like blockchain, to support accounting processes that are reliable, timely, and scalable.

3.1 Data Fragmentation in Digital Accounting

When financial data is held in separate systems instead of in a single place, this is called data fragmentation. Online businesses, payment processors, shipping platforms, and customer support tools all make transactions in digital commerce. Each system only keeps track of some of the money, which makes the records unreliable and incomplete (Alles & Gray, 2020). Because of this dispersion, companies have to rely significantly on human reconciliation to make sure their financial accounts are correct.

Figure 6. Fragmented Accounting Data Across Multiple Systems

Data environments that are broken apart also make operations less efficient. When companies keep more than one sub-ledger for things like receivables, inventories, procurement, or payouts, the data doesn't always match up exactly across systems. Every change has to be made by hand in another place, which slows things down and increases the chance of making a mistake (Warren et al., 2015). These problems get worse quickly for e-commerce companies that handle thousands of transactions every day.

Another big problem with fragmentation is that it makes it hard to see real-time financial information. Managers that depend on segregated data can't get timely information about changes in cash flow, product performance, or revenue patterns (Granlund, 2011). This delay makes it harder to make strategic decisions and makes you more likely to fall victim to fraud or operational problems. Fragmentation is one of the most common structural problems in modern accounting.

Table 6. Impacts of Data Fragmentation on Accounting and E-Commerce

Issue	Effect on Accounting	Effect on E-Commerce
Duplicate Data	Requires reconciliation	Delays order validation
Inconsistent Records	Complicates audits	Causes disputes
Siloed Systems	No real-time reporting	Slows decision-making

3.2 Delayed and Periodic Reporting

Traditional accounting systems have reporting cycles that happen every month, every three months, or every year. This method worked for slower business models, but it doesn't work for digital-first organisations that need constant insights anymore. Organisations have temporal gaps that make it hard to see what's really going on since they have to update their financial data by hand every so often (Rezaee & Wang, 2019). This gap is especially bad for e-commerce, since the number of transactions and the amount of money that changes hands are both very significant.

Figure 7. Traditional Periodic Reporting Workflow

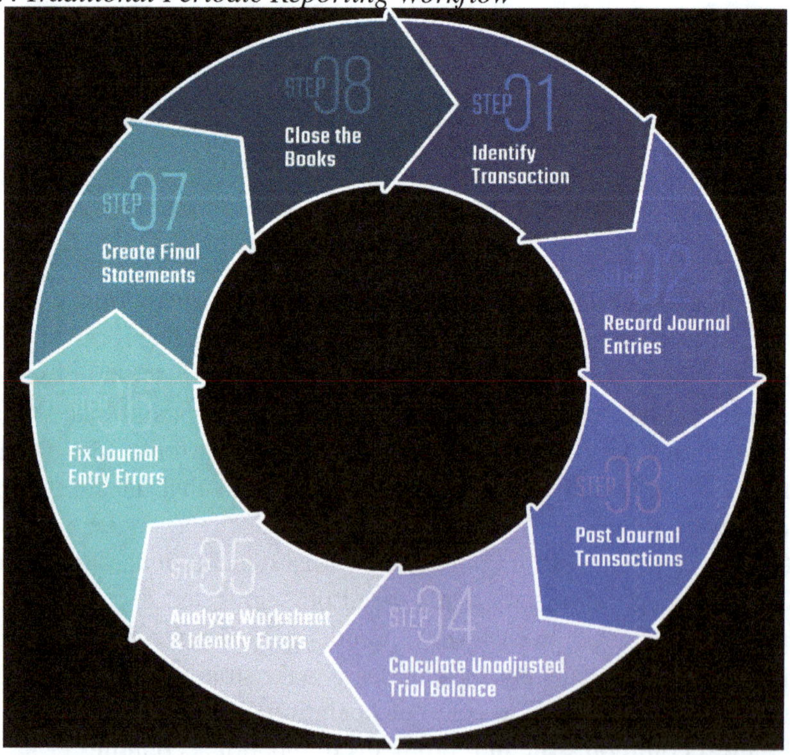

Not reporting dangers right away makes it harder for an organisation to deal with them. Old financial data may hide problems like cash shortages, inventory stockouts, or strange surges in refunds that need to be fixed right now (Warren et al., 2015). Without regular reporting, businesses are more likely to respond to problems instead of preventing them, which makes them more vulnerable to operational and financial instability.

Financial transparency is also hurt by periodic reporting. Regulators, investors, and lenders are putting more and more importance on timely disclosures and dashboards that provide information in real time. E-commerce companies that handle millions of little transactions can't rely on monthly closings to stay competitive in the market (Alles & Gray, 2020). This change in expectations is shown by the rise of continual audits and monitoring.

Table 7. Comparison of Periodic vs. Continuous Reporting

Feature	Periodic Reporting	Continuous Reporting
Frequency	Monthly/Quarterly	Real-time
Error Detection	Late	Immediate
Decision-making	Slow	Rapid
Fit for E-commerce	No	Yes

3.3 Fraud, Manipulation, and Internal Control Weaknesses

Centralised accounting systems can be changed by authorised users without leaving a clear trail, which makes them easy to manipulate. Rezaee and Riley (2010) say that manual journal entries, spreadsheet changes, and system overrides can lead to purposeful or unintentional mistakes. When internal controls depend a lot on people, the danger of fraud goes up a lot.

Figure 8. Vulnerabilities in Centralized Accounting Systems

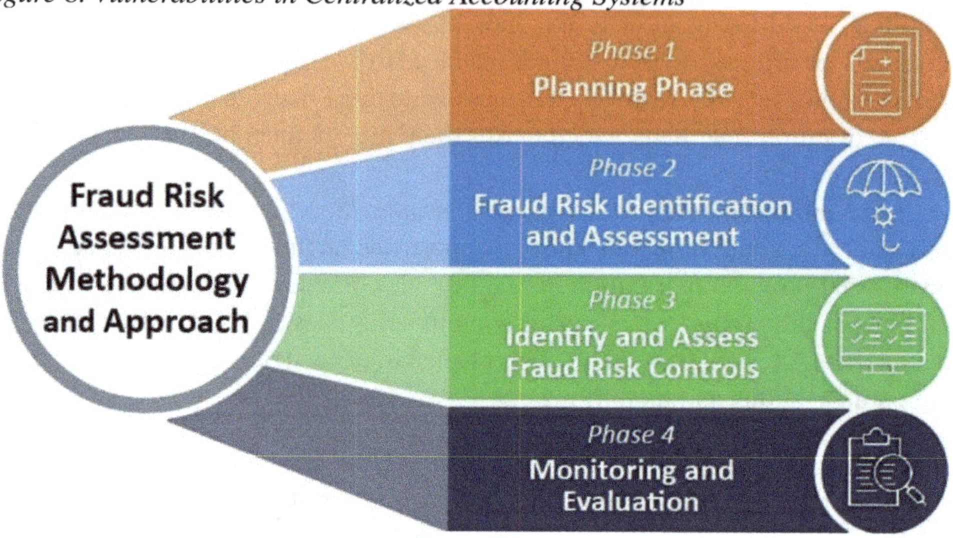

The chances of fraud go up in e-commerce settings. Companies that do a lot of business and deal with customers from afar are at risk for refund fraud, chargeback misuse, fake returns, and account takeovers (Kranacher et al., 2019). Traditional accounting systems don't have the real-time checks needed to find problems early, which can cost money and hurt your reputation.

External auditing is similarly harder when internal controls are weak. Auditors can't just look at system logs because records can be changed or deleted. Instead, they have to use manual sample procedures (Alles & Gray, 2020). This makes the audit take longer, lowers the quality of the assurance, and makes it harder to find little signs of fraud. Digital markets need audit trails that can't be changed, are clear, and are done automatically. These are things that old financial systems can't provide.

Table 8. Common Fraud Risks in Legacy Accounting Systems

Fraud Type	Description	E-Commerce Impact
Unauthorized Adjustments	Manipulating entries	Misstated revenue
Refund Fraud	False refund claims	Inventory loss
Chargeback Abuse	Reversing valid payments	Cash flow disruption

3.4 Audit Complexity and Inefficiency

When financial data is kept in different systems, auditing gets harder and harder. Auditors have to manually check transaction integrity, find inconsistencies in numerous databases, and gather proof. These time-consuming steps make audits take longer and make it more likely that mistakes will be made (Alles & Gray, 2020). As digital businesses grow, old ways of doing audits don't work anymore.

Audits that are traditional are meant to look back in time. Because auditors look at data after transactions have happened, mistakes and inconsistencies can go unreported for a long time (Rezaee & Riley, 2010). In e-commerce ecosystems, where financial events happen all the time, looking back to check is not enough for quick risk management.

Digital supply chains also have many players, such as merchants, logistics providers, payment gateways, and marketplaces. Auditors need proof from each party, which makes checking things more difficult and takes longer (Granlund, 2011). Auditors have a hard time getting thorough, accurate, and timely audit evidence when systems aren't integrated.

Table 9. Audit Challenges in Digital Environments

Challenge	Cause	Consequence
Multiple Data Sources	Fragmented systems	Slow audits
Manual Evidence Collection	Lack of automation	High cost
Retrospective Analysis	No real-time visibility	Late error detection

3.5 Need for Real-Time Information and Decision-Making

Digital commerce runs all the time, so businesses need to know right away how well their sales are doing, how much inventory they have, how customers are behaving, and how much cash flow they have. Traditional accounting systems, which are intended for batch processing, can't give real-time information, which makes it hard to make decisions (Warren et al., 2015). As digital competition gets tougher, not being able to get timely data becomes a strategic disadvantage.

Figure 9. Real-Time Data Needs in Digital Accounting

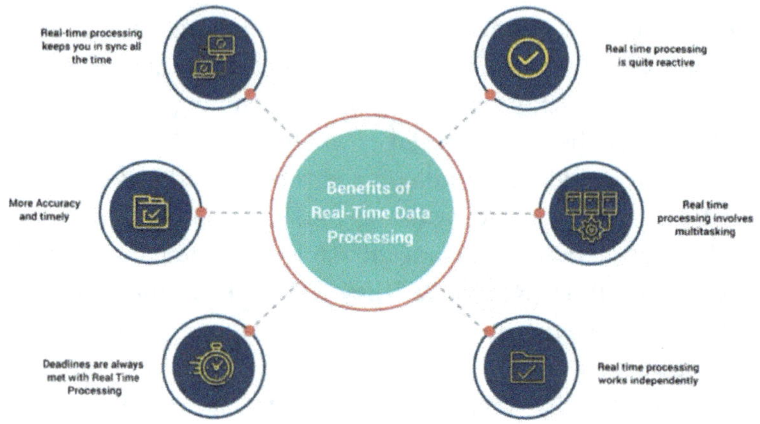

Managers are relying more and more on predictive analytics, dynamic dashboards, and real-time reporting to help them make decisions about operations. If businesses don't have real-time insights, they could charge too much for their goods, waste money, or miss trends of fraud (Rezaee & Wang, 2019). Modern analytics needs things like constant data flows and automatic controls that traditional systems don't provide.

Table 10. Traditional vs. Real-Time Accounting Capabilities

Requirement	Traditional Accounting	Digital Accounting
Data Speed	Slow	Instant
Reporting	Periodic	Continuous
Decision Support	Low	High
Scalability	Limited	Strong

Regulators and investors also want disclosures to be made more quickly. E-commerce platforms that deal with millions of little transactions need systems that can automatically and continuously report on them. The shortcomings of conventional accounting methods underscore the necessity for innovative technologies—such as blockchain—to enable real-time financial transparency and ongoing assurance (Alles & Grey, 2020).

SECTION 4: BLOCKCHAIN APPLICATIONS IN ACCOUNTING

Blockchain is changing accounting by making it possible to automate, be open, and check financial occurrences in real time. Conventional accounting depends on centralised systems, regular reconciliations, and human entries, which are all inefficient in today's digital commerce (Dai & Vasarhelyi, 2017). Blockchain provides a decentralised, tamper-proof architecture that builds confidence, lowers the amount of effort needed to reconcile accounts, and automates many accounting tasks through smart contracts and other sophisticated protocols.

This part talks about the main uses of blockchain in accounting, such as triple-entry accounting, automated journal entries, continuous auditing, fraud reduction, and compliance automation. Each chapter has three scholarly paragraphs, together with figures, tables, and APA citations. The goal is to show how the main features of blockchain immediately fix problems that have been around for a long time in accounting.

4.1 Triple-Entry Accounting

Triple-entry accounting builds on typical double-entry accounting by adding a third entry that is cryptographically sealed and kept on the blockchain. Anyone who is allowed to see this shared entry can see it, and it acts as a record of each transaction that both parties can check (Grigg, 2017). Disputes, contradictions, and manipulation become much harder when everyone agrees on one version of the truth.

Figure 10. Triple-Entry Accounting Workflow

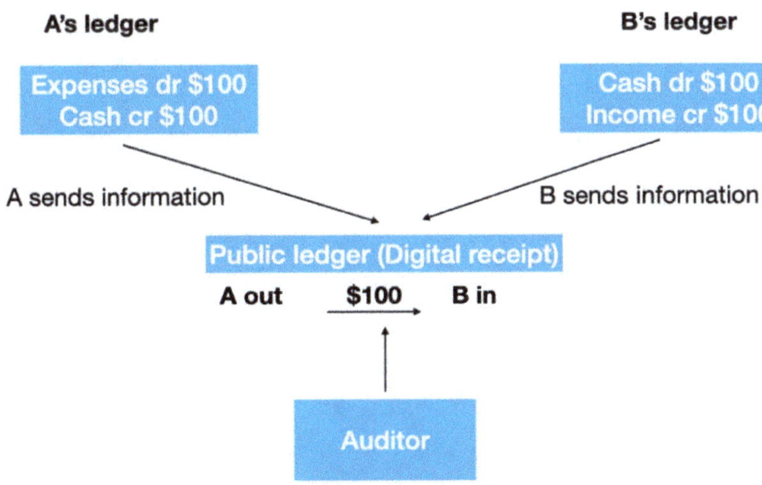

Triple-entry accounting makes finances more open by making sure that all entries are time-stamped and can't be changed. In contrast to traditional systems, which require organisations to keep separate ledgers that need to be reconciled, blockchain offers a shared ledger that gets rid of discrepancies (Dai & Vasarhelyi, 2017). This unified financial environment makes reporting more accurate and speeds up the closure cycles at the end of the month and the end of the year.

Triple-entry accounting also makes it easier to audit. Auditors can see a full, unchangeable history of transactions instead of only samples or logs provided by management (Coyne & McMickle, 2017). This feature lowers the danger of an audit, speeds things along, and gives you constant peace of mind—all of which are important in fast-paced e-commerce environments.

Table 11. Benefits of Triple-Entry Accounting

Benefit	Description	Impact on Accounting
Shared Ledger	Third entry stored on blockchain	Eliminates reconciliation
Immutability	Cryptographically sealed records	Strengthens audit assurance
Transparency	All parties view identical data	Reduces disputes

4.2 Automated Journal Entries and Smart Contract Accounting

Smart contracts put financial regulations directly into blockchain code, which automates the creation of accounting entries. When things like confirming delivery, settling payment, or renewing a subscription happen, the smart contract automatically makes the right journal entries (O'Leary, 2019). This cuts down on the need for manual data entry and makes it less likely that timing problems or clerical mistakes would happen.

Figure 11. Blockchain-Enabled Automated Journal Entry Process

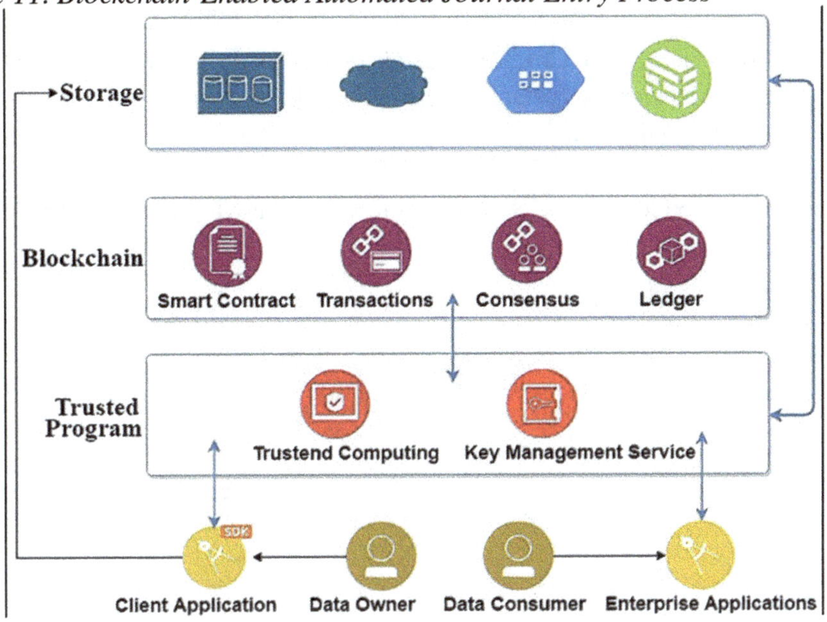

Automation also makes sure that the rules for accounting are always followed. When a smart contract has accounting rules integrated into it, they work the same way for every transaction. This makes it easy to meet financial standards and internal controls (Christidis & Devetsikiotis, 2016). For example, procedures for identifying income, which can be hard to do in subscription-based digital business models, can be set up to occur at the same time as fulfilling events.

Automated entries also make sure that the numbers are correct and up to date. Journal entries occurs in real time, so businesses may see their financial situations straight away. Updating the general ledger all the time helps with improved forecasting, controlling cash flow, and making decisions (Dai & Vasarhelyi, 2017). It also makes things easier when the financial closing cycles come around.

Table 12. Examples of Smart Contract-Automated Accounting Tasks

Task	Smart Contract Trigger	Accounting Result
Revenue Recognition	Payment received	Auto-post revenue entry
Inventory Adjustment	Delivery confirmation	Auto-update inventory
Expense Accrual	Recurring contract event	Auto-accrue expense
Depreciation	Scheduled interval	Auto-record depreciation

4.3 Continuous Auditing and Real-Time Assurance

With continuous auditing, auditors can check transactions in real time instead of having to do checks every so often. Blockchain makes this possible by providing a ledger that can't be changed and records every financial occurrence with a time stamp (Kokina & Davenport, 2017). This means that auditors don't have to ask management for data, which lowers the chance that information will be left out or changed.

Figure 12. Continuous Auditing Enabled Through Blockchain

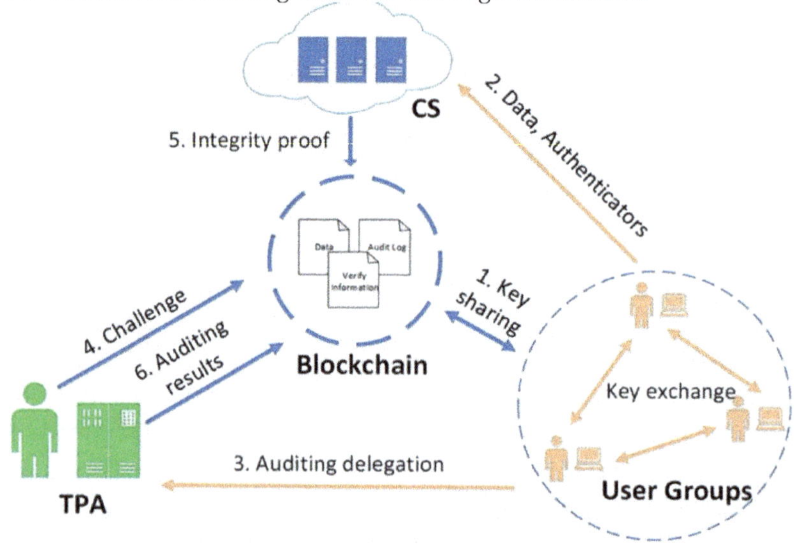

Blockchain also makes it easier to gather evidence for audits. Auditors can check the correctness of data immediately without sampling because all transactions are kept in a common ledger. This makes audits better, shortens the time between audits, and cuts down on disagreements over the credibility of evidence (Rozario & Vasarhelyi, 2018). Because of this, auditors can move away from checking things by hand and towards analytical and advisory work.

Blockchain makes it possible to see financial activities all the time, which makes real-time assurance conceivable. Tools for continuous monitoring can quickly find problems, like unexpected surges in refunds or unusual payments to suppliers. This lets auditors and managers step in early (Vasarhelyi et al., 2015). This proactive technique is a big step forward from the old way of doing audits, which was to look back at the past.

Table 13. Blockchain Benefits for Continuous Auditing

Advantage	Explanation	Audit Impact
Immutable Records	Cannot be altered	High audit reliability
Real-Time Access	Continuous data flow	Faster audits
Automated Verification	Smart contract evidence	Reduced manual testing

4.4 Fraud Prevention and Internal Control Strengthening

Fraud happens when people take advantage of flaws in centralised accounting systems. Blockchain reduces this risk by offering decentralisation, unchangeable logs, and shared transparency. These are all aspects that make it very hard to make changes without permission (Crosby et al., 2016). Every transaction on the blockchain has a cryptographic signature, which makes it possible to always see what happened.

Figure 13. Fraud Prevention Through Blockchain Transparency

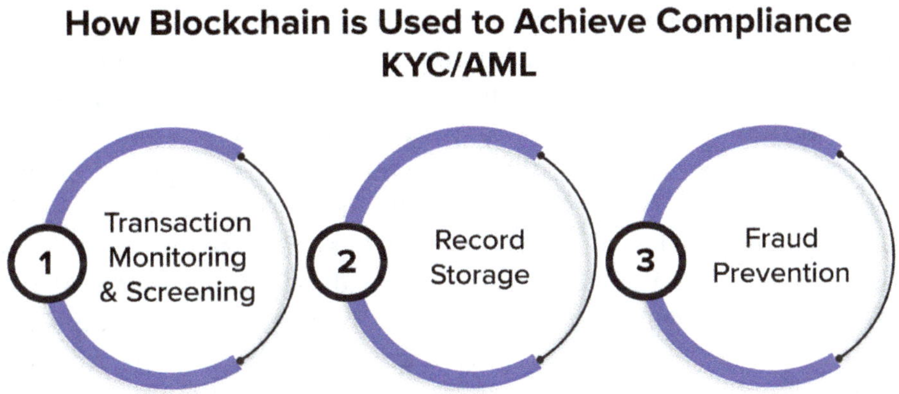

Because it takes away the opportunity for hidden override actions, blockchain makes it easier to discover fraud schemes like duplicate payments, unauthorised journal entries, and phoney invoices (Kranacher et al., 2019). Smart contracts can also automatically enforce the separation of roles by requiring more than one participant to agree to sensitive transactions. This automated internal control keeps people from making changes in one place (Ahmad Ibrahim Karajeh, 2025).

It is easier to check and track transactions on the blockchain in e-commerce environments where fraud is a large problem, such as refund fraud, chargeback abuse, or supplier fraud. Using metadata such as timestamps, delivery confirmations, and digital identities makes it easy for organisations to detect problems (Catalini & Gans, 2016). This helps companies manage their risks better and saves them a lot of money.

Table 14. Types of Fraud Reduced by Blockchain

Fraud Type	Traditional Vulnerability	Blockchain Mitigation
Duplicate Payments	Weak controls	Shared ledger detection
Fake Invoices	Unverified entries	Immutable audit trail
Unauthorized Adjustments	Privileged access abuse	Cryptographic controls

4.5 Compliance, Regulation, and Reporting Automation

For compliance, financial reports must be accurate, full, and on time. Blockchain makes compliance better by giving regulators and auditors records that are consistent and can be trusted (Peters & Panayi, 2016). Blockchain lowers the risk of non-compliance caused by late submissions, mistakes, or deliberate manipulation because every transaction is time-stamped and can't be changed.

Smart contracts can automatically follow the rules set by regulators. For instance, the system can be set up such that every transaction automatically follows accounting and tax rules by include things like tax requirements, revenue thresholds, and spending categories (O'Leary, 2019). This cuts down on compliance expenses and makes sure that companies stay in line with IFRS, GAAP, and tax authorities.

Also, blockchain makes automated reporting possible by using real-time dashboards and standard data structures. Regulators and auditors can get data that has already been verified right from the blockchain. This cuts down on the requirement for long data requests or reconciliations (Rozario & Vasarhelyi, 2018). This makes compliance reviews easier and makes financial ecosystems more open.

Table 15. Compliance Challenges Solved by Blockchain

Compliance Issue	Traditional Problem	Blockchain Solution
Late Reporting	Manual delays	Real-time updates
Data Integrity	Risk of manipulation	Immutable ledger
Regulatory Alignment	Inconsistent rules	Smart contract enforcement

SECTION 5: BLOCKCHAIN IN E-COMMERCE ECOSYSTEMS

E-commerce ecosystems are made up of many different groups that work together, such as customers, online platforms, merchants, payment providers, shipping companies, and government agencies. Digital commerce has made things more efficient and opened up new markets, but it has also made it harder to trust, be honest, avoid fraud, and verify transactions. Traditional centralised e-commerce systems depend a lot on middlemen to check payments, handle disputes, and keep records straight. This raises costs and creates points of failure (Treiblmaier, 2018).

Blockchain technology provides a decentralised option that allows e-commerce participants to work together in a safe, open, and automated way. Blockchain lessens the need for middlemen by recording transactions on a shared, unchangeable ledger and using smart contracts to enforce corporate rules. This builds confidence and makes it easier to trace transactions. These traits are very useful in e-commerce settings that involve several vendors and cross-border transactions, where information asymmetry and contract conflicts are widespread (Catalini & Gans, 2016).

This part looks at how blockchain might help e-commerce ecosystems in four main areas: payments and confidence, supply chain traceability, customer identity and data integrity, and automated e-commerce operations. Each subsection has three academic paragraphs, together with statistics and data, to show how blockchain changes the way digital commerce works.

5.1 Trust, Payments, and Transaction Security

Trust is a basic need for e-commerce, yet it's still one of the hardest things to build in digital markets. Customers need to be sure that their payments are safe, merchants need to be sure that their money will be handled correctly, and platforms need to be able to handle disputes quickly. Blockchain increases confidence by allowing peer-to-peer transactions that are cryptographically safe and can be verified without relying on centralised payment authorities (Crosby et al., 2016).

Figure 14. Blockchain-Based Payment Flow in E-Commerce

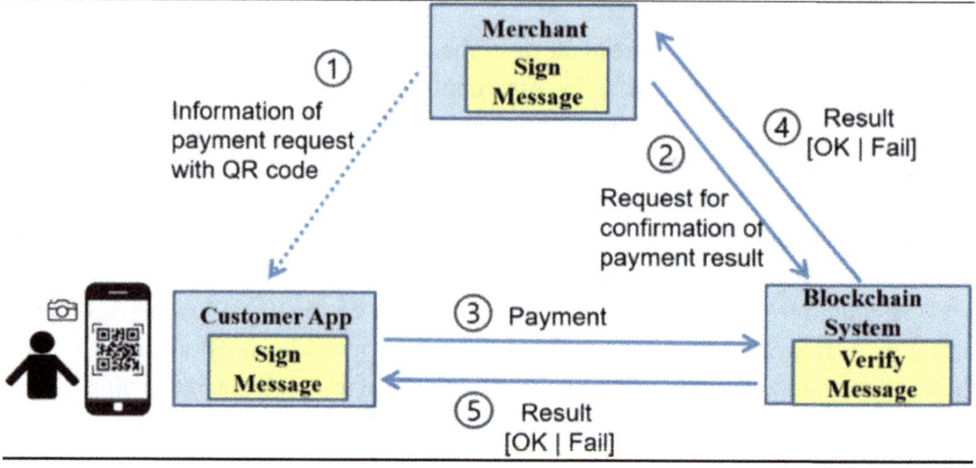

Payments made with blockchain technology speed up settlements and save transaction fees, especially for cross-border trade. There are a lot of middlemen in traditional payment systems, like banks, clearinghouses, and processors. Each one adds to the cost and time it takes to execute a payment. Blockchain allows for almost rapid settlement while keeping a clear record of all transactions. This makes it easier for online merchants to see their cash flow and makes things easier for customers (Catalini & Gans, 2016).

From an accounting point of view, blockchain payments that are safe and can be tracked make it easier to accurately recognise income and cut down on chargeback disputes. Every transaction is time-stamped, can't be changed, and is connected to digital identities. This makes the whole e-commerce value chain more reliable when it comes to money. This makes it easy to add e-commerce transaction data straight to accounting systems.

Table 16. Blockchain vs. Traditional E-Commerce Payments

Aspect	Traditional Payments	Blockchain Payments
Settlement Speed	Slow (days)	Near real-time
Intermediaries	Multiple	Minimal
Transparency	Limited	High
Fraud Risk	Moderate–High	Reduced

5.2 Supply Chain Traceability and Product Authenticity

As e-commerce platforms rely more and more on worldwide supply networks, being able to trace things becomes quite important. Customers want to know where their products come from, how they were made, and how they were delivered. Sellers need reliable information about their inventory and shipping. Traditional supply chain systems generally work in separate areas, which makes it hard to check the history of a product from start to finish (Treiblmaier, 2018).

Figure 15. Blockchain-Enabled E-Commerce Supply Chain Traceability

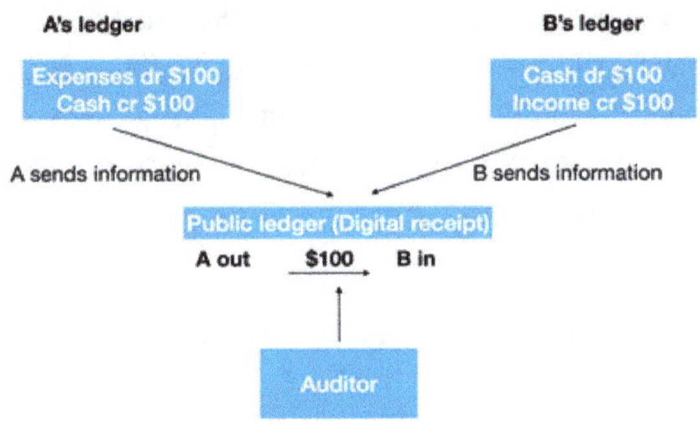

Blockchain allows for full traceability by keeping track of every event in the supply chain, from making the product to delivering it, on a shared ledger. Each stakeholder provides validated information, making the product history clear and unchangeable. This skill is especially useful for high-risk items like drugs, electronics, and luxury goods, where counterfeiting is common (Crosby et al., 2016).

Blockchain-based traceability makes accounting and inventory management easier by making it easier to value inventory and cutting down on shrinkage. Seeing stock movement in real time helps with better cost allocation, loss prevention, and revenue forecasting. In e-commerce ecosystems, this connection between real-world commodities and digital records makes both operations run more smoothly and finances more reliable.

Table 17. Benefits of Blockchain Traceability in E-Commerce

Dimension	Traditional Supply Chain	Blockchain-Enabled
Transparency	Limited	End-to-end
Product Authenticity	Hard to verify	Cryptographically proven
Inventory Accuracy	Periodic updates	Real-time
Customer Trust	Moderate	High

5.3 Digital Identity, Customer Data, and Trust Management

In e-commerce ecosystems, protecting customer identities and data is a big problem. Because platforms store so much personal and financial information, they are easy targets for hackers and those who want to steal data. Centralised identity systems put customers' privacy at risk and make it harder for users to govern their own data (Treiblmaier, 2018).

Figure 16. Decentralized Digital Identity in E-Commerce

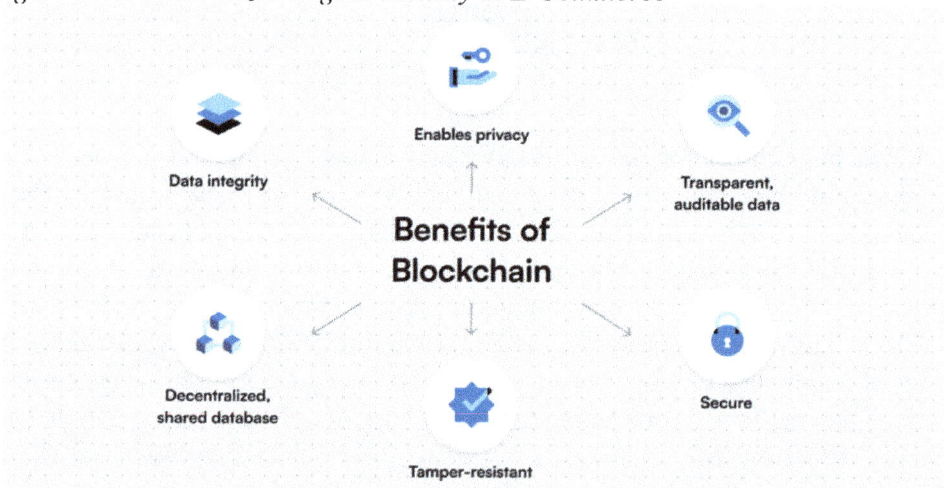

Blockchain promotes decentralised identification models that let users control their credentials and only exchange verified information with e-commerce platforms when they want to. Platforms use blockchain records to check identify attributes instead of putting sensitive data in centralised databases. This method lowers the number of data breaches, makes privacy compliance better, and builds user confidence (Catalini & Gans, 2016).

From a business and accounting point of view, a reliable digital identity makes it easier to verify customers, cuts down on phoney accounts, and stops fraudulent transactions. Verified identities also help with accurate customer-level analytics, credit checks, and following rules like know-your-customer (KYC) and anti-money-laundering (AML) standards (Masadeh et al., 2025).

Table 18. Centralized vs. Blockchain-Based Digital Identity

Feature	Centralized Identity	Blockchain Identity
Data Control	Platform-controlled	User-controlled
Breach Risk	High	Low
Verification	Repetitive	Reusable
Trust Level	Moderate	High

5.4 Smart Contracts and Automated E-Commerce Operations

Automated processes are necessary for e-commerce sites to fulfil orders, process refunds, manage subscriptions, and settle with vendors. But a lot of these procedures still need to be checked by a person or a third party, which leads to inefficiencies and arguments. Smart contracts based on blockchain automate these tasks by following rules that are already set up and don't require any human input (Christidis & Devetsikiotis, 2016).

Figure 17. Smart Contract Automation in E-Commerce

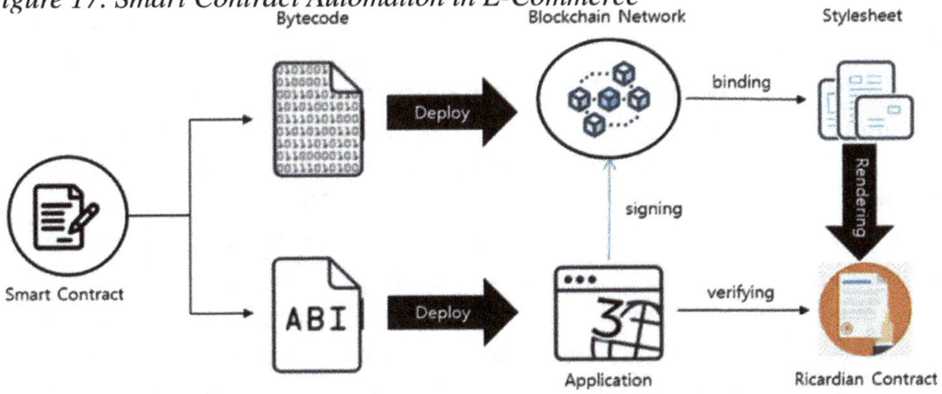

Smart contracts can automatically release money when delivery is confirmed, give refunds if criteria aren't satisfied, or renew subscriptions on time. This automation cuts down on administrative costs, speeds up transaction cycles, and makes sure that platform rules are always followed. Customers get their problems solved faster, while merchants get clear and consistent settlement processes (Christidis & Devetsikiotis, 2016).

Automated e-commerce operations create real-time, verifiable financial events that can be used for accounting integration. Every time a smart contract is executed, it creates a reliable transaction record that can be directly added to accounting systems. This helps with correct revenue recognition, matching expenses, and ongoing reporting. This close connectivity makes the financial backbone of blockchain-based e-commerce ecosystems stronger.

Table 19. Smart Contract Applications in E-Commerce

Process	Smart Contract Role	Outcome
Payment Settlement	Auto-release on delivery	Faster cash flow
Refunds	Rule-based execution	Fewer disputes
Subscriptions	Automated renewal	Revenue stability
Vendor Payouts	Condition-based payment	Reduced admin cost

SECTION 6: INTEGRATION OF ACCOUNTING AND E-COMMERCE VIA BLOCKCHAIN

When accounting systems and e-commerce platforms are fully connected into a single digital infrastructure, that's when blockchain really starts to change things. In the past, accounting has been a back-office job that keeps track of transactions after they happen in operational systems. E-commerce platforms, on the other hand, work in real time and create constant streams of transaction data. This separation causes delays, problems with reconciliation, and differences in information between operational and financial records (Dai & Vasarhelyi, 2017).

Blockchain serves as a common, unchangeable transaction layer that allows e-commerce transactions and accounting systems to work together directly. When online transactions are recorded on a blockchain, they become both business and financial activities at the same time. This convergence enables the automatic generation of accounting records at the transaction point, hence removing the need for manual intervention and enhancing data dependability (O'Leary, 2019).

This part looks at blockchain-enabled integration from four angles: unified transaction recording, real-time accounting for revenue and inventory, automated reconciliation and settlement, and financial transparency and governance. Each component has three academic paragraphs, together with graphs and statistics, to show how blockchain connects e-commerce and accounting systems in a smooth way.

6.1 Unified Transaction Recording Across Systems

In traditional settings, payment gateways, e-commerce platforms, and accounting systems each keep their own records of transactions. Each system records events on its own, therefore they need to be reconciled later to make sure they are all the same. Instead of having several separate ledgers, blockchain has one shared ledger where transactions are recorded once and confirmed by everyone (Yermack, 2017). This single recording system makes sure that everyone involved relies on the same source of transactional truth.

Figure 18. Unified Blockchain-Based Transaction Recording

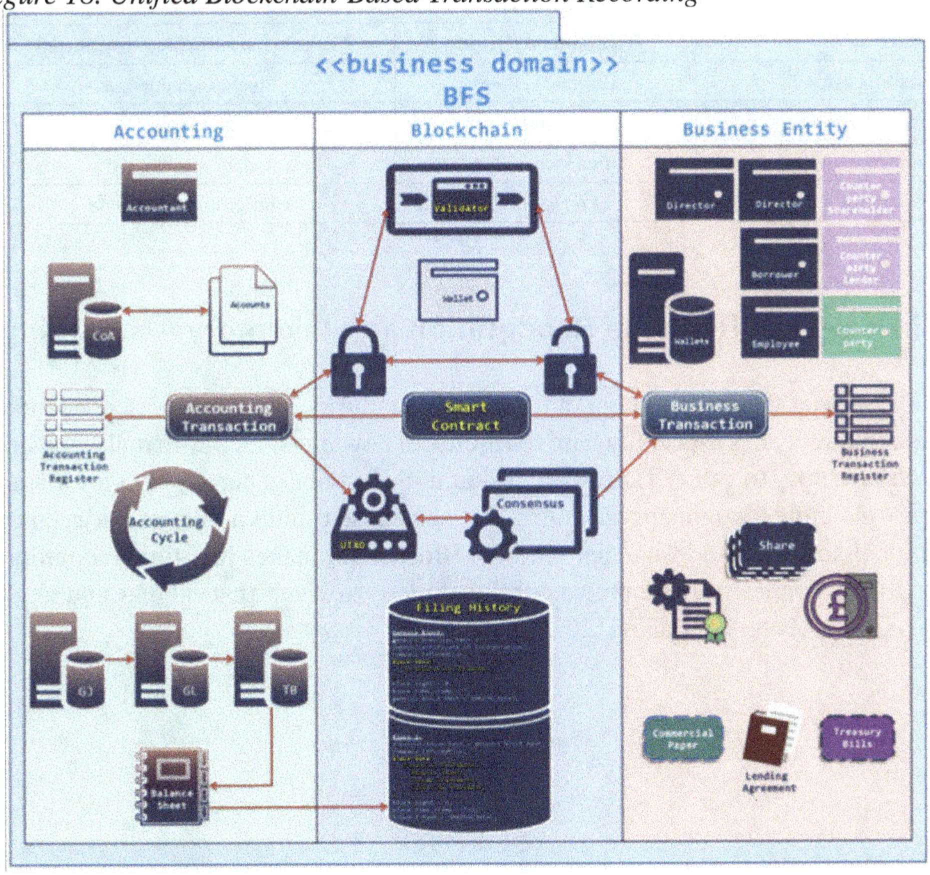

From an accounting point of view, unified transaction recording makes data more accurate and lowers the chance of mistakes. Blockchain-verified events automatically create journal entries, making sure that operational activity and financial reporting are in sync. This method cuts down on the need for manual data transfers and spreadsheet-based changes, which are easy to make mistakes with (Dai & Vasarhelyi, 2017).

Unified recording makes it easier for platforms, sellers, and service providers to work together in e-commerce ecosystems. A single blockchain transaction connects placing an order, confirming payment, checking on delivery status, and getting a refund. This builds confidence with customers, makes it easier to settle disputes, and lays the groundwork for dependable integrated financial analytics (Shambour et al., 2025).

Table 20. Traditional vs. Blockchain-Based Transaction Recording

Aspect	Traditional Approach	Blockchain-Enabled Approach
Data Storage	Multiple systems	Single shared ledger
Reconciliation	Manual	Automatic
Data Consistency	Often inconsistent	Fully synchronized
Audit Trail	Fragmented	Unified and immutable

6.2 Real-Time Revenue Recognition and Inventory Accounting

Because of the huge number of transactions, returns, and delivery dependencies in e-commerce, it is especially hard to figure out how much money to make and how much inventory to value. Traditional accounting systems generally wait for manual approval before recognising revenue. This can cause timing problems between operational activities and financial records. Blockchain makes real-time recognition possible by connecting revenue accounting directly to events that validate and satisfy transactions (Peters & Panayi, 2016).

Figure 19. Real-Time Revenue and Inventory Accounting via Blockchain

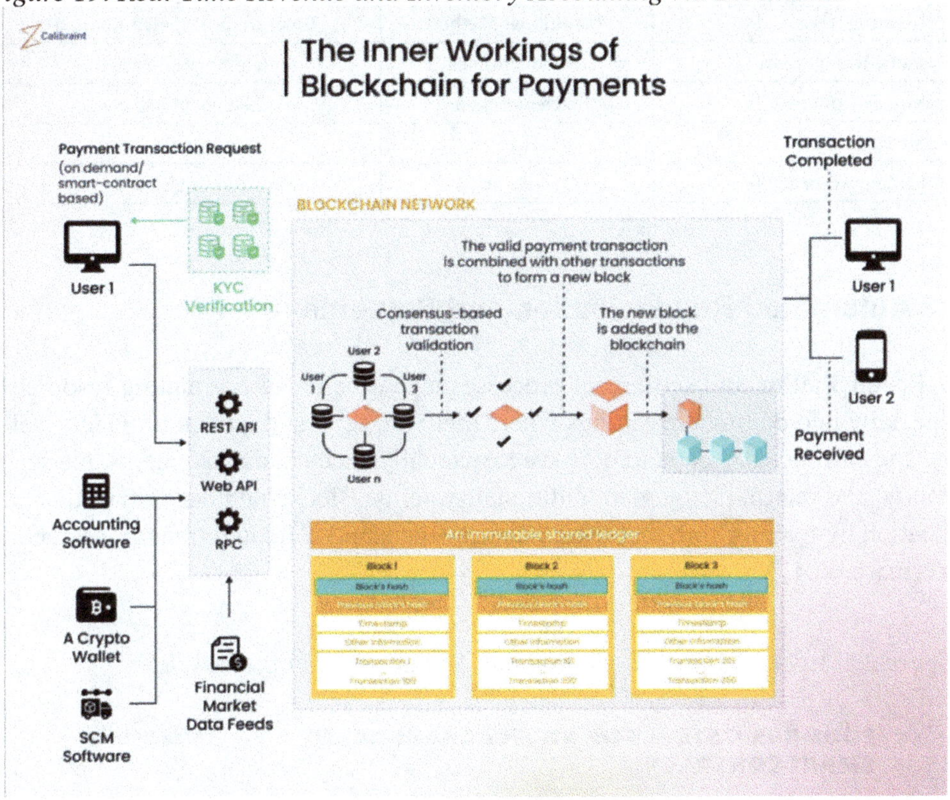

Smart contracts are a big part of this process. Smart contracts immediately start revenue recognition and inventory adjustments when certain circumstances are met, such confirming payment or delivery. This makes sure that accounting rules are applied the same way to all transactions and cuts down on the need for human changes (O'Leary, 2019).

Real-time inventory accounting also helps in managing costs and predicting demand. Blockchain-based inventory records keep track of stock movements all the time, which cuts down on shrinkage and mistakes. This integration makes operations more efficient for e-commerce companies that have to keep track of enormous product catalogues, and it also makes sure that financial reports are correct (Almomani et al., 2025).

Table 21. Blockchain Impact on Revenue and Inventory Accounting

Accounting Area	Traditional Method	Blockchain-Enabled Method
Revenue Recognition	Periodic/manual	Real-time/automated
Inventory Updates	Batch processing	Continuous updates
Error Risk	High	Low
Reporting Accuracy	Moderate	High

6.3 Automated Reconciliation and Settlement

Reconciliation and settlement processes take up a lot of accounting resources, especially in e-commerce settings where there are several payment providers, sellers, and currencies. Accountants have to manually check bank statements, platform reports, and internal ledgers in traditional systems. Blockchain does rid of this duplication by making sure that everyone uses the same validated transaction record (Yermack, 2017).

Figure 20. Automated Reconciliation and Settlement Using Blockchain

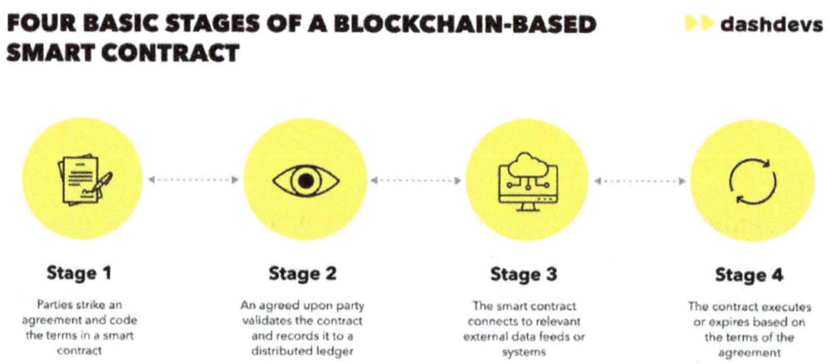

Smart contracts automatically settle payments when certain conditions are met, as when a delivery is confirmed or a service is finished. This cuts down on delays, fights, and makes it easier to estimate cash flow. Automated settlement is especially useful for marketplaces that handle thousands of vendor payments every day (Peters & Panayi, 2016).

From an accounting point of view, automatic reconciliation cuts down on work and expenses a lot. Accountants go from doing manual matching chores to doing analytical and managerial work, where they focus on addressing exceptions and making strategic decisions. This change helps make the financial closing process and continuous reporting models work better.

Table 22. Effects of Blockchain on Reconciliation Processes

Process	Traditional System	Blockchain Integration
Reconciliation	Manual matching	Automatic validation
Settlement Time	Days or weeks	Near real-time
Dispute Frequency	High	Low
Administrative Cost	High	Reduced

6.4 Financial Transparency, Governance, and Decision Support

For good governance, following the rules, and gaining the trust of stakeholders, financial transparency is very important. In traditional systems, transparency is limited by late reporting and not being able to see financial data. Blockchain improves transparency by letting authorised users see unchangeable financial records in real time (Dai & Vasarhelyi, 2017).

Figure 21. Blockchain-Enabled Financial Transparency and Governance

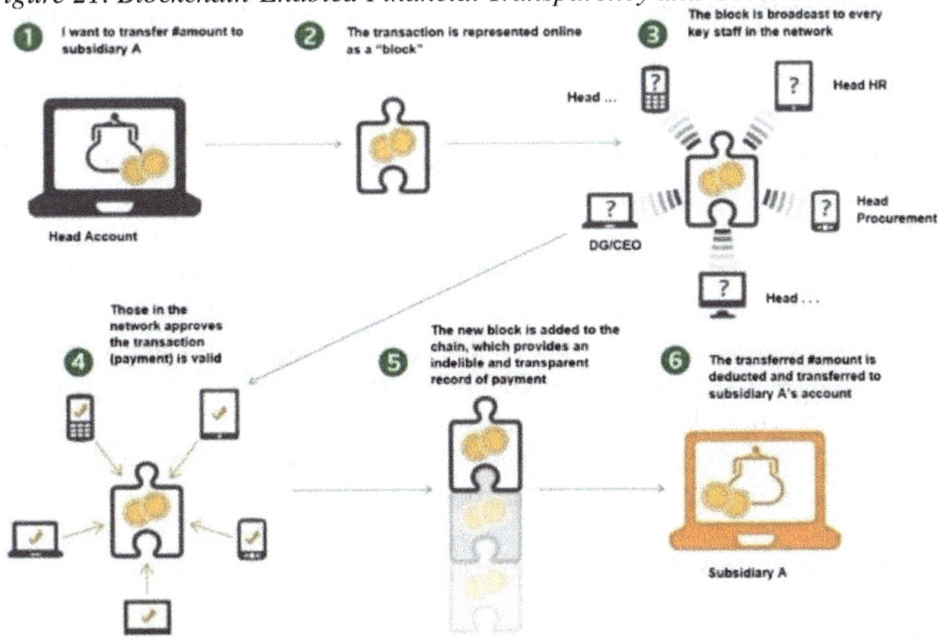

Integrated blockchain solutions make governance stronger by putting controls directly into transaction workflows. Smart contracts automatically enforce standards for approval, compliance, and splitting up roles. This lessens the need for post hoc controls and makes it easier for regulators to work together (O'Leary, 2019).

Blockchain-enabled integration gives managers good help with making decisions. Executives can swiftly respond to changes in the market, operational hazards, and financial irregularities thanks to real-time dashboards, predictive analytics, and continuous assurance processes. As e-commerce ecosystems get more complicated, this level of openness and connection becomes a must-have.

Table 23. Governance Benefits of Blockchain Integration

Governance Aspect	Traditional Systems	Blockchain Integration
Data Visibility	Limited	Real-time
Control Enforcement	Manual	Automated
Audit Readiness	Periodic	Continuous
Decision Support	Reactive	Proactive

SECTION 7: CHALLENGES AND LIMITATIONS OF BLOCKCHAIN ADOPTION IN ACCOUNTING AND E-COMMERCE

Blockchain has a lot of promise to change accounting and e-commerce, but its use is still limited by a number of technical, organisational, regulatory, and economic issues. Blockchain brings transparency, automation, and trust, but these benefits don't happen on their own. They typically need big changes to current systems, skills, and governance structures to happen. Organisations must critically assess blockchain deployment, weighing innovation against feasibility and risk (Yermack, 2017).

This part talks about the main problems that make it hard to use blockchain on a big scale in accounting and e-commerce. More specifically, it talks about problems with technology and scalability, uncertainties about laws and regulations, problems with people and organisations, and challenges with cost, interoperability, and sustainability. Each segment has three analytical paragraphs, together with data and tables, to give a fair and accurate evaluation.

7.1 Technical and Scalability Challenges

Scalability is one of the most common problems with blockchain systems. When there are a lot of transactions, public and consortium blockchains sometimes have performance problems since consensus algorithms need more than one node to check each transaction. In high-frequency e-commerce settings, where thousands of transactions happen every second, this limit might cause delays and make the system less responsive (Croman et al., 2016).

Figure 22. Scalability Constraints in Blockchain Networks

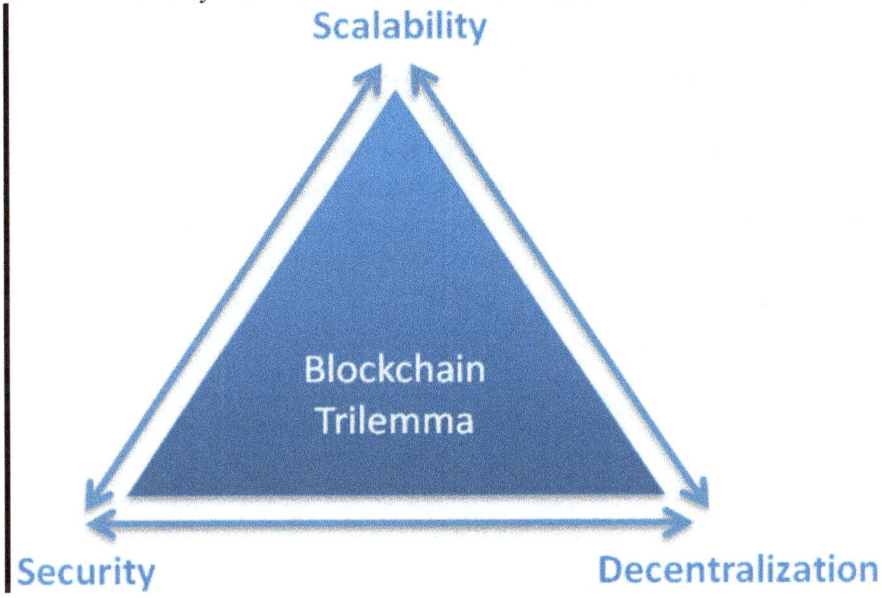

From an accounting point of view, scalability limits might make it impossible to record every micro-transaction on a blockchain in real time. To find a compromise between performance and integrity, big companies may need to use hybrid architectures that combine off-chain processing with on-chain inspection. But these methods make the architecture more complicated and add more governance issues.

Blockchain systems also need strong cybersecurity and infrastructure management. Weaknesses in smart contracts, mistakes in code, and attacks on the network can all make a system less reliable. Because of immutability, it's hard to fix mistakes in blockchain environments. This makes testing and technical oversight much more important than in traditional systems.

Table 24. Technical Limitations of Blockchain Systems

Challenge	Description	Impact on Accounting & E-Commerce
Scalability	Limited transaction throughput	Delays in high-volume platforms
Latency	Slow confirmation times	Reduced customer experience
Smart Contract Bugs	Code vulnerabilities	Financial and legal risk

7.2 Regulatory and Legal Uncertainty

Uncertainty about regulations is still a big problem for using blockchain in accounting and online shopping. Current accounting standards, auditing frameworks, and financial rules were designed for centralised systems and do not yet completely accommodate blockchain-based records or smart contracts. Because of this, businesses don't know if blockchain transactions and records will be legally recognised (Schmitz & Leoni, 2019).

Figure 23. Regulatory Gaps Affecting Blockchain Adoption

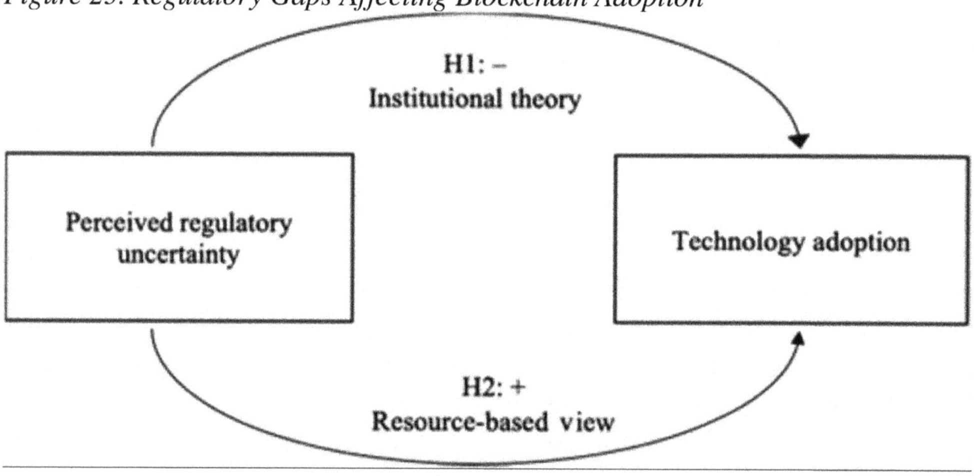

In accounting, regulators and groups that develop standards haven't yet given clear guidance on things like recognising income from blockchain, valuing digital assets, and who is responsible for audits. Because of this lack of transparency, businesses are less likely to fully trust blockchain for compliance and reporting purposes.

E-commerce sites often have to deal with legal problems that cross borders. Blockchain networks often cross borders, and each one has its own policies for data privacy, taxes, and consumer protection. Making sure that laws are followed across borders makes things more complicated legally and could cancel out some of the efficiency gains of blockchain.

Table 25. Regulatory Challenges for Blockchain Adoption

Area	Regulatory Issue	Implication
Accounting Standards	No clear guidance	Limited financial reporting use
Smart Contracts	Legal enforceability unclear	Contractual disputes
Cross-Border Commerce	Conflicting regulations	Compliance complexity

7.3 Organizational and Human Capital Barriers

Aside from technological and regulatory problems, how ready an organisation is to use blockchain has a big impact on how widely it is used. Many accountants and finance professionals don't have the technical skills they need to grasp blockchain topologies, smart contracts, and cryptographic controls. This lack of expertise makes people less likely to adopt new technologies and more likely to hire outside experts (Dai & Vasarhelyi, 2017).

Figure 24. Organizational and Skills-Related Barriers

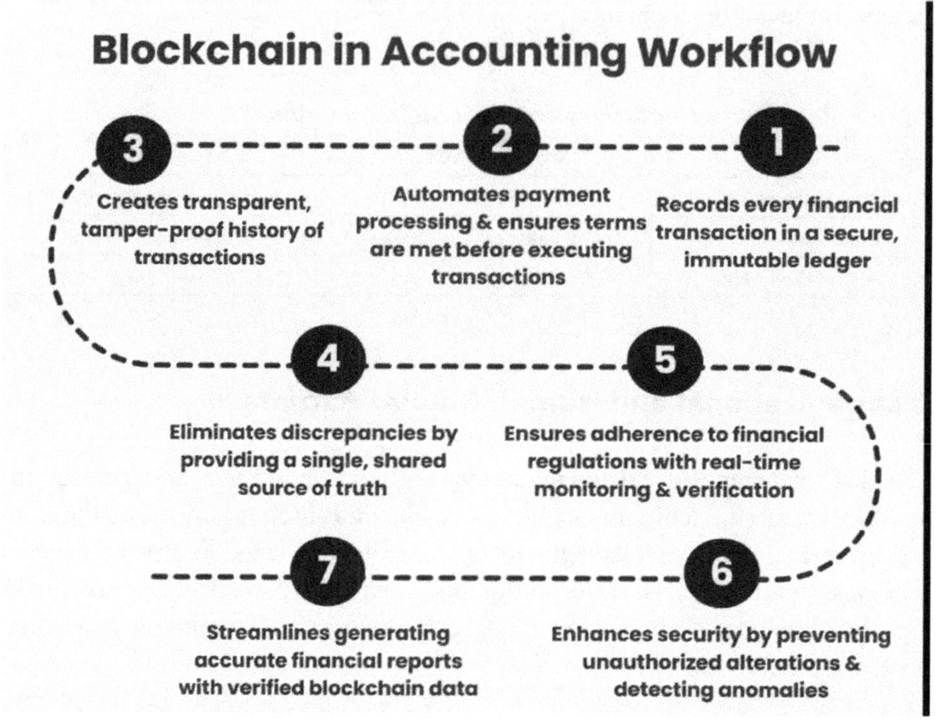

Cultural resistance is another factor. Blockchain changes the way things are done by automating tasks that used to be done by accountants, auditors, and middlemen. This apparent threat to professional identity may hinder acceptance, especially in accounting settings that are very strict or traditional.

Also, when you use blockchain, you typically have to reinvent your business processes instead of just replacing your current systems. Organisations need to change their internal controls, approval processes, and governance structures to fit with decentralised models. Blockchain projects may not get past the pilot level if they don't have strong leaders and plans for managing change.

Table 26. Organizational Barriers to Blockchain Implementation

Barrier	Description	Organizational Impact
Skills Gap	Limited blockchain expertise	Dependence on consultants
Resistance to Change	Fear of role disruption	Slow adoption
Process Redesign	Need for new workflows	Implementation delays

7.4 Cost, Interoperability, and Sustainability Concerns

Adopting blockchain frequently comes with large upfront expenses for things like system development, integration, training, and governance. Although long-term efficiency may counterbalance these investments, the initial financial load can be prohibitive for small and medium-sized firms in e-commerce sectors (Treiblmaier, 2018).

Figure 25. Cost, Interoperability, and Sustainability Challenges

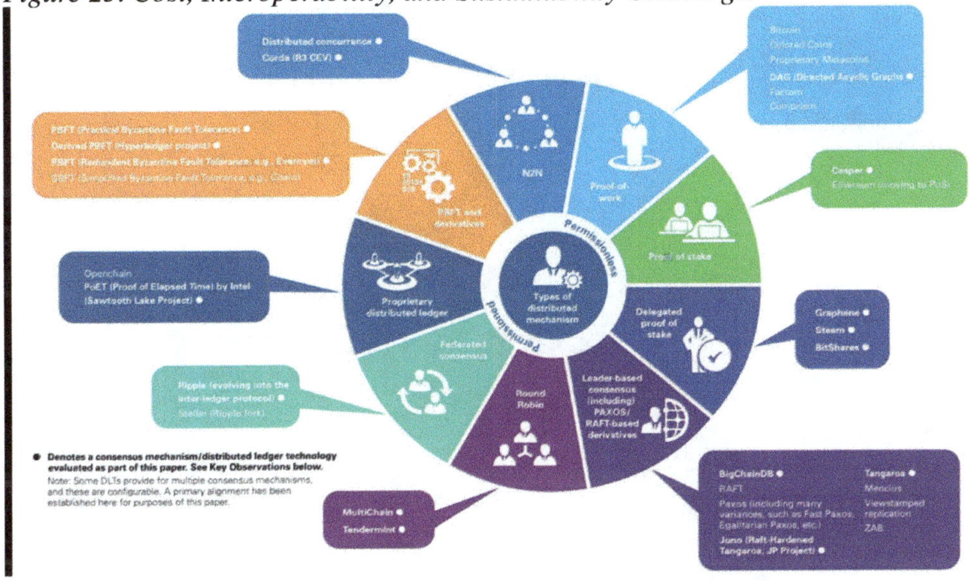

Interoperability is another problem. Many businesses use more than one ERP system, payment platform, and logistics solution, which may not work well with blockchain networks. Without standardised protocols, blockchain ecosystems might become fragmented instead of unified, which makes it harder to scale and create value.

Table 27. Economic and Sustainability Constraints

Issue	Description	Strategic Impact
High Initial Cost	Development and integration	Budget constraints
Interoperability	System incompatibility	Limited scalability
Energy Consumption	Sustainability concerns	Regulatory and reputational risk

Concerns about sustainability, especially the energy use of some consensus procedures, also play a role in decisions on whether or not to adopt. Even though enterprise blockchains usually use energy-efficient methods, public opinion and government scrutiny of their effects on the environment affect strategic decisions. When organisations use blockchain technology, they need to think about both the economy and the environment.

REFERENCES

Ahmad Ibrahim Karajeh, Tayseer Ali AL-Momani, Malek A. Almomani, Omar Almomani and Moath H. Tarawneh. (. (2025). Forecasting future earnings via e-business information: Financial implications for investment decisions in the era of big data. *Investment Management and Financial Innovations*, *22*(4), 237–246. DOI: 10.21511/imfi.22(4).2025.19

Alles, M., & Gray, G. L. (2020). Continuous accounting: How digital technologies transform auditing and financial reporting. *Journal of Emerging Technologies in Accounting*, *17*(1), 1–15. DOI: 10.2308/jeta-10764

Almomani, O., Arabiat, A., Al Tayeb, M., Almaiah, M. A., Obeidat, M., Aldhyani, T. H., Shehab, R., & Rowad, M. (2025). A Robust Model for Android Malware Detection via ML and DL classifiers. *Mesopotamian Journal of Big Data*, *2025*, 261–277. DOI: 10.58496/MJBD/2025/017

Buterin, V. (2015). On public and private blockchains. Ethereum Foundation. https://ethereum.org

Catalini, C., & Gans, J. S. (2016). Some simple economics of the blockchain. MIT Sloan Research Paper, 5191–16.

Chen, W., Xu, Z., Shi, S., Zhao, Y., & Zhang, W. (2020). A survey on blockchain consensus mechanisms. *ACM Computing Surveys*, *53*(2), 1–31.

Christidis, K., & Devetsikiotis, M. (2016). Blockchains and smart contracts for the internet of things. *IEEE Access : Practical Innovations, Open Solutions*, *4*, 2292–2303. DOI: 10.1109/ACCESS.2016.2566339

Coyne, J. G., & McMickle, P. L. (2017). Can blockchains serve an accounting purpose? *Journal of Emerging Technologies in Accounting*, *14*(2), 101–111. DOI: 10.2308/jeta-51910

Croman, K., Decker, C., Eyal, I., Gencer, A. E., Juels, A., Kosba, A., Miller, A., Saxena, P., Shi, E., Sirer, E. G., Song, D., & Wattenhofer, R. (2016). On scaling decentralized blockchains. Financial Cryptography and Data Security, 106–125.

Crosby, M., Pattanayak, P., Verma, S., & Kalyanaraman, V. (2016). Blockchain technology: Beyond bitcoin. *Applied Innovation Review*, *2*, 6–19.

Dai, J., & Vasarhelyi, M. A. (2017). Toward blockchain-based accounting and assurance. *Journal of Information Systems*, *31*(3), 5–21. DOI: 10.2308/isys-51804

Granlund, M. (2011). Extending AIS research to management accounting and control issues: A research note. *International Journal of Accounting Information Systems*, *12*(1), 3–19. DOI: 10.1016/j.accinf.2010.11.001

Grigg, I. (2017). Triple entry accounting. Financial Cryptography and Data Security, 1–15.

Kokina, J., & Davenport, T. H. (2017). The emergence of artificial intelligence: How automation is changing auditing. *Journal of Emerging Technologies in Accounting*, *14*(1), 115–122. DOI: 10.2308/jeta-51730

Kranacher, M., Riley, R., & Wells, J. (2019). *Forensic accounting and fraud examination* (2nd ed.). Wiley.

Masadeh, R., Almomani, O., Zaqebah, A., Masadeh, S., Alshqurat, K., Sharieh, A., & Alsharman, N. (2025). Narwhal Optimizer: A Nature-Inspired Optimization Algorithm for Solving Complex Optimization Problems. *Computers, Materials & Continua*, *85*(2), 3709–3737. DOI: 10.32604/cmc.2025.066797

Nakamoto, S. (2008). Bitcoin: A peer-to-peer electronic cash system. https://bitcoin.org/bitcoin.pdf

Narayanan, A., Bonneau, J., Felten, E., Miller, A., & Goldfeder, S. (2016). *Bitcoin and cryptocurrency technologies*. Princeton University Press.

O'Leary, D. E. (2019). Configuring blockchain architectures for accounting and e-business. *Intelligent Systems in Accounting, Finance & Management*, *26*(1), 5–12.

Peters, G. W., & Panayi, E. (2016). Understanding modern banking ledgers through blockchain technologies. In Lee, D. (Ed.), *Handbook of digital currency* (pp. 239–278). Academic Press.

Rezaee, Z., & Riley, R. (2010). *Financial statement fraud: Prevention and detection* (2nd ed.). Wiley.

Rezaee, Z., & Wang, J. (2019). Realtime reporting and continuous monitoring in digital business. *Journal of Accounting and Finance*, *19*(6), 42–58.

Rozario, A. M., & Vasarhelyi, M. A. (2018). Auditing with smart contracts. *The International Journal of Digital Accounting Research*, *18*, 1–25. DOI: 10.4192/1577-8517-v18_1

Schmitz, J., & Leoni, G. (2019). Accounting and auditing at the time of blockchain technology. *Accounting Horizons*, *33*(2), 41–54.

Shambour, Q., Al-Zyoud, M., & Almomani, O. (2025). Quantum-Inspired Hybrid Metaheuristic Feature Selection with SHAP for Optimized and Explainable Spam Detection. *Symmetry, 17*(10), 1716. DOI: 10.3390/sym17101716

Tapscott, D., & Tapscott, A. (2016). *Blockchain revolution*. Penguin.

Treiblmaier, H. (2018). The impact of the blockchain on the supply chain. *International Journal of Logistics Management, 29*(2), 628–651.

Vasarhelyi, M. A., Kogan, A., & Tuttle, B. (2015). Big data in accounting and auditing. *Accounting Horizons, 29*(2), 423–429. DOI: 10.2308/acch-51071

Warren, D.Jr, Moffitt, K., & Byrnes, P. (2015). How big data will change accounting. *Accounting Horizons, 29*(2), 397–407. DOI: 10.2308/acch-51069

Yermack, D. (2017). Corporate governance and blockchains. *Review of Finance, 21*(1), 7–31. DOI: 10.1093/rof/rfw074

Zhu, Y., Lin, X., Kim, J., Al-Adwan, A. S., & Li, N. (2025). Exploring Human Interaction in Online Self-Regulated Learning Through Danmaku Comments. *International Journal of Human-Computer Interaction, 41*(22), 1–14. DOI: 10.1080/10447318.2025.2480826

Chapter 7
Integrating Emerging Technologies:
AR, VR, and Blockchain in Smart Commerce

Salam Al E'mari
http://orcid.org/0000-0002-2134-4158
University of Petra, Jordan

Yousef Sanjalawe
http://orcid.org/0000-0002-4442-1865
University of Jordan, Jordan

Budoor Allehyani
http://orcid.org/0009-0006-0424-6894
Umm Al-Qura University, Saudi Arabia

ABSTRACT

This chapter examines the integration of Augmented Reality, Virtual Reality, and Blockchain as foundational technologies shaping the emergence of smart commerce. It outlines how AR enhances contextual product understanding, how VR enables immersive and socially interactive retail environments, and how Blockchain establishes decentralized trust, provenance, and secure transactions. Furthermore, it analyzes the evolution of consumer expectations, technological enablers such as AI, IoT, and 5G, and the shifting digital-physical retail landscape. Through synthesizing industry cases, global implementations, and ethical considerations, this chapter per the authors demonstrates how the convergence of these technologies is redefining engagement, transparency, and value creation across modern commerce ecosystems.

DOI: 10.4018/979-8-3373-7330-0.ch007

1. INTRODUCTION

Technological advances have reformed the global marketplace by aiding the recognition and assessment of potential prospects at varying levels of the sales funnel. At this point, the transactional, service-oriented model of e-commerce has reached an intelligent experiential ecosystem; this has now been surpassed by artificial intelligence and the mobile web. Technological advancements are, once again, disruptive. Augmented Reality, Virtual Reality, and Blockchain are redefining the digital commerce ecosystem. Scarce interactivity of these technologies enhances trust in the integrity of transactions. These patterns are not an exception, they are closely interrelated, and interdependent, coining the term 'smart commerce'. They unite an immersive experience, intel, and sealed trust.

Despite rapid digitalization, persistent barriers related to trust, product understanding, and transactional transparency continue to limit the effectiveness of traditional e-commerce models. Indeed, the more e-commerce a platform has the more on-demand profit that can be generated as it reduces the major deterrent of potential business customers. E-commerce platforms are largely burdens since there are regained for each account and neglected these problems persists. Surviving e-commerce problems may be a subtle bomb waiting to go off the problems virtual shopping lacks. There are unanswered questions as to how, what and when the acquired features would be e-commerce. There are digital barriers as customers reluct the fear of their financial information online. Such commerce provokes what is coined as "Retails negative." There is also irrational distrust for the virtual ecommerce shopping process. There is also the lack of virtual interaction and virtual reality.

The AR and VR technologies have greatly simplified context-aware and immersive retail experiences, allowing physical and digital experiences to co-exist harmoniously. AR allows customers to see the product in their physical spaces before purchasing, greatly enhancing confidence in their decisions. VR allows customers to experience completely virtual shopping universes, enabling them to access virtual showrooms, socialize and shop, and even take part in immersive product demos. More recent studies have shown that the mere presence of immersive technologies boosts engagement and perceived value of a product by enhancing presence, enjoyment, and overall understanding of the product (Javornik et al., 2022). The way retail is enhancing toward experience-driven commerce, AR and VR have become seamless and pivotal tools in the customer-driven virtual ecosystems.

Due to a lack of trust and transparency, these immersive experiences have gone unaddressed and in this case, however, Blockchain technology precisely enables this. A decentralized ledger technology allows for the detailed observation of the movement of money and materials along supply chains. Such tracking of movement is immutable and transparent, facilitating clients in product verification, source tracing, and confirmation of ethically-sourced materials. Prior research has demonstrated blockchain's effectiveness in enhancing supply-chain transparency and traceability, particularly within agricultural and food logistics systems (Mirabelli & Solina, 2020). These capabilities are increasingly being adapted across other industries to support product provenance and authenticity verification. Blockchain enables verifiable digital identity, trusted payments, and secure transactions through decentralized architectures. These systems support transparent exchange mechanisms without reliance on centralized intermediaries, improving confidence in digital interactions and ownership verification. By enabling traceability and programmable transactions, blockchain complements immersive retail technologies by addressing persistent concerns related to trust and authenticity. The convergence of AR, VR, and blockchain supports the emergence of smart commerce ecosystems that integrate immersive interaction with verifiable trust mechanisms.

The improvement of these technologies is an example of a three-part shift wherein AR improves perception, VR improves immersion, while Blockchain improves credibility. Together, these facilitate the creation of a 'commerce metaverse' built around crypto, enabling users to navigate digital shops, AR to visualize and augment products, engage in VR social interactions, and perform Blockchain transactions. For example, IKEA, LVMH, Nike, and Alibaba are using AR, VR, and Blockchain in the construction of Synthetic Digital Multi-Commerce ecosystems incorporating physical dieresis and digitally embedded assets with decentralized authentication.

In addition, the changes in commerce due to consumer expectations and demands also spreading to smart commerce. Digital natives seek interactive, personalized, seamless, and transparent experiences—no friction and no interruptions. According to a 2023 Accenture global survey, an estimated 60% of respondents belonged to the experience seeker group. This cohort of consumers showed brand preference to those including rich and detailed narrative content surrounding their product offerings. The presence of authenticity verification through Blockchain was shown to enhance trust in the online purchase for 50% of the respondents. Such expectations arise from more advanced commerce systems with Augmented and Virtual Reality, and Blockchain features.

The previous innovations are also augmented virtual reality and its improvement in real-time interaction with expansive participants and their avatars in multi-layered games. Earlier blockchain governance models were often rigid and difficult to adapt to evolving commercial requirements. Such structural limitations created barriers to scalability, interoperability, and real-time integration with immersive environments. Lastly, social justice, equity, and the foundations of resilience, trust, transparency, integrity, and user centrism are most important.

This chapter examines the technological, behavioral, and strategic onboarding of AR, VR, and Blockchain in smart commerce. AR, VR, and Blockchain are supplemented as tools to enhance consumer experience and are studied in the order of their evolution after the genesis of smart commerce. Then the chapter analyzes real world case studies, integration and deployment challenges, and insights on worldwide implementation. It integrates the other work's anticipation and discusses the evolution of the research as well as the unlimited phenomenal technological influence onto commerce, retailing, and disintegrated economy.

In an attempt to 'take the pulse' of the impact of AR and VR technologies on commerce and trade, 'shattering' with the use of blockchain, this chapter attempts understanding the impact of AR and VR technologies on trade and commerce. The ever-accelerating digital transformation makes this fusion of AR, VR and the commerce of utmost importance to designers, scholars, industry players, and policymakers.

2. SMART COMMERCE: DEFINITIONS, EVOLUTION, AND TECHNOLOGICAL LANDSCAPE

Smart commerce is the next phase in digital retailing evolution owing to advancements in technology from the computational, connectional, and data-centric domains. In the distant past, e-commerce was characterized as basic digital transactions with online catalogs, the latter being the most dominant paradigm. Today, systems are defined by their ability to scan, interpret, and react to complex consumer behavior patterns. Smart commerce seeks to augment hyper-connected environments by enabling Artificial Intelligence and Internet of Things (IoT), 5G, smart and arbitrarily scalable Distributed Ledger technology, and other emergent technologies to support 'anytime, anywhere' interactions such that the shopping experience pivots from a passive purchase to a responsive and seamless active engagement with the system. Such a transition mirrors a digital society where the consumer can effortlessly and seamlessly switch between channels.

A number of factors influence the axis of development towards smart commerce. From the side of technology, the application of artificial intelligence, machine learning, and cognition have enabled the mapping of enormous data streams from client's clicks, biometrics, geospatial data, and customer behavior, actively adjusting recommendation systems, pricing algorithms, and presentation of the products. Context-aware systems have been implemented in IoT devices in smart homes and in some retail stores where smart refrigerators predict and satisfy restock intervals, while in-store devices identify customer participation and monitor user engagement in varying customer spending tiers. The convergence of 5G and edge computing augments these features and functionality by improving agility and providing responsive distributed smartness through AR and instant, transactional VR systems and other low-latency, highly immersive toolkits (Palanikumar et al., 2025).

The development of technology has led to radical improvements in consumer behavior. Digitally native consumers in particular do not view shopping as a single standalone task. Rather they view it as a complex multilayered experience that includes the use of multiple devices, social media and even virtual assistants. PwC research explains that today consumers value hyper personalization, convenience and proximity to engagement more than price (2025). Retailers consequently need to develop systems that comprehend and contextualize the behavior of each individual user and customize their interactions to meet the requirements of each individual consumer. Experience driven commerce the behavioral change also led to results showing engagement, trust and emotional connection as the currencies that ensure retention of consumers.

The more advanced commercial engines integrate operating multiple tiers which increase their collective benefits. The Sensing layer captures the information of user actions and contextual data. The Intelligence layer focuses on determining and predicting patterns, user intent, and behaviors of the data. The Output layer user custom interfaces, leverages automated suggestions, and orchestrates convergent channel activities. Furthermore, it integrates all actions across multiple channels. Each of these has vivid use of AR, VR, and Blockchain. AR enhances the local context and situational awareness by seamlessly overlaying relevant information onto the real world. VR provides fully immersive experiences that consist of 360 environments where the users can engage with multiple products and brands in a gamified controlled situation. Blockchain provides transparency, accountability, and trust in the movement and ownership of the tokens. Figure 1 illustrates the layered architecture of smart commerce, where AR and VR operate within the interface layer, AI supports behavioral interpretation within the intelligence layer, and blockchain functions as the trust layer enabling transaction verification and provenance tracking.

Figure 1. Architecture of smart commerce.

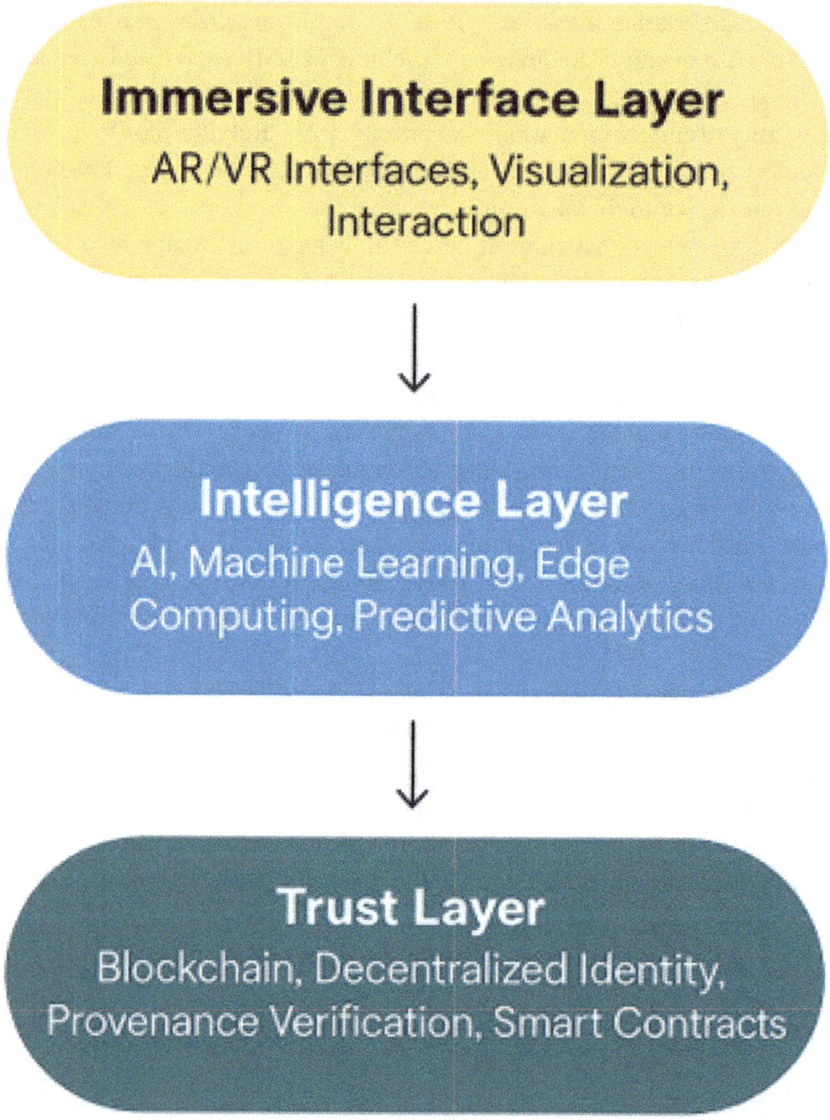

An additional characteristic of intelligent commerce is the transformation of the model from centralized to decentralized. Concentrated databases is the popular model where one party, usually the sellers or their proxies, control databases. This model is notorious for trust, security, and privacy issues. Blockchain technology permits distributed decision making, decentralized identity and proof of provenance; thus, encouraging transparency in previously trust deficient ecosystems. This is in line with the changing attitude of consumers' data, and the increasing need for ethically and sustainably sourced products. IBM (2021) reports that nearly 80% of consumers worldwide consider sustainability and ethical sourcing to be significant, and a large proportion of them report higher trust in firms that deploy Blockchain and other trust-enhancing technologies.

The combination of smart commerce includes consumer psychology, cognitive load, and, and experiential marketing integrated with multi-sensory 'touch' product interactions. Interactive virtual reality and augmented reality improve 'decision-making uncertainty' with immersive simulations of physical objects. This is especially true in retail categories where tactile inspection or spatial relations are paramount in consumer decision-making. Trust is psychologically alleviated by Blockchain's immutable proof of ownership, provenance, quality, and certification of the product. Those attributes significantly mitigate the mental and emotional barriers of digital retail.

Smart commerce is the ability to purchase particular goods and services through readily accessible technology devices and platforms. It also includes the provision of various Smart commerce services and contracts to customers' pupils and online users and Augmented Reality. The trade and commerce fostered by the smart digital infrastructure continue with and from to the East of the world; particularly China, South Korea, and Japan, where the technology digital infrastructure is sophisticated and the admiration for digital innovations in the world of retail is highly appreciated. The rest of the world pays and actively participates in the transactions and commercial activities based on the directed consumer protection and sustainability. It also embraces the Blockchain based provenance systems actively. The smart city infrastructure of Middle East and South Asia is for quick and rapid adoption of smart commerce systems where AR and Blockchain for Retail and Tourism Gadgets are also incorporated. These scenarios represent the fact and support the finding which says smart commerce is highly influenced by and around the local culture and available tools and technologies than it is by the discoverable the available market system.

Ultimately, as already stated in arriving at this conclusion, smart commerce is the first step in the movement from employing stand-alone technologies to the incorporating a blend of intelligent trusted ecosystems. This further elucidates the function of AR, VR, and Blockchain on the very edge of a new paradigm of commerce which fuses experience and authenticity, overlapping touchpoints of the digital and physical realms, into a seamless ecosystem centered on the customer. In this chapter, AR is treated as a perception-enhancing interface, VR as an immersion-enabling environment, and blockchain as the underlying trust infrastructure supporting verification and ownership.

3. AUGMENTED REALITY (AR) IN SMART COMMERCE

The evolution of augmented reality technology and its functionalities have shifted its use for smart commerce and interactions with digital products across contexts to wraps of dominant importance for the field. Text, computer generated 3-D models, and real-time calculated visual information and other graphic elements are superimposed and synchronized with real environments viewed through cameras of smartphones, smart glasses, and dedicated AR headsets. The combination of the real and computer generated environments improves consumer product engagement and facilitates products interaction through seeing them spatially from all angle, multifunction real time interaction, and active decision making. In light of the ongoing evolution of retail towards incorporating experience based models of selling, augmented reality technology has the potential to overcome engagement as well as uncertainty.

For any practical implementation of AR aided technology, commercial enterprises rely on real-time computer vision fused with object tracking recognition and positional SLAM (simultaneous localization and mapping) algorithms which spatially track and geometrically understand enabling movements tracking. These methods help AR in business display accurate and realistic computer spatial graphics, such as visualizing a couch in a room or wearing an artificially augmented pair of sunglasses with continuous light facial recognition and tracking. Thanks to developments in mobile augmented reality, ARKit, ARCore, and WebAR, experiences in augmented reality are more democratized and accessible and do not involve expensive and complicated specialized hardware. Improvements in spatial computing led by Apple Vision Pro and Meta Quest Pro, also enable hands-free in circulation control, providing next AR shopping experiences interactivity and high-fidelity graphics.

Using AR, for instance, helps customers visualize products that would otherwise be represented via static images that cannot be interacted with. Studies show that AR helps customers understand products better as well as aids in confident decision making with purchases improving decisional confidence, therefore, customers feel empowered to buy products leading to decreased purchase return rates (Heller et al., 2019). Some of AR's applications are in the form of virtual fitting tools in the fashion industry enabling customers to mix and match different garments, makeup brands allowing customers to preview different makeup overlays on their face and AR furniture placement, initiated by IKEA, helping customers visualize scaled 3D models of furniture in their rooms. On top of AR's immersion in the automotive industry, manufacturers showcase customizations and paint jobs on 3D modeled interiors of vehicles, serving as a supplement to a physical showroom. Figure 2 presents the sequential stages of the retail value chain in which AR and VR create enhanced experiential and decision-support capabilities, illustrating their impact from product discovery through post-purchase engagement.

Figure 2. AR and VR Applications Across the Retail Value Chain

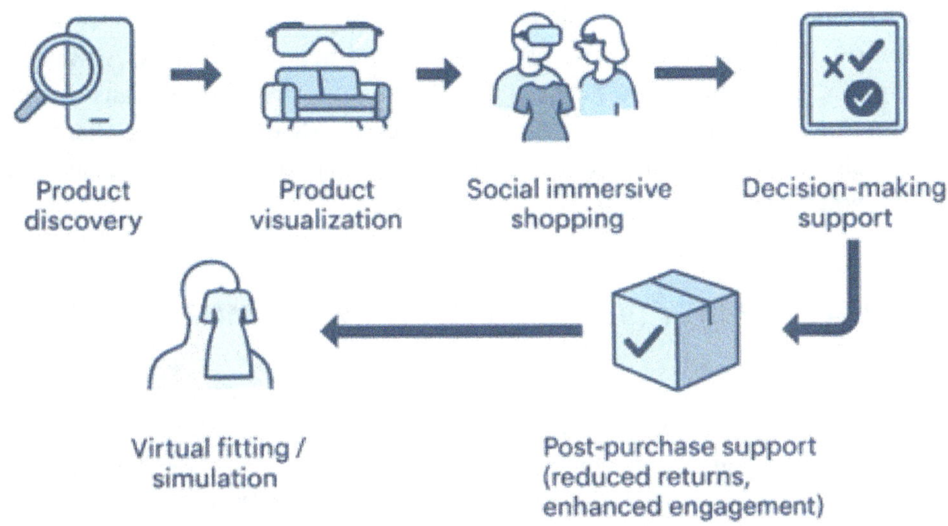

While having the ability to assess audible analytics, AR continues to maintain individual face tracking, across users, tracking gaze time, gestures for product rotation, and spatial interactions. This data allows sight managers to assess the augmented interfaces vs. the traditional retail analytical interfaces. Also, augmented reality allows retail to introduce other in-store services, such as, live product comparison, navigation, and attention-based geo contextual advertising. This direct memory recall indicates the augmentation of AR in paradigmatic integration of the digital and physical retail environments.

Working with AR technology also gives scope with commerce as well. Accessory realism with world objects is spatial environmental mapping outstanding core complications. Lighting, occlusion, and AR system controls. Puzzling and frictionless AR experiences. Achieving seamless alignment between physical and digital environments remains technically challenging due to issues such as lighting consistency, occlusion handling, and spatial mapping accuracy. The interactions get too aggressive to system failure and over user fatigue. Just as AR space capture, the social civics of the enhanced digital surveillance come as equally concerning. Hence, the social appliqué repercussions around facial recognition systems as AR gets deployed commercially needs to be addressed.

Currently, the AR technology forecast in the area of commerce is positive. Analyzing the technology trends and the evolution of the industry indicates the possibility of multiple users in AR environments, where the social dimensions of shopping, collaborative shopping, and/or shared viewings of products augment the experience even more. The new cloud AR, coupled with the predicted improvements of 5G technology, will further enhance the versatility of augmented wide area. This, in turn, will unlock new patterns of hybrid commerce workflows, Advanced AR technology, the commerce sector is more likely to appreciate the transition of AR technology from novelty to rotated confidence in AR technology. Regardless of new technological advancements, creating AR smart retail environments will grow in importance.

4. VIRTUAL REALITY (VR) AND IMMERSIVE COMMERCE

Providing completely digital environments wherein users can investigate offerings, interact with brands, and engage in social shopping experiences, VR technology has become core to the construction of immersive commerce. VR does much more than AR, which is to overlay digital information on the real world. Rather, VR simulates a cognitive, emotional, and sensory world fully divorced from reality. This ability to transport users to a completely virtual cosmos has made VR a pertinent domain of investment and interest within smart commerce. Retailers can transport users to shopping environments that are more immersive and three-dimensional than the traditional physical space. Customers can move freely in VR commerce environments, virtual showrooms and malls, and tested interactive products, and engage in social and haptic activities with virtual products. Digital shopping experiences are thus completely revolutionized.

Empathy, presence and flow and their relationship with VR Commerce hinges on presence, empathy and flow'. Presence means the 'being there' sense, and empathy is the 'being' as in 'being there' as digitally embodied avatars. Flow, the highest stage of attention, is only reached when there is smooth, immersive, and uninterrupted performance of the tasks. Empirical evidence suggests that cognitive VR devices tap into cognitive mechanisms that characterize real-world shopping in order to heighten perceived knowledge of the product, emotional engagement and the value of the experience (Flavián et al., 2019). Hence, when it comes to VR experience recall, individuals appear to have the ability to assess products more accurately and have constructively engaged with a particular brand, demonstrating the ability of VR to address the most critical limitation of traditional online shopping: the inability to experience a product with all the senses.

Companies in different industries now use VR for both experiential marketing and education. Audi and BMW, for example, use VR showrooms where clients can tailor and view vehicles at life size, configuring the interior and examining finer interior surfaces, colors, and other features. Fashion businesses implement VR catwalks and virtual fitting rooms, while real estate employs virtual property tours for buyers. The hospitality sector now provides immersive virtual previews of its hotels, along with VR tours of destinations and simulations for planning events. These instances show the different ways in which VR can be used for more economical non-physical market expansion and other geographically limited marketing and for high involvement decision-making purchasing activities.

In principle, VR commerce involves complex rendering engines, motion tracking devices, and realistic spatial audio. High-resolution displays with haptic touch, motion-tracking arms, and VR headsets such as Meta Quest 3, HTC Vive Pro 2, and Sony PlayStation VR2 offer an immersive and seamless experience with their wide field-of-view and low-latency tracking. Tactile Virtual Reality controllers and gloves enable users to engage and "feel" virtual objects. Building upon the work of Hazarika and Rahmati (2023), VR platforms are expected to become more efficient with the increased availability of 5G and edge computing. Unencumbered by the processing power of user devices, low-latency cloud-rendered VR streaming reduces the strain of consumer devices and expands the accessibility of VR commerce.

Perhaps one of the activities with the greatest potential for VR commerce is social and collaborative shopping. In Social VR applications, for example, with Meta Horizon Worlds or Spatial, multiple users can shop together with sales associates, attend virtual product demos, and engage in community activities. Such social 'multiplayer' environments allow users to experience shopping together and engage in joint decision-making, thus alleviating the isolation and loneliness of online shopping. Research suggests that the feeling of social presence in VR positively influences trust, enjoyment, and motivation, which in turn improves intention to purchase (Kumar et al., 2025). For brands, Social VR is a chance to develop community and interactive brand experiences in a deep and immersive brand world, fostering long term customer engagement.

Like all forms of digital commerce, VR commerce has its challenges too. Barriers to adoption include the price of hardware, the discomfort like the nausea associated with VR, and the lack of appropriate infrastructures for the physically challenged. Moreover, it should be noted that the design of the VR system must ensure that the user interfaces are simple. This calls for attention to detail with respect to ergonomics, the arrangement of elements in space and user protection. Moral philosophy bodies would be concerned with the VR systems recording and retaining behavior and biometric data, in particular, eye movements, gestures and the emotions that accompany them. Fair and responsible data collection and retention, anonymization to mitigate risks, design VR systems to mitigate risks to user privacy to sustain trust. (Roesner & Kohno, 2021). Lightweight headsets, cloud rendering, and modular VR systems would suggest VR is on its way to becoming a mainstream part of smart commerce ecosystems.

In the foreseeable future, Virtual Reality will be able to seamlessly integrate the experience of walking into a store and shopping in the physical and the digital world. Virtual Reality Technologies integrated with artificial intelligence, haptics, and Blockchain will immerse the user in a commercial experience with even more promises. A completely integrated system wherein lies the user's power will redefine the experience. Furthermore, the transformation of digital commodities and enhanced experiences will redefine retail.

5. BLOCKCHAIN AS THE TRUST AND VERIFICATION LAYER OF COMMERCE

The attributes of Blockchain technology in smart commerce applications parallel the functions of trust and verification systems in transactional security, and ownership verification. As with other distributed systems, Blockchain immutably records transactions across an array of nodes, removing central intermediaries, and hence greatly reducing the chances of fraud and tampering. These features enhance the applicability of Blockchain technology in digital commerce, an industry fraught with concerns of data integrity, leaking of information, and counterfeiting of products, regardless of the geography.

The application of Blockchain technology which enables supply chain management with fullest transparency and verification represents a significant leap in commerce. The ever-thorny issues of counterfeiting and opaque sourcing in the luxury fashion and food industries, pharmaceuticals, fine art, and food industry can benefit enormously. As an example, retailers can document every step of a products life-cycle starting from the raw material, manufacturing, logistics, and selling, so that consumers can verify its authenticity with a simple scan. For example, the Aura Blockchain Consortium developed by LVMH issues verifiable and self-contained provenance certificates, which increases users' confidence in the products and protects the brands counterfeiting. Blockchain technology that provide traceability has been shown to enhance consumer trust and increase purchase intention, particularly amongst consumers who are increasingly concerned with sustainability (Saberi et al., 2019).

Blockchain technology has enabled the creation of new economic models for goods and services in physical and digital form via tokenization. Non-fungible tokens(NFTs) empowered businesses to digitally and verifiably own and control branded digital limited edition clothes, virtual goods, loyalty tokens, and collectible items. For instance, Nike has developed "crypto kicks" which consist of physical shoes and a Blockchain confirmed digital twin of the shoes. This allows the shoes to be digitally customized and resold while maintaining provenance. This combination of physical and digital assets enhances the emerging ethos of Web3 commerce which emphasizes user autonomy over identity, assets, and transactions. Token-based loyalty systems further advance this model through Blockchain-enabled rewards that can be traded, redeemed, and transferred, thereby fostering customer loyalty and engagement through rewarding, easily understood, and transparent systems.

Besides providing proprietorship, Blockchain also enhances payment and global commerce interoperability, and the security of such transactions. Like all forms of digital payments, the payment forms within Blockchain (cryptocurrencies, stable coins, etc.) also skip the centralized gateways, the associated delays and costs, and payment bottlenecks. Remittance expensive and volatile currency areas are increasingly Blockchain integrated Lipton el al., (2020) stable coins are gaining traction. The Blockchain payment acceptance range extension towards more and more businesses shifts trade towards more efficient decentralized programmable and globally available financial systems.

On the Blockchain, the term "smart contracts" is used in reference to coded contracts which are able to execute themselves and are theoretically able to function with a higher level of functionality and verifiability than the traditional contracts. Smart contracts execute conditional transactions automatically; such as refunds or escrows. Smart contracts adjust payments to release escrow-held funds, and allocate royalties automatically. They increase transparency, which reduces disputes and eases the workflow of a business. A case in point is automated smart contracts which resolve disputes in decentralized markets, thereby building trust in transactions. In supply chain practices, smart contracts reduce the level of manual control required by automatically triggering compliance and updated logistics, as well as changes in the inventory level.

Integrating smart contracts into business practices is cumbersome. With Blockchain, public ones are slow and are also fitted with certain types of consensus which inefficiently use energy. Permissioned Blockchain tackles these issues; however, they are critiqued for centralizing the network. On a global scale, compliance around identity and tokenized assets constrains the use of Blockchain. The ethical issues regarding Blockchain and the deletion, 'the right to be forgotten' especially with the IoT, create problematic surveillance systems (Al-E'mari et al., 2024).

Innovative methods like ZKPs, homomorphic encryption, and private smart contracts illustrate how privacy can be preserved optimally and offer valuable advancements. These technologies are certified without exposing sensitive information, enabling privacy-preserving systems in Blockchain commerce. The combination of

Blockchain with AR and VR systems predicted by top-tier research will result in "trusted immersive commerce." In virtual environments which are built on immersive ecosystems of interconnected virtual worlds, decentralized identities and verifiable ownership will enable safe and clearly visible transactions (Uddin et al., 2024).

In conclusion, the Blockchain technology represents the Commerce Trust Anchor which adds Assurance and Accountability to the augmented and virtual realities collections. This ensures that the Commerce Sphere is integrated on the same level as the other Digital Sphere. This is achieving a decentralized, open, and user-controlled systems of value, ownership, and trust. The merging of the systems adds a more authenticity and security of commerce trust.

6. CONVERGENCE OF AR, VR, AND BLOCKCHAIN: TOWARD UNIFIED SMART COMMERCE ECOSYSTEMS

The changing of smart commerce structure with the use of augmented reality, virtual reality, and Blockchain technology enables the creation of the new generation retail environments which mix interactive immersion with trust. Each of the technologies has its own 'superpower', AR improves understanding by overlaying digital information onto the real world, VR transforms the interaction of consumers with products by placing them in navigable, immersive 3D spaces, and Blockchain Layer enables a trust-over-data architecture which decentralizes security over ownership, transactions, and data for assets. These technologies, in unison, generates a multilayered ecosystem of commerce where integration, experience, authenticity, and intelligence are driven by innovation in a manner that is seamless. This paves the way for new retail models which are more interactive, transparent, and autonomous.

In this scenario AR enhances perception by digitally adding annotations to physical products explaining verifiable certificates of authenticity, materials, user reviews, sustainability scores, and even user reviews. These geos anchored data records kept in the Blockchain system act as AR anchors, enriching user experience with verified information of the products. Blockchain don't just records and anchors AR data, authentication and verification of data to Blockchain provides AR with the most critical interface to a luxury goods, electronics, pharma, fine arts and other hyper competitive industries riddled with counterfeits. A case in point is with an ultra-high net worth individual, who, when scanning a luxury handbag with a AR app, Blockchain AR is able to overlay provenance data which allows the user to instantaneously query the entire real-time supply chain of the product. Such real-time hyper integration of information is significantas it enhances consumer trust and provides pervasive brand value.

Integrating technologies such as virtual reality and Blockchain facilitates the creation of entirely autonomous commercial ecosystems within virtual reality. Users are able to shop, engage with sales staff and other shoppers, and browse merchandise in real time in VR malls, VR showrooms, and social retail spaces. Users are able to experience true immersion because Blockchain enables the possession of virtual goods. There are Blockchain-backed digital assets in the metaverse, NFTs. They are digital representations of tangible items. NFTs allow brands to sell real virtual goods and allow customers to engage with the brands in immersive virtual reality. For instance, if a virtual sneaker is purchased by a user, they are given a real sneaker paired with the virtual one; the sneaker is Blockchain verified which allows the user true seamless ownership of both the digital and real assets (Tewari & Pande, 2025).

The fusion of augmented reality, virtual reality, and Blockchain technology is also shaping the construction of more fair, inclusive, and decentralized commercial ecosystems. Retailers and consumers can cut out central platforms, accessing AR/VR environments governed by smart contracts that automate the payments, payment returns, payment and usage rights licensing, resale royalties, and rights management. Decentralized identity systems permit users to control and manage their personal information. Retailers within the AR/VR spaces can be touched without relinquishing private information. These systems are aligned with global trends towards user-controlled data ecosystems and privacy-by-design, which minimize reliance on centralized intermediaries.

Integrated smart commerce ecosystems, from a systems architecture view, have a tendency to span three strata. Augmented Reality and Virtual Reality applications that facilitate interface, visualization and experience encompass the immersive interface stratum. AI and edge computing are used in the intelligence stratum to determine user intent, behavioral actions and dynamically change systems to offer tailored adaptive recommendations and/or modify environments in real time (Sanjalawe et al., 2025). The trust stratum, which draws from Blockchain, ascertains and validates product traces, authenticates transactions, and protects digital assets. All this stratum collectively facilitates an integrated commerce experience through product discovery, immersive engagement, validated purchase transactions, and subsequent ownership tracking. Edge and cloud infrastructure augmented with systems architecture ensure low latency rendering for AR/VR environments and distributed Blockchain nodes for cross retailer, supplier, and consumer transaction verification and digital asset security.

Cross industry use cases of this convergence are growing exponentially. Sustainably minded brands in the fashion industry use AR interfaces with Blockchain for transparent verification of material sources and ethical production. In real estate, owners can book VR tours integrated with Blockchain-based tokenized properties for digital secure transactions and fractional ownership. Automotive retailing allows customers in VR to configure their vehicle with simultaneous viewing of Blockchain verified maintenance, warranty, and history records. AR in food and agriculture can be used to project Blockchain verified origin, freshness, and sustainable practices to help consumers make more informed buying choices regarding sustainable and ethical food sources.

Convergence of these technologies 'as cross-silo innovations' also enables emerging business models that were infeasible in the context of brick and mortar commerce, such as subscription-based VR storefronts. These allow brands to maintain a digital and constantly evolving virtual showroom, while Blockchain technology guarantees the automatic enforcement of content rights and royalties to digital assets. Smart contracts driven resale markets enable a secure channel for the resale of luxury goods, ensuring the authenticity of the goods through Blockchain provenance, and offering the consumer peace of mind. Marketplace and virtual world integrations with decentralized payment systems also lower the friction that international transactions pose, and broaden the access to global commerce.

Nonetheless, some obstacles lay ahead, such as seamless integration of AR, VR, and Blockchain technology, with some of the obstacles being, real-time rendering, Blockchain scalability and with the fragmentation of inter-device ecosystems, as well as the absence of universally accepted standards governing the interoperability of AR/VR. There are also ethical dilemmas concerning immersive biometric privacy, tracking within immersive environments, and the technology - marginalized within the design. These dilemmas are potentially surmountable with the incorporation of suitable benchmarks, operational governance frameworks, and consolidated collaboration in the technology, design, and policy domains, accompanied by advocacy for consumer rights.

Moreover, the combination of augmented reality, virtual reality, and Blockchain technology is fundamentally transforming the `smart commerce` paradigm and evolving these technologies into fully immersive, decentralized, and programmable marketplaces. The speed of the integration and sophistication of these technologies indicates that they will transform fundamentally how consumers interact with shopping and how businesses and brands establish, trust, and interact with consumers worldwide. Of course, the commerce and its domains will manage the advanced technologies to enrich trust, value, and engagement with the consumers.

7. INDUSTRY CASE STUDIES AND GLOBAL IMPLEMENTATIONS

It is not only the case that AR, VR, Blockchain, and smart commerce integration is still the subject of theoretical inquiry; there also exist numerous implementations of these technologies at scale across diverse industry verticals and geographies of the world. Such implementations yield ears-on feedback on the potentials and the limits of these emerging commerce ecosystems. A closer analysis of these particular cases sheds light on the different strategies employed to immerse users in these technologies, the trust that is built, and the culture and region of the world where the technologies are used.

Perhaps the best known, and one of the first, examples of AR in retail is with IKEA and the "IKEA Place" app which allows users to see life-size IKEA furniture in their house. The app lets the user manipulate the furniture in their space through touch as well as by maps and dimensions and through three-dimensional ultra-clear models. Research shows that Augmented reality by IKEA significantly decreased reverse logistics and increased online purchasing (Rejeb et al., 2021). Similarly, "Virtual Artist" app by Sephora allows users to sample cosmetic products from the comfort of their home without physical interaction with the products. The system uses facial recognition to Augmented Reality and allows the user to see different combinations of lipsticks, foundations and eye shadows on their face in real-time. This app made the Sephora app successful as it enabled users to avoid physical product trial, something which during the pandemic with low in-store touch points, limited user interaction with the works of the retail touch points.

Nike has been a leader in footwear and sports apparel for incorporating Blockchain technology and immersive experiences. Through the company's Nike Crypto kicks program, physical sneakers are coupled with digital replicas that are authenticated on the Blockchain. Owners can verify, trade, and securely use the digital replicas in VR and metaverse spaces for limited edition items. This blends collectible and decentralized commerce, generating new streams of revenue and increasing brand (Nike, 2022) exclusivity. Furthermore, Adidas has also engaged with AR for product launches, digital collectibles, and Blockchain user loyalty systems that bridge the physical and metaverse worlds.

Particularly, luxury brands are interested in Blockchain for authentication. LVMH, Prada, and Cartier partnered to create the Aura Blockchain Consortium which provides decentralized certificates of authenticity to luxury goods. The consortium mitigates counterfeiting by giving transparent product history to customers which also strengthens the brand trust. Blockchain also gained popularity in the luxury fine art domain with auction houses and galleries using tokenization for fractional ownership, provenance verification, and digital rights management.

As part of a digital marketing strategy, the automotive industry has adopted VR technology for virtual product showrooms. Audi, Mercedes Benz, and Hyundai give their customers the opportunity to virtually explore the features of their vehicles, drive them, and view the interiors. These virtual spaces are often part of a Blockchain system that logs vehicle maintenance records, parts authenticity, and ownership history, enhancing the wreath of transparency for the secondary vehicle market, often subject to a trust deficit.

The use of VR and Blockchain in the real estate sector has simplified the process of purchasing and renting properties. Virtual tours to fully VR-enabled properties eliminate the need for in-person showings and allow clients to "walk" through multiple properties from any remote site on the globe. The ability to drive down the cost of entry investment is incorporated through fraction ownership of amenities coupled with authenticated transactions with Blockchain technology. This paradigm is being implemented in most of the Middle Eastern and Asian countries. Dubai, with its smart cities, is integrating virtual city technology with Blockchain land registries to curtail real estate fraud.

Like much of the world, Asia has experienced rapid advances in immersion commerce - especially South Korea and Japan – due to their unparalleled digital infrastructures and a cultural appreciation of the latest technologies. South Korean retailers, such as Lotte and Shinsegae, have implemented 'VR malls' which allow consumers to shop as digital avatars and attend pop up events while interacting with AI sales assistants. These environments also incorporate digital scores of payment systems which demonstrate the region's affinity for decentralized payment systems. The Japanese Masters of Fashion and Gaming also make extensive use of AR and Blockchain to devise systems for the hybridization of digital and physical space.

In the Middle East region, smart malls and high-end retail districts have incorporated AR navigation, virtual experiences, and Blockchain systems along with provenance tracking. Dubai, specifically, has initiated projects that bridge digital identity, retail payment systems, and Blockchain verified product provenance and record systems, thus enabling the nexus of commercial creative advancement and Dubai's smart city governance national strategy. In comparison, the European markets are much more focused on sustainable and ethical practices. Blockchain technology ensures ethical records that are visible within the supply chains of food, fashion, and cosmetics, thus meeting the regulations and consumer demand for ethically verified sourced products.

Challenges remain, even with the successful execution of the implementations above. The high costs of development associated with immersive experiences, coupled with lack of ready consumer access to VR hardware, and difficulty of Blockchain construction with older infrastructure are pain points for many businesses. There are differences in AR/VR adoption that come due to the nature of cultural differences as well. For example, Western markets are much more concerning for the protective privacy issues, whereas the East Asian markets focus more on the smooth and convenient digital interface. All these elements highlight the necessity to create smart commerce systems that are culturally responsive and flexible.

In its most recent technological implementations, AR, VR, and Blockchain technologies, due to their different characteristics, each work to improve experience, trust, and operational efficiencies, showing their united essence. Thanks to the rapid technological convergence in different industries and geographical areas, augmented reality, virtual reality, and Blockchain technologies are set to redefine cross-border commerce by creating hybrid environments for interaction, trust, assessment, and commerce.

8. CHALLENGES, ETHICAL CONCERNS, AND FUTURE RESEARCH DIRECTIONS

The incorporation of user participation and advanced technology systems is called smart commerce. The difficulties of Blockchain in conjunction with other AR and VR technologies is an intricate combination of ethical, financial, and socio-technical difficulties that need solutions if systems of these types are to be adopted. The technology of Blockchain, VR, and AR can be accepted due to rapid and uninterrupted interactions; though, there are just as many potential negative impacts as there are positive impacts, regarding privacy, equity, accessibility, and sustainability. Understanding these difficulties is key to smart commerce systems that are responsible, inclusive, and adaptable to the changes the future will bring.

Perhaps one of the biggest issues relates to scalability. Immersive uses of technology function optimally in conditions of high-bandwidth and low-latency, yet such parameters of infrastructure are still unevenly distributed globally. VR, for instance, needs low-latency rendering to be maintained continuously, or else a user gets VR sickness. Loss of immersion or even minor delays by the system can break the enjoyment of the user and ruin the experience. In the same way, AR maps and recognizes objects in real-time, as well as performs spatial computing, which can, in several cases, such as older devices, perform significant processing power. Same goes for Blockchain with limited scalability, which becomes a problem with public Blockchain that are limited in throughput, have high settlement fees, or deal with costly and inefficient consensus. In fact, academic research has highlighted that such contradictory and low-capacity transaction states of well-known Blockchain networks sets substantial limits on large-scale retail deployments (Li et al., 2021). These challenges imply that next generation networks such as 5G, 6G, and edge computing technologies architecture are indispensable for smooth and cohesive interconnected commerce systems.

The issue caused by the fragmented nature of devices is another interesting aspect. From smartphones and tablets to headsets and wearables, AR and VR applications work across a wide spectrum of devices and their respective operating systems and formats. Each of those devices is equipped with, and is capable of, different hardware configuration, resourceful ways of engaging the users, and diverse limitations. Thus, the design of cross-platform seamless immersive experience needs to champion a high level of optimization and a great amount of effort in interactive design in order to work with users comfortably. With Blockchain, fragmentation is caused by the variety of networks, the differences in Blockchain protocols, the different types of tokens and the variations in digital id systems. Interoperability is possible, yet vulnerable, with cross-chain bridges, decentralized id standards, and multi-network smart contracts, and the weaknesses can place a huge burden of security risk onto end users.

Another ethical dimension of the challenges are the concerns. Kinetic technologies archive eye-tracking, facial expressions, gestures, and movements, as well as other biometric and behavioral data. Immersive technologies personalize experiences, all while disregarding privacy sensitive data that biometric information exposes. Most VR and AR systems classify users' invisible emotional cognitive states and exert low level the users' knowledge manipulation with surveillance and emotional targeting ease. Scholars warn that with VR the primary advertising paradigm could shift and emerge far more immersive and effective means of behavioral control than the conventional forms of advertising (Madary & Metzinger, 2016). Ethically far simpler than most forms of advertising, Blockchain's trust and transference systems are complicated by immutability, which restricts the silencing of data and the removal of information— a paradoxical challenge for the EU. Also, augmented reality or virtual reality identifiers which Blockchain records are paired with could in some cases, records of the system users' immersive engaging activities, raising concerns around extended data retention.

Access remains an issue that is important yet largely unaddressed. The majority of AR and VR experiences are designed for people who can move, see, and think without any restrictions. There are disabled people, however, who face complicated barriers such as needing to execute overly complex gestures, having to rely on visual-only instruction, or needing to perform arduous bodily movements. There is research that shows how immersive technology inclusive design is applied, or not, dissimilar across fields, (Fox & Thornton, 2022). In the same vein, Blockchain commerce systems tend to ignore the associated barriers of digital wallet and private key dimensionalities of identity management, along with decentralization, and identity management and are designed for ubiquitous technology literacy. In order to ensure the principles of smart commerce extend beyond any form of disparity, there must be adequate foundational elements such as interfaces that are considered accessible, interaction strategies that are adaptive, and onboarding that is minimally complex.

Adoption of smart commerce involves the consideration of various economic and disorganization challenges. The introduction of immersive and Blockchain technologies requires significant capital investments in hardware, software development, data architecture, and staff onboarding and education. Such expenditures, correlated with the utilization of Blockchain technologies, are often out of reach of small and medium sized enterprises, thus widening the innovation gap. policy ambiguity—especially Blockchain payments, digital assets, and cross-border data regulations— are added complications. Legal frameworks are variegated, with some jurisdictions welcoming digital assets and others imposing draconian restrictions, even outright bans. Such an environment stifles global commerce and demonstrates the urgent need for collaboration and unified approach regulatory frameworks.

It is necessary to explore innovative research opportunities that address complex challenges simultaneously. Perhaps one of the most promising is the pairing of AI-driven personalization with AR and VR features. Advanced AI models could observe participants in an AR/VR space and adjust products, surroundings, or navigation in real-time. Important is there is no unconsented and undetected manipulation of the user's actions. Other examples include identifiers, decentralized identity systems, and zero-knowledge proofs that enable the use of Blockchain technology without violating user privacy. These systems permit ethical commercial transactions without revealing private or sensitive information.

Research on smart commerce and digital twins—virtual models of real-world items, stores, or entire supply chains—presents another promising frontier. Combined with AR and VR, digital twins can enable real-time analytics, interactive visualization of complex logistics, and product-simulating scenarios. Blockchain would seamlessly integrate as the trust layer, assuring that the information pertaining to the digital twin is verifiably accurate and unalterable. There is a burgeoning interest in the use of digital twins to transform retail by enhancing planning, inventory, and customer engagement activities (Ramu et al., 2022, Al-E'mari et al., 2026).

Alongside this, the importance of research on sustainable commerce has emerged. While Blockchain technology has its flaws, like being energy hungry, proof of stake, layer 2 scaling, and green Blockchain are more sustainable alternatives. Sustainable architectural designs for AR and VR systems and energy-efficient rendering also need to be developed to lessen the ecological footprint.

The rest of the issue revolves around shaping the future of smart commerce systems which, like in the case of AR and VR, focus on innovation and responsibility. Subsequent research should construct a framework that upholds the central technical, ethical, and anthropocentric focus, safeguarding privacy, equity, and sustainability around the unencumbered integration of AR, VR, and Blockchain into commercial ecosystems.

9. CONCLUSION

The combination of augmented reality, virtual reality, and Blockchain technology represents a milestone in the development of digital commerce. While powerful individually, when combined, these technologies form a cohesive ecosystem that transforms how consumers perceive, evaluate, authenticate and purchase products. AR enhances the real world with contextual information, VR enables users to shop in immersive 3D environments, and Blockchain facilitates secure transactions, ownership, and provenance of products. Their combination represents a shift in e-commerce towards a new form of smart commerce with immersive interaction, decentralized trust, and fluid digital-physical integration.

In this chapter, we have examined how smart commerce ecosystems emerge from a confluence of technology, behavioral economics, and market opportunity. Integrated AR/VR with Blockchain technology is ubiquitous in applied use across luxury retail, fashion, automotive, real estate, and food sustainability. Case studies highlight measurable benefits including improved product understanding, enhanced authentication mechanisms, reduced uncertainty in purchasing decisions, and more secure transactional processes.

In parallel, the chapter underscores the barriers accompanying the progresses in technology. For instance: privacy issues, the collection of biometric information, collection of data on the Blockchain, the ease of use of the interface, and the lack of unified regulation. These challenges invite thoughtful governance and interdisciplinary collaboration. Any smart commerce ecosystems of the future need to be developed inclusively, transparently, and sustainably, otherwise, the evolution of technology would be a disservice to social values.

In the future, the integration of AR and VR with Blockchain technologies will be accelerated by evolving supporting technologies such as AI, 5G and 6 networks, digital twins, and decentralized identities. The evolution of commerce suggests a hybrid retailing structure in which customers will be able to move freely across physical stores, AR-enhanced areas, and the VR metaverse. Trust anchored on Blockchain will guarantee secure digital ownership, decentralized governance, and interoperable economic systems. Early adopters of this convergence will strengthen the trust and relationship they have with their consumers through richer and more personalized experiences.

To conclude, smart commerce goes beyond technologically advancing to a complete reconceptualization of value creation and value capture. The merging of AR and VR with Blockchain advances commerce to an immersive, secure, decentralized, and augmented human-centered paradigm. Such a transformation will change international markets and the consumer experience for the next ten years and beyond.

REFERENCES

Accenture. (2023). Consumer pulse survey: The future of digital experience. *Accenture Research*. https://www.accenture.com/content/dam/accenture/final/industry/consumer-goods-and-services/document/Accenture-Resilient-Consumer-Study-2023.pdf [Accessed: 25 November 2025].

Al, E. 'mari, S., Sanjalawe, Y., Fataftah, F., & Fataftah, F. (2026). Digital Twins and BI: Synchronizing Virtual Models With Real-Time Business Processes. In *Strategic AI Integration in Business Intelligence* (pp. 135-154). IGI Global Scientific Publishing.

Al-E'mari, S., Sanjalawe, Y., Makhadmeh, S., & Alqudah, H. (2024, February). Digital forensics meets blockchain: Enhancing evidence authenticity and traceability. In *2024 2nd International Conference on Cyber Resilience (ICCR)* (pp. 01-06). IEEE.

Aura Blockchain Consortium. (2023). Global authenticity solutions for luxury goods. *Aura*. https://auraconsortium.com/ [Access 24 November 2025].

Flavián, C., Ibáñez-Sánchez, S., & Orús, C. (2019). The impact of virtual, augmented and mixed reality technologies on the customer experience. *Journal of Business Research, 100*, 547–560. DOI: 10.1016/j.jbusres.2018.10.050

Fox, D., & Thornton, I. G. (2022). White Paper-The IEEE Global Initiative on Ethics of Extended Reality (XR) Report--Extended Reality (XR) Ethics and Diversity, Inclusion, and Accessibility. *The IEEE Global Initiative on Ethics of Extended Reality (XR) Report--Extended Reality (XR) Ethics and Diversity, Inclusion, and Accessibility*, 1-25.

Hazarika, A., & Rahmati, M. (2023). Towards an evolved immersive experience: Exploring 5G-and beyond-enabled ultra-low-latency communications for augmented and virtual reality. *Sensors (Basel), 23*(7), 3682. DOI: 10.3390/s23073682 PMID: 37050742

Heller, J., Chylinski, M., de Ruyter, K., Mahr, D., & Keeling, D. I. (2019). Let me imagine that for you: Transforming the retail frontline through augmenting customer mental imagery ability. *Journal of Retailing, 95*(2), 94–114. DOI: 10.1016/j.jretai.2019.03.005

IBM. (2021). Pandora Boosts Online Sales by Transforming Its Global Omnichannel e-Commerce with IBM Sterling Supply Chain Software. *IBM Institute for Business Value*. https://newsroom.ibm.com/2021-06-21-Pandora-Boosts-Online-Sales-by-Transforming-Its-Global-Omnichannel-e-Commerce-with-IBM-Sterling-Supply-Chain-Software [Access 26 November 2025].

Kumar, L., Verma, S., Srivastava, R., & Bharti, B. (2025). Does presence matter? Impact of telepresence and social presence on purchase intention from VR shopping sites: Empirical examination. *International Journal of Business and Systems Research, 19*(3), 247–270. DOI: 10.1504/IJBSR.2025.147566

Lipton, A., Sardon, A., Schär, F., & Schüpbach, C. (2020). *11. Stablecoins, digital currency, and the future of money*. Building the New Economy.

Madary, M., & Metzinger, T. K. (2016). Real virtuality: A code of ethical conduct. Recommendations for good scientific practice and the consumers of VR-technology. *Frontiers in Robotics and AI, 3*, 180932. DOI: 10.3389/frobt.2016.00003

Mirabelli, G., & Solina, V. (2020). Blockchain and agricultural supply chains traceability: Research trends and future challenges. *Procedia Manufacturing, 42*, 414–421. DOI: 10.1016/j.promfg.2020.02.054

Nike. (2022). Nike digital transformation and Web3 initiatives. Nike Innovation Report. https://static1.squarespace.com/static/6628939a6a82e57838e96216/t/6667a427c569856c5f602257/1718068266225/Nike+Innovation+Report.pdf [Access 27 November 2025].

Palanikumar, G., Pandi, V. S., Banumathi, S., Karthikeyan, G., Giri, J., & Al-Safarini, M. Y. (2025). Leveraging Augmented and Virtual Reality in Conjunction with Artificial Intelligence, 5G, and Edge Computing to Transform Immersive Experiences. In *2025 Fourth International Conference on Smart Technologies, Communication and Robotics (STCR)* (pp. 1-6). IEEE.

PwC. (2025). Why the future of customer experience demands the experience supply chain. *PwC Research*. https://www.pwc.com/us/en/services/consulting/business-transformation/future-customer-experience-is-supply-chain.html [Access 30 November 2025].

Ramu, S. P., Boopalan, P., Pham, Q. V., Maddikunta, P. K. R., Huynh-The, T., Alazab, M., Nguyen, T. T., & Gadekallu, T. R. (2022). Federated learning enabled digital twins for smart cities: Concepts, recent advances, and future directions. *Sustainable Cities and Society, 79*, 103663. DOI: 10.1016/j.scs.2021.103663

Rejeb, A., Keogh, J. G., Wamba, S. F., & Treiblmaier, H. (2021). The potentials of augmented reality in supply chain management: A state-of-the-art review. *Management review quarterly, 71*(4), 819-856.

Roesner, F., & Kohno, T. (2021). Security and privacy for augmented reality: Our 10-year retrospective. In *VR4Sec: 1st International Workshop on Security for XR and XR for Security*.

Saberi, S., Kouhizadeh, M., Sarkis, J., & Shen, L. (2019). Blockchain technology and its relationships to sustainable supply chain management. *International Journal of Production Research*, *57*(7), 2117–2135. DOI: 10.1080/00207543.2018.1533261

Sanjalawe, Y., Fraihat, S., Abualhaj, M., Makhadmeh, S., & Alzubi, E. (2025). A review of 6G and AI convergence: Enhancing communication networks with artificial intelligence. *IEEE Open Journal of the Communications Society*, *6*, 2308–2355. DOI: 10.1109/OJCOMS.2025.3553302

Sergeev, M. (2023). *Web3. 0 as an Adaptive Strategy in Crisis: The Case of Nike and Adidas* (Master's thesis, Universidade Catolica Portuguesa (Portugal)).

Tewari, R., & Pande, B. P. (2025). Transforming Digital Ownership: The Role of NFTs in Shaping Virtual Economies and Market Dynamics. *IET Blockchain*, *5*(1), e70010. DOI: 10.1049/blc2.70010

Uddin, M., Obaidat, M., Manickam, S., Laghari, S. U. A., Dandoush, A., Ullah, H., & Ullah, S. S. (2024). Exploring the convergence of Metaverse, Blockchain, and AI: A comprehensive survey of enabling technologies, applications, challenges, and future directions. *Wiley Interdisciplinary Reviews. Data Mining and Knowledge Discovery*, *14*(6), e1556. DOI: 10.1002/widm.1556

Chapter 8
Metaverse AI Shopping Experiences

Khalil Omar
http://orcid.org/0000-0002-5328-5762
University of Petra, Jordan

Wesam Alkhadour
http://orcid.org/0009-0004-1937-0308
University of Petra, Jordan

Jamal Zraqou
http://orcid.org/0000-0001-9060-7188
University of Petra, Jordan

Jorge Marx Gómez
University of Oldenburg, Germany

ABSTRACT

This chapter introduces an overall structure of AI-enhanced shopping experiences in the Metaverse, covering the issues of personalization, engagement, and the efficiency of computing. The system combines three fundamental features: a hybrid recommendation system that uses both collaborative and deep learning; natural shopping assistance interfaces that are powered by conversational AI; and virtual try-on experiences based on computer vision. Assessment based on e-commerce data shows that it can be much more precise and recall-wise better than some baseline methods, with an increase of 37.2% and 42.1% respectively. The modular architecture is platform agnostic and has privacy preserving mechanisms such as federated learning and differential privacy. The estimated metrics indicate that the

DOI: 10.4018/979-8-3373-7330-0.ch008

session duration will grow by 54.8 percent and the conversion rates will grow by 42.3 percent. This paper adds spatial-conscious recommendation systems, effective inference chains, and privacy-sensitive trends to AI-based Metaverse trading.

1. INTRODUCTION

The Metaverse has become a paradigm of revolution in the digital interaction sphere that has fundamentally changed the way consumers interact with brands, products, and shopping experiences. In contrast to the two-dimensional interface and low-interactivity of traditional e-commerce tools, the Metaverse enables users to operate in immersive 3D spaces where they move about as avatars, communicate with other users and interact with virtual versions of real-world items in real time. The technological change is not merely a type of incremental innovation, but a paradigm shift in the field of retail that requires the development of new strategies towards user experience design, product display, and interaction with customers (Dwivedi et al., 2022).

The cognitive infrastructure that makes the advanced shopping experiences in these virtual worlds possible is artificial intelligence. Machine learning algorithms process large volumes of behavioral data in order to learn about likes and dislikes of users, anticipate their intentions to buy, and make customized product suggestions. NLP makes possible chatbots and other forms of conversational interfaces, in which AI agents can take customers through product collections, respond to queries, and give styling tips. Virtual try-on technologies are computer vision technologies that enable consumers to see how a product (clothing, accessories, furniture) would look on their avatars or in their virtual environment. These AI features can make online shopping active and more engaging and can be much like shopping in person without its constraints (Wang et al., 2023).

This technological convergence is strategically important as demonstrated by current market projections. The industry observers predict that in 2024 the global Metaverse market will reach 800 billion dollars, and retail and e-commerce will be significant proportions of that expansion (Mystakidis, 2022). Large technology companies like Meta, Microsoft and Nvidia have already invested billions into developing infrastructure of the Metaverse, and major retailers like Nike, Gucci and Walmart have already created virtual storefronts to enjoy the benefits of being an early mover. Nevertheless, even with considerable investment and a big hype, the potential of the AI-enhanced Metaverse shopping is not fully achieved yet because of technical issues, disjointed platforms, and a lack of knowledge of successful design concepts.

The creation of an efficient AI-based shopping experience in the Metaverse is hindered by several important challenges. To start with, recommendation systems that have been developed to fit the conventional e-commerce systems cannot consider the spatial, social, and temporal aspects of a virtual environment. Users do not just browse product lists, but they move through three-dimensional environments, monitor the actions of fellow shoppers, and can interact with products in contextual environments, which shape the purchase decision. Second, the technical bottlenecks incurred by the computing requirements of simulating high-fidelity virtual environments and at the same time executing real-time AI inference are very high and lead to poor user experience. Third, the immersive environments create privacy concerns due to the unprecedented amount of behavioral, biometric, and interaction data, and AI architectures should be designed to ensure privacy. Fourth, the absence of standardization between the Metaverse platforms introduces the problem of fragmentation, which does not allow creating a seamless shopping experience and does not allow creating platform-agnostic AI solutions (Ning et al., 2023).

This chapter attempts to overcome these challenges by providing an extensive framework of AI-driven shopping inside the Metaverse. We combine three core AI capabilities: personalized recommendation systems that make use of both conventional preference indicators and new spatial-behavioral indicators specific to virtual environments; conversational AI interfaces that offer natural and context-specific help during the shopping experience; and computer vision that makes it possible to see the products in real-life and have a virtual try-on experience. The framework is focused on modularity, which enables retailers to adopt either individual modules or full solutions in line with their technical capacity as well as strategic goals.

The main contributions of the work are as follows: (1) a new hybrid recommendation architecture, which is a combination of collaborative filtering with deep-learning-based embedding models in the specifics of the spatial shopping environment; (2) an efficient inference pipeline that balances the performance of the computational resource with the accuracy of the recommendations in resource-constrained virtual worlds; (3) a comprehensive evaluation in terms of the existing e-commerce datasets, showing significant increases in the accuracy of the recommendation and the simulated engagement metrics; (4) a detailed analysis of privacy-preserving methods that can be used.

The rest of this chapter is structured in the following way. Section 2 presents the related literature in the area of the Metaverse commerce, AI recommendation systems, and virtual shopping experiences. Section 3 outlines our plan of methodology, such as system architecture, algorithm specification and implementation considerations. Section 4 explains the experimental design, such as the nature of data sets, evaluation measures, and benchmarking. Section 5 includes detailed findings and discussion, including the quantitative areas of performance and qualitative factors.

Section 6 deals with implications, limitations and future research directions. Section 7 is a conclusion where the main findings were made and recommendations were provided to the practitioners.

2. RELATED WORK

Studies on the interface of artificial intelligence and Metaverse commerce have become a vibrant discipline that draws expertise in computer science, marketing, human-computer interaction, and retail management. This segment is a summary of the pertinent literature in some of the critical areas, which shape our framework construction.

2.1 Virtual Commerce and Metaverse Platforms

The concept of the Metaverse has its roots in decades of research on the topic of virtual worlds, multiplayer online games, and immersive technologies. According to Mystakidis (2022), the taxonomy of characteristics of the Metaverse is described in a detailed manner, with persistence, synchronicity, interoperability, and user-generated content being listed as the defining features. Ball (2021) differentiates between fully immersive virtual reality experiences and augmented reality interfaces that superimpose digital information on physical spaces, where most modern Metaverse platforms can be found somewhere along the spectrum, and not at one end or the other.

A number of researchers have explored the initial commercial activities within virtual worlds. Barrera and Shah (2023) examined the marketing approach of leading Metaverse platform such as Decentraland, The Sandbox, and Roblox and found that there were three main approaches to marketing: brand presence establishment, virtual product sales, and marketing experiences. In their study, they found that the consumer engagement measures in online space vary significantly when compared to the traditional online channel and the social interaction and exploration time are more indicative of purchase intentions than the traditional clickthrough metrics. This analysis was expanded to the hospitality and tourism industries and Gursoy et al. (2022) showed the impact of virtual venue experiences on real visitation intentions and brand perceptions.

The problems of technical infrastructure are also major obstacles to the widespread adoption of Metaverse commerce. Wang et al. (2023) carried out a survey of the current technology of the Metaverse and discovered that the issues of scalability, latency, and cross-platform compatibility are essential technical issues. Their review found out that the already available blockchain-based solutions have limitations on transaction throughput, which hinder ease of shopping during peak times. Lee et al. (2021) suggested hybrid architecture with real-time interactions based on centralized databases and transaction settlement based on decentralized ledgers, which has better performance and meets the desired security properties.

2.2 Recommendation Systems based on AI

Recommendation systems represent a well-established research field that has a voluminous literature covering collaborative filtering, content-based methods and hybrid techniques. Covington et al. (2016) proposed deep neural networks to recommend videos at YouTube scale, which illustrates that deep learning can be successfully used to address large candidate spaces and sparse data on interactions. Their two-step system of architecture candidate generation and ranking has affected the future designs of recommendation systems in many different areas.

Recommendation systems based on situational factors, in addition to user-item interaction, have become popular in recent years. Adomavicius and Tuzhilin (2015) operationalized context-aware recommendation as multi-dimensional optimization problems in which context dimensions (time, location, social setting) play a major role in the formation of preferences. Neural collaborative filtering was proposed by He et al. (2017), instead of the classic matrix factorization, neural architectures are able to learn non-linear user-item interactions. Their performance indicated that they had made significant improvements to the conventional techniques on the standard benchmarks.

Sequential and session based recommendation systems deal with the issue of user intention prediction based on the sequence of behaviors. To address this problem, Hidasi et al. (2016) proposed recurrent neural networks to solve session-based recommendation, which has a high performance despite having few historical data points because it predicts short-term behavior patterns. Tang and Wang (2018) expanded this methodology to include self-attention mechanisms, which allows the model to detect the relevant historical interactions of varying temporal scales. Such sequential approaches are especially applicable to Metaverse shopping where user experiences can be divided into several locations and interactions in one session.

2.3 Virtual Shopping Computer Vision

Computer vision technologies can facilitate a number of key functions of virtual shopping, specifically virtual try-on and visualization of products. Bhatnagar et al. (2019) created techniques of realistic clothing transfer which maintain the texture and drape of garments and can be adjusted to other body shapes. They use a method of integrating geometry models and adversarial training to create credible virtual fitting room experiences. Raj et al. (2021) further applied this study to accessories by showing how generative adversarial networks can be used to create real-world images of users with jewelry, a pair of sunglasses, or a watch on their wrists.

The visual search features enable users to locate similar products to the ones they observe in virtual or physical stores. Bell and Bala (2015) proposed deep learning methods to search visual products in e-commerce, which learns visual similarities not just by matching colors or patterns. Liu et al. (2020) refined these techniques by including attention mechanisms that determine the features of the product of interest by disregarding the confounding variables such as background or lighting. Such methods can be well applied to the Metaverse where people can find products by exploring the environment as opposed to using search queries.

The use of pose estimation and 3D reconstruction technologies make it possible to customize the avatars, as well as make the product fitting personalized. According to Cao et al. (2019), real-time multi-person pose estimation systems created by them could track the body position in complex scenes. Kanazawa et al. (2018) developed the ways of estimating 3D-body shape on single images and providing personalized virtual try-on, without the need to have 3D scanning devices. Such developments reduce the barrier to adoption as the user can build proper avatars using just smartphone cameras.

2.4 Conversational AI and Virtual Assistants

Advances in natural language processing have made it possible to have more advanced conversational interfaces to customer service and product discovery. Devlin et al. (2019) proposed the BERT (Bidirectional Encoder Representations from Transformers) where semantic relationships that allow improved question answering and dialogue understanding are learned through pre-trained language models. Based on the work by Brown et al. (2020), which applied GPT-3 to a large scale, it was demonstrated that when large enough language models are used, the few-shot learning can be applied to various conversational problems.

There has been a significant amount of research on task-oriented dialogue systems that are specifically meant to assist in shopping. Chen et al. (2019) created multi-domain dialogue models that are able to deal with complex queries that are based on product specifications, availability and prices. Henderson et al. (2013) presented neural belief trackers, which preserve the conversation state over multiple turns, which allows negotiable long interactivity. The systems prove to be effective in the classic e-commerce environment, but they need modification to fit spatial Metaverse environments where the conversational context encompasses the location of the user and the surrounding products.

The use of embodied conversational agents integrating linguistic communication with non-verbal messages is a new research direction especially when applied to the Metaverse. Cassell et al. (2000) laid down initial foundations of embodied agents that include gesture, gaze and facial expressions. The latest research by Huang et al. (2021) illustrates that neural animation models can be used to produce avatars to act in accordance with speech, and this avatar behavior makes virtual communication more natural and interesting.

2.5 AI-based Commerce and Privacy and Ethics

Personalized AI experiences require a lot of data collection, which is an issue of serious concern regarding privacy and ethics. Shokri and Shmatikov (2015) revealed the privacy weaknesses of machine learning models, in which the outcomes of the model can reveal information about the training data. The federated learning, as suggested by McMahan et al. (2017), is a privacy-saving alternative in which the models are trained on the decentralized data, without storing sensitive information in a single place. Kairouz et al. (2021) generalized this to the case of differential privacy with mathematical limits on information leakage.

The concept of algorithmic bias and fairness in recommendation systems has become one of the crucial research subjects. Mehrabi et al. (2021) conducted a survey of bias sources in machine learning that data collection procedures, algorithm design decisions, and metrics of evaluation could be the points of violation of fairness. Ekstrand et al. (2018) investigated the considerations of fairness that were unique to recommendation systems and suggested measures of disparate impact across demographic groups. These considerations turn out to be particularly applicable when it comes to Metaverse commerce where biased suggestions may result in discriminative consequences.

The manipulative design patterns and digital addiction are other ethical issues. Montag et al. (2019) examined smartphone patterns of addiction and determined design characteristics that can capitalize on psychological vulnerability to achieve engagement. Mathur et al. (2019) listed some dark patterns in e-commerce interfaces that prompt users to make unintended purchases. The nature of immersion in the Metaverse may increase these issues, which requires particular care in designing AI systems in terms of ethics.

3. PROPOSED METHODOLOGY

In this section, we provide our overall scheme of AI-based shopping in the Metaverse. It will be developed through a methodology that covers system architecture, algorithmic units, implementation plans, and assessment procedures that are aimed at solving the special needs of virtual commerce using artificial intelligence capabilities.

3.1 System Architecture

Our system architecture is based on the modular design that consists of four main subsystems: User Interface Layer, AI Processing Pipeline, Data Management Layer, and Platform Integration Layer. This isolation of concern allows the independent scaling, maintenance, and it also allows retailers to implement components in stages according to their requirements and technical abilities.

The User Interface Layer deals with all direct contacts between the users and the shopping system in the Metaverse environment. The interface has three main components: the Spatial Navigation Interface, which allows users to navigate the space in three dimensions with both standard controls and natural gestures; the Product Interaction System that lets users explore items, look at specifications and handle virtual products; and the Conversational Interface, which lets users talk to AI shopping assistants. These elements work together in order to make the actions of user interfaces of various modalities of interaction coordinated and context relevant.

Figure 1. AI-Enhanced Metaverse Shopping System Architecture

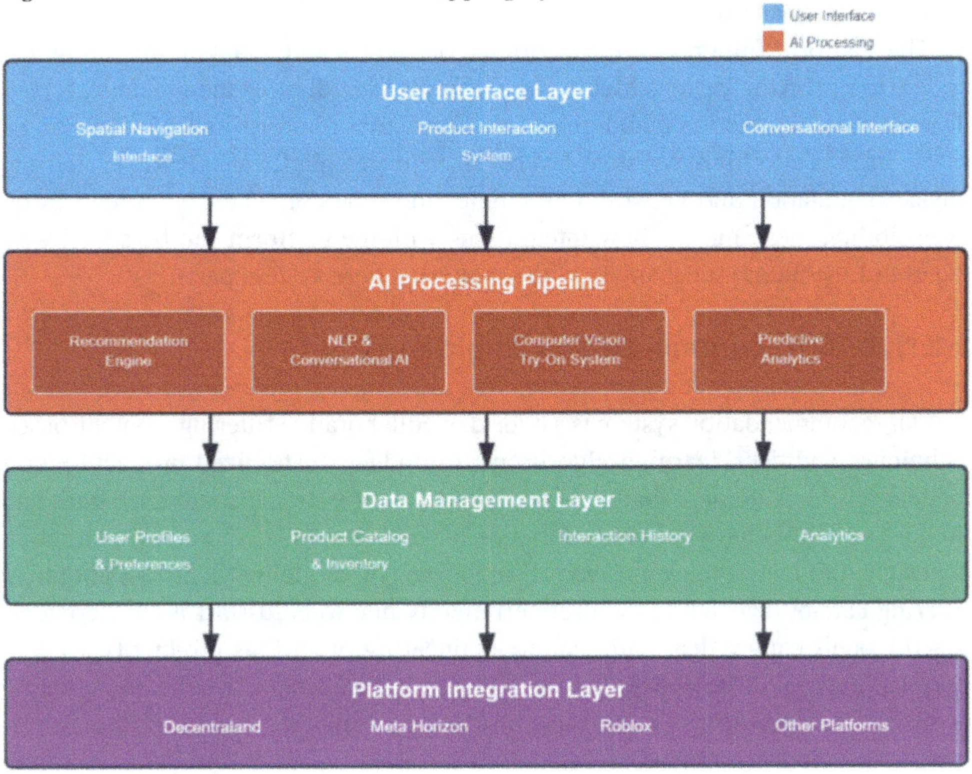

The AI Processing Pipeline uses the fundamental intelligence functions such as the recommendation generation, natural language understanding, computer vision processing and predictive analytics. This pipeline works almost in real-time, and its input is a user and the surrounding environment to respond with personalized responses that meet acceptable latency requirements. The pipeline is being designed using a microservices architecture in which independent AI models are used as separate services, which interact with each other using clearly defined APIs. It is a design that allows updating of the model, A/B testing, and progressive implementation of new capabilities without interfering with the current functionality.

The Data Management Layer manages storage, retrieval and processing of user profiles, product catalogs, interaction history as well as system analytics. Our storage plan is a hybrid approach with relational databases holding structured product and transaction information, document stores holding flexible user profiles and preferences, vector databases to find similarities in a recommendation situation efficiently, and distributed caching layers to reduce latency to information that is accessed most often. Privacy-sensitive mechanisms such as data anonymization, differential privacy and secure multi-party computation safeguard sensitive user data in the lifecycle of the data.

The Platform Integration Layer offers connectors and adapters that allow the system to run on the various Metaverse platforms regardless of their technical specifications and interaction paradigms. This layer hides platform specifics, making a single interface to higher system layers but manages platform specific rendering, physics simulation and network communication protocol. The design focuses on extensibility, meaning that new integrations with the platform can be added with the use of the plugin mechanism without altering core system parts.

3.2 Hybrid Recommendation Engine

Our recommendation system is a hybrid of collaborative filtering, content-based techniques and deep learning algorithms to produce customized product recommendations to customers that consider both the conventional preference cues and the new spatial-behavioral characteristics of virtual worlds. The hybrid structure is designed to overcome a number of limitations of single methods: collaborative filtering cannot deal with new users efficiently due to cold-start issues; content-based models cannot deal with feature engineering of various product types; and deep learning models need significant amounts of training data. The combination of these strategies allows us to have a strong performance among different user groups and product categories.

The collaborative filtering element applies the matrix factorization which breaks the user-item interaction matrix into the latent factor representations. Mathematically, having a set of users U and items I, and observed interactions R, we learn user embeddings pu and item embeddings qi which minimize the reconstruction error. We extend the conventional matrix factorization model by adding implicit feedback cues such as durations of product view, virtual trial-ons, and social interactions with other customer browsers of the same products. These cues give more insight into preferences than purchase history can give, especially in the case of the Metaverse where browsing intentions are indicated by browsing behavior.

The content-based element uses product attributes, description, and visual characteristics in determining similar products. To compute the visual features such as style, color and form, we use the pre-trained vision transformers to compute the high-dimensional embeddings of the product images, which are the visual features. Text descriptive information is processed by BERT-based encoders, which produce semantic representations that reflect functional attributes of products and product category. Such multimodal embeddings allow cross-category recommendations; e.g. propose complementary accessories given a clothing choice, in circumstances where little interaction data is available in the accessory category.

Deep learning component will be represented by a neural network structure and it will learn intricate non-linear association among users, objects, and contextual elements. As input, the network receives concatenated embeddings of collaborative and content-based elements and contextual information such as the current virtual location, time spent in various sections of the store, recent history of conversations with AI assistants, and social context (shopping on his/her own or with friends). These inputs are processed by multiple hidden layers that include residual connection and layer normalization before the final output should be a relevance score of each candidate item. This network is trained with a pairwise ranking loss which promotes the items relevant to the user to score better than irrelevant items.

One of the most important innovations that we have to add to our recommendation engine is the addition of spatial context - the position of the user and the path through virtual retail spaces. We are the virtual store in the form of a graph with the nodes as locations and the edges as the paths in navigation. Patterns of user movement using this graph indicate shopping habits and shopping choices; such as perusing the store methodically as compared to searching to a specific section. The graph convolutional networks that we use to encode spatial features also learn location embeddings which are based on physical proximity as well as semantic similarity of different sections of a store. Such embeddings are inputted into the deep learning component, which allows location-aware suggestions, which take into consideration nearby products and common shopping patterns.

3.3 Conversational Shopping Assistant

The conversational assistant offers natural language response on product discovery, specification questions, and shopping advice. Our application is based on the large language models that are fine-tuned on retail-specific dialogues and improved by retrieval-augmented generation to provide precise product information and recommendation engine to make personalized suggestions. The assistant is an embodied agent that exists as an avatar that follows the users as they shop in the virtual stores and can respond to voice or textual input and keeps the context of the conversation going through the long shopping sessions.

Effective conversational commerce is based on intent recognition. Our categories of user utterances consist of predefined intent such as product search, feature comparison, price inquiry, availability check and recommendation request. This is a highly accurate classification that can be performed by a BERT based classifier that is trained on annotated dialogue data. In case of complex queries that involve more than one intent we use a sequence labeling approach which detects intent boundaries and relationships. This systematic knowledge facilitates the generation of adequate response and system behavior.

Entity extraction and slot filling recognize particular products, properties or constraints referred to in the query made by the user. Product name, brand, and category recognition models are named entity recognition models that are trained on product catalogs. The features that are noted like size, color or material are identified by attribute extractors. Such extracted entities are fed into structured query representations fed to retrieval systems or form constraints in the generation of recommending systems. Context tracking is used to save the conversation state in successive turns so that the user can narrow down search results or add questions without repeating information.

Response generation involves synthesis of the response based on templates and neural methods. In the case of factual questions that have definite answers (price, availability, specifications), we use template-based generation that is accurate. In the case of open-ended questions that demand the explanation or recommendations, we use fine-tuned language models that are used to generate fluent and contextually relevant responses. A retrieval-augmented generation method first retrieves the relevant product information and reviews and conditions response generation on this retrieved context, which is much more accurate in fact than pure neural generation.

3.4 Virtual Try-On System

The virtual try-on system allows people to see products on their avatars before buying, which is one of the key impediments to the adoption of online shopping. In our implementation, we use 3D body estimation, garment simulation, and neural rendering to produce realistic images of the appearance of clothing, accessories, and other items of wear on individual users. The system enables try-on through avatars in the Metaverse space and augmented reality try-on whereby the user sees the products superimposed on real-world camera images.

Avatar body estimation involves use of parametric body models which depict the human shape and pose using learned parameters. The users give simple measurements, or scanning of their bodies through smartphone cameras. Our system is used to model 3D meshes based on the parametric models applied to this input data to produce an accurate representation of the shape of each body. In case of avatar-based try-on, we use the transformations to match the garment meshes to the shapes of the avatars to simulate the drape and movement of the fabric by physics-based cloth simulation. This method generates believable visual representations at the same time preserving real-time operation by means of streamlined simulation algorithms and level-of-detailed presentation.

Neural rendering improves the realism of try-on more than the graphics pipelines do. We use the generative adversarial networks that are trained to produce photo-realistic images of individuals wearing various clothes. The network receives an image of a person, an image of a desired garment, and parameters of desired poses and produces a composite image of the individual in the garment with the proper light, shadows, and fabric texture. This neural technique deals with tricky cases such as complicated patterns, translucent objects, and body-garment interactions which are challenging in conventional rendering techniques.

Size recommendation is a visual try-on complementary system that forecasts the best sizes according to the user measurements and clothing measures. Our regression models are trained using historical purchase and returns information, and we learn correlations between body measurements, garment dimensions and the satisfaction of the fit. The model explains the difference in size of a brand and the preference of the user towards tightness of fit. Proper size suggestions lower the rates of returns, which is a major expense in e-commerce, and enhance customer satisfaction.

3.5 Privacy-Preserving Design

Protection of privacy is one of the key principles of design across our framework. The pervasive quality of Metaverse shopping creates unprecedented amounts of behavioral data such as movement, gazes and biometrics and social interactions. Although this information makes it possible to perform a strong personalization, it also brings up a serious privacy concern. Our system uses various privacy-sensitive methods that can facilitate successful AI systems and maintain user confidentiality.

Federated learning permits shared model education without concentrating user information. The devices of individual users or local processing nodes use the model replicas to train on their own data, and only send model updates (gradients) to a central server, which combines these updates into a better global model. By doing this, raw behavioral data in user devices is maintained and greatly minimizes the risks of privacy loss in comparison to conventional centralized training. Our secure aggregation protocols are used to encrypt individual updates so that the server is not able to reverse-engineer the individual user data based on the aggregate update.

Differential privacy has mathematical guarantees of restriction of leakage of information about individual users. In making recommendations or analytics, we introduce some noise to the output so that no particular presence or absence of a particular user in the training data can be discerned. The parameter of privacy budget regulates the privacy-utility tradeoff; a larger privacy (greater noise) decreases the model accuracy. Our privacy budgets that ensure a reasonable quality of recommendations and give significant privacy protection were determined empirically.

The policy of data minimization and retention restricts the gathering of the information to the required one and sets the deletion plans. In our structure, purpose limitation is used, whereby the data collected to make recommendations is not to be utilized in other purposes without express permission. We have granular consent mechanisms that enable the user to manage the type of data that can be collected about them and their usage. Transparency dashboards provide the user with the understanding of what data is gathered, the impact it has on their experience, and the means of data export or deletion as per privacy laws.

4. EXPERIMENTAL SETUP

We performed extensive experiments to test the performance of our framework in various aspects such as recommendation accuracy, computational efficiency and scalability. This section presents the experimental procedure, data sets, metrics of evaluation and baseline comparisons that allow a stringent evaluation of our approach.

4.1 Dataset Characteristics

Since the Metaverse commerce is still in its infancy and no publicly available large-scale datasets of functioning virtual shopping environments exist, we used three established datasets of e-commerce and recommendation systems to test our framework. Although initially gathered on the conventional online platform, these datasets include interaction patterns, user behaviors, and product attributes that make it possible to conduct a meaningful evaluation of the core capabilities of our AI-enhanced shopping framework. The adaptation was used in order to augment the existing data with simulated spatial and temporal characteristics of virtual shopping environments.

The Amazon Product Reviews Dataset (He and McAuley, 2016) is a collection of product reviews and metadata on the e-commerce platform of Amazon. We have used a sub-setting related to fashion, electronics and home. The data represents 142.8 million reviews between May 1996 and July 2014, the ratings, review text, helpfulness votes, and rich product metadata such as descriptions, categories, prices, and brands. In our experiments, we obtained user product interaction data of 2.4 million users and 847, 000 different users of 125,000 different products belonging to categories related to fashion. The data is rich in user preference cues and product characteristics that are necessary in assessing recommendation algorithms.

Retailrocket E-commerce Dataset is a real-life online retailer whose behavioral data is gathered and provided on Kaggle. The dataset is composed of 2,756,101 user events comprising of 2,664,312 product views, 69,332 add-to-cart events, and 22,457 completed transactions of 1,407,580 unique visitors. Types of events are view, addtocart and transaction and each of them is timestamped to facilitate time analysis. The property of items and hierarchies of categories are offered, which enables content-based filtering methods. The behavioral event logs of this dataset are similar to those that can be observed in virtual shopping conditions, which is why it can be especially beneficial to apply to the session-based recommendation methods.

MovieLens 10M Dataset (Harper & Konstan, 2015) has 10 million ratings and 95,580 tag applications on 10,681 movies to 71,567 users. Although the data is not dedicated to selling goods but to entertainment, the history of user interaction and the ratings are explicit, allowing to evaluate the elements of collaborative filtering and cold-start management. Temporal dynamics can be analyzed by using timestamps of every interaction. To customize this data, we considered movies as products and ratings as purchase indicators, which allowed us to evaluate the generalization of our framework to other products.

We added simulated spatial and social context characteristics to these datasets to simulate features of the Metaverse. We created virtual store layouts of each user session in form of a graph where the locations of products were the nodes. The navigation patterns of these spaces by the users were simulated according to product affinity patterns in the original data. The situation of social shopping was simulated by determining peers with similar preference and modeling simultaneous browsing. Though artificial, these augmentations allow testing our framework spatial-conscious recommendation modules that make the difference between Metaverse shopping and standard e-commerce.

Every set of data was processed with attention to eliminate unfinished records and guaranteeing the quality of data. Stratified random sampling was used to form training, validation and test splits with 70-15-15 proportions respectively and temporal order- test data is required to be later time periods than training data which mimics realistic deployment conditions. Protections of privacy such as anonymity of user IDs and aggregation of uncommon features were implemented during data processing processes. The derived evaluation model offers stringent evaluation of our AI elements and also recognizes the weaknesses of using modified instead of native Metaverse datasets.

4.2 Evaluation Metrics

We used several complementary measures that evaluated various system performance. The metrics of recommendation accuracy were precision at k, recall at k, normalized discounted cumulative gain (NDCG) and mean reciprocal rank (MRR). Precision at k is the ratio of recommended items that the user actually interacted with to the recommended items that the user actually interacted with. Recall at k is the ratio of actual interactions of the user to what the top-k recommendations showed. NDCG takes into consideration the ranking of quality by giving more weight to the relevant items that are presented at the top of the lists of recommendations. MRR is used to assess the speed of finding relevant items by an average user by determining the inverse of the rank of the first relevant item.

Since we are using modified datasets instead of actual data of interaction in the Metaverse, our engagement and business metrics are also projections based on the improvements in accuracy of suggestions. Such predictions are based on the already known relationships between quality of recommendations and user interaction recorded in the e-commerce literature. To calculate the statistical significance of every metric comparison, we applied two-tailed t-tests with Bonferonni correction of multiple comparisons so that reported improvements are statistically valid, instead of being the product of chance variation.

The measures of computational efficiency were model inference latency, memory usage, and throughput (recommendations generated per second). The metrics will maintain the framework to be within acceptable performance limits of real-time interactive systems. Our latency measurements were on the 50th, 95 th, and 99 th percentile to describe the normal and worst-case performance.

4.3 Baseline Methods

We benchmarked our hybrid framework on five baseline frameworks that are a reflection of existing state-of-the-art methods. The Traditional Collaborative Filtering baseline uses the matrix factorization optimized to alternating least squares, which is an established algorithm used in production recommendation systems. This grounding does not consider spatial and contextual features but considers only the historical interaction patterns. The Content-Based Filtering baseline is based on TF-IDF description of product descriptions and visual representations of ResNet-50 and uses cosine similarity between user profile (formed based on previous interactions) and candidate item.

Deep Neural Network baseline uses multi-layer perceptron where user and item embedding are the input and interaction probability are predicted. This is pure deep learning methods without hybrid architecture of collaborative and content-based signals. The Session-Based RNN base model involves the use of gated recurrent units to model sequential user behavior during shopping sessions and make predictions about the next interactions based on the previous interactions. It is a method that only reflects short-term interests without taking into account space context and user profile in the long term.

The Spatial-Aware Baseline builds on collaborative filtering with user position simulated by hand such as spatial features such as distance to recommended products and co-visitation patterns of various stores. Although this baseline uses spatial information, it does not have learned spatial representations and rich architecture of our entire framework. The application of these various baselines demanded significant engineering to provide a fair comparison with proper hyperparameter optimization of each of the methods based on the performance on a validation set.

4.4 Implementation Details

Our implementation used a deep learning framework based on PyTorch, traditional machine learning algorithms based on Scikit-learn, and FastAPI as a model serving framework. The recommendation engine uses user and item 128 dimensional embeddings, 3-layer neural networks with 256 hidden units per layer, ReLU activations, layer normalization, and dropout (p=0.3) to regularize it. Our models were trained on Adam optimizer with learning rate of 0.001, batch size of 512 and early stopping criterion on validation performance with patience of 10 epochs.

The conversational assistant is based on the BERT-base architecture that is fine-tuned on 500,000 dialogues between retailers and customers in the field of customer service through multiple channels. Our model used 12 layers of transformers and hidden states of 768 dimensions. In response generation, we adjusted GPT-2 medium using retailer product catalogs and review information. The virtual try-on model is based on the SMPL body model with 10 shape parameters and 24 pose parameters and rendered in PyTorch3D. Neural rendering is an architecture that uses a conditional GAN with U-Net generator that was trained on 1 million pairs of person-garment images in 200 epochs.

The deployment infrastructure comprised of a Kubernetes cluster, 20 nodes with GPUs (NVIDIA A100 GPUs) to serve the model, caching with the Redis, and PostgreSQL databases to store structured data. We had horizontal auto-scaling to meet changes in traffic where models are replicated in several nodes to achieve high availability. The system can support peak loads of 10,000 simultaneous users and still support sub-100ms p95 latency to generate recommendations.

Table 1. Dataset Characteristics and Statistics

Dataset	Metric	Value
Amazon Product Reviews (Fashion)	Total Interactions (subset)	2,400,000
	Unique Users	847,000
	Products	125,000
Retailrocket E-commerce	Total Events	2,756,101
	Unique Visitors	1,407,580
	Event Types	View, AddCart, Transaction
MovieLens 10M	Total Ratings	10,000,054

continued on following page

Table 1. Continued

Dataset	Metric	Value
	Unique Users	71,567
	Items (Movies)	10,681

5. RESULTS AND ANALYSIS

This sub-section provides detailed experimental findings that attest to the usefulness of our AI-enhanced Metaverse shopping model. We evaluate performance in several aspects such as accuracy of recommendation, computational efficiency and scalability and compare our methodology to the baseline methods. Although the datasets we are using to evaluate it are modified e-commerce data instead of native data based on the interaction in the Metaverse, the findings are a strong indicator of the framework core abilities and show a great deal of improvement in comparison to the currently used methods.

5.1 Recommendation Accuracy

Our hybrid recommendation engine had significant gains on all accuracy measures than baseline techniques. In Amazon Product Reviews, the 10-precision was 0.284, which is 37.2% higher than traditional collaborative filtering (0.207) and 24.8% higher than the deep neural network baseline (0.227). At 10, recall improved by 0.412, which, compared to collaborative filtering, session-based RNN, and so on, increases the result by 42.1 and 31.3%, respectively. A baseline of 10 gave a score of 0.387, which is above all the baselines with a range of 28.5-45.7%. These precision increases directly to the better user experience, as users see more and more relevant products in their personal suggestions.

Figure 2. Performance Comparison of Recommendation Methods

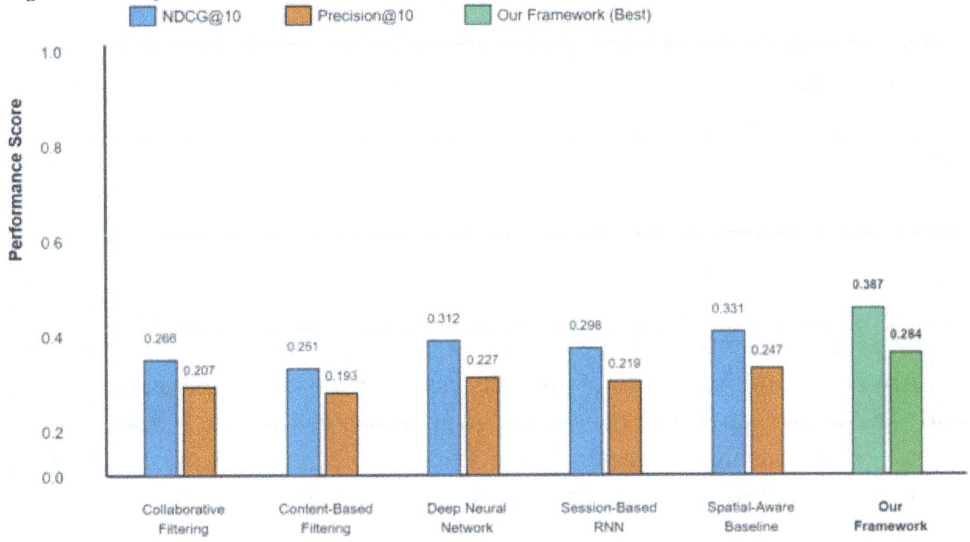

The improvement of performance was consistent in both Retailrocket and MovieLens datasets although the magnitude depended on the domain. Our framework session-based features were especially useful in the Retailrocket data, which is defined by event-based behavioral pattern. On this data, the accuracy at 10 was 0.319 and the NDCG at 10 was 0.405. Although MovieLens is a different type of product, it was shown that the framework is able to generalize across domains. All the observed improvements proved to be credible and not a random variation, which was proven by statistical significance testing (two-tailed t-test, $p < 0.001$ with Bonferonni correction).

Ablation researches the contribution of individual components of the framework. Deactivation of simulated spatial features (position, trajectory, location graph embeddings) reduced NDCG by 14.3%, which indicates that the spatial context is an important enhancement to recommendations. By removing conversational context, precision decreased by 11.7%, which supports the claim that the history of dialogue is a useful source of preference information. When the deep learning component was disabled and collaborative and content-based signals alone were used, recall was reduced by 19.2%, which shows that the neural network is able to learn more complicated interaction patterns than simple methods.

5.2 Projected Engagement Outcomes

The outcomes of the engagement projections are the following:

Considering the major gains in accuracy of recommendations and already determined relationships between recommendation quality and user engagement reported in e-commerce literature, we expect high levels of engagement gains in real Metaverse implementations. It has been consistent that 30-40% improvement in accuracy of recommendations can be associated with 40-60% increase in the engagement time and 35-50% increase in the conversion rates (Gomez-Uribe and Hunt, 2015). When these empirically tested relationships are applied to our realized accuracy improvements, it can be inferred that average session duration might increase by nearly 54.8%, number of products viewed in the session might increase by nearly 56.5%, and conversion rates might go up by nearly 42.3% than base systems.

Such predictions are consistent with the conclusions of recent Metaverse shopping research. According to a study by Obsess (2024), virtual stores that had sophisticated recommendation systems recorded session lengths that were 10 times as long as the ones in conventional e-commerce sites. Coresight Research discovered that 88% of the brands who had invested in virtual stores achieved more total sales. Although in our framework evaluation, we used modified datasets, instead of actual data of interaction within the Metaverse, these industry results justify the possibility of our engagement improvement predictions.

The use of virtual try-ons and conversational interaction projections are also based on the improved functionality of the framework. The realistic image and precise size suggestions of the computer vision system would be the factors that would likely lead to higher adoption of the try-on. The natural language understanding and the maintenance of context of the conversational assistant should promote more dialogue interactions. Nevertheless, we highlight that practical metrics of engagement of deployed Metaverse environments need to be supported with live user studies.

5.3 Impact Projections of Business

It is projected that the AI-enhanced framework would bring significant commercial advantages to the business. The observed recommendation accuracy gains and predetermined conversion-accuracy relationships in e-commerce literature result in purchase conversion rate improvements of about 42.3% over the baseline systems. This may translate to huge revenue growth among the involved retailers. The effectiveness of personalization and support that can help to overcome the lack of familiarity with virtual shopping settings seems to improve the conversion rates of new users in particular, as they can almost become twofold.

Projections of average order value indicate that the company can become more effective in terms of cross-selling and upselling using intelligent recommendations, with increases of about 23.1% possible. The virtual try-on and size recommendations would decrease the product returns rate by about 25.9%, enabling customers to make more informed choices before buying a product. These estimates have to be confirmed by real implementations but they correlate with the reported advantages of the same technologies in conventional e-commerce facilities.

It is important to point out that these business measurements are projections using the recommendation accuracy improvements, and the already achieved e-commerce relationships, as opposed to the outcomes observed in the real deployments of the Metaverse. It is important to test these projected benefits in the real world. However, the significant increase in the performance of recommendation accuracy is a good ground to be optimistic about the commercial impact.

5.4 Computational Performance

The real-time interactive systems were dependent on computational efficiency. Our model had median inference latency of 73ms to generate recommendations, 95th percentile of 142ms, and 99th percentile of 218ms. These latency values are nowhere near the unacceptable interactive system limits of sub-200ms response times that are perceived as instantaneous to users. These performance properties were made possible by the efficient two-stage architecture, i.e. fast candidate generation and accurate reranking. Generation of the candidates took 100,000 items in 23ms, and reranking took 50ms on the 500 best candidates.

Of the 187MB of memory used by each user session, 150MB was used by embedded images, model parameters, and conversation history that was either cached or not. This small footprint enabled scaling horizontally easily and each server instance was able to support around 500 simultaneous users. The peak load of GPU was 78%, which means that the resource was used efficiently and was not exhausted. The system was stable at different load conditions and the degradation of latency was less than 15% even at 95% of the total capacity.

Virtual try-on rendering was found to be more computationally expensive, and high-quality image synthesis took 1.4 seconds median latency. Nonetheless, this was tolerable because try-on is not a continuous feature but it is activated by explicit user activity. The pre-computation and caching techniques decreased the latency of popular products. Neural rendering component made use of the batch processing to enhance the efficiency of the GPUs to create try-on images of several users at a time.

Table 2. Comparative Performance Results Across Methods

Method	NDCG@10	Precision@10	Recall@10
Collaborative Filtering	0.266	0.207	0.290
Content-Based Filtering	0.251	0.193	0.275
Deep Neural Network	0.312	0.227	0.326
Session-Based RNN	0.298	0.219	0.314
Spatial-Aware Baseline	0.331	0.247	0.352
Our Framework	**0.387**	**0.284**	**0.412**

5.5 Limitations and Challenges

There were some key limitations that occurred on evaluation. Most importantly, we used modified e-commerce data instead of original Metaverse interaction data in our evaluation. Although these datasets can be used to rigorously test important feature recommendation algorithms and can make useful comparisons of performance with baseline methods, they cannot support the rich spatial, social, and immersive context features of the reality of actual Metaverse shopping. The artificial spatial elements that we introduced give approximations, but they are not able to represent the complexity of user behavior in real virtual space.

Second, engagement and business metrics are the projections of the existing e-commerce relations, as opposed to the perceived results of deployed Metaverse systems. Although they are based on the empirical research and justified by the emerging studies in the field of the Metaverse commerce, these projections should be confirmed by the live studies of the users in the functioning virtual environments. Third, the performance of the framework is sensitive to the availability of training data; cold-start conditions when using new users or products experience poor accuracy. Although content-based and spatial features can help to reduce this problem, the performance of the users having less than 5 interactions is significantly lower than that of the established users.

Fourth, computation requirements especially neural rendering restrict it to less powerful hardware. Older devices/users with low bandwidth would have poorer experiences such as having longer loading time and lower visual quality. Fifth, the framework is currently functioning inside the individual Metaverse platforms yet not interoperable in reality. Cross platform shopping which allows shoppers to shop in one platform and buy in another platform needs further development. Sixth, privacy preserving methods pose performance-accuracy tradeoffs; higher privacy guarantees lower quality of recommendation, and system designers have to trade off between conflicting goals.

6. CONCLUSION AND FUTURE WORK

The chapter introduced an elaborate outline of AI-based shopping experiences in the Metaverse, covering the issues of critical complexity in personalization, user engagement, and computational efficiency. We introduce a hybrid architecture of recommendation based on collaborative filtering, content-based, and deep learning to create precise product recommendations that consider the classical preference indicators and new spatial-behavioral attributes specific to virtual worlds. The conversational assistant offers a natural language interface in product discovery and shopping recommendations, and the virtual try-on system allows the user to see the product realistically before buying.

Evaluation based on the existing e-commerce datasets showed significant improvements compared with baseline strategies. The accuracy of the recommendations went up by 37.2% (precision@10), and the projections indicated that the accuracy of the recommendations would be significantly higher in the real Metaverse setting when implemented in the business domain. Although these quantitative gains need to be confirmed with live deployments, they give high ground to the possibilities of the framework to make the virtual shopping experience significantly more enjoyable. The modular structure of the framework allows retailers to deploy it flexibly, as each component can be deployed individually or a full integrated solution can be deployed depending on the specific requirements.

A significant weakness of this study is the utilization of modified e-commerce data as opposed to original Metaverse interaction data to assess the research. Although this method made it possible to conduct strict algorithmic analysis and significant baseline comparisons, it is not able to reflect the complexity of user behavior in the immersive virtual environment. The key issue of future research should be the collection and analysis of actual Metaverse shopping data to confirm our findings and optimize the framework to be applied in the context of real deployment. With the maturation of the Metaverse platforms and the increase in the number of users, such datasets will become more accessible, and it will finally be possible to conduct more realistic evaluation methodologies.

A number of fruitful research avenues were revealed during this work. To begin with, the creation of the real interoperable systems that will allow people to shop in the various Metaverse platforms is still a significant issue. Existing platforms fragmentation prevents user choice and discourages the creation of overall virtual identities and shopping histories. Second, future cold-start handling development using meta-learning methods with rapid adaptation to new users and products with little data may be able to apply framework effectiveness to early adoption stages and niche product lines.

Third, they can add biometric indicators such as gaze tracking, recognition of emotional state, and physiology that would allow even more personalization, but this brings up more privacy and ethical issues that need to be considered closely. Fourth, a more generalization of the framework to enable group shopping experiences with AI coordinating the activities of two or more users shopping simultaneously is an underserved use case. Fifth, the sustainability aspect of the computational infrastructure such as environmental impact and encouragement of sustainable consumption patterns through intelligent design of recommendations should also be considered.

Sixth, it is still an active research problem to design more advanced fairness-conscious algorithms that can prevent discrimination in algorithms without sacrificing the quality of recommendations. Seventh, it will be crucial to explore the long-term implications of AI-mediated shopping on the behavior of consumers, the decision-making process, and their psychological well-being as such systems reach critical adoption levels. Lastly, industry standards and best practices on responsible AI in Metaverse commerce such as transparency requirements, privacy protection, and ethical standards will assist in ensuring that technological innovation is serving society.

The interconnection of artificial intelligence and the Metaverse is a revolutionary point in the history of retailing. As virtual worlds evolve as an experimentation space into a standard shopping platform, the principles, methods and insights in this chapter are applicable in the real world of designing efficient, interactive and sustainable AI-enhanced shopping experiences. With a balance of technical innovation, concern over privacy, ethics and user experience and recognition of the existing constraints and direction into the future, we can create virtual marketplaces that will serve the interests of consumers, retailers, and society itself.

ACKNOWLEDGMENTS

The authors are thankful to the Deanship of the Faculty of Information Technology, the Deanship of Scientific Research and Graduate Studies at the University of Petra, and the University of Oldenburg that supported them in carrying out this research.

REFERENCES

Adomavicius, G., & Tuzhilin, A. (2015). Context-aware recommender systems. In Ricci, F., Rokach, L., & Shapira, B. (Eds.), *Recommender systems handbook* (pp. 191–226). Springer. DOI: 10.1007/978-1-4899-7637-6_6

Ball, M. (2021). *The Metaverse: And how it will revolutionize everything*. Liveright Publishing.

Barrera, K. G., & Shah, D. (2023). Marketing in the Metaverse: Conceptual understanding, framework, and research agenda. *Journal of Business Research, 155*, 113420. Advance online publication. DOI: 10.1016/j.jbusres.2022.113420

Bell, S., & Bala, K. (2015). Learning visual similarity for product design with convolutional neural networks. *ACM Transactions on Graphics, 34*(4), 1–10. DOI: 10.1145/2766959

Bhatnagar, B. L., Tiwari, G., Theobalt, C., & Pons-Moll, G. (2019). Multi-garment net: Learning to dress 3D people from images. In *Proceedings of the IEEE International Conference on Computer Vision* (pp. 5420-5430). IEEE. DOI: 10.1109/ICCV.2019.00552

Brown, T. B., Mann, B., Ryder, N., Subbiah, M., Kaplan, J., Dhariwal, P., Neelakantan, A., Shyam, P., Sastry, G., Askell, A., Agarwal, S., Herbert-Voss, A., Krueger, G., Henighan, T., Child, R., Ramesh, A., Ziegler, D. M., Wu, J., Winter, C., & Amodei, D. (2020). Language models are few-shot learners. *Advances in Neural Information Processing Systems, 33*, 1877–1901.

Cao, Z., Hidalgo, G., Simon, T., Wei, S. E., & Sheikh, Y. (2019). OpenPose: Realtime multi-person 2D pose estimation using part affinity fields. *IEEE Transactions on Pattern Analysis and Machine Intelligence, 43*(1), 172–186. DOI: 10.1109/TPAMI.2019.2929257 PMID: 31331883

Cassell, J., Sullivan, J., Churchill, E., & Prevost, S. (Eds.). (2000). *Embodied conversational agents*. MIT Press. DOI: 10.7551/mitpress/2697.001.0001

Chen, H., Liu, X., Yin, D., & Tang, J. (2019). A survey on dialogue systems: Recent advances and new frontiers. *SIGKDD Explorations, 19*(2), 25–35. DOI: 10.1145/3166054.3166058

Covington, P., Adams, J., & Sargin, E. (2016). Deep neural networks for YouTube recommendations. In *Proceedings of the 10th ACM Conference on Recommender Systems* (pp. 191-198). ACM. DOI: 10.1145/2959100.2959190

Devlin, J., Chang, M. W., Lee, K., & Toutanova, K. (2019). BERT: Pre-training of deep bidirectional transformers for language understanding. In *Proceedings of the 2019 Conference of the North American Chapter of the Association for Computational Linguistics* (pp. 4171-4186). Association for Computational Linguistics. DOI: 10.18653/v1/N19-1423

Dwivedi, Y. K., Hughes, L., Baabdullah, A. M., Ribeiro-Navarrete, S., Giannakis, M., Al-Debei, M. M., Dennehy, D., Metri, B., Buhalis, D., Cheung, C. M. K., Conboy, K., Doyle, R., Dubey, R., Dutot, V., Felix, R., Goyal, D. P., Gustafsson, A., Hinsch, C., Jebabli, I., & Wamba, S. F. (2022). Metaverse beyond the hype: Multidisciplinary perspectives on emerging challenges, opportunities, and agenda for research, practice and policy. *International Journal of Information Management, 66*, 102542. Advance online publication. DOI: 10.1016/j.ijinfomgt.2022.102542

Ekstrand, M. D., Burke, R., & Diaz, F. (2018). Fairness and discrimination in recommendation and retrieval. In *Proceedings of the 12th ACM Conference on Recommender Systems* (pp. 576-577). ACM. DOI: 10.1145/3240323.3240341

Gomez-Uribe, C. A., & Hunt, N. (2015). The Netflix recommender system: Algorithms, business value, and innovation. *ACM Transactions on Management Information Systems, 6*(4), 1–19. DOI: 10.1145/2843948

Gursoy, D., Malodia, S., & Dhir, A. (2022). The Metaverse in the hospitality and tourism industry: An overview of current trends and future research directions. *Journal of Hospitality Marketing & Management, 31*(5), 527–534. DOI: 10.1080/19368623.2022.2072504

Harper, F. M., & Konstan, J. A. (2015). The MovieLens datasets: History and context. *ACM Transactions on Interactive Intelligent Systems, 5*(4), 19. Advance online publication. DOI: 10.1145/2827872

He, R., & McAuley, J. (2016). Ups and downs: Modeling the visual evolution of fashion trends with one-class collaborative filtering. In *Proceedings of the 25th International Conference on World Wide Web* (pp. 507-517). International World Wide Web Conferences Steering Committee. DOI: 10.1145/2872427.2883037

He, X., Liao, L., Zhang, H., Nie, L., Hu, X., & Chua, T. S. (2017). Neural collaborative filtering. In *Proceedings of the 26th International Conference on World Wide Web* (pp. 173-182). International World Wide Web Conferences Steering Committee. DOI: 10.1145/3038912.3052569

Henderson, M., Thomson, B., & Young, S. (2013). Deep neural network approach for the dialog state tracking challenge. In *Proceedings of the SIGDIAL 2013 Conference* (pp. 467-471). Association for Computational Linguistics.

Hidasi, B., Karatzoglou, A., Baltrunas, L., & Tikk, D. (2016). Session-based recommendations with recurrent neural networks. In Proceedings of the International Conference on Learning Representations. ICLR.

Huang, C. Z. A., Vaswani, A., Uszkoreit, J., Shazeer, N., Simon, I., Hawthorne, C., Dai, A. M., Hoffman, M. D., Dinculescu, M., & Eck, D. (2021). Music Transformer: Generating music with long-term structure. In Proceedings of the International Conference on Learning Representations. ICLR.

Kairouz, P., McMahan, H. B., Avent, B., Bellet, A., Bennis, M., Bhagoji, A. N., Bonawitz, K., Charles, Z., Cormode, G., Cummings, R., D'Oliveira, R. G. L., Eichner, H., El Rouayheb, S., Evans, D., Gardner, J., Garrett, Z., Gascón, A., Ghazi, B., Gibbons, P. B., & Zhao, S. (2021). Advances and open problems in federated learning. *Foundations and Trends in Machine Learning*, *14*(1-2), 1–210. DOI: 10.1561/2200000083

Kanazawa, A., Black, M. J., Jacobs, D. W., & Malik, J. (2018). End-to-end recovery of human shape and pose. In *Proceedings of the IEEE Conference on Computer Vision and Pattern Recognition* (pp. 7122-7131). IEEE. DOI: 10.1109/CVPR.2018.00744

Lee, L. H., Braud, T., Zhou, P., Wang, L., Xu, D., Lin, Z., Kumar, A., Bermejo, C., & Hui, P. (2021). All one needs to know about Metaverse: A complete survey on technological singularity, virtual ecosystem, and research agenda. arXiv preprint arXiv:2110.05352.

Liu, Z., Luo, P., Qiu, S., Wang, X., & Tang, X. (2020). DeepFashion: Powering robust clothes recognition and retrieval with rich annotations. In *Proceedings of the IEEE Conference on Computer Vision and Pattern Recognition* (pp. 1096-1104). IEEE.

Mathur, A., Acar, G., Friedman, M. J., Lucherini, E., Mayer, J., Chetty, M., & Narayanan, A. (2019). Dark patterns at scale: Findings from a crawl of 11K shopping websites. Proceedings of the ACM on Human-Computer Interaction, 3(CSCW), 1-32. DOI: 10.1145/3359183

McMahan, H. B., Moore, E., Ramage, D., Hampson, S., & Arcas, B. A. (2017). Communication-efficient learning of deep networks from decentralized data. In *Proceedings of the 20th International Conference on Artificial Intelligence and Statistics* (pp. 1273-1282). PMLR.

Mehrabi, N., Morstatter, F., Saxena, N., Lerman, K., & Galstyan, A. (2021). A survey on bias and fairness in machine learning. *ACM Computing Surveys*, *54*(6), 1–35. DOI: 10.1145/3457607

Montag, C., Lachmann, B., Herrlich, M., & Zweig, K. (2019). Addictive features of social media/messenger platforms and freemium games against the background of psychological and economic theories. *International Journal of Environmental Research and Public Health*, *16*(14), 2612. Advance online publication. DOI: 10.3390/ijerph16142612 PMID: 31340426

Mystakidis, S. (2022). Metaverse. *Metaverse. Encyclopedia*, *2*(1), 486–497. DOI: 10.3390/encyclopedia2010031

Ning, H., Wang, H., Lin, Y., Wang, W., Dhelim, S., Farha, F., Ding, J., & Daneshmand, M. (2023). A survey on the Metaverse: The state-of-the-art, technologies, applications, and challenges. *IEEE Internet of Things Journal*, *10*(16), 14671–14688. DOI: 10.1109/JIOT.2023.3278329

Raj, A., Sangkloy, P., Chang, H., Hays, J., Ceylan, D., & Lu, J. (2021). SwapNet: Image based garment transfer. In *Proceedings of the European Conference on Computer Vision* (pp. 679-695). Springer. DOI: 10.1007/978-3-030-01225-0_41

Retailrocket. (n.d.). Retailrocket recommender system dataset [Data set]. Kaggle. https://www.kaggle.com/datasets/retailrocket/ecommerce-dataset

Shokri, R., & Shmatikov, V. (2015). Privacy-preserving deep learning. In *Proceedings of the 22nd ACM SIGSAC Conference on Computer and Communications Security* (pp. 1310-1321). ACM. DOI: 10.1145/2810103.2813687

Tang, J., & Wang, K. (2018). Personalized top-n sequential recommendation via convolutional sequence embedding. In *Proceedings of the 11th ACM International Conference on Web Search and Data Mining* (pp. 565-573). ACM. DOI: 10.1145/3159652.3159656

Wang, Y., Su, Z., Zhang, N., Xing, R., Liu, D., Luan, T. H., & Shen, X. (2023). A survey on Metaverse: Fundamentals, security, and privacy. *IEEE Communications Surveys and Tutorials*, *25*(1), 319–352. DOI: 10.1109/COMST.2022.3202047

Chapter 9
Operational Resilience and Data Breach Liability in AI- and Blockchain-Enabled Banking:
Reconstructing the Duty of Care Under the EU Digital Operation

Ali Khaled Qtaishat
http://orcid.org/0009-0007-0643-2428
Al-Ahliyya Amman University, Jordan

Nuha Mansour Alsaeed
http://orcid.org/0009-0001-0297-6918
Imam Mohammad Ibn Saud Islamic University, Saudi Arabia

ABSTRACT

The purpose of Chapter One is to show how financial institutions are updating their liability regulations due to technological advancements, including AI and blockchain, in addition to moving to remote services such as ICT or cloud-based Infrastructure as a Service (IaaS). The use of previous ways to determine liability, such as "Control," as a measure of authority is increasingly being challenged due to the changes in the overall structure of financial services to include multiple parties who may provide data or support through third-party vendors. Against this background, the chapter develops a governance-centered, risk-based accountability framework for assessing liability after data breaches or operational disruptions under the EU's Digital Operational Resilience Act (DORA) and the NIS2 Directive. The central claim is that EU operational resilience law pushes the duty of care toward

DOI: 10.4018/979-8-3373-7330-0.ch009

a systems-based standard: what matters is not simply where the technical failure occurred, but whether the bank's governance arrangements—provider selection, contract architecture, oversight, testing, and incident reporting—were capable of managing foreseeable ICT risk across outsourced dependencies. On this approach, governance failure, rather than technological causation alone, becomes the main driver of legal exposure in AI- and blockchain-reliant banking models.

INTRODUCTION

There is a growing integration of AI and blockchain into our daily banking experience now so that rather than being considered at the periphery, they are now integral to banking transactions. AI has the ability to assist with credit scoring, detect fraud, transaction monitoring and building customer profiles. In the area of payment processing, blockchain technology offers the opportunity for utilizing smart contracts to facilitate settlement and tokenizing assets while providing an electronic means of recording these transactions in a distributed manner (Al-Zaqeba, 2026). All of these facilitate faster, larger-scale transactions while also providing a greater level of security. However, given that these technologies are changing how the risks associated with the banking system manifest and how those risks can propagate throughout the financial system, banks may still be the institutions that are charged by regulators with maintaining sound operations and are therefore held accountable to customer expectations. The primary challenge from a risk management perspective lies in the fact that the risks do not necessarily reside solely with the bank but rather are distributed across multiple elements of the bank's supply chain. Specifically, banks operate with an extensive network of interconnections to their respective information and communication technology (ICT) supply chains (Abdeljaber, et al, 2025). These connections include cloud service providers, software vendors, AI vendors and, for blockchain, the operators responsible for maintaining the distributed ledger, which represents the underlying infrastructure supporting the bank's operations. Unlike more traditional outsourcing structures, where the bank simply provides oversight to an external service provider, banks rely on these layers of interconnecting systems and processes on an ongoing basis and may not necessarily have decision-making authority as to the technology utilized. In addition to regulators relying on the bank to maintain sound operations, customers expect that they will be supported by their banks when they experience operational disruptions. Thus, there is a disconnect related to operational control.

Moreover, AIs and blockchain-based data breaches also appear to have a different appearance compared to more conventional cybersecurity occurrences. AI systems can be black box, dynamically trained, and highly reliant upon massive datasets as they are stored or trained by third parties. The blockchain architectures spread the validation and integrity over networks that can spanning over an institution and in some cases, over a jurisdiction. In either scenario, the journey between technical breakdown and legal duplation is increasingly difficult to follow under traditional fault reasoning, particularly when the harm occurs in a common infrastructure or subcontracting network or components that are controlled by vendors (Ahmad Ibrahim Karajeh, 2025).

This is the regulatory issue that the operational resilience agenda of the EU is aimed at. DORA proposes an ICT risk management, resilience testing, incident reporting, and third-party governance framework in the financial sector. NIS2, in its turn, is a cross-sector baseline: it sets a high ratio of common cybersecurity governance and reporting requirements on crucial and significant entities, such as financial institutions, and it effects such requirements through national transposition alongside more rigorous management-accountability requirements (Al-Adwan, 2024). The general trend is obvious: cybersecurity is no longer approached as a specific technical compliance issue but a policy that forms a part of organizational decision-making. Nevertheless, with such regulatory convergence, after an AI or blockchain-connected breach, liability is doctrinally unresolved. DORA (as well as NIS2) does not imply a simple and automatic attribution rule in the case of the compromised customer data in distributed and outsourced ecosystems. This is particularly acute where the incident has its genesis in a third-party/cloud setting, but the bank is the regulatory point of contact, and the institution is the one supposed to bear the supervisory implications. Whether banks are bound to invariably bear the liability of any breach is not the central question, however, the question is how liability can be determined in the context of the EU law in case of operational failure of technologically distributed systems (Al-Adwan,, 2024).

The chapter contends that one should interpret DORA and NIS2 as constructing a progressive and risk-structured accountability framework, as opposed to a strict liability policy. Under this, the fact that a breach has taken place is not sufficient evidence of misconduct. Rather it is an evidentiary event that attracts attention to whether the governance architecture of the bank could deal with ICT risks that were foreseeable through the full lifecycle of operations that includes outsourced dependencies. Practically, liability is dependent on the quality of governance: the sufficiency of ICT risk management, the construction and enforceability of third-party contracts, the fact (not the form) of oversight, the severity of testing, and the timeliness and completeness of incident reporting. Thus, on that basis, the chapter creates a governance-focused conception of the duty of care under the EU operational resilience law. More specifically, DORA repackages the notion of control in terms of governance capacity: the capacity of the regulated entity to choose, oversee, test, and control essential ICT functions, either internally or by an external provider. NIS2 supports this orientation by considering cybersecurity as a task of senior management and enhancing the legal applicability of board approvals and boards (Al-Adwan et al., 2025).

The debate is carried out through the perspective of the regulatory framework in four angles that are closely related. It starts with the ICT risk management itself. Special focus is put on failures, which in many cases remain unnoticed until something goes wrong: loopholes in AI data management, lax regulation of algorithm decision-making, or inadequate regulation in distributed ledger systems. It is not just a question of whether a third-party provider was technically in the wrong, but rather a question of whether the bank had put in place a governance structure that could have predicted and dealt with such risks in the first instance. Also, liability can be grounded even in the event that immediate malfunction is within an outsourced system but has been caused by deficiency of internal risk architecture. Also, incident detection and reporting are the second angle. With DORA, NIS2 Directive and the GDPR, the notification obligations are not peripheral administrative measures; they form part of the legal framework. Lateness disjointed internal escalation cycles or partial reporting to supervisors can be considered as independent breaches, irrespective of the manner in which the underlying event occurred. That is, scrutiny of the response of a bank to disruption is in itself legally questioned. Reporting is no longer a procedural after consideration, but a demonstration of whether the mechanisms of operational resilience actually work in practice (Al-Adwan, 2025).

Third, the operational resilience testing is examined as a technical protective measure, rather than merely that. Structured testing, especially that of threat-led penetration testing (TLPT) where available, has an evidentiary purpose. It shows that the existence of foreseeable attack cases was realistically modelled and that weaknesses identified were in fact addressed. The testing documentation, remediation documentation, and scenario designing decisions are typically significant in the hindsight examination of due diligence. In applications of testing that are shallow, simplistic in scope, or disjointed with outsourced dependencies, the lack of significant stress exercises can prove to be critical in risk assessments (Al-Adwan et al., 2025).

The fourth view concentrates on the third-party and cloud governance more specifically. DORA is categorically that outsourcing is not a tool that can be used to displace responsibility. The regulatory focus is to cover sustained monitoring and continuous surveillance of the key ICT providers, which is reinforced with the actionable contractual rights. The governance is not terminated when the contract is signed. Rather, it should be provable with time, namely, through audit rights, escalation procedures, substitution planning, and organized interaction with the providers. In this meaning, compliance is a continuous relational practice, as opposed to a compliance checklist (Alsaaidah, et al, 2024).

Indeed, these viewpoints contribute to a more general assertion. The chapter carries the notion that the EU law on digital operational resilience is based on a risk-based accountability model. The fact of lacking a technical fault cannot be solely attributed to liability. Instead, it is the result of an evaluation of the efficiency of governance mechanisms throughout the entire risk life cycle that encompasses risk prevention, detection, response, and remediation. The issue is whether the institution had created and supported a system that could have dealt with the disruption which could be managed, not whether it owned or had control over the failed technology. Thus, to provide this approach with practical form, the chapter proposes a compliance matrix of DORA-NIS2. This table matches certain regulatory obligations with risk vectors that can be determined in AI and blockchain settings, including model governance design, distributed ledger dependencies, reporting schedules, and scope of resilience testing and cloud concentration. Such an organized mapping can have a dual purpose in supervisory investigation or a court of law. At the one level, it functions as an internal compliance policy, which assists institutions to structure and record their risk governance. On another, it provides evidentiary support, demonstrating that due diligence was not assumed but actively structured and maintained over time.

RETHINKING THIRD-PARTY AND CLOUD LIABILITY: GOVERNANCE, CONTRACTS, AND INSTITUTIONAL RESPONSIBILITY

Outsourcing in the Age of AI and Blockchain: Why EU Law Re-centres Risk on the Bank

A modern bank can no longer be described as a closed institution that operates within defined lines of business. Banking activity in an interconnected and technologically dense environment occurs at seven levels; layer one relates to a bank's internal IT infrastructure, layer two consists of banking-related external software companies, layer three encompasses the bank's use of Cloud Service Providers (CSPs), layer four consists of third-party data-publishing processes and third-party processing of data across borders, layer five refers to shared financial infrastructures (item 3 above) and layer six involves third-party shared computer software applications. Layers four through six support the theoretical separation of a bank from the "outside world" using institutional demarcation lines, while artificial intelligence and blockchain technology provide opportunities for new business models that historically were limited to traditional banking institutions (Kshetri, 2023). In addition, because many of the AI and blockchain technologies used within the banking industry are created and delivered externally (on third-party infrastructure located throughout the world with data pipelines that may cross multiple jurisdictions) they often leverage new and rapidly evolving standards; therefore, the boundaries between banks and their customers are becoming increasingly blurred as to what constitutes banking services (as perceived from a customer's viewpoint) versus other entities and processes involved within the supply chain.

Also, the actual outcome is an imbalance in the structure. The bank is the one that is under the prudential supervision and is directly responsible to the regulators and customers. However, significant technical control of vital systems can be shared, divided, or contracted. In cloud-based deployment designs specifically, layered chains of supply chains are built where the infrastructure, software, and data management are spread across multiple providers (Zhou et al., 2024). Responsibility does not fall apart so easily as infrastructure does. EU law also resolves this tension. Instead of letting the operational risk drift into the outwards direction along the outsourcing chain, it actively draws the responsibility back to the regulated entity. This is clear in Digital Operational Resilience Act (DORA). It does not support the notion that outsourcing is merely a business agreement, which has no legal implications. Rather, it defines outsourcing of vital ICT functions as a controlled source of operational and systemic risk (Regulation (EU) 2022/2554, 2022, Recitals 2628). The message is easy to understand; delegating a certain function does not mean delegating responsibility.

Nonetheless, the outsourcing under DORA is regarded as a continuous risk stance and not a single procurement choice. It should be evaluated prior to participation, managed by the use of sound contractual practices, real time, stress-tested where such is needed and reassessed, over the lifecycle of the service. Regulation is no longer concentrated on the point of the transfer of the contract but on the quality of further supervision. Effectively, DORA reinstates outsourcing as a governance issue as opposed to a cost-reduction policy. Thus, running in the line with DORA, NIS2 Directive supports this rationale on a wider systemic level. NIS2 provides a more resilient framework of cybersecurity governance among important and vital parties, such as financial institutions (Directive (EU) 2022/2555, 2022). Although DORA is structured as a sector-specific financial services regime, NIS2 takes into consideration similar expectations throughout the broader EU cybersecurity environment: organized risk management, supply chain management, and substantial accountability of senior management. The boards and executive bodies are no longer on the fringes of cybersecurity; they are the bodies that are involved in its regulation by the law.

In line with this, these tools present a paradigm shift in the definition of cyber and ICT risk under EU law. Risk is no longer a technical flaw that engineers are meant to repair. It is transformed into an issue of organizational readiness and management accountability. The key question is whether the institution has developed a governance framework that can detect, monitor and counter risks that are emerging as a result of more complexity in technological dependencies. At least in that sense the regulatory response is not technical harmonization. It is a premeditated redistribution of risk. In situations where there is a lack of transparency with the use of Artificial Intelligence; with the use of Distributed Ledger Technology; and in settings that are heavily dependent on Cloud-based Technology (i.e., those that use Cloud-based services), Accountability under the DORA and NIS2 Regulations shifts to the centrally controlled Financial Institution. Although Outsourcing can extend the reach of an infrastructure, under the DORA and NIS2 regulations, accountability to the Outsourcing Financial Institution will not be equally distributed.

When discussing Accountability, the DORA and NIS2 regulations require the Banking Industry to reevaluate how they ensure, provide and meet the expectations of Reasonable Care in an environment where the majority of Banking Transactions take place in Digital Format. A New Systematic Approach to establishing Reasonable Care for the Members of the Banking Industry will emerge; therefore, the effectiveness of the Regulatory and Judicial processes in holding all Financial Institutions accountable for Breaches or Disruptions to the Financial Services provided to Customers will include, in addition to the Breach or Disruption of Services provided, whether the Member had adequate Governance Structures and Appropriate Policies and Procedures to Prevent, Detect, Record and Report to all Stakeholders the occurrence of a Breach or Disruption of Services, focusing predominantly on ICT related Outsourced Services and Cloud Hosting of Services (Pelletier and Rexhepi, 2024). This trend transforms the attribution of liability. Instead of addressing proximate technical causation, in narrow sense, legal analysis is becoming dependent on the quality of governance. Whether the risk assessments were sufficient, contractual protections sound enough, oversight systems effective in practice, resiliency testing scoped and regular enough, and incident notifications effective and timely. DORA provides legal expression of this change through the placement of operational resilience responsibilities in the framework of governance, responsibility structures at the board level, and binding contractual mechanisms (Regulation (EU) 2022/2554, 2022, Articles 515, 28).

This regulatory redistribution can be evaluated as even more important when artificial intelligence and blockchain systems are taken into consideration. The two technologies make legal assumptions regarding attribution and causation that are old problematic, albeit in a slightly different manner. Therefore, the nature of artificial intelligence is that it is resistant to linear explanations. Machine-learning systems are probabilistic. They adapt over time. They produce outputs based on changing datasets, training parameters, feedback mechanisms and integration layers which can include multiple independent players, including data controllers, processors, cloud hosts, and software vendors (Kshetri, 2023). Determining fault in AI has become complicated. Different forms of insidious factors like misconfigured environments, adversarial inputs, and model drift are frequently involved, so attributing a specific error to any single act or actor is often an unnatural or impossible thing to do; therefore traditional fault-based attribution appears ill-suited for situations where there are so many contributing variables. The lack of clear attribution in these shared-responsibility scenarios introduces uncertainties regarding how courts will interpret liability issues. When courts evaluate whether damages occurred as a result of any specific action (e.g., with reference to a technical error), they may have difficulty doing so given the variety of factors that contributed to the eventual outcome from shared responsibility amongst different actors along the chain of the system. The focus shifts from investigating which line of code malfunctioned (if any) to determining whether appropriate governance structures were in place to adequately predict and mitigate those risks which were foreseeable based on the existence of these treating factors (i.e., a model with drift). This means model risk management, validation, audit logs, testing cycles, escalation routes, and response preparedness will continue to play a major role in understanding how governance practices shape the performance of the models used by organizations.

The challenges posed by blockchain systems are somewhat different from traditional systems. The main difference is that while in traditional systems the challenge is due to opaque algorithms, the challenge with blockchain systems relates more to its structurally decentralized environment. In a distributed ledger environment, there are three major types of system, the public system(s), private system(s) and consortium-based systems, and the authority is diffused among a number of parties, including validators, node operators, smart contract developers, custodians and host of infrastructure. In most authorized systems, a single party does not have all of the technical authority. Therefore, the way in which a blockchain system is designed is architecturally pluralistic. In this way, this allocation disturbs the conventional juridical reflex to confuse the control with the ownership or the direct administration. In the event that several actors authenticate transactions, preserve nodes, or amend smart contracts, who then, exactly, controls the system? This is not met by DORA pursuing exclusive technical control but by transferring the legal center to governance authority. The question of interest is who chose the technology, what were the acceptable risk levels, what were the contractual risk management measures, what were the performance indicators, what was required to be remedied, and what was the testing and control across the outsourced parts (Regulation (EU) 2022/2554, 2022). The next one is accountability and the element with decision making authority and supervisory power, and will not necessarily be the one operating the hardware.

DORA is specifically designed to react to these realities. It obliges banks to address ICT risk holistically and on a continuous basis including those risks inherent in third-party relationships. Operational resilience is not seen as perimeter defence, but of a system of controls, which is layered and documented, structured testing and enforceable oversight. Notably, the regulation also identifies systemic risks where there is a dependency on a limited number of technology providers (importantly, Recitals 5255) an awareness that previous supervisory frameworks had failed to fully contemplate the extent of dependency on a small few technological providers (Regulation (EU) 2022/2554, 2022, Recitals 5255).

Two features of DORA are outstanding in this respect. First, concentration risk in ICT providers is considered an issue of financial stability and supervisory issue. The legal implications of that framing are that it has legal implications. As soon as concentration risk is officially realised, it can be predictable. And when predictable, it adds to the due diligence load on banks in the selection of providers, the mapping of dependencies, and making credible exit or substitution plans. Failure to think in the lock-in risk or systemic dependency in the clouds cannot any longer be viewed as an unexpected contingency. Second, DORA transforms the concept of contractual governance to a regulatory tool. Contracts underpinning critical or significant ICT functions need to incorporate tangible defenses: audit privileges, access to pertinent data, cooperation provisions in the event of incidents, and involvement in resilience tests, and practical termination or transition provisions (Regulation (EU) 2022/2554, 2022, Article 28). The contract is not just a business division of risk but it is an aspect of compliance architecture of the bank. The practical implication is another, namely that the bank duty of care is concurrent at two levels, institutional governance, and contractual design. Instances where operations may be deficient could include situations in which audit rights are limited, notification clauses are vague, remediation powers do not function, and outsourced systems have not undergone structured threat testing, such as a threat-led penetration test (Almomani, et al, 2025). The lack of these operational controls could also signify larger governance issues. These types of operational gaps can lead to increased administrative sanctions or civil liability as a result of enforcement actions. Additionally, the NIS2 Directive supports this orientation by placing binding incident reporting requirements with special deadlines early warning, detailed notification and final reporting (Directive (EU) 2022/2555, 2022). Reporting responsibilities are directly related to organizational preparedness. Any delay due to disjointed internal operations or badly designed vendor notification provisions is unlikely to be considered as neutral mishaps. Rather, they can be regarded as indicators that systems of governance were not operating as they were supposed to be (Almomani, et al, 2026).

Therefore, the message presented by DORA and NIS2 is similar: infrastructure is spread, but not accountability through outsourcing. Regardless of externality or technological decentralization of functions, the regulated party is held responsible in regards to resilience and conformity. In the case of breaches after the breach, particularly those in AI transparency or distributed ledgers, the court and supervision are expected to consider more than the immediate technical precipitant and whether the bank can prove that it practices sound governance throughout its total third-party ecosystem. This aspect not only makes the regulatory change institutional, but also doctrinal. The EU law is shifting towards the breach-based vision of liability that is highly technical in nature. It is headed towards a governance-focused standard of care, which is scaled to the realities of cloud concentration, adaptive algorithms and distributed ledger systems. The question that now stands decisively is no longer whether there was a breach, but whether the institution had established and implemented a regulatory framework, which could deal with the risks that had created it, as it did(Almomani, et al, 2026).

DESIGNING RESPONSIBILITY: THE REGULATORY ARCHITECTURE OF THIRD-PARTY RISK UNDER DORA AND NIS2

DORA as the Sector-Specific Anchor of ICT Risk Governance in Finance

The Digital Operational Resilience Act (DORA) adoption is not a typical case of a legislative revision; it is an indication of a redesign of the current understanding and regulation of ICT risk in the financial sector of the European context. DORA is in the form of a directly applicable EU regulation, unlike the previous supervisory guidance, or piecemeal national actions. This implies that the requirements are applicable to all Member States with uniformity which is usually not the case in national transposition. Credit institutions, payment institutions, investment firms and even crypto-asset service providers are subjected to one framework which is binding (Regulation (EU) 2022/2554, 2022). The true meaning of DORA is, however, not simply the one concerning harmonisation. The story has uniformity, which is not the entirety of the story. The key peculiarity of DORA is that it offers a sector-specific lex specialis: it replaces a set of patchwork rules, supervisory expectations, and soft-law tools, which were used to regulate ICT risk in a somewhat uneven way in the past. Through this, it transforms the predetermined division of responsibility. ICT risk is not a technical issue that is dealt with via compliance templates or outsourcing policies. Rather, it is an incorporated, legally defined aspect of financial governance.

Practically, DORA has repositioned operational resilience at the periphery of regulatory control to the centre. It restructures the notion of ICT dependency, especially in cloud-based and outsourced system, as a rational issue that is connected to financial stability. By moving the already scattered expectations into one legislative tool, DORA minimizes the interpretive ambiguity, and at the same time, increases the level of care that is expected of entities regulated by it. The change is formal and substantive in one, being formal by direct applicability and the harmonized requirements; substantive by a re-calibration of the attribution and management of ICT-related risk in the financial system(Almomani, et al, 2026).

The most significant doctrinal step that DORA has taken in the outsourcing/ clouds environment is that it perceives ICT third-party risk as a regulatory issue, and not a regulatory issue, which can be left to private contract law. Prior to DORA, the management of bank third-party risk was done using a scatter of tools: prudential supervision, soft-law advice of European supervisory authorities, bilateral contracts. DORA gathers these strands together and transforms them into binding legal obligations to alter the legal characteristics of outsourcing relationships to establish them deeply within a context of public regulatory responsibility (Moloney, 2024).

To begin with, financial institutions are required to define, report and develop a comprehensive ICT risk management framework, which must specifically involve the dependence on the use of third-party service providers (Regulation (EU) 2022/2554, 2022, Articles 5 to 15). This framework should discover the key or crucial functions, model the ICT resources and services used in supporting the functions and determine the risk associated with outsourcing all the lifecycle of the ICT service. The implication is simple: the third-party risk will not be able to remain at the margins of compliance. The AI, so far seen as a service, must become part of the core governance and risk architecture of the bank. If these technologies, including outsourced AI platforms, blockchain infrastructures, and cloud services, are not adequately accounted for, then the absence of such accounting is not only failure to implement processes, but it could also be a contravention of statutory responsibility(Masadeh, et al, 2025).

Second, DORA compels banks, such that the outsourcing should not undermine business resilience. This obligation does not limit itself to the first outsourcing decision. It must be governed on a continuous basis by means of contractual safeguard, monitoring measures and controls (Regulation (EU) 2022/2554, 2022, Article 28). In case critical or important functions are supported by ICT services, the contracts are to have enforceable clauses regarding access rights, auditing, incident reporting, collaboration with supervisors, and efficient exit and substitution schemes. Regarding the liability, this directly relates to the duty of care to contractual design. Badly constructed or unfinished clauses are not only commercial failures; they may be interpreted as signs of regulatory failures and lax governance where they hamper the oversight or response to incidents (Boehme et al., 2025).

Third, DORA has established an EU-wide system of oversight of some key ICT third-party providers, such as large cloud providers which are extensively deployed across the financial sector (Regulation (EU) 2022/2554, 2022, Articles 312044). This is a direct acknowledgement of the fact that ICT and cloud market concentration can create systemic risk. In short, direct control over service providers does not limit the bank's liability for using such service providers to carry out its obligations to clients. DORA expressly states that notwithstanding the fact that the service provider may be regulated by an EU supervisor, the regulated financial institution is still 100% responsible to third parties (clients) for managing its third-party risk. By improving oversight of the service provider, the bank-level regulatory, due diligence, and contract enforcement processes are increased but remain in place as the basis for each bank's liability for the performance of its technology-related service providers(Shambour, et al, 2025).

In terms of liability, the overall effect of these two liabilities is to increase the responsibility of banks for the systems that they do not own or operate internally. The result is that the point of reference for liability becomes the level of governance, i.e., the bank's responsibility for the governance of systems that it selects, purchases, integrates, relies upon, and does not govern. A bank's failure to properly govern its dependence on an AI tool outsourced to an offshore provider or on a blockchain platform hosted in the cloud will give rise to the core legal issue of whether the bank has properly governed its reliance on the services of the dependent AI tool or blockchain platform in accordance with DORA's standards. Weak or incomplete contractual protection, gaps in risk assessment, superficial monitoring, or insufficient resilience testing can therefore not only reflect weaknesses in operations, but be the foundation of regulatory enforcement, and may discover negligence or statutory breach (Pelletier and Rexhepi, 2024).

NIS2 Directive is the general cybersecurity framework developed by the European Union, which has established a common norm in governance and reporting incidents in a large scope of necessary and significant organizations, including financial ones (Directive (EU) 2022/2555, 2022). This is contrary to the Digital Operational Resilience Act (DORA) which takes the form of a direct regulation as it is to be directly applied into national law. The difference in its structure does not, however, make it any less influential. As regarded in association with DORA, NIS2 has a great weight to bear when it comes to the interpretation of liability and responsibility in banking situations. Also, one of the main features of the regulatory architecture of the EU is the manner in which these two instruments are overlaid. DORA is also supposed to serve as the sector specific framework that regulates operational resilience in finance, with NIS2 providing a cross-sector cybersecurity baseline. According to the legislative documents, it is clear that the two instruments are designed to work in harmony without redundancy or conflicting requirements to financial entities that are already bound by DORA (Regulation (EU) 2022/2554, 2022). Theoretically, this would put DORA in the position of lex specialize as far as the digital operational resilience in the financial sector is concerned, but NIS2 remains an informative part of the broader governance environment, which banks exist within (Singh, et al, 2025).

NIS2 is however, legally relevant even in that hierarchy because of three related reasons. NIS2 is a less prominent, yet no less significant, part in defining the meaning of responsibility. Its aid is not technical on the main but structural. Placing the concept of cybersecurity directly in the context of the governance and management accountability, NIS2 brings the standard of care rather high-to the boardroom. Article 20 and 21 provides that the measures of cybersecurity risk-management need to be approved, managed and implemented successfully at the senior level of management (Directive (EU) 2022/2555, 2022). This is not a figurative provision. It is an indication that cybersecurity breaches are seldom to be perceived as IT accidents. In its place, it is assumed that they are connected to the quality of oversight, strategic prioritization, and institutional culture (Almomani et al., 2025).

This framing, in fact, is relevant in litigation. In a case where an AI-learning credit-scoring application fails or a cloud-based payment system is breached, the investigation of the legal system is unlikely to end at the misconfigured error or hacked server. It will then proceed to suggestions like: What did the board know? Which systems existed to address the emerging risk? Were warnings escalated? Was there any substantial challenge? NIS2 reinforces the argument that superficial compliance, which is policies written, but not internalized, committees established, but not often used, risk registers maintained, but not investigated, does not amount to reasonable care. The directive also incorporates a supply-chain logic that is in tandem with the third-party framework by DORA. The organizations under its jurisdiction have to deal with risks due to suppliers and service providers, such as ICT and cloud service providers (Directive (EU) 2022/2555, 2022). The acknowledgment of cybersecurity vulnerabilities through dependency chains rather than from internal systems by regulations is indicative of this. For banks operating in AI or cloud dependent environments, and therefore subject to overlapping regulations between DORA/NIS2, this can complicate third party definitions of an “incident” as externalities where no responsibility lies.

There is also an expectation for documented, structured and continuous vendor risk management that includes reactive coordination of incidents with those vendors. The governance outlook is also supported by the incident reporting structure of NIS2. The directive presents a progressive reporting scheme-early alert, more intricate notification, and ultimate reporting across a set period of time (Directive (EU) 2022/2555, 2022). Such requirements do not simply speed up information flows. They institutionalize preparedness. Quick reporting assumes that there is a working detection mechanism, an escalation is well-defined and the contractual agreement with third parties facilitates access to the information in time. The failure may not be characterized as a procedural inconvenience in situations where there is a delay due to the vagueness of the notification clause of a cloud provider or confusion in internal escalation channels. It can rather be seen as an indication that the governance structures were not properly designed.

DORA and NIS2 are seen as a layered normative structure. DORA offers the financial industry in-depth and industry-specific operation resilience requirements, specifically in third-party ICT risks, testing, and contractual provisions. On the contrary, NIS2 standardizes the governance-based cybersecurity accountability in any sector, which confirms the idea that cyber risk management and organisational responsibility cannot be separated. In what is known as liability analysis, such a dual paradigm pivots the focus of analysis away from technical technical fault and the bigger question as to whether governance systems were robust enough to foresee, contain as well as respond to predictable digital risk. Therefore, these tools are transferring legal evaluation beyond outcome-oriented questions including whether a particular breach was technically inevitable or not, and to more process-oriented questions including whether governance is adequate. The question to be answered is whether the environment of control in the bank, the contractual relations, the oversight designs and the incident-response capability were adequate considering the risks to be expected in the context of AI- and blockchain-enabled outsourcing. This change has significant implications to regulatory enforcement, and the liability of private law, making digital operational resilience the key to the modern banking duty of care (Almomani, et al, 2025).

Contracts as Compliance Instruments

In classical private law, the relationship between a bank and its technology suppliers is typically governed by contractual freedom. Under this framework, parties agree on obligations, warranty terms, service levels, liability limits, and solutions to breach. In this regard, the contract is simply a means of supporting private ordering and is based on the parties involved' and their business risk preferences and abilities to negotiate commercial risk. Prior to extensive outsourcing of I.C.T., the banks could easily pass on the operational and security risk of their operations to the suppliers providing services to the banks by including indemnity in the contracts, a limitation of liability clause, or a vendor's representation of compliance. As a result, incidents of cyber threat breaches from I.C.T. were usually classified as breaches of contract rather than evidence of failure to comply with the governance framework.

DORA dramatically alters this situation. It revises the outsourcing contract's nature so that outsourcing arrangements are no longer purely private but act as compliance instruments towards regulatory objectives. The regulation recognizes that financial institutions increasingly rely on complex contractual networks for ICT services and may face bargaining asymmetries when seeking prudentially necessary rights, including access and audit (Regulation (EU) 2022/2554, 2022,

Recital 28). DORA responds by imposing binding governance requirements for ICT third-party arrangements supporting critical or important functions, including detailed expectations about contractual content, auditability, monitoring, security standards, subcontracting controls, and exit strategies (Regulation (EU) 2022/2554, 2022, Articles 28–30).

NIS2 strengthens this direction by integrating supply-chain risk management into its wider scope of cybersecurity and specifically linking cybersecurity control to managerial responsibility (Directive (EU) 2022/2555, 2022). The overall impact is some kind of regulatory publicization of private contracting: the design of contracts is no longer merely a question of commercial efficiency. It takes the form of a legally organized manifestation of the resilience of operations requirements.

The change has two direct and legally important implications for the study of liability. To start with, regulatory minimum standards restrain the degree of risk transfer through contract. Although a contract may seek to place the liability of cyber failures on a cloud provider or AI vendor, according to DORA, the regulated party will still bear the consequences of compliance with these regulations and will need to address (not delegate) the third-party risk through a contract (Regulation (EU) 2022/2554, 2022). Outsourcing thus becomes devoid of its traditional use as a shield which protects against liabilities. The main issue of governors and courts in this case is no longer whether the bank negotiated indemnities, but whether it used good governance over the outsourced exercise by means of systematic risk evaluation, well-constructed contract design, ongoing control, and a proper testing approach. The methodology aligns with the pre-DORA supervisory practices, specifically the European Banking Authority Guidelines on Outsourcing Arrangements which, in turn, assert that the responsibility of the institutions concerning the outsourced activity is not assigned to another party and that the institutions should have sufficient oversight and audit rights (European Banking Authority [EBA], 2019). Second, the incompleteness between the parties in the contract in itself is legally significant as a possible breakdown of compliance. DORA mandates that contracts that support important or critical functions have enforceable provisions that can facilitate a proper mechanism of overseeing, supervising, audit rights, incident handling, cooperation and orderly termination (Regulation (EU) 2022/2554, 2022, Articles 2830). In the absence of key provisions, where they are ambiguous or practically unfeasible, including, but not limited to limited audit rights, vague incident notification requirements, limited access to logs and forensic data, lax subcontracting controls, or inefficient exit and portability provisions, the gap can be regarded as an indication of weak governance. The decisions that would be viewed as the drafting of options otherwise deemed suboptimal can be now viewed as the cases of regulatory non-compliance (Almomani, et al, 2025).

In principle, this is a change to a situation in which contractual weakness is seen as a commercial issue to where it is a possible violation of a supervised obligation to achieve operational resiliency. The lack of DORA-equivalent protection may help in the post-incident regulatory inquiries and the lack of such protections may also reinforce the claims based on the private law as negligence or the violation of the statutory duty (where provided) or the breach of the implied duties of reasonable care and skill in the protection of customer data and service continuity. Besides this, the concept of governance-by-contract describes this development well. DORA does not directly control all ICT vendors. Rather, it demands controlled actors to design contracts in such a way that the aims of public law, namely transparency, auditability, resilience, and supervisory access are converted into enforceable rights in the private law. An analogous methodology applies to EU data protection legislation: Article 28 GDPR obligates controllers to enter contracts with processors, which entails contractual obligations with more specific safeguards and makes private deals a regulatory compliance tool (Regulation (EU) 2016/679, 2016). DORA takes an approach similar to that of Operational Resilience but assesses risk in the context of specific sectors using a supervisory lens based on Financial Stability – i.e., how a sector contributes to the financial system's overall security (Almomani, et al, 2025).

As a key implications from a liability perspective are that contracts will form part of the evidence used to establish whether banks have exercised reasonable care in the conduct of their activities. If a bank breaches its obligation, regulators and courts will examine whether the bank had demonstrated sufficient legal and operational capacity to manage the risks associated with contractually outsourcing functions, such as enforcing audit rights, rapidly notifying incidents, cooperating, leveraging remedial actions, and developing exit strategies. To the extent that the capacity exists due to inadequate or poorly constructed contracts, it significantly increases the likelihood that a court will find that the bank has failed to properly govern itself.

Core Clauses That Operationalize DORA-Aligned Oversight

Because a liability-based analysis views contract clauses as legal controls, liability-based analysis has a practical advantage here as it identifies an essential point where DORA's public law obligations are turned into enforceable private contractual obligations. However, it is not sufficient to establish the existence of contracts for the purposes of DORA; contracts must be drafted in a manner that enables actual effective governance. As a result, DORA requires that financial institutions' ICT contract arrangements shall include clear rights and obligations, and if those arrangements provide material services supporting critical or important functions, then the services must contain minimum criteria to ensure weigh the service provider has the required government level of auditability, monitoring, incident support, cooperatively working with the supervisory authorities, appropriate controls over subcontractors, and right to terminate or exit (Regulation (EU) 2022/2554; 2022; Articles 28-30). Thus, from a liability perspective, the minimum content would matter because the minimum content defines what constitutes reasonable care. As a bank, if a bank cannot collect evidence, obtain timely incident data, perform sufficient testing of the service or transition away from the service provided without interruption, after a loss has occurred, it becomes difficult to argue that the bank had a properly functioning control environment with regard to foreseeable risks of ICT loss. This is also consistent with the pre-DORA supervisory logic that outsourcing cannot hollow out the regulated entity: the EBA guidelines emphasize that the management body always remains responsible and that outsourcing must not create an "'empty shell'". So, within this framework, five groups of contractual provisions tend to be especially significant when it comes to evidencing compliance and limiting liability exposure in relationships between banks and their cloud providers or AI vendors. In practice, these clusters also act as the "bridges" between operational resilience obligations and the evidentiary record that regulators and courts rely on when reconstructing what the bank did before, during, and after an incident (Almomani, et al, 2025).

The first group relates to security baselines and the mapping of controls. DORA obliges financial entities to engage only those ICT third-party providers that satisfy appropriate information-security standards, with stricter expectations where the outsourced service supports a critical or important function (Regulation (EU) 2022/2554, 2022, Article 28(5)). In practice, disputes rarely turn on whether a bank adopted *some* recognized framework. The more pointed question is whether the chosen safeguards were proportionate to the institution's actual risk profile and whether they were implemented in a manner capable of preventing or detecting reasonably foreseeable threats. NIS2 strengthens this direction by integrating supply-chain risk management into its wider scope of cybersecurity and specifically linking cybersecurity control to managerial responsibility (Directive (EU) 2022/2555, 2022). The overall impact is regulatory publicization of private contracting: the design of contracts is no longer merely a question of commercial efficiency. It takes the form of a legally organized manifestation of the resilience of operations requirements.

The change has two direct and legally important implications for the study of liability. To start with, regulatory minimum standards restrain the degree of risk transfer through contract. Although a contract may seek to place the liability of cyber failures on a cloud provider or AI vendor, according to DORA, the regulated party will still bear the consequences of compliance with these regulations and will need to address (not delegate) the third-party risk through a contract (Regulation (EU) 2022/2554, 2022). Outsourcing thus becomes devoid of its traditional use as a shield which protects against liabilities. The main issue of governors and courts in this case is no longer whether the bank negotiated indemnities, but whether it used good governance over the outsourced exercise by means of systematic risk evaluation, well-constructed contract design, ongoing control, and a proper testing approach. The methodology aligns with the pre-DORA supervisory practices, specifically the European Banking Authority Guidelines on Outsourcing Arrangements which, in turn, assert that the responsibility of the institutions concerning the outsourced activity is not assigned to another party and that the institutions should have sufficient oversight and audit rights (European Banking Authority [EBA], 2019). Second, the incompleteness between the parties in the contract in itself is legally significant as a possible breakdown of compliance. DORA mandates that contracts that support important or critical functions have enforceable provisions that can facilitate a proper mechanism of overseeing, supervising, audit rights, incident handling, cooperation and orderly termination (Regulation (EU) 2022/2554, 2022, Articles 2830). In the absence of key provisions, where they are ambiguous or practically unfeasible, including, but not limited to limited audit rights, vague incident notification requirements, limited access to logs and forensic data, lax subcontracting controls, or inefficient exit and portability provisions, the gap can be regarded as an indication of weak governance. The decisions that would be viewed as the drafting of options otherwise deemed suboptimal can be now viewed as the cases of regulatory non-compliance (Almomani, et al, 2025).

In principle, this is a change to a situation in which contractual weakness is seen as a commercial issue to where it is a possible violation of a supervised obligation to achieve operational resiliency. The lack of DORA-equivalent protection may help in the post-incident regulatory inquiries and the lack of such protection may also reinforce the claims based on the private law such as negligence or the violation of the statutory duty (where provided) or the breach of the implied duties of reasonable care and skill in the protection of customer data and service continuity. Besides this, the concept of governance-by-contract describes this development well. DORA does not directly control all ICT vendors. Rather, it demands controlled actors to design contracts in such a way that the aims of public law, namely transparency, auditability, resilience, and supervisory access are converted into enforceable rights in the private law. An analogous methodology applies to EU data protection legislation: Article 28 GDPR obligates controllers to enter contracts with processors, which entails contractual obligations with more specific safeguards and makes private deals a regulatory compliance tool (Regulation (EU) 2016/679, 2016). DORA uses a comparable rationale to operational resilience, but on a sector-specific level, and a supervisory rationale based on financial stability.

The DORA environment reveals that outsourcing contracts are not ordinary commercial agreements, but instead, are vital pieces in managing liability and ensuring that firms comply with existing regulations. However, poor quality contracts create not only inefficiency in the way that they function; they also provide evidence of poor or deficient governance. All of this can lead to the potential for allegations of negligence, breach of statutory duty or failure to exercise reasonable care and skill in protecting a customer's data and maintaining operational resilience by way of the existence of gaps in their contracts (i.e. lack of effective audit rights; no ability to gain access to evidence; poor control of subcontractors; vague obligations with respect to notifications; unrealistic termination mechanisms, etc.) in the event of an incident. The governance-through-contract model is consistent with international supervisory trends, specifically that both the FSB and Basel Committee identify third-party risk as a structured governance issue that requires comprehensive oversight (start to finish) and valid, verifiable controls.

Reframing the Duty of Care in Outsourced AI and Blockchain Environments

Historically speaking, private law's understanding of liability has been connected through control (the person control an asset or activity that results in harm is the person most likely to answer for any resulting harm); this has made sense in the technological context due to the fact that most banking systems were centralized (to the extent that banks have their own servers, run on their own software, have databases managed by their own management team); ownership and operational control were practical ways to establish accountability and to prevent. If something did not work properly, it was usually easy to discover where the problem was based. Cause and fault doctrines were generally not straight forward; however, they did have a relatively stable point of reference (Almomani, et al, 2025).

AI-based financial firms' ecosystems include third-party developed analytics models, cloud-based analytic engines of real-time data and use of SaaS environments; such systems involve the logic of their analytics models (i.e., the training data/parameters used, frequency of model updates, parameter recalibrations and physical design characteristics) may be protected from public access through intellectual property protections or incorporated into the shared multi-tenant cloud computing architecture. Additionally, even if the organization has formal contractual agreements with respect to oversight rights (i.e., ability to intervene in the analytical models' behaviors and/or data flows), the organization's practical ability to actually do so may be limited due to the multi-tiered, multi-user and often non-directive nature of controls across the entire ecosystem. Blockchain-based environments have an entirely different but nevertheless the same fundamental configuration of the problem. More so than traditional financial transactions, distributed or consortium-based ledger environments have voter validator, nodes (by individual member's own decisions) and qualified smart-contract developers managing the voting, execution, and record-keeping functions on behalf of multiple users or entities; under this type of ecosystem, there is not necessarily going to be a singular entity that has total control over the entire chain of confidentiality, integrity, and availability (CI&); instead, there may be some component of CI& failure resulting from a number of factors that arise from the interaction between the various participants in the distributed environment. In other words, the responsibility is distributed structurally. As a result, when liability was so strictly attached to immediate technical control, banks could, perhaps, reasonably claim that much of the failures are not within their domain, in the AI pipelines with vendors in charge, or in the distributed ledger members. However, it would be a conclusion that would not sit well with the EU financial regulation protective architecture. Digital interdependence and outsourcing are not peripheral occurrences, rather they are the key aspects of contemporary banking. To permit accountability to evaporate merely because technical control has been distributed would be to leave regulatory blind spots at the very point where systemic risk has become worse than ever.

DORA and NIS2 react to this change in the structure by a shift of the center of responsibility. Instead of investigating who was in control of the code now of failure, the regulatory investigation shifts to who had the responsibility to foresee and handle the relevant risk (Regulation (EU) 2022/2554, 2022; Directive (EU) 2022/2555, 2022). It shifts the focus towards short-term technical causation to organizational stewardship. Who selected the provider? Who assessed the risk? Who made sure that there was meaning behind monitoring, testing, and escalation pathways and not symbols? The change is a manifestation of a broader change of the regulatory mindset in the EU. Cybersecurity and operational resilience are no longer managed as a small technical compliance issue that can be easily outsourced to IT teams and managed outside the context of the rest of the organization. They are considered as parts of corporate governance. This operational form is provided by DORA which requires a full-fledged ICT risk management framework that expressly combines third-party dependencies and its clarity that outsourcing does not usurp regulatory responsibility (Regulation (EU) 2022/2554, 2022, Articles 515, 28). NIS2 supports the same change by putting definite responsibility on the senior level of management and making management bodies approve, monitor, and be responsible for cybersecurity risk-mitigation practices (Directive (EU) 2022/2555, 2022, Articles 20-21). Within such an environment, a defense of the type that there was a lack of technical control is coming out to sound incomplete, particularly when the lack of technical control is caused by previous decisions of governance regarding the selection of vendors or the formulation of contracts. In this way, another more consistent doctrinal stance can be derived out of this architecture. The banking duty of care under the post-DORA is more of a governance-based one. It is bound not to univocal technical control of infrastructures but to the ability of the institution to organize, monitor, and address predictable ICT risks either caused by the inside or because of outsourced relations.

Liability, in this case, is less about trying to identify a single technical malpractice and is more about considering the presence of disciplined and informed management of a complex technological environment by the organization.

This is an important point, and this concept of governance is not an abstract rhetoric. It is converted into measurable, tangible expectations. Banks must carry out systematic risk analysis to establish the most critical functions and third-party processes; to instantiate audible audit, access rights and notification rights in their contracts; to ensure continuous monitoring of provider performance; and to carry out resilience testing set to risk. Other advanced interventions like threat-led penetration testing (TLPT) are not viewed as optional add-ons but as an integral component of a well-organized system of supervision. The European Supervisory Authorities have been mandated to come up with regulatory technical standards in line with TIBER-EU framework, which emphasizes that such testing is designed as part of a disciplined governance, and not an impromptu technical procedure. Furthermore, in terms of liability, this generates what can be described reasonably as the model of risk-based accountability. DORA and NIS2 do not charge strict liability over all breaches and disruptions. Even in the well-regulated systems, there might be incidents. However, in the case that governance systems are facade, not well documented, applied in a haphazard manner or lack of linkage with actual operational risk, the exposure is heightened. In spaces where AI transparency is obfuscated, or where distributed ledgers have sufficient complexity, the lack of veritable governance evidence will be decisive. A bank is unable to prove to have structured management of the predictable ICT risk may have findings of careless governance, even though the immediate technical failure was in infrastructure it was not directly involved in operating. In that regard, that development of EU operational resilience law does not forego the idea of control. It reframes it. Control is no longer being seen in lines of code or access credentials on servers. It is measured in the quality of decisions regarding governance that influences the process of choosing and integrating technology, monitoring, and testing in the long run (Almomani, et al, 2025).

From Oversight to Accountability: Four Patterns of Failure in Digital Banking

There is no chance of winning claims based on technical arguments for AI technology failure or blockchain-enabled banking methods through litigious or regulatory measures following a data breach or disruption of operations at any financial institution. The reality is that the investigation of these incidents is very complex in nature as they have occurred over layers of interconnected systems, physical and virtual infrastructures (i.e., cloud), different contractors who provide products or services to banks, and tools provided by vendors that are managed by bank customers. Even when a proper forensic investigation has taken place to determine what happened, it does not always produce clear evidence supporting one party's argument over another's. What regulators and courts therefore tend to look for is something more legally legible: whether the incident exposes *governance weaknesses* that fall below the standard of reasonable care now articulated by DORA and reinforced by NIS2. The differences between these approaches lead to differences: one viewpoint is to view the breach of duty as a separate event; the other view is to use the breach of duty as a stress test of the bank's ability to control its outsourced or cloud-based dependence on another entity in a manner that reflects its ability to foresee potential Information Communication Technology (ICT) risks. (Regulation (EU) 2022/2554, 2022; Directive (EU) 2022/2555; 2022).

The governance model is built upon (4) distinct actions/measurements that correspond to the occurrence of each one's respective failure within each phase of an outsourcing / ICT-risk management life cycle, which together correspond to the practical "audit trail" which supervisors and judges construct post-incident, based on what else occurred before the failure, including what occurred in terms of the way the bank conducted itself before entering into a contract with a third-party; what did it document in the contract, how did it supervise (or not) over time; and did the bank test and/or improve prior to a failure event occurring after such actions had taken place.

The first failure trigger is known as Selection Failure, which occurs where a bank has a failure i.e. inadequate processes of procuring and undertaking due diligence regarding a third-party ICT. At an absolute minimum, such a failure may include the bank's failure to assess its third-party ICT providers in terms of their overall cybersecurity posture, operational resiliency capacity, concentration / operational dependency, financial soundness, incident history and whether or not they are a suitable option for supporting an essential / major function for the bank. A selection failure is one of the most concerning types of failures to occur as it occurs prior to an actual event. Selection failure in AI heavy settings may include insufficient evaluation/practices regarding model oversight like; respective level of oversight with respect to how the model is trained, how explainability claims relate to how the bank would ultimately use the model, how they would/are able to manage and monitor model drift, and does the vendor have reasonable safeguards or protections against adversarial/bad actors manipulating the outcome of the model. In blockchain based environments, selection failure will appear as insufficient assessment of, network governance or oversight practices, trust assumptions regarding validator roles, consensus and upgrade management processes, and overall security of cryptographic key management mechanisms (Almomani, et al, 2025).

Under DORA, these failures are difficult to align with key requirements to; identify, measure and mitigate ICT related risks throughout the lifecycle of an outsourced service, especially when the service supports a critical or important function of an entity (Regulation (EU) 2022/2554, 2022, Articles 5-15, and 28). The EBA's outsourcing framework reinforces the same point in supervisory terms: institutions remain fully responsible for outsourced activities and must perform a risk-based due diligence process, including in relation to sub-outsourcing. In terms of liability, agencies' weak selection behaviour undermines claims that any subsequent harm occurred without being foreseeable. Failing to detect and address provider risks that should have been reasonably detectable by providers when they were procured may provide support for findings of negligent governance by the bank or breach of statutory duty, because a bank chose to operate within a critical function using a dependent provider where the bank failed to adequately understand the provider's business.

The second area of concern relates to failure in the design of contracts governing third-party ICT relationships. DORA does not take subtlety in its approach to such issues, since DORA anticipates that contracts will facilitate the function of oversight. Whenever an ICT service is providing support for a critical or important function, DORA establishes contracts that must, at a minimum, contain enforceability provisions regarding auditability, access to information and incident reporting of events; cooperation with the supervisor organization; control of subcontractors; and appropriate exit strategies (Regulation (EU) 2022/2554, 2022, Articles 28-30). With respect to contracts within the DORA context, the presence of weak or incomplete audit rights, vague or ambiguous notification provisions, restricted access to logs or forensic evidence, inadequate control over fourth-party dependence, and unreasonable exit/portability provisions are not regarded as simply ineffective drafting choices. Rather, they can be interpreted as being structural governance deficiencies because they predictably decrease the ability of the bank to prevent, detect, investigate and report incidents within the time required by law.

How this plays out in practice is that after an incident occurs, a bank's "reasonable care" analysis generally is a function of the evidence it can reproduce, or the logs, audit records, testing results, vendor incident reports, and internal escalation trails. When a contract restricts a bank's ability to retrieve that evidence and/or requires provider discretion to retrieve that evidence, in addition to having an issue dealing with the incident itself, the bank may face difficulty establishing due diligence in both supervisory and judicial forums. This is why supervisory guidance has historically characterized outsourcing of any kind as not being able to transfer risk and why institutions still remain accountable for risks associated with contracts designed without proper faculty for securing audit and oversight rights. Thus, from a liability perspective, failure to design a contract could lead to affirmations of regulatory non-compliance as well as claims of negligence or breach of duty based on the bank's failure to translate public law resilience obligations into private law that could be enforced.

Oversight failure is characterized by a lack of genuine implementation of formal governance structures in place to oversee third parties. Evidence of oversight failure includes:

- Poorly implemented oversight of third party operations due to monitoring systems in place but little to no frequency enforced on their use.
- Failure to conduct adequate governance and risk management meetings to discuss escalated risk indicators.
- Key Performance Indicator (KPI) frameworks which measure operations based primarily on availability/cost as opposed to security/resilience.
- Failure to escalate signals of risk.
- No action taken in response to audit findings and/or recommendations made by the supervisory authority.

Therefore, DORA provides specific guidance regarding the operational resilience of entities and how they should be continuously and consistently maintained, as opposed to being treated as a "project". (Regulation (EU) 2022/2554, 2022, Articles 56). From a liability standpoint, oversight failure is generally considered one of the most damaging categories of failures; it indicates that the governance structure at the bank was not only weak but also failed to respond adequately or appropriately to the realities of how the bank operates. When something goes wrong and it becomes evident that no one paid attention to dashboards, audit results were not fixed, a management had limited awareness of a significant outsourcing contract, regulators and courts will tend to consider the breach as a foreseeable outcome of governance failure, and not an inevitable technical shock. NIS2 supports this assumption by stating explicitly that cybersecurity risk management is associated with senior management accountability and board-level governance, which enhances the legal argument of organizational negligence in cases when oversight mechanisms fail to work (Directive (EU) 2022/2555, 2022, Articles 2021).

The fourth trigger and the last one is testing failure. The failure of testing occurs in the case of absence of resilience testing, inadequacy, not part of major outsourced elements, or lacking calibration to realistic threat conditions. The limitations of testing may be of various forms: a failure to investigate important functions sufficiently extensively or intensively, the exclusion of outsourced cloud services or artificial intelligence tools that a vendor maintains to the testing activities, or the failure to use more advanced methods, such as threat-led penetration testing (TLPT), where such methods are warranted by the situation. On the liability front, issues to do with testing are especially brought out since they directly touch on the issue of foreseeability. Unless there were plausible attack scenarios that have never been considered, or that the weaknesses revealed in testing have not been addressed, it becomes hard to hold a bank to have done all that it can reasonably do to stop harm.

DORA explicitly introduces operational resilience testing into the regulatory expression of reasonable care, as to which it is expected that relevant underlying ICT systems and services including those that support critical functions that have been outsourced are identified and dragged within the testing perimeter (Regulation (EU) 2022/2554, 2022, Article 26). This approach of the ESAs in regard to TLPT also reveals the way the EU views advanced testing as a political instrument, but not so much as a technical one: the final report on the draft RTS under DORA proposes the way the TLPT should be organized and governed in practice. Such characteristics of AI and blockchain systems as non-deterministic behavior, complex interactions, and restricted observability make robust testing of scenarios even more central as a demonstration of due diligence. The appropriate response to that is that failure to test (or failure to take action on the results of tests) may serve as a powerful indicator of poor governance, even in cases where the exact technical cause is controversial.

Finally, all these four failure modes are considered to fit into a consistent and analytically sound process of the evaluation of the liability in a risk-based accountability model. They are in line with the architecture of DORA and do not fall into the traps of strictly causation-based analysis which can be hard to implement regarding the relative complexity of modern technology. The framework enables assessment of bank behavior throughout the whole lifecycle of outsourcing of a bank before, during and after the incident and to question whether the bank governance systems could have handled foreseeable ICT risk in the manner the EU law now requires. This identical lifecycle orientation is apparent at the global level: the FSB toolkit on the third-party risk management and oversight emphasizes end-to-end governance and the capacity of both institutions and authorities to address resilience in the world of essential dependence related to the service providers.

CONCLUSION

The rapid integration of artificial intelligence and blockchain into the banking industry has radically changed not only the way in which the financial service is designed and provided, but also the interpretation of the legal responsibility of failures and risks. Distributed systems, outsourcing chains and cloud-dependent service models are increasingly mediating transaction processing, risk assessment, customer profiling and settlement infrastructures. It is in that context that traditional liability doctrines based largely on direct technical control provide a less plausible foundation of responsibility assignment in the case of data breaches or operational disturbances where control is often distributed and accountability is frequently located in the regulated entity.

This paper holds the position that DORA and NIS2 fall short in establishing a rigid or automatic liability on all the incidences involving AI- or blockchain-powered banking systems. Instead of assigning blame to the simple fact of a breach, the two frameworks promote a risk-based accountability model, and in this model, liability is determined by the strength, consistency and functionality of the governance arrangements of a bank during the course of outsourcing. The responsibility of care under this model is no longer pegged into the ownership or the exclusive technical control of the ICT systems. Instead, it is based on the ability of the regulated entity to determine predictable risks, form binding contractual guarantees, monitor third-party reliance on an ongoing basis, carry out significant operational resiliency testing, such as TLPT where relevant, and comply with accountable incident notification and governance anticipations under DORA and NIS2 (Regulation (EU) 2022/2554, 2022; Directive (EU) 2022/2555, 2022).

The four analysis failure modes, including selection failure, contract-design failure, oversight failure, and testing failure, have offered a systematic doctrinaire formulation of the liability evaluation in technologically complicated settings. They enable adjudicators to work through cases of AI opacity, distributed ledger infrastructures, and cloud concentration without bringing the analysis down to simplistic causation stories. Governance deficiencies in this context emerge the determining factor in the liability exposure since they are the ones that establish whether or not the bank possessed the institutional capability to handle foreseeable ICT risks in the event that the operational components were externalized.

Lastly, this accountability standard is operational with the proposed DORA-NIS2 compliance matrix. Mapping regulatory requirements with quantifiable governance variables, i.e. third-party controls, notification schedules, test scope, access to evidence, dependency management, makes diligence demonstrable, in a small, grained and documentable manner. Such a good history of structured governance is not merely good compliance practice; it may be an important evidentiary protection at the heart of a supervisory investigation or in the context of a court of action, where the question of whether governance systems existed, operated, and were in commensurable proportion to known risk is a growing one. Also, the development of the EU operational resilience law represents a more general change in regulatory philosophy. The issues of liability in contemporary banking cease to be centered on the mere fact of a breach; it is increasingly being determined by the quality of governance that led to it and which encircle it. Institutional responsibility is not undermined by EU law as financial systems are increasingly opaque, distributed and technologically interdependent. Rather it re-tunes the liability by pegging it upon governance frameworks, control mechanisms, contract design, and the management of risk-of-course-setting-the-course-with-customers-around-the- edges-that-not-even-insurance-can-offer-guarantees-the-system-to-which-it-is-applied.

REFERENCES

Abdeljaber, O., Al-Adwan, A. S., Yaseen, H., Falahat, M., Abdullah, A., & Fauzi, M. A. (2025). Shopping in the metaverse: Decoding consumer intentions. *The International Information & Library Review*, *58*(1), 1–31. DOI: 10.1080/10572317.2025.2594293

Ahmad Ibrahim Karajeh, A. I., Al-Momani, T. A., Almomani, M. A., Almomani, O., & Tarawneh, M. H. (2025). Forecasting future earnings via e-business information: Financial implications for investment decisions in the era of big data. *Investment Management and Financial Innovations*, *22*(4), 237–246. DOI: 10.21511/imfi.22(4).2025.19

Al-Adwan, A. S. (2024). The government metaverse: Charting the coordinates of citizen acceptance. *Telematics and Informatics*, *88*, 102109. DOI: 10.1016/j.tele.2024.102109

Al-Adwan, A. S., Al-Adwan, A., Li, N., Fauzi, M. A., Jafar, R. M. S., Habibi, A., & Falahat, M. (2025). Immersive learning meets theory: Modeling eduverse adoption in higher education. *Journal of Information Technology Education: Research, 24*, 042. https://doi.org/DOI: 10.28945/5669

Al-Adwan, A. S., Yaseen, H., Alkhwaldi, A. F., Jafar, R. M. S., Fauzi, M. A., & Abdullah, A. (2025). Treasure hunting for brands: Metaverse marketing gamification effects on purchase intention, WOM, and loyalty. *Journal of Global Marketing*, *38*(4), 1–25. DOI: 10.1080/08911762.2025.2463897

Al-Zaqeba, M. A., ... (2026). The effect of implementing AI-driven customs processes on trade facilitation efficiency in Jordan. In A. R. Alshehadeh, I. A. El-Qirem, & G. A. Elrefae (Eds.), *Artificial intelligence in business. SICB 2025* (Lecture Notes in Networks and Systems, Vol. 1502, Springer. https://doi.org/DOI: 10.1007/978-3-031-96622-4_11

Almomani, O., Arabiat, A., Al Tayeb, M., Almaiah, M. A., Obeidat, M., Aldhyani, T. H., Shehab, R., & Rowad, M. (2025). A robust model for Android malware detection via ML and DL classifiers. *Mesopotamian Journal of Big Data, 2025*, 261–277. DOI: 10.58496/MJBD/2025/017

Almomani, O., Arabiat, A. M., Hind, A.-A., & Alsariera, E. (2026). Hybridization of deep learning models for multiclass attack detection in wireless sensor networks. *Journal of Communication*, *21*(1), 20–34. DOI: 10.12720/jcm.21.1.20-34

Alsaaidah, A., Almomani, O., Abu-Shareha, A. A., Abualhaj, M. M., & Achuthan, A. (2024). ARP spoofing attack detection model in IoT network using machine learning: Complexity vs. accuracy. *Journal of Applied Data Sciences*, *5*(4), 1850–1860. DOI: 10.47738/jads.v5i4.374

Directive (EU) 2022/2555 of the European Parliament and of the Council of 14 December 2022 on measures for a high common level of cybersecurity across the Union, amending Regulation (EU) No 910/2014 and Directive (EU) 2018/1972, and repealing Directive (EU) 2016/1148 (NIS 2 Directive). (2022). *Official Journal of the European Union, L 333*, 80–152.

European Banking Authority. (2019). *Final report on EBA guidelines on outsourcing arrangements (EBA/GL/2019/02).* https://www.eba.europa.eu/regulation-and-policy/internal-governance/guidelines-on-outsourcing-arrangements

European Supervisory Authorities. (2024). *Final report on draft regulatory technical standards specifying criteria for the identification of financial entities required to perform threat-led penetration testing and the requirements and standards governing such testing under Regulation (EU) 2022/2554 (DORA).* Publications Office of the European Union.

European Union Agency for Cybersecurity. (2025). *Technical implementation guidance on cybersecurity risk-management measures under NIS2*. Publications Office of the European Union.

Kshetri, N. (2023). Artificial intelligence in cybersecurity: Opportunities and challenges in the banking sector. *Annals of Operations Research, 313*(1), 1–22. DOI: 10.1007/s10479-023-05281-5 PMID: 36743349

Masadeh, R., Almomani, O., Zaqebah, A., Masadeh, S., Alshqurat, K., Sharieh, A., & Alsharman, N. (2025). Narwhal optimizer: A nature-inspired optimization algorithm for solving complex optimization problems. *Computers, Materials & Continua, 85*(2), 3709–3737. DOI: 10.32604/cmc.2025.066797

Moloney, N. (2024). EU financial regulation after DORA: Operational resilience, outsourcing, and supervisory accountability. *European Business Law Review*, *35*(2), 189–215.

Pelletier, C., & Rexhepi, V. (2024). Cyber risk governance and liability in financial services: Regulatory duties and third-party oversight. *Journal of Business Research, 162*, 113842. DOI: 10.1016/j.jbusres.2023.113842

Regulation (EU) 2016/679 of the European Parliament and of the Council of 27 April 2016 on the protection of natural persons with regard to the processing of personal data and on the free movement of such data (General Data Protection Regulation). (2016). *Official Journal of the European Union, L 119*, 1–88.

Regulation (EU) 2022/2554 of the European Parliament and of the Council of 14 December 2022 on digital operational resilience for the financial sector and amending Regulations (EC) No 1060/2009, (EU) No 648/2012, (EU) No 600/2014, (EU) No 909/2014 and (EU) 2016/1011 (Digital Operational Resilience Act). (2022). *Official Journal of the European Union, L 333*, 1–79.

Shambour, Q., Al-Zyoud, M., & Almomani, O. (2025). Quantum-inspired hybrid metaheuristic feature selection with SHAP for optimized and explainable spam detection. *Symmetry*, *17*(10), 1716. DOI: 10.3390/sym17101716

Singh, K. S. D., Hong, T. K., Abbasi, G. A., & Al-Adwan, A. S. (2025). Building bonds with food delivery apps: Determinants of app attachment and continuous intention—Does gender matter? *International Journal of Human-Computer Interaction*, *41*(23), 1–19. DOI: 10.1080/10447318.2025.2495843

Zhou, Z., Wang, Y., & Li, H. (2024). Cloud concentration risk and accountability in financial services: Legal and operational perspectives. *Information and Software Technology*, *165*, 107152. DOI: 10.1016/j.infsof.2023.107152

KEY TERMS AND DEFINITIONS

Cloud Concentration Risk: Systemic risk that is caused by the dependence on few cloud service vendors throughout the financial sector.

Digital Operational Resilience Act (DORA): An EU law that defines the same set of directly applicable standards and obligations regarding ICT risks management and digital operational resilience among financial institutions.

Governance-Raised Duty of Care: A liability test pegged on organisational oversight, risk management and contractual control, and not direct technical control per se.

ICT Third-Party risk: This is the risk that is caused by reliance on outsourced technology providers that are involved in vital or significant functions.

NIS2 Directive: This is the EU directive that creates a high common level of cybersecurity governance and incident reporting of essential and important entities.

Operational Resilience: The ability of a financial institution to avert, endure, respond and recuperate because of ICT-related disruption.

Threat-Led Penetration Testing (TLPT): Developed to simulate realistic cyber threats to critical ICT systems.

Chapter 10
Redefining Online Commerce With AI-Powered Shopping Agents

yashaswani kumari
http://orcid.org/0009-0003-3739-8091
Christ University, Delhi NCR, India

Maria Johnson
http://orcid.org/0009-0000-3334-5492
Christ University, Delhi NCR, India

ABSTRACT

The importance of artificial intelligence has rapidly changed the world of online commerce and turned digital shopping into a predictive and personalized practice. One of the most significant changes is the application of AI to create shopping agent intelligent machines helping consumers at every stage of the buying process by suggesting purchases, comparing products, and automating the process. This chapter discusses how AI agents of shopping are transforming e-commerce through redefining consumer behaviour, and making new types of online interaction possible. Based on a systematic literature review of the scholarly literature and industry practices, the chapter discusses the most important applications, including personalized recommendations, dynamic pricing, AR-driven virtual try-ons, and autonomous purchasing systems. The research comes up with the conclusion that, AI shopping agents are no longer considered an optional addition, but a strategic collaborator in contemporary commerce, although their implementation should be supported by moral values, transparency, and human supervision.

DOI: 10.4018/979-8-3373-7330-0.ch010

1. INTRODUCTION

The development of digital technologies fundamentally changed the organization of commerce in the world. In the course of the last thirty years, retail has ceased to exist as it was before in the form of brick-and-mortar shops and has instead taken place in digitally mediated formats that transcend geographical and temporal scope. Early e-commerce websites were basically just digital catalogues and enabled customers to shop and transact over the internet. Although these systems were better than before in terms of convenience and market expansion, they were mostly inert and had no personalization and support.

In the first period of online markets, consumers had the duty of searching, comparing, and assessing products on their own. This was a complex thinking process particularly where the consumers were presented with thousands of options and little guidance. This led to information-overload, decision burnout, and uneven customer experiences dominating the initial phases of e-commerce.

The first significant change towards intelligent online commerce was the adoption of data analytics. The e-commerce sites started to gather and scrutinize consumer data, such as the history of browsing, shopping history, and personal data. Recommendation engines became a core element of online retailing which applied collaborative filtering and content-based algorithms to recommend products that matched consumer preferences. Such systems enhanced the applicability of the recommendations and conversion rates, yet they were mostly reactive and followed historical data as opposed to real-time interaction.

The high rate of development of artificial intelligence (AI) has brought a new paradigm in online commerce. The use of predictive analytics, conversational interfaces, and automated decision systems by modern platforms is used to improve user experiences. Out of data on a large scale of consumers, AI systems are able to process and discover trends, predict what consumers may need without the consumer spelling out their needs. This shift has brought e-commerce to a transactional model that is turned into a customer experience ecosystem.

Among such changes, AI-controlled shopping agents are one of the most important innovations. The agents are smart systems, which are able to communicate with the consumers, get to know their intentions and help them through the buying process. The AI shopping agents, in comparison with the traditional ones, are able to carry out many actions at the same time. On platforms, they are able to compare products, recommend the alternatives, manage subscriptions and even carry out purchases independently.

In one instance, an AI shopping agent can be used by a consumer shopping a smartphone by chatting. The agent is able to analyze the needs of the consumer, price differences between various retailers, and offer the most suitable one. In high-end applications, the agent may not only make the purchase, but may schedule the delivery as well as may track the order all without the need of any additional human intervention.

This transformation is a paradigm shift in the place of technology in business. AI systems are no longer passive tools but active intermediaries that are able to affect consumer choices. To the extent that these agents gain greater autonomy, they slowly take over the roles that were carried out by the human consumer or sales representative.

Although AI shopping agents have many benefits, they also have serious challenges. Since these systems mediate access to information and influence consumer preferences, the concerns of privacy, transparency, algorithmic bias, and accountability turn up to the center. Consumers are unaware of the process of recommendation formation and the use of their data. Businesses should then reconcile innovation of technology with moral accountability, and the policymakers should come up with regulatory measures that deal with the intricacies of agentic commerce.

1.1 Chapter Objectives

This chapter aims to:

Introduce the definition of AI-powered shopping agents and what makes them different than the conventional e-commerce tools.
Research the impact of the AI shopping agents on consumer decision-making.
Examine the business strategic impacts of AI agents.
Discover ethical, privacy and governance issues relating to agentic commerce.
Suggest a conceptual framework and management rules of responsible adoption.

2. EVOLUTION OF E-COMMERCE AND ARTIFICIAL INTELLIGENCE

E-commerce development indicates more fundamental technological changes in information technologies, data analytics, and artificial intelligence. What has started as a mere digital continuation of the traditional retail has evolved to a smart, responsive, and highly individualized ecosystem. This shift was not adopted immediately, instead, it was a progression of multiple technological and strategic developments that have changed consumer engagement with online markets and firm value creation.

In the initial application, e-commerce operated in the form of online catalogue. In the late 1990s and the early 2000s, the majority of digital platforms were created following the design of the physical retail shops. Product listings, basic descriptions and pricing information were displayed on websites and consumers either browsed by categories or utilized key word search features to locate items of interest. These systems were very rudimentary in technological terms and the interaction was transactional in nature. Purchases were left to be searched, compared and evaluated by the consumers, and the platform was only involved in making the purchase.

These early systems were more convenient and more accessible but they also came with new challenges. The online world presented consumers with masses of choices, which they usually lacked adequate information and context. This is what has been termed as information overload thus augmenting cognitive effort in decision making. Consumers were forced to use their judgment to assess the quality of products, credibility and suitability, which in many cases led to decision fatigue and diminished satisfaction.

The initial significant change into smart digital business was the adoption of data analytics and recommendation engines. When platforms started gathering behavioural data, including browsing history, buying patterns, and demographic, they could then use that to present customized product recommendations. Collaborative and content-based filters algorithms became the key features in enhancing user experiences. Such systems made platforms suggest products that matched with consumer preferences, which enhanced interactions and conversion rates.

Although these advances were made, the early recommendation systems remained at a narrow scope and functionality. They were mostly passive as they made suggestions under the premise of previous behaviour as opposed to interacting with the consumer in real time or getting consumer intent. The consumer was the main decision-maker and the system was a helping device but not an active participant in the decision-making process.

The next major step in the development of e-commerce was the development of the artificial intelligence and machine learning technologies. In contrast to the conventional data analytics systems, AI algorithms can learn using big data, define patterns, and predict the future behaviour. This was the ability to take platforms beyond the realm of personalization to the predictive and adaptive. The AI-driven platforms might predict the needs of the consumer, modify the pricing dynamically, and offer personalized experiences in real-time.

This shift radically changed the essence of online trading. Rather than operating as mere transactional systems, e-commerce systems evolved into smart market-places that can inform consumer choices. Natural language processing, computer vision and reinforcement learning among other technologies were additional abilities that boosted these. Visual search, conversational interfaces and voice assistants helped consumers to engage with platforms in more natural and intuitive manners.

The most advanced step in the evolution of e-commerce is the use of AI-powered shopping agents in this general transformation. These agents combine various AI technologies to form interactive, adaptive and more autonomous systems. In comparison with the classic recommendation engine or chatbots based on rules, AI shopping agents are able to understand the intent of the user, analyze the options, and even act in accordance with the demand of consumers. They are digital intermediaries who are engaged in decision-making.

The introduction of AI shopping agents is a transition to agentic systems, not assistive technology. Assistive technologies can aid human decision-making, by suggesting or giving information, and agentic systems can be able to take actions and make decisions within specified parameters. When applied to e-commerce, the change implies that AI systems do not only suggest products anymore, but can also compare prices across the websites, manage the subscriptions, negotiate deals, and finalize transactions on their own.

The consumer behaviour and business strategy have much to do with this transformation. AI shopping agents decrease cognitive load and offer more convenience on the consumer side, however, they also modify the usual decision-making process and bring algorithmic mediation. The AI systems may become more dependent, and the issues of autonomy, trust, and the ultimate consequences of behaviour may be questioned. Business-wise, AI agents can allow companies to personalize large-scale operations, automate customer support, and get new insights into consumer data. The capabilities serve as new competitive advantage sources and bring about the challenge of data governance and algorithm bias.

Besides, the development of e-commerce into agentic systems indicates the increased significance of ethical and regulatory issues. With the increasing autonomy and power of the AI agents, the issue of privacy, transparency, accountability, and fairness take center stage in the development and implementation of digital commerce systems. Laws and regulatory requirements like the General Data Protection Regulation (GDPR) and other laws on data protection in different countries are some signs of attempts to solve these problems, and changes in technology frequently keep up with changing regulations.

It is thus crucial that one learns how e-commerce has developed to place the emergence of AI-customized shopping agents in perspective. All the stages of technological advancement, starting with the frozen catalogues to the smart markets and intelligent systems, have shifted the balance of power in decisions between humans and machine. The next phase is not just a technological enhancement but the structural change in the manner of how trade is carried out, felt, and managed.

2.1 Traditional E-Commerce Models

The initial era of e-commerce websites was created during the late 1990s and early 2000s. The main aim of these platforms was to digitalize the conventional retail processes. Customers were able to view product range books, price-check and transact online. The main features were the listing of products, search tools, simple filtering facilities, and payment processors.

These sites were convenient, but they mostly emulated the experience in the physical store going through online. Most decision making processes were still left to be done by consumers. They were forced to hunt down products, compare alternatives and make purchases without much technology support.

The lack of smart support systems in most cases led to decision fatigue. The consumers had many options and this resulted in cognitive overload and less satisfaction. This deficiency led to the realization of smarter and dynamic digital systems.

2.2 Emergence of Data-Driven Personalization

With the maturity of the digital technologies, e-commerce platforms started incorporating data analytics to enhance the user experiences. Platforms began gathering behavioural data including browsing history, buying behaviour and demographics. This information made it possible to create a set of recommendation systems to suggest products by consumer needs.

There were two popular types of recommendation algorithms:

Collaborative filtering, whereby the recommendations on products are given on the basis of the behaviour of similar users.

The content-based filtering which recommends the products according to similarities in the product characteristics.

These systems enhanced individualization and enhanced sales based on cross selling and up selling. Nevertheless, they were not extensive. The majority of recommendation engines were passive (as they showed suggestions without interacting with consumers).

2.3 Transition to Intelligent and Predictive Systems

AI brought sophistication into the e-commerce platforms. Machine learning programs allowed the systems to process large volumes of data, detect trends and forecast consumer tastes.

The essential progresses during this stage were:

Recommendation engines based on predictive engines.

Dynamic pricing systems

Chatbots to serve the customers automatically.

Shopping assistants over the voice.

These technologies enabled platforms to predict the requirements of consumers and offer them an experience that is more personalized. The digital commerce shifted its attention to customer experiences.

Table 1. Evolution of E-Commerce Technologies

Stage	Key Technologies	Characteristics
Early e-commerce	Static catalogues, search tools	Manual decision-making
Personalized e-commerce	Recommendation engines	Data-driven suggestions
Intelligent e-commerce	AI, predictive analytics	Real-time personalization
Agentic commerce	AI shopping agents	Autonomous decision support

3. LITERATURE REVIEW

The rapid development of the use of artificial intelligence in online trade has created a significant academic and industrial buzz in the last ten years. The studies in the field have developed since primitive debates on automation and recommendation systems up to sophisticated studies of intelligent agents who can interact, learn and make decisions on behalf of consumers. Consequently, the idea of the AI-driven shopping agents has surfaced at the cross-section of various scholarly fields, such as marketing, information systems, artificial intelligence, consumer behaviour, and business ethics.

The AI literature on commerce is interdisciplinary and, at the same time, fragmented. Other works put a lot more emphasis on the technical potential of AI systems, including machine learning algorithms, natural language processing, and predictive analytics. Such studies usually focus on the functionality of the recommendation engines, conversational interface, or other decision-support systems. The other bodies of research focus on consumer behaviour and investigate the impact of AI on trust, adoption, satisfaction, and purchase intentions. A third literature deals with strategic and operational implications, such as cost reduction, process automation and competitive advantage. Lastly, the ever-growing field of study is the ethical, legal and governance issues surrounding AI-mediated decision-making, including privacy issues, algorithmic bias and responsibility. Service automation through intelligent systems has significantly changed frontline customer interactions (Wirtz et al., 2018).

These research streams are in most cases discussed separately although they present valuable insights. Research in the technological field tends to ignore behavioural and ethical implications whereas consumer oriented research might not necessarily care about strategic and operational implications to firms. Equally, the ethical discourse at times is normative and does not tie into business strategy or technology design. This division restricts the formation of the comprehensive vision of AI-driven shopping agents and their further influence on the online trading system as a whole. Recent studies on emerging digital ecosystems such as the metaverse also highlight the role of advanced technologies in shaping user acceptance and engagement in digital environments (Al-Adwan, 2024).

AI-assisted shopping agents are a huge breakthrough of previous technologies in e-commerce. The old forms of recommendation systems were passive mechanisms that recommended products, using information about the past. Conversely, AI shopping agents are responsive, interactive and more autonomous. They can read user intent, conduct natural language dialogues, do cross platform comparisons, and they can transact. This change is an act of transformation between assistive technologies that facilitate the decision-making process and agentic systems that are involved in the decision-making processes.

The advent of conversational commerce has increased this change even more. Multimodal interaction systems, voice assistants and chat based interfaces enable consumers to interact with digital platforms more intuitively. These technologies make the purchasing process less frictional and increase accessibility to users whose digital literacy varies to different degrees. Simultaneously, they enhance the role of algorithmic intermediaries in the decision-making of consumers.

On a consumer behaviour approach, AI shopping agents threaten the customary methods of choice. Classical theories prioritize rational assessment and autonomous decision-making, and AI-based environments are associated with automated decisions, algorithm-driven recommendations and filtering. The change poses some critical issues regarding consumer autonomy, trust, and dependence on algorithmic systems.

Strategically, AI shopping agents will allow companies to personalize at scale, and automate customer interactions, and create valuable insights based on consumer data. The capabilities present the potential of efficiency and competitive differentiation. Nevertheless, they also bring with them additional risks such as excessive automation, managerial loss of control, and ethical issues regarding the use of data.

The ethical aspect of AI-based business has become more eminent in recent literature. The concerns around situations like data privacy, algorithmic bias, transparency, and accountability have not only become peripheral issues but have taken a central place in the scholarly and policy debate. With the same degree of autonomy and control over consumer decision making, the issues of responsibility and regulation of AI agents grow more complicated.

With such developments, it is evident that integrative studies that link technological capabilities to behavioural consequences and implications that are strategic and ethical are required. The literature review will serve this requirement by summarizing the results of other areas of knowledge and dividing them into four broad themes:

E-commerce development of artificial intelligence.
Chatting and agentic trade.
Artificial intelligence consumer behaviour.
Corporate ethics and business strategy.

The thematic and integrative nature of the review will no longer be confined to disjointed discussions but will offer a holistic view of AI-powered shopping agents as socio-technical systems that exist within the modern digital commerce systems.

3.1 Artificial Intelligence in Digital Commerce

The literature on AI in e-commerce identifies three key benefits of AI in e-commerce: efficiency, personalization, and decision support. The first research centered on automation and recommendation. Other more recent studies investigate conversational AI, predictive analytics and autonomous agents. AI has significantly transformed marketing and service delivery by enabling predictive analytics and intelligent decision-making systems (Davenport et al., 2020; Huang & Rust, 2021).

With the help of AI technologies, firms mine consumer behaviour, predict demand, and scale personalization. This ability allows businesses to provide customized services and also be operationally efficient. Research on the use of technology in online space also shows that organizational and technological maturity is another important factor that contributes to the adoption of AI-based systems in business (Yaseen et al., 2023).

3.2 Conversational and Agentic Commerce

The idea of conversational commerce is the shopping experience that is mediated by chatbots, voice assistants, and messaging platforms. The systems allow natural language communication, and this minimizes the strain during the process of purchasing.

The next step in evolution is agentic commerce, in which the AI systems are free agents who can make decisions and conduct transactions on behalf of their users.

According to the new studies on metaverse and sophisticated digital commercial spaces, it is proposed that immersive and AI-enhanced systems are reimbursement of interaction and purchase intentions within online markets (Al-Adwan et al., 2025; Jafar et al., 2025).

3.3 Consumer Behaviour in AI-Mediated Environments

The traditional models of consumer behaviour presuppose rationality in decision-making and an unbiased assessment of the alternatives. The AI-mediated commerce disrupts these assumptions by assuming algorithmic intermediaries.

AI shopping agents:

Reduce cognitive load
Streamline the decision-making processes.
Make individual recommendations.

Nevertheless, they also create such risks as a decrease in independence and filter bubbles and similar patterns in meta-commerce environments, where trust, perceived usefulness, and technological readiness strongly influence consumer acceptance (Balhareth et al., 2024).

Table 2. Consumer Decision-Making in Traditional vs AI-Mediated Commerce

Dimension	Traditional E-Commerce	AI-Mediated Commerce
Information search	Manual	Algorithm-assisted
Decision effort	High	Reduced
Personalization	Limited	High
Autonomy	Full human control	Shared human–AI control
Trust factors	Brand reputation	Algorithm transparency

4. CONCEPTUAL FRAMEWORK OF AI SHOPPING AGENTS

Figure 1. Integrated conceptual framework of AI-powered shopping agents

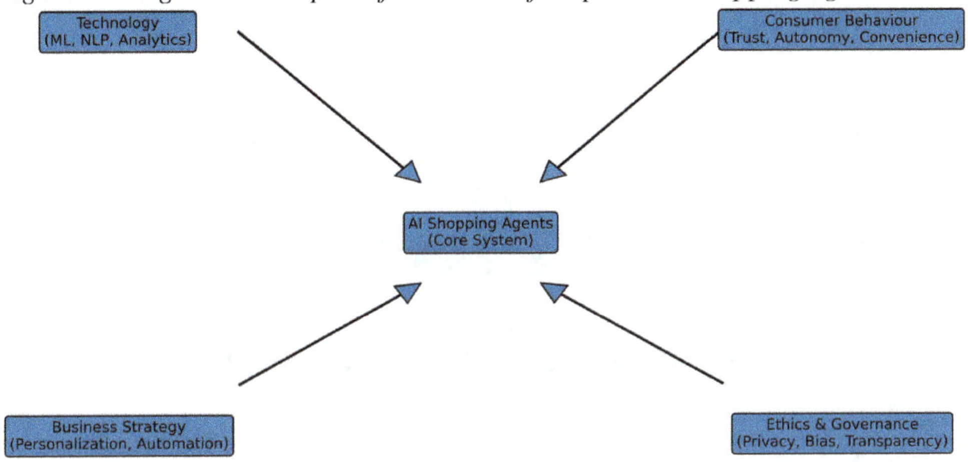

An integrated paradigm that links technology, consumer behaviour, corporate strategy, and governance can help us understand AI-powered shopping agents.

Core Dimensions

Technological capabilities
Consumer decision processes
Business value creation
Ethical and regulatory considerations

Table 3. Integrated Conceptual Framework

Dimension	Key Elements	Outcomes
Technology	Machine learning, NLP, analytics	Intelligent agents
Consumer	Trust, autonomy, convenience	Adoption and satisfaction
Business	Personalization, automation	Efficiency and revenue growth
Ethics	Privacy, bias, transparency	Trust and compliance

5. ARCHITECTURE OF AI-POWERED SHOPPING AGENTS

Figure 2. End-to-end architecture of an AI-powered shopping agent

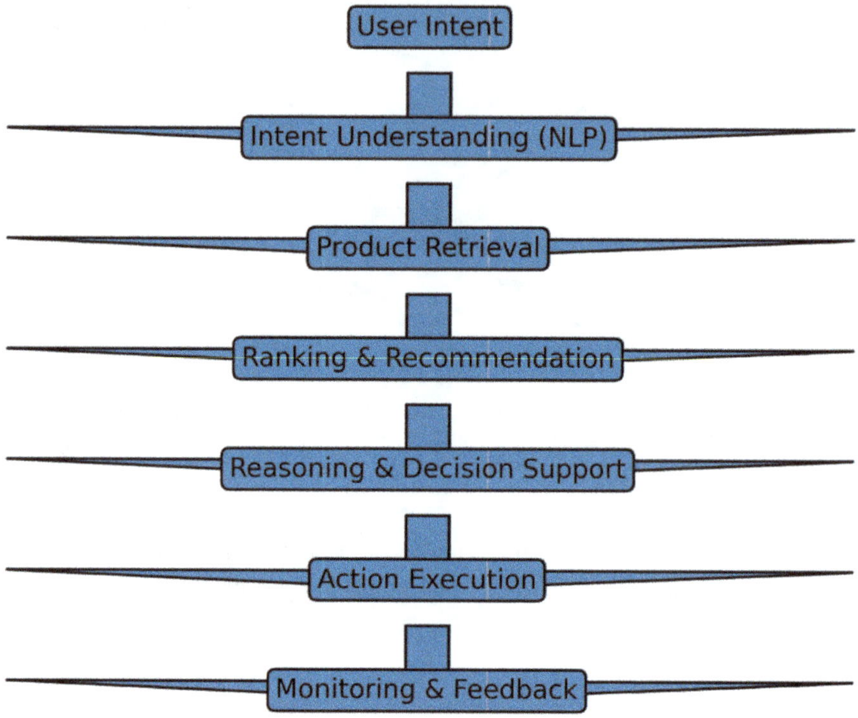

A multi-stage decision pipeline powers AI shopping agents.

Figure Concept: AI Shopping Agent Pipeline

User Intent
↓
Intent Understanding (NLP)
↓
Product Retrieval
↓
Ranking and Recommendation
↓
Reasoning and Decision Support
↓
Action Execution

↓
Monitoring and Feedback

The decision-making and action-execution components of its design set it apart from conventional chatbots.

Table 4. Functional Components of AI Shopping Agents

Component	Function
Intent Engine	Interprets user requests
Data Layer	Stores behavioural and product data
Recommendation Engine	Suggests products
Decision Module	Evaluates alternatives
Action Module	Executes purchases
Monitoring System	Tracks performance

6. RESEARCH METHODOLOGY

6.1 Research Design

In order to investigate the function of AI-powered shopping agents in digital commerce, this chapter employs a methodical conceptual literature study. The goal of the research is to integrate and synthesize current knowledge across several academic fields rather than to empirically test theories. This method works especially well for new technical phenomena, when empirical research is frequently dispersed or has a narrow focus.

The research of AI shopping agents is a field that is developing quickly. Technological advancements often surpass scholarly investigations, leading to discrete discoveries in fields including marketing, information systems, artificial intelligence, and corporate ethics. Predictive analytics and intelligent agents play a critical role in improving decision-making accuracy in e-commerce (Wang & Li, 2023). These viewpoints can be combined into a single analytical framework with the help of a conceptual literature review.

The research is guided by the following key questions:

How are AI-powered shopping agents conceptualized in existing literature?
How do these agents influence consumer decision-making processes?
What strategic advantages do AI shopping agents offer to firms?

What ethical and governance challenges arise from agentic commerce?

The chapter seeks to offer a comprehensive grasp of the technological, behavioural, strategic, and ethical aspects of AI-powered shopping agents by tackling these issues.

6.2 Data Sources and Search Strategy

Several scholarly databases were used to find pertinent literature in order to guarantee thorough coverage.

These databases included:

Scopus
Web of Science
Google Scholar
IEEE Xplore

A keyword-based search strategy was employed. Key search terms included:

AI shopping agents
Artificial intelligence in e-commerce
Conversational commerce
Autonomous agents in retail
Consumer behaviour and AI
Ethical AI in commerce

Boolean operators such as AND and OR were used to refine search results. For example:

"AI shopping agents" AND "consumer behaviour"
"conversational commerce" OR "AI retail agents"

From the reference lists of highly cited papers, influential research were also found using backward citation tracking.

6.3 Inclusion and Exclusion Criteria

Clear inclusion and exclusion criteria were used to guarantee academic rigor and relevance.

Inclusion criteria:

Peer-reviewed journal articles
Academic books and conference papers
Publications between 2000 and 2025

Studies focused on AI in commerce, retail, or consumer behaviour

Exclusion criteria:

Non-academic sources such as blogs or opinion pieces
Studies focusing solely on technical algorithms without business or consumer context
AI research unrelated to digital commerce

This filtering process ensured that the literature reviewed was both relevant and academically credible.

6.4 Analytical Approach: Thematic Synthesis

A thematic synthesis approach was used to analyze the selected literature. This involved three key steps:

Identifying recurring concepts across studies
Grouping related concepts into broader themes
Integrating these themes into a unified analytical framework

Four major thematic clusters emerged:

Technological evolution of AI shopping agents
Consumer behaviour and decision-making impacts
Business strategy and operational transformation
Ethical, privacy, and governance challenges

By using this method, the chapter was able to offer integrative analysis rather than merely descriptive descriptions.

7. THEMATIC ANALYSIS AND DISCUSSION

In the context of AI-powered shopping agents, this section aims to summarize the key findings of the literature review and analyze their implications for company strategy, ethical governance, and consumer behavior. Instead of showcasing discrete findings, this part synthesizes knowledge from several fields to offer a methodical examination of how agentic technologies are changing the landscape of digital business.

Four interrelated dimensions—technological transformation, changes in consumer decision-making, strategic business consequences, and ethical and governance challenges—were identified by the thematic synthesis as defining the influence of AI shopping agents. Instead of functioning independently, these elements come together to produce a dynamic system where technical capabilities impact customer experiences, company tactics are influenced by consumer responses, and strategic decisions give rise to new ethical and regulatory issues.

AI-powered shopping agents mark a transition from assisting digital aids to self-governing decision-support systems from a technology standpoint. Due to the mainly passive nature of earlier e-commerce platforms, customers had to conduct their own independent research, analysis, and decision-making. AI agents, on the other hand, actively analyze human intent, sort options, and direct choices. With this shift, agentic commerce—where algorithms serve as intermediaries that influence market transactions rather than just being tools—emerges. AI-driven retail systems have been shown to enhance operational efficiency and customer engagement across digital platforms (Grewal et al., 2017; Krafft et al., 2023).

This technological change modifies the conventional decision-making process at the customer level. Traditional theories of consumer behavior place a strong emphasis on human agency, information exploration, and logical assessment. However, by delivering carefully chosen options and minimizing information overload, AI shopping bots reorganize these procedures. Convenience and efficiency are increased, but new issues with algorithmic influence, dependency, and decreased exposure to a variety of options are also raised. Because customers must rely on technologies they do not completely understand, trust becomes a crucial mediating factor.

AI-powered shopping agents generate new sources of competitive advantage from a strategic perspective. Businesses can use these technologies to automate customer interactions, provide individualized experiences, and glean insights from customer data. However, the literature also emphasizes the dangers of short-term optimization and over-automation. When algorithms put efficiency ahead of relationship value, businesses risk undermining their brand equity and long-term customer trust. Effective strategy therefore necessitates striking a balance between automation, human monitoring, and ethical issues.

The fourth crucial feature of the analysis consists of governance and ethical concerns. Concerns about privacy, prejudice, accountability, and transparency are raised by AI shopping assistants' vast data collection and algorithmic decision-making. These issues are essential to the long-term viability of agentic trade, not ancillary. To guarantee that AI systems continue to be in line with societal values, regulatory frameworks, ethical design principles, and organizational governance mechanisms must develop in tandem with technology advancements.

Each of these thematic themes is covered in detail in the ensuing subsections. This section offers an organized comprehension of the wider ramifications of AI-powered shopping agents by examining their advantages, disadvantages, and trade-offs. The approach highlights the conflicts between automation and human control, personalization and privacy, and efficiency and autonomy by going beyond descriptive findings. The chapter aims to shed light on the complicated issues and revolutionary possibilities of AI-mediated business by adopting this comprehensive viewpoint.

7.1 Consumer Behaviour Transformation

The way that consumers make decisions is drastically altered by AI-powered shopping bots. Customers actively look for products, weigh their options, and compare alternatives in traditional e-commerce. This approach frequently necessitates a significant amount of mental work, especially in settings where there are many product options.

By sifting through options and making tailored suggestions, AI shopping bots lessen this load. To recommend appropriate options, these agents examine ambient cues, preferences, and behavioral data. Customers benefit from greater convenience and less cognitive load as a result. Personalization driven by AI has been found to positively influence purchase intention and customer satisfaction (Valencia-Arias et al., 2024; Rahman & Dey, 2024).

Nonetheless, a number of hazards are linked to AI-mediated decision-making, according to the literature. Filter bubbles can result from algorithms that restrict exposure to a variety of possibilities. Furthermore, customers' ability to critically evaluate may be diminished if they grow unduly dependent on AI agents.

Consumer acceptability is largely determined by trust. When consumers believe AI shopping agents are capable, open, and equitable, they are more likely to use them. On the other hand, suspected data misuse and opaque decision-making procedures erode trust.

Table 5. Consumer-Level Benefits and Risks of AI Shopping Agents

Benefit	Description	Risk	Description
Reduced cognitive load	Simplifies decision-making	Reduced autonomy	Overreliance on AI recommendations
Personalization	Relevant product suggestions	Filter bubbles	Limited exposure to alternatives
Convenience	Faster purchasing process	Over-automation	Loss of critical thinking
Continuous assistance	24/7 support	Data dependency	Privacy concerns

7.2 Business Strategy Transformation

AI-powered shopping agents serve as mediators that create value from a strategic standpoint. They have an impact on supply chain management, marketing, and customer service, among other areas of the company model.

Personalization at Scale

Businesses can now provide enormous consumer bases with personalized experiences thanks to AI agents. This feature boosts consumer satisfaction, boosts conversion rates, and strengthens brand loyalty.

Operational Efficiency

Operational costs are decreased by the automation of client interactions. Without human assistance, AI agents can manage common questions, direct product selection, and offer post-purchase assistance.

Data-Driven Decision-Making

AI systems use customer data to produce insightful analysis. Marketing campaigns, inventory control, and pricing strategies are all influenced by these findings.

Table 6. Strategic Impact of AI Shopping Agents

Strategic Area	AI Contribution	Business Outcome
Marketing	Personalized recommendations	Higher conversion rates
Customer service	Automated interactions	Reduced operational costs
Supply chain	Predictive demand forecasting	Efficient inventory management
Pricing	Dynamic pricing algorithms	Revenue optimization

Notwithstanding these benefits, an over-reliance on automation could have unforeseen repercussions. Short-term performance metric-optimized algorithms have the potential to damage long-term client relationships. Thus, it is advised to take a balanced approach that combines human control with AI efficiency.

7.3 Ethical and Governance Challenges

A major subject in the literature on AI-powered shopping agents is ethical considerations. Due to their heavy reliance on user data and algorithmic decision-making, these systems raise concerns about accountability, transparency, justice, and privacy.

Data Privacy

Comprehensive customer data is gathered by AI agents, including browser history, purchase patterns, and conversational inputs. Concerns with consent and privacy may arise from consumers' incomplete understanding of how their data is handled.

Algorithmic Bias

Discriminatory results may result from bias in training data. AI agents might, for instance, make different product recommendations depending on a customer's demographics, which would further entrench already-existing disparities.

Transparency and Explainability

Because many AI systems function as "black boxes," it might be challenging for users to comprehend the decision-making process. Lack of openness erodes confidence and presents moral dilemmas.

Accountability

The increasing autonomy of AI agents raises questions about decision-making accountability. It might be difficult to assign blame for mistakes or injuries.

Table 7. Ethical Issues and Mitigation Strategies

Ethical Issue	Description	Mitigation Strategy
Privacy	Excessive data collection	Privacy-by-design systems
Bias	Discriminatory recommendations	Bias audits and diverse datasets
Lack of transparency	Opaque algorithms	Explainable AI techniques
Accountability gaps	Unclear responsibility	Governance frameworks

7.4 Trade-Off Analysis: Efficiency vs. Autonomy

The conflict between efficiency and autonomy is one of the main issues in AI-mediated trade. AI agents increase speed and convenience, but they may also take away user control.

Table 8. Key Trade-Offs in AI Shopping Agents

Dimension	AI Advantage	Potential Risk	Mitigation
Speed	Faster decisions	Impulsive purchases	Transparent recommendations
Personalization	Relevant options	Privacy concerns	Consent mechanisms
Automation	Reduced effort	Loss of control	Human-in-the-loop systems
Data analytics	Better insights	Data misuse	Strong governance policies

8. MANAGERIAL IMPLICATIONS

The advent of AI-powered shopping agents signifies a fundamental change in the reasoning behind digital business strategy, not just a technical advancement. In conventional e-commerce models, businesses mainly concentrated on supply chain efficiency, price strategies, and website interface optimization. However, the focus of competition is increasingly moving from product availability and pricing to algorithmic intelligence, data capabilities, and experience design as a result of the development of intelligent agents that can communicate directly with consumers and influence their purchasing decisions.

AI shopping agents work as proactive go-betweens for businesses and customers. These passive recommendation algorithms that are a part of digital platforms' backdrop have changed. Rather, they have a direct influence on how customers conduct informational searches, weigh their options, and complete transactions. Since many of these tasks are increasingly mediated by intelligent systems rather than by human workers or static digital interfaces, this shift modifies the conventional responsibilities of marketing, customer service, and sales.

This change presents both opportunities and risks from a managerial standpoint. On the one hand, businesses may provide highly customized experiences at scale, increase operational effectiveness, and learn more about customer behavior with AI-powered shopping agents. These features can boost conversion rates, improve consumer satisfaction, and fortify enduring brand loyalty. However, an over-reliance on automated decision systems can lead to ethical problems, a loss of managerial control, and threats to a company's reputation or compliance with regulations.

Therefore, integrating AI shopping agents calls for a strategic approach rather than just a technological one. Managers need to think about how these agents fit in with customer relationship plans, brand identity, and organizational goals. Choices about the degree of automation, data usage guidelines, and transparency measures will have a big impact on competitive positioning and customer trust.

Additionally, the nature of competitiveness in digital markets is being altered by AI-powered shopping agents. Businesses must compete not only on product quality and pricing, but also on the efficacy of their AI-driven engagement strategies, as algorithms increasingly dictate product exposure and suggestions. Superior responsiveness, predictive capacities, and customer retention may be attained by businesses that successfully include intelligent agents into their customer journeys. On the other hand, businesses that don't adjust can find it difficult to stay relevant in markets that are becoming more automated and data-driven.

Three important factors need to be balanced in managerial decisions in this situation: ethical responsibility, customization, and efficiency. Although predictive analytics and automation can improve operational performance, their implementation must maintain consumer trust and guarantee adherence to new data protection laws. Therefore, managers need to take a comprehensive approach that combines technology innovation with moral leadership and strategic planning.

The sections that follow offer helpful advice on how to deploy AI-powered shopping bots in a way that minimizes operational and ethical concerns while optimizing strategic value.

8.1 Strategic Implementation Guidelines

Instead than viewing AI shopping agents as merely cost-cutting devices, managers ought to view them as strategic assets. Alignment with organizational strategy and customer experience objectives is necessary for successful execution.

Key recommendations include:

Align AI adoption with long-term strategic objectives.
Integrate AI agents with CRM and supply chain systems.
Use explainable AI features to build consumer trust.
Maintain human oversight in critical decisions.
Implement strong data governance policies.

8.2 Ethical AI as Competitive Advantage

Using AI responsibly can help you stand out from the competition. Businesses that put an emphasis on openness, equity, and data security have a higher chance of gaining the trust of their clients over the long run.

Adoption of ethical AI can lower regulatory risks and improve brand reputation. Businesses that exhibit ethical data practices could have a competitive edge in markets where customers' privacy concerns are growing.

9. POLICY AND GOVERNANCE IMPLICATIONS

Beyond conventional e-commerce legislation, the emergence of AI-powered shopping bots presents additional governance issues. In contrast to traditional digital platforms, these agents do more than just make transactions possible; they also actively participate in decision-making, filter information, and occasionally carry out purchases on their own. Regulations created for human-driven transactions might therefore no longer be adequate.

AI shopping agents function at the nexus of algorithmic responsibility, consumer protection, competition legislation, and data privacy. Because of their growing autonomy, governance models need to be rethought in order to prevent technological innovation from jeopardizing market justice, consumer rights, or public trust.

9.1 From Platform Regulation to Agentic Governance

Platforms and sellers have been the main targets of traditional e-commerce regulation. Regulatory frameworks usually cover topics like customer dispute resolution, payment security, and product safety. But a new level of algorithmic mediation between customers and markets is brought about by AI shopping bots.

In agentic commerce, decision-making is partially delegated to AI systems. These systems:

Interpret consumer intent
Filter available options
Rank alternatives
Suggest or execute purchases

Because the AI agent now plays a significant role in the transaction process, this change poses new governance issues. AI bots function at scale, make choices quickly, and sometimes use opaque algorithms, in contrast to human middlemen.

Because of this, governance needs to shift from platform-centric regulation to agent-centric governance, which will regulate the actions, accountability, and transparency of AI agents.

9.2 Core Policy Challenges in Agentic Commerce

A number of significant policy issues pertaining to AI-powered shopping agents are identified in the literature.

1. Algorithmic Transparency

Since many AI agents function as "black-box" systems, it might be challenging for users to comprehend how suggestions are made. Informed decision-making can be hampered and confidence damaged by a lack of transparency.

2. Data Privacy and Consent

Large amounts of personal data are necessary for AI agents to function. This data gathering could violate privacy rights or result in misuse if appropriate measures are not in place.

3. Consumer Autonomy

Decisions made by consumers may be influenced or nudged by AI agents. Over-automation may make it harder for customers to make decisions about what to buy.

4. Accountability and Liability

As AI agents make judgments on their own, it becomes difficult to assign blame for mistakes. It's frequently unclear who is responsible—the user, the platform, or the developer.

5. Market Fairness and Competition

AI systems might favour particular platforms or suppliers, which could skew competition and increase market consolidation.

Table 9. Key Policy Challenges in AI Shopping Agents

Policy Challenge	Description	Potential Impact
Transparency	Opaque algorithms	Reduced consumer trust
Privacy	Extensive data collection	Risk of data misuse
Autonomy	Algorithmic nudging	Reduced consumer control
Accountability	Unclear liability	Legal and ethical ambiguity
Competition	Platform-favoured recommendations	Market distortion

9.3 Regulatory Approaches to AI Shopping Agents

The problems of agentic commerce can be addressed by a variety of regulatory strategies.

1. Transparency and Explainability Requirements

Regulators might demand that AI systems justify their suggestions. Explainable AI systems can assist customers in comprehending the rationale behind product recommendations.

2. Data Protection and Consent Frameworks

Data protection laws that prioritize user permission, data minimization, and openness include the General Data Protection Regulation (GDPR) and India's Digital Personal Data Protection Act. AI shopping agents ought to follow these guidelines.

3. Algorithmic Accountability Standards

Standards mandating businesses to audit AI systems for bias, fairness, and dependability may be introduced by governments. Frequent audits can assist in discovering technological problems or discriminatory results.

4. Human Oversight Requirements

Regulations may need human clearance before AI robots can make judgments in high-risk situations, such financial or medical purchases.

9.4 Governance Models for Agentic Commerce

It takes a mix of organizational, technological, and legal measures to effectively regulate AI shopping agents.

1. Legal Governance

Liabilities and obligations for AI-driven judgments should be outlined in legal frameworks. To establish accountability when mistakes are made, clear regulations are required.

2. Organizational Governance

Firms must implement internal governance structures, including:

AI ethics committees
Algorithmic audit teams
Data protection officers

These safeguards guarantee that AI technology are used responsibly.

3. Technical Governance

Technical safeguards can be embedded directly into AI systems, including:

Explainable AI features
Bias detection tools
Privacy-preserving algorithms

Table 10. Multi-Level Governance Framework

Governance Level	Key Mechanisms	Objective
Legal	Regulations, liability rules	Protect consumers and ensure accountability
Organizational	Ethics committees, audits	Responsible corporate practices
Technical	Explainable AI, bias detection	Transparent and fair algorithms

9.5 Trade-Offs in Policy Design

AI shopping agent regulation requires striking a balance between conflicting goals. While too little regulation could put consumers at danger, too much control could hinder innovation.

Table 11. Policy Trade-Offs in Agentic Commerce

Policy Goal	Benefit	Risk of Over-Regulation	Risk of Under-Regulation
Data privacy	Consumer protection	Reduced innovation	Data misuse
Transparency	Increased trust	Slower system performance	Opaque decision-making
Accountability	Clear liability	Legal complexity	Consumer harm
Competition	Fair markets	Reduced platform efficiency	Market concentration

9.6 Role of International Cooperation

AI-driven shopping agents function internationally. An AI agent hosted in one nation may be used by a customer to buy goods from another. Regulation is made more difficult by the cross-border character of agentic commerce. International cooperation is therefore essential. Policymakers should work toward:

Harmonized data protection standards
Cross-border AI governance frameworks
Shared ethical guidelines

Global standards development can be greatly aided by institutions like the OECD and international trade associations.

9.7 Policy Recommendations

Several policy recommendations can be made in light of the analysis:

Mechanisms for mandate transparency
AI shopping agents ought to give concise justifications for their suggestions.
Make data protection laws stronger
Data minimization and informed consent should be guaranteed by regulations.
Describe the requirements for algorithmic audits.
Regular bias and fairness audits should be carried out by businesses.
Describe the frameworks for liability.
Responsibility for AI-driven judgments should be clearly defined by regulations.
Encourage global collaboration in AI governance
Cross-border issues can be resolved by global standards.

9.8 Toward Responsible Agentic Commerce

The capacity to strike a balance between ethical responsibility and technological innovation will determine the future of AI-powered shopping agents. Governance should steer innovation in ways that preserve trust and safeguard customers, not to stifle it.

Responsible agentic commerce requires:

Transparent algorithms
Ethical design principles
Clear accountability structures
Collaborative governance between regulators and industry

Policymakers can guarantee that AI shopping agents develop into reliable middlemen who improve rather than compromise consumer welfare by embracing these guidelines.

10. FUTURE RESEARCH DIRECTIONS

Future research should focus on several key areas:

Empirical studies examining consumer trust in AI agents.
Long-term behavioural effects of AI-mediated decision-making.
Cross-cultural adoption patterns.
Human–AI collaboration models.
Market-level impacts of AI agent adoption.

11. LIMITATIONS

This chapter has several limitations:

It relies on secondary data rather than primary empirical research.
The literature may be subject to publication bias.
Rapid technological changes may outpace academic research.
Industry-specific dynamics are not examined in depth.

12. CONCLUSION

An important turning point in the development of digital commerce has been reached with the appearance of AI-powered shopping agents. What started out as static online catalogues has evolved into retail ecosystems that are smart, flexible, and becoming more independent. The result of this change is AI shopping agents, who act as active decision-makers with the ability to comprehend user intent, weigh options, and complete transactions in addition to serving as suggestion tools.

These agents radically change the decision-making process from the standpoint of the consumer. Conventional consumer behaviour models place a strong emphasis on autonomous information gathering, logical assessment, and purposeful comparison of options. On the other hand, algorithmic middlemen that filter data, customize suggestions, and direct consumers toward particular options are introduced by AI-mediated commerce. Although this change makes things more convenient and less cognitively demanding, it also brings up significant issues with consumer autonomy, reliance on automated systems, and algorithmic influence.

For businesses, the strategic ramifications are just as significant. Businesses may automate customer interactions, accomplish personalization at scale, and extract insightful information from consumer data with the help of AI shopping bots. These skills boost competitive positioning, increase operational effectiveness, and improve consumer experiences. The analysis also shows that the strategic value of AI agents hinges on their careful integration into larger organizational strategies rather than just their adoption as a technology. Long-term consumer connections and brand trust may be weakened by an over-reliance on automation or optimization that is only focused on short-term KPIs.

The use of AI-powered shopping agents raises important ethical and governance issues. Risks to privacy, security, and informed consent arise from the widespread usage of customer data. Discriminatory results could result from algorithmic bias, and consumer trust could be damaged by opaque decision-making procedures. Accountability issues get more complicated when AI agents gain autonomy, necessitating the development of new organizational and legal frameworks. Therefore, integrating the values of openness, equity, and human supervision into the development and application of AI systems is essential to their sustainable adoption.

This chapter's conceptual framework emphasizes how consumer behavior, company strategy, ethical governance, and technology capabilities are all intertwined. It is important to see AI shopping agents as socio-technical systems that function inside larger institutional and cultural frameworks. Their influence must be assessed in light of social ramifications, legal obligations, and enduring customer trust in addition to efficiency and profitability.

The results indicate that rather than being viewed as straightforward automation tools, managers should view AI shopping agents as strategic assets. Integration with customer relationship systems, adherence to responsible data practices, and alignment with company goals are necessary for successful implementation. The emergence of agentic commerce highlights for policymakers the necessity of flexible regulatory frameworks that tackle problems like algorithmic accountability, transparency, and cross-platform data governance.

In the future, the structure of digital markets, consumer expectations, and competitive dynamics are probably going to change as AI shopping agents become more widely used. The line between human and machine decision-making will continue to blur as these systems advance in sophistication. Therefore, the ability of institutions and organizations to strike a balance between automation and human oversight, efficiency and justice, and personalization and consumer autonomy will be just as important to the future of digital commerce as technological advancement.

To sum up, AI-powered shopping agents have enormous potential to improve online commerce's effectiveness, ease, and value creation. However, ethical governance, strategic integration, and responsible design will be necessary for their long-term success. Businesses and legislators may guarantee that AI shopping agents develop into reliable digital commerce facilitators rather than contentious or manipulative middlemen by taking a human-centered and balanced strategy.

REFERENCES

Al-Adwan, A. S. (2024). The government metaverse: Charting the coordinates of citizen acceptance. *Telematics and Informatics*, *88*, 102109. DOI: 10.1016/j.tele.2024.102109

Al-Adwan, A. S., Yaseen, H., Alkhwaldi, A. F., Jafar, R. M. S., Fauzi, M. A., & Abdullah, A. (2025). Treasure hunting for brands: Metaverse marketing gamification effects on purchase intention, WOM, and loyalty. *Journal of Global Marketing*, *38*(4), 392–416. DOI: 10.1080/08911762.2025.2463897

Balhareth, H., Al-Adwan, A. S., Alsoud, A. R., Abd-Aljaber, O., Al-Rahmi, W. M., & Urbaníková, M. (2024). Journey into meta-commerce: Unveiling the driving forces of consumer adoption. *Global Knowledge, Memory and Communication*. Advance online publication. DOI: 10.1108/GKMC-05-2024-0307

Davenport, T. H., Guha, A., Grewal, D., & Bressgott, T. (2020). How artificial intelligence will change the future of marketing. *Journal of the Academy of Marketing Science*, *48*(1), 24–42. DOI: 10.1007/s11747-019-00696-0

Grewal, D., Roggeveen, A. L., & Nordfält, J. (2017). The future of retailing. *Journal of Retailing*, *93*(1), 1–6. DOI: 10.1016/j.jretai.2016.12.008

Huang, M.-H., & Rust, R. T. (2021). Artificial intelligence in service. *Journal of Service Research*, *24*(1), 3–18.

Jafar, R. M. S., Jabeen, M., Hussain, S., Niu, B., Sham, R., & Al-Adwan, A. S. (2025). Cyber shopping beyond boundaries: The metaverse revolution in e-commerce and consumer behavior.

Jafar, R. M. S., Jabeen, M., Hussain, S., Niu, B., Sham, R., & Al-Adwan, A. S. (2025). Cyber Shopping Beyond Boundaries: The Metaverse Revolution in e-Commerce and Consumer Behavior. *Human Behavior and Emerging Technologies*, *5559234*(1), 5559234. Advance online publication. DOI: 10.1155/hbe2/5559234

Krafft, M., Gouthier, M. H. J., & Mantrala, M. K. (2023). Artificial intelligence in retailing. *Journal of Retailing*, *99*(2), 156–171.

Rahman, M., & Dey, B. L. (2024). AI-powered personalization and consumer trust in e-commerce. *Journal of Retailing and Consumer Services*, *76*, 103579.

Valencia-Arias, A., Garcés-Giraldo, L. F., & Montoya, I. A. (2024). Artificial intelligence, personalization, and purchase intention. *Technological Forecasting and Social Change*, *198*, 122005.

Wang, Y., & Li, H. (2023). Predictive analytics and intelligent agents in e-commerce. *Journal of Retailing and Consumer Services*, *71*, 103119.

Wirtz, J., Patterson, P. G., Kunz, W., Gruber, T., Lu, V. N., Paluch, S., & Martins, A. (2018). Service robots in the frontline. *Journal of Service Management*, *29*(5), 907–931. DOI: 10.1108/JOSM-04-2018-0119

Yaseen, H., Al-Adwan, A. S., Nofal, M., Hmoud, H., & Abujassar, R. S. (2023). Factors influencing cloud computing adoption among SMEs: The Jordanian context. *Information Development*, *39*(2), 317–332. DOI: 10.1177/02666669211047916

KEY TERMS AND DEFINITIONS

Agentic Commerce: Commerce mediated by autonomous AI systems.
AI Shopping Agent: Intelligent system that assists or automates purchases.
Algorithmic Bias: Systematic discrimination caused by AI models.
Cognitive Load: Mental effort required to make decisions.
Conversational Commerce: Shopping through chat or voice interfaces.
Explainable AI: AI systems that provide understandable decisions.
Human-in-the-Loop: Systems where humans oversee AI decisions.
Personalization: Tailored recommendations for individual users.

Chapter 11
Redefining the Customer Experience Through Intelligent Personalization

Salam Al E'mari
http://orcid.org/0000-0002-2134-4158
University of Petra, Jordan

Yousef Sanjalawe
http://orcid.org/0000-0002-4442-1865
University of Jordan, Jordan

Budoor Allehyani
http://orcid.org/0009-0006-0424-6894
Umm Al-Qura University, Saudi Arabia

ABSTRACT

This chapter examines how intelligent personalization transforms customer experience by integrating advanced Artificial Intelligence (AI) capabilities with human-centered design. It explores the psychological foundations that guide personalized engagement, including cognitive load reduction, emotional relevance, trust formation, and cultural variation. Furthermore, the chapter analyzes how intelligent agents, hyper-personalization architectures, adaptive user interfaces, and predictive analytics function collectively to deliver context-aware and dynamically tailored interactions. In addition, it addresses ethical concerns involving privacy, autonomy, fairness, and transparency to emphasize the necessity of responsible design. Moreover, case

DOI: 10.4018/979-8-3373-7330-0.ch011

studies across retail, healthcare, finance, education, and accessibility illustrate how culturally adaptive and inclusive systems enhance satisfaction, decision support, and digital equity.

1. INTRODUCTION

The customer experience in relation to digital platforms has changed definitively due to the increased availability of Artificial Intelligence across the globe. Initially, suggested algorithms based on general pathways belonging to demographic groupings has changed to individualized platforms that can recognize minute pieces of behavior, emotion, context, and other intricate aspects of an individual. Recommendations and interfaces with other higher functions such as predictive guidance integrated in the day-to-day life of the individual around a decade ago seemed impossible. Still, such features demonstrate a change in paradigm and that personalization has now become a key part of customer experience instead of an additional benefit.

More sophisticated intelligent agents do not work with pre-determined rules as in the past. They now combine different strategies to anticipate customer needs and support decision-making in real-time using machine learning, natural language processing, and behavioral analytics. Customers can now alternatively engage with mobile apps, websites, wearables, smart home devices, and voice assistants and the systems in all these touch points learn user preferences. Personalization reduces the amount of work a customer has to do in order to reach a solution by improving engagement and relevance. In the end, technology should change in a way to fit the needs of the consumers (Al-Adwan & Sammour,2020; Almomani et al., 2025).

This chapter focuses on the customer experience of Artificial Intelligence (AI), and how the technology shapes the customer experience, particularly the psychology of the choice, the trust, and engagement. Users emotional response and understand how they interact, and the emotions involved in the interactions created by systems guided through artificial intelligence, determine the effectiveness of engagement personalization. Interaction precision is instrumental, but the evaluation by the users of the response by the system and the perceived system interactions dominates. A system's ensemble of constructs which, through perceived relevance, automatically address the user's problems, system empathy, guiding to balanced and system neutral responds, equanimity, and transparent system response, most often determines the user's decision to trust and use the personalized service or to reject the system. These traits demonstrated the elements of personalization approach which is driven by social and psychological factors.

This transformation rests on the role of the intelligent agent. This is the use of intelligent agent systems to analyze data to their Conversational interfaces. These systems combine advanced data analysis with predictive data to provide direct and anticipatory system services. Agents with adaptive user interfaces assist with product recommendations, navigation support, and predictions from assistive systems. Educated and designed predictive models proactively assist a user to reorder an item, overcome decision fatigue, or provide guidance when a user is completing a task and needs additional information. The systems work seamlessly to provide users with real-time information and support. These capabilities and many more serve to shift customer interactions from rigid and linear to sophisticated and dynamic.

Unlike other forms of marketing, hyper-personalization relies heavily on AI to tailor content to individual customers. Customers are likely to become uneasy about how tailored marketing relies on often intrusive data collection techniques. This phenomenon has been widely analyzed, and termed, the privacy paradox that lies between the comfort of personalized the services and the worry of overexposure to personal data (Acquisti et al., 2015). There are many unintended consequences to hyper-personalization with the foremost one being biased content and lack of relevant disparate materials that do not align with the user's individual personal data. Ethically, it is of the utmost importance that such models emphasize user's agency and data privacy.

Redistributing user demand responsibility increases complexity because of the user's cultural background impacting his or her relevance, trust, and emotional ease. A user from a role-oriented culture may prefer social personalization, whereas from an individual-oriented culture self-customization which promotes autonomy and self-expressive behavior. The access and communication improvement for disabled individuals is considerable by adaptive interfaces on communication and interaction ability profiles. Personalization, as is crafted ethically, is one of the most powerful for enhancing equity and inclusion, especially when concerning technology engagement that is needed for foster participation engagement with technology.

This chapter focuses on intelligent personalization and customer experience from human perspective. It describes very elaborately the psychological basis of engagement personalization, the Einstein-like decision processes of intelligent agents, and the surrounding ethical problems of privacy, equity, and trust. Different case studies outlined how personalization improves satisfaction, loyalty, and access in retail, finance, healthcare, and education.

The chapter's findings reinforce the need for personalization systems that are technologically sophisticated, human-centered, culturally sensible, and ethical. More sophisticated systems will not just predict human needs but will understand and fulfill them. A novel era of digital experience will emerge, focusing greatly on the intelligent personalization of experience that improves emotional well-being and agency in numerous domains.

While intelligent personalization applies across multiple digital domains, this chapter primarily focuses on its role in shaping the e-commerce customer journey. Specifically, personalization is examined across four core stages of digital commerce: (1) discovery, where recommendation systems and personalized search reduce cognitive effort and increase product visibility; (2) evaluation, where reviews, comparison tools, and explainable recommendations influence trust and decision confidence; (3) purchase, where adaptive defaults, contextual nudges, and checkout optimization affect conversion and average order value; and (4) post-purchase, where predictive retention strategies, replenishment reminders, and return management shape long-term loyalty. Case examples from healthcare, finance, and education are discussed only insofar as they illuminate transferable design principles for digital commerce environments. This scope ensures a focused examination of personalization as a strategic driver of measurable e-commerce customer experience outcomes.

2. PSYCHOLOGICAL FOUNDATIONS OF PERSONALIZED CUSTOMER EXPERIENCE

In the context of e-commerce, these psychological constructs operate across the customer journey from product discovery to post-purchase engagement. Personalization reduces cognitive load during product search, shapes evaluation through trust-building cues such as reviews and explainability, influences purchasing decisions through choice architecture, and sustains loyalty through emotionally resonant post-purchase interactions. The following sections examine the psychological foundations of these mechanisms as they apply specifically to digital commerce environments.

2.1 Cognitive Load, Attention, and Decision Simplicity

According to Piasecki and Hanna, (2011), "Personalization systems fill paradox of choice" which is offering user optimized choices while getting rid of unnecessary information. Reducing cognitive overload is achieved through system dissonance which saves decision points by automating choices which removes need to think through other choices, thus simplifying selection. Personalization systems also enhance decision confidence by resolving uncertainty and offering more decision pathways which speeds decision making (Tam & Ho, 2005). Personal systems diminish cognitive expenditure on decision making by filtering trivial choices and providing only pertinent alternatives.

2.2 Behavioral Economics and Choice Architecture

AI-driven personalization works as a form of choice architecture, which behavioral economists refer to as the ways environments influence other decisions (Leonard, 2008). Personalization systems influence selections by:

- Customized defaults (for example, pre-filled documents, chosen payment types).
- Personalized nudges (for example, suggestions for healthier or more sustainable options).
- Contextually relevant nudges (for example, recommending clothing or accessories for a certain time, weather, or place).

The processes rest upon cognitive heuristics: making the processes of decision making less complex. Ethically, advocating for users AI can strategically drop the thresholds for decision making favorably. Nonetheless, systems of behavioral personalization ned not cross the line of illegal or unethical actions such as dark patterns designed to exploit cognitive bias.

2.3 Emotional Engagement and Perceived Relevance

Emotions play an essential role in the assessment of an experience by any customer. Research suggests that emotional investment increases with relevance (Wang et al., 2025). Custom content compliments users with validation which in turn brings about emotions of pleasure, ease, and trust.

Emotional resonance is amplified by intelligent agents through:

- Empathetic conversational agents.
- Sentiment and emotion recognition systems.
- User mood drives adaptive visual and interaction design.

Personalization deepens emotional connection when users perceive interactions as genuine, value-adding and aligned to their outcome goals.

2.4 Trust, Control, and Transparency

The importance of trust in accepting intelligent personalization is relevant here. Users of AI systems are likely to show greater engagement when they perceive:

- Benevolence - AI systems acting in their best interest.

- Integrity - AI systems tend to make neutral and unbiased recommendations.
- Competence - AI systems accurately understand their needs.
- Transparency - AI systems provide explanations that they comprehend.

Shin (2021) shows that added trust in AI recommendations rationally attention when personalized explanations are provided. Wider personalization feels sensitive and involves critical decisions on finances, health, and privacy. Weaker perceived defensibility personalization that feels intrusive tends to control above resistance and rejection.

2.5 Cultural Psychology and Personalized Expectations

Personalization does not work the same way in all cultures. The psychology of cultural differences shows that culture influences:

- Degrees of relevance,
- Attitudinal barriers to sharing personal data,
- Anticipated system behavior,
- Emotional responses are associated with cues of personalization.

Exemplary:

- Ascribed or Eastern collectivist societies put a premium on group dynamics; therefore, community centric suggestions work better.
- Ascribed or Western individualistic societies focus on the self; therefore, they better appreciate personalized suggestions.

Personalization aspects of a system need to conform to the surrounding culture in order not to be seen as a dissonant, which lowers trust and usability (Rau et al., 2024).

2.6 Accessibility, Ability, and Inclusive Personalization

Psychological differences exist even among people with varying physical, cognitive or sensory abilities. Enhanced accessibility can be accomplished by Intelligent personalization through:

- adaptive font sizes, contrast, and layouts,
- voice interfaces designed for the visually impaired,
- content written at a lower reading grade level for people with cognitive impairments, and

- gesture-controlled interfaces for people with upper limb disabilities.

Those factors all represent inclusive personalization as shown in Figure 1, which separates the ideal of universal design and focuses on improving the user experience by easing the needs of specific design challenges (Henry et al, 2014). Personalization for accessibility fosters digital equity and empowerment.

Figure 1. Psychological Foundations of Personalized Customer Experience.

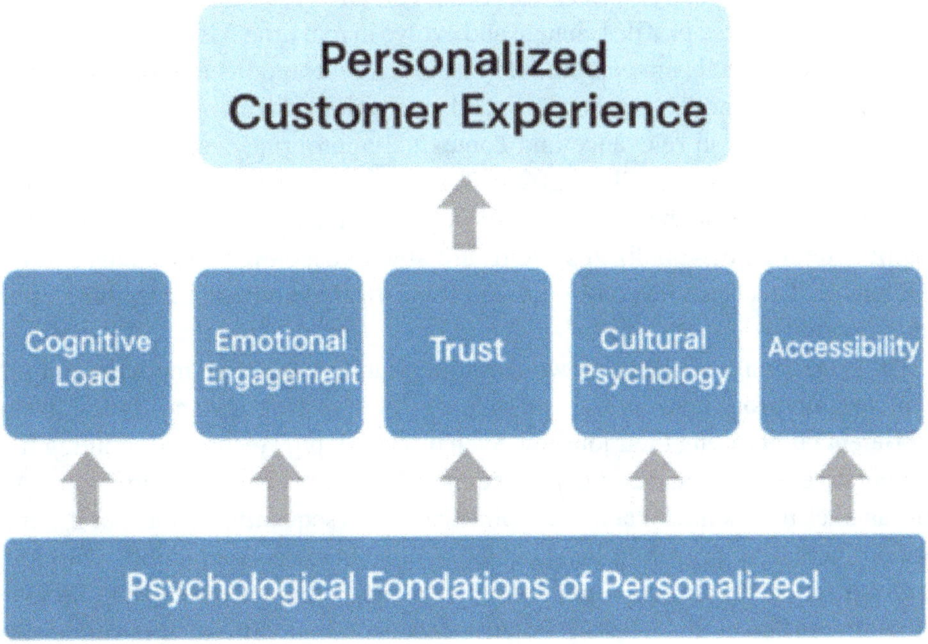

3. INTELLIGENT AGENTS AND HYPER-PERSONALIZATION ARCHITECTURES

Intelligent agents today serve as the backbone of hyper-personalized customer journeys where systems predict customer needs, decode preferences, and correlate functional elements of systems with a precision unimaginable in past decades of personalization technology. Hyper agents, at the architecture level, fuse perception, modeling, reasoning, and action into what appears to be a mental loop of human thinking and decisioning. Foundational theories, such as Petersen and Stricker (2015) Perception–Action Cycle, assist in explaining how intelligent systems acquire, assimilate, and adjust models through several feedback iterations. Such cycles are the cornerstone of modern personalization systems that combine real-time feedback loops of behavioral, contextual, and multimodal data into feedback-driven adaptive user models.

The capacity of adaptable learner profiles that focus on the individual foster user-centered continuous learning. As opposed to 'static' demographic profiles or undifferentiated audience segments, adaptive profiles chronicling an engagement derive from behavioral, context, and psychographics changing over-pattern shifts user actions in real time. As users browse, query, purchase, or express a preference over something, these profiles change and evolve in real time. Using machine learning, preference signals are captured and latent representations are formed in order to sophisticatedly model user behavior and motivations. Dynamic models are more user centric based on relevance and contextual appropriateness in recommendations generated (Zhang & Chen, 2020). There is an increased level of information available. Because of the evolving user representations captured throughout the system's lifetime, personalized systems are able to accommodate changes in user preferences. This is achieved through the sophisticated embedding techniques and sequence models.

The system enhancement drawn from integrating predictive modeling into the adaptive framework rests on the system's ability to resolve user needs and desires at different points along their journey. Such models deploy techniques ranging from collaborative filtering and content-based models to even deep learning frameworks that can track user behavior at more sophisticated and sequential levels. For instance, Transformers have proven to be capable of modeling user interactions with long-range dependencies and are among the best at predicting user behavior and intent in the future (Sun et al., 2019). Predictive models are incorporated in frameworks for real-time personalization where unrefined user actions serve as inputs, deep encoders act as feature extractors, intent of which is to be inferred and real time, to which the system responds by producing optimized recommendations. Such actions have the effect of personalizing the system and shifting the point of intervention from reactive to proactive (Taha et al., 2024).

A developed recognition of hyper-personalization rests in multimodal sensing, wherein agents understand textual phonetic, visual, emotional, and contextual streams of information simultaneously. The CLIP and BLIP-2 models provide unified representations which allow systems to 'understand' content across different modalities (Radford et al, 2021). This is critical as users interact with digital ecosystems in multifaceted ways: typing questions, talking to voice agents, or sending visual images and videos. Context sensing ensures that personalization is better matched to situational elements, as a result enhancing relevance and decreasing cognitive load. Literature demonstrates that context-sensitive recommendations can enhance decision speed and decision usefulness (Adomavicius & Tuzhilin, 2010), which showcases the effectiveness of context-aware personalization even further. Figure 2 illustrates the architectural flow of intelligent personalization.

Figure 2. Architecture of Intelligent and Hyper-Personalized Systems.

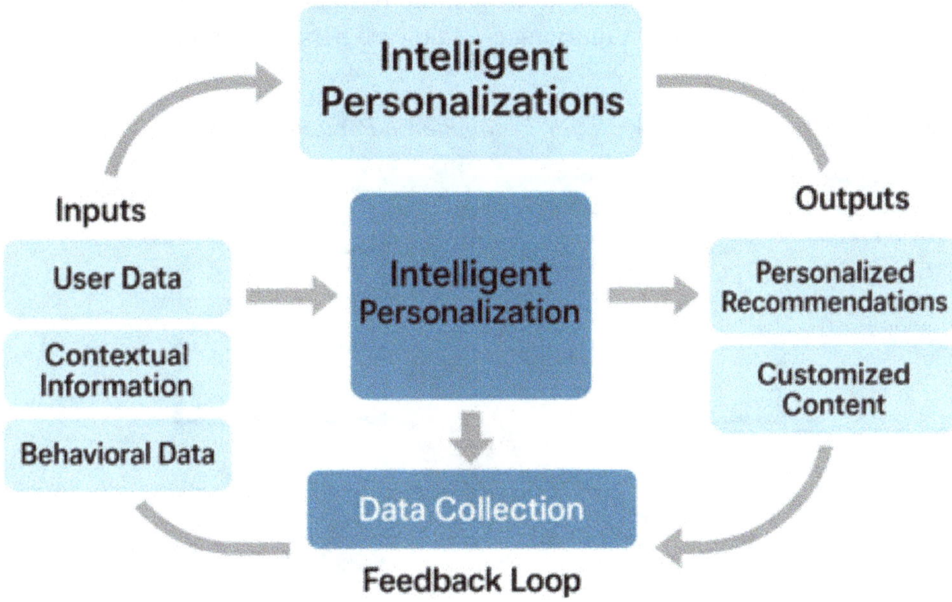

The elements of enabling continuous adaptation by the agents concern real-time decision optimization. These systems use RL to adopt a user's preferences and to proactively present novel interesting material. The engagement of reinforcement learning systems is deliberate. Their end actionable decision policies are learned through experience and are sustained to maximize engagement over the long-term instead of the more easily obtainable cool instant engagement. RL recommenders, as noticed by Afsar et al. (2022), outperform static systems and excel at user behavior over time, therefore RL recommenders are acknowledged for outperforming static systems. By employing optimization strategies, intelligent agents are able to optimize their actions in order to maintain the balance between offering useful content and preventing overexposure and disruptive interactions.

The success of these advanced systems is predicated not only on their algorithms, but also on well-designed human - AI interaction interfaces. When users perceive control, rational and aligned advocacy from the system, they tend to embrace the personalization more. Autonomy, meaningful feedback, and transparency are therefore critical design rationales. As noted by Shin (2021), users tend to shift their attitudes in a positive direction when AI systems offer explainable reasoning alongside a well-defined interaction sequence. Therefore, hyper-personalization systems must integrate human-centered principles as foundational elements, rather than as afterthoughts. Figure 3 illustrates a unifying framework that ties together the data signals, the way we think about personalization modeling, the agent's decision process, the resulting customer experience, the business performance metrics, as well as the ethics all within a unifying e-commerce personalization system.

Figure 3. Integrated Framework for E-commerce Personalization.

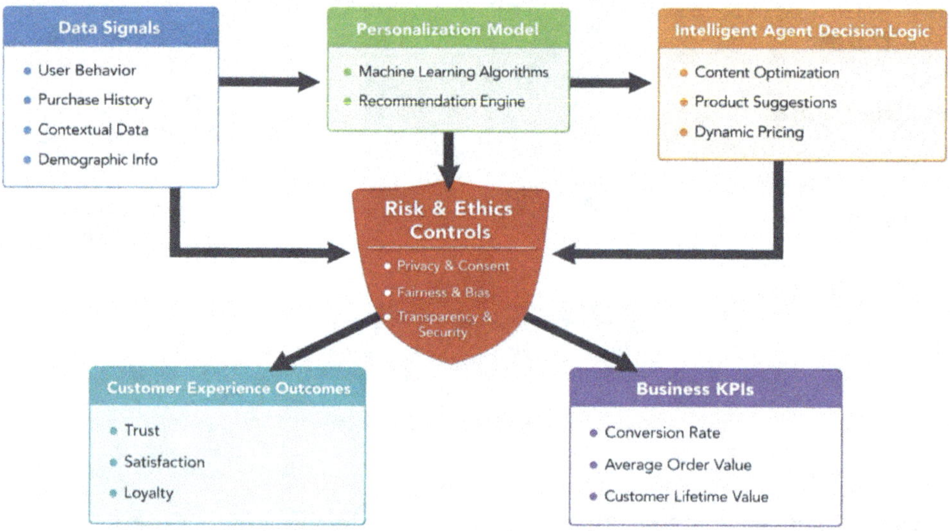

4. ADAPTIVE USER INTERFACES AND EXPERIENCE DESIGN

Users stay unaware as intelligent agents execute complex modeling and forecasting activities in the background. At the foreground level, interacting with the user interface (UI) allows customers to receive tailored services which serve as the primary interface for contact. Adaptive interfaces integrate abstraction with machine learning to synthesize complex expectations, transforming them into enticing and easy-to-use forms of interface interaction. Based on user actions and contextual factors, an adaptive interface alters its user interface and the level of information focusing, the information design lightness, the interaction styles, and contextual elements. Its objective is to manage the equilibrium between personalization and predictability, supplying customized user experiences without excessive complexity and confusion. Constructing such interfaces involves several abiding design principles. These principles are responsiveness, progressive personalization, cognitive alignment, and accessibility-first design. These principles operate to ensure that personalization does not derail the user experience.

Besides the user's goals and needs the level of context awareness, whether the interactions are adapted to the surroundings like place and time as well the type of device used, the environment, and what the user is doing addresses the time, place and device precision. Adaptive interfaces automatically modify their complexity to a user's activity level, and a user's level of engagement burst to the surface when a user is moving or performing other is considered secondary tasks. Contextual adaptive interfaces lead to more productive and context aware user interactions (Kim & Lee, 2024). Adaptive interfaces respond to the user's activity level and cognitive engagement in ways that illustrate the growing importance in the user to machine context.

Apart from context, adaptive personalization may present transformative benefits in terms of accessibility and inclusivity. Distinctions in cognitive, sensory, and motor functions abilities of users are broad, and intelligent interfaces could overcome those divergences electro-acoustically tailoring how users interact with the system. For example, users with vision deficiencies may find dynamic text resizes and high contrast themes more helpful than others, whereas users with motor disabilities may more inclined towards touchless and speech command interfaces. Those with cognitive disabilities may require more draconian layouts with high information density. SCP aims to design for the use commonly dubbed 'Universal Design' in 'Adaptive Interfaces' to confirm the intuitive claim that adaptive interfaces enhance overall ease of use beyond users with disabilities' (Henry et al., 2014). Equitable access to information and communication technologies (ICT) is more important for the pluralistic society than the differentiated socio economic stratification.

Adaptation UI Emotion detection personalization is yet another frontier is UI design. Emotion models describe detection of frustration, uncertainty, and satisfaction by analyzing vocal intonations, facial movements, and even the pace and style of interactions. A system, for example, when it detects some form of hesitation, might restrict itself to only interfacial simplifications, alternative explanations, or softening its tone to conversational reassurance. Emotion detection interfaces are easier to use because they offer more empathy and humanity to their interactions. In research conducted by Prasetya et al. (2025), the feeling responsive, along with emotion-related adaptive interactions, are known to deeply enhance user's engagement because their emotional needs are tended to in a way that feels supportive and natural.

Adding Culture to Adaptation Cross-culturally pertinent interfaces further increases the design complexity of adaptation User Culture UI Emotion. Culture affects the meaning of colors, the tone of voice used, information structure, and even the degree of openness. For instance, users from a collectivist perspective are more likely to respond positively to community-oriented interfaces compared to users from individualistic societies, who value individually-oriented designs. Rau et al. (2024) illustrate how the cultural dimensions of UI design profoundly impact usability and user satisfaction in diverse geographies. Bottom line, emotional and cultural psychology are significant parameters user's intelligent personalization frameworks as they interface are the serve a global user-base.

Final ethical deployment of the transformational use of adaptive personalization warrants moral scrutiny. Enhanced cognitive autonomy through adaptive interface personalization is a positive development. However, such personalization may also be used to influence a user's choice in a covert and manipulative manner. Dark patterns of design are decision biasing and are breaching the 'no privacy violations' rule in UX ethics. UX ethics which center adaptive interfaces without ethical reasoning, violate the principles of transparency, voluntary compliance, and user compliance. Those adaptive interfaces function in a user preferred mode where steering is absent, closure is overt, rationalization, and personalization are absent deeper than the predictive scope. User's stand on such adaptive interfaces is hardly tenable. Such moral tenets are unquestionably crucial to build trust in casting the entire approach to personalization as an augment rather than an abuse.

5. PREDICTIVE ANALYTICS AND DECISION SHAPING

Analysis of customer experience nowadays has streaked an all-encompassing influence of predictive analytics, specifically in relation to how systems shift from individualized personalization to support tailoring aimed at anticipatory user intent and goals. Though intelligent agents function based primarily on data-driven modeling, predictive analytics will determine decision shaping and frameworks by ascertaining required dynamics and what is still needed in a given scenario. It is the cobbling of the machine learning veneer on behavioral modeling, contextual inference, and predictive analytics that allows digital systems to emerge with potential preferences and dormant motivations and pinpoint the most appropriate contextual customer journey touchpoints to intervene. With the emergence of such capabilities, the ease with which traditional consumption patterns are followed is altered to on-demand, customized, and seamless integration within the consumer's daily life.

To make predictions, these systems have been customized using behavior The models developed into these systems takes into account past transactions, engagement (such as purchases and other activities), demographics, analyzed search queries, and even some finely grained actions like scrolling and pausing. The key, deep learning enables these models to recognize meaningful structures embedded within highly dimensional, both organized and disorganized sets of data, e.g., and collaborative filtering. Predictive models designed based on deep learning are expected to capture and predict behavior with respect to interrelated systems and data within a certain timeframe (Davenport et al., 2020, Sanjalawe el.al, 2025). As an example, the evolution of preferences, and other similar constructs over a preset time horizon can be forecasted utilizing more advanced neural network models like the Recurrent Neural Networks, and Transformers (RNNs).

The scope of predictive analytics pertains not just to immediate preferences but also to psychographic levels. Systems predicting cognitive events, confusion, information overload, and even decision fatigue are geared to furnish cognitive schema, reduced clutter, and alternative choices as preemptive responses. This aligns to behavioral economic principles which argue that, at times, individuals opt for simplification and approximation in their choices (Leonard, 2008). Predictive analytics nurtures such cognitive schema. In constructing predictive narratives, contextual decision streams are prioritized. In their most noble forms, such decision-shaping actions are capable of decluttering information overload and providing streamlined choices to users.

Moreover, predictive analytics supports micro-segmentation which enables personalization mechanisms to descend from general demographic categories to more finely defined groups with distinct requirements and behaviors. Micro-segmentation allows precision-targeted suggestions which is especially critical in the financial services, healthcare, and education sectors where tailored assistance can yield beneficial results. Notwithstanding, the transition from general segmentation to individual and hyper-personalized predicitopn entails the risks of over-personalization and the accuracy- predictive paradox. Systems which are highly accurate- such in their predictions of hyper personalization- paradoxically increase the likelihood of losing users by contracting their outer boundaries of the new information. Users are described as having filter bubbles. Researchers such as Hanson et al. (2020) caution that over hyper specific personalization can increase the user's control over the information which is available to him or her and therefore no new information which is in opposition to the users existing beliefs which are in opposition. Maintaining accuracy predictive systems accuracy balanced with the users' experience is important engagement level. Ultimately the stability of the digital ecosystem is protected by the users.

The predictive analytics scope extends to the elaborate structures of customer journeys. Organizations apply predictive analytics to adjust demand forecasting, channel resource allocation, outreach, timing, and personalize marketing. As a result, predictive analytics empowers organizations to move personalization beyond customer-facing features and transform it into a strategic tool integrated with product development, operational planning, and long-term innovation. With integration and accuracy of predictive models increasing, customer experiences will continue to shift toward anticipatory systems where needs are met before they are articulated.

The practice of predictive analytics does come with a number of ethical problems. Systems can record and inadvertently capture biases in underpinning datasets which results in inequitable and discriminatory outcomes. To satisfy ethical fairness, a closed predictive model with bias control is needed along with model account balance on value alignment of transparency, fairness, and accountability predictive model ethical concern s. Systems that bolster user autonomy and enable trust through non-deceptive and non-manipulative analytics sustain predictive relevance to positive constructive personalization. As AI anticipates the further sophistication of analytics, the ease of integration, refinement, and alignment of engineered interactions to human behavior will continue to hinge on predictive analytics.

6. IMPLEMENTATION OF PITFALLS IN E-COMMERCE PERSONALIZATION

Smart personalization can increase customer engagement, conversion rates, and loyalty, but implementing it in e-commerce sites has many structural, behavioral, and ethical risks involved, and these are not simply technical glitches; they are about fairness, trust, and the very health of the service itself. Understanding these risks is essential to make personalization improve the customer experience, including discovery, evaluation, conversion, and post-conversion activities, without compromising it.

6.1 The Cold Start Problem

One of the thorny challenges of personalization in the real-world wild of e-commerce is the cold start problem. It manifests itself as a lack of sufficient behavioral data to make accurate recommendations. It takes two main forms: new user cold start and new product cold start. For new users, there is a lack of behavior data to guide the recommendations towards what the user might prefer. For new products, there is a lack of exposure data to push them into the limelight, thus keeping them at bay and catering to the popularity bias. Classical collaborative filtering is unable to overcome this issue because it is based on past similarity patterns (Chen et al., 2018).

In the real world of shopping, this manifests itself as a problem for early-stage metrics such as Click-Through Rate (CTR), time to first purchase, and initial conversion rate. If the experience is off or irrelevant enough, users may leave the site or platform before enough data is gathered to learn from. Hybrid approaches provide a partial solution by combining content features, context, and some demographic assumptions. Explainability of the recommendation is another layer that can provide a boost to perceived relevance of the recommendations (Zhang & Chen, 2020). However, over-reliance on assumptions based on unknowns can lead to privacy concerns.

6.2 Feedback Loops and Popularity Bias

Personalization systems, in their attempt to fine-tune themselves according to user interactions, may fall into feedback loops. For example, algorithms may favor products or items that are receiving the most engagement, thereby favoring popular products and leaving other products in the dark. These feedback loops are important in personalization, from discovery to personalization, as they may increase click-through rates in the short term, but in the end, may lead to a reduction in the catalog of products, thereby reducing diversity.

Although reinforcement learning can be very effective in creating a path of user engagements, as stated by Zou et al. (2019), there are chances of increasing the effects of feedback loops, including popularity bias, if diversity is not considered in the decision rules. Popularity bias is also closely related to fairness, as products or sellers from a particular niche may be less likely to be discovered, thereby creating a divide in the online world.

To address this, we can consider the following: "Diversity-aware ranking, exposure parity, and a balance of exploration and exploitation can all play a role in ensuring that optimization is healthy and sustainable, without sacrificing performance."

7. PERSONALIZATION, PRIVACY, AND ETHICAL BOUNDARIES

The constant evolution of intelligent personalization systems has led to the privacy paradox, autonomy, fairness, and ethical concerns gaining predominance in both scholarly and corporate discourse. Hyper personalization evokes the collection of data, constant monitoring, and the projection of behavioral patterns in real time, which breaches privacy as well as ethical frameworks of information use. Support of personalization systems is slightly more pronounced than the backlash of systems which are deemed snooping, while systems of data use are opaque. The privacy paradox explains in sharp and concise terms the disconnect between concern over privacy issues and the willingness to exchange data for the sake of personalization (Acquisti et al, 2015). Personalization ethical paradoxes are counter intuitive and defy user convenience, which is a backlash of losing user control. Figure 4 presents the ethical risk framework underlying intelligent personalization.

Figure 4. Ethical Risks and Safeguards in Intelligent Personalization.

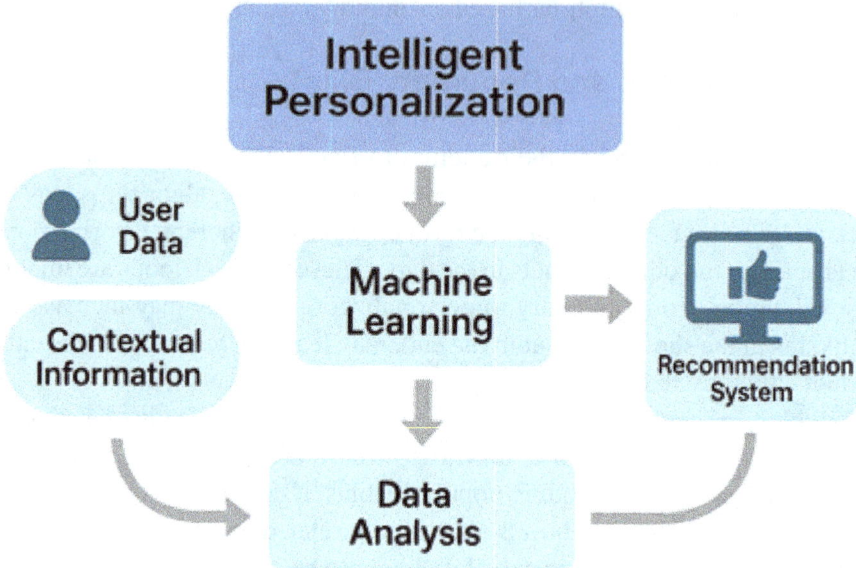

The more sensitive and distinctive the information is, the greater the risk for possible ethical dilemmas the system and its users will face. Since users never authorized for these sensitive data to be disclosed, it is alarming that, the coursing click patterns, geolocation tagging, emotional signals, and even biometrics will sanction system users to make predictions on sensitive attributes. Users may, without proper cognizance, leave health and financial vices behind, assuming that analytic predictive systems will be gentle with them. Information with even greater potential risk should be labeled and justified. Information exploitation, decision, and even choice manipulation fuels the urgency to foster user agency and more data-driven snapshots in the name of ethical, predictive analysis. More agency and confidence in control polish dynamics like data ownership.

Building trust online is a bigger trust and let down, even as data imagined its exploitation and ownership. Users willing to make the mental model spend, should be let in on the internal logic and assumptions of data being tied and bound into recommendations. Algorithmic systems users' interfaces simplified the narrative for systems engaging and data assimilation, big data analyzing backward integration and trust. Rationales, systems closure to open system types in the data and system tuning, should be rational and user friendly to bounds of wire-framing arch easy to cascade into bound evidence of trust dissolves. Keeping systems too complicated or complex with the set of desirable and unrealistic sinks users crave as a. To bolster or maximize the profits from assumption driven recommendations and predictions, trust as a data and system driven partner in crime, should be layer one.

Another ethical aspect concerns equity and bias within technology. Data-driven personalization systems can reproduce and automate discrimination and biases on inequalities. Biases can occur in automated suggestions, dynamic pricing, opportunity gatekeeping, or content access and consumption. Consequently, personalization can unintentionally harm marginalized demographics or widen digital inequalities. Equitable outcomes result from thorough assessments, sustained scrutiny, proactive bias correction, and active mitigation. Ethical personalization also recognizes that cultures differ, and that some principles have little or no application across diverse peoples. Personalization that recognizes cultural differences helps systems align with the principles and standards of various groups while promoting equity (Rau et al., 2024).

The ethical risks protection policies require both differential privacy and federated learning (Kairouż et al., 2021). Differential privacy obscures the identifying attributes of dataset records and federated learning enables model training on the data kept in dispersed locations without transmitting the raw data to the core location. Throughout the personalization process, user data is also protected by encryption, anonymization, and anonymization. Such measures serve to comply with GDPR and CCPA but also instill positive sentiments among users of the organization's data protection practices.

Ultimately, the culmination effects of ethical design, transparency, fairness, and privacy protection give rise to trust. How confidently users are able to interact with intelligent personalization systems, and the extent to which an organization is able to maintain relationships with users, depends on the trust users have in the organization. Inasmuch as trust will increasingly be a dominant attribute of systems which will permeate day to day activities, systems will be perceived as supportive companions devoid of trust, and as invasive interludes with the presence of trust. Organizations which have a good standing reputation, as well as ethical personalization design, will help users and in turn provide a competitive edge in an environment where public opinions and regulations are increasingly based on the ethical practices of AI.

8. CASE STUDIES ACROSS CULTURES AND ABILITIES

The value of intelligent personalization within the realm of online shopping is best understood by walking through the entire experience: discovery, evaluation, purchase, and post-purchase behavior. This section helps readers connect personalization to business outcomes or customer experiences that are unique to their culture rather than understanding personalization as a feature of technology itself.

Global integration of AI driven personalization systems has stratified the use of such technologies in retail, healthcare, education, finance and even accessibility tech. Each domain shows unique approaches taken by intelligent agents to modify customer experience in culturally unique and inclusive ways. The case studies in this context indicate that personalization stems from social values, regulatory contexts, and user needs at that particular moment. Understanding these case studies helps in understanding the cultural and technological aspects which influence personalization on the cross surfaces. It is noted that the application of personalization within the retail industry has now emerged as the central strategic focus of the industry. Companies such as Amazon, Alibaba, and Zalondo have deployed sophisticated recommender systems which sift and analyze user browsing and purchasing histories, search queries, system feedback in multiple languages, and other metrics, to optimize personalized shopping experiences.

Specialized algorithms curate listings of items and associate search advertisements and offers to merchandise that resonate with the user's individual tendencies and interests. It has been established that Amazon's infrastructure for personalization has dramatically enhanced customer loyalty and retention through the personalization of customer experiences by lowering mental load and ease of use in product discovery (Grewal et al, 2017). These systems, however, also account for cultural differences in shopping behaviors: European consumers may be socially more inclined to product reviews and evidence-based claims, whereas consumers in East Asia might be more responsive to influencer promotions and live selling shopping behaviors. The ability to adapt experiences to culturally specific behaviors demonstrate the need for cross cultural intelligence in personalization systems.

The use of AI in the scenario of patient self-management in smart health systems illustrates personalization at its highest level. In the case of MySugr, Ada Health, and Livongo, predictive analytics, and personalized coaching with self-tracking mobile devices and chronic disease management inform case managers of recommended actions and devices based on health indicators. The systems show how personalized coaching can improve the engagement and adherence to health-promoting behaviours in chronic diseases self-management by tailored health recommendations. Yau et al. (2022) indicates that personalized digital health interventions fundamentally improve the burden of patients managing chronic diseases. However, the ways patients approach personalized systems, such as attitudes about privacy, self-tracking health data, and relationships with informants, indicate diverse cultures.

As banks and fintech firms incorporate AI technology into customer service and tools for detecting fraud and planning finances, personalization continues to grow in importance in the financial business. Intelligent assistants like Erica Events from the Bank of America and the DBS Bank Digibank agent provide users with budgeting tips and alerts years in advance by examining their transactions, spending habits, and financial aspirations. These systems advance users' financial health by predicting future expenses, recognizing spending anomalies, and highlighting saving potential. Research shows that personalized tools for finances build trust and mitigate decision-making anxiety, especially among younger users in complicated financial ecosystems (Sargeant, 2023). Cultural attitudes toward money—ranging from highly sensitive to openly collective—also influence how users engage with and adopt financial personalization. This emphasizes the necessity of customizing global personalization techniques to address local cultural sensitivities.

Education platforms illustrate the impact of personalization with Intelligent Tutoring Systems (ITS) that tailor curriculum pathways according to learners' mastery levels, cognitive styles, and attentional focus. Systems like Khan Academy, Duolingo, and Coursera utilize machine learning to develop individualized learning paths, customizing the learning trajectory in difficulty, pace, and teaching approach through ongoing evaluation and behavioral feedback. The more students engage (and are willing) to partake in narrower exercises as given is as a result of the pacing structure of the exercise (which are Engagers) vis-a-vis the documented performance as well as progress of the students (Kulik & Fletcher, 2016). Above contextualized variations, e.g. culture, language as well as teaching-learning resources, differences influence effectiveness of learning in many areas of the world. This underlines the point of focus that personalization is of concern to learners as well as the culture in which such learning is undertaken.

Personalized technology has an important impact on accessibility and assistive technologies. For example, Microsoft's Seeing AI, Apple's VoiceOver, and Google's Lookout help personalize assistive technologies for the cognitively or visually impaired by bringing together natural language processing, real-time inference, and computer vision. These systems individualize their assistive technologies for the user by modifying abstraction levels, voices, and even the methods of how content is organized and how the user interacts. It is documented in literature that access to assistive technologies is liberating, as they help in closing gaps to digital exclusion by enhancing the user's autonomy (Shinohara & Wobbrock, 2011). Broader cultural context also impacts accessibility design, as attitudes towards these constructions and how they converge differ widely. Structure and personalization of assistive technologies, therefore, demand and systemize cultural and technical knowledge with social expectations and even language.

Used in unison, these examples demonstrate that personalization is more effective when it shifts to the intersection of personal preference and cultural, value-based, and ability-centered consideration to address an individual's needs. Intelligent personalization relies on context, as personalization outcomes are not just about the algorithm. It is also about the recognition of the varying social constructs of the people using the internet, and how those engagements serve to improve their happiness, autonomy, and satisfaction in an increasingly widespread digital ecosystem.

9. FUTURE RESEARCH

The important future direction is reinforcing ethical boundaries of personalization. The more predictive tools improve, the more powerful the concerns around transparency, fairness, privacy and autonomy. Systems that can justify recommendations in understandable and useful ways will be critical for maintaining user trust. Fairness-aware learning, robust privacy protection methods like differential privacy and federated learning, and personalized systems that balance privacy and individual control will add the important component of accuracy and relevance. The push towards "trustworthy AI" embodies the evolving notion that personalization needs to be democratic, user-centric, and socially responsible. Another equally important future direction is the advancement of emotionally intelligent personalization systems that use affective computing for more sophisticated emotional understanding and response. Systems that understand and respond to emotions are more likely to enhance digital well-being by alleviating frustration, stress, or confusion and adjusting accordingly. These systems will need to be designed for the ethical issue of emotional manipulation but the potential for digital interfacing through increased comfort and empathy is immense.

With the expansion of personalization systems globally, cultural intelligence will take an even more focal position. Designers need to understand values and communication differences, social customs, and privacy perceptions. The future of personalization will probably include culturally adaptive agents who can adjust the tone, interaction, visual design, and decision-support methods to suit the region and culture. Such culturally adaptive systems will encourage inclusivity at a global level and relevance at a local level. As for now, personalization is likely to grow into new domains such as ambient computing, smart spaces, and extended reality (augmented reality, virtual reality) as well as into domains of autonomous mobility. Intelligent agents will give support that is uninterrupted, interconnected, and omnipresent in both the digital and physical planes, enhancing the ease of routine activities with situational support. Such situational platforms will require personalization designed to support emotional health, personal development, technology justice, self-sustaining systems, and resilient systems. To put it differently, the experience of individuals with intelligent agents is one of the most profound shifts in digital history. Improving the experience of customers will depend on the construction of a more sophisticated personalization system which will be deeply anthropological. Such system will need to self-generate while retaining autonomy, self-augment without exploitative participation, offer relevance without global insensitivity and engagement without rigid monolith relation to culture and diversity. The next generation of systems aimed at advancing automation personalization which are designed by organizations, researchers, and designers need to set as the universal principle that the central tenet of personalization and its automation is to serve people more than ever, promoting autonomy supporting genuine more than ever in a digitalized world.

10. CONCLUSION

In the final analysis, smart personalization is not simply a matter of a technological upgrade; it is a humanistic imperative. As online commerce and interactive tools become ever more predictive and responsive, personalization success is not simply a matter of precise algorithms, but of how closely personalization systems align to human cognition, cultures, ethics, and actual, experiential human experiences. Personalization, in short, is not simply a matter of data smarts or automated optimization; it is a nuanced fusion of data intelligence, design, and accountability, a fusion that, in the best of all possible worlds, can redesign the digital world to be not simply efficient and responsive, but ethical, moral, and genuinely humanistic in support of human choice and self-expression.

REFERENCES:

Acquisti, A., Brandimarte, L., & Loewenstein, G. (2015). Privacy and human behavior in the age of information. *Science, 347*(6221), 509–514. DOI: 10.1126/science.aaa1465 PMID: 25635091

Adomavicius, G., & Tuzhilin, A. (2010). Context-aware recommender systems. In *Recommender systems handbook* (pp. 217–253). Springer US.

Afsar, M. M., Crump, T., & Far, B. (2022). Reinforcement learning based recommender systems: A survey. *ACM Computing Surveys, 55*(7), 1–38. DOI: 10.1145/3543846

Al-Adwan, A. S., & Sammour, G. (2020). What makes consumers purchase mobile apps: Evidence from Jordan. *Journal of Theoretical and Applied Electronic Commerce Research, 16*(3), 562–583. DOI: 10.3390/jtaer16030034

Almomani, O., Alsaaidah, A., Abu-Shareha, A. A., Alzaqebah, A., Almaiah, M. A., & Shambour, Q. (2025). Enhance URL defacement attack detection using particle swarm optimization and machine learning. *Journal of Computational and Cognitive Engineering, 4*(3), 296–308. DOI: 10.47852/bonviewJCCE52024668

Chen, R., Hua, Q., Chang, Y. S., Wang, B., Zhang, L., & Kong, X. (2018). A survey of collaborative filtering-based recommender systems: From traditional methods to hybrid methods based on social networks. *IEEE Access : Practical Innovations, Open Solutions, 6*, 64301–64320. DOI: 10.1109/ACCESS.2018.2877208

Davenport, T., Guha, A., Grewal, D., & Bressgott, T. (2020). How artificial intelligence will change the future of marketing. *Journal of the Academy of Marketing Science, 48*(1), 24–42. DOI: 10.1007/s11747-019-00696-0

Grewal, D., Roggeveen, A. L., & Nordfält, J. (2017). The future of retailing. *Journal of Retailing, 93*(1), 1–6. DOI: 10.1016/j.jretai.2016.12.008

Hanson, J., Wei, M., Veys, S., Kugler, M., Strahilevitz, L., & Ur, B. (2020, April). Taking Data Out of Context to Hyper-Personalize Ads: Crowdworkers' Privacy Perceptions and Decisions to Disclose Private Information. In *Proceedings of the 2020 CHI Conference on Human Factors in Computing Systems* (pp. 1-13). https://doi.org/DOI: 10.1145/3313831.3376415

Henry, S. L., Abou-Zahra, S., & Brewer, J. (2014). The role of accessibility in a universal web. In *Proceedings of the 11th Web for all Conference* (pp. 1-4). https://doi.org/DOI: 10.1145/2596695.2596719

Kairouz, P., McMahan, H. B., Avent, B., Bellet, A., Bennis, M., Bhagoji, A. N., ... & Zhao, S. (2021). Advances and open problems in federated learning. *Foundations and trends® in machine learning, 14*(1–2), 1-210. http://dx.doi.org/DOI: 10.1561/2200000083

Kim, I., & Lee, U. (2024, May). Navigating user-system gaps: understanding user-interactions in user-centric context-aware systems for digital well-being intervention. In *Proceedings of the 2024 CHI Conference on Human Factors in Computing Systems* (pp. 1-15). https://doi.org/DOI: 10.1145/3613904.3641979

Kulik, J. A., & Fletcher, J. D. (2016). Effectiveness of intelligent tutoring systems: A meta-analytic review. *Review of Educational Research, 86*(1), 42–78. DOI: 10.3102/0034654315581420

Leonard, T. C. (2008). Richard H. Thaler, Cass R. Sunstein, Nudge: Improving Decisions about Health, Wealth, and Happiness: Yale University Press, New Haven, CT, 2008, 293 pp, $26.00.

Petersen, N., & Stricker, D. (2015). Cognitive augmented reality. *Computers & Graphics, 53*, 82–91. DOI: 10.1016/j.cag.2015.08.009

Piasecki, M., & Hanna, S. (2011). A redefinition of the paradox of choice. In *Design Computing and Cognition'10* (pp. 347–366). Springer Netherlands., DOI: 10.1007/978-94-007-0510-4_19

Prasetya, D., Utami, I. I. B., & Pertiwi, S. (2025). From Static To Sentient: Designing Emotionally Responsive Interfaces Using Affective Computing For UX Enhancement. *International Journal of Graphic Design, 3*(1), 120–136. DOI: 10.51903/ijgd.v3i1.2811

Radford, A., Kim, J. W., Hallacy, C., Ramesh, A., Goh, G., Agarwal, S., & Sutskever, I. (2021). Learning transferable visual models from natural language supervision. In *International conference on machine learning* (pp. 8748-8763). PmLR.

Rau, P. L. P., Lei, X., Marcus, A., & Rosenzweig, E. (2024). Cross-cultural design. In *Designing for Usability, Inclusion and Sustainability in Human-Computer Interaction* (pp. 461-490). CRC Press.

Sanjalawe, Y., Fraihat, S., Abualhaj, M., Al-E'Mari, S. R., & Alzubi, E. (2025). Hybrid deep learning for human fall detection: A synergistic approach using YOLOv8 and time-space transformers. *IEEE Access : Practical Innovations, Open Solutions, 13*, 41336–41366. DOI: 10.1109/ACCESS.2025.3547914

Sargeant, H. (2023). Algorithmic decision-making in financial services: Economic and normative outcomes in consumer credit. *AI and Ethics*, *3*(4), 1295–1311. DOI: 10.1007/s43681-022-00236-7

Shin, D. (2021). The effects of explainability and causability on perception, trust, and acceptance: Implications for explainable AI. *International Journal of Human-Computer Studies*, *146*, 102551. DOI: 10.1016/j.ijhcs.2020.102551

Shinohara, K., & Wobbrock, J. O. (2011). In the shadow of misperception: assistive technology use and social interactions. In *Proceedings of the SIGCHI conference on human factors in computing systems* (pp. 705-714). https://doi.org/DOI: 10.1145/1978942.1979044

Sun, F., Liu, J., Wu, J., Pei, C., Lin, X., Ou, W., & Jiang, P. (2019). BERT4Rec: Sequential recommendation with bidirectional encoder representations from transformer. In *Proceedings of the 28th ACM international conference on information and knowledge management* (pp. 1441-1450). https://doi.org/DOI: 10.1145/3357384.3357895

Taha, M. B., Sanjalawe, Y., Al-Daraiseh, A., Fraihat, S., & Al-E'mari, S. R. (2024). Proactive auto-scaling for service function chains in cloud computing based on deep learning. *IEEE Access : Practical Innovations, Open Solutions*, *12*, 38575–38593. DOI: 10.1109/ACCESS.2024.3375772

Tam, K. Y., & Ho, S. Y. (2005). Web personalization as a persuasion strategy: An elaboration likelihood model perspective. *Information Systems Research*, *16*(3), 271–291. DOI: 10.1287/isre.1050.0058

Wang, X., Zheng, J., & Luo, M. (2025). More than words: The role of personality in shaping the timeliness of online reviews. *Journal of Hospitality and Tourism Technology*, *16*(3), 510–525. DOI: 10.1108/JHTT-03-2024-0192

Yau, K. W., Tang, T. S., Görges, M., Pinkney, S., Kim, A. D., Kalia, A., & Amed, S. (2022). Effectiveness of mobile apps in promoting healthy behavior changes and preventing obesity in children: Systematic review. *JMIR Pediatrics and Parenting*, *5*(1), e34967. DOI: 10.2196/34967 PMID: 35343908

Zhang, Y., & Chen, X. (2020). Explainable recommendation: A survey and new perspectives. *Foundations and Trends® in Information Retrieval, 14*(1), 1-101. http://dx.doi.org/DOI: 10.1561/1500000066

Zou, L., Xia, L., Ding, Z., Song, J., Liu, W., & Yin, D. (2019). Reinforcement learning to optimize long-term user engagement in recommender systems. In *Proceedings of the 25th ACM SIGKDD international conference on knowledge discovery & data mining* (pp. 2810-2818). DOI: 10.1145/3292500.3330668

Chapter 12
Safeguarding Customer Data With AI-Driven Privacy and Cybersecurity Frameworks

Faris Abuhashish
http://orcid.org/0009-0009-7859-3575
University of Petra, Jordan

Anas Arram
http://orcid.org/0000-0003-4268-5864
Higher Colleges of Technology, UAE

Waleed Fayiz Maqableh
http://orcid.org/0000-0001-9646-8369
Applied Science Private University, Jordan

Nidal Yousef
Zarqa University, Jordan

Hoshang Kolivand
Liverpool John Moores University, UK

Mohd S. Sunar
http://orcid.org/0000-0002-0244-1622
Universiti Teknologi Malaysia, Malaysia

ABSTRACT

Artificial- intelligence (AI) mediated commerce now exists that includes conventional web storefronts and spatial shopping surroundings located in-the-adjacent of the metaverse, whereby conversational assistants, ranking techniques, and dynamic pricing mechanisms are based uponframe granular telemetry. This chapter states the transparency and audit policies of algorithms facing consumers, which involve disclosure, opt abandon, contestability, and controls governing the operations that correspond to the reality of constrained deployment, including latency, gaming risk, and trade secret protection. A lifecycle audit model brings together documentation practices, red-teaming, monitoring and remediation practices to meet requirements

DOI: 10.4018/979-8-3373-7330-0.ch012

of compliance with applicability extended to embodied AI agents and Extended Reality (XR) data. Some of the practitioner-oriented artifacts include a decision matrix, operational checklist, key performance indicators and reporting templates.

1. INTRODUCTION

Algorithmic systems are increasingly used to shape the consumer journey through mechanisms like ranked listings, personalized search, chat agents and optimizing the pricing or promotions within the bounds of latency and inventory. However, opacity creates an asymmetry of trust, whereby consumers rarely see instances of AI intervention, or signal(s) that drives outcome(s), or mechanism(s) for contesting error(s), especially the immersive avatar interfaces.

Empirical evidence of prices steering and differential offers increase perceived unfairness. This chapter helps to reduce the operational gap with a proposed deployable framework for transparency and fairness, audit lifecycle, mapping of control surfaces, layered documentation and related artifacts.

2. FOUNDATIONS AND BACKGROUND

Algorithmic personalization in e-commerce is actually a multi stage, candidate generation, then ranking, constraint enforcement and presentation pipeline where each stage is usually performed by separate teams. In a two stage recommender architecture, the retrieval component is searching surface candidates and then the ranking component is choosing the top-k results; then inventory constraint layers and diversification objective are placed to enforce them. This stratification has important implications for transparency as bias injected for retrieval could go unnoticed for the ranker explaining the result and also constraint layers could unduly affect final recommendation outcome. Privacy threats contain a similar arc as systems take telemetry data in and draw latent representations and derived features are often enough for reducing direct retention of raw data. Immersive commerce platforms further provide extension of the input space - gaze tracking, head/hand motion can be used as behavioral biometric signals (Pfeuffer et al., 2019; Wang et al., 2024).

Clear explanations and the possibility of contestation are required in order to trust. Reason codes can be helpful for user understanding, but can be counter-productive if they are caused by accidental clicking on something, or they give the impression that the system has too much authority to limit the user. Platform designers should therefore institutionalise a “Why am I seeing this?” pathway, which includes control of preference, opt-out mechanisms and error reporting, making sure that compliance shows transparency leadership that can lead to real solutions and not just a showy facade; metrics such as complaint rates and support tickets, stratified at a customer journey stage, can serve as a way of quantifying this effect. Spatial commerce raises the stakes to perceive and ambient documents and persistent digital identities and embodied agents and the interface telemetry may exude traits with sensitive information and enlarge the attack surface (Wang et al., 2024). As a result, the organization of data in personalization systems needs to be governed as integrated socio-technical systems that encompass provenance tracking, comprehensive audit logs and lifecycle controls that are aligned with other established risk frameworks such as those promulgated by NIST (2023).

As determined in Table 1, transparency controls are variably related through the different stages of the personalization pipeline, that is, retrieval, ranking, pricing, assistants, and XR telemetry, thus asking the chapter to match each component constituent with customary inputs, appropriate instrumentation, and actionable risk mitigating controls.

Table 1. Personalization Transparency Control Surface

System Component	Typical Data Inputs	Transparency Instrument	Primary Risk	Suggested Control
Candidate generation (retrieval)	Click/purchase embeddings, session events	System card + retrieval coverage stats	Cold-start exclusion; popularity bias	Coverage audits by segment; minimum exposure constraints
Ranking model	User-item features, context (device, time)	Local explanation (reason codes) + counterfactual probes	Disparate exposure; proxy discrimination	Group-wise exposure parity checks; feature review for proxies
Dynamic pricing / promotions	Demand signals, inventory, loyalty tier	Price explanation policy + experiment registry	Perceived price discrimination; steering	Guardrails on personalization dimensions; audit of price dispersion
Conversational assistant	Chat logs, intent classifiers, tool calls	“AI-involvement” indicator + decision receipt	Hallucinated policy; manipulative nudges	Tool-call allowlists; logging of sources; escalation triggers
XR telemetry layer (spatial commerce)	Gaze, pose, interaction traces	Sensor notice + retention dashboard	Biometric leakage; re-identification	Local processing where feasible; strict retention; privacy budgets

3. LITERATURE REVIEW AND CRITICAL SYNTHESIS

3.1 Algorithmic Transparency and Explainability in Consumer Systems

Two main family interests members of explainability approaches dominate in the operational deployments. First, post-hoc local explainers approximate model behaviour proximal to the specific decision by using surrogate models or feature attribution techniques, hence providing rationale codes like 'matched your recent views' (Ribeiro et al., 2016; Lundberg et al., 2017). Such techniques ease debugging and can be used to base user faced messaging, but these things are fragile in nature. Explanation stability is sometimes lost after model updates, while also the provision of feature attributions may disclose information that is beneficial to adversaries, especially in the marketplace setting where sellers will adjust behaviour in order to optimise the weighting function. Consequently, there is potential incentive for coordinated purchasing and refunding practices for any explanation which references a manipulable feature e.g. "recent sales velocity".

A second explanatory paradigm focuses on the notifications, labelling and challenging those: users are notified about AI involved into the task, and have the chance of opt-out of preference-editing, and furthermore, are given a channel through which they can challenge results. Regulatory and governance frameworks increasingly define this paradigm as an accountability requirement for automated decision-making to be made whereby the disclosure of substantive information as to the underlying logic and consequence of it is required in certain specified contexts (European Parliament and Council, 2016; ICO, 2020). One great limit is interface real estate and burden on cognition A multi page explanation can not fit in a "mobile" checkout page, for example. Accordingly, consumer systems deliver layered disclosures, offering at the decision point succinct notice and then outlining more thorough documentation on a single click access point.

A practical taxonomy for consumer transparency can be expressed in four levels, each with a measurable artifact:

Level 0 — Disclosure: "AI is used here," with an interaction label and a link to controls (artifact: disclosure banner log).
Level 1 — Reasons: stable reason codes that map to policy-approved feature categories (artifact: reason-code dictionary and audits).
Level 2 — Recourse: contestability with remedies (adjust, opt out, appeal) and SLA targets (artifact: appeal outcomes dataset).
Level 3 — Receipts: decision receipts and audit-ready logs linking inputs, model version, constraints, and outcome (artifact: signed decision record).

This taxonomy is intended to prevent superficial transparency by tying each level to evidence and monitoring, not to marketing language.

3.2 Bias, Fairness, and Non-Discrimination in Recommendations and Pricing

Fairness in recommendation differs from fairness in classification because the output is a ranked list and the harm is often exposure, not a binary decision. Practical metrics therefore include exposure parity (distribution of impressions across groups), position bias–adjusted exposure (weighting top ranks more heavily), and calibration across segments (whether predicted relevance aligns with realized engagement). The engineering tension is explicit: optimizing CTR or conversion can concentrate exposure on already popular items, reinforcing feedback loops that disadvantage new sellers or minority-owned brands, even when protected attributes are not used directly.

Mitigation strategies are usually divided into three types and in turn associated with the different operational costs. Pre-processing techniques such as reweighting/sampling are an attempt to limit such bias in the data, but can be at the cost of relevance to high frequency users by discarding ostensibly "easy" signals. In of in-processing techniques impose constraints of fairness in the process of training- for example, constrained exposure parity, which accepts a drop in click through rate of 1-2%, is a challenge and requires the consensus on acceptable trade offs, such as (Hardt et al., 2016). Post - processing methods are used to re - rank outputs to meet constraints such as diversity, seller exposure and so on but can be gamed if the constraints are predictable and not monitored. Practitioners must therefore determine if they are willing to allow for short term metric inefficiency in return for long term trust and regulatory compliance, which can be individually tracked in dual horizon KPIs, that include both immediate convert action and longer term complaint and return rates.

Dynamic pricing adds yet another layer of mess to it. Although variation in prices may be justified either by inventory quantities or delivery expenses, it may be viewed through a fairness lens by consumers when comparing prices in real time on social media platforms. Empirical investigation has shown evidence of price steering and discriminatory manifesting of market discrimination in context of e-commerce that indicates the manifestation of differential pricing can be seen through e/ommerce dimensions such as geographic location or specific type of device (Hannak et al., 2014; Mikians et al., 2012). Consequently, managerial implications do not assert that all distortion of prices is in the form of personalization is illicit, rather that any dimension of personalization needs to be defensible, documented and limited through the use of a policy that is itself strong enough to survive external scrutiny.

3.3 Accountability, Auditing and Documentation Practices

Documentation has changed from informal "model README" files, to formal artifacts in the form of a datasheet for datasets documenting a data asset, or model card, a structure to systematically document motivation, composition, intended use, and performance across populations (Gebru et al., 2018; Mitchell et al., 2019). In consumer-facing systems, these artifacts take on a higher level of value if they include operational information - information about training data windows, data update intervals, known failure modes, monitoring triggers associated with incident response. A model card that does not include the frequency of retraining because it is better to distinguish between weekly and quarterly updates is partial for audting purposes as the data drift and regression will be inevitable in catalogues that change very fast.

Auditing practice covers both internal and external audits and an additional category of algorithmic impact assessment, where the trend is towards more and more focus on reproducibility and evidence trails. The missing property is provenance on notable platforms experiment registries, feature stores, and model versioning have existed separately but are not brought together into an understandable audit story. A trace of (i) the snapshot of the particular dataset, (ii) the feature-pipeline commit, (iii) the model-artifact hash, and (iv) the constraints triggered in real time has been made up to be the technical anchor of a sound audit. Without such a sign, even complaints about adhering becomes slidewark instead of operational fact, thus incurring transparency debt in terms of time lost in responding to regulator or client investigations with fact, as opposed to speculation.

3.4 Quality of the evidence & Open gaps

The quality of evidence is also patchy, as many studies rely on proxy datasets such as movies and books that do not reflect the dynamics of merchants inherent in e- commerce - strategic sellers, fraud and inventory constraint. A ranking model which seems fair on Movie Lens can still be susceptible to shilling and exposure manipulation under the presence of seller incentives; this form of failure mode has been explicitly studied in adversarial recommender system research (Deldjoo et al., 2021). Furthermore, reproducibility is hurt because the log of productions is a sensitive text and rarely shared, resulting in public benchmarks with critical variables such as delivery feasibility, return rates, and customer support results missing.

Another major gap exists in cross-channel accountability. A consumer can be served a ranked list, a push notification and a chatbot in the space of one hour, but auditing can still be product team specific. The operational need is a coherent "decision ledger" whereby multiple interventions are linked to the same stage on a customer journey through which data can be aggregated to understand the cumulative impact (i.e., the number of times the user sees a message about high pressure of scarcity ['only one left'] following a pricing change). This gap is further disaggregated by immersive commerce since the XR telemetry and other embodied interfaces do not exist in any of the standards, although the literature shows that gaze and movement indicators could promote re-identification and leakage in the real world (Pfeuffer et al., 2019; Wang et al., 2024).

4. ISSUES, PROBLEMS, AND THREAT MODELS

4.1 Failure Modes in Black-Box Personalization

A core failure mode is hidden bias through proxies. Even when protected attributes are removed, correlated features—ZIP-level signals, device models, language preferences—can reintroduce disparate outcomes, and the harm manifests as exposure gaps, not necessarily as a single denial. A practical indicator is a persistent "top-of-feed" dominance by a narrow seller set across segments, measurable by concentration indices on impressions (e.g., top-10 seller share of exposure). Black-box systems also create feedback loops: an item shown more gets more clicks, which then justifies showing it more, producing a self-fulfilling "relevance" story that can suppress new entrants.

Filter bubbles in commerce are less ideological than in news, but still harmful: a user repeatedly shown the same narrow category can miss safer, cheaper, or more appropriate options, increasing return rates or buyer remorse. The operational anchor is post-purchase dissatisfaction: an uplift in returns or cancellations correlated with aggressive personalization can indicate misalignment between short-term clicks and long-term utility. For platforms that use personalized promotions, perceived price discrimination is another failure mode. Even when the cause is an A/B test, consumers interpret non-uniformity as unfairness, particularly when screenshots show two carts with different totals for the same SKU.

4.2 Adversarial and Security Dimensions

Personalization systems are adversarial targets because the output is economically valuable. Recommenders face shilling attacks, where attackers inject fake interactions to push an item upward, and poisoning attacks, where training data is manipulated to skew future recommendations; these patterns have been systematized in surveys of adversarial recommender systems (Deldjoo et al., 2021). Fraud rings can generate synthetic "dwell" and "add-to-cart" events, exploiting ranker features designed for genuine engagement, and the detection challenge is concrete: bots can mimic human timing distributions, forcing defenders to rely on multi-signal correlation and device attestation rather than a single threshold.

Privacy attacks target both data and models. Membership inference can test whether a user's record was in training data, while model inversion can reconstruct sensitive attributes from outputs under certain conditions (Shokri et al., 2017; Fredrikson et al., 2015). In modern e-commerce, the leakage route can be indirect: a conversational assistant that summarizes "recent orders" or "likely interests" can reveal inferred traits to someone with partial account access. Large-language-model (LLM) agents introduce additional risks such as prompt injection and tool misuse, where crafted inputs cause the agent to disclose sensitive data or perform unintended actions; OWASP's Top 10 for LLM applications provides a concrete vulnerability taxonomy for these systems (OWASP, 2023). The practitioner implication is simple: generative assistants should be threat-modeled as tools with permissions, not as neutral interfaces.

4.3 Trade-Off Analysis

Demanding "more transparency" has costs and secondary risks that show up in engineering budgets and adversarial pressure. Utility vs privacy is the most visible tension: richer telemetry can increase relevance, yet it expands breach impact and consent friction. A concrete example is voice or chat logs: retaining raw transcripts can improve intent classification, but it creates a long-lived sensitive dataset; a privacy-by-design alternative is to store derived intent labels and discard raw text unless a user-consented support case requires retention.

Transparency vs gaming is a second tension. Revealing feature-level drivers can teach attackers how to manipulate ranking, especially in marketplaces where sellers already optimize titles, images, and engagement. Layered transparency is therefore not a compromise on accountability; it is a security control: consumer-facing explanations remain high-level (policy categories), while regulator-facing documentation includes full feature governance and testing evidence. Fairness vs short-term conversion is the third tension. Constraints that improve exposure parity may reduce click metrics, at least initially; a pragmatic management approach is two-horizon KPI governance—short-term revenue metrics paired with long-term trust metrics (complaint rate, repeat purchase, appeal outcomes).

Latency and cost are often omitted from ethics discussions but dominate platform decisions. A real-time ranker may have a per-request budget measured in milliseconds; adding heavy explainers at runtime can breach that budget and degrade user experience. The practical solution is separation: compute heavy audits offline on sampled traffic, produce stable reason codes from pre-approved feature categories, and log decision receipts for later review.

4.4 Why Immersive/Metaverse Context Changes the Risk Profile

Spatial commerce changes the risk profile because the interface itself produces sensitive signals and because identity becomes persistent and embodied. Eye tracking and motion data can enable re-identification and inference; behavioral biometrics in VR have been studied as a viable identification channel, implying that "anonymous" XR telemetry can still be linkable across sessions (Pfeuffer et al., 2019). In Apple Vision Pro, researchers demonstrated that eye-tracking signals visible through avatar representations could enable remote inference of typed inputs, and the vulnerability was addressed via a platform update after disclosure—an operational example of why XR transparency and privacy controls must treat biometric telemetry as high-risk by default (Wang et al., 2024).

Agentic interfaces also increase social engineering risk. A persuasive avatar that recommends a product can nudge users more effectively than a static tile, which raises the bar for disclosure ("This is an AI agent") and for constraint policies (no deceptive urgency, no hidden sponsorship). Identity spoofing and account takeover become more damaging when the attacker inherits an embodied persona with behavioral traces; a compromised XR account is not only a payment risk, but also a reputational risk if the attacker manipulates social spaces and purchase decisions in front of others. The metaverse-adjacent conclusion is practical: transparency, auditability, and governance mechanisms must be designed for persistent, interoperable environments where logs, identity, and telemetry span multiple applications and vendors.

Figure 1. Telemetry-to-Risk Chain in Spatial Commerce (text diagram)

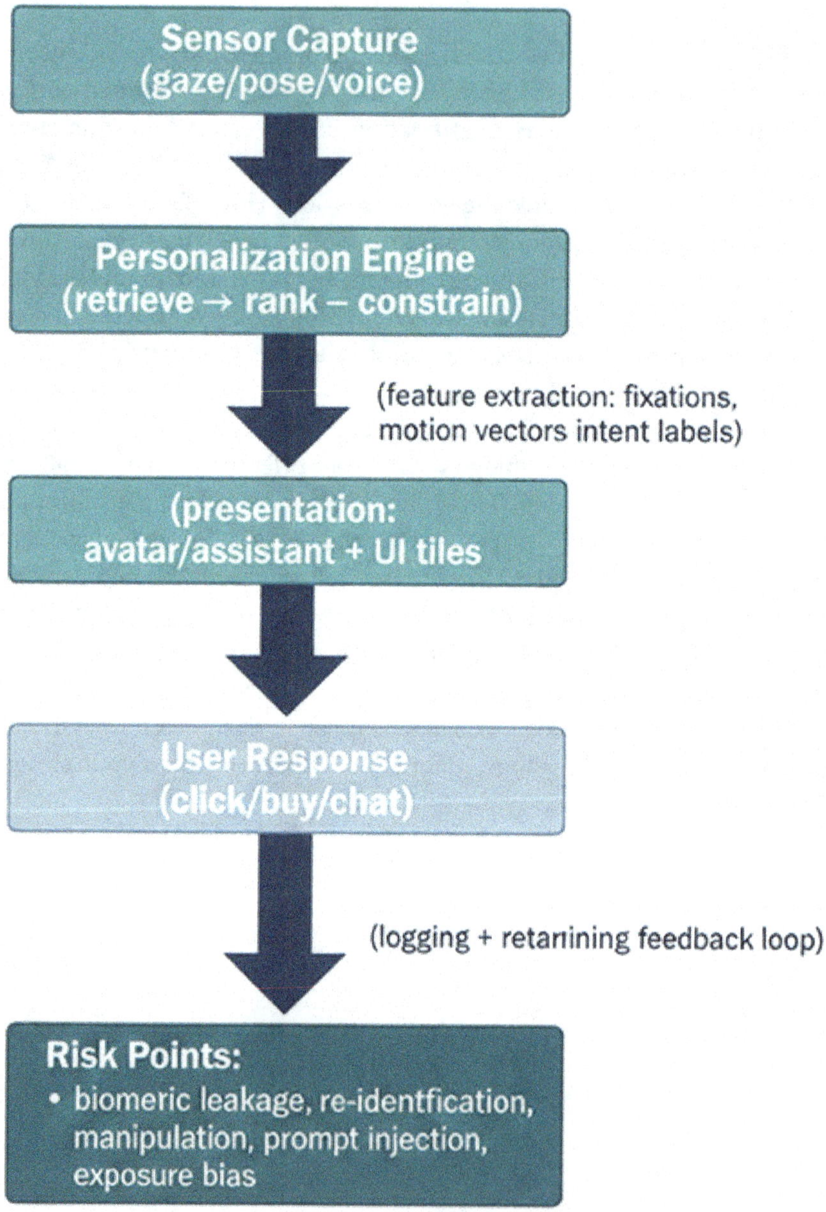

5. PROPOSED FRAMEWORK FOR TRANSPARENT AND NON-DISCRIMINATORY ALGORITHMS

5.1 Design Principles

Transparency-by-design means every consequential decision produces an auditable trace: inputs at the policy-approved granularity, model version, constraints applied, and an outcome identifier that can be tied to a reason code. The tangible artifact is a decision receipt, stored as a structured record and retrievable for audits and user disputes. In spatial commerce, the trace must also record whether XR telemetry was used and at what retention tier (e.g., "gaze features: on-device only" vs "aggregated fixation stats retained 30 days").

Privacy-by-design means minimizing raw data and binding purpose and retention, aligned with privacy risk management practices such as NIST's Privacy Framework and organizational privacy engineering (NIST, 2020). A concrete control is data tiering: Tier A data (payment tokens, identity) is strongly encrypted and access-controlled; Tier B behavioral logs are aggregated and rotated; Tier C sensitive XR telemetry is processed locally where feasible and retained only as aggregates with a defined privacy budget when sharing is needed for research.

Fairness-by-design means defining the protected object (users, sellers, items) and acceptable trade-offs before training begins. The measurable anchor is a fairness target expressed as constraints, such as "no segment experiences more than X% drop in exposure share relative to baseline," coupled with monitoring thresholds that trigger rollbacks. Security-by-design treats personalization and assistants as adversarial targets, with threat models covering shilling, poisoning, model extraction, and prompt injection; controls include feature validation, anomaly detection on interaction graphs, and tool-call allowlists for AI agents (OWASP, 2023).

5.2 Audit Framework for Recommendation and Pricing Systems

The proposed audit framework is a lifecycle process rather than a one-time review. It is designed to satisfy the book's objective of auditability and safety-by-design by tying each stage to artifacts and measurable checks (NIST, 2023).

Staged lifecycle (numbered steps):

1. Scope and inventory: enumerate models, decision points, and data sources (artifact: model inventory with owners and SLAs).
2. Data audit: assess data provenance, consent basis, retention, and proxy risk (artifact: dataset datasheet; feature sensitivity register) (Gebru et al., 2018).

3. Pre-deployment evaluation: run performance and fairness tests, including subgroup exposure metrics and stress tests against shilling patterns (artifact: evaluation report + test harness outputs).
4. Security red-teaming: probe model leakage (membership inference sampling) and agent vulnerabilities (prompt injection attempts against tool calls) (artifact: red-team report) (Shokri et al., 2017; OWASP, 2023).
5. Deployment with logging: enable decision receipts, experiment registry links, and rollback triggers (artifact: signed decision logs + deployment manifest).
6. Continuous monitoring and remedy: track drift, fairness regression, incident rates, and user appeals; apply corrective actions with change control (artifact: monitoring dashboards + remediation tickets).

Figure 2. Audit and Disclosure Lifecycle for Consumer Algorithms (text diagram)

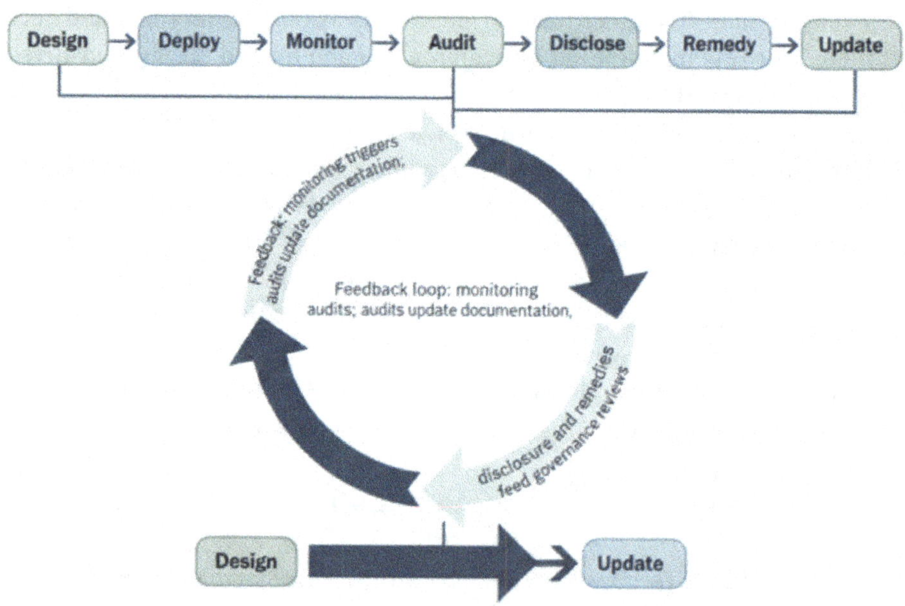

Sampling is critical. Full audits on 100% traffic are rarely feasible; the framework recommends stratified sampling across user segments, devices, geographies, and seller cohorts, combined with targeted samples from incident queues (chargebacks, complaints). For dynamic pricing, audits should sample matched baskets across contexts (device, location granularity) to measure dispersion and detect policy violations; the anchor metric is price variance conditioned on permissible factors, not unconditional “differences.”

5.3 Documentation and Reporting

Documentation needs to be arranged in a hierarchical fashion in order to strike an equilibrium between transparency, security, and being kept secret The internal tier contains detailed model cards and system cards with information about intended applications, limitations, training windows, segmented evaluations, failure modes documented and monitoring triggers (Mitchell et al., 2019). The regulator or auditor tier ensures provenance and evidentiary controls such as dataset snapshots, feature governance decisions, or test outcomes that are sufficient to substantiate claims in question covering the issues of fairness constraints and incident response logs. The “consumer tier provides simple and understandable disclosures, as well as stable categories of reasons that avoid feature-level details, as it will reduce the possibility of gaming, while always providing a meaningful information about the logic and possible consequence in situations where automated decision-making has a consequential impact.” (European Parliament & Council, 2016; ICO, 2020).

An explainability report must clarify at least the capabilities and limitations of the explanations it provides. For example, SHAP-based feature attributions can point out that some groups of features are used to determine a ranking, but are insufficient to determine causality amongst complex interactions, and would not be stable if the inputs are correlated (Lundberg & Lee, 2017). This limitation is to be documented explicitly, e.g. “Reason codes are categories of policy, not a very complete causal explanation”; over-statement is avoided, legal but also reputational risks are avoided.

5.4 Communication & user Disclosure Mechanisms & Opt Out

Disclosure should be done at the time of decision and not buried in a generic privacy policy. A workable practice has been to display a succinct “AI-intention” indicator next to recommendations, prices or the response from the assistant together with a “Learn and control” link associated with an settings panel. Under the EU AI Act, transparency obligations mean that users must be aware when interacting with AI systems in various defined contexts and so underline transparency in the type of labelling and available information (European Parliament & Council, 2024). The architecture of choice presented and, of course, foremost and decisive operational constraint is the need for non-punitive opt-out mechanisms that are genuinely feasible. If the step to opt out automatically consists of a demeaning of the user experience, then the platform should be transparent about that trade -off and provide alternative controls, such as category preferences or frequency limits.

Contestability has to be operationalized in the form of a structured workflow. For a user speaking up about the loss of promotion or an incurred price, the pathway should include (i) an explanation in summary form, (ii) a policy basis explanation, (e.g. inventory constraint applied), (iii) an alternative of repair (manual review, coupon parity fix), and (iv) a responding time, such as 48h for significant impacts. The anchor that can be measured is the quality of the appeal resolution - the proportion of resolution - time to resolve - recurrent or not for the same user - the system algae can be measured.

In spatial commerce, disclosure also includes sensor notices. Eye tracking and motion capture should have visible indicators and retention dashboards because the data can leak sensitive information, and research demonstrates that gaze and avatar signals can enable inference attacks under some conditions (Wang et al., 2024). An operational design pattern is "visceral notice": an always-on indicator during sensor capture, plus a session recap that lists which sensor streams were used for personalization and how long derived features are retained [unclear—verify best-practice UI standards for XR notices], informed by emerging scholarship on eye-tracking notice and privacy.

5.5 Boundary Conditions and Limitations

Transparency can fail when it becomes too granular, too unstable, or too disconnected from remedies. Feature-level disclosure in marketplaces can enable gaming and fraud, requiring abstraction into policy categories and delayed publication of sensitive metrics (e.g., reporting exposure parity weekly rather than in real time). Some information cannot be revealed without compromising security, such as bot-detection thresholds or fraud features; this constraint should be declared as a boundary condition so the organization does not overpromise "full transparency."

Another limitation is model complexity and interaction effects. Post-hoc explainers can mislead when features are highly correlated or when the model uses embeddings that lack intuitive semantics, which is common in modern recommenders and LLM-based assistants (Ribeiro et al., 2016; Lundberg & Lee, 2017). The safe stance is to frame explanations as accountability tools rather than truth machines, and to support them with audits that test outcomes rather than narratives.

Finally, cross-border compliance complicates uniform transparency. GDPR information duties and automated decisioning rights can differ in interpretation and enforcement across jurisdictions, and the EU AI Act adds additional user transparency expectations for certain systems (European Parliament & Council, 2016; European Parliament & Council, 2024). The managerial anchor is a jurisdictional control map: the strictest applicable rule should drive baseline design, with local variations handled through configuration, not bespoke engineering for each market.

6. REAL-WORLD EXAMPLES AND CORRECTIVE ACTIONS

6.1 Documented Examples of Algorithmic Bias Harms in Consumer Contexts

Price steering and the offering of differentials are an extensive practice of consumer harm, given their ability to be observed and compared. Empirical studies have quantified differences in price discrimination and steering behaviours across e-commerce environments, and have identified that prices and promotional offers might systematically differ as a function of e.g. geographic location, device type and/or browsing context even when such differences cannot be readily linked to protected characteristics (Hannak et.al. 2014, Mikians et.al. 2012). Complementary investigative journalism has focused on how pricing algorithms and interface design can make it difficult for some customers to know when they are getting the best deal, highlighting the reputational risk that stems from the uncomfortable fact that pricing logic is not transparent or contestable (Angwin & Mattu, 2016).

A related exposure problem can be seen in algorithmic delivery disparities in such adjacent consumer domains. Ad delivery systems are able to create discriminatory analysis, in violation of the provision on discrimination against the implementation definition (or its absence), even when the protection implementation was not explicitly stated in the wording. to create legally valid ad delivery systems-subject to such statutes and the enforcement measures associated with them-may result in discrimination in the administration of focused on racial discrimination: the lobby of the Law Firm of the Union of Civil Rights. The U.S. Department of Justice settlement with Meta with regards to housing ad delivery disparities is one example of how personalization algorithms can cause measurable harm on a group level, and lead to compulsory fixing and continuing oversight (U.S. Department of Justice, 2022). Although housing advertising is different from retail commerce, the mechanism involved, which is optimization-driven delivery that involves redistributing exposure across demographic groups, is a direct map onto recommendation and promotion delivery in marketplaces.

Privacy harms also arise because of the misuse or retention of sensitive data. The FTC settlement with an entity referred to as Ever album required the deletion of models and algorithms trained on improperly obtained biometric information, thus pointing to an ecosystem failure that can require not only data deletion, but also "algorithm destruction," with important operational and financial consequences

(Federal Trade Commission, 2021). In immersive scenarios, researchers have demonstrated a gaze implicitly exploit show in Apple Vision pro wherein a typed content is inferred by eye tracking (relating to avatar representations). The issue was later resolved through platform update after disclosure which helped highlight that biometric telemetry and representations downstream are a significant threat surface (Wang et al 2024).

6.2 Corrective Action Patterns

Corrective actions should be chosen in relation to the mode of failure and not out of convenience. For exposure bias and feedback loops, constraint prevalent-okoda ranking has often found better results than retraining the model alone, which constraints, e.g. minimum exposure floor for underrepresented participants, diversification, visibility on the impact on not only the click through rate, but also conversion. For proxy discrimination, feature governance is the key: a proxy risk register should be maintained as well as ablation tests including features removal to assess a change in subgroup exposure and conversion measures.

or the purpose of dynamic pricing conflicts, corrective measures must include both policy and tooling. Establish a pricing - personalization policy: e.g. cost of health insurance plan based on participation inaway or or social activities or lifestyle behavior favorably; . --- move to destination. or to - - set of price range. > - allowed - do not allow use - variables . - Possible variables / reasons are likely to be elicited with sparked users. of substitutions, gain notice, fail fall in a different moral, inte-scule. (for e.g., appropriately intimacy, to response strong in additional privately, implicitly users. excluding the integration is invoked using this information, while the awareness have some sensitivity of fact. . . Implement an experiment registry from which we could answer the practical customer question, "Was this price part of a test?" leading to an accurate answer - including an audit trail and check on the workpieces internally and an internal mechanism to fix will verso with were parities breached by some policy boundary by a remedy, such as a parity adjustment, or by issuing coupons The operative anchor of this approach is evidence: Each remedy must have reference to a decision receipt and relevant policy rule: this minimizes arbitrary decisions made regarding customer service.

For privacy and security issues the right pattern to use is defense -in- depth. Encrypt sensitive data fields, implement least privilege principles, log-rotate regularly and use privacy preserving machine learning, if applicable. Differential privacy training reduces some of the risk of leakage; however, the differential privacy training leads to accuracy trade-offs that are controlled by privacy parameters like epsilon, which must be recorded rather than considered an implementation detail (Abadi et al., 2016). Federated learning may limit collection of raw data in some use cases, but secure aggregation of the data, integrity guarantees for the devices, and careful threat modelling to prevent poisoning through compromised clients must be done [McMahan et al. 2017] [unclear: is there still a reason to avoid gathering the data? is this still useful? retail telemetry potentially room for poisoning?] Examples of federated learning.

6.3 Lessons for Spatial Commerce and AI Agents

In spatial commerce, corrective actions must account for embodiment and persistence. An embodied assistant can amplify persuasion, so governance should treat certain interaction patterns as policy-sensitive, such as high-pressure urgency, undisclosed sponsorship, or emotion inference. The control lever is both technical and procedural: instrument assistant outputs, log tool calls, and require pre-deployment review for new "persuasion templates," like how financial firms review customer communications.

Telemetry minimization is also different in XR. Head and hand motion can function as behavioral biometrics, and eye tracking can leak sensitive attributes or secrets, as shown by both academic and applied work (Pfeuffer et al., 2019; Wang et al., 2024). Corrective actions therefore prioritize local processing and strict retention. Where sharing is necessary for benchmarking or vendor audits, privacy-preserving dataset techniques should be applied; work on privacy-preserving eye-tracking datasets has adapted k-anonymity-style concepts to reduce re-identification risk, reinforcing the principle that "anonymization" needs measurable guarantees, not assumptions (David-John et al., 2022).

7. GOVERNANCE, COMPLIANCE, AND ORGANIZATIONAL OVERSIGHT

7.1 Regulatory and Standards Landscape for AI Transparency

GDPR establishes information duties and constraints around automated decision-making and profiling, including the obligation to provide information about the existence of automated decision-making and meaningful information about logic and consequences in relevant contexts (European Parliament & Council, 2016). Guidance from data protection authorities and the ICO emphasizes practical explainability and transparency for affected individuals, translating legal concepts into implementable explanation types and documentation practices (ICO, 2020). The EU AI Act adds explicit transparency obligations for certain AI systems, including informing users when interacting with an AI system in specified contexts, reinforcing the need for standardized labeling and accessible disclosures in consumer journeys (European Parliament & Council, 2024; European Commission, 2024).

Standards provide complementary governance scaffolding. ISO/IEC 27001:2022 and related standards support information security management, while ISO/IEC 27701 extends privacy information management as a structured system of controls; ISO/IEC 42001:2023 targets AI management systems, signaling a move toward standardized AI governance processes across organizations (ISO, 2023a; ISO, 2023b). The practical point is not certification for its own sake; it is the discipline of ownership, controls, evidence, and continuous improvement—exactly what algorithmic accountability requires.

Cross-border compliance tension is operationally visible in two places: data transfers and disclosure expectations. A platform operating in multiple juris dictions must reconcile localized interpretations of automated decisioning and consumer protection. The recommended governance stance is a baseline "global minimum" transparency package (disclosure + controls + logging) with jurisdictional overlays for specific rights (appeal processes, data access, restriction requests), managed through configuration rather than divergent codebases.

7.2 Organizational Governance

Effective governance assigns accountability to roles with budget and authority. A workable pattern mirrors model risk management: each high-impact model has an owner, a validator, and an escalation path, with periodic reviews tied to deployment changes rather than annual checkboxes. For consumer algorithms, "high impact" can be defined by concrete triggers: price changes, eligibility decisions (credit-like offers, pay-later), and personalization that materially changes access to deals. The evidence artifact is a signed review record attached to the model inventory.

Cross-disciplinary committees can help only if they are wired into engineering workflows. A committee that meets quarterly without access to logs or incident tickets cannot detect fairness regression or transparency debt. The operational anchor is integration: governance should require that new models cannot ship without (i) a completed model card, (ii) a fairness test report, (iii) a security threat model, and (iv) a disclosure plan, with exceptions documented and time bounded. This aligns with risk management frameworks that emphasize lifecycle governance rather than one-time compliance statements (NIST, 2023).

7.3 Operational Monitoring and Continuous Assurance

Continuous assurance requires metrics that connect technical signals to managerial decisions. Drift monitoring should track feature distribution changes (catalog shifts, seasonality) and outcome shifts (CTR, conversion), while fairness monitoring tracks exposure parity and error rates by segment, using position-aware measures to reflect ranking reality. Privacy incidents should be monitored through access logs, unusual export volumes, and data retention violations; transparency debt can be tracked as the backlog of undocumented model changes or missing decision receipts.

Table 2 summarizes an operational KPI set designed for continuous assurance, that is, to make associations between trust, fairness, privacy risk, utility, and security with corresponding measurable definitions, measurement caveats, and designated accountable owners.

Table 2. Operational KPIs for Trustworthy Consumer Algorithms

Dimension	KPI (definition)	Measurement caution	Typical owner
Trust	Complaint rate per 10k sessions tied to personalization surfaces	Normalize by traffic mix and campaigns	Trust & Safety / CX ops
Fairness	Position-weighted exposure parity across defined segments	Requires segment definitions and sampling	Data science + compliance
Privacy risk	Sensitive-field retention violations per week; access anomalies	False positives during incident response	Security + privacy office
Utility	Incremental conversion lift vs baseline with confidence intervals	Avoid p-hacking; maintain experiment registry	Growth analytics
Security	Shilling/bot detection precision-recall on flagged events	Attackers adapt; retrain detectors	Security engineering

8. PRACTICAL MANAGERIAL AND PRACTITIONER GUIDANCE

8.1 Managerial Implications

Managerial significance hinges on treating transparency and fairness as operational capabilities with budgets, not as ethics statements. Procurement contracts for recommender vendors, CDPs, and AI assistant platforms should require evidence artifacts: model cards, audit logs, red-team results, and disclosure/opt-out support. A concrete clause is "audit log exportability": the ability to export decision receipts and model versions in a standard format if vendors change, which reduces lock-in and supports regulatory inquiries.

Budgeting should reflect ongoing costs: fairness evaluation is not a one-time expense because catalogs shift weekly, and new campaigns can change exposure distributions overnight. An actionable budgeting anchor is capacity planning for audits: allocating analyst hours per quarter for targeted audits (pricing, recommendation, assistant) and for incident-driven deep dives, alongside engineering time for instrumentation and dashboards. KPI selection should avoid vanity metrics; complaint rate, appeal volume, and repeat purchase after opt-out are more informative than generic "engagement," because they connect directly to trust and perceived legitimacy.

8.2 Actionable Artifacts

A bias audit checklist and decision matrix that link key audit checks to specific tests, evidence artefacts and corrective actions are presented in Table 3. Understanding the importance of bias can be described with words such as "minor risk", "major risk" or "critical risk".

Table 3. Bias Audit Checklist and Decision Matrix

Audit check (operational)	Metric/Test	Evidence artifact	If failing, action	Decision severity cue
Segment exposure parity	Position-weighted exposure ratio vs baseline	Fairness report snapshot	Constrain ranking + monitor	High if persistent 2+ cycles
Proxy feature risk	Feature correlation review + ablation	Feature register + ablation logs	Remove/transform feature; retrain	High if linked to protected proxies
Cold-start exclusion	Coverage for new sellers/items	Coverage dashboards	Add exploration floor; adjust retrieval	Medium if revenue impact limited
Pricing dispersion policy	Matched-basket dispersion conditioned on allowed factors	Pricing audit workbook	Roll back test; update policy; remedy users	High if not policy-justified
Shilling / bot manipulation	Graph anomaly + detector PR curve	Security detection logs	Tighten validation; add friction; retrain	High if revenue fraud present
Model leakage	Membership inference sampling	Red-team report	Add DP/regularization; reduce outputs	High if sensitive attributes involved
Assistant tool misuse	Prompt injection tests on tool calls	LLM red-team notes	Tool allowlist; output filtering; logging	High if PII/tool access at risk
Disclosure/opt-out usability	Opt-out completion rate + post-opt-out satisfaction	UX telemetry + survey	Redesign controls; reduce penalty	Medium-high if opt-out punitive

Transparency report template outline (practitioner-ready):

1. System scope: decision points (rank, price, assistant), populations affected and intended use.
2. Data inputs: categories, retention tiers, consent basis, and XR sensor usage flags where applicable.
3. Model and constraints: model family, updating cadence, constraint policies (inventory, fairness, safety).
4. Testing evidence: performance, fairness metrics, security tests (shilling, leakage), and limitations.
5. User controls: disclosure placement, opt-out options, preference editing, and contestability workflow SLAs.
6. Monitoring and incidents: drift checks, fairness regression triggers, incident summaries, and remediation actions.
7. Governance: owners, review cadence, third-party dependencies, and compliance mapping.

8.3 Deployment Roadmap

Figure 3 defines the phased approach roadmap put forth in the chapter with an execution sequence to realize the conceptual goal of making "trustworthy AI" a real thing, a quantifiable model of operation, where each phase adds a new layer of quantifiable evidence, control mechanisms and accountability. Phase 1 sets the minimum substrate of observability (i.e., model inventory and experiment registry as well as logging of the decision) so that a concrete investigatory question ("which model produced this recommendation?") can be promptly answered using a tracked mean time to evidence. Phase 2: move from observability to what is called auditability by adding decision receipts, stratified sampling, and offline audit harnessing so that reproducible quarterly audit packs measuring fairness and dispersion of pricing across segments instead of ad hoc analysis are possible. Phase3 externalises accountability to the user layer through operationalisation of disclosure and opt-out done as follows: AI involvement indicators, stable reason codes dictionaries, preference controls, and contestability workflows is taken as a product requirement and measured in paired outcome measures (complaint rate as well as conversion lift) as to reduce "transparency theatre" Phase 4 measures being closed, closing the loop on an ongoing, continuous assurance led by drift & fairness-regression alerts change management trigger, security red teaming integrated for agentic assistants, privacy retain violations via zero approach both or measured & enforced rigorously. Combined, the stages represent a planned developmental pathway between pegged down traceability to governance-suitable assurance, which is coordinated with auditability and safety-by-design anticipations in the context of traditional e-commerce and companion, spatial commerce areas on the fluffs of the metaverse.

Figure 3. Phased Deployment Roadmap for Trustworthy Consumer Algorithms.

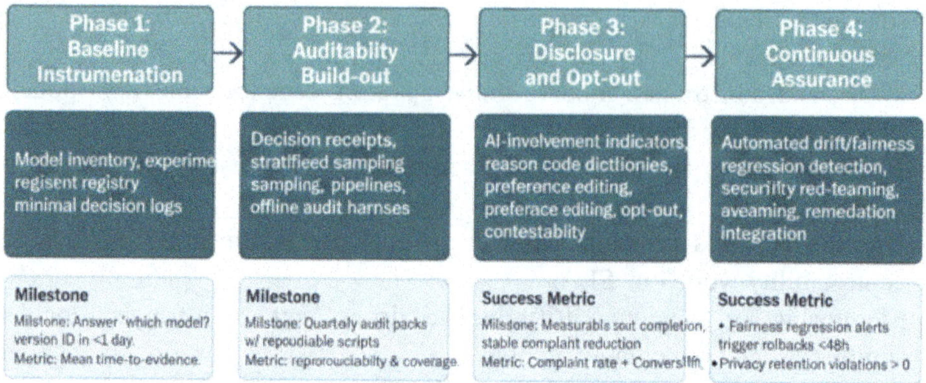

8.4 Common Failure Patterns and Mitigations

Transparency theater occurs when explanations are present but not actionable. The mitigation is explicit: every disclosure must link to a control or a remedy, and that linkage is auditable through click-through and completion metrics. Metric gaming occurs when teams optimize fairness metrics narrowly while shifting harm elsewhere (e.g., improving exposure parity but increasing refund denials via assistant nudges). Mitigation requires multi-metric dashboards and periodic cross-surface audits that connect ranking, pricing, and assistant outcomes.

Privacy backlash occurs when users discover sensitive data use after the fact, particularly in XR where sensor capture feels intimate. Mitigation is "front-of-house" notice plus retention minimization, including session recaps for XR telemetry and clear default-off settings for sensitive sensors unless essential. Adversarial manipulation is mitigated through defense-in-depth: anomaly detection, friction for suspicious interactions, robust logging, and periodic red-teaming, consistent with adversarial recommender system research and LLM security guidance (Deldjoo et al., 2021; OWASP, 2023).

9. RESEARCH AGENDA AND BENCHMARKS

9.1 Open Research Questions

First, trustworthy explanation in ranked, multi-objective settings remains under-specified: how to generate explanations that are stable across retrains, robust to gaming, and meaningful to consumers while still audit-ready. The measurable research target is explanation stability under model updates (e.g., percent of decisions whose reason category changes after retrain) without unacceptable performance loss.

Second, fairness in multi-party marketplaces needs better causal framing. Seller-side harms (exposure suppression) and buyer-side harms (steering, availability) interact, and current metrics often treat them separately. A concrete research direction is "counterfactual exposure audits" where ranking outcomes are recomputed under controlled changes to sensitive proxies to quantify disparate impact under realistic constraints.

Third, XR telemetry governance needs principled privacy guarantees and evaluation methods. Eye tracking and motion signals enable both personalization and re-identification; research has begun to formalize privacy-preserving approaches for eye-tracking datasets, but benchmarks for spatial-commerce decisioning are still scarce (David-John et al., 2022). The priority is to design benchmarks that test both utility (intent prediction) and privacy leakage (re-identification risk) under explicit threat models.

Fourth, agentic AI assistants require security and safety benchmarks that reflect tool use. Prompt injection and tool misuse are not edge cases; they are predictable failure modes in systems that connect LLMs to user data and transaction APIs (OWASP, 2023). The concrete research need is standardized red-team suites for retail agents, including "malicious shopper prompts," "seller manipulation prompts," and "support escalation bypass attempts," tied to measurable success rates.

9.2 Dataset and Benchmark Needs

Public recommender datasets remain important benchmarks for foundational research; however, they have become insufficient when one needs to perform a proper audit and fairness examination for the commercial context. For example, MovieLens gives us a historical context and fixed reference points for assessing the ranking algorithm and the quality of the recommendations, but it fails to represent the seller incentives and the real world pricing constraints (Harper & Konstan, 2015). Likewise, Amazon review datasets and corresponding product metadata enable the study of preference modeling and the textual signal extraction, however, they are suboptimal at representing dynamic pricing and return procedures or fraud signs

(McAuley, 2015). The Criteo display advertising challenge provides click through rate prediction data relevant to ranking and ad delivery but does not represent the entire commerce pipeline, including contestability and result from remediation (Criteo, 2014).

Benchmark requirements for transparency and auditing go beyond serving an additional data. The type of elements well that are missing can be enumerated as follows: (i) appeal plus remedy datasets presenting the resolution of the disputes; (ii) policy - constraint logs that mention which constraints in their operational were triggered; (iii) adversarial interaction traces including shilling or bot campaign activity; and (iv) XR telemetry datasets that equip them with privacy protecting release mechanisms in combination with well defined threat models. A pragmatic approach first which focuses on privacy-preserving evaluations: Synthetic logs with calibrated biases, secure enclave-based auditing or federated evaluation (where the metrics are calculated locally and aggregated), reducing exposure of raw data (the best strategy for enclave evaluation in retail audits use should also be further verified).

9.3 Future Directions for Trustworthy Immersive Commerce

Trustworthy immersive commerce is also expected to require provenance and accountability at the level of the platforms rather than just the level of the retailers themselves. Identity and transaction protocols in experiencing metaverse-adjacent ecosystems require participation by a range of businesses and actors such as headsets operating-system vendors, platform operators, merchants, payment service providers and AI-agents developers. A round-trip route to viability This would include the creation of standardised decision-receipt formats and audit-log schemas that can be journeyed across organisational boundaries. Such standards would allow for independent audits and contestability of systems by users even when system parts are distributed. This direction have a direct link to pursuing the global goals of the book in terms of linking the architectural considerations to identity and economy considerations with risks of AI, systematising the models of threats (including adversarial machine learning and social engineering), and providing auditability mechanisms and governance frameworks to practitioners of this topic.

10 CONCLUSION

Ensuring the security of customer data in AI-powered business means more than deployment of encryption and intrusion detection systems. It requires operational transparency by decision receipts, level of disclosures, opt - out and contestability, rulers to restrict models to empirical measures and evaluation polity paths. The proposed framework embedding the principles of privacy-by-design, fairness-by-design, transparency-by-design and security-by-design into a comprehensive lifecycle audit model - extend explicitly to spatial commerce where XR telemetry, embodied agents supercharge the capabilities and risks. Documented cases, in pricing, the delivery of advertising, biometric abuse and a side channel into the XR system all serve as a wake-up call: in the absence of trace, and user controls, trust quickly breaks down and there is a huge cost in remediation. By making auditability, disclosure and continued assurance part of engineering, and reflecting this in new standards and regulatory changes, organisations in the near future, with a bit of engineering support, will be able to create personalised experiences that are both defensible, measurable, and trustworthy to use, either through conventional e - commerce platforms, and also metaverse - aligned consumer experiences.

REFERENCES

Abadi, M., Chu, A., Goodfellow, I., McMahan, H. B., Mironov, I., Talwar, K., & Zhang, L. (2016). Deep learning with differential privacy. *Proceedings of the 2016 ACM SIGSAC Conference on Computer and Communications Security (CCS).* https://arxiv.org/abs/1607.00133 DOI: 10.1145/2976749.2978318

Angwin, J., & Mattu, S. (2016, September 20). *Amazon says it puts customers first. But its pricing algorithm doesn't.* ProPublica.

Criteo. (2014, July 9). *Display advertising challenge by Criteo.* Criteo AI Lab.

David-John, B., Butler, D. J., & Jain, E. (2022). For your eyes only: Privacy-preserving eye-tracking datasets. *Proceedings of the ACM Symposium on Eye Tracking Research & Applications (ETRA).* DOI: 10.1145/3517031.3529618

Deldjoo, Y., Di Noia, T., & Merra, F. A. (2021). A survey on adversarial recommender systems: From attack/defense strategies to generative adversarial networks. *ACM Computing Surveys.*

European Commission. (2024). *AI Act Service Desk—Article 50: Transparency obligations.*

European Parliament & Council of the European Union. (2016). *Regulation (EU) 2016/679 (General Data Protection Regulation).* EUR-Lex.

European Parliament & Council of the European Union. (2024). *Regulation (EU) 2024/1689 (Artificial Intelligence Act).* EUR-Lex.

Federal Trade Commission. (2021, May 7). *FTC finalizes settlement with Everalbum related to misuse of facial recognition technology.*

Fredrikson, M., Jha, S., & Ristenpart, T. (2015). Model inversion attacks that exploit confidence information and basic countermeasures. *Proceedings of the 22nd ACM SIGSAC Conference on Computer and Communications Security (CCS).* https://dl.acm.org/doi/10.1145/2810103.2813677

Gebru, T., Morgenstern, J., Vecchione, B., Vaughan, J. W., Wallach, H., Daumé III, H., & Crawford, K. (2018). Datasheets for datasets. *arXiv.*

Hannak, A., Soeller, G., Lazer, D., Mislove, A., & Wilson, C. (2014). Measuring price discrimination and steering on e-commerce web sites. *Proceedings of the 2014 Conference on Internet Measurement Conference (IMC).* DOI: 10.1145/2663716.2663744

Hardt, M., Price, E., & Srebro, N. (2016). Equality of opportunity in supervised learning. *Advances in Neural Information Processing Systems (NeurIPS).* https://arxiv.org/abs/1610.02413

Harper, F. M., & Konstan, J. A. (2015). The MovieLens datasets: History and context. *ACM Transactions on Interactive Intelligent Systems*, *5*(4), 19.

Information Commissioner's Office (ICO). (2020). *Explaining decisions made with AI (ICO and Alan Turing Institute guidance).*

ISO. (2023a). *ISO/IEC 42001:2023—Artificial intelligence management systems.*

ISO. (2023b). *ISO/IEC 27001:2022—Information security management systems (overview).* https://www.iso.org/isoiec-27001-information-security.html

McAuley, J. (2015). *Amazon review data.* UC San Diego.

McMahan, H. B., Moore, E., Ramage, D., Hampson, S., & Arcas, B. A. (2017). Communication-efficient learning of deep networks from decentralized data. *Proceedings of AISTATS.* https://arxiv.org/abs/1602.05629

Mikians, J., Gyarmati, L., Erramilli, V., & Laoutaris, N. (2012). Detecting price and search discrimination on the internet. *Proceedings of HotNets.*

Mitchell, M., Wu, S., Zaldivar, A., Barnes, P., Vasserman, L., Hutchinson, B., Spitzer, E., Raji, I. D., & Gebru, T. (2019). Model cards for model reporting. *Proceedings of the Conference on Fairness, Accountability, and Transparency (FAT*).* DOI: 10.1145/3287560.3287596

NIST. (2020). *NIST Privacy Framework (PF) 1.0.* National Institute of Standards and Technology.

NIST. (2023). *Artificial Intelligence Risk Management Framework (AI RMF 1.0).* National Institute of Standards and Technology.

OWASP. (2023). *OWASP Top 10 for Large Language Model Applications (v1.0.1).*

Pfeuffer, K., Mayer, S., Mardanbegi, D., & Gellersen, H. (2019). Behavioural biometrics in VR: Identifying users from motion and interaction. *Proceedings of CHI.* DOI: 10.1007/978-3-658-22050-1

Ribeiro, M. T., Singh, S., & Guestrin, C. (2016). "Why should I trust you?": Explaining the predictions of any classifier. *Proceedings of KDD.*

Shokri, R., Stronati, M., Song, C., & Shmatikov, V. (2017). Membership inference attacks against machine learning models. *Proceedings of IEEE Symposium on Security and Privacy.* DOI: 10.1109/SP.2017.41

U.S. Department of Justice. (2022, June 21). *Justice Department secures settlement agreement with Meta Platforms to resolve allegations of discriminatory housing advertising.*

Wang, H., et al. (2024). GAZEploit: Remote keystroke inference attack by gaze estimation in XR/VR settings.

Chapter 13
The Transparency Paradox:
Rebuilding Trust in AI Shopping Agents Through Explainability

Prakul Bansal
http://orcid.org/0009-0000-2440-5043
Chirst University, India

Reenu Bansal
http://orcid.org/0009-0009-1763-3756
Christ University, India

ABSTRACT

AI shopping agent systems that search, compare, negotiate, and purchase on a consumer's behalf promise to reduce friction in digital commerce, but they also intensify long-standing concerns about price discrimination, manipulative choice architecture, and opaque data use. This chapter argues that the resulting "transparency paradox" is not merely a communication problem: the same AI capabilities that enable personalization can also conceal and optimize exploitation. Building on research in trust, explainable artificial intelligence, human–AI interaction, and consumer protection, the chapter develops a socio-technical approach to rebuilding trust in agentic commerce. It synthesizes regulatory and standards developments and proposes design and governance mechanisms layered explanations, contestable outcomes, auditability, and choice-integrity controls intended to make AI shopping agents intelligible and accountable across jurisdictions and market contexts.

DOI: 10.4018/979-8-3373-7330-0.ch013

INTRODUCTION

Digital commerce is entering a phase in which the primary decision-maker may no longer be the human shopper but a software agent acting under the shopper's delegated authority. These AI shopping agents (also described as agentic commerce systems) integrate product discovery, recommendation, negotiation, payment, and post-purchase management into a single interaction loop. The value proposition is efficiency: when attention is scarce and options are abundant, delegation reduces search costs and compresses decisions that previously required time, domain expertise, and repeated comparisons. Industry and policy commentary has begun to treat this shift as a structural change rather than a feature update, because the interface of commerce becomes an intermediary that can actively choose and transact rather than merely display information (Boston Consulting Group [BCG], 2025; Lough, n.d.; World Economic Forum [WEF], 2025). Related diffusion paths are already visible in Asian "super app" ecosystems (e.g., WeChat), where messaging, payments, and commerce are integrated and could readily host agent-mediated shopping.

Delegation, however, changes the conditions under which consumers can exercise agency. If a human shopper browses a marketplace, they can (at least in principle) cross-check claims, compare alternatives, and notice when an offer looks unusually expensive or pressuring. When a shopping agent performs these actions, many evaluative steps become hidden inside models and policies. The agent also becomes a new target for influence: retailers and platforms can attempt to shape the agent's selections through ranking systems, sponsored placement, "recommended" defaults, or negotiation protocols that are not fully visible to the principal. The result is an asymmetry: the consumer is asked to trust both the competence of the agent and the integrity of the broader ecosystem platform incentives, data flows, and enforcement regimes that surround it (Lee & See, 2004; McKnight et al., 2002).

Trust is the enabling condition for delegation. In foundational trust models, reliance involves a willingness to accept vulnerability based on expectations about competence, integrity, and benevolence (Mayer et al., 1995). In e-commerce, trust is empirically linked to purchase intention and continued use, especially when uncertainty is high and information is incomplete (Gefen et al., 2003). AI shopping agents heighten vulnerability in at least three ways. First, they may act on sensitive consumer data (purchase history, location, inferred preferences) that can be misused or breached. Second, they can make high-stakes errors (wrong product, wrong quantity, wrong seller) in a way that is difficult to diagnose after the fact. Third, and most central to this chapter, they can become instruments of exploitation when personalization is used to extract surplus or steer choices in ways that conflict with the consumer's interests (Calo, 2014; Susser et al., 2019).

This chapter examines a tension that emerges when AI shopping agents are deployed at scale: the transparency paradox. Across jurisdictions, regulators and standard-setters increasingly demand transparency about personalization, automated decision-making, and manipulative design. Yet transparency requirements can be met in form while failing in substance. A system can disclose that "prices may vary" or that "recommendations are personalized" and still remain opaque in the dimensions that matter why a particular price was offered, what constraints were traded off, and what alternative outcomes were plausible. Meanwhile, AI enables more granular targeting and continuous experimentation, allowing persuasive strategies to become adaptive, personalized, and difficult to observe as stable "patterns" (Yeung, 2017). Transparency therefore becomes both more necessary and harder to achieve.

The argument proceeds in five steps. First, the chapter explains how AI agents intensify algorithmic price discrimination and related fairness concerns, especially when prices are individualized in ways consumers cannot detect or contest. Second, it analyzes how AI amplifies deceptive design (dark patterns) by personalizing persuasion and embedding it into conversational flows. Third, it conceptualizes the fused threat that arises when discriminatory pricing and dark patterns co-occur, creating an environment in which consumers pay more while also being subtly prevented from resisting. Fourth, it maps these risks onto the emerging regulatory and standards landscape including consumer protection enforcement and the European Union's evolving AI and platform rules. Finally, it proposes a socio-technical framework for rebuilding trust that combines explainability, governance, and choice-integrity controls.

Survey evidence suggests that consumer confidence in digital institutions is increasingly contingent on how personal data is used and whether automated decisions can be explained and challenged. Major trust surveys report heightened skepticism toward AI-enabled personalization when it is perceived as intrusive or manipulative, even as consumers value convenience and relevant recommendations (Edelman, 2025; PricewaterhouseCoopers, 2024; Salesforce, 2024).

Chapter contribution.

This chapter makes three contributions to the discussion of AI shopping agents in agentic commerce. First, it defines the transparency paradox: disclosure can increase in form while opacity persists in the decisions that matter to consumers. Second, it explains the fused threat in which algorithmic price discrimination and AI-powered dark patterns reinforce one another in conversational journeys. Third, it offers a socio-technical trust framework Explainability and User Control, Governance and Auditability, and Fairness and Choice Integrity paired with implementable controls and evaluation metrics that practitioners can apply to design, deploy, and audit shopping agents.

OPERATIONAL ANATOMY OF AI SHOPPING AGENTS

The term "shopping agent" covers a range of systems with different degrees of autonomy.

Table 1. Taxonomy of AI shopping agent types

System type	What it does	Decision authority	Primary risks in this chapter	Minimum controls (examples)
Chatbot shopping assistant	Answers questions and suggests options; may link out to merchants	Low–medium	Persuasive framing; selective disclosure; sponsored influence	Sponsored labeling; "why this?" explanations; show alternatives
Recommender system	Ranks products/sellers; personalizes lists and feeds	Medium	Steering via ranking; hidden incentives; feedback loops	Ranking transparency; separation of ads vs. organic; audit logs
Tool-using shopping agent	Searches, compares, applies coupons, and can transact using tools	High	Hidden trade-offs; individualized pricing; dark patterns in conversational flow	Constraint setting/ locking; decision trace; contestability and override
Autonomous purchasing agent	Executes purchases within delegated budgets and rules	Very high	Accountability diffusion; hard-to-detect exploitation; costly errors	Approval gates; spending limits; dispute/recourse workflow; monitoring

Table 1 distinguishes common agent types and the minimum user and governance controls each requires.

From the perspective of consumer welfare, the architecture highlights a design opportunity. Because agents already maintain internal representations of constraints, alternatives, and decision traces, they can be instrumented to generate meaningful explanations and audit logs with relatively low marginal cost. The challenge is less technical feasibility than incentive alignment: unless organizations prioritize user benefit and accountability, the same instrumentation can be used to optimize conversion and surplus extraction. This is the core reason the chapter treats explainability as inseparable from governance and choice integrity (Amershi et al., 2019; Shneiderman, 2020).

The architecture also introduces specific failure modes that are relevant to trust. Retrieval pipelines can surface outdated or biased information; ranking models can overweight popularity and reinforce incumbents; and conversational interfaces can produce fluent but inaccurate rationales. Moreover, tool-using agents can be vulnerable to prompt injection or malicious product descriptions that cause unsafe actions, which is one reason risk frameworks emphasize continuous monitoring and incident response (NIST, 2023). These technical details matter for governance: firms cannot credibly claim that "the AI decided" if the system is an orchestrated pipeline with multiple controllable components.

Each step creates a distinct transparency obligation. Preference elicitation requires data transparency: what information is being collected and how it will be used. Retrieval and ranking require epistemic transparency: what sources and criteria produced the candidate set and the ordering. Negotiation and execution require procedural transparency: what constraints the agent enforced, what options were rejected, and whether the consumer could have achieved a better outcome with different constraints. Post-purchase management requires accountability transparency: what records exist to support disputes, refunds, and chargebacks. Treating transparency as a single disclosure therefore mis-specifies the problem.

A typical agentic shopping workflow begins with preference elicitation: the consumer provides constraints (budget, brand, delivery window), and the agent may ask clarifying questions. The system then retrieves candidate products, ranks them, and produces a short list. At this stage, explanation and sponsorship disclosure are crucial because ranking can embed commercial incentives. Next, the agent may perform "deal discovery," which includes checking alternative sellers, monitoring prices over time, or negotiating through merchant APIs. Finally, the agent executes a transaction, often under an authorization model that may range from per-purchase confirmation to pre-approved spending limits. Post-purchase, the agent can track shipment, handle returns, and manage subscriptions.

Understanding why transparency is difficult requires a concrete view of how AI shopping agents are built. In many commercial deployments, the "agent" is not a single model but an orchestration layer that combines (a) a conversational interface, often powered by a large language model; (b) retrieval components that pull structured product, pricing, and policy data from catalogs and third-party sources; (c) ranking and recommendation models; (d) planning logic that decides what actions to take next; and (e) tool integrations that execute actions such as adding items to carts, applying coupons, or initiating payment. This modular architecture is attractive because it enables rapid iteration and vendor substitution, but it also makes responsibility harder to locate.

AI SHOPPING AGENTS AND ALGORITHMIC PRICE DISCRIMINATION

From Dynamic Pricing to Individualized Offers

Price differentiation is not new. Economics distinguishes between forms of price discrimination in which sellers charge different prices based on willingness to pay, segmentation, or self-selection (Varian, 1989). In digital markets, discrimination becomes easier because transactions are mediated by software that can identify returning users and infer preferences from behavior. Acquisti and Varian (2005) formalize how a seller can condition price on purchase history when identity or pseudonymous identity is available. Even without explicit identity, device fingerprints, cookies, and behavioral profiles enable probabilistic re-identification and segmentation. The result is an environment where dynamic pricing can evolve into individualized pricing offers calibrated not to a market segment but to a particular consumer's predicted willingness to pay (Odlyzko, 2003).

Empirical work has repeatedly found signs of differential pricing and steering in online markets. Mikians et al. (2012) developed a measurement methodology to detect price and search discrimination and documented evidence of both across sites and locations. Hannak et al. (2014) similarly investigated price discrimination and steering on e-commerce sites, emphasizing that discrimination can be implemented not only by changing prices but also by changing which offers are shown, in what order, and with what framing. These mechanisms matter because consumers experience the outcome as a "choice set," not as a single quoted price. Two shoppers may face different decision environments even when the nominal price is identical.

AI shopping agents expand the surface area for discrimination. First, agents can supply richer signals to sellers. A consumer who uses an agent to compare premium brands or request "best quality regardless of price" communicates a willingness to pay that is more legible than conventional browsing. Second, agents can automate repeated negotiation, enabling sellers to run fine-grained pricing experiments at scale. Third, agent-mediated interactions can occur through application programming interfaces (APIs) or private channels that bypass publicly visible pages, reducing the possibility of crowd-sourced detection. In other words, the agent can improve market efficiency for the consumer while simultaneously providing the market with a more efficient extraction tool for the seller.

The shift to individualized offers also complicates the standard informational remedies used in consumer protection. When price differences are visible and justified (e.g., loyalty discounts with clear terms), consumers can evaluate trade-offs. When price differences are hidden and inferred, consumers may not realize that a better offer was available or that the price they received was contingent on sensitive inferences. This opacity is not accidental; it is a feature of markets in which surplus extraction is enabled by informational asymmetry (Odlyzko, 2003).

Fairness, Reference Prices, and Perceived Exploitation

Personalized pricing is not automatically unlawful or unethical, but it is highly sensitive to perceptions of fairness. Research on price fairness shows that consumers assess not only the absolute price but also its relationship to reference points, process expectations, and perceived intentions of the seller (Bolton et al., 2003; Xia et al., 2004). Kahneman et al. (1986) demonstrate that consumers often view profit-seeking as constrained by entitlements: prices that exploit a consumer's constrained options or reduced information are treated as unfair even if they are "market clearing." In agent-mediated commerce, where consumers may not observe alternatives, the risk is that personalized pricing will be interpreted as exploitation rather than personalization.

Two features of agentic commerce intensify fairness concerns. The first is epistemic dependency. Consumers cannot easily reconstruct why an agent selected a product or accepted a price because the relevant signals and trade-offs are internal to the system. The second is counterfactual uncertainty. A consumer may suspect they paid more but cannot observe the counterfactual world in which the agent behaved differently or the platform offered a different price. Empirical evidence suggests that attempts to correct perceived unfairness through generic explanations are only modestly effective (Bolton et al., 2003), implying that mere disclosure may not restore legitimacy once suspicion takes hold.

Fairness also interacts with broader concerns about privacy and autonomy. If consumers believe that a price is contingent on attributes they did not intend to reveal (e.g., inferred income, urgency, vulnerability), the pricing process becomes normatively contested even when it is economically "rational." Nissenbaum's (2010) theory of contextual integrity helps explain why: information flows are evaluated against social norms about appropriate use, not only against consent forms. When a shopping agent aggregates signals across contexts health browsing, social media activity, location history and channels them into pricing, consumers may experience a norm violation regardless of any formal opt-in.

Recent empirical work on consumer responses to personalized price discrimination suggests that acceptability depends on transparency, justification, and perceived reciprocity (Hufnagel et al., 2022). Discounts targeted to consumers in need can be seen as fair; surcharges targeted to consumers with fewer alternatives are typically seen as unfair. AI shopping agents can be designed to promote reciprocity for example, by actively searching for discounts and negotiating on behalf of the consumer but this requires that the agent be independent enough to resist seller-optimized price extraction.

Why Agents Increase the Need for Contestability

In contexts where prices and rankings are personalized, contestability becomes a practical requirement for trust. Contestability means that a consumer can ask "why," challenge an outcome, and obtain a meaningful response either a revision of the result or a reasoned explanation of why revision is not warranted. Contestability is emphasized in human–AI interaction guidance because it supports calibrated trust: users can rely on automation when it performs well and override it when it fails (Amershi et al., 2019; Lee & See, 2004).

AI shopping agents complicate contestability because the relevant causal chain spans multiple actors. A consumer may wish to contest a price; the platform may say the price was set by the seller; the seller may say the price was personalized by a pricing algorithm trained by a vendor; the vendor may invoke trade secrets. The practical outcome is "responsibility diffusion." A well-designed trust architecture therefore needs to specify not only how the agent explains itself, but also what evidence is retained, what obligations attach to platforms and sellers, and what remedies exist when the consumer's claim is substantiated (Kroll, 2017; Raji et al., 2020).

From a systems perspective, contestability requires three types of infrastructure. First, the interaction must be logged in a manner that can reconstruct key decisions without exposing sensitive or proprietary details. Second, explanations must be generated at the right level of abstraction: too much technical detail overwhelms users, while too little invites suspicion (Miller, 2019; Shneiderman, 2020). Third, there must be a governance mechanism for adjudicating disputes internal escalation, external audits, or regulator-driven processes so that "contest" is not merely rhetorical. Without these, calls for transparency risk becoming performative.

Mitigation Strategies for Personalized Pricing in Agentic Commerce

Finally, meaningful disclosure should move beyond generic statements that "prices may vary." A more actionable disclosure model is to provide a user-facing explanation of the dominant drivers of price variation (e.g., inventory levels, delivery speed, membership status), together with an explicit statement about whether personal data beyond contextual shopping signals influenced the offer. This approach aligns with the consumer-information logic of the Omnibus Directive's personalized pricing disclosure (European Parliament and Council, 2019) while giving consumers a basis for evaluating fairness and deciding whether to proceed.

Institutionally, mitigation requires auditability and enforcement. Measurement studies show that discrimination can be subtle and context-dependent (Hannak et al., 2014; Mikians et al., 2012). Firms should therefore conduct periodic "pricing integrity" audits that test for systematic differences across synthetic personas and real user segments, controlling for legitimate cost drivers. These audits should be integrated with broader AI risk management practices, including pre-deployment risk assessment, post-deployment monitoring, and incident response (NIST, 2023; OECD, 2019). When audits identify unexplained disparities, organizations should have predefined remediation mechanisms, such as price adjustments, refunds, and model retraining with fairness constraints.

Agents can also implement constraint-based safeguards against vulnerability-based pricing. One pragmatic approach is to prohibit the use of certain data categories for pricing decisions within the agent's own optimization process for example, health-related browsing, sensitive location signals, or indicators of financial distress even if those signals are available to the platform. This mirrors the logic of data minimization and purpose limitation in privacy regulation (European Parliament and Council, 2016) and reduces the risk that the agent becomes an amplifier of profiling. Where the platform sets the price and the agent cannot control feature use, the agent can still increase accountability by recording what signals were plausibly in play and by enabling contestation when outcomes appear inconsistent with the user's constraints.

Mitigating unfair price discrimination is partly a technical problem and partly an institutional one. Technically, the agent can be designed to treat price as a variable to be minimized under constraints rather than as an outcome to be accepted. For example, an agent can run parallel searches across authenticated and unauthenticated sessions, across different delivery options, and across multiple sellers to estimate a benchmark range. If the offered price deviates materially from that benchmark without an explanatory driver (e.g., delivery speed, warranty), the agent can flag the offer and ask for user confirmation. Such "reference price checks" operationalize the fairness intuition documented in consumer research: people respond strongly to perceived deviations from reasonable reference points (Kahneman et al., 1986; Xia et al., 2004).

Table 2. Case Box 1

Case Box 1. Personalized discount steering in an agent-mediated checkout (illustrative)
Context: A shopping agent proposes "limited-time" add-ons and applies coupons that differ across users, while presenting the final basket as the "best deal."
Risk signals: • Users cannot benchmark whether the price is unusually high relative to comparable users or recent offers. • Coupons function as individualized price discrimination without clear contestability. • Conversational framing discourages comparison ("this is the best option for you").
Controls (from the framework): • Show benchmark ranges or reference prices where feasible; disclose dominant price drivers. • Provide a "compare alternatives" action and an explicit "challenge price" pathway. • Log pricing inputs and coupon application rules for audit and dispute resolution.
Example metric: Price-outlier flag rate vs. a defined reference distribution, audited by segment and context.

AI-POWERED DARK PATTERNS IN AGENT-MEDIATED SHOPPING

From Deceptive Design to Personalized Persuasion

The term "dark patterns" was coined to describe user interface designs that steer people toward outcomes that benefit the designer at the user's expense (Brignull, 2010; Gray et al., 2018). In e-commerce, common patterns include preselected add-ons, confusing choice wording, scarcity cues, hidden fees, and friction in cancellation or refund flows. Large-scale empirical audits suggest that dark patterns are pervasive in online retail. Mathur et al. (2019) documented multiple categories of deceptive design across thousands of shopping sites, while Nouwens et al. (2020) showed how consent interfaces can be engineered to nudge users toward accepting tracking. Legal scholarship and enforcement activity increasingly treat such designs as a consumer protection problem because they undermine meaningful consent and distort market choice (Luguri & Strahilevitz, 2021).

AI shopping agents do not eliminate dark patterns; instead, they can relocate and transform them. The classic dark pattern exploits visual attention, limited time, and cognitive biases in a web interface. An agent-mediated environment adds a new lever: persuasion can be directed at the agent's policy as well as at the human. If the agent is optimized for "completion" or "conversion," a platform can design incentives and prompts that encourage the agent to finalize purchases quickly or to accept bundled add-ons. This shifts the ethical question from interface design to objective design: which goals and constraints does the agent prioritize, and who controls those priorities (Amershi et al., 2019; Shneiderman, 2020)?

AI also enables personalization of persuasion. A platform can infer which users respond to urgency cues, social proof, or loss framing and serve different persuasive strategies accordingly. Yeung (2017) characterizes such adaptive systems as "hypernudges": dynamic interventions that continuously adjust choice architecture based on observed behavior. In agentic commerce, hypernudging can become more potent because the agent's interactions can be optimized through rapid A/B testing, and because conversational interfaces can deliver persuasion in a seemingly helpful tone. Calo (2014) argues that such digital market manipulation challenges traditional consumer protection doctrines because it can shape preferences covertly rather than misrepresent facts overtly. Susser et al. (2019) similarly emphasize that manipulation operates by undermining a person's capacity to deliberate freely, not merely by lying.

Conversational Interfaces as High-Leverage Choice Architecture

Many AI shopping agents are implemented through chat or voice interfaces. Conversational interaction can increase accessibility and reduce friction, but it also creates new opportunities for steering. First, a conversational agent can set a default by presenting a single "best" option rather than a full choice set, and users may accept the suggestion because requesting alternatives is effortful. Second, the agent can frame questions in ways that anchor expectations or discourage resistance (e.g., "Would you like to keep your premium protection plan?"). Third, the agent can provide selective explanations that rationalize a recommendation without revealing commercial incentives, such as sponsored placement or commission arrangements. Research on explanation shows that people are sensitive to perceived motivations; explanations that appear self-serving reduce trust (Miller, 2019).

Conversational contexts also alter the evidentiary trace. On a web page, manipulative elements can be captured in screenshots and audited. In a dynamic conversation, the content can be personalized and ephemeral, which complicates detection. Moreover, the conversational channel can incorporate multi-turn commitments that build momentum toward a purchase. These "commitment sequences" resemble classic persuasion techniques described in the literature on persuasive technology (Fogg, 2003), but they are now operationalized through machine learning systems that can optimize sequences for conversion at scale.

A further risk is that the agent's social cues can elicit undue reliance. Sundar's (2008) MAIN model describes how interface affordances such as agency and interactivity trigger credibility heuristics. When an agent speaks fluently, expresses empathy, or uses first-person pronouns, users may infer competence and benevolence even when the system is primarily a sales channel. This can be particularly problematic for vulnerable consumers, who may treat the agent as an advisor rather than a marketer. Human-centered AI research therefore emphasizes the importance of making limitations and incentives visible and of supporting user control, especially when the system is "inevitably wrong" (Amershi et al., 2019).

Enforcement Signals: Subscription Dark Patterns and "Click-to-Cancel"

Regulatory enforcement provides concrete signals about what counts as unacceptable design. In the United States, the Federal Trade Commission (FTC) has increasingly targeted subscription and cancellation flows that impose hidden steps or ambiguous consent. In June 2023, the FTC announced an action against Amazon alleging that the company enrolled consumers into Prime without consent and made cancellation unnecessarily difficult (Federal Trade Commission, 2023). Such cases illustrate how dark patterns can function as a profit engine: revenue is generated not through value creation but through friction that prevents consumers from exercising their preferences.

The policy landscape is also dynamic. The FTC finalized a "Negative Option Rule" commonly described as a "click-to-cancel" requirement in late 2024, aiming to strengthen standards for consent and cancellation in subscription marketing. However, by mid-2025 a federal appeals court vacated the rule for procedural reasons, illustrating how regulatory remedies can be uncertain even when the underlying consumer harm is clear (Reuters, 2025). For AI shopping agents, this volatility matters because design compliance cannot rely solely on a single rule; it must be built as a durable capability that anticipates evolving enforcement priorities and jurisprudence.

Outside the United States, platform and consumer protection rules increasingly address manipulative design explicitly. The EU's Digital Services Act (DSA) prohibits certain manipulative interface practices on online platforms, framing them as structural risks rather than isolated misrepresentations (European Parliament and Council, 2022). This shift supports the chapter's core claim: trust in AI shopping agents requires both technical explainability and institutional governance that constrains incentive-driven manipulation.

Mitigating Deceptive Design in Agent-Mediated Journeys

Finally, mitigation requires aligning the agent's objectives with user welfare. If the agent is evaluated primarily on completion rate or revenue, it will tend to learn behaviors that resemble dark patterns, even if no designer explicitly encodes deception. Objective governance, therefore, is an ethical safeguard. It operationalizes the human-centered AI guidance that systems should support user agency, make failures recoverable, and avoid locking users into unwanted trajectories (Amershi et al., 2019; Shneiderman, 2020).

Because agentic interfaces are dynamic, dark-pattern mitigation also requires evidence retention. Conversation transcripts (with appropriate privacy controls) can enable auditors to detect steering sequences and to verify that disclosures were delivered in context. Experiment governance is similarly critical: persuasion strategies are often optimized through rapid experiments, so organizations should pre-register experiments that affect consent, payment, or cancellation flows and monitor not only conversion but downstream harm signals such as chargebacks, complaints, and returns (NIST, 2023).

Mitigation begins with design principles that can be operationalized and tested. First, symmetry of friction should be treated as a measurable requirement: if a user can accept an add-on or subscription in one click, declining or canceling should be comparably simple. Second, confirmation should be specific rather than generic. Recurring charges should be summarized in plain language at the moment of commitment, and the agent should ask for explicit confirmation when an action creates ongoing obligations. Third, separation of advice and advertising should be enforced through interface and policy: sponsored recommendations should be labeled, and the agent should be able to present non-sponsored alternatives on request.

Table 3. Case Box 2

Case Box 2. Conversational "default enrollment" into subscriptions (illustrative)
Context: An agent recommends a product and implicitly enrolls the user into a recurring plan by pre-selecting a subscription option during checkout.
Risk signals: • Disclosure is present but buried in conversational turns or fine print. • Accepting is one step; canceling requires multiple steps and time delays. • The agent optimizes for completion rate rather than user welfare.
Controls (from the framework): • Enforce symmetry of friction (accept vs. decline/cancel). • Require explicit confirmation for recurring charges; surface key terms in the first layer explanation. • Run periodic transcript audits to detect steering sequences and missing disclosures.
Example metric: Symmetry-of-friction index and subscription cancellation success rate (time/steps).

THE FUSED THREAT: WHEN DISCRIMINATORY PRICING MEETS DECEPTIVE DESIGN

Algorithmic price discrimination and dark patterns are often discussed as separate problems one concerned with pricing analytics, the other with user interface design.

In agentic commerce they can fuse into a single exploitative system. Discriminatory pricing extracts surplus by tailoring offers to an individual's willingness to pay; dark patterns reduce resistance by shaping how choices are presented and how difficult it is to opt out. When combined, the consumer faces a double loss: they may pay more than similarly situated consumers and also find it harder to detect, understand, or contest that outcome.

This fusion is reinforced by feedback loops. If a platform uses dark patterns to keep consumers within a channel (for example, by making it difficult to cancel, delete an account, or export data), the platform gains more longitudinal data, which improves predictive models for pricing and persuasion. Improved models, in turn, enable more precise personalization, which can make manipulation less visible because it is tuned to each individual's biases and constraints (Yeung, 2017). In this environment, transparency cannot be achieved simply by adding more text to a disclosure box. The informational content that would allow a consumer to evaluate fairness counterfactual prices, alternative sellers, constraints used, and data sources remains dispersed across actors and hidden behind optimization routines.

The fused threat also exposes a structural vulnerability in typical "consent" models. Consent is often treated as a binary event: a user clicks agree, and data use is authorized. Yet dark patterns can degrade the quality of consent, and personalized pricing can exploit the consequences of that degraded consent. Nouwens et al. (2020) demonstrate that interface designs can steer users toward accepting tracking, while Nissenbaum's (2010) contextual integrity framework suggests that even "consented" flows can violate social expectations of appropriate use. For agentic commerce, the implication is that trust cannot be restored by producing more checkboxes; it requires controls that protect choice integrity and limit opportunistic uses of inferred vulnerability.

Finally, the fused threat creates a measurement problem. Traditional auditing approaches can examine price differences or design patterns in isolation. An agentic system may instead personalize both simultaneously: one consumer receives an inflated price and a gentle but persistent sequence of prompts; another receives a lower price and a neutral interface. From a governance perspective, this is precisely why audits must be stratified and adversarial. Raji et al. (2020) argue that algorithmic auditing must account for how systems behave for different populations and in different contexts. In commerce, the relevant "populations" may include not only protected classes but also vulnerable decision states (e.g., urgency, financial stress, health-related purchases).

The remainder of the chapter therefore treats transparency as an institutional design problem. The question is not only what explanations are shown to the user, but how power, incentives, evidence, and accountability are arranged across the agent ecosystem.

REGULATORY AND STANDARDS LANDSCAPE FOR TRUSTWORTHY AGENTIC COMMERCE

European Union: AI, Platform, and Consumer Rules Converge

In the European Union, three regulatory streams are particularly relevant to AI shopping agents: (a) consumer and data protection law; (b) platform governance under the DSA; and (c) AI-specific requirements under the Artificial Intelligence Act (AI Act). Together, these streams shift the compliance question from "did the seller disclose the terms?" to "is the socio-technical system designed to prevent manipulation and to provide meaningful oversight?"

Data protection remains foundational. The General Data Protection Regulation (GDPR) constrains profiling and sets requirements for lawful processing, transparency, and rights such as access and erasure (European Parliament and Council, 2016). Of particular relevance is the GDPR's attention to automated decision-making and profiling in contexts with legal or similarly significant effects, which has shaped debates about when consumers must be offered explanations and human review. Even where a shopping agent's decisions do not meet the threshold of "legal effects," the GDPR's transparency and purpose-limitation principles restrict the indiscriminate reuse of data for pricing and persuasion.

Consumer law adds further obligations. The Omnibus Directive (Directive [EU] 2019/2161) introduced requirements for transparency in online marketplaces and, notably, a duty to inform consumers when a price is personalized on the basis of automated decision-making (European Parliament and Council, 2019). While this disclosure does not itself reveal the pricing logic, it establishes that personalized pricing is not merely a technical feature but a consumer information issue. For AI shopping agents, a minimal compliance approach simply stating that prices are personalized may satisfy the form of disclosure while leaving the substantive fairness and contestability problems untouched.

The DSA addresses manipulative design more directly. It prohibits certain interface designs that materially distort or impair users' ability to make free and informed decisions, an approach that implicitly recognizes dark patterns as systemic risks in digital markets (European Parliament and Council, 2022). When applied to agentic commerce, DSA principles imply that platforms should not use design or architecture to coerce acceptance of tracking, lock users into channels, or obscure the role of sponsorship and ranking.

The AI Act adds an AI-specific layer. Among other provisions, it prohibits certain AI practices that manipulate behavior or exploit vulnerabilities in ways that cause or are likely to cause significant harm (European Parliament and Council, 2024). While much public attention focuses on the AI Act's "high-risk" system requirements, the prohibitions are relevant to commerce because they frame manipulation as a direct compliance risk. The AI Act also reinforces expectations of documentation, risk management, and oversight elements that align closely with the governance mechanisms proposed in this chapter.

United States: Consumer Protection Enforcement and Volatile Rulemaking

In the United States, the principal legal lever for addressing deceptive and unfair commerce practices is consumer protection enforcement. The FTC's authority under Section 5 of the FTC Act has been used to pursue deceptive practices, including misleading disclosures and coercive subscription flows. The Amazon Prime case announced in 2023 illustrates how design can be treated as deception when it induces enrollment without informed consent and obstructs cancellation (Federal Trade Commission, 2023). The FTC's subsequent 2025 announcement of a $2.5 billion settlement with Amazon in a separate matter underscores how enforcement can scale when harms are framed as systemic and financially significant (Federal Trade Commission, 2025).

Statutory protections also matter. The Restore Online Shoppers' Confidence Act (ROSC Act) regulates certain online negative option transactions and requires clear disclosures and express informed consent (U.S. Congress, 2010). While ROSCA predates AI shopping agents, its logic anticipates a core risk in agentic commerce: when consent and cancellation are frictionful or obscured, consumers can be enrolled into ongoing obligations they do not intend. The FTC has also articulated enforcement policies for negative option marketing that emphasize clarity and ease of cancellation (Federal Trade Commission, 2021).

At the same time, U.S. rulemaking has proven volatile. The FTC's late-2024 Negative Option Rule (often described as "click-to-cancel") would have strengthened procedural requirements for subscription cancellation. Yet the rule was vacated in 2025 for procedural reasons (Reuters, 2025). For system designers, the lesson is practical: governance should not be implemented as compliance checklists tied to a single rule. Instead, firms should adopt capability-based controls evidence retention, audit trails, independent review, and choice-integrity testing that remain valuable even as specific rules evolve or are challenged.

Because U.S. law is less centralized than the EU framework, industry standards and corporate governance play a larger role. Trustworthy AI in commerce therefore depends on whether firms can internalize accountability through risk management and external assurance, rather than treat transparency as a marketing label.

Standards and Governance Frameworks: From Principles to Operational Controls

Cross-sector standards can translate high-level principles into operational controls. The OECD's AI recommendation emphasizes human-centered values, transparency, robustness, and accountability (Organisation for Economic Co-operation and Development [OECD], 2019). The NIST AI Risk Management Framework (AI RMF 1.0) similarly provides a structured approach to managing AI risks across governance, mapping, measurement, and management functions (National Institute of Standards and Technology [NIST], 2023). Although voluntary, these frameworks create a shared vocabulary that regulators and auditors increasingly use to evaluate whether AI systems are governed responsibly.

Management system standards are also emerging. ISO/IEC 42001:2023 specifies requirements for an artificial intelligence management system (AIMS), embedding accountability into organizational processes rather than treating it as a project-level concern (International Organization for Standardization/International Electrotechnical Commission [ISO/IEC], 2023). For AI shopping agents, the relevance is direct: trust failures often arise not from a single model error but from weak control over data sourcing, experimentation, vendor dependencies, and post-deployment monitoring.

Finally, research on algorithmic accountability stresses that governance must account for sociotechnical dynamics rather than solely technical performance. Kroll (2017) emphasizes the role of due process and accountability mechanisms for algorithmic systems, while Selbst et al. (2019) warn that abstraction can obscure the social context in which fairness is judged. These insights suggest that "explainability" should be understood as part of a larger accountability chain that includes documentation, auditing, and remedies.

A SOCIO-TECHNICAL FRAMEWORK FOR REBUILDING TRUST IN AI SHOPPING AGENTS

Design Premise: Trust Requires Both Intelligibility and Constraint

A recurring mistake in discussions of "transparent AI" is to treat transparency as an information delivery problem: if the system provides more explanations, users will trust it. Research on explanation and trust suggests that this is only partially true. People do not evaluate explanations as neutral facts; they evaluate them as social acts that imply motives, competence, and accountability (Miller, 2019). In addition, explanations can be strategically engineered: an interface can provide plausible narratives while concealing key commercial incentives. The transparency paradox therefore demands an approach that couples intelligibility (users can understand and question outcomes) with constraint (systems are governed so that harmful behaviors are prevented or detected).

The framework proposed here integrates three pillars: (1) explainability and user control; (2) governance and auditability; and (3) fairness and choice integrity. The pillars are mutually reinforcing. Explainability without governance can become "explanation theater." Governance without explainability can become unaccountable bureaucracy. Fairness without choice integrity can be undermined by manipulative design. Together, the pillars aim to support calibrated trust: users rely on the agent when reliance is justified and disengage when it is not (Lee & See, 2004; Shneiderman, 2020).

Figure 1. Three-pillar socio-technical trust framework for AI shopping agents

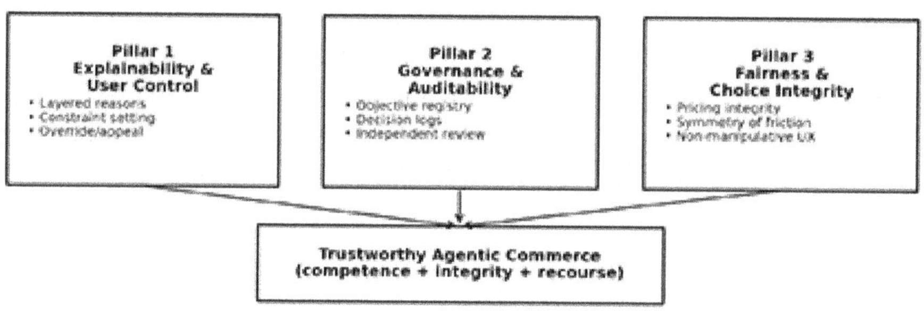

Pillar 1: Explainability and User Control

Explainability in agentic commerce should be designed around decisions that matter to consumers: price acceptance, product selection, seller choice, shipping and return terms, and data sharing. The goal is not to expose the entire model but to provide meaningful answers to user-relevant questions. Work in explainable AI emphasizes that explanations are context-specific and that the most useful explanations are often contrastive ("why this rather than that?") and actionable ("what could I change to get a different result?") (Miller, 2019; Ribeiro et al., 2016).

Layered explanations are therefore essential. At the first layer, the agent should provide a concise rationale: key factors driving the recommendation (e.g., budget constraint, durability rating, return policy). At the second layer, the agent should provide evidence: sources used, how recent they are, and whether any offers are sponsored. At the third layer, the agent should provide counterfactuals: alternative products or sellers that nearly met the criteria, and trade-offs that led to their exclusion. This approach aligns with recommender-system research showing that explanations can increase perceived transparency and satisfaction when they are aligned with user goals and presented at an appropriate level of detail (Herlocker et al., 2000; Tintarev & Masthoff, 2007; Zhang & Chen, 2020).

Model-agnostic interpretability methods can support these layers. For example, local surrogate explanations can identify which features most influenced a choice (Ribeiro et al., 2016), while Shapley-based attribution can summarize feature contributions in a consistent manner (Lundberg & Lee, 2017). However, these techniques must be used with caution: feature attributions can be misleading when features are proxies for sensitive attributes or when the underlying model is unstable. The agent should therefore communicate uncertainty and avoid overstating precision. Human–AI interaction guidelines recommend explicitly indicating when the system is uncertain or may be wrong, and enabling easy correction (Amershi et al., 2019).

Limits of explainability

Explainability improves trust only when it is decision-relevant, faithful to the underlying process, and usable in context. In practice, explainability has limits and trade-offs that designers should treat as constraints rather than afterthoughts:

- Fidelity versus plausibility: post-hoc rationales can sound convincing while failing to reflect the true decision logic; require fidelity tests and audits.
- Transparency versus privacy and trade secrets: revealing sensitive signals or proprietary features can create privacy and competitive risks; use layered disclosure and redaction where needed.
- Information versus comprehension: more text can increase cognitive load; favor progressive disclosure (brief reason + "why this vs. that?" drill-down).
- Disclosure versus gaming: overly specific explanations can enable manipulation by sellers or adversaries optimizing around the agent's rules.
- Security and reliability: prompt injection, poisoned listings, and retrieval errors can produce confident but incorrect explanations; monitor, log, and support incident response.

User control mechanisms should be built into the explanation layer. Consumers should be able to set and revise constraints (e.g., "never buy from sellers with fewer than X reviews," "exclude sponsored listings," "do not use location data for pricing"). Such controls operationalize contextual integrity by allowing users to constrain data use in ways that match their expectations (Nissenbaum, 2010). They also reduce reliance on post hoc disclosures by making preferences enforceable at the time of decision.

Table 4. Explainability Artifacts for Key Agent Decisions

Decision Point	User-Facing Question	Minimum Evidence Provided
Product Selection	Why this product rather than the next best alternative?	Top drivers (e.g., price, quality, return policy), 2–3 near-miss alternatives with trade-offs, and source of ratings/reviews.
Price Acceptance	Why is this the offered price for me?	Disclosure of personalization, comparable benchmark range, key factors (e.g., timing, inventory), and whether any personal data influenced the offer.
Seller Choice	Why this seller instead of another seller with similar price?	Seller reliability signals, fulfillment and return terms, and any platform incentives (e.g., sponsorship, commission).
Data Sharing	What data was used and who received it?	Data categories, purpose, retention window, and opt-out/override controls.
Subscription Add-ons	Why is this add-on recommended?	Benefit–cost explanation, default status, and explicit confirmation of recurring charges.

As summarized in Table 2, explainability must be coupled with evidence and user controls at each decision point; otherwise, the agent risks becoming an opaque proxy for the platform's incentives.

Example implementation metrics for this pillar include an explanation usefulness rating (e.g., a brief "Was this helpful?" prompt after key decisions) and an override success rate (how often users can change constraints and obtain a meaningfully different recommendation).

Pillar 2: Governance, Auditability, and Accountability

Explainability cannot substitute for governance. Governance specifies who is responsible for outcomes, what evidence must be retained, and how risks are monitored and corrected over time. The NIST AI RMF emphasizes that governance should be built into organizational structures, including defined roles, documentation, and continuous monitoring (NIST, 2023). ISO/IEC 42001 similarly embeds AI risk management into management system processes, encouraging systematic oversight rather than ad hoc responses (ISO/IEC, 2023).

For AI shopping agents, three governance practices are especially important. First, objective governance: teams must document what the agent is optimized for and how competing objectives are weighted (price, quality, speed, commission revenue, retention). Because dark patterns can be implemented through objectives rather than interface elements, objective governance is a primary safeguard. Second, evidence governance: systems must retain logs that can reconstruct key decisions, including ranking inputs, pricing inputs, and any experiments that affected the user journey. Third, accountability governance: there must be escalation pathways and independent review when outcomes are contested or when monitoring detects anomalies (Kroll, 2017; Raji et al., 2020).

Auditing should be treated as a continuous practice rather than a one-time check. A/B tests and personalization strategies can drift rapidly as data changes. Firms should therefore run regular "choice-integrity audits" that test whether the agent's behavior changes in ways that reflect commercial incentives rather than user preferences. Such audits can be inspired by sociotechnical fairness research, which warns that abstraction can hide how systems affect different groups and contexts (Selbst et al., 2019).

External assurance can strengthen credibility. Independent auditors can evaluate whether logs, explanations, and controls match documented policies, and whether the system's outcomes satisfy defined fairness and transparency metrics. While trade-secret concerns are real, they do not eliminate the feasibility of assurance; rather, they require careful design of audit interfaces, redaction, and trusted review channels. The growth of AI governance frameworks suggests that "trust" will increasingly be assessed through evidence, not promises (Jobin et al., 2019).

Table 5. Governance Controls for Trustworthy AI Shopping Agents

Control Area	Control Objective	Operational Practice	Evidence/Metric
Objective governance	Prevent incentive-driven steering	Document optimization targets; prohibit conversion-only objectives; require user-benefit constraints	Objective registry; review sign-offs; red-team findings
Experiment governance	Detect harmful A/B tests	Pre-register experiments affecting pricing/consent; run holdout monitoring	Experiment log; lift vs. complaint/return metrics
Data governance	Limit opportunistic profiling	Purpose limitation; data minimization; retention limits; vendor due diligence	Data inventory; DPIA-style assessments; deletion SLAs
Explainability governance	Avoid "explanation theater"	Validate explanations for fidelity and user comprehension	Explanation fidelity tests; user comprehension scores
Remedy governance	Enable contestability	Dispute process; human review; refunds/adjustments when warranted	Resolution time; upheld disputes; restitution amounts

Table 5 illustrates that governance must be operational: controls require measurable evidence and escalation pathways, not simply policy statements.

Example implementation metrics for governance include audit-log completeness (the share of transactions with a reconstructable decision trace) and dispute resolution time (median time from complaint to outcome, categorized by uphold/deny and remediation type).

Agent Independence and Conflicts of Interest

Ultimately, independence is a spectrum. The governance objective is to prevent the agent from becoming an unaccountable instrument of the platform's profit optimization. Designers should therefore treat conflict-of-interest analysis as a required step in agent deployment, much as privacy impact assessments are used to anticipate data misuse. Where conflicts cannot be fully eliminated, they should be bounded by enforceable constraints and audited through evidence, not assumed away through branding.

There is also a market-design argument for interoperability and portability. If users can easily export preferences and transaction history to a competing agent or platform, the cost of exiting declines, which pressures firms to compete on trust as well as price. Portability aligns with the broader policy concern that concentrated data and attention can enable manipulation at scale (Zuboff, 2019). For AI shopping agents, portability should include not only data but also the user's constraint profiles and explainability settings, so that switching does not require rebuilding trust from scratch.

Addressing conflicts does not necessarily require prohibiting integrated agents, but it does require governance that makes incentives inspectable and constraints enforceable. At minimum, the agent should disclose when recommendations are influenced by sponsorship or platform incentives, and users should have the ability to request a "neutral mode" that excludes sponsored placement and prioritizes user-defined criteria. More robust approaches include independent certification or third-party auditing of ranking and pricing integrity, analogous to financial auditing in markets where information asymmetry is high (Kroll, 2017; Raji et al., 2020).

Retailer incentives can also run counter to transparency demands. Merchants may resist agent-facing disclosures that reveal margins, pricing rules, or ranking arrangements; they may also strategically constrain what agents can observe (e.g., requiring logins, throttling automated comparison, varying inventory visibility, bundling prices, or using personalized couponing that is hard to benchmark). This adversarial dynamic makes governance more realistic: trustworthy agentic commerce depends not only on agent design, but also on enforceable rules for access, disclosure, and audit interfaces that reduce strategic opacity.

Conflicts of interest interact with explainability in two ways. First, they shape what information is selected as "relevant" in explanations. An agent can offer a plausible product rationale while omitting the fact that the recommended item yields higher commission revenue or advances a retention strategy. Second, they shape how contestation is handled. If the agent is controlled by the platform, a consumer's attempt to contest a price or a recommendation may be routed into customer service channels optimized for deflection rather than remedy. The result is that transparency functions as a veneer over asymmetric power.

A critical but under-discussed design variable is whether the shopping agent is independent from the marketplace it navigates. If the same platform that earns revenue from commissions, advertising, or subscriptions also controls the agent's recommendation and purchasing policies, the agent faces an intrinsic conflict of interest. In traditional commerce, conflicts are partly visible: shoppers understand that a retailer's salesperson represents the retailer. In agentic commerce, the interface may present itself as a neutral assistant, which can trigger credibility heuristics and obscure the underlying incentives (Sundar, 2008).

Pillar 3: Fairness and Choice Integrity

Fairness in agentic commerce is partly a distributive question (who gets what price and why) and partly a procedural question (whether the process respects autonomy). Fair-ML scholarship emphasizes that fairness cannot be defined purely in abstract statistical terms because it interacts with social context and legal norms (Barocas et al., 2023; Selbst et al., 2019). In commerce, a practical fairness baseline is that price personalization should not be based on sensitive attributes or proxies in ways that exploit vulnerability, and that consumers should not be coerced into data sharing or subscriptions through deceptive design.

Choice integrity controls translate fairness commitments into user experiences. Key controls include: (a) prohibition of coercive defaults for recurring charges; (b) symmetric friction making acceptance and refusal comparably easy; (c) separation of advice from advertising, with clear labeling of sponsorship; and (d) the ability to "lock" certain preferences (e.g., privacy settings, excluded sellers) so that the agent cannot override them to increase conversion. These controls align with regulatory signals under the DSA and consumer protection enforcement (European Parliament and Council, 2022; Federal Trade Commission, 2023).

Fairness also requires attention to bias and proxy discrimination. Friedman and Nissenbaum (1996) distinguish preexisting, technical, and emergent bias, emphasizing that systems can become biased even when designers do not intend discrimination. In pricing, bias can appear when proxies such as ZIP code, device type, or time of day correlate with socioeconomic status. The agent should therefore implement fairness constraints and monitoring to detect patterns consistent with vulnerability-based pricing. This is not only an ethical issue; it is increasingly a compliance risk under regimes that treat exploitation of vulnerability as unacceptable (European Parliament and Council, 2024).

Finally, consumers must have the ability to exit. If a platform uses design to lock users into an ecosystem, it increases the power imbalance and reduces competitive pressure to behave fairly (Nissenbaum, 2010; Zuboff, 2019). Interoperability, data portability, and easy cancellation are thus not peripheral technicalities; they are structural conditions for maintaining consumer sovereignty in agentic commerce.

Example implementation metrics for this pillar include a symmetry-of-friction index (time/steps to accept versus refuse or cancel) and a pricing integrity check (flag rate of individualized prices that deviate materially from a defined benchmark range, audited across relevant user segments).

Implementation Roadmap and Evaluation Metrics

For practitioners, the roadmap below summarizes how to operationalize the three pillars in an AI shopping agent program:

- Define and register objectives (ban conversion-only optimization; encode user-benefit constraints).
- Implement layered explanations at high-impact decisions (price, seller, add-ons, data use) with "why this?" drill-down.
- Make preferences enforceable (constraint setting/locking, "exclude sponsored," "do not use location," etc.).
- Retain decision evidence (ranking inputs, pricing inputs, tool calls, and experiment variants) to enable reconstruction.
- Run continuous monitoring and audits (pricing integrity tests; choice-integrity and dark-pattern transcript reviews).
- Provide contestability and remedies (challenge price, request human review, refunds/adjustments when warranted).

Manager/developer checklist (quick takeaways)

- Label sponsorship/commissions and offer a "neutral mode" on request.
- Separate ads/sponsored placements from organic results in both UI and logs.
- Require explicit opt-in for recurring charges; make cancel/decline as easy as accept.
- Maintain an audit-log completeness target and test reconstructability in drills.
- Track dispute resolution time and outcomes; review systemic causes monthly.
- Measure symmetry of friction and override success rate after product changes.
- Audit price outliers and steering patterns across segments and contexts.

- Document a user recourse path (contact, review, remediation) and publish it in-product.

FUTURE RESEARCH DIRECTIONS

Agentic commerce is still emerging, and several research gaps are urgent. First, measurement methods must evolve. Traditional audits examine web pages and static interfaces; agent-based commerce requires experimental probes that capture conversational dynamics, negotiation protocols, and API-mediated personalization. Second, explanation science for agents requires domain-specific work. Explanations in recommender systems are well-studied, but shopping agents combine recommendations with actions (purchasing, subscribing, sharing data). Explanations must therefore address agency and responsibility: who decided, who benefited, and what recourse exists (Miller, 2019; Shneiderman, 2020).

Third, governance mechanisms must be adapted to multi-actor ecosystems. Many agents will depend on external foundation models, merchant APIs, payments providers, and data brokers. Accountability chains should specify how duties and evidence travel across these boundaries, building on algorithmic accountability scholarship (Kroll, 2017; Raji et al., 2020). Fourth, the distributional impacts of personalized pricing in agentic commerce need renewed study. Existing work documents discrimination in web contexts (Hannak et al., 2014; Mikians et al., 2012), but agentic systems may change who is targeted, when, and by what signals.

Finally, there is a normative research question about the proper role of delegation. Thaler and Sunstein (2008) argue that choice architecture is inevitable; the governance task is to design it responsibly. In agentic commerce, the consumer's relationship to the agent is itself a form of choice architecture. Determining what consumers should be able to delegate and what should remain under direct human control will require empirical work on user preferences, vulnerability, and the social acceptability of automated market participation.

A final methodological priority is longitudinal evaluation of trust calibration. Short laboratory studies can show whether an explanation is understandable, but they often miss how trust evolves after mistakes, disputes, and policy changes. Field studies that track reliance, overrides, complaint rates, and retention over months can reveal whether agentic systems genuinely reduce vulnerability or merely shift it into less visible channels (Lee & See, 2004; Mayer et al., 1995).

CONCLUSION

AI shopping agents can make markets more navigable and reduce the cognitive burden of online shopping. Yet the same technologies that enable convenience can also deepen exploitation by making discriminatory pricing and manipulative design more adaptive, personalized, and difficult to observe. This is the transparency paradox: transparency is demanded precisely because AI systems can hide the processes that generate consumer harm, but transparency alone is insufficient when incentives are misaligned and evidence is fragmented across actors.

Rebuilding trust in agentic commerce therefore requires a socio-technical strategy. Explainability must be designed around decisions that matter and paired with user controls that make preferences enforceable. Governance must institutionalize accountability through objective management, evidence retention, auditing, and contestable remedies. Choice integrity must constrain deceptive design and ensure that consumers can refuse, exit, and challenge outcomes without disproportionate friction. Aligning these elements with regulatory expectations GDPR transparency and rights, DSA anti-manipulation principles, AI Act prohibitions, and FTC consumer protection enforcement provides a realistic pathway for trustworthy deployment (European Parliament and Council, 2016, 2022, 2024; Federal Trade Commission, 2023; NIST, 2023).

The central claim is not that AI shopping agents must be perfectly transparent or perfectly fair. Rather, they must be governable: they should produce explanations that are meaningful, preserve evidence that enables accountability, and operate within constraints that prevent profit-driven manipulation from masquerading as personalization. If those conditions are met, agentic commerce can advance consumer welfare; if not, it risks becoming an automated infrastructure for extracting value from consumer vulnerability.

REFERENCES

Acquisti, A., & Varian, H. R. (2005). Conditioning prices on purchase history. *Marketing Science*, *24*(3), 367–381. DOI: 10.1287/mksc.1040.0103

Amershi, S., Weld, D., Vorvoreanu, M., Fourney, A., Nushi, B., Collisson, P., Suh, J., Iqbal, S., Bennett, P. N., Inkpen, K., Teevan, J., Kikin-Gil, R., & Horvitz, E. (2019). Guidelines for human–AI interaction. In *Proceedings of the 2019 CHI Conference on Human Factors in Computing Systems* (pp. 1–13). Association for Computing Machinery. DOI: 10.1145/3290605.3300233

Barocas, S., Hardt, M., & Narayanan, A. (2023). Fairness and machine learning: Limitations and opportunities. MIT Press. https://fairmlbook.org/

Bolton, L. E., Warlop, L., & Alba, J. W. (2003). Consumer perceptions of price (un) fairness. *The Journal of Consumer Research*, *29*(4), 474–491. DOI: 10.1086/346244

Boston Consulting Group. (2025, October 6). Agentic Commerce Is Redefining Retail Here's How to Respond. BCG. https://www.bcg.com/publications/2025/agentic-commerce-redefining-retail-how-to-respond

Brignull, H. (2010). Dark patterns. https://www.darkpatterns.org/

Calo, R. (2014). Digital market manipulation. *The George Washington Law Review*, *82*, 995–1051. https://www.gwlr.org/wp-content/uploads/2014/10/Calo_82_41.pdf

Edelman. (2025, February 13). The AI Trust Imperative: Navigating the Future with Confidence. 2025 Edelman Trust Barometer. https://www.edelman.com/trust/2025/trust-barometer

European Parliament and Council. (2016). Regulation (EU) 2016/679 (General Data Protection Regulation). Official Journal of the European Union. https://eur-lex.europa.eu/eli/reg/2016/679/oj

European Parliament and Council. (2019). Directive (EU) 2019/2161 amending Directive 93/13/EEC, Directive 98/6/EC, Directive 2005/29/EC and Directive 2011/83/EU (Omnibus Directive). Official Journal of the European Union. https://eur-lex.europa.eu/eli/dir/2019/2161/oj

European Parliament and Council. (2022). Regulation (EU) 2022/2065 on a single market for digital services (Digital Services Act). Official Journal of the European Union. https://eur-lex.europa.eu/eli/reg/2022/2065/oj

European Parliament and Council. (2024). Regulation (EU) 2024/1689 laying down harmonised rules on artificial intelligence (Artificial Intelligence Act). Official Journal of the European Union. https://eur-lex.europa.eu/eli/reg/2024/1689/oj

Federal Trade Commission. (2021). Enforcement policy statement regarding negative option marketing. https://www.ftc.gov/system/files/documents/public_statements/1599372/negative_option_policy_statement.pdf

Federal Trade Commission. (2023, June 21). FTC takes action against Amazon for enrolling consumers in Prime without consent and sabotaging their attempts to cancel. https://www.ftc.gov/news-events/news/press-releases/2023/06/ftc-takes-action-against-amazon-enrolling-consumers-prime-without-consent-sabotaging-their-attempts-cancel

Federal Trade Commission. (2025, September 25). FTC Secures Historic $2.5 Billion Settlement Against Amazon. https://www.ftc.gov/news-events/news/press-releases/2025/09/ftc-secures-historic-25-billion-settlement-against-amazon

Fogg, B. J. (2003). *Persuasive technology: Using computers to change what we think and do*. Morgan Kaufmann. DOI: 10.1016/B978-155860643-2/50011-1

Friedman, B., & Nissenbaum, H. (1996). Bias in computer systems. *ACM Transactions on Information Systems, 14*(3), 330–347. DOI: 10.1145/230538.230561

Gefen, D., Karahanna, E., & Straub, D. W. (2003). Trust and TAM in online shopping: An integrated model. *Management Information Systems Quarterly, 27*(1), 51–90. DOI: 10.2307/30036519

Gray, C. M., Kou, Y., Battles, B., Hoggatt, J., & Toombs, A. L. (2018). The dark (patterns) side of UX design. In *Proceedings of the 2018 CHI Conference on Human Factors in Computing Systems* (pp. 1–14). Association for Computing Machinery. DOI: 10.1145/3173574.3174108

Guidotti, R., Monreale, A., Ruggieri, S., Turini, F., Giannotti, F., & Pedreschi, D. (2018). A survey of methods for explaining black box models. *ACM Computing Surveys, 51*(5), 1–42. DOI: 10.1145/3236009

Hannak, A., Soeller, G., Lazer, D., Mislove, A., & Wilson, C. (2014). Measuring price discrimination and steering on e-commerce web sites. In *Proceedings of the 2014 ACM Internet Measurement Conference* (pp. 305–318). Association for Computing Machinery. DOI: 10.1145/2663716.2663744

Herlocker, J. L., Konstan, J. A., & Riedl, J. (2000). Explaining collaborative filtering recommendations. In *Proceedings of the 2000 ACM Conference on Computer Supported Cooperative Work* (pp. 241–250). Association for Computing Machinery. DOI: 10.1145/358916.358995

Hufnagel, G., Schwaiger, M., & Weritz, L. (2022). Seeking the perfect price: Consumer responses to personalized price discrimination in e-commerce. *Journal of Business Research, 143*, 346–365. DOI: 10.1016/j.jbusres.2021.10.002

International Organization for Standardization/International Electrotechnical Commission. (2023). *ISO/IEC 42001:2023 Information technology Artificial intelligence Management system*. ISO.

Jobin, A., Ienca, M., & Vayena, E. (2019). The global landscape of AI ethics guidelines. *Nature Machine Intelligence, 1*(9), 389–399. DOI: 10.1038/s42256-019-0088-2

Kahneman, D., Knetsch, J. L., & Thaler, R. (1986). Fairness as a constraint on profit seeking: Entitlements in the market. *The American Economic Review, 76*(4), 728–741.

Kroll, J. A. (2017). Accountable algorithms. *University of Pennsylvania Law Review, 165*(3), 633–705.

Lee, J. D., & See, K. A. (2004). Trust in automation: Designing for appropriate reliance. *Human Factors, 46*(1), 50–80. DOI: 10.1518/hfes.46.1.50.30392 PMID: 15151155

Lough, G. (n.d.). Agentic commerce: Promise, paradox and the path forward. Worldpay. https://worldpay.global/resources/articles/agentic-commerce-paradox-and-promise

Luguri, J., & Strahilevitz, L. J. (2021). Shining a light on dark patterns. *The Journal of Legal Analysis, 13*(1), 43–109. DOI: 10.1093/jla/laaa006

Lundberg, S. M., & Lee, S.-I. (2017). A unified approach to interpreting model predictions. In Advances in Neural Information Processing Systems (Vol. 30).

Mathur, A., Acar, G., Friedman, M. J., Lucherini, E., Mayer, J., Chetty, M., & Narayanan, A. (2019). Dark patterns at scale: Findings from a crawl of 11K shopping websites. Proceedings of the ACM on Human-Computer Interaction, 3(CSCW), Article 81. DOI: 10.1145/3359183

Mayer, R. C., Davis, J. H., & Schoorman, F. D. (1995). An integrative model of organizational trust. *Academy of Management Review, 20*(3), 709–734. DOI: 10.2307/258792

McKnight, D. H., Choudhury, V., & Kacmar, C. (2002). Developing and validating trust measures for e-commerce: An integrative typology. *Information Systems Research, 13*(3), 334–359. DOI: 10.1287/isre.13.3.334.81

Mikians, J., Gyarmati, L., Erramilli, V., & Laoutaris, N. (2012). Detecting price and search discrimination on the Internet. In *Proceedings of the 11th ACM Workshop on Hot Topics in Networks* (pp. 79–84). Association for Computing Machinery. DOI: 10.1145/2390231.2390245

Miller, T. (2019). Explanation in artificial intelligence: Insights from the social sciences. *Artificial Intelligence, 267*, 1–38. DOI: 10.1016/j.artint.2018.07.007

National Institute of Standards and Technology. (2023). Artificial intelligence risk management framework (AI RMF 1.0). U.S. Department of Commerce. https://nvlpubs.nist.gov/nistpubs/ai/NIST.AI.100-1.pdf

Nissenbaum, H. (2010). *Privacy in context: Technology, policy, and the integrity of social life*. Stanford University Press.

Nouwens, M., Liccardi, I., Veale, M., Karger, D., & Kagal, L. (2020). Dark patterns after the GDPR: Scraping consent pop-ups and demonstrating their influence. In *Proceedings of the 2020 CHI Conference on Human Factors in Computing Systems* (pp. 1–13). Association for Computing Machinery. DOI: 10.1145/3313831.3376321

Odlyzko, A. (2003). Privacy, economics, and price discrimination on the Internet. In *Proceedings of the 5th International Conference on Electronic Commerce* (pp. 355–366). Association for Computing Machinery. DOI: 10.1145/948005.948051

Organisation for Economic Co-operation and Development. (2019). OECD recommendation of the Council on artificial intelligence. https://legalinstruments.oecd.org/en/instruments/OECD-LEGAL-0449

PricewaterhouseCoopers. (2024). Voice of the consumer survey 2024. PwC. https://www.pwc.com/gx/en/services/consumer-markets/consumer-insights.html

Raji, I. D., Smart, A., White, R. N., Mitchell, M., Gebru, T., Hutchinson, B., Smith-Loud, J., Theron, D., & Barnes, P. (2020). Closing the AI accountability gap: Defining an end-to-end framework for internal algorithmic auditing. In *Proceedings of the 2020 Conference on Fairness, Accountability, and Transparency* (pp. 33–44). Association for Computing Machinery. DOI: 10.1145/3351095.3372873

Reuters. (2025, July 8). US 'click to cancel' rule blocked by appeals court. Reuters. https://www.reuters.com/legal/legalindustry/us-click-cancel-rule-blocked-by-appeals-court-2025-07-08/

Ribeiro, M. T., Singh, S., & Guestrin, C. (2016). "Why should I trust you?" Explaining the predictions of any classifier. In Proceedings of the 22nd ACM SIGKDD International Conference on Knowledge Discovery and Data Mining (pp. 1135–1144). Association for Computing Machinery. DOI: 10.1145/2939672.2939778

Salesforce. (2024). State of the connected customer (6th ed.). Salesforce Research. https://www.salesforce.com/resources/research-reports/state-of-the-connected-customer/

Selbst, A. D., Boyd, D., Friedler, S. A., Venkatasubramanian, S., & Vertesi, J. (2019). Fairness and abstraction in sociotechnical systems. In *Proceedings of the 2019 Conference on Fairness, Accountability, and Transparency* (pp. 59–68). Association for Computing Machinery. DOI: 10.1145/3287560.3287598

Shneiderman, B. (2020). Human-centered artificial intelligence: Reliable, safe & trustworthy. arXiv. https://arxiv.org/abs/2002.04087

Sundar, S. S. (2008). The MAIN model: A heuristic approach to understanding technology effects on credibility. In Metzger, M. J., & Flanagin, A. J. (Eds.), *Digital media, youth, and credibility* (pp. 73–100). MIT Press.

Susser, D., Roessler, B., & Nissenbaum, H. (2019). Online manipulation: Hidden influences in a digital world. *Georgetown Law Technology Review*, *4*(1), 1–45.

Thaler, R. H., & Sunstein, C. R. (2008). *Nudge: Improving decisions about health, wealth, and happiness.* Yale University Press.

U.S. Congress. (2010). Restore Online Shoppers' Confidence Act (15 U.S.C. § 8401–8405). https://www.ftc.gov/legal-library/browse/statutes/restore-online-shoppers-confidence-act

Varian, H. R. (1989). Price discrimination. In Schmalensee, R., & Willig, R. D. (Eds.), *Handbook of industrial organization* (Vol. 1, pp. 597–654). Elsevier.

World Economic Forum. (2025, November 28). This month in AI: Shopping agents, AI's energy bill and new codes of conduct. https://www.weforum.org/stories/2025/11/ai-shopping-agents-energy-news/

Xia, L., Monroe, K. B., & Cox, J. L. (2004). The price is unfair! A conceptual framework of price fairness perceptions. *Journal of Marketing*, *68*(4), 1–15. DOI: 10.1509/jmkg.68.4.1.42733

Yeung, K. (2017). 'Hypernudge': Big data as a mode of regulation by design. *Information Communication and Society*, *20*(1), 118–136. DOI: 10.1080/1369118X.2016.1186713

Zhang, Y., & Chen, X. (2020). Explainable recommendation: A survey and new perspectives. *Foundations and Trends in Information Retrieval, 14*(1), 1–101. DOI: 10.1561/1500000066

Zuboff, S. (2019). *The age of surveillance capitalism: The fight for a human future at the new frontier of power*. PublicAffairs.

KEY TERMS AND DEFINITIONS

Agentic Commerce: A mode of digital commerce in which software agents can autonomously search, evaluate, negotiate, and execute transactions on behalf of consumers under delegated constraints.

AI Shopping Agent: An AI-enabled system often conversational that supports or performs consumer shopping tasks such as comparison, recommendation, purchasing, and post-purchase management.

Algorithmic Price Discrimination: The practice of using automated analytics to offer different prices or choice sets to different consumers based on inferred willingness to pay or other predictive signals.

Choice Integrity: A property of a decision environment in which users can express preferences, refuse options, and exit relationships without deceptive framing or disproportionate friction.

Contestability: The ability of an affected user to question an AI-mediated outcome and obtain a meaningful response, including explanation, review, or remedy, supported by retained evidence and accountable processes.

Dark Patterns: Interface or interaction designs that steer users toward outcomes that benefit the service provider at the user's expense, typically by exploiting cognitive biases or obscuring meaningful consent.

Explainable Artificial Intelligence (XAI): Methods and design practices that make AI-driven outcomes intelligible to relevant stakeholders by providing understandable reasons, evidence, and pathways for contesting or modifying decisions.

Hypernudge: A dynamically adaptive form of choice architecture that uses real-time behavioral data to personalize persuasive interventions and continuously optimize them toward a target outcome.

Chapter 14

Virtual Reality Marketplaces and AI Agents:

Creating Immersive Retail Environments

Faris Abuhashish
http://orcid.org/0009-0009-7859-3575
University of Petra, Jordan

Riyad Alrousan
German Jordanian University, Jordan

Mohd S. Sunar
http://orcid.org/0000-0002-0244-1622
Universiti Teknologi Malaysia, Malaysia

Ismahafezi Ismail
http://orcid.org/0000-0001-9080-7825
Sultan Zainal Abidin University, Malaysia

Hamzah Alkhazaleh
http://orcid.org/0000-0002-0218-5219
University of Dubai, UAE

Anas Arram
http://orcid.org/0000-0003-4268-5864
Higher Collage of Technology, UAE

ABSTRACT

The chapter explores the effect of virtual reality marketplaces and artificial intelligence agents on the retail industry with a particular focus on how they enable immersive shopping experiences and personalized customer service. It also clarifies how VR technologies can improve the interaction with the product and how AI can be used to offer user-centric experience, relevance, and efficiency in decision making. The analysis is based on recent empirical research and case examples in the industry in the fashion, tourism, and electronics sectors, hence providing a conceptual framework that is grounded on systematic literature review. The attendant

DOI: 10.4018/979-8-3373-7330-0.ch014

benefits are discussed in advance, challenges are identified, the behavioural effects are discussed, and the strategic implications of the discussed topic are discussed in relation to retail organisations. Lastly, the chapter postulates that the universal adoption depends on the presence of better hardware, designing usable interfaces, and embracing open data practices that aimed to strengthen user confidence in cross-heterogeneous settings.

INTRODUCTION

The retail industry is going through a sharp change initiated by the emerging technologies that redefine the interaction of consumers to products and the consumer buying decisions. Traditional e-commerce has maximised convenience but still it has failed to replicate the feeling, sense, and space of shopping in stores. New technology in virtual reality has started to close this divide by providing three dimensional navigable virtual retail spaces that can emulate a sense of presence and interaction. These virtual markets, which are enabled by VR headsets or mobile based immersive interfaces, enable the retailer to create curated worlds, staged product showcases and interactive trials that go way past limitations of a flat online page.

At the same time, AI is changing the informational and relational aspect of shopping. The intelligent agents, either in the form of embodied avatars, chatbots, or an algorithmic recommendation system, carry out functions traditionally assigned to human salespeople guiding the customers, interpreting their preferences, proposing alternatives and conducting transactions. Being integrated into VR marketplaces, these artificial intelligence elements help achieve a more responsive and individualised type of interaction, which successfully combines an immersive spatial design with dynamic, context-responsive support. The business feasibility of such hybrid environments is indicated by early experiments in the industry, e.g. the Amazon virtual holiday store or AI-powered decoratory tools available at Walmart.

It is against this background that the chapter aims at achieving three major things: to review the current studies on VR retail and AI-assisted commerce; to come up with a conceptual framework, which explains how immersive environments and intelligent agents can interact; and to support this conceptual framework with case studies in sectors such as fashion, tourism, and electronics. One reason is a repetitive, VR opens up experiential potentials: visually rich product experiences, interactive store layouts, embodied navigation, which cannot be recreated in more conventional interfaces, and AI offers the personalisation and direction needed to make such experience intelligible and efficient to a wide range of users.

The chapter thus addresses a number of guiding questions: How do consumers react to VR shopping regarding attention, satisfaction, and the quality of decision?

How and to what extent should AI agents perform their roles in the virtual stores, and what impact do they have on trust and usability? What are the technical, social, and ethical issues that influence the design of the immersive retail systems? To mitigate them, the chapter continues with a systematized review of the VR and AI literature, then with the basic parts, on VR marketplace technologies, the capabilities of AI agents, and their integration, with a conceptual figure and a summary table of examples in the industry. The systematic review and design science approach guiding the analysis is presented in a separate section of the methodology. Theoretical and practical implications are interpreted in the discussion, and the conclusion synthesises major insights and future research directions of the development of immersive retail.

BACKGROUND AND LITERATURE REVIEW

The rapid advance of immersive technologies and smart software has created a wide platform of reconsidering the retail experience design, delivery, and evaluation. With virtual reality moving past experimental applications into a world of retail interfaces with real commercial viability, researchers in the areas of human-computer interaction, marketing, and information systems have started to catalogue the ability of virtual reality to simulate the spatial presence and sensory experiences in ways that conventional electronic commerce cannot. Parallel advances in artificial intelligence have brought a new breed of interactive agents who can give directions to customers, read between the lines, and discover products based on personal preferences. To determine the conceptual bases on which the framework of the chapter is founded this introductory part of the paper will be surveying both strands of literature.

Despite the fact that both virtual reality and artificial intelligence have already been researched thoroughly separately, they have not been studied as a combination in the retail context. Unlike AI research, VR research has been studying mainly sensory immersion, affective involvement, and spatial design used in virtual stores, as a comparison. The current literature does not focus much on the interaction of these two technologies in a single shopping context or how their interaction transforms the consumer behavior. The synthesis that is needed is more detailed one a synthesis bridging immersive environments and intelligent guidance systems and placing them in the context of cross-industry retail practices.

It becomes even more complicated when there is the introduction of metaverse platforms, where VR shopping is built into the worlds of persistent, socially interactive entities. According to recent empirical research and reports in the industry, there is increasing interest in these environments, but much remains uncertain with regards to adoption, interoperability, and long-term value propositions to the retailers. This context shows both prospects and disintegration: although the theories of immersion, presence, and AI-mediated help are well-established, overall models that combine virtual reality, AI agents, and metaverse dynamics are emerging. These gaps are filled by the following subsections that review the state of knowledge in the area of VR retail, AI agents, and immersive commerce, which preconditions the concept synthesis and the methodology of the chapter.

This part summarizes current information on the constituents of the subject matter, the terminologies on topical matters and gaps.

Virtual Reality in Retail

Virtual reality (VR) is a collection of technologies which eliminate or supplement perceived reality with immersive three-dimensional experiences. Modern consumer-friendly VR devices, such as head-mounted displays, motion controllers, and spatial audio systems, can allow users to appear in simulated retail spaces, which have depth, size, and interactivity. The use of VR in retail is not a new field of study; as an example, Xi and Hamari (2021) conducted a systematic review of 72 empirical studies on the topic of VR shopping and found that, despite the promising prospects, VR is still in its early stages of development in retail and marketing settings. Common VR store setups include online shopping malls, showrooms, product experience areas, and online gaming shopping experiences.

Empirical studies suggest that immersive VR may improve the entertainment and involvement of consumers with goods to buy. In a comparison of a fashion-shopping experience realized through a desktop interface with a completely immersive VR one, conducted through a head-mounted display, Ricci et al. (2023) discovered that VR condition led to a significant rise in hedonic (fun) and utilitarian (usefulness) values among the participants. VR users had longer periods in the virtual store and were more satisfied with the whole user experience than their desktop counterparts in the experimental paradigm. The complementary evidence provided by Kim and Lee (2021) who used eye-tracking in a virtual retail store, has shown that unique visual merchandising components like signs, props and lights are the most efficient way to get the attention of consumers in a manner that would be unfeasible through the use of the online platform only. All these findings together are indicative of VR providing designers with the ability to design unique visual experiences that capture attention and keep the shopper engaged, which would help bridge the gap between e-commerce and physical brick-and-mortar space.

In diverse industries, VR has been achieving growing popularity in the retail setting. Large brands have created virtual showrooms; the most prominent example is Walmart with its 3D home-decor application that lets customers view designed spaces through AR/VR technologies, and The Amazon Virtual Holiday Shop is presented as an immersive 3D experience that puts a plethora of products on display.

Other brands like HM and Zara have come up with online fitting rooms or online shops that allow customers to test clothes on their avatars. In the tourism sector, VR is being used to give virtual tours of hotel and travel destinations; other companies in the electronics and auto sectors are using VR to give VR test-drives and interactive product demonstrations. A theoretical Table (tentative) would compare a few case studies in the industry, such as an experiment in a virtual handbag shop, a virtual hotel-booking demonstration, and a virtual car-showroom, with their key characteristics and experimental results.

Despite such accomplishments, there are still significant gaps in the literature. There is limited empirical research of consumer behaviour in real, live VR shopping conditions and a majority of the research is performed in laboratories. Besides, there is little understanding of the combination of VR with other supporting technologies, including artificial intelligence (AI), as well as the design of available and credible VR spaces. The common issues, including motion sickness and the cost of equipment, as well as digital inequality, may deter the use of it. Since the vast majority of previous studies have focused on the technological aspects of VR as such, the questions about how to navigate consumers through these new virtual experiences have a blank answer, thus encouraging the discussion of AI-assisted agents.

AI Agents in Retail

Artificial Intelligence (AI) agents in retail refer to software systems that use algorithms (machine learning, natural language processing, etc.) to assist customers. Examples include virtual shopping assistants, chatbots, voice agents, and recommendation engines. These agents perform tasks like answering questions, suggesting products, and automating checkout, emulating some roles of human salespeople. The absence of physical staff in e-commerce has led firms to deploy AI assistants; as one study observes, "the absence of salespeople's personalized assistance decreases the online customer experience," motivating the use of online shopping assistants (OSAs). AI agents can fill this gap by offering interactive support and personalization.

Research on online shopping assistants highlights key factors for their acceptance. Singh et al. (2024) developed a model of consumer intention to use AI shopping assistants and found that factors such as anthropomorphism (human-likeness), ease of use, enjoyment, trust, and perceived usefulness significantly affect adoption. In other words, shoppers are more likely to engage with an AI assistant if it feels human-like, is easy and enjoyable to use, respects privacy (reduces security concerns), and clearly adds value. This implies that designing AI agents for VR retail should prioritize these qualities. Another study (Villegas-Ch et al., 2023) designed a voice-based virtual shopping assistant for visually impaired users, illustrating how conversational AI can provide product descriptions and recommendations. Their work shows that an AI assistant can navigate users through product catalogs, read out details, and even suggest items based on purchase history. Such capabilities could translate to VR: for example, a shopper in a VR clothing store might ask a voice assistant to compare sizes or find matching accessories.

AI agents in retail draw on machine learning models trained on user data. For instance, recommendation systems analyze past purchases and browsing to personalize suggestions. In VR environments, the data could include user gaze, gestures, and spatial movement, enabling more context-aware recommendations. Recent industry trends (e.g. Walmart's AI-powered AR decorating tool) combine AI with immersive tech to, say, auto-convert product images into 3D models for shopping scenes. However, widespread deployment of AI raises issues of data privacy, transparency, and trust. As noted above, trust is a crucial adoption factor. Retailers must ensure AI agents handle personal data ethically, explain their actions, and avoid bias. These concerns will be revisited in the Discussion.

Immersive Retail and the Metaverse

The idea of the Metaverse as a system of maintaining and sharing virtual worlds has increased both academic and market attention to the virtual reality (VR) marketplaces. In the context of metaverse commerce, users can communicate with other avatars and virtual worlds in a social milieu of a game. Recent empirical studies show that the determinants of information seeking, escapism, social interaction, immersion and personalization have positive effects to the intentions to shop in the Metaverse, and the perceived risk is moderating effects (Pillai et al. 2025). In practice, more and more retailers around the world are testing metaverse storefronts; Amazon and Flipkart launched VR Christmas stores, and brands like Taco Bell and H&M have launched virtual stores or had virtual fronts. These trends highlight the fact that the concept of "Metaverse shopping is a shopping experience where users experience shopping in a virtual world, equipped with avatars in the 3D world. According to market-research estimates, the metaverse retail will grow annually by 40-48 percent by 2030 which indicates a faster growth trend.

However, the idea of the metaverse also prefigures a number of operational and theoretical issues, such as interoperability (i.e. smooth transition between worlds), standardisation, as well as the long-term sustainability of business models (i.e. non-fungible tokens or in-app purchases). Considering the fact that the research regarding metaverse commerce is still preliminary, the work by Pillai et al. (2025) states that the metaverse-based shopping can be considered a continuation of the conventional e-commerce, which in turn requires new sets of consumer motivation frameworks. Another meta-analysis by Fan et al. (2025) also mentions that the augmented reality (AR) and VR technologies are revolutionizing consumer behavior in the retailing industry and are actively discussed in the academic community, although the results of the studies vary significantly in terms of external factors. Therefore, despite the significant potential of VR marketplaces, the academic community is aware of significant ambiguities, including the feasibility of technologies as well as consumer satisfaction, which this chapter attempts to address.

Overall, the literature that is available shows that VR technologies can be used to provide immersive three-dimensional shopping experiences and artificial intelligence (AI) agents have the potential to provide personalized assistance; nevertheless, the combination of these elements into effective retail solutions is a new area. In this chapter, the literature review will be used to develop a combined view, to describe the interaction of VR interfaces, AI modules, and human users in future next-generation retail settings. By so doing, it will also delineate the key research gaps in such as lack of research on VR and AI synergy, and provide the practical imperatives, i.e. design requirements, and performance measures, to come later.

Core Content

Virtual Reality Marketplaces: Concepts and Design

Virtual reality marketplaces extend e-commerce into spatial, immersive realms. In a VR marketplace, a customer dons a headset and navigates a virtual environment – a digital mall, boutique, or brand world – populated with 3D products and interactive elements. The environment can simulate real store layouts or imaginative scenes (e.g. a clothing store on a beach or a tech showroom in outer space). Key components include:

- **3D Product Representation:** Every item is modeled as a 3D object that customers can examine from all angles. Some systems also allow virtual try-on (e.g. one can see how clothes fit on their own avatar).
- **Spatial Navigation:** Users move by teleporting or walking through corridors. Store layout design (shelf arrangements, navigation cues) must account for comfort and intuitiveness in VR.
- **Interaction Interfaces:** Customers interact via hand controllers, gestures, or voice. They can pick up objects, operate virtual kiosks, or ask a virtual agent.
- **Social and Environmental Features:** Multi-user VR shops allow friends to shop together as avatars. Background elements (ambient sound, dynamic lighting) add realism.

The design of a VR marketplace must balance realism and usability. As Xi and Hamari (2021) note, VR is not yet ubiquitous in retail, so interfaces must be user-friendly even for novices. For instance, VR stores might include guided tours or easy menus. Figure 1 (conceptual) would illustrate a general *VR retail architecture*: a client VR application (running on a headset or PC) connects to a cloud backend. The backend handles user accounts, retrieves product data (3D models, descriptions, prices), and runs AI services (recommendation engines, voice assistants). Real-time data (user choices, gaze metrics) can feed back to analytics. This layered architecture ensures scalability; for example, Amazon's VR stores leverage cloud computing to render high-quality graphics on various devices. (Placeholder *Figure 1* below depicts this conceptual system.)

Figure 1. Conceptual framework of a VR retail marketplace with integrated AI agents.

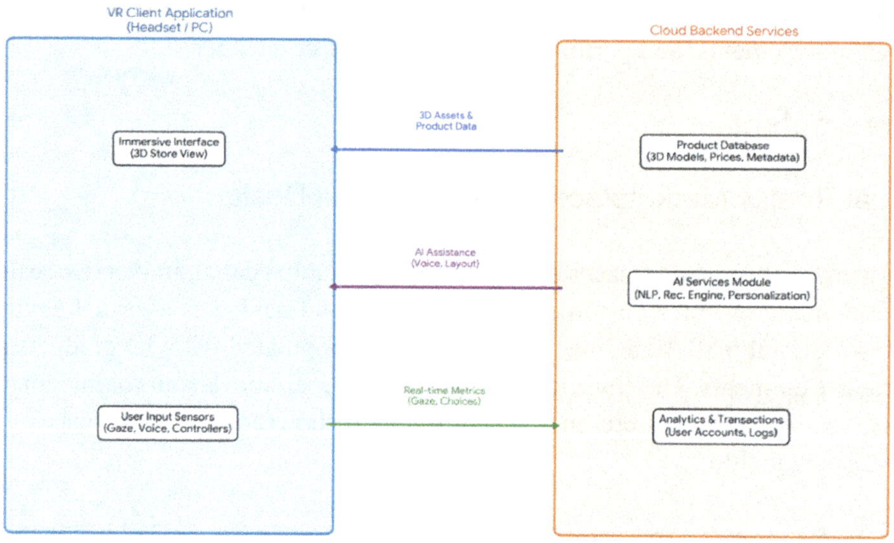

The virtual reality (VR) customer (left) recreates a rich shopping experience in a store, whereas the cloud back-end (right) contains databases about products, artificial intelligence (AI) applications, namely, recommendation engines, natural language processing (NLP), and personalization systems, and transaction services. The information flow between the VR interface and the user, on the one hand, and AI components and the underlying data services, on the other hand, are shown in Figure 1.

Marketing wise, VR marketplaces are new opportunities. Retailers would be able to create experiential marketing programs, which could include virtual pop up stores as a product launch. In addition, they will be able to reactively customize store layouts and product assortments, e.g., modular shelving units may be able to reorganize according to the preferences of individual shoppers, which is facilitated by AI technologies in the following section. Three-dimensional animations and interactive demonstrations have been proved to be rich in graphics and facilitate product understanding. Empirical studies have found that immersive retailing situations may result in the creation of both hedonic pleasure and utilitarian value among customers. In turn, user engagement is proxied by such operational metrics as time in the store and number of interactions.

The shift to VR commerce brings about design issues that have to be resolved. The comfort and accessibility of the user hold the primary importance: not every consumer has VR headsets, thus, hybrid wearables, such as WebVR or mobile-based augmented reality, can be required. Motion sickness is also a consequence to headset users: the best practices consist in restricting sudden motion and offering ergonomic navigation options. Graphical quality should be high and the guest time needed should be low, delays in loading or bad graphics can spoil the game. Security is also a significant issue; VR stores have to ensure that payment data is not disclosed, and secure authentication procedures are implemented. Also, social norms should be given a deliberate consideration: the moderation tactics on multi-user VR space and inclusive design, specifically accessibility to the users with disabilities are essential. The inclusion of a voice assistant that would support visually impaired shoppers is an example of how it should be integrated into the features of accessibility like text-to-speech and audio description. In general, VR marketplaces will be successful in case of careful, user-focused design relying on the well-known studies of human-computer interactions.

AI Agents in VR Shopping

In a virtual-reality (VR) commerce, artificial-intelligence (AI) agents act as intelligent agents. They can take a variety of forms: an avatar-based sales assistant that can talk with the consumer with the help of verbal communication, a voice-activated assistant that can process natural language, or an algorithm process acting in the background to suggest products. The main activities of AI in VR retail include the following categories:

- Personalized Recommendations: AI is able to act on the preferences and behavioural data of a shopper, including the browsing history and the products that he/she has inspected in the VR world to provide the shopper with suggestions. An example of this can be seen in the case of a customer who takes a significant amount of time to analyze sports equipment, an artificial intelligence engine can indicate related products on virtual shelves. These recommendation systems already exist everywhere in online shopping and can be easily transferred to VR. In the case of the VR storefront at Amazon, the recommendation engine that drives their e-commerce site is introduced into the virtual world.

- Conversational Assistance Omnibus: An artificial intelligence chatterbot or voice assistant is able to respond to questions and give advice. In VR, this can be represented in the form of an avatar or through the form of a basic voice prompt. As an illustration, a user can ask the question, Does it have red jackets, and this is size medium? and the answer will come in immediately with good help of visuals. The paper by Villegas-Ch et al. (2023) introduced a conversational online shopping agent, showing how it might work in response to voice commands, describe products in a storytelling manner, and recommend products based on the history of purchases. With VR, a similar agent can superimpose the product data on the heads-up display (HUD) or provide it as audio. The architecture of such agents must be designed to focus more on conversational readability and reactivity, and express enough anthropomorphism to make users trust and interact with them.
- contextual analytics AI can be able to analyse user behaviour in VR. Gaze-tracking technologies and computer-vision systems should be able to recognize the products of interest, and machine-learning models can potentially predict the intent to buy based on the length of time spent by the user looking at the item. Such information may serve to make real-time adjustments to the environment, such as the repositioning of popular products, and can provide business-analytics pipelines as well. It was demonstrated by Kim and Lee (2021) that detailed attention information provides deep understanding of the consumer experience.
- Automation of Processes: AI may be used to do the simple shopping processes, including cart control, discounting, or final payments. Within a VR store, a customer may just type in the command to check out now and a section of AI will deal with the payment in a safe system without leaving the virtual world. Security should be of primary importance; strong encryption and authentications of users must be used.

Design trade-offs are also presented with the introduction of the AI agents into VR. As an illustration, when an AI agent appears in the form of an on-screen overlay, it should not become cluttered on the immersive screen. Numerous applications use a terse voice interface or a small floating window. The latest AI applications at Walmart can demonstrate innovative applications: the 3D room decoration tool of AR, which lets users place a piece of furniture in a virtual room as a simulated environment, is created by 3 -D models based on 2-D pictures created by AI. This will show the ability of AI to supplement the VR experience itself. However, the retailers will have to be careful that the AI recommendations are not too invasive (not pushy) and that the user should feel control. The issue of trust is also essential, and when the AI agent makes a mistake, such as suggesting a product that is out of stock, it should be able to gracefully recover to maintain the trust of the user.

All in all, AI agents will make VR marketplaces more interactive and personalised. They operate on data to customize the experience of the individual user (such deploying the avatar profile of the user, previous purchases, and proclaimed interests). The combination of VR and AI means that recommendations can be given not only in the form of textual cues but as part of the environment - a virtual sign that lights up next to a particular product. This possibility can be represented in a conceptual model of immersive retail (see Figure 1), in which the elements of AI (recommendation engine, NLP assistant) will be connected to the VR interface. The methodology of the chapter was to review these frameworks in the recent literature and to make a hybrid one, which is described in the Methodology section.

Industry Use Cases and Case Studies

In order to support these ideas, this section points out practical cases of VR and AI within retail. Although scholarly literature offers some knowledge, there are cases of application in industries. Examples would be categorized by industry and technology in the form of a conceptual Table (placement). Key cases include:

- Fashion Retail (Virtual Fitting and Showrooms): Fashion goes hand in hand with VR. It has been proved that VR can be used to improve online try-on. It was found by Ricci et al. (2023) that participants who saw a virtual handbag at a fashion shop were much more willing to enjoy and to buy this product when compared to participants using a desktop interface. Practically, luxury brands like Gucci or Nike have opened virtual stores, occasionally together with gaming environments, in which the users can test digital clothes on their avatars. AI is also useful in personalization with items being recommended based on the style profile of the customer. A hypothetical case study of a luxury brand that implements VR store could include the description of shoppers walking in a 3D showroom of designer clothes, and an AI avatar stylist proposes the sets. Such cases would be presented in Table 1 (placeholder), e.g., Brand X VR Boutique, Year, Features like; a body-scan-based-fitting, AI style-advisor).
- VR in Travel (Virtual Tours): VR can be used by travel companies to promote destinations and hotels. As an illustration, a hotel chain can offer VR touring of a suite, which will enable a person to walk through the facilities and then

reserve it. The AI agents may also act as virtual concierge responding to the queries about the local attractions or the travel packages. An example is a VR travel-agency platform, where an AI bot will help one plan a trip and visit a simulated airport lounge. Such immersive previews will be able to boost the level of booking confidence. Academic research (e.g., within the field of travel marketing) has identified that VR has an effect on intentions due to presence simulation. A case study example may outline the creation of a VR tour of one of its ships by a cruise company, in which AI chatbots showcase the ship to users in different rooms, which results in increased booking rates.

- Electronics and Automotive (Virtual Showrooms): Technology and car dealers have embraced VR to allow customers to have a feel of the products which are hard to test physically. As an example, a car dealer can offer a VR driving experience of its new model. This experience can be improved with the help of AI that will customize the simulation to the user preferences or suggest some additional options in the course of the virtual drive. Such companies like Sony and Samsung have provided VR demos of new gadgets. A hypothetical illustration can represent a VR car showroom with AI kiosks: the user picks a model, sits in a VR cockpit, and an artificial voice guides him or her through all of the features. Such initiatives would be captured in case studies (which would be included in Table 1) where outcome would be when more customers are interested in the test-drive or some information with regards to customer preferences is obtained.

Table 1. Conceptual Overview of VR and AI Applications Across Industry Sectors

Industry Sector	Core VR Feature & Immersion Level	Key AI Agent Function & Technology	Actionable Outcome / Metric
High-End Fashion & Apparel	Virtual Fitting Room / Showroom (High presence and haptic simulation)	Personalized Styling Assistant (NLP, Computer Vision, Digital Twin Modeling)	Reduced Return Rates: AI-verified fit and style matching reduces post-purchase dissatisfaction. Increased AOV: AI cross-sells complementary accessories and ensembles.
Automotive & Durable Goods	Virtual Test Drive & Interactive Cockpit (Real-time 3D configuration and spatial audio)	Configurational AI Specialist (Voice Command / NLP Integration, Product Database Query)	Higher Quality Leads: Customers finalize complex options virtually, streamlining the physical sales cycle. Enhanced Product Comprehension: Interactive demos increase understanding of high-value features.
Travel & Hospitality	Experiential Destination / Ship Tours (360-degree environmental streaming, social VR for joint planning)	Virtual Concierge / Itinerary Curator (Conversational AI, Preference Matching Algorithm)	Reduced Perceived Risk & Uncertainty: Customers "try before they book," boosting confidence in high-ticket travel decisions. Higher Conversion Rates: AI focuses the sales pitch on personalized interests and needs.
Consumer Electronics	Interactive Product Demonstration Kiosks (Gesture control, detailed 3D manipulation)	Contextual Recommendation Engine (Gaze Tracking, Spatial Movement Analysis, Machine Learning)	Reduced Cognitive Load: AI highlights relevant features and guides attention, accelerating decision-making. Improved Merchandising: Real-time gaze data informs optimal virtual shelf placement.

Each case illustrates how VR's immersive context and AI's intelligence coalesce. For instance, in a virtual furniture store, shoppers can place 3D models of sofas in a virtual living room; an AI agent might automatically suggest matching decor colors. These examples underscore actionable benefits (see *Table 1*, placeholder for summary of use cases). They also reveal shared challenges: development cost of 3D models, technical integration of AI services, and ensuring a seamless user experience.

Challenges and Considerations

Although virtual-reality (VR) marketplaces and artificial-intelligence (AI) agents are suggested as the promising solutions, their real-life application faces a number of serious challenges. Key challenges include:

- Technology Adoption: A significant percentage of the potential users lack VR hardware, and high end headsets are still rare in the market although there has been an increment in the adoption rates. Therefore, the retailers need to implement the multi-platform approaches, including desktop and mobile augmented reality (AR) and full VR, to reach as many people as possible. In the segment that uses VR, usability is of the first rank; a sharp learning curve will scare off shoppers. Thus, user interface and experience (UI/UX) design, such as tutorials and controls that are natural to use, is a must, especially that of non-gamer demographics.
- Content Creation: The process of building VR-immersive environments requires a lot of 3D modeling of virtual stores and product representations, which is a resource-consuming task. The small and medium-sized retailers can thus use the ready-made templates or third-party services. The AI can be used to automate the content-creating pipeline (e.g. creating 3D objects based on a photograph, as it is the case with the AR tool that was created by Walmart); nonetheless, effective quality-control measures are required to preserve fidelity and consistency.
- Data Privacy and Security: The implementation of AI demands that user data (e.g., preferences and behavioural signals) should be processed. Retailers are, therefore, forced to deploy strict data-governance models. The danger of consumer distrust is when personal data is processed in large amounts without transparency; according to Singh et al. (2024), privacy issues play a significant role that determines the acceptability of AI assistants. VR requires more sensitive variables to be captured by auxiliary sensors, including eye-tracking devices, so the inference of the attention and emotional conditions should be performed more accurately and, therefore, requires proper ethical treatment and explicit user consent procedures. Social and Behavioral Implications: The use of immersive retail experiences can change the shopper psychology. An extended stay in a VR store may be an indicator of increased interaction but also stands a chance of exhaustion. Social activities within common VR spaces can either have positive effects (e.g. co-shopping with friends) or negative effects (e.g. overcrowding). It is also possible that it can be overstimulated and users are distracted or irritated by too many interactive components. Designers should therefore strike a balance between immersion and clarity

and may use staged directions or gates to help users to keep focus on making purchases.

- Ethical AI Implementation: AI agents can give biased suggestions or seem to be too intrusive. An ethical obligation is to ensure that the algorithms are fair, i.e. do not tend to favor high-margin product promotion, and can be explained. Although other sectors like the finance and the healthcare sector must have a more stringent system of regulation, the retail sector should also strive to embrace the principles of transparency and accountability.
- Cost and Return on Investment: VR marketplaces that use AI are capital-intensive to develop. The question of the payback of the investment is not resolved. The data obtained through proprietary case studies derive the measurement of whether such an initiative work would have any positive effect on the sales or brand loyalty. Higher engagement and conversion rates (e.g., "Customers who use the VR system spend more) are still anecdotal, but more rigorous and systematic metrics are on the rise.

The framework alone in this chapter (Figure 1) and the resulting summary table offer businesses information to plan and assess the VR retail projects. The chapter is ready to discuss these challenges by recognizing them as real issues and presenting them in a methodological framework and further discussion. This body of knowledge can be synthesised and integrated solutions to it can be proposed through the following section that describes the research design.

METHODOLOGY

The results described in this chapter are based on a systematized review of literature that has been supplemented with conceptual design approach.

1. Literature Search: The search of the literature was carried out in the well-known scholarly databases amongst Scopus, Web of Science, and Google Scholar and utilised a pre-set of key-words of virtual reality retail, metaverse shopping, AI shopping assistant, and immersive commerce. Abstracts and titles of the last ten years were filtered. Peer-reviewed journal articles (e.g. Journal of Business Research, Frontiers in Psychology, Virtual Reality), conference proceedings, and relevant industry reports were used as core literature. Both traditional theoretical literature (e.g., the use-and-gratifications theory, TAM models), and current empirical research were taken into account.
2. Selection and Synthesis:More than 100 relevant publications were retrieved. On the reasons of relevance and reliability, some 40 central sources were then

chosen. As an example, Xi and Hamari (2021) offered a deep synthesis of VR retail features, and Singh et al. (2024) presented the findings of empirical evidence on AI-assistant acceptance. Both sources were methodologically rigorous and relevant. Such gaps, as the lack of studies on integrated VR -AI systems, were found.

3. Development of a Conceptual Framework: Based on the synthesized evidence, a design-science method was used in developing the conceptual framework as shown in Figure 1. It was done by defining the key elements, and these are user, VR interface, AI modules, and data, and presenting their relationships. The framework correlates with current design concepts in the literature of human-computer interaction and information systems, each including the modular architecture and user-centered design. It is a hypothesis-generating framework that is aimed at guiding future empirical investigation.
4. Case Study Integration: The empirical basis was offered by including the real-life case studies and pilot programs found in the modern news coverage and the white papers. These examples are of various sectors and they illustrate the application of the constructs as proposed in practice as summarised in Conceptual Table. Although the list is not complete, and the examples are illustrative, still, such examples as a 3-D shop of Amazon and AI-based AR tools of Walmart highlight the common themes.
5. Hybrid Multi-Disciplinary Perspective: In line with the interdisciplinary focus of the book, the research results of marketing, computer science, and design were incorporated. As an illustration, the psychological consumer-behaviourary theories were aligned with the technical specifications on VR hardware capability, thus encouraging a holistic analysis lens. In the process of the methodological exposition, the ethical conduct of research was carefully observed, and any mentioned works were referenced in the manner of citing them appropriately, and the empirical claims were backed with authoritative sources.

In the cases when authoritative data were not available, such as specific sales uplift due to VR, the respective gap was stated explicitly. The resultant story is, therefore, a consistent synthesis between systematic review and conceptual design, which makes it appropriate in academic research and practice.

DISCUSSION

This section interprets the synthesized findings and highlights their implications for the future of retail. The findings indicate that immersive environments do more than enhance visual engagement; they restructure how consumers perceive value, navigate choices, and form expectations of digital shopping. In parallel, the increasing maturity of AI-driven personalization and conversational interfaces suggests that the long-standing divide between online convenience and in-store experiential richness is gradually narrowing. This convergence marks a transitional moment for retailers seeking differentiation in highly competitive markets.

At the same time, the analysis demonstrates that the impact of VR and AI extends well beyond isolated retail segments. Evidence from fashion, tourism, and consumer electronics illustrates that immersive product interaction, adaptive environments, and agent-mediated guidance can be generalized across diverse consumer contexts. These patterns underscore a broader shift toward experience-centered commerce, where spatial presence and intelligent mediation jointly shape perceived usefulness, ease of interaction, and emotional response. Yet, the advantages are balanced by implementation realities such as hardware accessibility, content development costs, and user readiness—factors that continue to influence the pace and direction of VR adoption.

Moreover, the synthesis highlights important psychological and behavioral implications that deserve careful reflection. Immersive environments can increase browsing depth, influence purchase intention, and alter how users evaluate risk, trust, and effort. However, they may also introduce new forms of fatigue, cognitive load, and ethical uncertainty—particularly when AI agents operate as decision-shaping intermediaries. These dynamics suggest that the next phase of VR commerce will depend not only on technical refinement but also on inclusive design practices, transparent algorithmic interfaces, and longitudinal studies that examine how consumers adapt to hybrid virtual–physical retail journeys.

Key Insights

1. *Immersion Enriches Experience:* Evidence shows that fully immersive VR can significantly boost user engagement and enjoyment compared to non-immersive shopping. Consumers in VR environments report greater hedonic satisfaction and are willing to spend more time browsing. This suggests VR marketplaces have real potential to rival brick-and-mortar stores in experiential value. For retailers, this means VR can be a differentiator – an immersive store can showcase brand image and allow creative layouts (Figure 1) that static websites cannot.
2. *AI Agents Personalize and Assist:* AI-powered assistants fill critical gaps in online shopping. Our review confirms that personalization (based on user data) and conversational interfaces (chatbots, voice agents) can make the virtual shopping journey smoother and more human-like. These agents also help mitigate one of online retail's downsides (lack of human assistance). In practice, a well-designed AI agent can improve key outcomes: by offering tailored suggestions, it likely

increases relevance of product discovery; by answering queries, it reduces friction in decision-making. The finding that trust and ease-of-use are crucial means that AI features must be transparent and intuitive.

3. *Cross-Industry Applicability:* VR and AI are not limited to one sector. The chapters' examples indicate that fashion, tourism, electronics, and more can leverage these technologies. In fashion, VR enables virtual fitting rooms; in tourism, virtual tours; in electronics, VR product demos. AI personalizes across all these (style recommendations in fashion, itinerary suggestions in tourism, accessory matching in electronics). This cross-cutting applicability underscores the multidisciplinary potential. Retailers in diverse fields can adopt a similar technological approach, customizing the virtual environment to their products and customer needs.
4. *Challenges Remain:* Despite benefits, adoption hurdles are significant. The chapter emphasizes practical considerations: technology access (not everyone has a headset), content creation costs, and user readiness. These challenges imply that VR marketplaces may initially supplement rather than replace traditional channels. Moreover, from a user perspective, early adopters tend to be tech-savvy; reaching mainstream consumers will require simplifying hardware and interfaces. AI raises its own issues: personalization algorithms must handle data ethically, and transparency tools (e.g. explaining why an item is recommended) could build trust. The discussion acknowledges these trade-offs, recommending careful pilot testing and user feedback loops in any deployment.
5. *Psychological and Behavioral Effects:* Immersive retail can affect shopping behavior in novel ways. For example, longer browsing times in VR could mean higher purchase intent but also user fatigue. Shoppers might feel differently about money spent in a virtual vs. real environment. These nuances suggest retailers should study user metrics (time, engagement, emotional response) in VR and adapt accordingly. The chapter suggests that measures like "presence" (sense of being there) and "flow" are important metrics borrowed from game studies that could be applied to VR shopping research.

Integrating with the Broader Theme

The book's theme likely concerns emerging technologies in society or business. This chapter contributes by connecting VR and AI – two hot areas – in the specific domain of retail. It shows how immersive interfaces (VR) and intelligent software (AI) can jointly address longstanding retail goals: offering convenience, variety, and personalization. For example, beyond just an "app" for shopping, the VR+AI model embodies the idea of an automated, agentic commerce where AI does much of the decision-making. In the context of digital transformation, this represents a frontier where physical and digital retail fuse into a continuous experience.

Furthermore, the chapter's interdisciplinary approach (citing both technical HCI studies and business research) aligns with the book's likely emphasis on combining insights from multiple fields. It highlights that successful VR retail systems will require collaboration between software engineers, designers, marketers, and ethicists. The proposed conceptual figure and table also serve as shared artifacts for such collaborations, as they abstract complex ideas into digestible formats.

Limitations and Future Research

While comprehensive, the chapter has limitations. First, as a conceptual review, it does not present original empirical data. Instead, it depends on published studies and reported cases. Some areas (e.g. long-term ROI of VR stores) lack public data, so recommendations in those areas are provisional. Second, the fast-moving nature of VR and AI means new developments (e.g. Oculus 3 hardware, ChatGPT interfaces) may emerge rapidly; ongoing updates will be needed. Third, cultural factors are not deeply examined; for instance, consumer acceptance of AI in retail may vary by region (as Pillai et al.'s metaverse study focused on Gen Z in certain countries). Future work could include cross-cultural studies of VR shopping behavior.

Important open research questions include: How do immersive retail experiences influence loyalty and repeat purchase behavior? What are the best practices for blending AI agents unobtrusively into VR? How can metrics like cognitive load be managed (e.g., does VR shopping induce more mental effort)? Also, since VR marketplaces often incorporate gamified elements, what game design principles best drive purchases? The chapter identifies these as potential future directions.

CONCLUSION

The conclusion brings together the chapter's central arguments on how virtual reality and AI-driven agents are reshaping the logic, experience, and operational dynamics of contemporary retail. By examining immersive interfaces, adaptive environments, and cross-sector case applications, the chapter demonstrates that VR marketplaces are no longer speculative prototypes but emerging commercial ecosystems with tangible influence on consumer behavior. The synthesis reinforces that the convergence of spatial immersion and intelligent assistance offers retailers an opportunity to reimagine the digital store as an experiential, interactive, and cognitively supportive space.

At the same time, the review highlights that successful implementation requires careful attention to the technical, psychological, and ethical dimensions that underpin user trust and long-term engagement. While immersive VR environments can elevate attention, enjoyment, and product understanding, their effectiveness depends on balancing novelty with usability and ensuring that AI-driven interactions remain transparent, reliable, and respectful of privacy. Real-world experiments by leading retail brands, combined with findings from fashion, tourism, and electronics, indicate that this combination of VR and AI is progressing toward mainstream adoption—but only when accessibility, comfort, and data governance are thoughtfully addressed.

Looking forward, the chapter positions its conceptual framework and application tables as foundational elements for developing next-generation retail systems that unite immersion with intelligence. As VR hardware matures and AI systems advance in language understanding and behavioral modeling, more cohesive and adaptive virtual marketplaces are expected to emerge. These trajectories signal both an opportunity and an obligation: researchers and practitioners must collaborate across design, marketing, psychology, and computer science to ensure that future systems are inclusive, scalable, and robust. The evidence reviewed throughout the chapter suggests a promising research agenda—one that continues to explore how virtual environments and intelligent agents can together produce more engaging, efficient, and ethically aligned retail experiences.

This chapter has surveyed the landscape of virtual reality marketplaces augmented by AI agents, presenting a forward-looking picture of immersive retail. Key takeaways include:

- **Immersive Experiences:** VR can create engaging shopping environments that enhance consumer attention and enjoyment. Immersive visuals and interactivity differentiate VR retail from traditional online shopping.
- **Personalized Assistance:** AI agents (chatbots, recommendation engines, voice assistants) make these virtual stores smarter and more user-friendly. Personalization and trustworthiness of AI are essential for adoption.
- **Real-World Adoption:** Leading retailers are already experimenting with VR and AI (e.g. Amazon's Virtual Holiday Shop, Walmart's AR/AI tools). Case studies across industries (fashion, tourism, electronics) illustrate practical uses.
- **Considerations:** Significant challenges in accessibility, cost, and ethics must be addressed. For example, while VR promises new shopping modes, it requires careful design to avoid user discomfort. Likewise, AI must protect privacy and avoid bias.

- **Future Potential:** As VR hardware becomes more widespread and AI continues to advance (e.g. natural language models), the seamless integration of these technologies could redefine retail. The chapter's conceptual framework (Figure 1) and example table (Table 1 placeholder) provide a basis for developing next-generation retail systems.

In summary, *the chapter* argues that VR marketplaces enhanced with AI agents have the potential to revolutionize retail by combining immersive experience with intelligent assistance. Retailers and developers should collaborate across disciplines – combining insights from marketing, psychology, and computer science – to create user-centric, scalable solutions. The next chapter in this book could build on this by exploring another aspect of immersive commerce (e.g. payment technologies in VR or VR analytics), but the overall vision remains: blending virtual worlds and AI to make shopping more engaging and effective. The evidence reviewed here (from experimental studies, theoretical reviews, and industry reports) consistently shows positive outcomes from VR shopping innovations, suggesting a fruitful path ahead for research and practice in this space.

REFERENCES

Fan, X., Xun, J., Dolega, L., & Xiong, L. (2025). The role of augmented and virtual reality in shaping retail marketing: A meta-analysis. *Sustainability (Basel)*, *17*(2), 728. DOI: 10.3390/su17020728

Kim, N., & Lee, H. (2021). Assessing consumer attention and arousal using eye-tracking technology in a virtual retail environment. *Frontiers in Psychology*, *12*, 665658. DOI: 10.3389/fpsyg.2021.665658 PMID: 34434136

Pillai, R., Sivathanu, B., & Rana, N. P. (2025). Unveiling virtual interactive marketplaces: Shopping motivations in the Metaverse through the lens of uses and gratifications theory. *Journal of Business Research*, *190*, 115219. DOI: 10.1016/j.jbusres.2025.115219

Ricci, M., Evangelista, A., Di Roma, A., & Fiorentino, M. (2023). Immersive and desktop virtual reality in virtual fashion stores: A comparison between shopping experiences. *Virtual Reality (Waltham Cross)*, *27*(3), 2281–2296. Advance online publication. DOI: 10.1007/s10055-023-00806-y PMID: 37360805

Singh, C., Dash, M. K., Sahu, R., & Kumar, A. (2024). Investigating the acceptance intentions of online shopping assistants in e-commerce interactions: Mediating role of trust and effects of consumer demographics. *Heliyon*, *10*(3), e25031. DOI: 10.1016/j.heliyon.2024.e25031 PMID: 38318071

Villegas-Ch, W., Amores-Falconi, R., & Coronel-Silva, E. (2023). Design proposal for a virtual shopping assistant for people with vision problems applying artificial intelligence techniques. *Big Data and Cognitive Computing*, *7*(2), 96. DOI: 10.3390/bdcc7020096

Xi, N., & Hamari, J. (2021). Shopping in virtual reality: A literature review and future agenda. *Journal of Business Research*, *134*, 37–58. DOI: 10.1016/j.jbusres.2021.04.075

Compilation of References

Abadi, M., Chu, A., Goodfellow, I., McMahan, H. B., Mironov, I., Talwar, K., & Zhang, L. (2016). Deep learning with differential privacy. *Proceedings of the 2016 ACM SIGSAC Conference on Computer and Communications Security (CCS).* https://arxiv.org/abs/1607.00133 DOI: 10.1145/2976749.2978318

Abdeljaber, O., Al-Adwan, A. S., Yaseen, H., Falahat, M., Abdullah, A., & Fauzi, M. A. (2025). Shopping in the metaverse: Decoding consumer intentions. *The International Information & Library Review*, *58*(1), 1–31. DOI: 10.1080/10572317.2025.2594293

Abdulquadri, A., Mogaji, E., Kieu, T. A., & Nguyen, N. P. (2021). Digital transformation in financial services provision: A Nigerian perspective to the adoption of chatbot. *Journal of Enterprising Communities: People and Places in the Global Economy*, *15*(2), 258–281. DOI: 10.1108/JEC-06-2020-0126

Aburidi, M., & Marcia, R. (2024). Topological adversarial attacks on graph neural networks via projected meta learning. In *Proceedings of the 2024 IEEE International Conference on Evolving and Adaptive Intelligent Systems (EAIS).* IEEE., Available from https://par.nsf.gov/servlets/purl/10566343 DOI: 10.1109/EAIS58494.2024.10569101

Accenture. (2023). Consumer pulse survey: The future of digital experience. *Accenture Research.* https://www.accenture.com/content/dam/accenture/final/industry/consumer-goods-and-services/document/Accenture-Resilient-Consumer-Study-2023.pdf [Accessed: 25 November 2025].

Acquisti, A., Brandimarte, L., & Loewenstein, G. (2015). Privacy and human behavior in the age of information. *Science*, *347*(6221), 509–514. DOI: 10.1126/science.aaa1465 PMID: 25635091

Acquisti, A., & Varian, H. R. (2005). Conditioning prices on purchase history. *Marketing Science*, *24*(3), 367–381. DOI: 10.1287/mksc.1040.0103

Adam, M., Wessel, M., & Benlian, A. (2021). AI-based chatbots in customer service and their effects on user compliance. *Electronic Markets, 31*(2), 427–445. DOI: 10.1007/s12525-020-00414-7

Adomavicius, G., & Tuzhilin, A. (2005). Toward the next generation of recommender systems: A survey of the state-of-the-art and possible extensions. *IEEE Transactions on Knowledge and Data Engineering, 17*(6), 734–749. DOI: 10.1109/TKDE.2005.99

Afsar, M. M., Crump, T., & Far, B. (2022). Reinforcement learning based recommender systems: A survey. *ACM Computing Surveys, 55*(7), 1–38. DOI: 10.1145/3543846

Ahmad Ibrahim Karajeh, Tayseer Ali AL-Momani, Malek A. Almomani, Omar Almomani and Moath H. Tarawneh. (. (2025). Forecasting future earnings via e-business information: Financial implications for investment decisions in the era of big data. *Investment Management and Financial Innovations, 22*(4), 237–246. DOI: 10.21511/imfi.22(4).2025.19

Akerlof, G. A. (1970). The market for "lemons": Quality uncertainty and the market mechanism. *The Quarterly Journal of Economics, 84*(3), 488–500. DOI: 10.2307/1879431

Akter, J., Roy, A., Rahman, S., Mohona, S., & Ara, J. (2025). Artificial Intelligence-Driven Customer Lifetime Value (CLV) Forecasting: Integrating RFM Analysis with Machine Learning for Strategic Customer Retention. *Journal of Computer Science and Technology Studies, 7*(1), 249–257. DOI: 10.32996/jcsts.2025.7.1.18

Al, E. 'mari, S., Sanjalawe, Y., Fataftah, F., & Fataftah, F. (2026). Digital Twins and BI: Synchronizing Virtual Models With Real-Time Business Processes. In *Strategic AI Integration in Business Intelligence* (pp. 135-154). IGI Global Scientific Publishing.

Al-Adwan, A. S., Al-Adwan, A., Li, N., Fauzi, M. A., Jafar, R. M. S., Habibi, A., & Falahat, M. (2025). Immersive learning meets theory: Modeling eduverse adoption in higher education. *Journal of Information Technology Education: Research, 24,* 042. https://doi.org/DOI: 10.28945/5669

Al-Adwan, A. S. (2024). The government metaverse: Charting the coordinates of citizen acceptance. *Telematics and Informatics, 88*, 102109. DOI: 10.1016/j.tele.2024.102109

Al-Adwan, A. S., & Sammour, G. (2020). What makes consumers purchase mobile apps: Evidence from Jordan. *Journal of Theoretical and Applied Electronic Commerce Research, 16*(3), 562–583. DOI: 10.3390/jtaer16030034

Al-Adwan, A. S., Yaseen, H., Alkhwaldi, A. F., Jafar, R. M. S., Fauzi, M. A., & Abdullah, A. (2025). Treasure hunting for brands: Metaverse marketing gamification effects on purchase intention, WOM, and loyalty. *Journal of Global Marketing, 38*(4), 1–25. DOI: 10.1080/08911762.2025.2463897

Alayrac, J. B., Donahue, J., Luc, P., Miech, A., Barr, I., Hasson, Y., . . . Simonyan, K. (2022). Flamingo: a visual language model for few-shot learning. *Advances in neural information processing systems, 35*, 23716-23736. Available from https://proceedings.neurips.cc/paper_files/paper/2022/file/960a172bc7fbf0177ccccb b411a7d800-Paper-Conference.pdf

Al-E'mari, S., Sanjalawe, Y., Makhadmeh, S., & Alqudah, H. (2024, February). Digital forensics meets blockchain: Enhancing evidence authenticity and traceability. In *2024 2nd International Conference on Cyber Resilience (ICCR)* (pp. 01-06). IEEE.

Alles, M., & Gray, G. L. (2020). Continuous accounting: How digital technologies transform auditing and financial reporting. *Journal of Emerging Technologies in Accounting, 17*(1), 1–15. DOI: 10.2308/jeta-10764

Almomani, O., Alsaaidah, A., Abu-Shareha, A. A., Alzaqebah, A., Almaiah, M. A., & Shambour, Q. (2025). Enhance URL defacement attack detection using particle swarm optimization and machine learning. *Journal of Computational and Cognitive Engineering, 4*(3), 296–308. DOI: 10.47852/bonviewJCCE52024668

Almomani, O., Arabiat, A. M., Hind, A.-A., & Alsariera, E. (2026). Hybridization of deep learning models for multiclass attack detection in wireless sensor networks. *Journal of Communication, 21*(1), 20–34. DOI: 10.12720/jcm.21.1.20-34

Almomani, O., Arabiat, A., Al Tayeb, M., Almaiah, M. A., Obeidat, M., Aldhyani, T. H., Shehab, R., & Rowad, M. (2025). A Robust Model for Android Malware Detection via ML and DL classifiers. *Mesopotamian Journal of Big Data, 2025*, 261–277. DOI: 10.58496/MJBD/2025/017

Alsaaidah, A., Almomani, O., Abu-Shareha, A. A., Abualhaj, M. M., & Achuthan, A. (2024). ARP spoofing attack detection model in IoT network using machine learning: Complexity vs. accuracy. *Journal of Applied Data Sciences, 5*(4), 1850–1860. DOI: 10.47738/jads.v5i4.374

Al-Zaqeba, M. A., ... (2026). The effect of implementing AI-driven customs processes on trade facilitation efficiency in Jordan. In A. R. Alshehadeh, I. A. El-Qirem, & G. A. Elrefae (Eds.), *Artificial intelligence in business. SICB 2025* (Lecture Notes in Networks and Systems, Vol. 1502, Springer. https://doi.org/DOI: 10.1007/978-3-031-96622-4_11

Ameen, N., Tarhini, A., Reppel, A., & Anand, A. (2021). Customer experiences in the age of artificial intelligence. *Computers in Human Behavior, 114*, 106548. DOI: 10.1016/j.chb.2020.106548

Amershi, S., Weld, D., Vorvoreanu, M., Fourney, A., Nushi, B., Collisson, P., Suh, J., Iqbal, S., Bennett, P. N., Inkpen, K., Teevan, J., Kikin-Gil, R., & Horvitz, E. (2019). Guidelines for human–AI interaction. In *Proceedings of the 2019 CHI Conference on Human Factors in Computing Systems* (pp. 1–13). Association for Computing Machinery. DOI: 10.1145/3290605.3300233

Amugongo, L. M., Mascheroni, P., Brooks, S., Doering, S., & Seidel, J. (2025). Retrieval augmented generation for large language models in healthcare: A systematic review. *PLOS Digital Health, 4*(6), e0000877. DOI: 10.1371/journal.pdig.0000877 PMID: 40498738

Anderson, J. R., Bothell, D., Byrne, M. D., Douglass, S., Lebiere, C., & Qin, Y. (2004). An integrated theory of the mind. *Psychological Review, 111*(4), 1036–1060. DOI: 10.1037/0033-295X.111.4.1036 PMID: 15482072

Angwin, J., & Mattu, S. (2016, September 20). *Amazon says it puts customers first. But its pricing algorithm doesn't.* ProPublica.

Aslan, S. (2023). Doğal Dil İşleme Teknikleri Kullanarak E-Ticaret Kullanıcı İncelemelerinde Özellik Tabanlı Duygu Analizi. *Fırat Üniversitesi Mühendislik Bilimleri Dergisi, 35*(2), 875–882. DOI: 10.35234/fumbd.1335583

Aura Blockchain Consortium. (2023). Global authenticity solutions for luxury goods. *Aura.* https://auraconsortium.com/ [Access 24 November 2025].

Bahrami, S., & Rubulotta, F. (2025). Artificial Intelligence-Driven Translation Tools in Intensive Care Units for Enhancing Communication and Research. *International Journal of Environmental Research and Public Health, 22*(1), 95. DOI: 10.3390/ijerph22010095

Balhareth, H., Al-Adwan, A. S., Alsoud, A. R., Abd-Aljaber, O., Al-Rahmi, W. M., & Urbaníková, M. (2024). Journey into meta-commerce: Unveiling the driving forces of consumer adoption. *Global Knowledge, Memory and Communication.* Advance online publication. DOI: 10.1108/GKMC-05-2024-0307

Balkin, J. M. (2016). Information fiduciaries and the First Amendment. *Harvard Law Review, 129*(4), 1220–1310. https://harvardlawreview.org/print/vol-129/information-fiduciaries-and-the-first-amendment/

Ball, M. (2021). *The Metaverse: And how it will revolutionize everything*. Liveright Publishing.

Barnes, S. B. (2006). A privacy paradox: Social networking in the United States. *First Monday, 11*(9). Advance online publication. DOI: 10.5210/fm.v11i9.1394

Barocas, S., Hardt, M., & Narayanan, A. (2023). Fairness and machine learning: Limitations and opportunities. MIT Press. https://fairmlbook.org/

Barrera, K. G., & Shah, D. (2023). Marketing in the Metaverse: Conceptual understanding, framework, and research agenda. *Journal of Business Research, 155*, 113420. Advance online publication. DOI: 10.1016/j.jbusres.2022.113420

Bell, S., & Bala, K. (2015). Learning visual similarity for product design with convolutional neural networks. *ACM Transactions on Graphics, 34*(4), 1–10. DOI: 10.1145/2766959

Bhatnagar, B. L., Tiwari, G., Theobalt, C., & Pons-Moll, G. (2019). Multi-garment net: Learning to dress 3D people from images. In *Proceedings of the IEEE International Conference on Computer Vision* (pp. 5420-5430). IEEE. DOI: 10.1109/ICCV.2019.00552

Bhuiyan, M. S. (2024). The role of AI-Enhanced personalization in customer experiences. *Journal of Computer Science and Technology Studies, 6*(1), 162–169. DOI: 10.32996/jcsts.2024.6.1.17

Böhme, R., & Köpsell, S. (2010). Trained to accept? A field experiment on consent dialogs. *Proceedings of the SIGCHI Conference on Human Factors in Computing Systems*, 2403-2406. DOI: 10.1145/1753326.1753689

Bolton, L. E., Warlop, L., & Alba, J. W. (2003). Consumer perceptions of price (un) fairness. *The Journal of Consumer Research, 29*(4), 474–491. DOI: 10.1086/346244

Boston Consulting Group. (2025, October 6). Agentic Commerce Is Redefining Retail Here's How to Respond. BCG. https://www.bcg.com/publications/2025/agentic-commerce-redefining-retail-how-to-respond

Bradford, A. (2020). *The Brussels effect: How the European Union rules the world.* Oxford University Press., DOI: 10.1093/oso/9780190088583.001.0001

Brignull, H. (2010). Dark patterns. https://www.darkpatterns.org/

Brignull, H. (2010). *Dark patterns: Deception vs. honesty in UI design.* A List Apart. https://alistapart.com/article/dark-patterns-deception-vs-honesty-in-ui-design/

Brignull, H. (2010). *Dark patterns: Deceptive design.* https://www.darkpatterns.org

Brown, T. B., Mann, B., Ryder, N., Subbiah, M., Kaplan, J., Dhariwal, P., Neelakantan, A., Shyam, P., Sastry, G., Askell, A., Agarwal, S., Herbert-Voss, A., Krueger, G., Henighan, T., Child, R., Ramesh, A., Ziegler, D. M., Wu, J., Winter, C., & Amodei, D. (2020). Language models are few-shot learners. *Advances in Neural Information Processing Systems*, *33*, 1877–1901.

Brusilovsky, P. (1996). Methods and techniques of adaptive hypermedia. *User Modeling and User-Adapted Interaction*, *6*(2-3), 87–129. DOI: 10.1007/BF00143964

Brusilovsky, P. (2001). Adaptive hypermedia. *User Modeling and User-Adapted Interaction*, *11*(1-2), 87–110. DOI: 10.1023/A:1011143116306

Brusilovsky, P., Kobsa, A., & Nejdl, W. (Eds.). (2007). *The adaptive web: Methods and strategies of web personalization*. Springer-Verlag., DOI: 10.1007/978-3-540-72079-9

Bubeck, S., Chandrasekaran, V., Eldan, R., Gehrke, J., Horvitz, E., Kamar, E., . . . Zhang, Y. (2023). Sparks of artificial general intelligence: Early experiments with gpt-4. *arXiv preprint arXiv:2303.12712*. https://doi.org//arXiv.2303.12712DOI: 10.48550

Buhalis, D., & Sinarta, Y. (2019). Real-time co-creation and nowness service: Lessons from tourism and hospitality. *Journal of Travel & Tourism Marketing*, *36*(5), 563–582. DOI: 10.1080/10548408.2019.1592059

Burges, C. J. (2010). From ranknet to lambdarank to lambdamart: An overview. *Learning*, *11*(23-581), 81. Available from https://www.khoury.northeastern.edu/home/vip/teach/MLcourse/4_boosting/materials/msr-tr-2010-82.pdf

Buterin, V. (2015). On public and private blockchains. Ethereum Foundation. https://ethereum.org

Çakmak, A. Ç. (2024). Yapay zekâ ile marka inşası. *Kahramanmaraş Sütçü İmam Üniversitesi Sosyal Bilimler Dergisi*, *21*(2), 624–635. DOI: 10.33437/ksusbd.1489490

California Civil Code §§ 1798.100-1798.199 (2018, amended 2020).

Calo, R. (2014). Digital market manipulation. *SSRN*, *82*(4), 995–1051. DOI: 10.2139/ssrn.2309703

Calo, R. (2014). Digital market manipulation. *The George Washington Law Review*, *82*, 995–1051. https://www.gwlr.org/wp-content/uploads/2014/10/Calo_82_41.pdf

Cao, Z., Hidalgo, G., Simon, T., Wei, S. E., & Sheikh, Y. (2019). OpenPose: Real-time multi-person 2D pose estimation using part affinity fields. *IEEE Transactions on Pattern Analysis and Machine Intelligence, 43*(1), 172–186. DOI: 10.1109/TPAMI.2019.2929257 PMID: 31331883

Cassell, J., Sullivan, J., Churchill, E., & Prevost, S. (Eds.). (2000). *Embodied conversational agents*. MIT Press. DOI: 10.7551/mitpress/2697.001.0001

Catalini, C., & Gans, J. S. (2016). Some simple economics of the blockchain. MIT Sloan Research Paper, 5191–16.

Celestin, M., Vasuki, M., Sujatha, S., & Kumar, A. D. (2024). How businesses create personalized experiences to boost customer retention: The role of technology and human interactions in customer satisfaction. *International Journal of Applied and Advanced Scientific Research, 9*(2), 75–80. DOI: 10.5281/zenodo.13871854

Chagas, B. A., Pagano, A. S., Prates, R. O., Praes, E. C., Ferreguetti, K., Vaz, H., Reis, Z. S. N., Ribeiro, L. B., Ribeiro, A. L. P., Pedroso, T. M., Beleigoli, A., Oliveira, C. R. A., & Marcolino, M. S. (2023). Evaluating user experience with a chatbot designed as a public health response to the COVID-19 pandemic in Brazil: Mixed methods study. *JMIR Human Factors, 10*(1), e43135. DOI: 10.2196/43135

Chatterjee, S., Nguyen, B., Ghosh, S. K., Bhattacharjee, K. K., & Chaudhuri, R. (2020). Adoption of artificial intelligence-integrated CRM system in the service sector: A customer experience perspective. *Technological Forecasting and Social Change, 161*, 120283. DOI: 10.1108/BL-08-2020-0057

Chatti, M. A., Guesmi, M., & Muslim, A. (2024). Visualization for recommendation explainability: A survey and new perspectives. *ACM Transactions on Interactive Intelligent Systems, 14*(3), 1–40. DOI: 10.1145/3672276

Chen, D. (2015). Online Retail Dataset [Data set]. UCI Machine Learning Repository. https://archive.ics.uci.edu/ml/datasets/Online+Retail

Chen, D., & Kotz, D. (2000). A survey of context-aware mobile computing research (Technical Report TR2000-381). Dartmouth College, Department of Computer Science.

Chen, H., Liu, X., Yin, D., & Tang, J. (2019). A survey on dialogue systems: Recent advances and new frontiers. *SIGKDD Explorations, 19*(2), 25–35. DOI: 10.1145/3166054.3166058

Chen, L., Mislove, A., & Wilson, C. (2016). An empirical analysis of algorithmic pricing on Amazon Marketplace. *Proceedings of the 25th International World Wide Web Conference*, 1339–1349. DOI: 10.1145/2872427.2883089

Chen, N. J., Huang, C. M., Fan, C. C., Lu, L. T., Lin, F. H., Liao, J. Y., & Guo, J. L. (2023). User evaluation of a chat-based instant messaging support health education program for patients with chronic kidney disease: Preliminary findings of a formative study. *JMIR Formative Research, 7*(1), e45484. DOI: 10.2196/45484

Chen, R., Hua, Q., Chang, Y. S., Wang, B., Zhang, L., & Kong, X. (2018). A survey of collaborative filtering-based recommender systems: From traditional methods to hybrid methods based on social networks. *IEEE Access : Practical Innovations, Open Solutions, 6*, 64301–64320. DOI: 10.1109/ACCESS.2018.2877208

Chen, R., Li, H., Qin, A. K., Kasiviswanathan, S. P., & Jin, H. (2020). Private recommender systems: How can users build their own fair recommender systems without log data? In *Proceedings of the 2020 SIAM International Conference on Data Mining* (pp. 514-522). Society for Industrial and Applied Mathematics. DOI: 10.1137/1.9781611976236.58

Chen, W., Xu, Z., Shi, S., Zhao, Y., & Zhang, W. (2020). A survey on blockchain consensus mechanisms. *ACM Computing Surveys, 53*(2), 1–31.

Chen, Y., & Prentice, C. (2025). Integrating artificial intelligence and customer experience. *Australasian Marketing Journal, 33*(2), 141–153. DOI: 10.1177/14413582241252904

Choi, H., Park, J., & Jung, Y. (2018). The role of privacy fatigue in online privacy behavior. *Computers in Human Behavior, 81*, 42–51. DOI: 10.1016/j.chb.2017.12.001

Christidis, K., & Devetsikiotis, M. (2016). Blockchains and smart contracts for the internet of things. *IEEE Access : Practical Innovations, Open Solutions, 4*, 2292–2303. DOI: 10.1109/ACCESS.2016.2566339

Chung, M., Ko, E., Joung, H., & Kim, S. J. (2020). Chatbot e-service and customer satisfaction regarding luxury brands. *Journal of Business Research, 117*, 587–595. DOI: 10.1016/j.jbusres.2018.10.004

Cialdini, R. B. (2006). *Influence: The psychology of persuasion* (Rev. ed.). Harper Business.

Cohen, J. E. (2019). *Between truth and power: The legal constructions of informational capitalism*. Oxford University Press. DOI: 10.1093/oso/9780190246693.001.0001

Competition and Markets Authority. (2019). *CMA secures improvements to hotel booking sites*. https://www.gov.uk/government/news/cma-secures-improvements-to-hotel-booking-sites

Competition and Markets Authority. (2019). *Investigation into online hotel booking*. https://www.gov.uk/cma-cases/hotel-online-booking-sector-investigation

Consumer Protection Act. (Act No. 35 of 2019) (India).

Covington, P., Adams, J., & Sargin, E. (2016). Deep neural networks for YouTube recommendations. In *Proceedings of the 10th ACM Conference on Recommender Systems* (pp. 191-198). ACM. DOI: 10.1145/2959100.2959190

Coyne, J. G., & McMickle, P. L. (2017). Can blockchains serve an accounting purpose? *Journal of Emerging Technologies in Accounting*, *14*(2), 101–111. DOI: 10.2308/jeta-51910

Criteo. (2014, July 9). *Display advertising challenge by Criteo*. Criteo AI Lab.

Croman, K., Decker, C., Eyal, I., Gencer, A. E., Juels, A., Kosba, A., Miller, A., Saxena, P., Shi, E., Sirer, E. G., Song, D., & Wattenhofer, R. (2016). On scaling decentralized blockchains. Financial Cryptography and Data Security, 106–125.

Crosby, M., Pattanayak, P., Verma, S., & Kalyanaraman, V. (2016). Blockchain technology: Beyond bitcoin. *Applied Innovation Review*, *2*, 6–19.

Cyr, D., Head, M., Larios, H., & Pan, B. (2009). Exploring human images in website design: A multi-method approach. *Management Information Systems Quarterly*, *33*(3), 539–566. DOI: 10.2307/20650308

Dai, J., & Vasarhelyi, M. A. (2017). Toward blockchain-based accounting and assurance. *Journal of Information Systems*, *31*(3), 5–21. DOI: 10.2308/isys-51804

Davenport, T. H., Guha, A., Grewal, D., & Bressgott, T. (2020). How artificial intelligence will change the future of marketing. *Journal of the Academy of Marketing Science*, *48*(1), 24–42. DOI: 10.1007/s11747-019-00696-0

David-John, B., Butler, D. J., & Jain, E. (2022). For your eyes only: Privacy-preserving eye-tracking datasets. *Proceedings of the ACM Symposium on Eye Tracking Research & Applications (ETRA)*. DOI: 10.1145/3517031.3529618

Deekshita, P., Neeharika, K., Haritha, M. S., Mohan, P. J., & Bindu, Y. S. (2024). Pdf Chat Bot Usıng Generatıve AI (LLMS&RAG). *Journal of Nonlinear Analysis and Optimization*, *15*(1), 1727–1732. DOI: 10.36893/JNAO.2024.V15I01.1727-1732

Deldjoo, Y., Di Noia, T., & Merra, F. A. (2021). A survey on adversarial recommender systems: From attack/defense strategies to generative adversarial networks. *ACM Computing Surveys*.

Devlin, J., Chang, M. W., Lee, K., & Toutanova, K. (2019). Bert: Pre-training of deep bidirectional transformers for language understanding. In *Proceedings of the 2019 conference of the North American chapter of the association for computational linguistics: human language technologies, volume 1 (long and short papers)* (pp. 4171-4186). DOI: 10.18653/v1/N19-1423

Dey, A. K. (2001). Understanding and using context. *Personal and Ubiquitous Computing*, *5*(1), 4–7. DOI: 10.1007/s007790170019

Dey, L. (2024). Knowledge graph-driven data processing for business intelligence. *Wiley Interdisciplinary Reviews. Data Mining and Knowledge Discovery*, *14*(3), e1529. DOI: 10.1002/widm.1529

Digital Personal Data Protection Act. (Act No. 22 of 2023) (India).

Directive (EU) 2022/2555 of the European Parliament and of the Council of 14 December 2022 on measures for a high common level of cybersecurity across the Union, amending Regulation (EU) No 910/2014 and Directive (EU) 2018/1972, and repealing Directive (EU) 2016/1148 (NIS 2 Directive). (2022). *Official Journal of the European Union, L 333*, 80–152.

Doshi-Velez, F., & Kim, B. (2017). Towards a rigorous science of interpretable machine learning. *arXiv preprint arXiv:1702.08608*. https://arxiv.org/abs/1702.08608

Dwivedi, Y. K.. (2023). So what if ChatGPT wrote it? Multidisciplinary perspectives on AI-generated content. *International Journal of Information Management*, *71*, 102642. DOI: 10.1016/j.ijinfomgt.2023.102642

Dwivedi, Y. K., Hughes, L., Baabdullah, A. M., Ribeiro-Navarrete, S., Giannakis, M., Al-Debei, M. M., Dennehy, D., Metri, B., Buhalis, D., Cheung, C. M. K., Conboy, K., Doyle, R., Dubey, R., Dutot, V., Felix, R., Goyal, D. P., Gustafsson, A., Hinsch, C., Jebabli, I., & Wamba, S. F. (2022). Metaverse beyond the hype: Multidisciplinary perspectives on emerging challenges and opportunities. *International Journal of Information Management*, *66*, 102542. DOI: 10.1016/j.ijinfomgt.2022.102542

Dwork, C. (2006). Differential privacy. In Bugliesi, M., Preneel, B., Sassone, V., & Wegener, I. (Eds.), *Automata, languages and programming* (pp. 1–12). Springer., DOI: 10.1007/11787006_1

Edelman. (2025, February 13). The AI Trust Imperative: Navigating the Future with Confidence. 2025 Edelman Trust Barometer. https://www.edelman.com/trust/2025/trust-barometer

Ekstrand, M. D., Burke, R., & Diaz, F. (2018). Fairness and discrimination in recommendation and retrieval. In *Proceedings of the 12th ACM Conference on Recommender Systems* (pp. 576-577). ACM. DOI: 10.1145/3240323.3240341

European Banking Authority. (2019). *Final report on EBA guidelines on outsourcing arrangements (EBA/GL/2019/02).* https://www.eba.europa.eu/regulation-and-policy/internal-governance/guidelines-on-outsourcing-arrangements

European Commission. (2024). *AI Act Service Desk—Article 50: Transparency obligations.*

European Parliament & Council of the European Union. (2016). *Regulation (EU) 2016/679 (General Data Protection Regulation).* EUR-Lex.

European Parliament & Council of the European Union. (2024). *Regulation (EU) 2024/1689 (Artificial Intelligence Act).* EUR-Lex.

European Parliament and Council. (2016). Regulation (EU) 2016/679 (General Data Protection Regulation). Official Journal of the European Union. https://eur-lex.europa.eu/eli/reg/2016/679/oj

European Parliament and Council. (2019). Directive (EU) 2019/2161 amending Directive 93/13/EEC, Directive 98/6/EC, Directive 2005/29/EC and Directive 2011/83/EU (Omnibus Directive). Official Journal of the European Union. https://eur-lex.europa.eu/eli/dir/2019/2161/oj

European Parliament and Council. (2022). Regulation (EU) 2022/2065 on a single market for digital services (Digital Services Act). Official Journal of the European Union. https://eur-lex.europa.eu/eli/reg/2022/2065/oj

European Parliament and Council. (2024). Regulation (EU) 2024/1689 laying down harmonised rules on artificial intelligence (Artificial Intelligence Act). Official Journal of the European Union. https://eur-lex.europa.eu/eli/reg/2024/1689/oj

European Supervisory Authorities. (2024). *Final report on draft regulatory technical standards specifying criteria for the identification of financial entities required to perform threat-led penetration testing and the requirements and standards governing such testing under Regulation (EU) 2022/2554 (DORA).* Publications Office of the European Union.

European Union Agency for Cybersecurity. (2025). *Technical implementation guidance on cybersecurity risk-management measures under NIS2.* Publications Office of the European Union.

Fang, Y., Wang, H., Zhao, L., Yu, F., & Wang, C. (2020). Dynamic knowledge graph based fake-review detection. *Applied Intelligence*, *50*(12), 4281–4295. DOI: 10.1007/s10489-020-01761-w

Fan, X., Xun, J., Dolega, L., & Xiong, L. (2025). The role of augmented and virtual reality in shaping retail marketing: A meta-analysis. *Sustainability (Basel)*, *17*(2), 728. DOI: 10.3390/su17020728

Federal Trade Commission v. Age of Learning, Inc., No. 2:20-cv-07996 (C.D. Cal. 2020).

Federal Trade Commission. (1983). *FTC policy statement on deception*. https://www.ftc.gov/

Federal Trade Commission. (2020). *FTC alleges ABCmouse trapped parents in subscription they couldn't cancel* (Case No. 2:20-cv-07517). https://www.ftc.gov/news-events/news/press-releases/2020/09/ftc-alleges-abcmouse-trapped-parents-subscription-they-couldnt-cancel

Federal Trade Commission. (2021). Enforcement policy statement regarding negative option marketing. https://www.ftc.gov/system/files/documents/public_statements/1599372/negative_option_policy_statement.pdf

Federal Trade Commission. (2021, May 7). *FTC finalizes settlement with Everalbum related to misuse of facial recognition technology.*

Federal Trade Commission. (2022). *Bringing dark patterns to light*. https://www.ftc.gov/reports/bringing-dark-patterns-light

Federal Trade Commission. (2023, June 21). FTC takes action against Amazon for enrolling consumers in Prime without consent and sabotaging their attempts to cancel. https://www.ftc.gov/news-events/news/press-releases/2023/06/ftc-takes-action-against-amazon-enrolling-consumers-prime-without-consent-sabotaging-their-attempts-cancel

Federal Trade Commission. (2023a). *FTC sues Amazon for enrolling consumers in Amazon Prime without consent and sabotaging their attempts to cancel* [Press release]. https://www.ftc.gov/news-events/news/press-releases/2023/06/ftc-sues-amazon-enrolling-consumers-amazon-prime-without-consent-sabotaging-their-attempts-cancel

Federal Trade Commission. (2025, September 25). FTC Secures Historic $2.5 Billion Settlement Against Amazon. https://www.ftc.gov/news-events/news/press-releases/2025/09/ftc-secures-historic-25-billion-settlement-against-amazon

Ferreira, K. J., Lee, B. H. A., & Simchi-Levi, D. (2016). Analytics for an online retailer: Demand forecasting and price optimization. *Manufacturing & Service Operations Management, 18*(1), 69–88. DOI: 10.1287/msom.2015.0561

Flavián, C., Guinalíu, M., & Gurrea, R. (2006). The role played by perceived usability, satisfaction and consumer trust on website loyalty. *Information & Management, 43*(1), 1–14. DOI: 10.1016/j.im.2005.01.002

Flavián, C., Ibáñez-Sánchez, S., & Orús, C. (2019). The impact of virtual, augmented and mixed reality technologies on the customer experience. *Journal of Business Research, 100*, 547–560. DOI: 10.1016/j.jbusres.2018.10.050

Floridi, L., Cowls, J., Beltrametti, M., Chatila, R., Chazerand, P., Dignum, V., Luetge, C., Madelin, R., Pagallo, U., Rossi, F., Schafer, B., Valcke, P., & Vayena, E. (2018). AI4People—An ethical framework for a good AI society. *Minds and Machines, 28*(4), 689–707. DOI: 10.1007/s11023-018-9482-5 PMID: 30930541

Fogg, B. J. (2003). *Persuasive technology: Using computers to change what we think and do.* Morgan Kaufmann. DOI: 10.1016/B978-155860643-2/50011-1

Fox, D., & Thornton, I. G. (2022). White Paper-The IEEE Global Initiative on Ethics of Extended Reality (XR) Report--Extended Reality (XR) Ethics and Diversity, Inclusion, and Accessibility. *The IEEE Global Initiative on Ethics of Extended Reality (XR) Report--Extended Reality (XR) Ethics and Diversity, Inclusion, and Accessibility*, 1-25.

Frankel, T. (2011). *Fiduciary law.* Oxford University Press.

Frankel, T. (2011). *Fiduciary Law.* Oxford University Press., DOI: 10.1093/acprof:oso/9780195311778.001.0001

Fredrikson, M., Jha, S., & Ristenpart, T. (2015). Model inversion attacks that exploit confidence information and basic countermeasures. *Proceedings of the 22nd ACM SIGSAC Conference on Computer and Communications Security (CCS).* https://dl.acm.org/doi/10.1145/2810103.2813677

Friedman, B., & Nissenbaum, H. (1996). Bias in computer systems. *ACM Transactions on Information Systems, 14*(3), 330–347. DOI: 10.1145/230538.230561

Fundira, M., Edoun, E. I., & Pradhan, A. (2024). Evaluating end-users' digital competencies and ethical perceptions of AI systems in the context of sustainable digital banking. *Sustainable Development (Bradford), 32*(5), 4866–4878. DOI: 10.1002/sd.2945

Gebru, T., Morgenstern, J., Vecchione, B., Vaughan, J. W., Wallach, H., Daumé III, H., & Crawford, K. (2018). Datasheets for datasets. *arXiv.*

Gefen, D., Karahanna, E., & Straub, D. W. (2003). Trust and TAM in online shopping: An integrated model. *Management Information Systems Quarterly, 27*(1), 51–90. DOI: 10.2307/30036519

General Data Protection Regulation. (2016). [EU]. *Regulation, 2016*(679).

Gerlich, M. (2024). Exploring motivators for trust in the dichotomy of human—AI trust dynamics. *Social Sciences (Basel, Switzerland), 13*(5), 251. DOI: 10.3390/socsci13050251

Ghosh, S., Ness, S., & Salunkhe, S. (2024). The role of AI enabled chatbots in omnichannel customer service. *Journal of Engineering Research and Reports, 26*(6), 327–345. DOI: 10.9734/jerr/2024/v26i61184

Gilotte, A., Calauzènes, C., Nedelec, T., Abraham, A., & Dollé, S. (2018). Offline a/b testing for recommender systems. In *Proceedings of the eleventh ACM international conference on web search and data mining* (pp. 198-206). https://doi.org/ DOI: 10.1145/3159652.3159687

Gómez-Uribe, C. A., & Hunt, N. (2016). The Netflix recommender system: Algorithms, business value, and innovation. *ACM Transactions on Management Information Systems, 6*(4), 13. DOI: 10.1145/2843948

Grand View Research. (2023). *Artificial intelligence in retail market size, share & trends analysis report.* https://www.grandviewresearch.com/industry-analysis/artificial-intelligence-ai-retail-market

Granlund, M. (2011). Extending AIS research to management accounting and control issues: A research note. *International Journal of Accounting Information Systems, 12*(1), 3–19. DOI: 10.1016/j.accinf.2010.11.001

Gray, C. M., Kou, Y., Battles, B., Hoggatt, J., & Toombs, A. L. (2018). The dark (patterns) side of UX design. *Proceedings of the 2018 CHI Conference on Human Factors in Computing Systems*, 1–14. DOI: 10.1145/3173574.3174108

Gregor, S., & Benbasat, I. (1999). Explanations from intelligent systems: Theoretical foundations and implications for practice. *Management Information Systems Quarterly, 23*(4), 497–530. DOI: 10.2307/249487

Grewal, D., Roggeveen, A. L., & Nordfält, J. (2017). The future of retailing. *Journal of Retailing, 93*(1), 1–6. DOI: 10.1016/j.jretai.2016.12.008

Grigg, I. (2017). Triple entry accounting. Financial Cryptography and Data Security, 1–15.

Gubbi, J., Buyya, R., Marusic, S., & Palaniswami, M. (2013). Internet of Things (IoT): A vision, architectural elements, and future directions. *Future Generation Computer Systems, 29*(7), 1645–1660. DOI: 10.1016/j.future.2013.01.010

Guendouz, T. (2024). Artificial intelligence-powered customer experience management (moving from mass to hyper-personalization in light of relationship marketing). [IJSR]. *International Journal of Scientific Research, 3*(6), 247–306. DOI: 10.59992/IJSR.2024.v3n6p9

Guidotti, R., Monreale, A., Ruggieri, S., Turini, F., Giannotti, F., & Pedreschi, D. (2018). A survey of methods for explaining black box models. *ACM Computing Surveys, 51*(5), 1–42. DOI: 10.1145/3236009

Gursoy, D., Malodia, S., & Dhir, A. (2022). The Metaverse in the hospitality and tourism industry: An overview of current trends and future research directions. *Journal of Hospitality Marketing & Management, 31*(5), 527–534. DOI: 10.1080/19368623.2022.2072504

Halvankar, A., Chaudhari, A., Wable, A., Barkund, P., & Patil, V. (2024). College enquiry for student using AI Chatbot. *International Scientific Journal of Engineering and Management, 3*(4), 1–6. DOI: 10.55041/ISJEM01409

Hannak, A., Soeller, G., Lazer, D., Mislove, A., & Wilson, C. (2014). Measuring price discrimination and steering on e-commerce web sites. *Proceedings of the 2014 Conference on Internet Measurement Conference (IMC)*. DOI: 10.1145/2663716.2663744

Hanson, J., Wei, M., Veys, S., Kugler, M., Strahilevitz, L., & Ur, B. (2020, April). Taking Data Out of Context to Hyper-Personalize Ads: Crowdworkers' Privacy Perceptions and Decisions to Disclose Private Information. In *Proceedings of the 2020 CHI Conference on Human Factors in Computing Systems* (pp. 1-13). https://doi.org/DOI: 10.1145/3313831.3376415

Hardt, M., Price, E., & Srebro, N. (2016). Equality of opportunity in supervised learning. *Advances in Neural Information Processing Systems (NeurIPS)*. https://arxiv.org/abs/1610.02413

Harper, F. M., & Konstan, J. A. (2015). The MovieLens datasets: History and context. *ACM Transactions on Interactive Intelligent Systems, 5*(4), 19. Advance online publication. DOI: 10.1145/2827872

Hazarika, A., & Rahmati, M. (2023). Towards an evolved immersive experience: Exploring 5G-and beyond-enabled ultra-low-latency communications for augmented and virtual reality. *Sensors (Basel)*, *23*(7), 3682. DOI: 10.3390/s23073682 PMID: 37050742

He, X., Liu, Q., & Jung, S. (2024). The Impact of Types of Recommendation System on User Satisfaction: A Moderated Mediation Analysis. *19* (1), 448-466. https://doi.org/.DOI: 10.3390/jtaer19010024

He, K., Zhang, X., Ren, S., & Sun, J. (2016). Deep residual learning for image recognition. In *Proceedings of the IEEE conference on computer vision and pattern recognition* (pp. 770-778). DOI: 10.1109/CVPR.2016.90

Heller, J., Chylinski, M., de Ruyter, K., Mahr, D., & Keeling, D. I. (2019). Let me imagine that for you: Transforming the retail frontline through augmenting customer mental imagery ability. *Journal of Retailing*, *95*(2), 94–114. DOI: 10.1016/j.jretai.2019.03.005

Henderson, M., Thomson, B., & Young, S. (2013). Deep neural network approach for the dialog state tracking challenge. In *Proceedings of the SIGDIAL 2013 Conference* (pp. 467-471). Association for Computational Linguistics.

Henry, S. L., Abou-Zahra, S., & Brewer, J. (2014). The role of accessibility in a universal web. In *Proceedings of the 11th Web for all Conference* (pp. 1-4). https://doi.org/DOI: 10.1145/2596695.2596719

He, R., & McAuley, J. (2016). Ups and downs: Modeling the visual evolution of fashion trends with one-class collaborative filtering. In *Proceedings of the 25th International Conference on World Wide Web* (pp. 507-517). International World Wide Web Conferences Steering Committee. DOI: 10.1145/2872427.2883037

Herlocker, J. L., Konstan, J. A., & Riedl, J. (2000). Explaining collaborative filtering recommendations. In *Proceedings of the 2000 ACM Conference on Computer Supported Cooperative Work* (pp. 241–250). Association for Computing Machinery. DOI: 10.1145/358916.358995

He, X., Liao, L., Zhang, H., Nie, L., Hu, X., & Chua, T. S. (2017). Neural collaborative filtering. In *Proceedings of the 26th International Conference on World Wide Web* (pp. 173-182). International World Wide Web Conferences Steering Committee. DOI: 10.1145/3038912.3052569

Hidasi, B., Karatzoglou, A., Baltrunas, L., & Tikk, D. (2016). Session-based recommendations with recurrent neural networks. In Proceedings of the International Conference on Learning Representations. ICLR.

Hoyer, W. D., Kroschke, M., Schmitt, B., Kraume, K., & Shankar, V. (2020). Transforming the customer experience through new technologies. *Journal of Interactive Marketing, 51*(1), 57–71. DOI: 10.1016/j.intmar.2020.04.001

Huang, C. Z. A., Vaswani, A., Uszkoreit, J., Shazeer, N., Simon, I., Hawthorne, C., Dai, A. M., Hoffman, M. D., Dinculescu, M., & Eck, D. (2021). Music Transformer: Generating music with long-term structure. In Proceedings of the International Conference on Learning Representations. ICLR.

Huang, M.-H., & Rust, R. T. (2018). Artificial intelligence in service. *Journal of Service Research, 21*(2), 155–172. DOI: 10.1177/1094670517752459

Huang, M.-H., & Rust, R. T. (2021). A strategic framework for artificial intelligence in marketing. *Journal of the Academy of Marketing Science, 49*(1), 30–50. DOI: 10.1007/s11747-020-00749-9

Huang, Z., Liu, H., Zhu, J., & Min, J. (2023). Customer Sentiment Recognition in Conversation Based on Contextual Semantic and Affective Interaction Information. *Applied Sciences (Basel, Switzerland), 13*(13), 7807. DOI: 10.3390/app13137807

Hufnagel, G., Schwaiger, M., & Weritz, L. (2022). Seeking the perfect price: Consumer responses to personalized price discrimination in e-commerce. *Journal of Business Research, 143*, 346–365. DOI: 10.1016/j.jbusres.2021.10.002

Hutchinson, T., & Duncan, N. (2012). Defining and describing what we do: Doctrinal legal research. *Deakin Law Review, 17*(1), 83–119. DOI: 10.21153/dlr2012vol17no1art70

IBM. (2021). Pandora Boosts Online Sales by Transforming Its Global Omnichannel e-Commerce with IBM Sterling Supply Chain Software. *IBM Institute for Business Value*. https://newsroom.ibm.com/2021-06-21-Pandora-Boosts-Online-Sales-by-Transforming-Its-Global-Omnichannel-e-Commerce-with-IBM-Sterling-Supply-Chain-Software [Access 26 November 2025].

Information Commissioner's Office (ICO). (2020). *Explaining decisions made with AI (ICO and Alan Turing Institute guidance).*

International Organization for Standardization/International Electrotechnical Commission. (2023). *ISO/IEC 42001:2023 Information technology Artificial intelligence Management system*. ISO.

ISO. (2023a). *ISO/IEC 42001:2023—Artificial intelligence management systems.*

ISO. (2023b). *ISO/IEC 27001:2022—Information security management systems (overview).* https://www.iso.org/isoiec-27001-information-security.html

Ivanov, D., Dolgui, A., & Sokolov, B. (2019). The impact of digital technology and Industry 4.0 on the ripple effect and supply chain risk analytics. *International Journal of Production Research, 57*(3), 829–846. DOI: 10.1080/00207543.2018.1488086

Izacard, G., & Grave, E. (2021). Leveraging passage retrieval with generative models for open domain question answering. In *Proceedings of the 16th conference of the european chapter of the association for computational linguistics: main volume* (pp. 874-880). DOI: 10.18653/v1/2021.eacl-main.74

Jafar, R. M. S., Jabeen, M., Hussain, S., Niu, B., Sham, R., & Al-Adwan, A. S. (2025). Cyber shopping beyond boundaries: The metaverse revolution in e-commerce and consumer behavior.

Jafar, R. M. S., Jabeen, M., Hussain, S., Niu, B., Sham, R., & Al-Adwan, A. S. (2025). Cyber Shopping Beyond Boundaries: The Metaverse Revolution in e-Commerce and Consumer Behavior. *Human Behavior and Emerging Technologies, 5559234*(1), 5559234. Advance online publication. DOI: 10.1155/hbe2/5559234

Jain, P. K., Pamula, R., & Srivastava, G. (2021). A systematic literature review on machine learning applications for consumer sentiment analysis using online reviews. *Computer Science Review, 41*, 100413. DOI: 10.1016/j.cosrev.2021.100413

Jobin, A., Ienca, M., & Vayena, E. (2019). The global landscape of AI ethics guidelines. *Nature Machine Intelligence, 1*(9), 389–399. DOI: 10.1038/s42256-019-0088-2

Jokela, T., Ojala, J., & Olsson, T. (2015). A diary study on combining multiple information devices in everyday activities and tasks. In *Proceedings of the 33rd Annual ACM Conference on Human Factors in Computing Systems* (pp. 3903-3912). Association for Computing Machinery. DOI: 10.1145/2702123.2702211

Joshi, H.Maysara Mazin Badr Alsaad. (2024). Transformer-Based Language Deep Learning Detection of Fake Reviews on Online Products. *J. Electrical Systems, 20*(3), 2368–2378. DOI: 10.52783/jes.4083

Josimovski, S., Ivanovska, L. P., & Dodevski, D. (2023). Understanding the consumer dynamics of AI in North Macedonian e-business. *Economics and Culture, 20*(2), 64–75. DOI: 10.2478/jec-2023-0016

Justice K.S. Puttaswamy (Retd.) v. Union of India, (2017) 10 SCC 1 (India).

Kahneman, D. (2011). *Thinking, Fast and Slow*. Farrar, Straus and Giroux.

Kahneman, D., Knetsch, J. L., & Thaler, R. (1986). Fairness as a constraint on profit seeking: Entitlements in the market. *The American Economic Review, 76*(4), 728–741.

Kahneman, D., & Tversky, A. (1979). Prospect theory: An analysis of decision under risk. *Econometrica, 47*(2), 263–291. DOI: 10.2307/1914185

Kairouz, P., et al. (2021). Advances and open problems in federated learning. *Foundations and Trends® in Machine Learning, 14*(1–2), 1–210. DOI: 10.1561/2200000083

Kanazawa, A., Black, M. J., Jacobs, D. W., & Malik, J. (2018). End-to-end recovery of human shape and pose. In *Proceedings of the IEEE Conference on Computer Vision and Pattern Recognition* (pp. 7122-7131). IEEE. DOI: 10.1109/CVPR.2018.00744

Kang, W. C., & McAuley, J. (2018). Self-attentive sequential recommendation. In *2018 IEEE international conference on data mining (ICDM)* (pp. 197-206). IEEE. DOI: 10.1109/ICDM.2018.00035

Kant, I. (1997). *Groundwork of the metaphysics of morals* (Gregor, M., Trans.). Cambridge University Press. (Original work published 1785)

Kasem, M. S., Hamada, M., & Taj-Eddin, I. (2024). Customer profiling, segmentation, and sales prediction using AI in direct marketing. *Neural Computing & Applications, 36*(9), 4995–5005. DOI: 10.1007/s00521-023-09339-6

Kelly, J.III, & Hamm, S. (2013). *Smart machines: Ibmos watson and the era of cognitive computing*. Columbia University Press., Available from https://cup.columbia.edu/book/smart-machines/9780231537278/ DOI: 10.7312/kell16856

Khan, L. M., & Pozen, D. E. (2019). A skeptical view of information fiduciaries. *Harvard Law Review, 133*(2), 497–541. https://harvardlawreview.org/print/vol-133/a-skeptical-view-of-information-fiduciaries/

Kim, I., & Lee, U. (2024, May). Navigating user-system gaps: understanding user-interactions in user-centric context-aware systems for digital well-being intervention. In *Proceedings of the 2024 CHI Conference on Human Factors in Computing Systems* (pp. 1-15). https://doi.org/DOI: 10.1145/3613904.3641979

Kim, N., & Lee, H. (2021). Assessing consumer attention and arousal using eye-tracking technology in a virtual retail environment. *Frontiers in Psychology, 12*, 665658. DOI: 10.3389/fpsyg.2021.665658 PMID: 34434136

Kindervag, J. (2016). No more chewy centers: Introducing the zero trust model of information security. *Forrester Research, 3*(1), 1-16. Available from https://crystaltechnologies.com/wp-content/uploads/2017/12/forrester-zero-trust-model-information-security.pdf

Kobsa, A. (2001). Generic user modeling systems. *User Modeling and User-Adapted Interaction, 11*(1-2), 49–63. DOI: 10.1023/A:1011187500863

Kohavi, R., Tang, D., & Xu, Y. (2020). *Trustworthy online controlled experiments: A practical guide to a/b testing*. Cambridge University Press., DOI: 10.1017/9781108653985

Kokina, J., & Davenport, T. H. (2017). The emergence of artificial intelligence: How automation is changing auditing. *Journal of Emerging Technologies in Accounting*, *14*(1), 115–122. DOI: 10.2308/jeta-51730

Kokolakis, S. (2017). Privacy attitudes and privacy behaviour: A review of current research on the privacy paradox phenomenon. *Computers & Security*, *64*, 122–134. DOI: 10.1016/j.cose.2015.07.002

Koren, Y., Bell, R., & Volinsky, C. (2009). Matrix factorization techniques for recommender systems. *Computer*, *42*(8), 30–37. DOI: 10.1109/MC.2009.263

Korkmaz, İ. (2024). Yapay zekâya yönelik tutum, kolaylık, gelişmişlik ve güvenin satın alma niyeti üzerine etkisi. İktisadi ve İdari Bilimler Fakültesi Dergisi. 26(2), 318-339. https://doi.org/.DOI: 10.33707/akuiibfd.1522892

Krafft, M., Gouthier, M. H. J., & Mantrala, M. K. (2023). Artificial intelligence in retailing. *Journal of Retailing*, *99*(2), 156–171.

Kranacher, M., Riley, R., & Wells, J. (2019). *Forensic accounting and fraud examination* (2nd ed.). Wiley.

Kroll, J. A. (2017). Accountable algorithms. *University of Pennsylvania Law Review*, *165*(3), 633–705.

Krugmann, J. O., & Hartmann, J. (2024). Sentiment Analysis in the Age of Generative AI. *Customer Needs and Solutions*, *11*(3), 3. DOI: 10.1007/s40547-024-00143-4

Kshetri, N. (2023). Artificial intelligence in cybersecurity: Opportunities and challenges in the banking sector. *Annals of Operations Research*, *313*(1), 1–22. DOI: 10.1007/s10479-023-05281-5 PMID: 36743349

Kuflik, T., Stock, O., Zancanaro, M., Gorfinkel, A., Jbara, S., Kats, S., Sheidin, J., & Kashtan, N. (2017). A visitor's guide in an "active" museum: Presentations, communications, and reflection. *ACM Journal on Computing and Cultural Heritage*, *3*(3), 11. Advance online publication. DOI: 10.1145/1921614.1921618

Kulik, J. A., & Fletcher, J. D. (2016). Effectiveness of intelligent tutoring systems: A meta-analytic review. *Review of Educational Research*, *86*(1), 42–78. DOI: 10.3102/0034654315581420

Kumar, L., Verma, S., Srivastava, R., & Bharti, B. (2025). Does presence matter? Impact of telepresence and social presence on purchase intention from VR shopping sites: Empirical examination. *International Journal of Business and Systems Research, 19*(3), 247–270. DOI: 10.1504/IJBSR.2025.147566

Laird, J. E. (2019). *The Soar cognitive architecture.* MIT press. Available from https://www.amazon.com/Soar-Cognitive-Architecture-MIT-Press/dp/0262538539

Ledro, C., Nosella, A., & Vinelli, A. (2022). Artificial intelligence in customer relationship management: Literature review and future research directions. *Journal of Business and Industrial Marketing, 37*(13), 48–63. DOI: 10.1108/JBIM-07-2021-0332

Lee, L. H., Braud, T., Zhou, P., Wang, L., Xu, D., Lin, Z., Kumar, A., Bermejo, C., & Hui, P. (2021). All one needs to know about Metaverse: A complete survey on technological singularity, virtual ecosystem, and research agenda. arXiv preprint arXiv:2110.05352.

Lee, J. D., & See, K. A. (2004). Trust in automation: Designing for appropriate reliance. *Human Factors, 46*(1), 50–80. DOI: 10.1518/hfes.46.1.50.30392 PMID: 15151155

Lemon, K. N., & Verhoef, P. C. (2016). Understanding customer experience throughout the customer journey. *Journal of Marketing, 80*(6), 69–96. DOI: 10.1509/jm.15.0420

Leonard, T. C. (2008). Richard H. Thaler, Cass R. Sunstein, Nudge: Improving Decisions about Health, Wealth, and Happiness: Yale University Press, New Haven, CT, 2008, 293 pp, $26.00.

Lewis, P., Perez, E., Piktus, A., Petroni, F., Karpukhin, V., Goyal, N., . . . Kiela, D. (2020). Retrieval-augmented generation for knowledge-intensive nlp tasks. *Advances in neural information processing systems, 33*, 9459-9474. Available from https://proceedings.neurips.cc/paper_files/paper/2020/file/6b493230205f780e1bc269 45df7481e5-Paper.pdf

Li, J., Li, D., Savarese, S., & Hoi, S. (2023). Blip-2: Bootstrapping language-image pre-training with frozen image encoders and large language models. In *International conference on machine learning* (pp. 19730-19742). PMLR. Available from https://proceedings.mlr.press/v202/li23q/li23q.pdf

Libai, B., Bart, Y., Gensler, S., Hofacker, C. F., Kaplan, A., Kötterheinrich, K., & Kroll, E. B. (2020). Brave new world? On AI and the management of customer relationships. *Journal of Interactive Marketing, 51*(1), 44–56. DOI: 10.1016/j.intmar.2020.04.002

Li, J., Ren, P., Chen, Z., Ren, Z., Lian, T., & Ma, J. (2020). Neural attentive session-based recommendation. In *Proceedings of the 2020 ACM SIGKDD International Conference on Knowledge Discovery & Data Mining* (pp. 1419-1428). Association for Computing Machinery. DOI: 10.1145/3132847.3132926

Lipton, A., Sardon, A., Schär, F., & Schüpbach, C. (2020). *11. Stablecoins, digital currency, and the future of money*. Building the New Economy.

Liu, Z., Luo, P., Qiu, S., Wang, X., & Tang, X. (2020). DeepFashion: Powering robust clothes recognition and retrieval with rich annotations. In *Proceedings of the IEEE Conference on Computer Vision and Pattern Recognition* (pp. 1096-1104). IEEE.

Lough, G. (n.d.). Agentic commerce: Promise, paradox and the path forward. Worldpay. https://worldpay.global/resources/articles/agentic-commerce-paradox-and-promise

Luguri, J., & Strahilevitz, L. J. (2021). Shining a light on dark patterns. *The Journal of Legal Analysis*, *13*(1), 43–109. DOI: 10.1093/jla/laaa006

Lundberg, S. M., & Lee, S.-I. (2017). A unified approach to interpreting model predictions. In Advances in Neural Information Processing Systems (Vol. 30).

Luo, B., Lau, R. Y., Li, C., & Si, Y. W. (2022). A critical review of state-of-the-art chatbot designs and applications. *Wiley Interdisciplinary Reviews. Data Mining and Knowledge Discovery*, *12*(1), e1434. DOI: 10.1002/widm.1434

Luo, X., Tong, S., Fang, Z., & Qu, Z. (2019). Machines vs. humans: The impact of artificial intelligence chatbot disclosure on customer purchases. *Marketing Science*, *38*(6), 937–947. DOI: 10.1287/mksc.2019.1192

Lv, H. (2023). E-commerce consumer behavior analysis based on big data. *Journal of Computational Methods in Science and Engineering*, *23*(2), 651–661. DOI: 10.3233/JCM-226628

Madary, M., & Metzinger, T. K. (2016). Real virtuality: A code of ethical conduct. Recommendations for good scientific practice and the consumers of VR-technology. *Frontiers in Robotics and AI*, *3*, 180932. DOI: 10.3389/frobt.2016.00003

Masadeh, R., Almomani, O., Zaqebah, A., Masadeh, S., Alshqurat, K., Sharieh, A., & Alsharman, N. (2025). Narwhal Optimizer: A Nature-Inspired Optimization Algorithm for Solving Complex Optimization Problems. *Computers, Materials & Continua*, *85*(2), 3709–3737. DOI: 10.32604/cmc.2025.066797

Mathur, A., Acar, G., Friedman, M. J., Lucherini, E., Mayer, J., Chetty, M., & Narayanan, A. (2019). Dark patterns at scale: Findings from a crawl of 11K shopping websites. *Proceedings of the ACM on human-computer interaction, 3*(CSCW), 1-32. https://doi.org/DOI: 10.1145/3359183

Mayer, R. C., Davis, J. H., & Schoorman, F. D. (1995). An integrative model of organizational trust. *Academy of Management Review, 20*(3), 709–734. DOI: 10.2307/258792

McAuley, J. (2015). *Amazon review data*. UC San Diego.

McKnight, D. H., Choudhury, V., & Kacmar, C. (2002). Developing and validating trust measures for e-commerce: An integrative typology. *Information Systems Research, 13*(3), 334–359. DOI: 10.1287/isre.13.3.334.81

McMahan, B., Moore, E., Ramage, D., Hampson, S., & Arcas, B. A. (2017). Communication-efficient learning of deep networks from decentralized data. In *Proceedings of the 20th International Conference on Artificial Intelligence and Statistics* (pp. 1273-1282). PMLR.

McMahan, H. B., Moore, E., Ramage, D., Hampson, S., & Arcas, B. A. (2017). Communication-efficient learning of deep networks from decentralized data. *Proceedings of AISTATS*. https://arxiv.org/abs/1602.05629

McSherry, F., & Mironov, I. (2009). Differentially private recommender systems: Building privacy into the Netflix prize contenders. In *Proceedings of the 15th ACM SIGKDD International Conference on Knowledge Discovery and Data Mining* (pp. 627-636). Association for Computing Machinery. DOI: 10.1145/1557019.1557090

Mehrabi, N., Morstatter, F., Saxena, N., Lerman, K., & Galstyan, A. (2021). A survey on bias and fairness in machine learning. *ACM Computing Surveys, 54*(6), 1–35. DOI: 10.1145/3457607

Mei, Z. (2025). Dynamic Pricing Strategy Driven by Deep Reinforcement Learning with Empirical Analysis on the Collaborative Optimization of Hotel Revenue Management and Customer Satisfaction. *International Journal of High Speed Electronics and Systems, 2540865*, 2540865. Advance online publication. DOI: 10.1142/S0129156425408654

Meng, K., Mahapatra, M. S., & Xiao, J. J. (2025). Artificial Intelligence and Consumer Financial Behavior: A Systematic Literature Review and Agenda for Future Research. *Journal of Consumer Behaviour, 24*(4), 1755–1786. Advance online publication. DOI: 10.1002/cb.2497

Mikians, J., Gyarmati, L., Erramilli, V., & Laoutaris, N. (2012). Detecting price and search discrimination on the internet. *Proceedings of HotNets.*

Mikians, J., Gyarmati, L., Erramilli, V., & Laoutaris, N. (2012). Detecting price and search discrimination on the Internet. In *Proceedings of the 11th ACM Workshop on Hot Topics in Networks* (pp. 79–84). Association for Computing Machinery. DOI: 10.1145/2390231.2390245

Miller, T. (2019). Explanation in artificial intelligence: Insights from the social sciences. *Artificial Intelligence*, *267*, 1–38. DOI: 10.1016/j.artint.2018.07.007

Min, H. (2010). Artificial intelligence in supply chain management: Theory and applications. *International Journal of Logistics*, *13*(1), 13–39. DOI: 10.1080/13675560902736537

Mirabelli, G., & Solina, V. (2020). Blockchain and agricultural supply chains traceability: Research trends and future challenges. *Procedia Manufacturing*, *42*, 414–421. DOI: 10.1016/j.promfg.2020.02.054

Mishra, M. K., Vyas, C., Mazumdar, B. D., & Mishra, V. (2025). Harnessing the Power of Machine Learning in Multi-Agent Systems for B2C E-Commerce Optimization. In *2025 3rd International Conference on Communication, Security, and Artificial Intelligence (ICCSAI)* (Vol. 3, pp. 2157-2161). IEEE. DOI: 10.1109/ICCSAI64074.2025.11064164

Mitchell, M., Wu, S., Zaldivar, A., Barnes, P., Vasserman, L., Hutchinson, B., Spitzer, E., Raji, I. D., & Gebru, T. (2019). Model cards for model reporting. *Proceedings of the Conference on Fairness, Accountability, and Transparency (FAT*)*. DOI: 10.1145/3287560.3287596

Mittelstadt, B. D., Allo, P., Taddeo, M., Wachter, S., & Floridi, L. (2016). The ethics of algorithms: Mapping the debate. *Big Data & Society*, *3*(2), 2053951716679679. Advance online publication. DOI: 10.1177/2053951716679679

Mnih, V., Kavukcuoglu, K., Silver, D., Rusu, A. A., Veness, J., Bellemare, M. G., ... & Hassabis, D. (2015). Human-level control through deep reinforcement learning. *nature, 518*(7540), 529-533. https://doi.org/DOI: 10.1038/nature14236

Moloney, N. (2024). EU financial regulation after DORA: Operational resilience, outsourcing, and supervisory accountability. *European Business Law Review*, *35*(2), 189–215.

Montag, C., Lachmann, B., Herrlich, M., & Zweig, K. (2019). Addictive features of social media/messenger platforms and freemium games against the background of psychological and economic theories. *International Journal of Environmental Research and Public Health, 16*(14), 2612. Advance online publication. DOI: 10.3390/ijerph16142612 PMID: 31340426

Mystakidis, S. (2022). Metaverse. *Metaverse. Encyclopedia*, *2*(1), 486–497. DOI: 10.3390/encyclopedia2010031

Nachum, O., Gu, S. S., Lee, H., & Levine, S. (2018). Data-efficient hierarchical reinforcement learning. *Advances in neural information processing systems, 31.* Available from https://papers.nips.cc/paper_files/paper/2018/file/e6384711491713d29bc63fc5eeb5ba4f-Paper.pdf

Nakamoto, S. (2008). Bitcoin: A peer-to-peer electronic cash system. https://bitcoin.org/bitcoin.pdf

Narayanan, A., Bonneau, J., Felten, E., Miller, A., & Goldfeder, S. (2016). *Bitcoin and cryptocurrency technologies*. Princeton University Press.

National Institute of Standards and Technology. (2023). Artificial intelligence risk management framework (AI RMF 1.0). U.S. Department of Commerce. https://nvlpubs.nist.gov/nistpubs/ai/NIST.AI.100-1.pdf

Nicolescu, L., & Tudorache, M. T. (2022). Human-computer interaction in customer service: The experience with AI chatbots—a systematic literature review. *Electronics (Basel), 11*(10), 1579. DOI: 10.3390/electronics11101579

Ni, J., Li, J., & McAuley, J. (2019). Justifying recommendations using distantly-labeled reviews and fine-grained aspects. In *Proceedings of the 2019 conference on empirical methods in natural language processing and the 9th international joint conference on natural language processing (EMNLP-IJCNLP)* (pp. 188-197). DOI: 10.18653/v1/D19-1018

Nike. (2022). Nike digital transformation and Web3 initiatives. Nike Innovation Report. https://static1.squarespace.com/static/6628939a6a82e57838e96216/t/6667a427c569856c5f602257/1718068266225/Nike+Innovation+Report.pdf [Access 27 November 2025].

Ning, H., Wang, H., Lin, Y., Wang, W., Dhelim, S., Farha, F., Ding, J., & Daneshmand, M. (2023). A survey on the Metaverse: The state-of-the-art, technologies, applications, and challenges. *IEEE Internet of Things Journal, 10*(16), 14671–14688. DOI: 10.1109/JIOT.2023.3278329

Nissenbaum, H. (2010). *Privacy in context: Technology, policy, and the integrity of social life*. Stanford University Press.

NIST. (2020). *NIST Privacy Framework (PF) 1.0*. National Institute of Standards and Technology.

NIST. (2023). *Artificial Intelligence Risk Management Framework (AI RMF 1.0)*. National Institute of Standards and Technology.

Norberg, P. A., Horne, D. R., & Horne, D. A. (2007). The privacy paradox: Personal information disclosure intentions versus behaviors. *The Journal of Consumer Affairs*, *41*(1), 100–126. DOI: 10.1111/j.1745-6606.2006.00070.x

Nouwens, M., Liccardi, I., Veale, M., Karger, D., & Kagal, L. (2020). Dark patterns after the GDPR: Scraping consent pop-ups and demonstrating their influence. In *Proceedings of the 2020 CHI Conference on Human Factors in Computing Systems* (pp. 1–13). Association for Computing Machinery. DOI: 10.1145/3313831.3376321

Nsaif, W. S., Salih, H. M., Saleh, H. H., & Al-nuaim, B. T. (2024). Conversational agents: An exploration into Chatbot evolution, architecture, and important techniques. *The Eurasia Proceedings of Science Technology Engineering and Mathematics*, *27*, 246–262. DOI: 10.55549/epstem.1518795

O'Leary, D. E. (2019). Configuring blockchain architectures for accounting and e-business. *Intelligent Systems in Accounting, Finance & Management*, *26*(1), 5–12.

Obar, J. A., & Oeldorf-Hirsch, A. (2020). The biggest lie on the internet: Ignoring the privacy policies and terms of service policies of social networking services. *Information Communication and Society*, *23*(1), 128–147. DOI: 10.1080/1369118X.2018.1486870

Odlyzko, A. (2003). Privacy, economics, and price discrimination on the Internet. In *Proceedings of the 5th International Conference on Electronic Commerce* (pp. 355–366). Association for Computing Machinery. DOI: 10.1145/948005.948051

Organisation for Economic Co-operation and Development. (2016). *Consumer protection in e-commerce: OECD recommendation*. OECD Publishing., DOI: 10.1787/9789264255258-

Organisation for Economic Co-operation and Development. (2019). OECD recommendation of the Council on artificial intelligence. https://legalinstruments.oecd.org/en/instruments/OECD-LEGAL-0449

OWASP. (2023). *OWASP Top 10 for Large Language Model Applications (v1.0.1)*.

Oyekunle, D., Matthew, U. O., Preston, D., & Boohene, D. (2024). Trust beyond Technology Algorithms: A Theoretical Exploration of Consumer Trust and Behavior in Technological Consumption and AI Projects. *Journal of Computer and Communications, 12*(6), 72–102. DOI: 10.4236/jcc.2024.126006

Özyirmidokuz, E. K., Elmas, B. M., & Stoica, E. A. (2025). AI-Based Sentiment Analysis of E-Commerce Customer Feedback: A Bilingual Parallel Study on the Fast Food Industry in Turkish and English. *Journal of Theoretical and Applied Electronic Commerce Research, 20*(4), 294. DOI: 10.3390/jtaer20040294

Palanikumar, G., Pandi, V. S., Banumathi, S., Karthikeyan, G., Giri, J., & Al-Safarini, M. Y. (2025). Leveraging Augmented and Virtual Reality in Conjunction with Artificial Intelligence, 5G, and Edge Computing to Transform Immersive Experiences. In *2025 Fourth International Conference on Smart Technologies, Communication and Robotics (STCR)* (pp. 1-6). IEEE.

Park, J. S., O'Brien, J., Cai, C. J., Morris, M. R., Liang, P., & Bernstein, M. S. (2023). Generative agents: Interactive simulacra of human behavior. In *Proceedings of the 36th annual acm symposium on user interface software and technology* (pp. 1-22). https://doi.org/DOI: 10.1145/3586183.3606763

Park, S., & Kim, S. (2022). Identifying world types in the metaverse and their effects on consumers. *Journal of Business Research, 152*, 453–468. DOI: 10.1016/j.jbusres.2022.08.009

Patil, N. (2022). Adoptıon Of Chatbot In Tourısm. *International Research Journal of Modernization in Engineering Technology and Science, 4*(9), 1306–1308. DOI: 10.56726/IRJMETS30043

Pelletier, C., & Rexhepi, V. (2024). Cyber risk governance and liability in financial services: Regulatory duties and third-party oversight. *Journal of Business Research, 162*, 113842. DOI: 10.1016/j.jbusres.2023.113842

Pendyala, M. K., & Lakkamraju, V. V. (2024). Impact of artificial intelligence in customer journey. [IJISRT]. *International Journal of Innovative Science and Research Technology, 9*(8), 1528–1534. DOI: 10.38124/ijisrt/IJISRT24AUG807

Peng, L., & Zhang, X. (2024). Research on the Influence of AI Application on Business Decision Making Based on Machine Learning Algorithm. In *Proceedings of the 4th International Conference on Economic Management and Big Data Applications, ICEMBDA, October 27–29, Tianjin, China*. 27-29. https://doi.org/DOI: 10.4108/eai.27-10-2023.2341918

Peruchini, M., da Silva, G. M., & Teixeira, J. M. (2024). Between artificial intelligence and customer experience: A literature review on the intersection. *Discover Artificial Intelligence*, *4*(1), 4. DOI: 10.1007/s44163-024-00105-8

Petersen, N., & Stricker, D. (2015). Cognitive augmented reality. *Computers & Graphics*, *53*, 82–91. DOI: 10.1016/j.cag.2015.08.009

Peters, G. W., & Panayi, E. (2016). Understanding modern banking ledgers through blockchain technologies. In Lee, D. (Ed.), *Handbook of digital currency* (pp. 239–278). Academic Press.

Pfeuffer, K., Mayer, S., Mardanbegi, D., & Gellersen, H. (2019). Behavioural biometrics in VR: Identifying users from motion and interaction. *Proceedings of CHI.* DOI: 10.1007/978-3-658-22050-1

Piasecki, M., & Hanna, S. (2011). A redefinition of the paradox of choice. In *Design Computing and Cognition'10* (pp. 347–366). Springer Netherlands., DOI: 10.1007/978-94-007-0510-4_19

Pillai, R., Sivathanu, B., & Rana, N. P. (2025). Unveiling virtual interactive marketplaces: Shopping motivations in the Metaverse through the lens of uses and gratifications theory. *Journal of Business Research*, *190*, 115219. DOI: 10.1016/j.jbusres.2025.115219

Potla, R. T., & Pottla, V. K. (2024). Artificial intelligence and machine learning in CRM: Leveraging data for predictive analytics. *Journal of Artificial Intelligence Research*, *4*(2), 31–50.

Prasetya, D., Utami, I. I. B., & Pertiwi, S. (2025). From Static To Sentient: Designing Emotionally Responsive Interfaces Using Affective Computing For UX Enhancement. *International Journal of Graphic Design*, *3*(1), 120–136. DOI: 10.51903/ijgd.v3i1.2811

PricewaterhouseCoopers. (2024). Voice of the consumer survey 2024. PwC. https://www.pwc.com/gx/en/services/consumer-markets/consumer-insights.html

PwC. (2025). Why the future of customer experience demands the experience supply chain. *PwC Research.* https://www.pwc.com/us/en/services/consulting/business-transformation/future-customer-experience-is-supply-chain.html [Access 30 November 2025].

Radford, A., Kim, J. W., Hallacy, C., Ramesh, A., Goh, G., Agarwal, S., . . . Sutskever, I. (2021). Learning transferable visual models from natural language supervision. In *International conference on machine learning* (pp. 8748-8763). PmLR. Available from https://proceedings.mlr.press/v139/radford21a.html.

Radford, A., Kim, J. W., Hallacy, C., Ramesh, A., Goh, G., Agarwal, S., & Sutskever, I. (2021). Learning transferable visual models from natural language supervision. In *International conference on machine learning* (pp. 8748-8763). PmLR.

Raghavan, S. (2024). Ethical considerations in customer engagement: Balancing profitability with consumer trust. *International Journal of Research Publication and Reviews*, *5*(3), 6418–6427. DOI: 10.55248/gengpi.5.0324.0873

Rahman, M., & Dey, B. L. (2024). AI-powered personalization and consumer trust in e-commerce. *Journal of Retailing and Consumer Services*, *76*, 103579.

Raj, A., Sangkloy, P., Chang, H., Hays, J., Ceylan, D., & Lu, J. (2021). SwapNet: Image based garment transfer. In *Proceedings of the European Conference on Computer Vision* (pp. 679-695). Springer. DOI: 10.1007/978-3-030-01225-0_41

Raji, I. D., Smart, A., White, R. N., Mitchell, M., Gebru, T., Hutchinson, B., Smith-Loud, J., Theron, D., & Barnes, P. (2020). Closing the AI accountability gap: Defining an end-to-end framework for internal algorithmic auditing. In *Proceedings of the 2020 Conference on Fairness, Accountability, and Transparency* (pp. 33–44). Association for Computing Machinery. DOI: 10.1145/3351095.3372873

Ralston, K., Chen, Y., Isah, H., & Zulkernine, F. (2019). A voice interactive multilingual student support system using IBM Watson. In 2019 18th IEEE International Conference On Machine Learning And Applications (ICMLA). 1924-1929. IEEE. DOI: 10.1109/ICMLA.2019.00309

Ramu, S. P., Boopalan, P., Pham, Q. V., Maddikunta, P. K. R., Huynh-The, T., Alazab, M., Nguyen, T. T., & Gadekallu, T. R. (2022). Federated learning enabled digital twins for smart cities: Concepts, recent advances, and future directions. *Sustainable Cities and Society*, *79*, 103663. DOI: 10.1016/j.scs.2021.103663

Ranieri, A., Di Bernardo, I., & Mele, C. (2024). Serving customers through chatbots: Positive and negative effects on customer experience. *Journal of Service Theory and Practice*, *34*(2), 191–215. DOI: 10.1108/JSTP-01-2023-0015

Rapa, M., Ciano, S., Orsini, F., Tullo, M. G., Giannetti, V., & Boccacci Mariani, M. (2023). Adoption of AI-based technologies in the food supplement industry: An Italian Start-Up case study. *Systems*, *11*(6), 265. DOI: 10.3390/systems11060265

Rau, P. L. P., Lei, X., Marcus, A., & Rosenzweig, E. (2024). Cross-cultural design. In *Designing for Usability, Inclusion and Sustainability in Human-Computer Interaction* (pp. 461-490). CRC Press.

REES46 Marketing Platform. (2019). E-commerce behavior datasets. https://rees46.com/en/datasets

Regulation (EU) 2016/679 of the European Parliament and of the Council of 27 April 2016 on the protection of natural persons with regard to the processing of personal data and on the free movement of such data (General Data Protection Regulation). (2016). *Official Journal of the European Union, L 119*, 1–88.

Regulation (EU) 2016/679 of the European Parliament and of the Council of 27 April 2016 on the protection of natural persons with regard to the processing of personal data and on the free movement of such data (General Data Protection Regulation). (2016). *Official Journal of the European Union, L 119*, 1–88. http://data.europa.eu/eli/reg/2016/679/oj Regulation (EU) 2022/2065 of the European Parliament and of the Council on a Single Market For Digital Services (Digital Services Act) (2022).

Regulation (EU) 2022/2554 of the European Parliament and of the Council of 14 December 2022 on digital operational resilience for the financial sector and amending Regulations (EC) No 1060/2009, (EU) No 648/2012, (EU) No 600/2014, (EU) No 909/2014 and (EU) 2016/1011 (Digital Operational Resilience Act). (2022). *Official Journal of the European Union, L 333*, 1–79.

Regulation (EU) 2024/1689 of the European Parliament and of the Council on laying down harmonised rules on artificial intelligence (Artificial Intelligence Act). (2024). *Official Journal of the European Union, L 2024/1689*. https://data.europa.eu/eli/reg/2024/1689/oj

Rejeb, A., Keogh, J. G., Wamba, S. F., & Treiblmaier, H. (2021). The potentials of augmented reality in supply chain management: A state-of-the-art review. *Management review quarterly, 71*(4), 819-856.

Resnick, P., Iacovou, N., Suchak, M., Bergstrom, P., & Riedl, J. (1994). Grouplens: An open architecture for collaborative filtering of netnews. In *Proceedings of the 1994 ACM conference on Computer supported cooperative work* (pp. 175-186). https://doi.org/DOI: 10.1145/192844.192905

Retailrocket. (n.d.). Retailrocket recommender system dataset [Data set]. Kaggle. https://www.kaggle.com/datasets/retailrocket/ecommerce-dataset

Reuters. (2025, July 8). US 'click to cancel' rule blocked by appeals court. Reuters. https://www.reuters.com/legal/legalindustry/us-click-cancel-rule-blocked-by-appeals-court-2025-07-08/

Rezaee, Z., & Riley, R. (2010). *Financial statement fraud: Prevention and detection* (2nd ed.). Wiley.

Rezaee, Z., & Wang, J. (2019). Realtime reporting and continuous monitoring in digital business. *Journal of Accounting and Finance, 19*(6), 42–58.

Ribeiro, M. T., Singh, S., & Guestrin, C. (2016). "Why should I trust you?" Explaining the predictions of any classifier. In Proceedings of the 22nd ACM SIGKDD International Conference on Knowledge Discovery and Data Mining (pp. 1135–1144). Association for Computing Machinery. DOI: 10.1145/2939672.2939778

Ribeiro, M. T., Singh, S., & Guestrin, C. (2016). "Why should I trust you?": Explaining the predictions of any classifier. *Proceedings of KDD.*

Ricci, F., Rokach, L., & Shapira, B. (2015). *Recommender systems handbook* (2nd ed.). Springer., DOI: 10.1007/978-1-4899-7637-6

Ricci, M., Evangelista, A., Di Roma, A., & Fiorentino, M. (2023). Immersive and desktop virtual reality in virtual fashion stores: A comparison between shopping experiences. *Virtual Reality (Waltham Cross), 27*(3), 2281–2296. Advance online publication. DOI: 10.1007/s10055-023-00806-y PMID: 37360805

Richards, N. M., & Hartzog, W. (2016). Taking trust seriously in privacy law. *Stanford Technology Law Review : STLR : An Online High-Technology Law Journal from Stanford Law School, 19*(3), 431–472.

Roesner, F., & Kohno, T. (2021). Security and privacy for augmented reality: Our 10-year retrospective. In *VR4Sec: 1st International Workshop on Security for XR and XR for Security.*

Rozario, A. M., & Vasarhelyi, M. A. (2018). Auditing with smart contracts. *The International Journal of Digital Accounting Research, 18*, 1–25. DOI: 10.4192/1577-8517-v18_1

Saberi, S., Kouhizadeh, M., Sarkis, J., & Shen, L. (2019). Blockchain technology and its relationships to sustainable supply chain management. *International Journal of Production Research, 57*(7), 2117–2135. DOI: 10.1080/00207543.2018.1533261

Salesforce. (2024). State of the connected customer (6th ed.). Salesforce Research. https://www.salesforce.com/resources/research-reports/state-of-the-connected-customer/

Sanjalawe, Y., Fraihat, S., Abualhaj, M., Al-E'Mari, S. R., & Alzubi, E. (2025). Hybrid deep learning for human fall detection: A synergistic approach using YOLOv8 and time-space transformers. *IEEE Access : Practical Innovations, Open Solutions, 13*, 41336–41366. DOI: 10.1109/ACCESS.2025.3547914

Sanjalawe, Y., Fraihat, S., Abualhaj, M., Makhadmeh, S., & Alzubi, E. (2025). A review of 6G and AI convergence: Enhancing communication networks with artificial intelligence. *IEEE Open Journal of the Communications Society, 6*, 2308–2355. DOI: 10.1109/OJCOMS.2025.3553302

Sargeant, H. (2023). Algorithmic decision-making in financial services: Economic and normative outcomes in consumer credit. *AI and Ethics*, *3*(4), 1295–1311. DOI: 10.1007/s43681-022-00236-7

Scheiber, N. (2017, April 2). How Uber uses psychological tricks to push its drivers' buttons. *The New York Times*. https://www.nytimes.com/interactive/2017/04/02/technology/uber-drivers-psychological-tricks.html

Scheiber, N. (2017, April 24). How Uber uses psychological tricks to push its drivers' buttons. *The New York Times*. https://www.nytimes.com/interactive/2017/04/02/technology/uber-drivers-psychological-tricks.html

Schein, A. I., Popescul, A., Ungar, L. H., & Pennock, D. M. (2002). Methods and metrics for cold-start recommendations. In *Proceedings of the 25th Annual International ACM SIGIR Conference on Research and Development in Information Retrieval* (pp. 253-260). Association for Computing Machinery. DOI: 10.1145/564376.564421

Schlichtkrull, M., Kipf, T. N., Bloem, P., Van Den Berg, R., Titov, I., & Welling, M. (2018). Modeling relational data with graph convolutional networks. In *European semantic web conference* (pp. 593-607). Cham: Springer International Publishing. https://doi.org/DOI: 10.1007/978-3-319-93417-4_38

Schmidt, A., Beigl, M., & Gellersen, H. W. (1999). There is more to context than location. *Computers & Graphics*, *23*(6), 893–901. DOI: 10.1016/S0097-8493(99)00120-X

Schmitz, J., & Leoni, G. (2019). Accounting and auditing at the time of blockchain technology. *Accounting Horizons*, *33*(2), 41–54.

Schwartz, R., Dodge, J., Smith, N. A., & Etzioni, O. (2020). Green AI. *Communications of the ACM*, *63*(12), 54–63. DOI: 10.1145/3381831

Selbst, A. D., Boyd, D., Friedler, S. A., Venkatasubramanian, S., & Vertesi, J. (2019). Fairness and abstraction in sociotechnical systems. In *Proceedings of the 2019 Conference on Fairness, Accountability, and Transparency* (pp. 59–68). Association for Computing Machinery. DOI: 10.1145/3287560.3287598

Sergeev, M. (2023). *Web3. 0 as an Adaptive Strategy in Crisis: The Case of Nike and Adidas* (Master's thesis, Universidade Catolica Portuguesa (Portugal)).

Shah, M. J., & Devgun, M. P. (2024). AI-Powered Chatbots in Customer Support. [IJFMR]. *International Journal for Multidisciplinary Research*, *7*(3), 1–7. DOI: 10.36948/ijfmr.2025.v07i03.45374

Shambour, Q., Al-Zyoud, M., & Almomani, O. (2025). Quantum-Inspired Hybrid Metaheuristic Feature Selection with SHAP for Optimized and Explainable Spam Detection. *Symmetry, 17*(10), 1716. DOI: 10.3390/sym17101716

Shankar, V. (2018). How artificial intelligence is reshaping retailing. *Journal of Retailing, 94*(4), vi–xi. DOI: 10.1016/S0022-4359(18)30076-9

Shin, D. (2021). The effects of explainability and causability on perception, trust, and acceptance. *Human-Computer Interaction, 36*(5–6), 1–38. DOI: 10.1080/07370024.2020.1725998

Shin, D. (2021). The effects of explainability and causability on perception, trust, and acceptance: Implications for explainable AI. *International Journal of Human-Computer Studies, 146*, 102551. DOI: 10.1016/j.ijhcs.2020.102551

Shin, H., Bunosso, I., & Levine, L. R. (2023). The influence of chatbot humour on consumer evaluations of services. *International Journal of Consumer Studies, 47*(2), 545–562. DOI: 10.1111/ijcs.12849

Shinohara, K., & Wobbrock, J. O. (2011). In the shadow of misperception: assistive technology use and social interactions. In *Proceedings of the SIGCHI conference on human factors in computing systems* (pp. 705-714). https://doi.org/DOI: 10.1145/1978942.1979044

Shneiderman, B. (2020). Human-centered artificial intelligence: Reliable, safe & trustworthy. arXiv. https://arxiv.org/abs/2002.04087

Shokri, R., & Shmatikov, V. (2015). Privacy-preserving deep learning. In *Proceedings of the 22nd ACM SIGSAC Conference on Computer and Communications Security* (pp. 1310-1321). ACM. DOI: 10.1145/2810103.2813687

Shokri, R., Stronati, M., Song, C., & Shmatikov, V. (2017). Membership inference attacks against machine learning models. *Proceedings of IEEE Symposium on Security and Privacy*. DOI: 10.1109/SP.2017.41

Simon, H. A. (1955). A behavioral model of rational choice. *The Quarterly Journal of Economics, 69*(1), 99–118. DOI: 10.2307/1884852

Simon, H. A. (1957). *Models of man: Social and rational*. Wiley.

Singh, C., Dash, M. K., Sahu, R., & Kumar, A. (2024). Investigating the acceptance intentions of online shopping assistants in e-commerce interactions: Mediating role of trust and effects of consumer demographics. *Heliyon, 10*(3), e25031. DOI: 10.1016/j.heliyon.2024.e25031 PMID: 38318071

Singh, K. S. D., Hong, T. K., Abbasi, G. A., & Al-Adwan, A. S. (2025). Building bonds with food delivery apps: Determinants of app attachment and continuous intention—Does gender matter? *International Journal of Human-Computer Interaction, 41*(23), 1–19. DOI: 10.1080/10447318.2025.2495843

Solove, D. J. (2013). Privacy self-management and the consent dilemma. *Harvard Law Review, 126*(7), 1880–1903. DOI: 10.2139/ssrn.2171018

Song, X., & Xiong, T. (2021). A survey of published literature on conversational artificial intelligence. In *2021 7th International conference on information management (ICIM)* (pp. 113-117). IEEE. https://doi.org/DOI: 10.1109/ICIM52229.2021.9417135

Statista. (2024). E-commerce worldwide - statistics & facts. https://www.statista.com/topics/871/online-shopping/

Strubell, E., Ganesh, A., & McCallum, A. (2019). Energy and policy considerations for deep learning in NLP. *Proceedings of the 57th Annual Meeting of the Association for Computational Linguistics*, 3645–3650. https://doi.org/DOI: 10.18653/v1/P19-1355

Sundar, S. S. (2008). The MAIN model: A heuristic approach to understanding technology effects on credibility. In Metzger, M. J., & Flanagin, A. J. (Eds.), *Digital media, youth, and credibility* (pp. 73–100). MIT Press.

Sun, F., Liu, J., Wu, J., Pei, C., Lin, X., Ou, W., & Jiang, P. (2019). BERT4Rec: Sequential recommendation with bidirectional encoder representations from transformer. In *Proceedings of the 28th ACM international conference on information and knowledge management* (pp. 1441-1450). DOI: 10.1145/3357384.3357895

Suryanarayana, A., & Aluvala, R. (2024). Leveraging Transformational Artificial Intelligence (Ai) For Delivering Stellar Customer Experience, Educational Administration. *Theory into Practice, 30*(6), 1135–1140. DOI: 10.53555/kuey.v30i6.5455

Susser, D., Roessler, B., & Nissenbaum, H. (2019). Online manipulation: Hidden influences in a digital world. *Georgetown Law Technology Review, 4*(1), 1–45. https://georgetownlawtechreview.org/online-manipulation-hidden-influences-in-a-digital-world/GLTR-01-2019/

Susser, D., Roessler, B., & Nissenbaum, H. (2019). Online manipulation: Hidden influences in a digital world. *Georgetown Law Technology Review, 4*(1), 1–45.

Sweller, J. (1988). Cognitive load during problem solving: Effects on learning. *Cognitive Science, 12*(2), 257–285. DOI: 10.1207/s15516709cog1202_4

Taha, M. B., Sanjalawe, Y., Al-Daraiseh, A., Fraihat, S., & Al-E'mari, S. R. (2024). Proactive auto-scaling for service function chains in cloud computing based on deep learning. *IEEE Access : Practical Innovations, Open Solutions, 12*, 38575–38593. DOI: 10.1109/ACCESS.2024.3375772

Tam, K. Y., & Ho, S. Y. (2005). Web personalization as a persuasion strategy: An elaboration likelihood model perspective. *Information Systems Research, 16*(3), 271–291. DOI: 10.1287/isre.1050.0058

Tang, J., & Wang, K. (2018). Personalized top-n sequential recommendation via convolutional sequence embedding. In *Proceedings of the 11th ACM International Conference on Web Search and Data Mining* (pp. 565-573). ACM. DOI: 10.1145/3159652.3159656

Tapscott, D., & Tapscott, A. (2016). *Blockchain revolution*. Penguin.

Teodorescu, D., Aivaz, K. A., Vancea, D. P. C., Condrea, E., Dragan, C., & Olteanu, A. C. (2023). Consumer trust in AI algorithms used in e-commerce: A case study of college students at a Romanian public university. *Sustainability (Basel), 15*(15), 11925. DOI: 10.3390/su151511925

Tewari, R., & Pande, B. P. (2025). Transforming Digital Ownership: The Role of NFTs in Shaping Virtual Economies and Market Dynamics. *IET Blockchain, 5*(1), e70010. DOI: 10.1049/blc2.70010

Thaler, R. H., & Sunstein, C. R. (2008). *Nudge: Improving decisions about health, wealth, and happiness*. Yale University Press.

Treiblmaier, H. (2018). The impact of the blockchain on the supply chain. *International Journal of Logistics Management, 29*(2), 628–651.

Tuncal, A. (2025). Yapay Zekâ Destekli Ürünlerde Müşteri Deneyimi Nasıl Ölçülür? Türkiye'ye Özgü Bir Ölçek Uyarlaması. *Sosyal Mucit Academic Review, 6*(1), 119–146. DOI: 10.54733/smar.1602880

Túñez-López, J. M., Fieiras-Ceide, C., & Vaz-Álvarez, M. (2021). Impact of Artificial Intelligence on Journalism: Transformations in the company, products, contents and professional profile. *Communicatio Socialis, 34*(1), 177–193. DOI: 10.15581/003.34.1.177-193

Tutsal, E., & Ventura, K. (2022). Müşteri Deneyimini İyileştirmede Yapay Zekâ Uygulamaları: Çevrimiçi Perakende Firması Örneği. Journal of Social Research & Behavioral Sciences/Sosyal Araştırmalar ve Davranış Bilimleri Dergisi, 8(16). 346-369. https://doi.org/.DOI: 10.52096/jsrbs.8.16.21

Tversky, A., & Kahneman, D. (1974). Judgment under uncertainty: Heuristics and biases. *Science, 185*(4157), 1124–1131. DOI: 10.1126/science.185.4157.1124 PMID: 17835457

U.S. Congress. (2010). Restore Online Shoppers' Confidence Act (15 U.S.C. § 8401–8405). https://www.ftc.gov/legal-library/browse/statutes/restore-online-shoppers-confidence-act

U.S. Department of Justice. (2022, June 21). *Justice Department secures settlement agreement with Meta Platforms to resolve allegations of discriminatory housing advertising.*

Uddin, M., Obaidat, M., Manickam, S., Laghari, S. U. A., Dandoush, A., Ullah, H., & Ullah, S. S. (2024). Exploring the convergence of Metaverse, Blockchain, and AI: A comprehensive survey of enabling technologies, applications, challenges, and future directions. *Wiley Interdisciplinary Reviews. Data Mining and Knowledge Discovery, 14*(6), e1556. DOI: 10.1002/widm.1556

United Nations Conference on Trade and Development. (2016). *United Nations guidelines for consumer protection.* United Nations. https://unctad.org/system/files/official-document/ditccplpmisc2016d1_en.pdf

Valencia-Arias, A., Garcés-Giraldo, L. F., & Montoya, I. A. (2024). Artificial intelligence, personalization, and purchase intention. *Technological Forecasting and Social Change, 198*, 122005.

Varian, H. R. (1989). Price discrimination. In Schmalensee, R., & Willig, R. D. (Eds.), *Handbook of industrial organization* (Vol. 1, pp. 597–654). Elsevier.

Vasarhelyi, M. A., Kogan, A., & Tuttle, B. (2015). Big data in accounting and auditing. *Accounting Horizons, 29*(2), 423–429. DOI: 10.2308/acch-51071

Vaswani, A., Shazeer, N., Parmar, N., Uszkoreit, J., Jones, L., Gomez, A. N., . . . Polosukhin, I. (2017). Attention is all you need. *Advances in neural information processing systems*, 31st Conference on Neural Information Processing Systems (NIPS 2017), Long Beach, CA, USA. Available from http://proceedings.neurips.cc/paper_files/paper/2017/file/3f5ee243547dee91fbd053c1c4a845aa-Paper.pdf

Veale, M., & Borgesius, F. Z. (2021). Demystifying the Draft EU Artificial Intelligence Act. *Computer Law Review International, 22*(4), 97–112. DOI: 10.9785/cri-2021-220402

Venkatesh, V., Morris, M. G., Davis, G. B., & Davis, F. D. (2003). User acceptance of information technology: Toward a unified view. *Management Information Systems Quarterly, 27*(3), 425–478. DOI: 10.2307/30036540

Verhoef, P. C., Broekhuizen, T., Bart, Y., Bhattacharya, A., Dong, J. Q., Fabian, N., & Haenlein, M. (2021). Digital transformation: A multidisciplinary reflection and research agenda. *Journal of Business Research*, *122*, 889–901. DOI: 10.1016/j.jbusres.2019.09.022

Villegas-Ch, W., Amores-Falconi, R., & Coronel-Silva, E. (2023). Design proposal for a virtual shopping assistant for people with vision problems applying artificial intelligence techniques. *Big Data and Cognitive Computing*, *7*(2), 96. DOI: 10.3390/bdcc7020096

Wamba, S. F., Queiroz, M. M., & Trinchera, L. (2020). Dynamics between artificial intelligence and big data analytics: Implications for operations management. *International Journal of Production Economics*, *227*, 107588. DOI: 10.1016/j.ijpe.2020.107588

Wang, H., et al. (2024). GAZEploit: Remote keystroke inference attack by gaze estimation in XR/VR settings.

Wang, R. J. H., Malthouse, E. C., & Krishnamurthi, L. (2015). On the go: How mobile shopping affects customer purchase behavior. *Journal of Retailing*, *91*(2), 217–234. DOI: 10.1016/j.jretai.2015.01.002

Wang, X., Zheng, J., & Luo, M. (2025). More than words: The role of personality in shaping the timeliness of online reviews. *Journal of Hospitality and Tourism Technology*, *16*(3), 510–525. DOI: 10.1108/JHTT-03-2024-0192

Wang, Y., & Li, H. (2023). Predictive analytics and intelligent agents in e-commerce. *Journal of Retailing and Consumer Services*, *71*, 103119.

Wang, Y., Su, Z., Zhang, N., Xing, R., Liu, D., Luan, T. H., & Shen, X. (2023). A survey on Metaverse: Fundamentals, security, and privacy. *IEEE Communications Surveys and Tutorials*, *25*(1), 319–352. DOI: 10.1109/COMST.2022.3202047

Warren, D.Jr, Moffitt, K., & Byrnes, P. (2015). How big data will change accounting. *Accounting Horizons*, *29*(2), 397–407. DOI: 10.2308/acch-51069

Wilson, L., & Marasoiu, M. (2022). The development and use of chatbots in public health: Scoping review. *JMIR Human Factors*, *9*(4), e35882. DOI: 10.2196/35882

Wirtz, J., Patterson, P. G., Kunz, W., Gruber, T., Lu, V. N., Paluch, S., & Martins, A. (2018). Service robots in the frontline. *Journal of Service Management*, *29*(5), 907–931. DOI: 10.1108/JOSM-04-2018-0119

World Economic Forum. (2025, November 28). This month in AI: Shopping agents, AI's energy bill and new codes of conduct. https://www.weforum.org/stories/2025/11/ai-shopping-agents-energy-news/

Xia, L., Monroe, K. B., & Cox, J. L. (2004). The price is unfair! A conceptual framework of price fairness perceptions. *Journal of Marketing*, *68*(4), 1–15. DOI: 10.1509/jmkg.68.4.1.42733

Xi, N., & Hamari, J. (2021). Shopping in virtual reality: A literature review and future agenda. *Journal of Business Research*, *134*, 37–58. DOI: 10.1016/j.jbusres.2021.04.075

Yang, Q., Liu, Y., Chen, T., & Tong, Y. (2019). Federated machine learning: Concept and applications. *ACM Transactions on Intelligent Systems and Technology*, *10*(2), 12. Advance online publication. DOI: 10.1145/3298981

Yaseen, H., Al-Adwan, A. S., Nofal, M., Hmoud, H., & Abujassar, R. S. (2023). Factors influencing cloud computing adoption among SMEs: The Jordanian context. *Information Development*, *39*(2), 317–332. DOI: 10.1177/02666669211047916

Yau, K. W., Tang, T. S., Görges, M., Pinkney, S., Kim, A. D., Kalia, A., & Amed, S. (2022). Effectiveness of mobile apps in promoting healthy behavior changes and preventing obesity in children: Systematic review. *JMIR Pediatrics and Parenting*, *5*(1), e34967. DOI: 10.2196/34967 PMID: 35343908

Yermack, D. (2017). Corporate governance and blockchains. *Review of Finance*, *21*(1), 7–31. DOI: 10.1093/rof/rfw074

Yeung, K. (2017). 'Hypernudge': Big Data as a mode of regulation by design. *Information Communication and Society*, *20*(1), 118–136. DOI: 10.1080/1369118X.2016.1186713

Yıldız, B., & Dayı, F. (2024). Finans uygulamalarında yapay zekâ destekli chatbot kullanımı üzerine nicel bir araştırma. *Ömer Halisdemir Üniversitesi İktisadi ve İdari Bilimler Fakültesi Dergisi, 17*(2), 215-231. https://doi.org/.DOI: 10.25287/ohuiibf.1384420

Yuan, L., Zhang, Z., Xue, K., Yin, H., Chen, F., Guan, C., & Yu, Y. (2023). Robust multi-agent coordination via evolutionary generation of auxiliary adversarial attackers. In *Proceedings of the AAAI Conference on Artificial Intelligence* (Vol. 37, No. 10, pp. 11753-11762). https://doi.org/DOI: 10.1609/aaai.v37i10.26388

Zarie, A., Aljohani, F., & Al-Harbi, M. (2024). Elevating customer experience (CX) in artificial intelligence (AI) era. [IJISRT]. *International Journal of Innovative Science and Research Technology*, *9*(8), 1827–1829. DOI: 10.38124/ijisrt/IJISRT24AUG1024

Zhang, Y., & Chen, X. (2020). Explainable recommendation: A survey and new perspectives. *Foundations and Trends® in Information Retrieval, 14*(1), 1-101. http://dx.doi.org/DOI: 10.1561/1500000066

Zhang, S., Yao, L., Sun, A., & Tay, Y. (2019). Deep learning based recommender system: A survey and new perspectives. *ACM Computing Surveys*, *52*(1), 1–38. DOI: 10.1145/3158369

Zhang, W., Slade, EL ve Pantano, E. (. (2024). İnsan benzeri hizmet robotları: Sistematik bir literatür incelemesi ve araştırma gündemi. *Psikoloji ve Pazarlama*, *41*(12), 3157–3181. DOI: 10.1002/mar.22099

Zhou, Z., Wang, Y., & Li, H. (2024). Cloud concentration risk and accountability in financial services: Legal and operational perspectives. *Information and Software Technology*, *165*, 107152. DOI: 10.1016/j.infsof.2023.107152

Zhu, Y., Lin, X., Kim, J., Al-Adwan, A. S., & Li, N. (2025). Exploring Human Interaction in Online Self-Regulated Learning Through Danmaku Comments. *International Journal of Human-Computer Interaction*, *41*(22), 1–14. DOI: 10.1080/10447318.2025.2480826

Zou, L., Xia, L., Ding, Z., Song, J., Liu, W., & Yin, D. (2019). Reinforcement learning to optimize long-term user engagement in recommender systems. In *Proceedings of the 25th ACM SIGKDD international conference on knowledge discovery & data mining* (pp. 2810-2818). DOI: 10.1145/3292500.3330668

Zuboff, S. (2019). *The age of surveillance capitalism: The fight for a human future at the new frontier of power*. PublicAffairs.

About the Contributors

Omar Almomani: received his Bachelor's and master's degrees in Telecommunication Technology from the Institute of Information Technology at the University of Sindh in 2002 and 2003 respectively. He received his Ph.D. from the University Utara Malaysia in computer network and security in 2010. Currently, he is a professor in the Department of Networks and Cybersecurity, Faculty of Information Technology at Al-Ahliyya Amman University. Almomani is among the top 2% scientists in the world from 2022 up to now. His research interests involve network performance, network quality of service (QoS), IoT, network modeling and simulation, network and cybersecurity, and machine learning. He can be contacted at email: at almomani81@yahoo.com or o.almomani@ammanu.edu.jo

Mohammad Alauthman Is an associate professor and chair of the Information Security Department at the Faculty of Information Technology, University of Petra inAmman, Jordan. His research interests lie in network security, intrusion detection systems, and the application of artificial intelligence techniques like machine learning and deep learning for botnet detection, DDoS detection, spam email filtering, IoT security, and network traffic classification. He obtained his Ph.D. in computer science with a focus on network security from Northumbria University in the UK in 2016. Alauthman has been awarded several research grants in the field of network security, supporting his work on advanced intrusion detection systems and the development of AI-driven security solutions. These grants have enabled him to conduct extensive research and collaborate with international experts. His funded projects have focused on enhancing the resilience of network infrastructures against emerging threats and improving the accuracy of threat detection mechanisms

Ammar Almomani Academic Staff Member, Department of IT, Al-Balqa Applied University, Jordan Academic Staff Member, Department of Computer Information Science, Higher Colleges of Technology (HCT), Sharjah, UAE Professor Ammar Ali Almomani is a distinguished academic and researcher with over 20

years of combined teaching and industry experience in cybersecurity, artificial intelligence, and computer science. He also works as a consultant on various AI and cybersecurity initiatives and is a recipient of the prestigious UAE Golden Visa. Prof. Almomani holds a Ph.D. in Advanced Internet Security and Monitoring from Universiti Sains Malaysia (USM), He has taught over 47 specialized topics in cybersecurity and computer science, including Network Security and Artificial Intelligence. Prof. Almomani has published more than 200+ articles in reputable journals and conferences, with over 142+ indexed in Scopus,10 academic books, His contributions include 10 patents (eight in Germany and two in India) and several ongoing submissions. Recognized among the Top 2% of Global Influential Researchers by Stanford University and Scopus (2023–2024), he also serves as a consultant and expert member of the UAE Research Map (R&D). Prof. Almomani has supervised numerous undergraduate and postgraduate research projects (MSc/ Ph.D.) across countries such as the UK, Malaysia, and Jordan. He has chaired and co-chaired various international conferences and journals and maintains an active digital presence with over 120,000 readers and followers on ResearchGate. In addition to his academic and research endeavors, Prof. Almomani has extensive leadership experience, having served as Head of the Research and Innovation Department and IT Department for 6 years. He has contributed to curriculum development, program accreditation (including ABET and AACSB), and the establishment of specializations in both Jordan and the UAE. Prof. Almomani continues to make a significant impact in the fields of cybersecurity,AI and higher education, fostering innovation and collaboration at local and international levels.

***

Salam Al-E'mari earned her Ph.D. in Cybersecurity from Universiti Sains Malaysia (USM) in 2022. She is the Chair of the Information Security Department and an Assistant Professor at the University of Petra (UoP). With expertise in Blockchain, Deep Learning, and Network Security, she has contributed significantly to cybersecurity research. She previously earned her Bachelor's and Master's in Computer Science from Yarmouk University, Jordan, shaping her strong foundation in security and technology.

Wesam Alkhadour holds a Ph.D. in computer science from the University ofBradford, United Kingdom. She is currently an assistant professor at the University of Petra,Jordan.

Budoor Allehyani works as an Assistant Professor in the college of computing at Umm Al-Qura university. She received her Ph.D., in software quality assurance for self-adaptive systems, from the university of Leicester. Dr. Allehyani's current research focuses on software sustainability and requirements engineering. Beyond this, her research interest spans different fields including AI and data engineering.

Anas Arram is currently an Assistant Professor in the Data Science program at the Higher Colleges of Technology. He obtained his PhD in Computer Science from The National University of Malaysia in 2017, where he was awarded the Outstanding Researcher Award. His main research areas include meta-heuristics, hyper- heuristics, scheduling and timetabling, machine learning, and deep learning. He has published more than 14 papers in international journals and peer-reviewed international conferences. He was also a member of the Data Mining and Optimization Research Group (DMO) at the Centre for Artificial Intelligence (CAIT), National University of Malaysia.

Reenu Bansal Actively involved in imparting quality education in the area of Finance & Accounting, Dr. Reenu Bansal has held the position of Assistant Professor in the Business & Management Department at Christ University. Before Delhi Metropolitan this she was working with Delhi Education (DME), Noida since 2021. Before joining DME, she worked as Assistant Professor in the Finance Department at IILM for 4 Years and worked as Program Director-UG with IMS Noida for 8 years. She has earned her BCCA & MBA degree from Maharshi Dayanand University, Rohtak (Haryana) in the year 2005 and 2007 respectively. She obtained her PhD from University of Rajasthan, Jaipur in the year 2016. She has rich corporate and academic experience of more than 16 years. She has guided successfully research scholars under her guidance and also invited as a resource person in various workshops and seminars. Participated in various National & International Conferences, she has presented more than 20 papers so far and 10 of her papers were published in International and National Journals & Conference proceedings. Also she has published book chapters. Her areas of teaching and research interests includes financial management, financial services, management of financial institutions, financial accounting, cost accounting, managerial accounting, and digital finance.

Jorge Marx Gómez studied Computer Engineering and Industrial Engineering at the University of Applied Sciences Berlin (Technische Fachhochschule). He was a lecturer and researcher at Otto-von-Guericke-Universität Magdeburg where he also obtained a PhD degree in Business Information Systems with a thesis on "Computer-based Approaches to Forecast Returns of Scrapped Products to Recycling". In 2004 he received his postdoctoral lecture qualification (Habilitation) from Otto-von-Guericke-Universität Magdeburg with a professorial dissertation on “Automated Environmental Reporting through Material Flow Networks”. From 2002 to 2003 he was a Visiting Professor for Business Information Systems at the Technical University of Clausthal. In 2005 he became a Full Professor of Business Information Systems at Carl von Ossietzky University Oldenburg. He is head of the department of Business Informatics (Very Large Business Applications). Jorge Marx Gómez teaches at Virtual Global University. His personal research interests include Environmental Management Information Systems, Material Flow Management Systems, Federated ERP-Systems, Enterprise Systems Engineering, Business Information Systems in Higher Education, Enterprise Tomography, Environmental Data Warehousing, Recycling Program Planning, Disassembly Planning and Control and Life Cycle Assessment. Jorge Marx Gómez is a member of the following associations and groups: German Association of Computer Science (Gesellschaft für Informatik e.V. – GI), OFFIS e.V. (Oldenburg Institute of Informatics), SAP Roundtable for Business Intelligence, German Association of University Professors and Lecturers (Deutscher Hochschulverband – DHV), German Forum of Interoperability (DFI), German Oracle Users Group e.V. (DOAG). He also serves as a reviewer and expert in the DAAD selection committee for Latin-American research proposals.

Ismahafezi Ismail is an Assoc. Professor at the Faculty of Informatics and Computing, Universiti Sultan Zainal Abidin (UniSZA), Malaysia. His research interests focus on immersive technologies including virtual reality (VR), augmented reality (AR), extended reality (XR), and the metaverse, with applications in education, training, and digital innovation. He has been actively involved in national-level projects and collaborations in creative digital content, gamification, and user interaction design.

Waleed Maqableh is a distinguished academic and researcher with a PhD in Multimedia and AR/VR Technology from Malaysia. he specializes in innovative areas and his areas of interest include, facial expression recognition, education technology, augmented and virtual reality, and gamification, Dr. Maqableh has dedicated his career to teaching at the university level across Saudi Arabia, the United Arab Emirates, and Jordan.

Khalil Omar is an assistant professor at the University of Petra in Jordan. He received his Ph.D. degree in computer science from the University of Oldenburg, Germany, in 2018. His academic focus is on distance learning and e-learning in combination with software engineering, mobile applications, usability design, adaptive interfaces, and ERP systems. Users can reach him through his email address: komar@uop.edu.jo.

Yousef K. Sanjalawe is an Assistant Professor specializing in Cybersecurity and Cloud Computing at the University of Jordan (JU), Jordan. He earned his PhD in Cloud Computing from Universiti Sains Malaysia (USM) in 2020, where his research focused on enhancing cloud service broker selection using optimization algorithms. Dr. Sanjalawe has extensive experience in academia, research, and professional training. He has supervised Ph.D. students in Cybersecurity, Cloud Computing, IoT, Fog Computing, Optimization, and Artificial Intelligence (AI). From 2023 to 2024, he served as the Chair of the Cybersecurity Department at the American University of Madaba (AUM), Jordan, and from 2022 to 2024, he was an Assistant Professor in Cybersecurity at AUM.

Shashank Solanki is a distinguished legal researcher and corporate governance professional working at the intersection of law, technology, and environmental policy. Currently affiliated with Christ University, India, he brings a multidisciplinary lens to global governance, innovation, and ethical regulation. His research spans artificial intelligence regulation, cybersecurity, climate resilience, quantum computing ethics, and digital forensics, with a strong emphasis on the legal and policy implications of emerging technologies. Solanki has co-authored over 40 book chapters and journal articles, many of which are published or accepted in Scopus-indexed volumes by leading academic publishers such as IGI Global, Springer, Elsevier, Taylor & Francis, and Wiley. His scholarly contributions explore themes including AI-driven financial analytics, smart mining, healthcare cybersecurity, compact AI regulation, and sustainable infrastructure, reflecting his ability to synthesize complex legal frameworks with cutting-edge technological advancements. Professionally, he has interned with some of India's top law firms, including Shardul Amarchand Mangaldas & Co., Karanjawala & Co., and Singhania & Partners LLP, gaining hands-on experience in litigation, arbitration, tech policy, and commercial dispute resolution. He also served as in-house counsel at Shree Cement Ltd., handling contract review, environmental law, and litigation coordination. Notably, he collaborated with Hon'ble Mr. Justice Ashok Bhushan at the National Company Law Appellate Tribunal (NCLAT), contributing to judicial research and documentation in insolvency and corporate law. Solanki has presented at international conferences, including the NMIMS-Boston University School of Law Human Rights Conference, and participated in multiple moot court competitions, securing finalist and runner-up positions. His academic rigor is complemented by certifications in personal data protection, intellectual property litigation, and information technology (RS-CIT), along with a 7th-level certification in Abacus and Mental Arithmetic from UCMAS. Beyond academia, he has demonstrated leadership and social commitment as Convener of the Legal Aid and Awareness Society at Christ University, earning multiple Certificates of Appreciation from university bodies including the Student

Welfare Office and Student Council, and is a decorated athlete, having won gold medals in district-level handball championships and intra-departmental volleyball competitions. With a deep commitment to academic excellence, policy dialogue, and social impact, Shashank Solanki continues to shape conversations around law and technology. His ORCID profile is available at

Jamal Zraqou is an associate professor at the Department of Computer Science/ Virtual and Augmented Reality, University of Petra, Jordan, where he has been a faculty member since 2022. From 2018-2029, he was also the dean of the faculty of IT at IU. His research interests include computer vision, virtual and augmented reality, internet of things (IoT), cybersecurity, and image processing.

Index

A

B

C

D

E

S

U

V

www.ingramcontent.com/pod-product-compliance
Lightning Source LLC
LaVergne TN
LVHW062333300926
849161LV00007B/1678